Forbidden Texts
on the
Western Frontier

Forbidden Texts
on the
Western Frontier

The Christian Apocrypha in North American Perspectives

Proceedings from the 2013 York University
Christian Apocrypha Symposium

Edited by
TONY BURKE

Foreword by
CHRISTOPH MARKSCHIES

CASCADE *Books* • Eugene, Oregon

FORBIDDEN TEXTS ON THE WESTERN FRONTIER
The Christian Apocrypha in North American Perspectives
Proceedings from the 2013 York University Christian Apocrypha Symposium

Copyright © 2015 Wipf and Stock Publishers. All rights reserved. Except for brief quotations in critical publications or reviews, no part of this book may be reproduced in any manner without prior written permission from the publisher. Write: Permissions, Wipf and Stock Publishers, 199 W. 8th Ave., Suite 3, Eugene, OR 97401.

Cascade Books
An imprint of Wipf and Stock Publishers
199 W. 8th Ave., Suite 3
Eugene, OR 97401

www.wipfandstock.com

ISBN: 978-1-4982-0982-3

Cataloging-in-Publication data:

Forbidden texts on the western frontier : the Christian apocrypha in North American perspectives : proceedings from the 2013 York University Christian Apocrypha Symposium / edited by Tony Burke ; foreword by Christoph Markschies.

xxx + 370 p. ; 23 cm. Includes bibliographical references and indexes.

ISBN: 978-1-4982-0982-3

1. Apocryphal books (New Testament). 2. Apocryphal Gospels. 3. Jesus Christ—Biography—History and criticism. 4. Paul, the Apostle, Saint. 5. Church history—Primitive and early church, ca. 30–600. I. Burke, Tony (1968–). II. Markschies, Christoph. III. Title.

BS2850 F25 2015

Manufactured in the U.S.A.   07/22/2015

Scripture quotations are from the New Revised Standard Version Bible, copyright 1989, Division of Christian Education of the National Council of the Churches of Christ in the United States of America. Used by permission. All rights reserved.

*To François Bovon and Helmut Koester,
two giants upon whose shoulders we stand.*

Contents

List of Illustrations and Tables | ix
Foreword by Christoph Markschies | xi
Preface | xix
Abbreviations | xxi
Contributors | xxix

1. Introduction | 1
   —Tony Burke

2. North American Approaches to the Study of the Christian Apocrypha on the World Stage | 19
   —Jean-Michel Roessli
       Appendix—The AELAC (Association Pour L'étude de la Littérature Chrétienne): A Brief Historical Survey | 52

3. The "Harvard School" of the Christian Apocrypha | 58
   —Brent Landau

4. Excavating Museums: From Bible Thumping to Fishing in the Stream of Western Civilization | 78
   —Charles W. Hedrick

5. Scriptural Trajectories through Early Christianity, Late Antiquity, and Beyond: Christian Memorial Traditions in the *longue durée* | 95
   —Pierluigi Piovanelli

6. Jesus at School among Christians, Jews, and Muslims | 111
   —Cornelia Horn

7 Nag Hammadi, Gnosticism, Apocrypha: Bridging Disciplinary Divides | 132
   —Nicola Denzey Lewis

8 Canon Formation: Why and Where Scholars Disagree | 145
   —Lee Martin McDonald

9 Apocryphal Gospels and Historical Jesus Research: A Reassessment | 173
   —Stephen J. Patterson

10 Apocryphal Gospels and Historical Jesus Research: A Response to Stephen Patterson | 186
   —John S. Kloppenborg

11 Apocryphal Gospels and Historical Jesus Research: A Response to Stephen Patterson | 192
   —Mark Goodacre

12 The Distinctive Sayings of Jesus Shared by Justin and the Pseudo-Clementines | 200
   —F. Stanley Jones

13 The *Tiburtine Sibyl*, the Last Emperor, and the Early Byzantine Apocalyptic Tradition | 218
   —Stephen J. Shoemaker

14 Confused Traditions? Peter and Paul in the Apocryphal Acts | 245
   —David L. Eastman

15 Digital Humanities and the Study of Christian Apocrypha: Resources, Prospects and Problems | 270
   —Kristian S. Heal
   Appendix—Select Digital Humanities Resources | 279

16 Conversions of Paul: Comparing Acts and *Acts of Paul* | 282
   —Glenn E. Snyder

Bibliography | 303
Ancient Texts Index | 345
Subject Index | 359
Modern Authors Index | 363

Illustrations and Tables

Figure 1: The standard iconography of Peter (left) and bald Paul (right). Vatican Museums inv. 60768. Photograph by David Eastman. | 266

Figure 2: Peter and Paul presented as the nearly-indistinguishable apostolic twins. Vatican Museums inv. 60798. Photograph by David Eastman. | 267

Figure 3: Peter and Paul as mirror images of each other. Vatican Museums inv. 60798. Photograph by David Eastman. | 267

Figure 4: Traditional apostolic iconography but with Peter and Paul reversed. Vatican Museums inv. 60717. Photograph by David Eastman. | 268

Table 1. Conversion Stories in Acts | 284

Table 2. The House of Judas in Damascus | 290

Foreword[1]

— Christoph Markschies —

THOSE OF US IN Europe who work with Christian apocrypha will appreciate this opportunity to reach for a volume documenting the current state of the question in the United States and Canada. In Europe, research on the apocrypha has been closely tied to the annual meetings of the *Association pour l'étude de la littérature apocryphe chrétienne* (AELAC), which until 2013 took place in Dole (Burgundy). Only few European scholars regularly travel to the great annual meetings of the Society of Biblical Literature in the United States or—as the unforgettable and as-kind-as-he-was-wise François Bovon (1938–2013) did—actually move to North America to teach and conduct research there. The lower intensity of transatlantic scholarly cooperation—at least in comparison to that of European countries—can be explained not only by the significant geographical distance, but also by the fact that European research on apocrypha is often published in French, a language which is not widely studied at a sufficient level everywhere (including, admittedly, Europe). Barely one tenth of the members of AELAC live and work in the U.S. and Canada; consequently, the contents of a volume such as the present one put together by Tony Burke should not only attract the interest of North American scholars, but also provide their counterparts in Europe with an excellent overview of the current research on apocrypha taking place in the United States and Canada.

Papers included in this volume can be roughly divided into four groups: first, there are a number of attempts to describe the characteristics and the history of American research on apocrypha; second, some representative examples of American research are provided, along with; third, American perspectives on European (and German) research on apocrypha; and fourth, papers which—as is to be expected with a subject as complex as

1. I would like to thank Slavomír Čéplö for translating this Foreword into English.

this one—grapple with the term "apocrypha" and its definition. Based on this division of the contents of this volume, I will now proceed with a few remarks on the individual papers.

First, the papers that aim to track the history of Christian apocrypha research in the United States and Canada. Some time ago, Elizabeth A. Clark demonstrated how European and especially German scholars and research paradigms helped promote the concept of Early Church History in nineteenth-century America.[2] One could continue her narrative of history well into the twentieth century, and I will only need to mention Edgar J. Goodspeed in Chicago who studied with Aldof Harnack in 1898 in Berlin, and later met Theodor Nöldecke in Tübingen.[3] It is hardly surprising, therefore, that it was not just the Harvard School that was influenced by German scholars or scholars who spent their formative years in Germany (as Brent Landau shows); the same and yet a fundamentally different story could be written for the Divinity School in Chicago, and several other institutions. However, it must be made clear that the German and Swiss scholars Helmut Koester and François Bovon repeatedly pointed out to what extent their move to America changed the fundamental paradigms of their research (and the same is, incidentally, true of Hans Dieter Betz in Chicago). One must also not underestimate the "strong local influences" of the department tradition in Harvard that Landau describes. This is made clear by, say, a comparison between scholars influenced by Bultmann from both sides of the Atlantic. Koester, as well as his Bonn colleague Wilhelm Schneemelcher,[4] were influenced by Rudolf Bultmann's form criticism—Koester obtained his doctorate in Marburg, the last place where Bultmann was academically active,[5] Schneemelcher was exposed to Bultmann's most significant works during his studies in 1920s Berlin.[6] But while Schneemelcher—who was active in the German Protestant Church (for example in its ecumenical dialogue with the Greek Orthodox Church)[7] all of his life—was influenced by Karl Barth's idea of church theology and therefore considered apocrypha to be relevant only for the history of Christian piety, but not for the history of Christian theology, Koester (together with James Robinson who

---

2. Clark, *Founding the Fathers*.
3. Cobb and Jennings, *Biography*, 1–2.
4. For more on Schneemelcher, see below, p. xv.
5. Koester, *Synoptische Überlieferung*.
6. Bultmann, *Geschichte der synoptischen Tradition*.
7. See the Foreword by the Patriarch of Constantinople Demetrios I (1972–1991), in Damaskinos Papandreou et al., eds., *Oecumenica et Patristica*, 7–9.

was also originally influenced by Karl Barth)[8] placed emphasis elsewhere. In other words, Koester drifted much further away from the paradigms of his German studies than Schneemelcher ever could. Maybe we could even speak anachronistically of a more conservative and a more radical reception of Rudolf Bultmann's theological as well as historical concerns. It is, after all, well-known that Bultmann himself did not do any work on Christian apocrypha, not even in his book reviews.[9] Consequently, his students and others he influenced could not follow in his footsteps—for example, when it comes to the question of the so-called historical Jesus. Additionally, as Stephen J. Patterson makes clear in his contribution, certain viewpoints held by classical German scholarly figures could have survived even without direct contact and tight routes of transmission—so, in some parts of the American search for the "historical Jesus," the idea of a "plain Jesus" was given precedence over any considerations of the age of tradition, which also assumes the central position in the message of the New Testament in Harnack's lectures on "The Essence of Christianity."[10] Patterson, and F. Stanley Jones with him, shows the effect this has on the reconstruction of the first decades of Christianity when such approaches shaped by the New Testament (or rather by a certain view of Jesus, whether derived from the *Gospel of Thomas* or the Synoptics) are abandoned and all texts are considered worthy and equal. The paper by Pierluigi Piovanelli makes it abundantly clear that for some time now (and perhaps increasingly so), scholars from other European countries than Germany have exercised influence over the debate in the United States and Canada, and the same can be said about the situation in Germany: the influence of research from the United States and Canada is increasing constantly. His enthusiastic defense of *longue durée* and objections to limiting Christian apocrypha research to texts from antiquity show how far has the discussion drifted from its original connection to the study of the New Testament: all versions of apocryphal texts, even the medieval ones, are of interest. Later editors are to be taken seriously and should never be considered mere reworkers of an original text sanctified by virtue of its age. Piovanelli also makes another excellent point by drawing attention to scholars with double qualifications, such as Bovon, who studied both ancient Christianity of the early imperial era as well as Byzantine Christianity and was thus able—just to give one example—to study the growth of the Stephen tradition.[11] Without such double qualifications,

---

8. Robinson, "Theological Autobiography."
9. Bultmann, *Theologie als Kritik*.
10. Osthövener, "Adolf von Harnack als Systematiker"; Osthövener, "Nachwort."
11. Bovon, "*Dossier* on *Stephen*"; Bovon and Bouvier, "La translation des reliques."

the study of the complex history of versions of many Christian apocrypha could only have been possible in teams. To the fields listed by Piovanelli, we must, naturally, add the knowledge of the languages of the Christian Orient which are indispensable to those who wish to study the material in its full scope or, alternatively, invoke wider cooperation such as that practiced by the AELAC through the many volumes of the series Corpus Christianorum.

A number of papers address the notoriously complicated issue of defining what "apocrypha" are and how to tell them apart from hagiographic or the so-called gnostic writings. Even a cursory look at the history of such attempts reveals[12] that there is no logically precise delineation of this material written down somewhere in the Platonic realm of ideas that waits to be correctly read. Any and all attempts at definition are based on conventions and pragmatic compromises and therefore must be tested in scholarly practice. The debate of the recent decades has only succeeded in showing that some of these attempts lead nowhere, as is the case with, say, those older definitions which presuppose such an early existence of a Christian biblical canon and that the term "apocrypha" is merely a label for those noncanonical writings that aspired to become a part of the canon, but were not accepted as such by the majority (or "orthodox") church. This definition of "apocrypha" which seeks to establish a dialectical relationship of such writings to the biblical canon (and which has become quite commonplace) is especially useless when extending the definition of the term to writings beyond antiquity and recognizing that many relevant textual traditions are only extant in medieval recensions (as Pierluigi Piovanelli rightly points out). But even the classic sociological delineation of apocrypha as mere witnesses to "popular piety" employed as a matter of course by Schneemelcher (who, in turn, follows Lietzmann)[13] can only be applied to a fraction of the material. Nicola Denzey Lewis is right to point to the oft-cited origin of the so-called apocryphal or gnostic literature in an anti-intellectual (or at least only partially educated) milieu or even as a part of folk religion, where in fact such an assessment is more likely to be a later legacy of a heresiologically-determined prejudice against both textual contexts. In fact, the vast majority of the so-called Christian gnostic texts (including, but not limited to, those found in Nag Hammadi) belong *per definitionem* to collections of Christian apocrypha. Often there are only pragmatic reasons—of ostensibly economic nature—that motivate publishers and booksellers to exclude Nag Hammadi texts from editions of Christian apocrypha. Additionally, Denzey Lewis has shown elsewhere that the unity of the Nag Hammadi texts, appar-

12. Markschies, "Haupteinleitung," 104–14.
13. Ibid., 75–80.

ently constructed on the basis of their relationship as a single archeological artifact, is not as solid as it would seem upon first glance.[14] And with that, any reason to treat and edit this corpus separately disappears.

For a European scholar working with Christian apocrypha, seeing European research traditions through the (critical) eye of an American-based colleague is naturally particularly interesting and the paper by Jean-Michel Roessli offers a number of fascinating insights. Roessli wonders why the field is so strongly focused on the two thick volumes assembled by a Hamburg secondary school teacher[15] named Johann Albert Fabricius. The reason for that is most likely the wide dissemination of these volumes which can be easily found in used books stores even today.[16] Roessli cites this focus on a baroque anthology as a mere example of how heavily the conflicts of the past three centuries weigh on European research. And so he also wonders why, when compiling collections of translations of early Christian apocrypha, Wilhelm Schneemelcher followed Edgar Hennecke and Christoph Markschies followed Wilhelm Schneemelcher. The truth in these cases, however, is slightly more complicated: one might say that the editors felt bound to follow in the tradition of their predecessors and did so also because their predecessors left them the *Neutestamentliche Apokryphen* (first published in 1904[17]) as a sort of inheritance. Inheritance binds. However, it does not bind the inheritors to slavishly continue the work of their predecessors. Consider the latest edition which came out in 2012 where the break with tradition is more than obvious: the title of the collection is *Antike christliche Apokryphen* ("Ancient Christian Apocrypha") because a large number of texts emerged at a time when there did not exist (at least in some areas under the influence of the "orthodox" church) any generally-recognized New Testament canon and so calling such writings "New Testament Apocrypha" would be absurd. The new title also serves to indicate agreement with certain common basic principles of the AELAC, which were expressed also in the critical review of one of Schneemelcher's editions by Éric Junod.[18] To put it bluntly: the new title of the new Schneemelcher edition recognizes that Junod is right and Schneemelcher wrong. The only, but seemingly decisive, point where Markschies maintained the classic architec-

14. Denzey Lewis and Blount, "Rethinking the Origins."

15. Though, in fact, the "secondary school" was something between a secondary school of our times and a university: a *Gymnasium illustre*.

16. Markschies, "Haupteinleitung," 11.

17. Hennecke, *Neutestamentliche Apokryphen*.

18. Junod, "'Apocryphes du Nouveau Testament': Une appellation erronée et une collection artificielle"; see also "Apocryphes du Nouveau Testament ou apocryphes chrétiens anciens?"

ture of Hennecke's and Schneemelcher's work is the form-critical structure based on the canonical New Testament writings: gospels, acts, epistles, and apocalypses. This is, incidentally, also the structure employed by Fabricius, who, however, organized his volume on Old Testament Pseudepigrapha strictly alphabetically by biblical figures. The approach adopted by Christoph Markschies and Jens Schröter in *Antike christliche Apokryphen* where apocryphal writings are ordered by form or genre should be understood in the same pragmatic terms. While Wilhelm Schneemelcher defended this arrangement of texts with a statement of research principles arguing that this form-critical structure is the crucial insight of German New Testament scholarship in the twentieth century,[19] the motivation for holding on to this arrangement until today is now purely pragmatic: a chronological arrangement of the texts would be extremely speculative since their dating is either controversial or it is, considering the fluidity of the repeatedly reworked material, outright impossible. The alternative, an alphabetical arrangement, would mix modern literary titles, manuscript abbreviations, and other titles often haphazardly selected from a host of titles extant in manuscript witnesses in a motley ensemble which would perhaps be appropriate for a loose series titled "Some More Apocrypha," but certainly does not seem fitting for a selection of the most important ancient and late antique texts comprising several thousand pages. The same applies here: there is nothing hiding behind the arrangement (any more) except for practical considerations which are in any case set aside in the planned subsequent volumes on biographical tradition and also in other places. After all, unlike "New Testament Apocrypha," the label "Ancient Christian Apocrypha" includes not only the apocryphal acts, but also various other forms of biographical tradition, such as *vitae* or testaments. Jean-Michel Roessli is naturally perfectly right when he says that the history of research on Christian apocrypha before Fabricius has been examined only cursorily[20] and that European scholarship [is] burdened by the past, at least in the sense that what is perceived as revolutionary in recent scholarship still runs within established tracks that are connected to certain normative traditions. Interestingly, when one looks at the work of American or Canadian scholars, it is obvious that research on Christian apocrypha is still too tied to the canonical writings, as clearly seen in the paper by Stephen J. Patterson. Even if it is true that for at least some apocryphal writings the relationship to the canonical writings or figures or

---

19. As said in a conversation on the occasion of the transfer of publishing responsibilities to Markschies, summer 1994 in Bad Honnef near Bonn.

20. So for example Markschies, "Haupteinleitung," 91–95, including more detailed comments on Michael Neander.

genres is their primary *raison d'être*, apocryphal writings as such must be treated and studied separately from canonical writings.

And finally, a number of papers in this volume focus on individual apocryphal writings and by doing so demonstrate the vigor of American and Canadian research. It is somewhat surprising, however, that most of these studies chose to employ a comparatively classic approach to the material. More often than not, new research paradigms can barely be seen on the horizon rather than applied to apocryphal texts. Lee Martin McDonald goes beyond summarizing his work on the formation of the biblical canon by extending it to the study of the material aspect of modes of transmission. As such, exploration of the material culture of the antique world and its relationship to the history of the formation of its scripture canon is a fascinating and promising avenue of research[21] that I would like to see discussed in much more detail in the future. Surprisingly, there is only one paper (by Kristian S. Heal) on the subject of Digital Humanities, which can be found at the end of the volume and focuses on a single (but admittedly characteristic) example. It is, after all, immediately obvious that this is an area where much needs to be done for the so-called apocryphal literature: the existing corpora, such as the *Thesaurus Linguae Graecae*, contain texts drawn from the now-obsolete nineteenth-century compilations edited by Tischendorf, Lipsius/Bonnet and others. Heal's paper describes an edition of the *Syriac History of Joseph* prepared for the Oxford-BYU Syriac Digital Corpus using the Classical Text Editor developed by the Wiener Akademie der Wissenschaften. But it is perhaps a common task of American and European apocrypha research (and not just a challenge related to certain specific texts) to shift their focus away from books to the digital presentation of the fruits of their work. This applies especially to critical editions, since newly-discovered manuscripts can be easily converted to a digital edition and digitalized photographs of the manuscript can be linked with the edition or transliteration. Hardcopy publications can even be linked to digital editions, as is the case with Peter Schäfer's latest edition of the *Toledot Jeshu*.[22] It is desirable to engage with leading experts in the field of Digital Humanities in a discussion about whether a digital corpus of apocryphal literature (with appropriate links to other corpora) could and should be built. This fluid literature, which mostly exists in various translations and editions and thus constitutes a perfect example of "living literature,"[23] is especially

---

21. I myself have attempted to draw conclusions about the Sitz im Leben of the so-called apocryphal gospels from their material aspect, in Markschies, "Was wissen wir über den Sitz im Leben?"

22. Meerson and Schäfer, eds., *Toledot Yeshu*.

23. Markschies, "Haupteinleitung," 9–10.

amenable to digital presentation: with a push of a button, one can focus on a single version in a synoptic presentation, but one can also step back and see the text in the multitude of its recensions and editions. The digital medium helps to avoid especially the type of pseudocanonization typical of the nineteenth-century editions, which artificially filtered out certain texts from a rich and varied current of transmission. They thus created compiled texts, texts which had never been attested, texts that are the product of the philological fantasy of a modern editor or rather their desperate attempt to control a nearly unmanageable abundance of witnesses and versions—a problem that modern technology may be better equipped to handle.[24]

But this introduction should certainly not end with a note of this excellent volume's shortcomings, even if those shortcomings are in fact a roadmap to a mighty task. I hope that these lines are but an opening salvo of a renewed and close transatlantic cooperation in the field of Christian apocrypha research which seeks to build on the work begun in the twentieth-century by European scholars such as Helmut Koester and François Bovon, as well as Bultmann's student James M. Robinson, but also to critically evaluate and transform it for the needs of a changed research landscape. The papers in this volume which critically reflect upon American research are—or at least will be, once European scholars undergo such self-reflection—an excellent point from which to start anew and work together. In that sense, Tony Burke and Brent Landau should be congratulated and thanked for their efforts to organize the York Christian Apocrypha Symposium and publish the expanded proceedings in this volume.

---

24. Some fundamental observations can be found as early as Ritter, *Stemmatisierungsversuche zum Corpus Dionysiacum Areopagiticum*.

Preface

THE PAPERS IN THIS volume were presented at the York Christian Apocrypha Symposium, "Forbidden Texts on the Western Frontier: The Christian Apocrypha in North American Perspectives," held from September 24–25, 2013 at York University in Toronto, Canada. The Symposia Series began in 2011 with the goal of strengthening the field of Christian Apocrypha Studies in North America through fostering collaboration between scholars and raising awareness of the results of their investigations. The 2011 Symposium gathered together experts on the controversial *Secret Gospel of Mark*, a text that many scholars consider a modern forgery. The papers from that event were published by Cascade Books in early 2013 as *Ancient Gospel or Modern Forgery? The Secret Gospel of Mark in Debate*.

The 2013 Symposium, organized by Tony Burke and Brent Landau, examined the past, present, and future of Christian Apocrypha Studies in North America—looking back at the defining moments and voices in scholarship, looking around at what makes our approaches unique and what has come to define us on the world stage, and looking forward at new methodologies and new opportunities for collaboration. The gathering was made possible by a generous grant from the Social Sciences Humanities Research Council of Canada and by contributions from several funding bodies within York University. We wish to thank Martin Lockshin and Savitri Ramjattan in the Department of the Humanities, the Office of the Vice-President Research and Innovation, the Faculty of Graduate Studies, and the Faculty of Liberal Arts and Professional Studies. Particular thanks go to Janet Friskney, Research Officer for the Faculty of Liberal Arts and Professional Studies, who patiently guided us through the grant-writing process.

Additional thanks go to our panelists who contributed their time and expertise to the Symposium, and to the students who assisted in the administration of the conference: Robert Loughton, Joe Oryshak, and Sarah Veale, and to Jason Chartrand for helping compile the indices. We are grateful also to all those who attended the Symposium and participated in the discussions that arose. Special appreciation goes to Christoph Markschies who brings an international voice to the project with his foreword, to Slavomír Čéplö for last-minute translation assistance, to Pierluigi Piovanelli, Timothy Pettipiece, and John Kloppenborg for their feedback on the introduction, and to K. C. Hanson and Matthew Wimer at Wipf and Stock Publishers for their continued support of the Symposium. Finally, my personal thanks go to Brent Landau for his invaluable assistance planning the symposium; unfortunately, work and family responsibilities prevented him from serving as co-editor of this collection.

For information on future symposia in the York Christian Apocrypha Symposium Series, look for announcements on the Apocryphicity blog (http://www.apocryphicity.ca) or visit the Symposium's web page (www.apocryphicity.ca/york-christian-apocrypha-symposium-series/).

April 2015
Tony Burke

Abbreviations

ANCIENT

1 Clem.	1 Clement
2 Clem.	2 Clement
Acts Pet. Paul	Acts of the Holy Apostles Peter and Paul
Acts John	Acts of John
Acts Paul	Acts of Paul
Acts Pet.	Acts of Peter
Acts Pet. 12 Apos.	Acts of Peter and the Twelve Apostles
Acts Thom.	Acts of Thomas
Apoc. Elijah	Apocalypse of Elijah
Apoc. Ps.-Meth.	Apocalypse of Pseudo-Methodius

Aphrahat
Dem.	Demonstrations

Arm. Gos. Inf.	Armenian Gospel of the Infancy

Aristotle
Rhet.	Rhetorica

Augustine
Conf.	Confessions
Doctr. chr.	De doctrina christiana

Clement of Alexandria
Exc.   *Excerpta ex Theodoto*

Ep. Apos.   *Epistle of the Apostles*

Epiphanius
De mens. et pond.   *De mensuribus et ponderibus (On Weights and Measures)*

Pan.   *Panarion*

Eusebius
Dem. ev.   *Demonstratio evangelica*

Hist. eccl.   *Historia ecclesiastica*

Gos. Phil.   *Gospel of Philip*

Gos. Thom.   *Gospel of Thomas*

Herm. Mand.   Shepherd of Hermas, Mandate(s)

Hippolytus
Haer.   *Refutatio omnium haeresium*

Hist. Virg.   *History of the Blessed Virgin Mary*

Inf. Gos. Thom.   *Infancy Gospel of Thomas*

Irenaeus
Haer.   *Adversus haereses*

Isidore of Seville
Orig.   *Origenes*

Jerome
Epist.   *Epistulae*

Vir. ill.   *De viris illustribus*

Josephus
Ag. Ap.	*Against Apion*
Ant.	*Jewish Antiquities*
J.W.	*Jewish War*

Jos. Asen.	*Joseph and Aseneth*
Jub.	*Jubilees*

Justin
1 Apol.	*1 Apology*
Dial.	*Dialogue with Trypho*

Mart. Pet.	*Pseudo-Linus, Martyrdom of Blessed Peter the Apostle*
Pass. Holy	*Passion of the Holy Apostles Peter and Paul*

Origen
Princ.	*De principis*

Philo
Congr.	*De congressu eruditionis gratia (On the Preliminary Studies)*
Legat.	*Legatio ad Gaium (On the Embassy to Gaius)*

Prudentius
Perist.	*Peristephanon*

Pseudo-Clementines
Ps.-Clem.	*Pseudo-Clementines*
Hom. (KlH)	*Homilies (Klementia)*
Rec. (R)	*Recognitions (Recognition)*

Rufinus
Orig. Hom. Jon.	*Origenis in Jonam homiliae*
Orig. Hom. Num.	*Origenis in Numeros homiliae*

Socrates Scholasticus
Hist. eccl.	*Historia ecclesiastica*

Sozomen
Hist. eccl.	*Historia ecclesiastica*

Tertullian
Marc.	*Adversus Marcionem*
Praescr.	*De praescriptione haereticorum*

Theodoret
Hist. eccl.	*Historia ecclesiastica*

Tib. Sib.	*Tiburtine Sibyl*

MODERN

ABD	The Anchor Bible Dictionary. 6 vols. Edited by David Noel Freedman. New York: Doubleday, 1992
AH	Art History
AHR	American Historical Review
AnBoll	Analecta Bollandiana
ANRW	Aufstieg und Niedergang der römischen Welt
ASSR	Archives de sciences sociales des religions
Aug	Augustiniaum
BAR	Biblical Archaeology Review
BASP	Bulletin of the American Society of Papyrologists
BETL	Bibliotheca ephemeridum theologicarum lovaniensium
BGBE	Beiträge zur Geschichte der biblischen Exegese
BRev	Bible Review

ByzZ	*Byzantinische Zeitschrift*
BZNW	Beihefte zur Zeitschrift für die neutestamentliche Wissenschaft
CBET	Contributions to Biblical Exegesis and Theology
CCSA	Corpus Christianorum: Series Apocryphorum
CCSL	Corpus Christianorum: Series Latina
CP	*Classical Philology*
CSCO	Corpus Scriptorum Christianorum Orientalium
CSEL	Corpus Scriptorum Ecclesiasticorum Latinorum
EHPR	Études d'histoire et de philosophie religieuses
ETR	*Études théologiques et religieuses*
GCS	Die griechische christliche Schriftsteller der ersten [drei] Jahrhunderte
HDR	Harvard Dissertations in Religion
HR	*History of Religions*
HTR	*Harvard Theological Review*
JBL	*Journal of Biblical Literature*
JECS	*Journal of Early Christian Studies*
JEH	*Journal of Ecclesiastical History*
JRAS	*Journal of the Royal Asiatic Society*
JSJ	*Journal for the Study of Judaism in the Persian, Hellenistic, and Roman Periods*
JSJSup	Journal for the Study of Judaism Supplements
JSNT	*Journal for the Study of the New Testament*
JSNTSup	Journal for the Study of the New Testament Supplement Series
JSP	*Journal for the Study of the Pseudepigrapha*
JTS	*Journal of Theological Studies*
LCL	Loeb Classical Library
LSJ	Henry George Liddel, Robert Scott, Henry Stuart Jones. *A Greek-English Lexicon*. 9th ed. with revised supplement. Oxford: Clarendon Press, 1996.
LTP	*Laval théologique et philosophique*
Mus	*Muséon: Revue d'études orientales*
NAWG	Nachrichten (von) der Akademie der Wissenschaften in Göttingen

NedTT	*Nederlands theologisch tijdschrift*
NHS	Nag Hammadi Studies
NHMS	Nag Hammadi and Manichean Studies
NICNT	New International Commentary on the New Testament
NovT	*Novum Testamentum*
NovTSup	Supplements to Novum Testamentum
NTS	*New Testament Studies*
OECT	Oxford Early Christian Texts
OLA	Orientalia Lovaniensia Analecta
OLP	*Orientalia Lovaniensia Periodica*
Or	*Orientalia*
OrChr	*Oriens Christianus*
OrChrAn	Orientalia Christiana Analecta
P. Oxy.	*The Oxyrhynchus Papyri*. Edited by B. P. Grenfell et al. London: Egypt Exploration Society, 1898–
PO	Patrologia Orientalis
PRSt	*Perspectives in Religious Studies*
RB	*Revue biblique*
RBL	*Review of Biblical Literature*
REJ	*Revue des études juives*
RHPR	*Revue d'histoire et de philosophie religieuses*
RTAM	*Recherches de théologie ancienne et médiévale*
RTP	*Revue de théologie et de philosophie*
SAC	Studies in Antiquity and Christianity
SBLDS	Society of Biblical Literature Dissertation Series
SBLHBS	Society of Biblical Literature History of Biblical Studies
SBLSP	Society of Biblical Literature Seminar Papers
SBLTT	Society of Biblical Literature Texts and Translations
SBS	Stuttgarter Bibelstudien
SC	Sources chrétiennes
SecCent	*Second Century*
SHR	Studies in the History of Religions (supplements to Numen).
SNTSMS	Society for New Testament Studies Monograph Series

SNTW	Studies of the New Testament and Its World
SR	*Studies in Religion*
StOR	Studies in Oriental Religions
StPatr	Studia patristica
SVTP	Studia in Veteris Testamenti Pseudepigraphica
TENTS	Texts and Editions for New Testament Study
ThTo	*Theology Today*
TJT	*Toronto Journal of Theology*
TSAJ	Texte und Studien zum antiken Judentum
TU	Texte und Untersuchungen
TUGAL	Texte und Untersuchungen zur Geschichte der altchristlichen Literatur
VC	*Vigiliae Christianae*
VCSup	Supplements to Vigiliae Christianae
WGRW	Writings from the Greco-Roman World
WGRWSup	Writings from the Greco-Roman World Supplement Series
WMANT	Wissenschaftliche Monographien zum Alten und Neuen Testament
WUNT	Wissenschaftliche Untersuchungen zum Neuen Testament
ZNW	Zeitschrift für die neutestamentliche Wissenschaft und die Kunde der älteren Kirche

Contributors

Tony Burke is Associate Professor of Early Christianity at York University in Toronto, Ontario.

Nicola Denzey Lewis is Visiting Associate Professor at Brown University in Providence, Rhode Island.

David Eastman is Associate Professor of Religion and teaches in the Ancient, Medieval and Renaissance Studies Program at Ohio Wesleyan University.

Mark Goodacre is Professor of New Testament and Christian Origins at Duke University, Durham, North Carolina.

Kristian Heal is Director of the Center for the Preservation of Ancient Religious Texts at Brigham Young University.

Charles W. Hedrick is Distinguished Emeritus Professor at Missouri State University, Springfield, Missouri.

Cornelia B. Horn is Senior Researcher in the Faculty of Philosophy, University of Tübingen, a Heisenberg Fellow in the Department of Greek and Latin, Freie Universität (Berlin), and a research fellow at the Institute of Christian Oriental Research, Catholic University of America, Washington.

F. Stanley Jones is Professor of Religious Studies and Director of the Institute for the Study of Judaeo-Christian Origins at California State University, Long Beach, California.

Contributors

John S. Kloppenborg is Professor and Chair of the Department for the Study of Religion at the University of Toronto.

Brent Landau is Lecturer in Religious Studies at the University of Texas at Austin.

Christoph Markschies is Professor of Ancient Church History (Patristics) at the Humboldt-Universität zu Berlin.

Lee Martin McDonald is President Emeritus and Professor of New Testament Studies at Acadia Divinity College, Acadia University in Nova Scotia.

Stephen J. Patterson is the George H. Atkinson Chair in Religious Studies at Willamette University, Salem, Oregon.

Pierluigi Piovanelli is Professor of Second Temple Judaism and Early Christianity at the University of Ottawa, Ottawa, Ontario.

Jean-Michel Roessli is an Associate Professor of Historical Theology in the Department of Theological Studies at Concordia University, Montreal.

Stephen Shoemaker is a Professor of the History of Christianity in the Department of Religious Studies at the University of Oregon, Eugene.

Glenn E. Snyder is a Visiting Assistant Professor of Classical Studies at Indiana University-Purdue University Indianapolis.

– 1 –

Introduction

— Tony Burke —

THE YORK CHRISTIAN APOCRYPHA Symposium Series was created in 2011 as a forum to showcase the work of North American scholars who study the Christian Apocrypha (CA). For the second symposium, titled "Forbidden Texts on the Western Frontier: The Christian Apocrypha in North American Perspectives," we decided to take that mandate seriously and look directly at ourselves, to consider what makes CA Studies in the U.S. and Canada unique, to celebrate our strengths, and reflect on our weaknesses.

North America has no shortage of accomplished scholars in the field, but it has lacked the visibility and prestige enjoyed by our European colleagues, due in part to their highly-regarded publishing initiatives and the collaborative synergy that made these initiatives possible. Since 1904, German scholars have worked together to produce the celebrated *Neutestamentliche Apokryphen in deutscher Übersetzung* volumes, currently being updated by the editorial team of Christoph Markschies and Jens Schröter.[1] The French and Swiss scholars who established the Association pour l'étude de la littérature apocryphe chrétienne (AELAC) have produced their own collection, the two-volume *Écrits apocryphes chrétiens*,[2] as well as a number of critical editions in the Corpus Christianorum Series Apocryphorum, the

---

1. Markschies and Schröter, eds., *Antike christliche Apokryphen*.
2. Bovon, Geoltrain, and Kaestli, eds., *Écrits apocryphes chrétiens*.

journal *Apocrypha*, and a series of pocketbook editions of individual texts (La collection de poche Apocryphes); they also meet regularly at an annual summer réunion and smaller meetings during the winter months. Readers looking for texts in English translation have been served with a number of collections by individual scholars, including J. K. Elliott's *The Apocryphal New Testament* (an update of the collection of M. R. James from 1924), and several compendia assembled by Bart Ehrman. But none of these are collaborative projects on the scale of the French and German collections. It must be acknowledged that membership in the AELAC has become increasingly international over the past decade and North American scholars have assembled with their European colleagues at the group's meetings and have contributed to their publishing endeavors—notably, Tony Burke, Kristian Heal, F. Stanley Jones, Brent Landau, Pierluigi Piovanelli, Jean-Michel Roessli, and Stephen Shoemaker are all members of the group and have published in their series' and/or the *Apocrypha* journal. Similarly, the first volume of the Markschies-Schröter collection includes work by three scholars based in Canada: Wolf-Peter Funk, Stanley Porter, and Wendy Porter. Nevertheless, North American scholarship can profit from gatherings that take place closer to home and from collaborating on scholarly endeavors that address the interests of North American readers.

Efforts have been made to satisfy these needs. U.S. and Canadian (and some international) CA scholars have met at annual meetings of the Society of Biblical Literature for decades, contributing papers to the Christian Apocrypha Section, as well as the Nag Hammadi and Gnosticism Section, and various sessions on such topics as ancient fiction, pseudepigraphy, and second-century Christianity. The North American Patristics Society is also a venue for work on CA texts. The first formal North American gathering focused entirely on CA scholarship took place at the University of Ottawa in 2006 at a workshop organized by Pierluigi Piovanelli entitled "Christian Apocryphal Texts for the New Millennium: Achievements, Prospects, and Challenges."[3] The papers presented at the workshop covered a variety of texts and topics, thus demonstrating the vibrancy and diversity of the field in North America. The workshop concluded with a discussion of collaborative projects and the possibility of forming an academic association, but after a failed attempt to mount a second workshop in 2007, the momentum begun in 2006 was temporarily lost.

Nearly ten years later, much has changed. The first York Christian Apocrypha Symposium, convened in 2011 by Tony Burke with assistance

---

3. Many of the papers presented at the workshop have been published in Piovanelli, Burke, and Pettipiece, eds., *Rediscovering the Apocryphal Continent*.

from Phil Harland, continued the efforts of the Ottawa workshop to bring together CA scholars from across the continent. This initial gathering had rather humble goals. Nine U.S. and Canadian scholars assembled for one day of discussion of a single text, one that has captured the attention of North American scholars and the wider public: the *Secret Gospel of Mark*.[4] Shortly after, Burke and Brent Landau began work on *New Testament Apocrypha: More Noncanonical Scriptures*, a collection of texts in translation with contributions primarily from North American scholars. The project, a sister to *Old Testament Pseudepigrapha: More Noncanonical Scriptures* compiled by Richard Bauckham, James Davila, and Alexander Panayotov, aims to supplement Elliott's *The Apocryphal New Testament* with new and neglected texts that have never-before appeared in English CA collections. Then, in 2013 Burke joined forces with Landau once again to mount this second York Symposium, this time on a much larger scale. They decided to construct a "state-of-the-art" for CA Studies in North America, with invited presenters looking at the past, present, and future of the field on the continent. Part of that future is the creation, at last, of a North American academic association devoted to the study of the CA. The objectives of collaboration and organization are on their way to being achieved but they are made possible only by the efforts of the many scholars working in the field today and by the perspectives that have shaped and continue to inform their work.

CHRISTIAN APOCRYPHA STUDIES IN THE UNITED STATES

CA Studies in the U.S. is characterized, chiefly by its critics, as having two propensities: the integration of noncanonical texts into the quest for the historical Jesus and the support of Walter Bauer's theory on the development of early Christianity. Both of these characteristics are said to be hallmarks of the so-called "Harvard School,"[5] but they infuse also the work of the controversial Jesus Seminar as well other scholars working throughout North America.

Brent Landau's essay in this volume traces the history of the Harvard School to Helmut Koester, who joined the faculty of Harvard Divinity

---

4. The papers were published in early 2013 as Burke, ed., *Ancient Gospel or Modern Forgery?*

5. Darrell Bock, one of the chief critics of U.S. Christian Apocrypha scholarship, also uses the term "new school" for those who champion these two perspectives, though this group is not limited to scholars from Harvard. See *Missing Gospels*, esp. 44–55; for a response to Bock's category, see Burke, "Entering the Mainstream," 22–24.

School in 1958. Koester's approach to the CA is marked by his reluctance to favour one category of texts, canonical or noncanonical, over another; all are representatives of early Christian literature, and all have the potential to provide insights into the origins of Christianity.[6] This perspective has led Koester to propose theories of the development of New Testament literature that incorporate apocryphal texts at an early stage in the process. Koester's legacy is observable in the work of his doctoral students—including Ron Cameron, Julian Hills, Bentley Layton, Elaine Pagels, and Richard Valantasis—but perhaps his impact is most observable in the work of the Jesus Seminar. The Seminar was formed in 1985 by Robert Funk, who assembled around 200 scholars, primarily North American, as well as non-scholars with academic training, with the twin goals of arriving at a consensus about the life and teaching of Jesus and then presenting these findings to a wide audience. The Seminar's methodological principles entailed examining all Christian texts composed before 300 CE, including noncanonical texts, as possible repositories of authentic Jesus traditions. Seminar member John Dominic Crossan, the author of several best-selling studies of the historical Jesus,[7] is particularly well-known for his early dating of noncanonical texts and became, for many people, the public face of the Seminar and thus the target of much of the criticism levelled against it.[8] Other Seminar members include Charles Hedrick, F. Stanley Jones, John Kloppenborg, and Stephen Patterson. The approach of the Seminar is reflected in the group's collection of texts, *The Complete Gospels*,[9] which places new translations of the canonical gospels side-by-side with select CA texts; the book is the closest North American scholarship has come before now to producing a multi-author CA collection. The Seminar has also published, through its imprint Polebridge Press, a number of CA texts in translation in the series Early Christian Apocrypha edited by Julian Hills.[10]

---

6. See particularly Koester, *Ancient Christian Gospels*.

7. Crossan, *Historical Jesus*, 427–66 carefully lays out his methodological approach to the sources; Crossan, *Cross That Spoke*, is somewhat notorious for its claim that the *Gospel of Peter* is a witness to a "Cross Gospel" that forms the basis for the Passion Narrative of the canonical Gospels.

8. For a survey of early responses to the work of the Seminar see Miller, *Jesus Seminar and Its Critics*.

9. Miller, ed., *Complete Gospels*. Contributors on the apocryphal texts include Crossan, Funk, Koester, Kloppenborg, and Patterson, along with Harold Attridge, Ron Cameron, Jon B. Daniels, Arthur J. Dewey, Julian V. Hills, Ronald F. Hock, Karen L. King, Marvin Meyer, Donald Rappé, and Philip Sellew.

10. A list of the books in the series that have appeared to date, as well as other CA-related books published by the Seminar, is provided in Burke, "Entering the Mainstream," 23.

Of course Helmut Koester is not the only scholar at Harvard who has contributed significantly to the study of the CA. François Bovon joined the school in 1993 from the University of Geneva, bringing with him European CA scholarship's interest in examining late apocryphal texts and its emphasis on conducting manuscript research. Bovon trained a number of young CA scholars, including Ann Graham Brock, Nicole Kelley, Brent Landau, Catharine Playoust, and Glenn Snyder. Harvard also is home to Karen L. King who joined the faculty in 1997. King works primarily with Coptic apocrypha and is best known for her work on the *Gospel of Mary* and for her challenge to the scholarly construct of "Gnosticism" in her monograph *What Is Gnosticism?*[11] Her students include Benjamin Dunning and AnneMarie Luijendijk. Both Bovon and King brought to Harvard Divinity School new approaches to the study of the CA. As influential as Koester has been to the field, it would be wrong to characterize the "Harvard School," indeed all study of the CA in the U.S., solely by Koester's developmental theories of early Christian literature.

Prominent also in CA Studies is Claremont Graduate University in California. There James M. Robinson established the Coptic Gnostic Library Project at the Institute for Antiquity and Christianity in 1966. The project initiated the publication of a facsimile edition of the Nag Hammadi codices, the first English translation of the library in 1977 (revised in 1988),[12] and a series of critical editions published by Brill as The Coptic Gnostic Library. Among the scholars who worked on the project were Charles Hedrick, who narrates some of his activities at Claremont in his scholarly autobiography in this volume, John D. Turner, Elaine Pagels, and Marvin Meyer. Meyer also was chief editor of the update to Robinson's collection in 2008 and published a series of popular-market books on individual Nag Hammadi and related texts;[13] in addition, he became well-known as a voice arguing for the authenticity of the *Secret Gospel of Mark*.[14] More recently, Claremont has been home to Dennis R. MacDonald, who joined the faculty in 1998 and became director of the Institute for Antiquity and Christianity in 2000. MacDonald is known for *The Legend and the Apostle*, a study of second-century Pauline traditions,[15] and for his interest in allusions to Greek literature in Christian texts, particularly the *Acts of Andrew*.[16] Other

11. King, *What Is Gnosticism?*; King, *Gospel of Mary of Magdala*.
12. Robinson, *Nag Hammadi Library*.
13. Meyer et al., eds., *Nag Hammadi Scriptures*.
14. See particularly Meyer, *Secret Gospel*.
15. MacDonald, *Legend and the Apostle*.
16. MacDonald, *Christianizing Homer*.

CA scholars who have led projects at the Institute include F. Stanley Jones (Jewish Christianity A. The Pseudo-Clementines) and Ronald F. Hock (The Chreia and Ancient Rhetoric and Education Project).

Two other U.S. institutions have become centres for the study of the CA. Princeton University is home to Elaine Pagels, whose participation in the Coptic Gnostic Library Project led to the writing of her best-selling examination of the texts, *The Gnostic Gospels*, in 1979. Pagels has remained active in the study of the texts and has worked in various capacities with a number of CA scholars, including Geoffrey Smith, Nicola Denzey Lewis, and Annette Yoshiko Reed. Bart Ehrman, another graduate of Princeton (though working under Bruce Metzger), also has done much to bring the CA to public attention, mostly due to his appearances in a rash of documentaries—including the *Secret Lives of Jesus* (National Geographic, 2006), *Bible Secrets Revealed* (The History Channel, 2014), and the series *Banned From the Bible* (The History Channel, 2003, 2007, and 2012)—created to capitalize on the curiosity about the texts occasioned by Dan Brown's popular novel *The Da Vinci Code*. Though most well-known for his work on textual criticism of the New Testament, Ehrman has contributed to CA scholarship through the editing of several collections of texts: *Lost Scriptures* (a companion to his study of early heretical groups, *Lost Christianities*), *The Apocryphal Gospels* (texts and translations, in collaboration with Zlatko Pleše), and *The Other Gospels* (a republishing of *The Apocryphal Gospels* without the texts in the original languages). He also was involved in the publication of the *Gospel of Judas*, contributing an essay to the National Geographic Society's popular-market translation of the text[17] and appearing in their 2006 documentary about the discovery. At the University of North Carolina at Chapel Hill, where he holds the James A. Gray Distinguished Professor of Religious Studies, Ehrman has supervised the work of a number of students who have published in the field, including Chris Frilingos, Catherine Burris, and Diane Lipsett.

Tying together scholars from all four of these schools, and indeed from various institutions throughout North America, is a fascination with the Bauer Hypothesis, named for Walter Bauer, author of *Rechtgläubigkeit und Ketzerei im ältesten Christentum*, published in 1934 but not translated into English until 1971, under the leadership of Robert Kraft.[18] Bauer challenged the classical articulation of the history of the early church, as set out by Eusebius of Caesarea and others, that Christianity spread out from Jerusalem,

---

17. Ehrman, "Christianity Turned on Its Head"; Ehrman later also wrote *The Lost Gospel of Judas Iscariot*, a popular-market book on the text.

18. English translation: Bauer, *Orthodoxy and Heresy*.

transforming no belief into correct belief (orthodoxy), imparted by Jesus to the apostles and then to the apostles' successors; that initial unity soon was compromised with the introduction of wrong belief (heresy), which the church, principally through the writings of the heresiologists, worked hard to eradicate. Against this view, Bauer argued that in some locations in the ancient world, heretical forms of Christianity, such as Marcionism, were established first and these were replaced later by orthodoxy. Bauer's position received mixed reviews in Germany, but it found a sympathetic hearing by Rudolf Bultmann and his students, particularly Helmut Koester, who took up a challenge issued by Bultmann to carry Bauer's hypothesis from the second century into the first,[19] and thus influenced a new generation of scholars in the U.S. to support and refine Bauer's ideas. Many of the details of Bauer's study have been proven wrong with the discovery of new primary sources, particularly the Nag Hammadi codices, but the essential arguments—that Christianity began in variety not unity and that what is orthodoxy lies in the eye of the beholder—continue to shape scholarship on the CA, so much that Bauer's supporters are often the target of attack for apologetic writers, who continue to advocate the pre-Bauer model of Christian origins, in their efforts to discourage interest in apocryphal texts. This interest is due, at least in part, to the popularity of Bart Ehrman's discussions of the material—some critics even refer now to Bauer's hypothesis as the "Bauer-Ehrman thesis."[20]

If critics of American approaches to the study of the CA are to be believed, then U.S. scholarship focuses on privileging noncanonical texts over the canonical and on demonstrating that orthodox Christianity has no claim to being the one, true, legitimate form of Christianity. Certainly, this characterization is accurate for some U.S. scholars, but it fails to take into account the European perspective, exemplified by Bovon's students at Harvard, that encourages the study of late, not early, apocrypha and thus skirts the issue of what can be learned from the texts about the historical Jesus and early Christianity. As the contributions of these scholars become more widely known, U.S. CA Studies will be less the target of caricature and future assessments will reflect its considerable variety.

---

19. Koester, "GNOMAI DIAPHORAI." On the support of Bauer by Bultmann and Koester see the appendix ("The Reception of the Book") in Bauer, *Orthodoxy and Heresy*, 306–10.

20. See, for example, Köstenberger and Kruger, *Heresy of Orthodoxy*. For an extended discussion of apologetic responses to U.S. scholarship on the Christian Apocrypha see Burke, "Heresy Hunting."

CHRISTIAN APOCRYPHA STUDIES IN CANADA

Any conversation, on any topic, about Canada and the U.S. makes apparent the greater strength of the southern nation over its neighbour to the north. Canada's national inferiority complex is an integral part of its identity. Certainly the number of Canadian scholars working in the CA is fewer than in the U.S. and their work is less well-known internationally. That said, Canadians have made a number of significant contributions to the field.

The one major centre for CA Studies in Canada is Université Laval in Quebec, home to the series Bibliothèque copte de Nag Hammadi (BCNH). Begun in 1974 by Jacques É. Ménard of the Université des Sciences humaines de Strasbourg, and Hervé Gagné and Michel Roberge of Université Laval, the BCNH produces critical editions, as well as concordances and studies, of the Nag Hammadi library and related texts for francophone readers—think of it as the French counterpart to The Coptic Gnostic Library at Claremont. The team published also in 2007 the first of a two-volume collection of translations of the entire corpus for Gallimard's Bibliothèque de la Pléiade;[21] this model of producing scholarly editions and a Pléiade collection for a wider audience is the same used by the AELAC (Association pour l'étude de la littérature apocryphe chrétienne), whose endeavours are discussed in detail in Jean-Michel Roessli's paper in this volume. The BCNH is currently under the direction of Louis Painchaud, Wolf-Peter Funk, and Paul-Hubert Poirier. Each of these scholars works also on texts beyond the Nag Hammadi corpus; Painchaud has published on the *Gospel of Judas*,[22] Funk is editing the Berlin portion of the Coptic Manichaean texts from Medinet Madi,[23] and Poirier has worked extensively on the *Acts of Thomas* and recently waded into the debate over defining "Christian Apocrypha."[24] Students of Laval who have made important contributions to CA Studies include Michael Kaler, Timothy Pettipiece, Tuomas Rasimus, and Alin Suciu.

To the west of Quebec City, Montreal's Concordia University features three scholars working in the CA: Lorenzo DiTommaso, André Gagné, and Jean-Michel Roessli. DiTommaso's research focuses on the Old Testament Pseudepigrapha, but he has published particularly on Christian-authored Daniel apocrypha.[25] Gagné works on the *Gospel of Thomas* and co-ordinates

---

21. Mahé and Poirier, eds., *Écrits gnostiques*.

22. Including Painchaud, "À Propos de la (re)découverte de l'Évangile de Judas," an important early critical appraisal of the reconstruction and interpretation of the text in the *editio princeps* in Kasser and Wurst, eds., *Gospel of Judas*.

23. Funk, *Kephalaia (I)*.

24. Poirier, "Vers une redéfinition."

25. DiTommaso, *Book of Daniel*.

the Nag Hammadi Seminar, a gathering of graduate and undergraduate students, sometimes featuring guest speakers from other Canadian universities. And Roessli, who was trained in Europe and moved to Canada in 2007, works on the Christian *Sybilline Oracles* and, as a member of the editorial team of the AELAC, is a friendly bridge between North American CA scholars and their European colleagues.

Farther west lies the University of Ottawa, home of Pierluigi Piovanelli, another European-trained scholar who has done much to advance the study of the CA in Canada. He organized the Ottawa workshop in 2006, has chaired the Christian Apocrypha Section of the Society of Biblical Literature, presented at the 2011 and 2013 York Christian Apocrypha symposia, and is a contributor to both series of More Canonical Scriptures (Old Testament Pseudepigrapha and New Testament Apocrypha). Also, as a longtime member of the AELAC, he has helped introduce North American scholars to the group and thereby increase its international profile. Like Bovon at Harvard, Piovanelli has brought European approaches to the study of the CA to North America, but, as Jean-Michel Roessli remarks, he has also exposed European scholars to a burgeoning North American interest in modern apocryphal texts. Piovanelli's specific research areas are the *Apocalypse of Paul* and Ethiopic texts, such as the *Book of the Rooster*, which he translated for *Écrits apocryphes chrétiens*.[26] Piovanelli is joined at the University of Ottawa by Dominique Côté, a former student of Paul-Hubert Poirier. Côté has worked extensively on the *Pseudo-Clementines*.[27]

The University of Toronto in Ontario is alma mater to Scott Brown, Tony Burke, and Mary Dzon. Brown is one of the principal voices in the debate over the authenticity of the *Secret Gospel of Mark*;[28] Burke and Dzon, working under Robert Sinkewicz in the Department of Medieval Studies/Department for the Study of Religion, both wrote their dissertations on apocryphal infancy traditions. Burke's dissertation, critical edition and commentary on the *Infancy Gospel of Thomas*,[29] was the first North American contribution to the Corpus Christianorum Series Apocryphorum, thus further forging links between European and North American scholarship. The European perspective guiding the Series Apocryphorum is reflected also in the late antique and medieval texts featured in Burke's *New Testament Apocrypha: More Noncanonical Scriptures* collection (co-edited with

---

26. Piovanelli, "Livre du coq."

27. See, for example, his monograph Côté, *Le theme de l'opposition*.

28. See Brown, *Mark's Other Gospel*, and his contributions to Burke, ed., *Ancient Gospel*.

29. Burke, *De infantia Iesu*.

Brent Landau) and in the breadth of texts discussed in his popular-market introduction to the CA, *Secret Scriptures Revealed*. Burke also is founder of the York Christian Apocrypha Symposium and co-ordinates a session on the CA at the annual meeting of the Canadian Society of Biblical Studies (in conjunction with Timothy Pettipiece for the Canadian Society of Patristic Studies). Though few other graduates of the University of Toronto work in the CA field, there are currently a number of doctoral students working with John Kloppenborg on CA texts, including Ian Brown, Callie Callon, and Anna Cwikla, all regular contributors to the CSBS/CSPS session.

Our cross-Canada survey ends in the Prairies at the University of Winnipeg with Zbigniew Izydorczyk. A lone voice in the wilderness, Izydorczyk has been working for decades on the manuscript tradition of the *Gospel of Nicodemus* and related texts and is known internationally as a prominent scholar of this material. Along with his own work, surveyed in Jean-Michel Roessli's essay, Izydorczyk has collaborated with Rémi Gounelle on bibliographical resources for the *Acts of Pilate*,[30] co-authored the entry on the *Vengeance of the Savior* for *Écrits apocryphes chrétiens*,[31] and contributed to a volume of the Instrumenta of the Series Apocryphorum.[32] In addition, Izydorczyk organized a workshop on the Pilate Cycle in October 2010 entitled "Editing the *Acts of Pilate* in Early Christian Languages: Theory and Practice," which included presentations by international (including Albert Frey, Rémi Gounelle, and Jean-Daniel Dubois) and Canadian scholars (including Burke, Poirier, and Roessli).[33]

To some extent, Canadian contributions to the study of the CA are obscured by the fact that a number of Canadian-born or Canadian-trained scholars—including Philip Tite, Nicola Denzey Lewis, and Mary Dzon—work in the U.S. This situation only underscores the international nature of CA Studies in North America, where some of the major developments in the field were made by European émigrés and where many of the scholars have made significant contributions to European publishing projects. It is hoped that the collaboration amongst North American CA scholars occasioned and encouraged by the York Christian Apocrypha Symposium Series will enhance awareness of our strengths and capabilities and lead to additional opportunities for international collaboration.

---

30. Izydorczyk and Gounelle, "Thematic Bibliography of the *Acts of Pilate*"; and Izydorczyk and Gounelle, "Thematic Bibliography of the *Acts of Pilate*. Addenda et corrigenda."

31. Bisson, Brossard-Dandré, and Izydorczyk, "Vengeance du Sauveur."

32. Izydorczyk and Wydra, eds., *Gospel of Nicodemus*.

33. Most of the papers from the workshop were published in *Apocrypha* 21 (2010).

THE 2013 SYMPOSIUM

"Forbidden Texts on the Western Frontier: The Christian Apocrypha in North American Perspectives" gathered together 19 CA scholars from the U.S. and Canada for two days of presentations, exchanging of ideas, and discussion of future collaborations.

The work of the Symposium began the morning of September 25 with our first session, "Christian Apocrypha in the 21st Century." The goal of the session was to present an overview of North American contributions to the field and to describe the research trajectories of North American CA scholarship. Jean-Michel Roessli (Concordia University) was asked to examine "North American Approaches to the Study of the Christian Apocrypha on the World Stage." His presentation included an account of the origins and scholarship of the AELAC, an organization with which many of the scholars participating in the Symposium are involved, and the impact of the group's work on North American scholarship, particularly via François Bovon and Pierluigi Piovanelli. Roessli took a bit of a detour at the end of his presentation, urging North American scholars to examine the origins of the study of the CA during the Enlightenment. This began a discussion of the "apocryphal canon" (that is, the decisions behind why certain apocryphal texts are selected for inclusion into scholarly collections) that many of the Symposium participants touched upon over the course of the weekend. Pierluigi Piovanelli (University of Ottawa) followed with "Trajectories through Early Christianity and Late Antiquity: The *longue durée* of Christian Memorial Traditions in American Scholarship," an informal discussion on approaches to the study of late antique and medieval apocrypha. The interest in understanding such material in the context of its time and place of composition is considered the hallmark of the European perspective brought to North America by Bovon and Piovanelli. Piovanelli used the example of his work on the *Book of the Rooster* (wisely renamed from its former title, the "Book of the Cock," an announcement that elicited giggles from the audience), to show how scholars can examine a late text with consideration of the possibility that it drew on earlier sources, but that the precise nature of these sources are impossible to recover. Piovanelli then surprised everyone with the announcement of a new apocryphal text in Ethiopic, the *Story of the Passion of Christ*, which entails a brief summary of a vision of the flogging and crucifixion of Jesus seen by the three women at the tomb. As it turns out, however, the text is actually a medieval devotional text which originally featured three medieval female saints as the visionaries. Though the *Story of the Passion of Christ* did not begin as an apocryphon, it was transformed into one by a later scribe. In his completed paper, Piovanelli ponders what this example may mean for the study of other CA texts that similarly appear to have reused and repurposed earlier sources. The discovery of new texts can be exciting, Piovanelli says, and though scholars often hope that they contain ancient materials, "in some cases manuscript hunters end up with unexpected surprises that can have, perhaps, the same relevance for the study of epochs and cultural areas other than the origins of Christianity" (p. 108).

The other two presentations in the session focused on two of the major centres for the study of the CA: Harvard University and Claremont Graduate University. The presenters delivered first-hand accounts of their own time spent at these institutions. First, Brent Landau (University of Texas at Austin) discussed "The 'Harvard School' of the Christian Apocrypha," which has become well-known (and much-criticized) due to Helmut Koester's arguments that certain noncanonical texts reveal much about stages in the development of the composition of the canonical Gospels. Landau drew attention also to the contributions to scholarship made by François Bovon and Karen King, and mentioned some important events in the Harvard school's prehistory: an 1838 address by Ralph Waldo Emerson and a collection of agrapha made by James Hardy Ropes in 1896. Landau noted the impact of the Harvard school on the field in North America, particularly through those who, like himself, graduated from the program. But he lamented also that the future of the school is uncertain—Koester is still teaching (in his 57th year at Harvard!), but Bovon and King, he said at the time, have suffered from very serious illnesses in recent years and none of the present junior faculty list the CA as a chief research interest. Landau was right to be concerned; Bovon succumbed to cancer a month after the Symposium. The second of the two presentations on centres for CA research was Charles Hedrick's (Missouri State University) scholarly autobiography, "Excavating Museums: From Bible Thumping to Fishing in the Stream of Western Civilization." Hedrick's long and accomplished career intersected with several major discoveries of the last century, including the publishing of the Nag Hammadi library (as a member of The Coptic Gnostic Library Project at Claremont), the *Gospel of the Savior*, and the *Gospel of Judas*. Hedrick mentions in his completed paper the conflict he had studying apocryphal texts while still being much involved in the Southern Baptist Church (he even served as pastor at several points in his early professional career). As a graduate student he came to the conclusion that, "in historical scholarship it is not possible to be a servant of the church and the discipline at the same time" particularly because "noncanonical literature presents a threat to the church" (p. 82). Not everyone in attendance at the Symposium agreed that a decision has to be made between church and scholarly study, but even today there have been some nightmare stories out of the U.S. of biblical scholars losing their positions because their work conflicts with the mandate of their institutions. The interplay between faith and historical investigation was another topic of discussion over the course of the Symposium.

The presentations in the first afternoon session, "New Frontiers in Christian Apocrypha Studies," looked at bridging gaps between CA and related disciplines. In "Jesus at School among Christians, Jews, and Muslims," Cornelia Horn (Catholic University of America) continued her work on Christian and Muslim use of Jesus and Mary infancy traditions. This time her discussion featured the story of Jesus in school from the *Infancy Gospel of Thomas* and looked at its transformations in the *Armenian Infancy Gospel*, the *Toledot Yeshu*, and the story of the Imam Muḥammad al-Bāqir in *Umm al-kitāb* (an eighth-century Shi'ite text). The new frontier opened up here, then, is the sharing of apocryphal traditions across the dividing lines of religions. In the conclusion of her presentation, Horn asked us to consider the status of texts like *Umm al-kitāb*—does its connection to apocryphal Jesus stories make it a Christian apocryphal text, or an Islamic apocryphal text, or something else? Nicola Denzey Lewis (Brown University) followed with a dynamic presentation entitled, "Nag Hammadi, Gnosticism, Apocrypha: Bridging Disciplinary Divides." The completed paper points out how scholars have segregated gnostic texts from other apocrypha—she writes, "the Christian apocrypha and our so-called gnostic texts have become the ugly, wicked stepsisters in the fairy tale of New Testament Studies—one silly, the other dangerous" (p. 132). The divide between the two bodies of texts is most apparent at conferences like the SBL Annual Meeting, which separates Nag Hammadi or Gnostic Studies from Christian Apocrypha, despite the fact that some Nag Hammadi texts are not gnostic (e.g., the *Acts of Peter and the Twelve Apostles*) and some gnostic texts are not from Nag Hammadi (e.g., the *Pistis Sophia*, the *Gospel of Mary*); one text in particular, the *Gospel of Thomas*, seems to transcend all of these boundaries. Denzey Lewis echoes the call by other scholars to redraw these boundaries, to classify all the texts as "early Christian literature" and then focus on sub-genres such as apocalypse, romance, or gospel. The final paper of the session was "Debating Canon Formation: Why and Where Scholars Disagree" by Lee Martin McDonald (Institute for Biblical Research). McDonald has written extensively on the canon, and seems to show no signs of slowing down; but his work has not been effectively brought into discussions of the CA, despite the fact that canon is very important for studying *noncanonical* texts, particularly since the various forms that the canon has taken over time and space has bearing on whether or not a text is declared noncanonical. McDonald's paper touches on several aspects of his previous work on canon that CA scholars should take into account, including his position that the Muratorian Canon is a product of the early fourth, not second, century, and his view of the development of the Western canon (it clearly was not settled in the fourth-century). He states (rightly) also, that a fixed text of the New Testament was never physically possible until "the invention of moveable text and the printing press" (p. 163), and makes the provocative point that, thanks to electronic media, we are living in a time much like the first few centuries when we can pick and choose the texts we value, and without any sense of having to limit a corpus to the mechanics of book production. The session concluded with a response by Lorenzo DiTommaso (Concordia University) to the two papers available in draft form (by Denzey Lewis and McDonald). In an early stage of the planning process, DiTommaso was invited to present on Christian Old Testament Pseudepigrapha—another category of texts rarely discussed in connection with the CA. Jim Davila, a Harvard graduate working at the University of St. Andrews in Scotland, has done much to open up this new frontier with his work on re-evaluating the authorship of the Pseudepigrapha,[34] thereby encouraging North American CA scholars to follow the path of their European colleagues in bringing Christian-authored Pseudepigrapha into CA scholarship. Unfortunately, DiTommaso's schedule did not allow him time to write a paper, but we were pleased to have him attend the Symposium and offer his thoughts on the other papers of the session.

The afternoon of the first day of the Symposium began with a session focused specifically on North American scholarship's interest in the CA for studying the historical Jesus. Stephen Patterson (Willamette University), who has worked extensively with the *Gospel of Thomas* and is known for his position on the text being an early repository of teachings of Jesus, provided a re-evaluation of work in this area, including his own previously-stated arguments. His presentation opened on a surprisingly skeptical note with the declaration that "the apocryphal gospels have had virtually no impact on the historical study of Jesus in North America," and adding later, "or on any other continent for that matter" (p. 176 in the completed paper). The Synoptic Jesus, he said, is still the focus of historical Jesus work. Nevertheless, Patterson spent the rest of his time making a case for a cluster of sayings of Jesus from the *Gospel of Thomas* that were not accepted by the Jesus Seminar: the sayings about primordial androgyny (e.g., log. 22, "When you make the two one. . ."). He remarked that scholars tend to dismiss the apocryphal gospels as "more speculative, mystical, ascetical, enigmatic, or just downright confusing" and asks "should this necessarily disqualify them completely from

---

34. See Davila, *Provenance of the Pseudepigrapha*.

the discussion?" (p. 178). In the end, Patterson advocated casting our nets wide when examining the historical Jesus, stating, "The question is not, after all, which of the gospels best represents the historical Jesus. The question for critical scholarship is how to imagine an historical figure from which could emanate all of the various traditions and interpretations that appear in the first century or so of nascent Christian development" (p. 185). Patterson's paper was followed by two responses (included in this volume), one from John Kloppenborg (University of Toronto), known particularly for his work on Q, and Mark Goodacre (Duke University), who has recently joined CA scholarship with his book *Thomas and the Gospels: The Case for Thomas's Familiarity with the Synoptics*.

Day one came to a close with a keynote address from Annette Yoshiko Reed (University of Pennsylvania). She titled her presentation, "The Afterlives of Christian Apocrypha." It touched on a range of topics, spanning from early scholarship on the texts to modern use of CA imagery in popular culture, particularly Manga (with examples from *Neon Genesis Evangelion* and others). Reed noted that the creators of Manga know little about Christianity and simply pluck from it whatever ideas they think useful for their stories. Only when Western distributors take issue with the content do the creators realize that they are using controversial apocryphal imagery. Reed's address, intended as an oral and visual presentation, is not included in this volume.

On day two of the Symposium we looked to the future. The first session featured several presentations by contributors to the anthology *New Testament Apocrypha: More Noncanonical Scriptures*, examining some little-known or under-appreciated texts and traditions. In the first presentation, F. Stanley Jones (California State University) investigated "The Distinctive Sayings of Jesus Shared by Justin and the Pseudo-Clementines." Jones contributed two pieces to the first *MNTA* volume: the Syriac epitome of the *Acts of Peter* and an Aramaic fragment of the *Toledot Yeshu*, neither of which had appeared earlier in English translation. The goal for the second volume is to include a translation of the entire *Pseudo-Clementines* corpus, since the currently-available English translation is now almost 150 years old. As for Jones's paper, it presents an argument against the view that the shared sayings derive from a gospel harmony; instead, Jones argues, the Basic Writer of the *Pseudo-Clementines* seems to have pulled them from Justin's lost work *Syntagma*, which Justin wrote to refute Marcion. The sayings thus have a distinct Marcionite or anti-Marcionite flavour. Jones was followed by Stephen Shoemaker (University of Oregon), presenting on "The *Tiburtine Sibyl*, the Last Emperor, and the Byzantine Apocalyptic Tradition." Shoemaker's paper draws on his translation of the *Tiburtine Sibyl* prepared for *MNTA*; he also has contributed a new translation of the *Apocalypse of the Virgin* to the volume. For many people in the room, Shoemaker's paper was their first exposure to this text, though it was widely popular in the Middle Ages and deeply influenced medieval culture (Shoemaker says it was "more influential on medieval eschatology than the canonical Apocalypse," p. 221). Nevertheless, the *Tiburtine Sibyl* is rarely included in CA collections (Erbetta's expansive collection is the exception), chiefly because it is a relatively recent composition (late fourth century). Shoemaker thus called the text, in his presentation, an example of "noncanonical apocrypha," and cautioned listeners to his presentation to be careful of allowing the CA collections to limit study to the standard texts. An important feature of the *Tiburtine Sibyl* is its description of the Last Emperor, a figure identified with Constantine who, the Sibyl says, will "devastate all the islands and cities of the pagans and destroy all the temples of idols" (*Tib. Sib.* 10). Shoemaker argues that the Sibyl's description of this figure may have influenced early Islamic eschatology.

The final two papers of the session were "Backstories of the Bandits: The Emergence, Submersion and Re-emergence of the Cult of Dysmas" by Mark Bilby (University of San Diego) and David Eastman's (Ohio Wesleyan University) "Confused Traditions? Peter and Paul in the Apocryphal Acts." Bilby, like Shoemaker, brought attention to a little-studied apocryphon, though this one is not a complete text but an "orphan story" with versions appearing in a variety of sources, including manuscripts of the *Gospel of Pseudo-Matthew* and the *Gospel of Nicodemus*. Orphan stories tend to be neglected because they are considered late additions to the texts; sometimes these additions appear in notes to editions or translations, but are otherwise rarely given much attention (though this may change with Bilby's contribution on the traditions to *MNTA*). Bilby demonstrated how widespread were these stories of the Good Thief and how important they are to medieval piety. Unfortunately, Bilby's paper could not be finished in time for inclusion in the volume. For his presentation, Eastman similarly juggled a wide assortment of texts to show how depictions of Peter and Paul tend to blend in later apocryphal acts, as well as in the *Toledot Yeshu* and iconography. Eastman is working on his own collection of these later acts, none of which have been translated into English. For *MNTA*, Eastman has contributed a new translation of the *Epistle of Pseudo-Dionysius the Areopagite to Timothy*, which features a story of Peter and Paul's martyrdoms, and a new translation of the *Acts of Xanthippe and Polyxena*. Among the interesting features of the blended stories of Paul and Peter is the tendency to place words of Paul in Peter's mouth; curiously, Eastman finds no case in the apocryphal texts of Peter where Peter quotes 1 or 2 Peter.

The afternoon session of day two considered new approaches to studying apocryphal texts. Kristian Heal (Brigham Young University) guided the audience through new research tools used in his efforts to create a critical edition and translation of the Syriac *History of Joseph*. His presentation, "Digital Humanities and the Textual Critic: Resources, Prospects and Problems," focused on tools for studying Syriac texts, but his handout (included here as an appendix to the completed paper) included a wider list of resources. The completed paper presents these resources in a text-editing travelogue similar to François Bovon's article "Editing the Apocryphal Acts," which details his efforts to find and edit Greek manuscripts of the *Acts of Philip*. Heal was followed by Mary Dzon (University of Tennessee) who discussed *incunabula* for her paper "'All the (Good) News That's Fit to Print?' Early Printings of Apocryphal Texts." *Incunabula* are rarely brought into research on the transmission of CA, yet several important texts (including the *Protevangelium of James* and the *Gospel of Nicodemus*) were first published as *incunabula* and, in some cases, these early printed books drew upon manuscripts that are no longer available. Dzon focused on early printings of the *Gospel of Pseudo-Matthew*, some of which contain stories of Jesus' childhood that have not previously appeared in scholarship. Unfortunately, Dzon's paper could not be finished in time for inclusion in the volume.

Glenn Snyder's (Indiana University-Purdue University Indianapolis) presentation, "The Conversion of Paul: The Production of a Model," reconsidered the direction of dependence of the *Acts of Paul* and the canonical Acts by focusing on one specific tradition: Paul's conversion. The *Acts of Paul* is particularly suited for such an approach as it is much debated whether an "*Acts of Paul*" ever truly existed as a complete text rather than as several separate stories. The audience raised objections to some of Snyder's conclusions, however; and there was an audible gasp when Snyder declared Galatians un-Pauline. The completed paper allows for a more careful evaluation of Snyder's detailed form-critical work; it is eye-opening to read the conversion stories this way, particularly if one considers Acts 9:10b–11, 17–18a (the story of Ananias) as a story separate from Acts 9:1–10a, as it brings attention to some of the episode's curious features, such as the house of Judas on Straight Street and the construction of Paul's name, translated by Snyder as "a stumbling man by the name Tarseus" (p. 293). Finally, the session came to a close with "Ordinary or Extraordinary? The Reception of the *Protevangelium of James* in the *History of the Blessed Virgin Mary*" by Lily Vuong (Valdosta State University). What makes this paper a "new approach" is Vuong's interest in the *History of the Blessed Virgin Mary*, a late reworking of the *Protevangelium of James* and other infancy traditions in Syriac known more widely in its further translation into the *Arabic Infancy*

Gospel. To her surprise (and everyone else's) Vuong found that *Hist. Virg.* tends to diminish Mary's special qualities, not enhance them as one might expect. Audience reaction to Vuong's paper was mixed; there was praise for bringing this development in Marian piety to our attention, but concerns were raised over her early dating of *Hist. Virg.* (fourth century, but eighth century is more likely) and her understanding of the complexities of the manuscript evidence. Vuong decided to continue working on the project, but it was not completed in time for inclusion in the volume.

The symposium finished with a session entitled "Christian Apocrypha in North America: Where Do We Go From Here?" The goal of this session was to consider new collaborative endeavours, including outreach projects, future gatherings, and publishing ventures. The most dramatic outcome of the session was the decision to form a new academic association dedicated to the study of the CA—a North American counterpart, of sorts, to the AELAC. After the conclusion of the Symposium, a board of directors was formed and a meeting took place in November 2014 to consider the group's mandate and to give the group a name: the North American Society for the Study of Christian Apocryphal Literature (NASSCAL). For news and information on the group visit its web site at NASSCAL.com.

It would appear from the success of the 2013 Symposium that the state of North American CA Studies is strong. There is much more variety in our scholarship than critics' assessments and popular culture representations indicate; its debt to the Bauer Hypothesis and its pursuit of the historical Jesus cannot be denied, but it also has more affinities with European approaches than has been acknowledged and this European connection continues to gain strength. The traditional centers for CA Studies—Harvard, Claremont, and Laval—remain vital but new ones are emerging, including the University of Texas in Austin, the University of North Carolina at Chapel Hill, the University of Ottawa, the University of Toronto, and York University. North America is also growing as a center for Digital Humanities research with such projects as the Hill Museum and Manuscript Library, and Coptic Scriptorium, created by Carolin Schroeder (University of the Pacific) and Amir Zeldes (Georgetown University). And new opportunities for collaboration are emerging through the *More New Testament Apocrypha* volumes, the York Christian Apocrypha Symposium, and NASSCAL. North American CA Studies is no one-trick pony. The 2013 York Christian Apocrypha Symposium Proceedings is a celebration of our accomplishments and an indicator of greater things ahead.

— 2 —

North American Approaches to the Study of the Christian Apocrypha on the World Stage

— Jean-Michel Roessli[1] —

TONY BURKE AND BRENT LANDAU kindly invited me to express my views on the North American approaches to the study of the Christian Apocrypha on the world stage, a challenging task that I imprudently accepted, even though I am not an expert on American scholarship and rather new in North America, having arrived in Canada, through Sudbury, Northern Ontario, only in August 2007. Moreover, I am not a member of the SBL Christian Apocrypha Section or of any North American Association of that type—at least not yet. Thus, I do not feel fully qualified to address this topic as an insider or a practitioner; what I can do, however, is offer an informed outsider's perspective on the recent trends in North American scholarship. In so doing, I will indicate some of the strengths and weaknesses of North American approaches and make a few suggestions about possible avenues and topics for further research.

---

1. I wish to thank warmly Dr. Tony Burke and Dr. Brent Landau for inviting me to this Symposium. My gratitude also goes to Dr. Tony Burke, Dr. Zbigniew Izydorczyk, and Hereward Senior for correcting and greatly improving the English of this text, and to Matthew Anderson, Anne-Catherine Baudoin, Alain Desreumaux, Jean-Daniel Dubois, Alain Le Boulluec, and Pierluigi Piovanelli for their generous comments on earlier drafts of this paper. All errors that may remain are mine.

TENDENCIES IN NORTH AMERICAN SCHOLARSHIP ON CHRISTIAN APOCRYPHA

In North America, as in Europe, interest in apocryphal literature is not new. It has enjoyed a considerable revival in North America since at least the first decades of the twentieth century. However, too often this interest has expressed itself through a strong tendency to read apocryphal literature through a biblical lens. To put it differently, North American scholarship has been frequently motivated by a desire to compare apocryphal with the canonical writings, assuming a necessary dependence of the noncanonical upon the canonical and trying to establish points of contact between them. The more-or-less conscious presupposition has been that noncanonical texts derived from the biblical ones, and this assumption can be seen in the continued use of phrases like "Apocrypha of the New Testament" or "Pseudepigrapha of the Old Testament," terms that were coined by Johann Albert Fabricius (1668–1736) in the early eighteenth century.[2] Although still occasionally employed today, these labels have now been seriously challenged and alternative terms have been proposed, such as "Christian Apocrypha," or "Jewish Pseudepigrapha," or simply "Christian and Jewish Apocrypha." I will come back to this terminology below. In North America, especially in the United States, the assumption that apocryphal texts depend on the canonical is reflected in a long-standing restrictive focus on those apocryphal writings—mainly some apocryphal gospels—that were perceived as valid sources for recovering the historical Jesus. This is the case with the *Gospel of Peter*, the *Gospel of Thomas*, and a few other early writings of that kind.[3]

Although this biblical perspective was widespread in Europe as well as in North America for decades and even centuries, "a growing conviction" has emerged in more recent years "that this literature should not simply be set aside as secondary and derivative documents, wholly dependent on the canonical writings for any tradition or data they may contain."[4] Without

---

2. For a biography of Fabricius, see Petersen, *Intellectum liberare*; Petersen, "Learned Communication"; and Reed, "Modern Invention."

3. E.g., the *Dialogue of the Savior*, the *Apocryphon of James*, the *Gospel of Truth*. John Dominic Crossan, for example, believes some Christian Apocrypha to be invaluable in reconstructing the life and teachings of Jesus (see, e.g., Crossan, *Historical Jesus*) whereas John Paul Meier (*Marginal Jew*) judges that they are worthless in Jesus research. Recently, Robert E. Van Voorst, in his *Jesus Outside the New Testament*, deliberately discusses noncanonical sources about Jesus, but he does so in order to corroborate some of the NT traditions about Jesus. We could multiply examples of scholars who follow the same approach. See, however, Aune, *Jesus*, 182–206; cf. Baudoin, Review of Aune, *Jesus*.

4. Smith, "John and the Apocryphal Gospels," 156. Interestingly, Smith goes so far

pretending to trace the full history of North American scholarship on Christian Apocrypha, I would like to point out that as far back as the 1920s, Percival Gardner-Smith (1888–1985; a Biblical scholar somewhat forgotten today), "who was to espouse the cause of the independence of the Gospel of John, argued, for example, that the *Gospel of Peter* was not dependent on, or derivative from, the canonical Gospels."[5] More recently, in his *Introduction to the New Testament*—the English translation of *Einführung in das Neue Testament im Rahmen der Religionsgeschichte und Kulturgeschichte der hellenistischen und römischen Zeit*—Helmut Koester has shown no inclination to regard canonical gospels as antecedent to, or as the source of, the apocryphal ones. Indeed, to him, the opposite seems to be the case, especially as far as such documents as the *Gospel of Thomas* and the *Gospel of Peter* are concerned.[6] For his part, John Dominic Crossan, in D. Moody Smith's words, "has argued that the *Gospel of Thomas*, Egerton Papyrus 2, the *Secret Gospel of Mark*, and the *Gospel of Peter* are independent witnesses to the forms of early Christianity they represent, not to be explained on the basis of the canonical Gospels, as if they were derivative from them."[7] Thus, certain experts interested in this literature have worked hard to free the apocryphal writings from the "biblical concepts and categories that have heretofore dominated their study and interpretation."[8] It must be stressed, however, that trying to understand the relationship between the canonical and the apocryphal writings is perfectly legitimate, and there is nothing wrong with such an enterprise. We can certainly learn much from a comparative study of these texts. It is rather the tendency to dismiss the value of the apocryphal literature just because of its noncanonical status that is a problem, at least

---

as to suggest that "the Gospel of John may be labeled the 'first apocryphal gospel' in the sense that it intermittently preserves Jesus traditions independent of the Synoptics, in a way similar to the apocryphal gospels" (as summarized in Charlesworth, *Authentic Apocrypha*, 31).

5. Smith, "John and the Apocryphal Gospels," 156. For a comprehensive and recent study of the latter gospel, see Foster, *Gospel of Peter*; note that the name of the series in which the volume appears (Texts and Editions for New Testament Study) shows once again the direct connection to studies of the canonical Bible.

6. In the same year (1980), Koester published his article "Apocryphal and Canonical Gospels." See also the magisterial survey of canonical and early apocryphal texts by the same author, *Ancient Christian Gospels*, and Koester, "Epilogue."

7. Smith, "John and the Apocryphal Gospels," 156. On these various texts, see also Marguerat, Norelli, and Poffet, eds., *Jésus de Nazareth*. For English introductions to the field of apocryphal literature in general, see Foster, *Apocryphal Gospels*; Klauck (a German scholar teaching at the Divinity School of the University of Chicago), *Die apokryphe Bibel*; Klauck, *Apocryphal Gospels*; Klauck, *Apocryphal Acts*; and, of course, Burke, *Secret Scriptures Revealed*.

8. Shoemaker, "Early Christian Apocryphal Literature," 521.

on a scholarly level, in the same way that it would be problematic to overrate Christian Apocrypha with regard to the study of the canonical Bible just because of their outcast status.[9] In terms of literary history, all texts found inside the Bible as well as all those falling outside of it belong to the Christian tradition and are parts of the history of Christian literature; they should be treated in the same manner, differentiated only by their supposed date of composition, when it can be approximated. Their theological status is only secondary and belongs to their reception history. In this respect, the reactions that followed the publication of Dan Brown's novel *The Da Vinci Code*, and the responses from scholars of the Bible and of early Christianity to the work,[10] demonstrate that too much time and ink has been wasted in fierce polemics between those open to the study of Christian Apocrypha and those who apologetically deny their usefulness and/or sometimes even denounce them as dangerous to believers. Even though disagreements and controversies are part of the academic debate and may help to clarify each position, they may also prevent scholarly debates from moving forward, as the parties involved in the discussion remain entrenched and do not really listen to the arguments of the opposing sides. Although this tendency is not absent from the European stage, it is much more widespread in North America, and particularly in the United States, probably because more experts in the disciplines of Theological and Religious Studies are themselves so committed to their own faith and denomination that they are not willing or able to assume a critical distance from their religious or anti-religious commitments and are, therefore, deeply biased in their approaches to canonical and noncanonical writings.

Consequently, although it is legitimate and tempting to scrutinize the relationship between canonical and noncanonical writings, it seems also important to study the apocryphal writings for themselves and understand them in their own way as texts produced and/or used by people or communities who sincerely believed they were relevant. In this respect, this literature probably teaches us more about those who produced it than about the historical Jesus or the Jesus movement itself.

9. Although his distinction between "false and genuine Christian Apocrypha" in his *Authentic Apocrypha* is disputable, in my view James H. Charlesworth is right when he writes: "It is inconsistent of New Testament specialists to relegate the New Testament Apocrypha and Pseudepigrapha to the status of discarded books because they are shaped by legends and myths, and then at the same time revere Matthew's use of legends and myths in his Infancy Gospel" (xi); and "It is a pity that the New Testament Apocrypha and Pseudepigrapha do not receive the attention they deserve in theological and academic circles and in theological and university curricular offerings" (29). See further comments below.

10. See the excellent survey offered by Burke, "Heresy Hunting."

Having said this, I must confess that I, too, in a paper on the Passion Narrative in the *Sibylline Oracles*,[11] deliberately engaged in comparing the way Jesus' Passion is recounted in these third-century apocryphal texts with the canonical Gospels, as well as with some other noncanonical writings (mostly the *Gospel of Peter*). Yet, even though I made this comparison with the assumption—in this case fully legitimate—that the Passion Narrative in the *Sibylline Oracles* relies heavily on the canonical Passion Narrative, I also tried to identify what is specific to the authors of the *Sibylline Oracles* and what makes them unique in our understanding of early Christian beliefs about the Passion of Jesus. Even the 2014 collection of essays I edited with Tobias Nicklas betrays in its very title—*Christian Apocrypha: Receptions of the New Testament in Ancient Christian Apocrypha*[12]—this tendency to look at the Christian Apocrypha through a biblical lens; however, this approach is only one among many possible approaches to adopt in the scholarship, and we do hope that readers will also find there texts that are both interesting and instructive.

THE PLACE OF NORTH AMERICAN SCHOLARSHIP IN THE HISTORY OF RESEARCH ON CHRISTIAN APOCRYPHA

In a 1988 paper titled "Research on the New Testament Apocrypha and Pseudepigrapha" and revised ten years later as *Authentic Apocrypha: False and Genuine Christian Apocrypha*,[13] James H. Charlesworth provides a short overview of previous research in the field and proposes to distinguish four phases of interest in the history of scholarship in what he calls New Testament Apocrypha and Pseudepigrapha.

In Charlesworth's opinion, the first of these phases began sometime in the Middle Ages and culminated in the publication of Johann Fabricius's monumental *Codex Apocryphus Novi Testamenti* (published in three volumes between 1703 and 1719). Without going into much detail here, we can say that research on the early modern reception of Christian Apocrypha

---

11. Roessli, "Passion Narrative."

12. Roessli and Nicklas, eds., *Christian Apocrypha*, with contributions by Tony Burke, André Gagné, et al.

13. Charlesworth, "Research," revised in Charlesworth, *Authentic Apocrypha*. The bibliography included in "Research" is a condensed version of the one published the year before (together with James R. Mueller), *New Testament Apocrypha and Pseudepigrapha*; for an assessment, see Elliott, Review of Charlesworth and Mueller, *New Testament Apocrypha and Pseudepigrapha*.

conducted by Irena Backus,[14] Anthony Grafton,[15] and Jean-Louis Quantin,[16] among others, as well as my own still ongoing and, therefore, still unpublished research on the reception of the *Sibylline Oracles*,[17] prove the situation to have been much more complicated. A variety of sub-phases in and motivations for the interest in Christian and Jewish apocrypha can be distinguished during the first phase identified by Charlesworth, not to mention the unacknowledged complexity of approaches to apocryphal texts during the Middle Ages.[18]

Charlesworth's second phase basically encompasses the nineteenth century, a time characterized "by the rise of rationalism, the pervasive critique of traditions, and the search for knowledge according to post-Enlightenment and post-Kantian mood [...]; hence faith in the reliability of apocryphal writings declined."[19] Among the numerous hallmarks of that period, Charlesworth rightly singles out as most significant: Jacques-Paul Migne's *Dictionnaire des Apocryphes, ou Collection de tous les livres apocryphes* (1856–1858), Constantin Tischendorf's *Acta Apostolorum Apocrypha* (1851), *Evangelia Apocrypha* (1853), and *Apocalypses Apocryphae* (1866); as well as Alfred Resch's four-volume *Aussercanonische Paralleltexte zu den Evangelien* (1893–1896), to which could be added also Resch's *Agrapha: Aussercanonische Schriftfragmente* (1906).[20]

The third phase of interest in apocryphal writings began, in Charlesworth's view, toward the end of the nineteenth and the beginning of the twentieth century with the discovery of the Oxyrhynchus papyri, which reawakened "a keen interest in the lost gospels and 'forgotten' sayings of Jesus,"[21] an interest made popular by several scholars, especially Joachim

14. Backus, "Renaissance Attitudes"; Backus, "Les apocryphes néo-testamentaires"; Backus, *Historical Method*; "Early Christianity"; Backus, "Jacques Lefèvre d'Etaples."

15. See, for example, Grafton, "Higher Criticism."

16. See, for example, Quantin, "Dodwell, Mill, Grabe."

17. For a short presentation of my project, see http://www.frqsc.gouv.qc.ca/upload/editeur/resume_Roessli.pdf.

18. On the Christian Apocrypha in the Middle Ages, see Gounelle, "Sens et usage d'*apocryphus*"; Rose, "Medieval Memories"; and Rose, *Ritual Memory*, esp. 42–78.

19. Charlesworth, *Authentic Apocrypha*, 38.

20. On this, see now Pesce, *Le parole dimenticate di Gesù*.

21. Charlesworth, *Authentic Apocrypha*, 39. In endnote 58, Charlesworth adds that "the new tendency, foreshadowed in Resch's books, breaks into the open in four publications by B. P. Grenfell and A.S. Hunt, namely *Sayings of Our Lord from an Early Greek Papyrus* (London, 1897), *New Sayings of Jesus and Fragment of a Lost Gospel from Oxyrhynchus* (with L.W. Drexel, London, 1897, repr. 1904), *Fragment of an Uncanonical Gospel from Oxyrhynchus* (Oxford, 1908), and *The Oxyrhynchus Papyri* (6 vols., London, 1908)."

Jeremias in his *Unbekannte Jesusworte*, printed at least three times in a quarter of a century (from 1948 to 1963) and translated into English in 1957.[22]

Without giving much explanation, Charlesworth places the beginning of the last and fourth phase of interest in the Christian Apocrypha in 1965. This date approximately coincides with the completion of the third edition of Edgar Hennecke and Wilhelm Schneemelcher's *Neutestamentliche Apokryphen* in two volumes (1959 and 1964) and, above all, with their English translation in 1963–1965.[23] In Charlesworth's view, this phase "is marked by a tendency to evaluate the texts critically as evidence (alongside the canonical gospels) for early forms of Christianity."[24] Yet, as Tony Burke rightly states,

> Charlesworth's identification of the fourth, and arguably still ongoing, phase of CA [i.e., Christian Apocrypha] research is undisputedly generalized—not all scholars view the CA as valuable texts for the study of early Christianity. The past few years in particular have seen a backlash from conservative scholars over the efficacy of using these texts to reconstruct early Christian history, particularly for recovering the life and teachings of Jesus.[25]

Moreover, as already emphasized above, Christian Apocrypha should not be read and used only "for recovering the life and teachings of Jesus." They deserve a better treatment, along with other products of early Christianity, whatever their canonical status. One of the major problems in Charlesworth's approach is his distinction between what he calls "authentic Apocrypha" and "forgeries," such as the *Letter of Lentulus* (or the *Secret Gospel of Mark*). I do not see how such a distinction can be defended. I do not see why the *Gospel of Nicodemus*, to take another example, could be considered as an authentic apocryphon and the *Letter of Lentulus* not. Outside of their content, the only difference between the latter, regarded as false, and the former, deemed genuine, is temporal, as Piovanelli and Burke have pointed out.[26] The only reason why Charlesworth takes the *Letter of Lentulus* for a

---

22. On this, see also Bauckham, "Study of Gospel Traditions."

23. Hennecke and Schneemelcher, eds., *New Testament Apocrypha*. It must be added that a fifth edition of *Neutestamentliche Apokryphen*, published this time under only the name of Wilhelm Schneemelcher, also was translated into English, after a sixth revised edition, in 1991–1992.

24. As summarized in Burke, "Entering the Mainstream," 19.

25. Ibid., 20.

26. On all this, I concur with Burke, "Entering the Mainstream," 21–22, citing also Piovanelli, "What Is a Christian Apocryphal Text?," 33–34; Piovanelli, "Qu'est-ce qu'un 'écrit apocryphe chrétien'?," 179–81.

false apocryphon is its late date of composition (the late Middle Ages), but this is not a valid argument, as the production of apocryphal texts never really came to an end. The most we are entitled to is to distinguish between ancient, medieval, modern, and even contemporary apocrypha. And should we deem that the *Secret Gospel of Mark* is a scholarly forgery by Morton Smith or an early modern humanist,[27] it could not be equated with the *Letter of Lentulus*, since the purpose of these two texts was completely different.

Recently, Paul-Hubert Poirier came back to the topic in a paper entitled "Vers une redéfinition du champ apocryphe: Aperçus de la recherche récente consacrée aux apocryphes," delivered at a conference of the ACÉBAC (Association catholique pour l'étude de la Bible au Canada)—the French-speaking counterpart of the CSBS (Canadian Society of Biblical Studies)—that was held in 2008 at Châteauguay, near Montreal, and published four years later.[28] Unlike Charlesworth, the Quebec scholar focuses mostly on the twentieth century and distinguishes two main phases in the study of apocryphal literature: prior to the 1970s and thereafter. According to Poirier, a kind of "Copernician" revolution occurred in the late 70s with the foundation of the AELAC (Association pour l'étude de la littérature apocryphe chrétienne)[29] and the renewed debate among scholars about this literature, the ways to define it, and the kinds of materials it is supposed to encompass.

So even though the revival of interest in Christian Apocrypha in North America is not new, it is obvious that for a few decades now this revival has taken on a much stronger tone than it had in the twentieth century. This is largely due to the passion and efforts of a handful of young active scholars in Early Judaism and Early Christianity, who chose to dedicate their doctoral research to early Christian texts not included in the biblical canon and who then continued to work on this literature once their PhDs were submitted. This is the case of our colleagues Tony Burke and Brent Landau, who organized this symposium and are possibly launching a new and promising trend in our field in North America. Burke is not only the author of the now-standard scholarly work on the *Infancy Gospel of Thomas*,[30] but he has also been very active in stimulating and disseminating discussions about

27. On this apocryphon, see the proceedings of the 2011 York Christian Apocrypha Symposium by Tony Burke, *Ancient Gospel or Modern Forgery?*; cf. Burnet, Review of Burke, *Ancient Gospel or Modern Forgery?*; and Miceli, "Account."

28. Poirier, "Vers une redéfinition."

29. See the brief historical account of the AELAC attached to this paper. Readers may also find updated information about the projects of this association on its website: www.aelac.org.

30. Burke, *De infantia Iesu*; cf. Andrist, Review of Burke, *De infantia Iesu*.

the Christian Apocrypha with his blog Apocryphicity, in organizing the York Symposium Series, as well as in providing English-speaking readers with an introduction to apocryphal literature: *Secret Scriptures Revealed. A New Introduction to the Christian Apocrypha* (2013). Landau, for his part, wrote his dissertation on a fascinating but little-known text: the *Revelation of the Magi*.[31] He published a book on the same text aimed at a broader audience in 2010,[32] and also contributed articles on other topics related to apocryphal literature.

Addressing North American scholarship on Christian Apocrypha, one must not forget the research of North American scholars in the field of Gnostic Studies. Most important in this respect are the contributions of the Claremont School of Theology, as well as the ongoing publication of the Coptic Library of Nag Hammadi (Bibliothèque copte de Nag Hammadi, BCNH), founded by a team of French Quebec scholars at Laval University.[33] In contrast to what some people think, the border between the study of gnostic and apocryphal texts is not clear, mostly because what these words refer to also is not clear, and, though not all apocryphal texts pertain to the "gnostic mindset or worldview," gnostic literature as a whole is certainly to be counted as part of the apocryphal "continent."[34] Therefore, the two areas of research should not be as sharply differentiated as they often are today. Fortunately, some scholars try to build bridges between these two fields of expertise: Jean-Daniel Dubois in France with his *Jésus apocryphe*,[35] Christoph Markschies and Jens Schröter in the seventh and latest edition of Hennecke-Schneemelcher[36] in Germany, or Nicola Denzey Lewis[37] and Philip Tite[38] in North America, to name just a few prominent scholars. But too many other scholars still tend to keep the two fields separate and do not encourage collaboration or dialogue.

---

31. Landau, "Sages and the Star-Child." The same year Landau published an article in *Apocrypha* based on his doctoral work, "Revelation of the Magi." More recently, he published "'One Drop of Salvation.'"

32. Landau, *Revelation of the Magi*. See also the reviews by Evans, Heal, and Reed.

33. See http://www.naghammadi.org/.

34. Expression borrowed from Picard, *Le continent apocryphe*.

35. Dubois, *Jésus apocryphe*.

36. Markschies and Schröter, eds., *Antike christliche Apokryphen*; cf. reviews by Böttrich, Heath, and Elliott, "The 'New' Hennecke."

37. See her paper in this volume and also Denzey Lewis, *Introduction to "Gnosticism"*; cf. van den Kerchove, Review of Denzey Lewis, *Introduction to "Gnosticism."*

38. See, in particular, Tite, *Valentinian Ethics*; and Tite, *Apocryphal Epistle to the Laodiceans*.

Finally, any discussion of North American scholarship on Christian Apocrypha should also mention the work of North American francophone scholars, or better: francophone scholars established in North America (particularly all those scholars working in Canada, and in the province of Quebec in particular). Among the most recent collection of essays on Christian and Jewish Apocrypha, I can mention *En marge du canon: études sur les écrits apocryphes juifs et chrétiens* edited by André Gagné and Jean-François Racine, published in 2012. Two of the nine contributions included in that volume have a more general character and are intended to offer a kind of survey of the field of apocryphal literature. The aforementioned essay by Paul-Hubert Poirier, "Vers une redéfinition du champ apocryphe" is perhaps the most relevant to the topic at hand. The other contributions deal with more specific subject matters pertaining to apocryphal texts.[39]

NORTH AMERICAN AND EUROPEAN APPROACHES TO THE STUDY OF APOCRYPHAL LITERATURE

To characterize roughly the main trends in North American and European approaches to the study of the apocryphal literature, I must first point out that a shift has occurred between the older and the younger generations of scholars on both sides of the ocean. Generally speaking, the founding scholars of the AELAC, the international Association for the Study of Christian Apocryphal Literature, were primarily interested in tracing the often very complex transmission history of the texts under study, trying to identify, collect and classify manuscripts in order to reconstruct the best possible text and to produce the best critical edition—considered to be the necessary starting point for a careful philological, literary, and religious or theological analysis. The North American scholars working on apocryphal literature during the same period seem to have been more interested in using these texts as documents to reconstruct the social environment of early

---

39. Gagné and Racine, eds., *En marge du canon*. Table of Contents: André Gagné and Jean-François Racine, "Avant-propos" (7–11); Jean-François Racine, "Écrits canoniques et écrits apocryphes: un couple bien assorti" (13–31); Jean-Pierre Michaud, "Jésus de l'histoire et écrits apocryphes chrétiens" (33–84); Poirier, "Vers une redéfinition"; Pierre Cardinal, "Le cours du temps selon l'Apocalypse syriaque de Daniel. Essai de compréhension fondée sur la structure du texte" (121–57); Roessli, "Le récit de la Passion"; Serge Cazelais, "L'Évangile de Judas cinq ans après sa (re)découverte. Mise à jour et perspectives" (201–24); André Gagné, "Lire un apocryphe en synchronie. Analyse structurelle et intratextuelle du *logion* 22 de l'Évangile selon Thomas" (225–49); Pierluigi Piovanelli, "L'Enoch Seminar. Quelques considérations rétrospectives et prospectives de la part d'un 'vétéran'" (251–78). For some reviews of the book, see, e.g., Gounelle, Junod, Létourneau, and Naïmi.

Christianity. Interestingly, the current generation of North American scholars, while still eager to reconstruct the social contexts that produced this literature, now seems to share also the concerns of the first generation of European members of the AELAC and is placing more emphasis on the preliminary philological work on the apocryphal texts. The same can be said, I think, about the attention given to the relationship between the Christian Apocrypha and Greco-Roman literature of classical and late antiquity. This is an area of research pursued mostly by European scholars trained in the humanities, and it is, if I am not mistaken, only more recently that North American scholars decided to explore this avenue of research. In contrast, European scholars of the former generation, and sometimes even of the current one, are rather slow, if not reluctant, to embrace gender studies and feminist approaches to the Christian Apocrypha. The German scholars are an exception, and their work was so inspirational in North America that some of them moved here to disseminate their ideas and to work in a more open environment. What is revealed here is a huge cultural gap between a large part of the European scholarship and that of North America, a gap that goes far beyond the field of apocryphal literature and has other causes and implications that cannot be addressed in this paper.[40]

So with all the caveats and acknowledgements of the diversity of scholarly profiles, training, and intellectual horizons, one can hazard the opinion that the European approach to apocryphal literature seems to have given preference, at least in its first stage, to the methods of the humanities, that is to say, to textual and artefactual analysis, whereas the North American approach of the same period seems to have prioritized the methods and tools of the social sciences, such as social-scientific models or quantitative analysis. Of course, the two approaches do not and/or should not exclude each other; on the contrary, they are clearly complementary. Both approaches can and should be combined. For this reason North American and European scholars have much to gain from closer collaboration.

A glance at the list of publications of the AELAC, available on the website of the association, reveals that the main purpose of this association has been: 1) to prepare volumes for the Series Apocryphorum, intended for specialists and 2) to disseminate this literature to a broader audience through the Pléiade volumes and the paperback series, La collection de poche Apocryphes (nicknamed the "red series"), whose editorial board I have been coordinating since 2010.[41] In this respect, I would like to take

40. Numerous are the examples of good gender studies applied to Christian Apocrypha, e.g., Brock, "Genre of the Acts of Paul."

41. The first volume of the series in English has just been published: Jones, *Syriac Pseudo-Clementines*. Other English volumes are in preparation. I also draw the attention

the opportunity to correct a misunderstanding surrounding the Pléiade volumes.[42] Although the two sumptuous volumes of the Pléiade, with their 2000 pages printed on "Bible paper" might give the impression of a "counter-Bible," that impression is misleading. The reason why the AELAC and its collaborators decided to publish selected Christian Apocrypha in this series is that, beyond the prestige attached to the name of the French publisher Gallimard in general and to its Pléiade series in particular, the Pléiade is entirely dedicated to what can be called "world literature." Indeed, the series includes French translations and occasionally bilingual editions of masterpieces of literary works from all over the world. So publishing apocryphal Christian writings in the Pléiade series—after the publication of *The Bible: The Écrits interestamentaires*,[43] including some texts from Qumran and a sample of the so-called Pseudepigrapha of the Old Testament,[44] and before the publication of the *Écrits gnostiques*[45]—merely means that apocryphal writings belong to the treasury of world literature and are, therefore, as worth reading as any other piece of literature.[46] In this regard, if contemporary North American interest in apocryphal literature has peaked after the publication of Dan Brown's best-selling novel *The Da Vinci Code* and best-selling scholarly books like Bart D. Ehrman's *Lost Christianities* or *Lost Scriptures*, in French-speaking Europe this awakening of interest was sparked, above all, by the publication of the *Écrits apocryphes chrétiens*, particularly the first volume,[47] with the translation of Dan Brown's novel helping to keep it in focus.

If we compare the AELAC list with the project of the North American series about to be launched by Tony Burke and Brent Landau, *New Testament Apocrypha: More Noncanonical Scriptures*, it appears that the main goal of the latter is to complement the repertory of apocryphal texts

---

of North American readers to the Studies on Early Christian Apocrypha series, edited by Jan Bremmer at Peeters, Leuven (10 volumes published so far). The titles are listed in Burke, "Entering the Mainstream," 26 n. 31.

42. *Écrits apocryphes chrétiens*, vol. 1 (eds. Bovon and Geoltrain), vol. 2 (eds. Geoltrain and Kaestli).

43. *La Bible. L'Ancien Testament*, trans. Dhorme, Guillaumont, and Michaéli; *La Bible. Le Nouveau Testament*, trans. Gros, Grosjean, and Léturmy.

44. Dupont-Sommer and Philonenko, eds., *La Bible. Écrits intertestamentaires*.

45. Mahé and Poirier, eds., *Écrits gnostiques*.

46. Poirier, "Vers une redéfinition," 101.

47. The number of volumes sold thus far goes beyond 30,000. It might seem very little in comparison with *The Da Vinci Code* or even with Erhman's books, but given the cost of these volumes and the rather highly-educated target-audience, as well as the critical mass of people reading French, it is an impressive number and rather unexpected from the editors and publishers.

already available in English and other modern languages with translations of a variety of neglected, little-known, forgotten, sometimes marginal, or newly-discovered texts that await translation, publication, commentary, and study.[48] Personally, I welcome this new series, which will definitely fill a gap in scholarship, and I trust the volumes of this series will inspire further studies in North America as well as in Europe.[49]

Whatever differences can be identified between the European and North American approaches to the Christian Apocrypha, I would avoid contrasting them too sharply. First, some experts who contributed to the scholarship in apocryphal literature in North America came from Europe. They had a European background and training, but became rapidly influenced by the North American style of inquiry and changed, or at least broadened, their horizons in the North American intellectual climate. For instance, Helmut Koester, came from Germany to Harvard Divinity School in 1958 and became the world-renowned scholar we all know; similarly, the late François Bovon, a Swiss French scholar, was appointed at the same institution in 1993 and has been extraordinarily active in both the fields of New Testament and Christian Apocrypha Studies, mostly in the area of the apocryphal acts.[50] Another, younger example, is Pierluigi Piovanelli, a Canadian scholar of Italian origin, trained both in Italy and in France, who worked for years with scholars like Jean-Daniel Kaestli at the Biblical Institute of the University of Lausanne in Switzerland, where the AELAC project was first conceived as a collaboration of French and Swiss scholars. Piovanelli came to Ottawa in late 1999, and since then he has proudly represented Canadian scholarship in North America and worldwide. If I may, I would like to share an interesting anecdote about Piovanelli. In June 2003, just a few years after his arrival at Ottawa, Piovanelli was invited to give a paper at the annual meeting of the AELAC held in Dole, in the French

48. Readers may find updated information about this project, which mirrors Richard Bauckham's, James Davila's, and Alexander Panayatov's series *Old Testament Pseudepigrapha: More Noncanonical Scriptures*, at the following link: http://www.apocryphicity.ca/resources/more-christian-apocrypha/.

49. Burke and Landau have decided to keep the classical, but disputed, label "New Testament Apocrypha" for the series, in part to indicate its kinship to Bauckham, Davila, and Panayatov's More Old Testament Pseudepigrapha volumes. However, to show that they have integrated elements of the recent terminological debate, they have added a broader and more inclusive sub-title: "More Noncanonical Scriptures." Readers will decide what to think about this choice. In my view, there is still a tension, if not a small contradiction, in insisting on speaking of Christian Apocrypha and cataloguing them under the umbrella-term "New Testament Apocrypha."

50. For an example of scholarship combining the study of manuscripts, the context of their production, and the use of apocryphal texts, see Bovon et al., eds., *Apocryphal Acts of the Apostles*.

Jura. Piovanelli chose to deliver a paper entitled "What is a Christian Apocryphal Text and How Does it Work? Some Observations on Apocryphal Hermeneutics." I remember the surprise of the audience at the new perspective on apocryphal texts presented by Piovanelli. What he proposed then was nothing less than a redefinition or, more precisely, a broadening of the definition of what should be included under the umbrella-term "Christian Apocrypha." Basically, and without doing full justice to his paper, what can be said is that Piovanelli questioned, among other things, "the arbitrary time limitations imposed by traditional definitions, arguing that the scope of Christian Apocrypha should include late medieval and even modern texts, as the religious impulse behind such works is the same."[51] He "advocated widening the scope of the field . . . to embrace all Christian Apocrypha, including examples as recent as Mel Gibson's *The Passion of the Christ* and L. H. Dowling's *The Aquarian Gospel of Jesus the Christ*."[52] Some of the audience at Dole were puzzled and rather skeptical, others were intrigued by Piovanelli's insights about the Christian Apocrypha. I also remember how Piovanelli responded to objections regarding these new boundaries. I do not know if *he* remembers this, but he replied along these lines: "It might sound strange or difficult for the Europeans to accept, but it is already a commonplace in North America," which does not mean that Piovanelli had nothing new to contribute, but that what he said was already part of the *Zeitgeist* of North American scholarship. The paper delivered in Dole in 2003 was first published in English two years later in a Dutch journal and finally in French in 2006 in a volume in honour of Pierre Geoltrain,[53] one of the founding figures of the AELAC. Piovanelli would probably agree that an update is needed—he was then quite reticent, for example, to include *The Da Vinci Code* among the contemporary apocryphal writings. In my view, his paper demonstrates the strong and positive influence of the North American mindset on a European scholar working on apocryphal literature in North America. Personally, I would nevertheless make a distinction between apocrypha that take their roots in a deep religious quest and those apocrypha that just exploit a taste for exotic in religious literature.

Second, we must keep in mind that the AELAC, although founded in Geneva-Lausanne and Paris in 1981 by Europeans, such as François

---

51. As summarized by Shepherd, "Early Christian Apocrypha," 41–42.

52. As summarized by Burke, "Entering the Mainstream," 21.

53. Piovanelli, "What Is a Christian Apocryphal Text?"; Piovanelli, "Qu'est-ce qu'un 'écrit apocryphe chrétien'?"

Bovon (1938–2013),[54] Pierre Geoltrain (1929–2004), Jean-Daniel Dubois,[55] Jean-Claude Picard (1943–1996), Alain Desreumaux, Éric Junod, and Jean-Daniel Kaestli, and in close collaboration with Brepols and the Institut des Sources chrétiennes, was originally conceived of as an international association, even if it took some time for North American scholars to join it and become more actively involved in its scholarly work. Moreover, most people involved in Christian Apocrypha Studies in North America today—many of whom attended the 2013 York Symposium—are either members or correspondents of the AELAC (members being those scholars who have contributed or are in the process of creating a volume in the Series Apocryphorum of the Corpus Christianorum, published by Brepols at Turnhout, as is the case with Tony Burke, Brent Landau, Stephen Shoemaker, Pierluigi Piovanelli, myself, and others). In this sense, it is not exaggerated to say that the AELAC has been playing a hugely important role in federating scholars interested in apocryphal literature all over the world.

To sum up, the strength of North American scholarship in the field of apocryphal literature, and more broadly in Early Christian or even Medieval Studies, lies, in my opinion, in the freedom to challenge some of the most persistent views and, therefore, in the ability to raise new sets of questions and open new avenues of research. This was the case with the so-called "parting of the ways," challenged in different ways almost simultaneously by Annette Yoshiko Reed[56] and Daniel Boyarin,[57] whose work forced European and non-European scholars to respond or to reconsider and refine their own views. At the risk of falling into a *cliché*, I wonder if the freedom enjoyed by North American scholarship may have something to do with its shorter history and the lighter burden of tradition compared to Europe. I leave this question open. I must add, however, that too often contemporary North American and European scholars deem it their duty to be original and challenge older views at any cost, without necessarily taking serious account of earlier scholarship, as if bringing up something supposedly new was the answer to all questions. This is probably one of the unfortunate consequences of the pressure to publish, typical of the current academic world both in North America and in Europe.

---

54. See Bovon's announcement of the origins of the Series Apocryphorum in "Vers une nouvelle édition."

55. Dubois provides a second account, this time for English audiences: "New 'Series Apocryphorum.'"

56. Becker and Reed, eds., *Ways That Never Parted*.

57. Boyarin, *Border Lines*.

NORTH AMERICAN CONTRIBUTIONS TO CURRENT ISSUES IN THE FIELD

Defining "Apocrypha"

One of the most challenging issues pertaining to the field of apocryphal literature is to define the word "Apocrypha" and to determine exactly what the word encompasses. The term's meaning has evolved greatly over the course of time, in early Christianity as well as in early modernity—that is to say, during the Reformation and the Counter or Catholic Reformation—to the point that its meaning is often strongly coloured by the confessional commitment of its user. This word is so problematic that Willy Rordorf, a Protestant scholar and an expert in early Christian literature, in his discussion of the phrase "New Testament Apocrypha," went so far as to suggest "completely abandoning the word Apocrypha and the phrase 'New Testament Apocrypha' and replacing it with 'anonymous or pseudepigraphical, extra-biblical Christian literature.'"[58] His suggestion was not adopted, probably because it is not fully satisfactory, but also because Éric Junod, the main actor in the debate with Wilhelm Schneemelcher, "resigned himself to keeping the appellation 'Apocryphal' but eliminating 'New Testament' to form the new phrase 'Écrits apocryphes chrétiens' (Christian Apocryphal Writings)."[59] I must admit, however, that if Rordorf's term were not so vague and broad, I would advocate something very similar, for example, "extra-canonical writings." In this respect, I would like to draw attention to a fascinating collection of noncanonical writings about Jesus compiled by a German-American Lutheran minister and scholar active in the U.S. in the late nineteenth and early twentieth centuries: Bernhard Pick (1842–1917),

---

58. Burke, "Entering the Mainstream," 21, citing Rordorf, "Terra Incognita," 146.

59. Burke, "Entering the Mainstream," 21. The discussion began with Éric Junod, "Apocryphes du Nouveau Testament ou apocryphes chrétiens anciens?" The same year, François Bovon ("Vers une nouvelle édition") raised similar questions as his Swiss colleague Junod. It was followed by Schneemelcher's answer to Junod in the introduction to the fifth edition of *Neutestamentliche Apokryphen*, to which Junod replied in turn with his decisive "'Apocryphes du Nouveau Testament': une appellation erronée et une collection artificielle." Jean-Daniel Kaestli also contributed to the debate: "Les écrits apocryphes chrétiens," in *Le mystère apocryphe*. In the previous article in the same volume ("Le mystère apocryphe"), Junod provides further thoughts about this literature; see also Herrenschmidt and Schmidt, "Présentation," and, of course, Bovon and Geoltrain, "Introduction générale," in *Écrits apocryphes chrétiens*, 1:xvii–lviii. German scholars have addressed this difficult issue again and again: Markschies, "Neutestamentliche Apokryphen'"; Nicklas, "Semiotik—Intertextualität—Apokryphität"; Nicklas, "'Écrits apocryphes chrétiens'"; and, of course, very recently in the Haupteinleitung to Markschies and Schröter, eds., *Antike christliche Apokryphen*, 1–180.

author of *The Extra-Canonical Life of Christ, Being a Record of the Acts and Sayings of Jesus of Nazareth Drawn from Uninspired Sources* (1903). His work was preceded by an earlier attempt of a similar nature, *The Life of Jesus according to Extra-Canonical Sources* (1887), and followed by another: *Paralipomena: Remains of Gospels and Sayings of Christ* (1908). Given his translations of the five great apocryphal acts, *Apocryphal Acts of Paul, Peter, John, Andrew and Thomas* (1909),[60] Pick can be regarded as a true pioneer of North American scholarship on apocryphal literature.[61] He is also an early example of the seminal influence of European, and more particularly German, scholarship in North America. Pick's preface to *The Extra-Canonical Life of Christ*, written in November 1902, gives a sense of his views on apocryphal literature. Pick starts by saying: "I make no apology for bringing a work of this kind before the public, because it fills a gap in the Jesus-Literature."[62] This opening statement shows that it was no less an unusual endeavour to write about Christian Apocrypha in his time than it has been these past decades and even to some extent today. He then explains that "our aim is to present the life, work and sayings of Jesus as we find them in the words which the Church never recognized as her own, and which by way of contrast are called acanonical and apocryphal."[63] To my knowledge, Pick is the only scholar to use the adjective "acanonical," and he does so more than once in his work. Pick nicely concludes his short preface by saying: "The author's only wish is: *tolle, lege*,"[64] taking over the famous Augustinian motto coined to exhort the reading of the Bible (*Conf.* 8.12.29) and applying it to apocryphal or "acanonical" literature. Although he titled his collection

---

60. The preface to the volume illustrates the author's intentions in publishing such a book: ". . . the critical edition of the Apocryphal Acts by Lipsius and Bonnet, [in particular, has] opened a large, but very little cultivated field of ancient Christian literature. The oldest of these Acts are those which are treated in the present volume. They give us a picture of Christianity towards the end of the second century. They are important for the history of the Christian cultus in the second and third century, and by their description of the divine service in the houses they supplement of picture delineated in the Acts of the Apostles. They are also important for the history of Christian poetry which commences among the Gnostics; in short: though these Acts contain both 'truth and fiction,' they cannot be ignored by the teacher and preacher, the missionary and historian. What has hitherto been a *terra incognita* generally speaking, has now been made accessible, especially by the beautiful edition of Lipsius and Bonnet, whose text must now be considered as *textus receptus*" (Pick, *Extra-Canonical Life of Christ*, iii).

61. Along with a number of articles (including "History of the Printed Editions" and "Vowel Points Controversy"), Pick is known also for several books: *Cabala*; *Talmud: What It Is*; *Jesus in the Talmud*; and his collaborative work on the *Ante-Nicene Fathers*.

62. Pick, *Extra-Canonical Life of Christ*, 5.

63. Ibid., 6.

64. Ibid., 7.

of texts *The Extra-Canonical Life of Jesus*, Pick refers to these writings as the New Testament Apocrypha in his introduction and organizes his collection according to the literary genre of the New Testament (gospels, acts, epistles, and apocalypses), that has been common since Fabricius, and, above all, since the work of his successor Johann Carl Thilo (1794–1853).[65] Typical of the attitude of the biblical scholars of that time and of many of our own contemporaries, Pick agreed with Christopher Woodsworth, who wrote: "It may be observed once for all that these Apocryphal Books are of great value and interest as confirming the substance of the gospels, and also as showing by contrast what the Evangelical Narrative *would* in all probability *have been* if it had been left to human annalists, unassisted by the Spirit of God."[66]

Also worth mentioning in the context of North American scholarship on the Christian Apocrypha is the interesting and little-known contribution of Edgar Johnson Goodspeed (1871–1962), a Biblical scholar and a great collector of manuscripts of the New Testament, born in Quincy (Illinois) and professor at the University of Chicago in the first half of the twentieth century. Beside his translations of the Bible and of the so-called deuterocanonical writings of the Old Testament (called "Apocrypha" by Protestants), Goodspeed wrote on a few curious nineteenth-century writings he labeled apocrypha. In 1931 he published at the University of Chicago Press a small book titled *Strange New Gospels*, expanded as *Modern Apocrypha* in 1956,[67] in which he deals with such texts as the *Unknown Life of Jesus Christ*, the *Aquarian Gospel*, the *Letter of Benan*, the *Letter from Heaven*, the *Long-Lost Second Book of Acts*, and the *Nazarene Gospel*, of which not all are truly "modern apocrypha." Further investigation of these writings should be pursued.

The Notion of "Corpus" and "Collection"

One of the main problems we are facing in our field is the notion of "corpus" or even of "collection" of apocryphal texts, often used in the scholarship on this literature. Actually, there never was a "corpus" or a "collection" of apocryphal texts, which would have lain next to the Bible or as an independent

---

65. Thilo, *Codex apocryphus Novi Testamenti*.

66. Wordsworth, *Four Gospels*, note at Luke 2:28, quoted by Pick, *Extra-Canonical Life of Christ*, 18. Walter Bauer (1877–1960), a disciple of Adolf von Harnack (1851–1930), shared this approach in his *Leben Jesu im Zeitalter der Neutestamentlichen Apokryphen*, esp. vi–vii. *Histoire de l'Église du Christ* (1948–1965), by French writer and academician Daniel-Rops (1901–1965), reflects a similar attitude a few decades later.

67. Goodspeed, *Strange New Gospels*; Goodspeed, *Modern Apocrypha*.

unit beside it. Moreover, all combinations of apocrypha compiled by scholars over the last century differ from each other. With the exception of the Nag Hammadi library in early Christianity and of some apocryphal acts of the apostles, such as the legends known today as *Pseudo-Abdias* (see below), which were brought together to form a kind of collection in the Middle Ages, most apocryphal texts have had their own life, generally independent from other apocryphal texts. Therefore, there is something almost self-contradictory and absurd about speaking of a "corpus" or a "collection" in reference to texts that simply did not make it into the Christian Bible—that is to say, to texts that are not considered to be parts of a "canon." The texts or writings that do not make it into a "canon" do not need to constitute a corpus, as if to counterbalance the canon. Not making it into the Bible does not guarantee that the rejected texts form a kind of counter-corpus, a "counter-canon." This misconception has inevitable and possibly unfortunate consequences for the selection of texts assembled in volumes of Christian Apocrypha and for their reception. So instead of speaking of a "corpus" or even of a "collection" of apocryphal texts, and instead of twisting definitions in order to fit texts into a defined "corpus" or "collection," it would probably be more appropriate to use a word like "florilegium" or "anthology,"[68] commonly employed in literature in a more or less neutral way. One advantage such usage might give the compiler or editor is greater freedom in the choice of material to include, perhaps based on subjective grounds. As will be shown below, the first attempts to bring together texts that did not make it into the Bible did indeed resemble more "anthologies" or "florilegia" than "collections" or "corpora."

What is striking in the debate about constituting "collections" of texts under the umbrella-term "Apocrypha" or "Pseudepigrapha" is a tendency to accept the paradigm presented by Fabricius in his *Codices*—the *Codex apocryphus Novi Testamenti* and the *Codex pseudepigraphus Veteris Testamenti*, as well as in his *Bibliotheca Graeca*—as *the* objective historical framework, without always realizing all the consequences for our understanding of these texts. However important and significant Fabricius is in the history of scholarship (and he certainly is), it is remarkable that most specialists in early Judaism and early Christianity do not give equal attention to works of earlier learned humanists of the Renaissance era in order to see how scholars of generations prior to Fabricius dealt with this literature, which principles guided their selection, how they classified or organized the chosen texts, and so forth. Such a broader approach would help to better understand

---

68. See, however, the reflections of David Stern regarding the use of this term for any kind of texts compilation in his *Anthology in Jewish Literature* (quoted by Reed, "Modern Invention," 408).

Fabricius's own contributions and to see alternatives to his approach. For, although Fabricius's achievements surpass the work of his predecessors in many ways and come closer to the standards of contemporary scholarship—probably one of the reasons why he has been regarded as *the* historical point of reference for cataloguing apocryphal literature—Fabricius was still a man of his time, with his own presuppositions, and was one of several scholars who brought together texts not found in the Bible. Moreover, as his classification of noncanonical Christian texts was based, as is well known, on their alleged connection to or dependence on the canonical Bible (the Old and the New Testaments) and their distinctive literary genres (gospels, acts, epistles, and apocalypses), Fabricius has influenced the way of reading this material for more than two centuries. So why not try to look for alternatives? And alternatives do, in fact, exist. The interest in and need for such anthologies of texts can be traced back to the period before Fabricius, to the early Reformation, and even earlier. Thanks to the development of printing, their number increased rapidly from the middle of the sixteenth century onwards. Historians can benefit highly by examining them, not necessarily in order to imitate them, but to understand the principles on which they relied and compare them with the categories we are still often unconsciously using today. Let me provide two or three examples.

Anthologies of Extrabiblical Texts in Early Modernity

I would like to begin with an anthology of Christian texts assembled in 1557 by Michael Neander, a Lutheran theologian and great erudite of his time, expert in Greek, Latin and even familiar with Hebrew. This anthology was included in the Latin translation of Luther's *Shorter Catechism*, a work brilliantly studied by Irena Backus, an expert in the reception of the Church Fathers and Christian Apocrypha in early modernity and from whom I am borrowing the following explanation.[69] Although the first edition of Neander's *Catechism* does not contain the word "Apocrypha," his selection nevertheless includes apocryphal pieces, which resurface in the second and third editions of 1564 and 1567, both of which use the word "Apocrypha" in the title. In his translation of Luther's *Shorter Catechism*, Neander sought to highlight early Christian values using extrabiblical material found in the works of famous Greek authors, such as Flavius Josephus, Eusebius of Caesarea, Theodoret of Cyrrhus, and others, as well as in anonymous writings. A comparison between the three editions of the *Catechism* shows that the selection of extrabiblical texts considerably expanded over the course of

---

69. Backus, "Early Christianity."

time. In its 1557 edition, the anthology is limited to fifteen 'pious' excerpts. Of those, only two, the Abgar story taken from Eusebius (*Hist. eccl.* 1.13), and the acrostic poem *Jesus Christ, Son of God, Saviour, Cross*—quoted from chapter 18 of Constantine's *Speech to the Assembly of Saints* that forms part of Book 5 of Eusebius's *Life of Constantine* and not from a manuscript of the *Sibylline Oracles*—would be labelled Christian Apocrypha today. As for the other excerpts, two have a clear connection with the person of Christ: the article "Jesus" from the *Suda* (tenth century) and the so-called *Testimonium flavianum* from Flavius Josephus's *Jewish Antiquities*.[70]

As Backus points out, "the title page of the second edition indicates quite clearly that at some point between 1557 and 1563 (the date of the preface) Neander's focus had shifted from short sapiential, pagan and patristic pieces, to the historical and didactic value of what we call nowadays Christian Apocrypha. Moreover, he had developed a particular conception of what the term 'Apocrypha' should cover."[71] The title of Neander's second edition, reproduced here from the English translation provided by Backus, reads as follows:

> *The short Catechism of Martin Luther in Greek and Latin, newly revised. To it are added some selected sayings of the Fathers and also apocryphal accounts of Christ, Mary, etc. and of Christ's relatives and family, non-Biblical, but found in the works of ancient approved authors, Church Fathers, historians, philologists and sundry other Greek writers.*[72]

This definition was further refined on a separate title page of the second part of the *Catechism*, the section that contains the apocryphal texts:

> *Apocrypha, that is accounts of Christ, Mary, Joseph, Christ's relatives and family, not in the Bible, but found in the works of ancient*

---

70. The other texts are two examples of firmness and courage in the Christian faith: the account of Basilius the Great reported in Theodoret, *Hist. eccl.* 4.19, and the story of the inhabitants of Edessa told in Sozomen, *Hist. eccl.* 6.18. The other pieces are a hymn attributed to Clement of Alexandria, hymns by Gregory of Nazianzus, two odes of Prodromus, an extract from Nonnos of Panapolis's *Paraphrase of the Gospel of John*, a Latin prayer composed by Victor Strigel (a writer contemporary with Neander), as well as an excerpt about the Essenes from Pseudo-Philo and a *Forma Confessionis fidei* taken from Epiphanius of Salamis's *Ancoratus*.

71. Backus, "Early Christianity," 202.

72. Ibid.: *Catechesis Martini Lutheri parua, Graecolatina, postremum recognita. Ad eam vero accesserunt sententiae aliquot Patrum selectiores Graecolatinae. Narrationes item apocryphae de Christo, Maria, etc. cognatione ac familia Christi, extra Biblia, sed tamen apud veteres probatos autores, Patres, historicos, philologos et multos alios Scriptores graecos repertae. Omnia Graecolatina, descripta, exposita et edita studio et opera Michaelis Neandri Sorauiensis.*

> Greek authors, Church Fathers, historians and philologists (including also the Proteuangelion of James, recently discovered in the East and hitherto unpublished), copied from the words of the Oracles and the Sibyls, also from pagan testimonies and from books of many ancient authors, set forth and published in Greek and Latin by Michael Neander of Sorau.[73]

In Neander's view, the value of Christian Apocrypha was not only pedagogical but also historical. Having defined the genre and considerably increased the apocryphal content of his appendix to Luther's *Catechism*, Neander expounds the nature and value of apocryphal literature in his preface of 10 April 1563, addressed to Seyfried von Promnitz (ca. 1534–1597). He begins by openly accepting oral tradition and saying that all the Old Testament patriarchs and prophets, as well as Christ and his disciples, actually said and did much more than any written account (biblical or not) would lead us to believe. If we consider Neander's elaboration on extrabiblical information concerning Christ, we can see that what interests him in particular are, first, the signs and portents accompanying the birth of Christ not found in the Gospel accounts but present in the works of ancient and medieval history, and, second, pagan announcements of Christ's birth such as the Pythia's prophecy, found in the *Suda* under "*Augustus.*" It is important to note that the links between Christian and pagan elements remain of central importance to Neander's concept of education and that these links can be found in apocryphal accounts of Christ's and his family's acts and sayings. Unlike Jacques Lefèvre d'Étaples (ca. 1455–1536), the only *major* figure to publish Christian Apocrypha in any quantity before Neander,[74] the Sorau schoolmaster is not at all interested in establishing a hierarchy of sacred texts. Apocryphal texts are of purely historical interest and are to be read in a pagano-Christian or a Judeo-Christian context. They are, moreover, to be kept apart from the Bible and are to be sharply divided into "good apocrypha," written down "pio studio" by the apostles or their disciples, and

---

73. Ibid. *Apocrypha, hoc est narrationes de Christo, Maria Ioseph, cognatione et familia Christi extra Biblia; apud veteres tamen Graecos scriptores, patres, historicos et philologos reperta (inserto etiam proteuangelio Iacobi grece, in Oriente nuper reperto, necdum edito hactenus) ex Oraculorum ac Sibyllarum vocibus, gentium etiam testimoniis denique multorum veterum autorum Libris descripta, exposita et edita Graecolatine, a Michaele Neandro Sorauiense.* In the 1567 edition, the title page contains the following addition: *His nunc primum accessit, praeter alia diui Prochori (qui ex septem ministris vnus fuit et Stephani protomartyris consobrinus) de Ioanne Euangelista et Theologo historia Graecolatina, nunquam antea in lucem edita, Sebastiano Castalione interprete.* The *Acts of John* by Prochorus indeed constituted the sole addition to Neander's 1567 edition.

74. On this learned humanist, see Backus, "Renaissance Attitudes."

"bad apocrypha," written down by heretics to legitimize their errors in the hope of seeing them defended.[75] So far as other New Testament categories are concerned, Neander does not seem to be at all interested in the apocryphal acts, which he could easily have added to his collection, as he must have known the Basel editions of *Pseudo-Abdias*.[76] Possibly, he thought, like Luther, that all necessary information about the apostles' lives was contained in the canonical accounts and that there was no need to add to them. Another reason could have been the nature of the accounts themselves, given that they were not always edifying and were full of rather spectacular miracles. Indeed, there were no sixteenth-century Lutheran editions of *Pseudo-Abdias*.

For Neander only Greek apocrypha could be historically useful and he included only a few non-Greek pieces which had either become a part of the tradition about Christ (such as the *Letter of Lentulus*) or which possessed equivalents in Greek (such as the *Sibylline Oracles*). Although he was limited in his conception of Christian Apocrypha as worthy of publication only as an appendix to Luther's *Catechism*, Neander had, in general, a more favorable attitude towards Christian Apocrypha than the *Decretum Gelasianum* or indeed the early medieval canonists. Therefore, he compiled his list of what he considered "good" apocrypha from a variety of sources, only one of which was the chapter *Romana ecclesia of* Gratian's *Decretum*.[77]

Clearly, Neander's attitude towards apocryphal literature is perfectly in line with the practice of some ancient Christian churches or communities who were open to the use and reading of apocryphal texts and who labelled them "apocrypha" not to condemn and reject them as heretical and dangerous but to distinguish them from the canonical writings yet still acknowledging their potential value for the spiritual edification of the faithful. The distinction made by Michael Neander between "good" and "bad" apocrypha mirrors the various connotations given to the word "apocrypha" in early Christianity, connotations that range from unfavorable to favorable. Not all Protestant theologians, however, were ready to go as far as Michael Neander to embrace apocryphal texts as part of Christian pedagogy. Reformed

---

75. This is a common medieval notion of Christian Apocrypha.

76. Lazius, ed., *Abdiae Babyloniae episcopi*. For a discussion of the other early editions of this collection of texts, among which is Friedrich Nausea's *1531 editio princeps, Anonymi Pilalethi Eusebiani*, see Backus, *Historical Method*, 295–320; for more on the *Pseudo-Abdias* collection, see the work of Els Rose—for example, Rose, *Ritual Memory*; and Rose, "Medieval Memories."

77. The above exposition on Neander owes much to Backus, "Early Christianity," 200–204.

theologians from the Calvinist tradition were often as prompt to reject them as their strongest opponents among the early Church Fathers.

It must be noted also that Neander's selection of texts labelled "apocryphal" did not rely on strictly biblical criteria, but more on their supposed usefulness for the spiritual edification of the faithful and on their pedagogical utility.[78] Moreover, his selection was not arranged according to the biblical literary genres, but thematically according to what they could say about Jesus and his family, whatever their literary genre. Their value as supposed historical documents was thus more important than their conformity to canonical sources.

Two years after the third edition of Neander's version of Luther's *Shorter Catechism* and before his conversion from Lutheranism to Calvinism, Johann Grynaeus (1540–1617) published his *Monumenta sanctorum Patrum orthodoxographa*, a large (2064 pages!) compilation of writings of minor "orthodox" writings which would later be called either apocrypha or pseudepigrapha. The *Monumenta* is actually the second and expanded edition of an earlier anthology of extrabiblical texts from various sources compiled in 1555 by Johannes Basilius Herold (1514–1567).[79] These volumes contain diverse texts, ranging from what would later be called "apostolic writings" to what came to be referred to as apocrypha or pseudepigrapha. Thus Clement of Rome's and Ignatius's letters and Hermas's *Shepherd* were placed side-by-side with the *Protevangelium of James*, the *Testament of the Twelve Patriarchs* (in the first Latin translation made by Robert Grosseteste [1175–1253], chancellor of the University of Oxford) and a bilingual "edition" of the *Sibylline Oracles* as it was available at this time.[80] These large anthologies provide no introductions to individual texts and practically no explanatory notes except for a general preface at the beginning of each volume; only the bare texts are made available to the reader. Given the broad range of these collections, it is not surprising that their editors did not follow any clear criteria of selection, which remained loose and eclectic.[81] What

---

78. This was also the view of the late François Bovon in one of his last contributions, "Beyond the Canonical and the Apocryphal Books"; cf. Van den Kerchove, Review of Bovon, *Emergence of Christianity*.

79. Herold, *Orthodoxographa*. See further Backus, *Historical Method*, 253–54.

80. That edition included eight of the twelve books in the revised Latin translation made by Sebastian Castalio in 1555, nine years after his first translation and ten years after Xystus Betuleius's *editio princeps* printed by Johannes Oporin, in the very city of Basel where Oporin's competitor, Heinrich Petri, published the *Monumenta*. With further details on the edition of the *Sibylline Oracles*, see Roessli, "Sébastien Castellion et les *oracula Sibyllina*."

81. Needless to say, all these compilations produced by Protestants were condemned and put on the index by the Roman Catholic Church almost as soon as they

this foregrounds is that early modern theologians and editors made no firm distinctions between apostolic, apologetic, patristic, and even apocryphal and pseudepigraphical writings. They were simply making available non-canonical texts that needed to be brought to light. For me, this is one of the most compelling aspects of those early anthologies. The anthologies confirm that the distinction between apocrypha and pseudepigrapha—i.e., Christian and Jewish apocrypha, and even the Apostolic Fathers—did not exist in the early modern period. They also serve as a reminder that one needs to be cautious when using these labels and, perhaps, to avoid separating the study of Jewish Pseudepigrapha from that of Christian Apocrypha as is often found in contemporary scholarship. In this connection, it may be pointed out that the international journal *Apocrypha*, published by Brepols since 1990 with the support of the AELAC, has been conceived as a journal dedicated to the study of all sorts of materials expressive of both Jewish and Christian imagination over more than two millennia, including what are nowadays commonly referred to as pseudepigrapha and apocrypha.

In this context, it is interesting to note that the first edition of the *Neutestamentliche Apokryphen* by Edgar Hennecke (1865–1951), a pupil and disciple of Adolf von Harnack (1851–1930), mirrors to some extent the approach of the early Lutheran tradition of blurring the distinction between what we call apostolic (Clement of Rome, Ignatius, Polycarp, etc.) and apocryphal writings, except that they are arranged according to the New Testament literary genres. It is only the later editions of Hennecke's *Neutestamentliche Apokryphen*, particularly the third one, prepared by both Hennecke and Wilhelm Schneemelcher (1914–2003),[82] that grew more restrictive and progressively less inclusive, the number of texts increasing only because new texts were brought to light.

Interestingly, Christoph Markschies and Jens Schröter, the two editors-in-chief of the seventh and latest edition of Hennecke-Schneemelcher,[83] wondered whether they should align themselves with the same tradition or "move forward in light of more recent research."[84] After discussing at length the notions of their predecessors, they finally chose a kind of middle path between continuity with the Lutheran tradition of their predecessors and the requirements of contemporary research. They decided to exclude

---

appeared; cf. *Index of Forbidden Books* (Louvain, 1588; Trent 1564; Liège, 1569). See Bujanda, ed., *Index des livres interdits*, vol. 2.

82. Hennecke and Schneemelcher, eds., *Neutestamentliche Apokryphen*. For a biographical note on Schneemelcher see Kinzig, "Wilhelm Schneemelcher."

83. Markschies and Schröter, eds., *Antike christliche Apokryphen*.

84. Heath, Review of Markschies and Schröter, *Antike christliche Apokryphen*, 240.

Hermas's *Shepherd* and other texts from the same category, and to focus more exclusively on what we call Christian Apocrypha nowadays.

I am alluding to these practices not only to broaden our perspectives on the early scholarship in the field of Christian Apocrypha Studies, but also to encourage my fellow North American colleagues to explore a similar approach to research in their own areas of interest. My own studies of the editorial history of the *Sibylline Oracles*, since their rediscovery in the mid-sixteenth century, has led me to scrutinize their role in the development of the science of philology and their theological status in the debates about Scripture and divine inspiration, as well as other relevant issues in early modernity. This experience was so rewarding that I strongly encourage all scholars working with texts—apocryphal or not—that circulated in the age of printing to investigate the critical and editorial work of our predecessors, as we have much to learn from them. They can, for instance, help us to become aware of our own thought paradigms or of shifts in the study of a particular text. Sometimes one can even discover a reading not attested to in any surviving manuscripts but preserved in a marginal note penned by an early theologian or exegete. This, too, happened to me when I fortuitously came upon an interesting variant reading for book 6 of the *Sibylline Oracles*—a wonderful Christological hymn dating from the late second or early third century—in an excursus about the *Sibylline Oracles* embedded in a commentary on Matthew 2:1–2 about the Magi by the Calvinist scholar Friedrich Spanheim the Elder (1600–1649).[85] This is just one small example of unexpected insights one can get from paying attention to the work of Renaissance humanists.

More Terminological Issues

In a paper entitled "Pseudepigraphy, Authorship, and the Reception of 'The Bible' in Late Antiquity" delivered in Montreal in 2006, but published two years later,[86] Annette Yoshiko Reed provides a very stimulating discussion of some central concepts of the field, such as canonicity, apocryphicity, and above all pseudepigraphy and authorship.[87] After pointing out the

---

85. Spanheim, *Dubia evangelicorum*, 373: "ἐκ δὲ μιᾶς πηγῆς ἄρτου κόρος ἔσσεται ἀνδρῶν," "Et ex una fonte satietas panis erit viris." This reading has been apparently unknown to all editors of the *Sibylline Oracles*. On Book 6 of the *Sibylline Oracles*, see Roessli, "Le VIe livre des *Oracles sibyllins*."

86. Reed, "Pseudepigraphy."

87. On the practice of pseudepigraphy in the ancient world, apart from the essays in von Fritz, *Pseudepigrapha I*, mentioned by the author, see also Aune, "Reconceptualizing the Phenomenon" and Baum, *Pseudepigraphie*, which updates the seminal work of

ambivalence of the word "pseudepigraphy" towards the end of her paper, Reed rightly noted that most scholars since the end of the nineteenth century have complained about the inadequacy and ambivalence of the term, and yet have continued to use it. Her remarks echo, apparently without being aware of it, Albert-Marie Denis's attempt to propose an alternative terminology in his *Introduction à la littérature religieuse judéo-hellénistique (Pseudépigraphes de l'Ancien Testament)*, where the Dominican scholar speaks of "religious Judaeo-Hellenistic" literature, adding the label "Old Testament Pseudepigrapha" in parenthesis in order for scholars to know what he means by the term. Reed returned to this topic in a later article already alluded to above, "The Modern Invention of 'Old Testament Pseudepigrapha,'" in 2009.[88] There she advocates, among other things, relinquishing or changing these early modern labels still in use *faute de mieux*. I whole-heartedly applaud such a proposal. I made a similar plea 13 years ago in an article review of Denis's volumes published in *Apocrypha*, where I suggested the use of a strictly historical label: "Jewish literature of the Hellenistic and Roman period," modelled on the German title given to a book series dedicated to this literature.[89] It is troubling that, although scholars have repeatedly advocated the rejection of old, inappropriate, and misleading vocabulary and its replacement by more accurate or, at least, more neutral terminology, the old habits are so deeply ingrained that so far they have proven impossible to change.

Thus, while I strongly support the calls for renaming the Jewish writings produced by Hellenized Jews, I strongly question the appropriateness and the scholarly seriousness of phrases such as "secret gospels" or "forbidden texts," whether they refer to Christian texts or not. As we all know, although the term "apocryphal" can mean "secret" or "hidden,"[90] its meanings and its connotations have changed over the course of time and only a minority of apocryphal texts were actually secret and forbidden; had it been otherwise, we would not have so many copies of some of them, copies that were made by monks who obviously deemed them worth copying. So, in my view only those texts that explicitly claim to disclose a secret or hidden message or revelation should be called "secret" or "hidden." I am aware that part of the motivation in expanding such terminology to all apocrypha is to attract people to texts that might remain outside their horizons. For sure, it

---

Speyer, *Die literarische Fälschung* (reviewed by Bickerman, "Faux littéraires").

88. Reed, "Modern Invention."

89. Roessli, "L'Introduction à la littérature judéo-hellénistique"; the model is Jüdische Schriften aus hellenistisch-römischer Zeit, abbreviated JSHRZ.

90. See, e.g., Le Boulluec, "Écrits contestés," (on the famous passage of Eusebius of Caesarea's *Hist. eccl.* 3.25).

sounds much catchier to speak of "secret gospels" or "forbidden texts" than to use the somewhat obscure and mysterious term "apocrypha," but is not a scholar's task to avoid falling into the trap of supermarket science? The challenge is, of course, both to make these texts available to non-specialists and thereby justify the time and money invested in researching them, and to maintain scholarly integrity in all scholarly and popularizing activities. Personally, I consider it more important to keep the terms or phrases that have been historically attested to, such as apocrypha, and to explain the diversity and evolution of their meanings through the centuries than to make concessions to marketing interest or to indulge in sensationalism. This is also the reason why I would not support claims such as the one put forth by Tony Burke that while "'Christian apocryphal literature' or 'anonymous or pseudepigraphical, extrabiblical Christian literature' may be more accurate terms, they are less likely to draw as many readers or tweak the interests of college and university students shopping for titillating electives."[91] First, I am not sure that the label "Christian apocryphal literature" is "less likely to draw as many readers," and second, I do believe that it is a scholar's responsibility to open the readers' minds to what is unfamiliar or unknown. In this regard, Burke's *Secret Scriptures Revealed* fortunately has the more neutral sub-title *A New Introduction to the Christian Apocrypha*.

Alternative terms have been proposed and used to refer to the literature in question: Bart Ehrman called his compendium *Lost Scriptures* and his survey of early Christian groups *Lost Christianities*,[92] titles deemed "poor" by Tony Burke and others, but that may have been inspired by *The Lost Books of the Bible*,[93] a public-domain reprint of William Hone's 1820 *Apocryphal New Testament* compilation of outdated translations of Christian Apocrypha originally published by Jeremiah Jones (1693–1724) and of Apostolic Fathers by William Wake (1657–1737).[94] Lee Martin McDonald refers to those early religious writings of both Judaism and Christianity that

---

91. Burke, "Entering the Mainstream," 25.

92. Ehrman, *Lost Christianities*; *Lost Scriptures*; note also *Lost Gospel of Judas*.

93. The book first appeared under this title, *The Lost Books of the Bible*, in 1926. Rutherford Hayes Platt Jr. reissued this compilation as *The Lost Books of the Bible and the Forgotten Books of Eden* in 1963. The second half of the book, *The Forgotten Books of Eden*, includes a number of items of Jewish Pseudepigrapha. For more on the history of this compilation, see Goodspeed, *Modern Apocrypha*, 106–14.

94. Under the names of William Wake and other learned scholars was also printed a compilation titled *Forbidden Books of the Original New Testament of Jesus Christ* in London in 1863. On Wake, see Sykes, *William Wake*.

are not parts of our Bible as "Forgotten Scriptures" and, more recently, as "Non-Canonical Religious Texts."[95]

AVENUES FOR FURTHER RESEARCH

As much as I am pleased to see signs of interest and research on the early printings of apocryphal literature on the part of some North American colleagues, I would also like to see more interaction with medievalists. Unless we want to focus on and limit ourselves to studying only ancient apocrypha, we should also recruit more medievalists interested in the reception, use, and production of apocryphal material in the history, literature, and art of the Middle Ages. We could all benefit from stronger interactions and collaborations. Facing the sometimes formidable complexity of the manuscript traditions, medievalists have developed new approaches to and new strategies for the art of editing ancient texts that can be extremely helpful also to scholars of early Christianity, since most of the manuscripts of apocryphal texts also date from the Middle Ages.[96] They could help us also to see how the apocryphal material is exploited in medieval sources, thus revealing the richness and diversity in the reception and survival of apocryphal traditions in later periods. Here I would like to draw the attention of the reader to the contributions of Zbigniew Izydorczyk to the study of Christian Apocrypha in North America. Izydorczyk's ongoing research on the *Gospel of Nicodemus* is paradigmatic of how a medievalist can contribute to the field of apocryphal literature. After having worked to collect, describe, and classify a wide range of manuscripts of the Latin *Gospel of Nicodemus*[97] for his dissertation on the harrowing of hell in Middle English literature, he then expanded his research, in close collaboration with other colleagues, to explore the translations of this authentic "bestseller" of the Middle Ages into most European vernaculars and their dissemination throughout Europe.[98] Izydorczyk also showed an interest in the earliest printed versions of the

---

95. McDonald, *Forgotten Scriptures*; McDonald and Charlesworth, eds., *Non-Canonical Religious Texts*.

96. See, e.g., Bédier, "La tradition manuscrite"; Pasquali, *Storia della tradizione* (cf. Ullmann, Review of Pasquali, *Storia della tradizione*); Cerquiligni, *Éloge de la variante*. See also the special issue of *Speculum* 65/1 (1990) dedicated to the New Philology, and Guignard, "Tradition horizontale et tradition verticale."

97. See Izydorczyk, *Manuscripts*.

98. Izydorczyk, ed., *Medieval Gospel of Nicodemus*. The editor published further studies about medieval renditions of the text; see Izydorczyk and Gounelle, "Thematic Bibliography of the *Acts of Pilate*"; and Izydorczyk and Gounelle, "Thematic Bibliography of the *Acts of Pilate*. Addenda et corrigenda."

Gospel of Nicodemus and their manuscript sources.[99] He went even further and investigated, with Charlotte Fillmore-Handlon, the survival of the *Gospel of Nicodemus* in the Canadian province of Manitoba.[100] In pursuing this research he gives a model of the perfect combination of European and North American training in both philological and cultural studies. The research of Mary Dzon, who specializes in the transmission of apocryphal literature in medieval England, offers another example of the emerging North American interest in combining scholarship on early Christianity with explorations of its reception and transformation during the medieval period.[101]

In the same way, the boundary between apocryphal literature and hagiography, particularly from the fourth century onwards, is not easy to determine and is subject to questioning. I fully agree with Éric Junod, Christoph Markschies, Els Rose, and Stephen Shoemaker that a solution to the problem has not yet been reached, perhaps because "the complex and uncertain relationship between apocryphal literature and hagiography has not yet been fully explored."[102] Els Rose, a Dutch member of the AELAC, goes even further and rightly proposes that Christian Apocrypha and hagiography should be a part of a "triangle" that would include liturgy as well.[103] It would definitely be worthwhile to initiate discussions among experts in apocrypha and specialists in liturgy and hagiography, especially since the latter are quite numerous in North America.

Yet another avenue of research that seems to be partly neglected or forgotten, at least to my knowledge, in North American studies on apocryphal literature is the presence of apocryphal themes and motifs in art and, particularly, in Christian iconography. Although never highly developed in Europe, this field was not totally absent from the AELAC conferences in 1986 and 1995, but it has dramatically declined in the last decades, especially after the retirement and the passing away of Nicole Thierry and Catherine Paupert, who were among its strongest francophone proponents. Since most scholars working with Christian Apocrypha are experts in the textual traditions and do not feel as comfortable with the visual arts, they should make an effort to establish collaborations with art historians. As pointed out by Jean-Daniel Dubois, some portraits of Christ in the Middle Ages could hardly be understood without a reference to the *Acts of John* or

99. Izydorczyk, "Earliest Printed Versions."

100. Izydorczyk and Fillmore-Handlon, "Modern Life of an Ancient Text."

101. See Dzon and Kenney, eds., *Christ Child in Medieval Culture*.

102. Shoemaker, "Early Christian Apocryphal Literature," 525. See also Schneemelcher (translated by Wilson), *New Testament Apocrypha*, 1:54, 58–61 and 69; Junod, "'Apocryphes du Nouveau Testament,'" 38–39; and Rose, *Ritual Memory*, 35–42.

103. Rose, *Ritual Memory*, 28, 34, and 35–42.

to the *Doctrine of Addai*.[104] How can we comment on these kinds of texts without acknowledging the impact they had on visual representation of the apostles or on the iconoclast controversy? In my opinion, North American researchers in Christian Apocrypha should actively pursue collaboration with art historians. Of course, there are books in English that deal with this topic dating back to 2001, such as *Art and the Christian Apocrypha* by David R. Cartlidge and James Keith Elliott. This is an excellent book, but the treatment of the subject remains rather broad and general. More specialized research remains to be done. In 1991, the late French art historian Catherine Paupert collaborated closely with the American medievalist Richard Landes, a specialist in messianism and millennialism in the Middle Ages, on a book dedicated to the *Vita* of Saint Martial de Limoges, a text dated around the year 1000 which raises the difficult issue of the frontier between "apocryphal" and "hagiographical" literature.[105] José María Salvador Gonzalez, to name one art historian working with apocryphal literature, wrote an important paper, available both in Spanish and in English, entitled "The Death of the Virgin Mary (1295) in the Macedonian Church of the Panagia Peribleptos in Ohrid. Iconographic interpretation from the perspective of three apocryphal writings."[106] The oracle of the *Tiburtine Sibyl*, of particular interest to Lorenzo DiTommaso, Stephen Shoemaker and me, inspired several visual representations during the medieval and Renaissance periods, which would be worth analysing in collaboration with art historians. These are just a few examples of apocryphal traditions that could benefit from an interaction between art historians and biblical scholars.

As far as I can judge, an area that seems to be strong and promising in North American scholarship on the Christian Apocrypha is the study of Oriental traditions and of texts preserved in Near Eastern languages, with contributions from Tony Burke, Cornelia Horn, Brent Landau, and Stephen Shoemaker, to name only a few.[107]

---

104. See Dubois, "L'AELAC," 28; and Dubois, "L'apport des chrétiens," 247–49.

105. Landes and Paupert, *Naissance d'Apôtre*.

106. The same author also published the following articles: "La Dormición de la Virgen María"; "La presentación de María"; and "El Fresco de La Dormición de María."

107. See, e.g., Burke, "*Infancy Gospel of Thomas* from an Unpublished Syriac Manuscript"; Horn, ed., *The Bible, the Qur'an, and Their Interpretation*; Landau, "Sages and the Star-Child"; and Shoemaker, "New Syriac Dormition Fragments."

CONCLUSION

North American approaches to the study of apocryphal literature have much to offer to the field in general. My hope is that the interaction between European and North American scholars continues and grows even stronger. To accomplish this, we need to fulfill one important condition: we need to read each other's research. The Europeans do tend to read North American scholarship, but not always; North Americans read whatever is published in English, but tend to ignore scholarship available in other languages. From my experience, this is where the main weakness of North American and, more broadly, of English-speaking scholarship, lies, not only in the field of apocryphal literature but also in a number of other areas of research, both in the humanities and social sciences. In my view and in the view of many other scholars, this is a recurring and increasing problem not only in the Anglo-Saxon world but also in Europe, although this tendency—I must admit—is much stronger and much more common in North America than elsewhere. When I attended the 2011 York Christian Apocrypha Symposium, the one dedicated to the *Secret Gospel of Mark*, I was extremely disappointed that except for Pierluigi Piovanelli, who is originally a European, none of the scholars who were in attendance seemed to be aware of work on the text by Alain Le Boulluec and Annick Martin. Even though the symposium was intended for North American scholars, I found this ignorance profoundly troubling. True and serious scholarship implies taking into account the scholarly work of colleagues working in other cultural and linguistic areas. I teach at an English-speaking university based in Montreal and even in such a bilingual environment it is extremely difficult to convince English-speaking students to use secondary literature that is not available in their mother tongue. Strangely, the need to read other languages, including English, seems generally obvious to French-speaking or German-speaking students. If scholars and professors who are supposed to model scholarly practice for future generations of researchers are exclusively Anglo-centric, how can they convince their students that it is necessary to pay attention to scholarship produced in other languages? If the younger generation of North American scholars does not reverse this tendency, there will be no meaningful exchange of ideas anymore between the English-speaking world and German, French, Italian, Spanish, Portuguese, Polish, or Russian scholars. And let us be clear, contrary to what some may think, the ones who will lose the most if things continue this way are not the Europeans, who can generally deal with more than one foreign language (at least passively), but the unilingual North American scholars. This might sound alarming, but I am indeed extremely worried about this situation as the ever-growing body of evidence does not seem to contradict my rather pessimistic view. Of course, there are some exceptions and they are among the best, but they are only exceptions. My concern is a serious one, because if the tendency to ignore what is published in other modern languages is allowed to continue, one can seriously question the reliability of Anglo-Saxon scholarship in ancient languages (Greek, Latin, Coptic, etc.), which are much more challenging than modern living tongues. This would have disastrous consequences for Biblical, Apocryphal, and Patristic Studies. As I heard from a specialist in the early Reformation— an Italian scholar who worked in a German context and who is a perfect polyglot—"in North America, as soon as you speak or understand more than one foreign language, you are a genius. Therefore, I am a genius, because I read scholarship in German, French, Spanish, and English, to name the main modern foreign languages I am practising." In European scholarship, this is simply normal, a well-understood and generally-accepted rule. I gently exhort my North American colleagues to remedy this weakness in their field and to follow the example of their European counterparts.

One of the main strengths of the European teams of the AELAC— particularly the Swiss team—is their regular meeting, two to three times a term, to discuss the current work of the members. I participated in these workshops for years and I remember how beneficial they were. Participants were invited to give papers that were more or less polished, or to submit their work-in-progress, and pose problems (philological, exegetical and so on) in hope of receiving some input from friends and colleagues. In most cases, what was discussed was a passage of an apocryphal text, but occasionally more general or theoretical issues were addressed as well. I am aware that, whereas it is rather easy for people living in such a small area such as the French part of Switzerland to travel for one hour or so to meet with colleagues, it is much more challenging, if not impossible, for North American scholars to meet regularly in person, just because of the huge size of the continent. However, in an age of highly sophisticated technology, other ways of working together, of discussing issues at stake in our respective research, and of sharing information could and should be explored, such as videoconferencing or using safe cloud platforms (such as Dropbox) to post works in progress. Such close collaborations are the key to future breakthroughs in the field of apocryphal literature as well as in individual scholarly careers.

– APPENDIX –

The AELAC (Association pour l'étude de la Littérature Chrétienne)

A Brief Historical Survey*

THE AELAC BEFORE THE AELAC

THE AELAC WAS FOUNDED in 1981 in Geneva and Paris. What led scholars from these two cities to create an association dedicated to the study of Christian apocryphal literature? The answer lies in the ten years previous to its foundation. Scholars working in the francophone faculties of theology in Switzerland discussed the opportunity of publishing an anthology of Christian apocryphal texts translated into French. At the time francophone scholars had access to the collections of texts edited by Hennecke-Schneemelcher in German, James in English, Erbetta in Italian, or Santos Otero in Spanish, but nothing comparable or equivalent was available in French[1]—thus the strong incentive to fill the gap. After an exchange of a few letters between specialists of early Christianity working in France and Switzerland, a small group of colleagues and friends, under the leadership of François Bovon in Geneva (Éric Junod, Jean-Daniel Kaestli, and the late Jean-Marc Prieur) and of Pierre Geoltrain in Paris (Alain Desreumaux, Jean-

---

1. There was, of course, the 1952 collection of Amiot, *La Bible Apocryphe*, with an introduction by Daniel-Rops, but it consists only of short excerpts without any introduction and comments. Prior to Amiot, there was the bilingual edition of Michel and Peeters, eds., *Évangiles apocryphes*.

Daniel Dubois, and Francis Schmidt), met in October 1971 and decided to produce a collection of Christian apocryphal texts translated into French. The idea was not to translate the latest edition of Hennecke-Schneemelcher, the widest and probably the best set of texts available at that time, but to assemble a team of scholars to establish new translations based on the search for new manuscripts.

The initiators of the project were probably not aware of its implications and consequences. More than 100 years had elapsed since the pioneering work of Tischendorf and Lipsius, to name but two of the giants of nineteenth-century scholarship in Biblical Studies, both canonical and non-canonical. The progress made in the field of discovering and editing Greek and Latin texts was huge. In addition, the search for manuscripts—some of which were already identified in catalogues, some entirely unknown and therefore not recorded—could not be limited to the Greek and Latin traditions, but had to be extended to include other Christian languages (Syriac, Armenian, Georgian, Coptic, Ethiopic, Arabic, and Slavonic, to name the most important ones). So, with this somewhat naïve ambition, the small team began to search for collaborators with competencies in the various fields and a strong interest in this literature. It was clear from the beginning that this could not be an individual enterprise. However, experts in these exotic languages are often strongly individualistic and it took well over ten years to convince and bring together specialists ready to work collectively and collaboratively on this project.

The initial team also had to face another challenge: finding a publisher who would be interested or open to such an adventure. In the French part of Switzerland, the few publishers available, such as Labor et Fides in Geneva, could not afford such a risk. In France, particularly in Paris where there is a greater number of publishers, the offer was rejected based on the assumption that there was very little interest in this literature. A discussion with Geuthner, an excellent publisher in Paris specializing in Oriental Studies, fell through. Beauchesne, also in Paris, had published a book by Luigi Cirillo and Michel Frémaux on the *Gospel of Barnabas*,[2] so it was thought that Beauchesne could be an option. This first publication, however, did not give rise to a series, as was hoped and expected. After these initial few years of navigating in the unknown, the publisher Brepols in Belgium was considered as a venue for this literature.

As the project grew, the need for an official meeting became stronger and the colleagues involved in the project decided to organize an annual meeting for two days near the end of June in a place located between

---

2. Cirillo and Frémaux, *Évangile de Barnabé*.

Lausanne-Geneva and Paris. The selected place was Dole in the French Jura. There the initial team of specialists started to meet in 1975. This annual meeting rapidly became a tradition and ever since colleagues have met year after year in Dole except for one year when the religious house hosting the annual meeting, the *Sanctuaire* Notre Dame de Mont Roland, was not available for the usual date and another location was sought. The Sanctuaire permanently closed its doors in late 2013, resulting in a change of venue for the annual meeting to the Centre Culturel Saint Thomas in Strasbourg in 2014 and the 2015 meeting will take place at the Centre international de séjour in Besançon.

THE FOUNDATION OF THE AELAC

It was during the course of the first discussions with Brepols that the idea of creating a scholarly association emerged; it became clear that this ambitious project needed to be rooted in a solid institutional structure. This structure is the AELAC, the Association for the study of Christian Apocryphal Literature, constituted in 1981 in St. Peter Abbey in the city of Bruges, the wonderful Venice of the North. In attendance were the editorial board of the AELAC, the board of Brepols with Laurent Bols at its head, and the most important members of the series Corpus Christianorum of the time, Dom Eligius Dekkers, Dom Louis Leloir, and Maurice Geerard, who were from the onset constant supporters of the project and remained generous in providing the young and inexperienced team with constructive criticism and advice. Also present at the foundational act of the AELAC were people from the Institut des Sources chrétiennes (Institute for Christian Sources) based in Lyon, who served as a kind of peer for the AELAC because of their interest and longterm experience in creating critical editions of Greek and Latin Christian texts.

From the very beginning, in order to assure continuity in the activities of those involved in the project, Brepols wanted the AELAC to be rooted in academic institutions. Thus, the AELAC was composed of two groups of scholars: one based in or connected with the Faculties of Theology of Geneva and Lausanne and the other connected with the Religious Studies section of the École pratique des hautes études (EPHE) in Paris. The Swiss team focused on the editions of Greek and Latin texts, studied from a Biblical or New Testament Studies perspective, whereas the Parisian team was motivated by research on the origins of Christianity from the context of the history of early Judaism considered in all its diversity. For the latter, research on the Christian Apocrypha was narrowly connected to research on the Jewish Pseudepigrapha dating from what is typically called the intertestamental period. The expertise of the Swiss team can be seen in a 1981 volume on the apocryphal acts edited by François Bovon and published by Labor et Fides in Geneva.[3] The Parisian team's capabilities and interests are illustrated in the preparation of the conference commemorating the centenary of the foundation of the EPHE in 1986 and in the publication of the proceedings of this conference under the suggestive title "La fable apocryphe" (The Apocryphal Fable) in the first two volumes of the newly-founded journal *Apocrypha* (1990).

One of the first tasks faced by the members of this small group of scholars was to provide the publisher with a kind of definition of their field and to delineate a program and a general outline of the work to be done by the Association. The early members of the group (Jean-Daniel Kaestli, Jean-Daniel Dubois, Éric Junod and others) remember the passionate and heated discussions that animated their meetings when they were trying to define the notion of "apocryphicity" and the idea of a "corpus" or "collection" of texts to be put together under the umbrella-term of "apocrypha." The heated debates of these early times set the general tone of the meetings of the Association, not only in Dole but also in three to four smaller gatherings held throughout the year in Switzerland (Lausanne, Bex) and in Paris. But the AELAC is not only a venue for debates and discussions; it is also an institution with editorial projects. The most important among these are the volumes of the Series Apocryphorum.

THE AELAC AND ITS EDITORIAL PROJECTS

On its website Brepols sums up the Series Apocryphorum's goal as:

> In much the same way as the Series Latina and the Series Graeca, a group of scholars from the universities of Geneva, Fribourg, Neuchâtel, Lausanne, and of the École Pratique des Hautes Études of Paris will publish all the pseudepigraphical or anonymous texts of Christian origin attributed to biblical characters or based on events reported or suggested by the Bible. The series' purpose is to enrich the knowledge of apocryphal Christian literature by supplying editions of often dispersed and even unedited texts. Besides the critical text, each volume contains a complete study of the Apocrypha edited, with commentary and translation into a modern language.

---

3. Bovon et al., eds., *Actes apocryphes des Apôtres*.

In the decades since its foundation, the AELAC has truly become an international association of scholars and welcomes collaborators from all over the world with various backgrounds and cultural horizons, as well as an utmost interest in apocryphal literature. Some of these scholars and collaborators teach and reside in North America, including Tony Burke, Mary Dzon, Peter Dunn, Cornelia Horn, Zbigniew Izydorczyk, F. Stanley Jones, Brent Landau, Robert Phenix, Pierluigi Piovanelli, Jean-Michel Roessli, and Stephen Shoemaker.

The first goal of the AELAC was and remains the publication of volumes for the Series Apocryphorum, a most demanding task. Originally the AELAC did not intend to work for the next two centuries, as was envisaged for the other projects of the Corpus Christianorum (Series Graeca et Latina, Corpus Scriptorum Christianorum Orientalium, etc.). The initial hope of Brepols was to see an average of one volume published every year by the Association. Now more than 30 years after the foundation, the total number of volumes published is just under 20. This means that between the intention and the reality there is often a gap due to various reasons, the difficulty and complexity of the task being certainly the most challenging.

At the beginning of the contract with Brepols, Pierre Geoltrain was forward-thinking enough to include in the editorial projects of the AELAC the possibility of publishing translations of apocryphal texts with shorter introductions and commentaries aimed at a broader audience. These volumes could be either shorter versions of a Series Apocryphorum volume already completed or conceived as a preliminary work for a forthcoming volume.[4] This is how the project of a wide anthology of texts came to light almost ten years after the foundation of the AELAC. The prestigious series La Pléiade published by Gallimard in Paris, reputed for its scholarly publications of literary works, was immediately seen as the most appropriate venue for an anthology that would incorporate the apocryphal literature as part of its series of volumes on world literature. At about the same time the paperback series Apocryphes was created with the same goal of presenting texts in translation to a wider audience. Some members of the AELAC were afraid these volumes would distract members of the association from their main goal of producing volumes for the Series Apocryphorum. Now more than 15 years has elapsed since the publication of the first of the two Pléiade volumes and it seems that the dynamics created by this project have positively influenced the collaborators of the association and encouraged

---

4. This is confirmed by a comparison between the list and date of publication of the volumes of the Series Apocryphorum and the texts published either in the Pléiade or in the paperback series Apocryphes—some were published after the Series, some beforehand.

them to keep focusing on the main task, although sometimes at a very slow pace. Considering that more than 20,000 copies of each of the Pléiade volumes have so far been sold, we can now affirm that this collection filled an important gap in our field.

Finally, after the publication of the first volumes of the Series Apocryphorum, the need for indices, concordances, and lexica emerged. To address this need, a complementary series to the Series Apocryphorum was conceived, the Instrumenta, of which only three volumes have appeared to date: a concordance of the *Acts of Philip*, and two volumes focusing on the transmission of the *Gospel of Nicodemus*.

Among the various editorial projects of the AELAC, one of the most popular is the *Bulletin de l'AELAC*, which serves as a bibliographical repertoire and an address book of members. The *Bulletin* is a very useful resource for reaching scholars working in the field of apocryphal literature and for disseminating information on their scholarly works and contributions. The *Bulletin* is complemented by the website of the AELAC (http://www3.unil.ch/wpmu/aelac/), which provides access to other sources of information, including descriptions of both published and forthcoming volumes in their various series, and details about the Association's meetings.

— 3 —

The "Harvard School" of the Christian Apocrypha

— Brent Landau —

INTRODUCTION

THE SUBJECT OF THIS paper is what I have termed the "Harvard School" of Christian Apocrypha Studies. What precisely this approach presumes will be stated momentarily, but at the outset, I characterize it as both the most dominant and the most controversial approach to the scholarly study of apocryphal Christian literature. By dominant, I mean that many of the specialists in the Christian Apocrypha (henceforth CA) currently working in North America have had some degree of substantial contact with scholars who have taught at Harvard Divinity School, or teach there presently. By controversial, I mean that the conclusions about the CA reached by members of the Harvard School have provoked viscerally positive and negative reactions among both specialists in the broader field of New Testament Studies and the general public. As regards the latter group, I would argue that many of the most sensational Bible-related media events in recent years—including and especially the ongoing strange affair of the *Gospel of Jesus' Wife*—have utilized the perspective of the Harvard School, and the ensuing controversy has paid off very handsomely for the creators of such media events.

In what follows, I will begin by offering two provisional definitions of the Harvard School: one adopted by its proponents, the other adopted by its detractors. Then, I will trace the study of the CA at Harvard. Although there was at least one earlier Harvard scholar who made a significant contribution to CA Studies, for all practical purposes, the "Harvard School" proper began with the arrival of Helmut Koester in 1958. I will devote a significant amount of this paper to Koester in particular, since he is by far the scholar most responsible for the development of the Harvard School approach to the CA. I will next address the ways in which François Bovon and Karen King, who both came to Harvard in the 1990s, have interacted with Koester's approach and have made their own distinctive contributions to and modifications of what constitutes the Harvard approach to the CA. Finally, I will conclude by assessing the current state of the study of the CA at Harvard and the fortunes of the Harvard School more generally.

PART ONE: DEFINING THE HARVARD SCHOOL AND ITS RELATIONSHIP TO THE STUDY OF RELIGION AT HARVARD

How may we best define the "Harvard School" of CA Studies? Rather than offer a single definition, I will offer two because of the polarizing effect of the Harvard School approach. In this way, CA Studies is rather like other highly controversial concepts, such as postmodernism, Marxism, or conservatism: how you define it will depend to some degree on whether you subscribe to or reject its tenets. In the framing of its proponents, the Harvard School approach to the study of early Christian literature does not succumb to the confessionally-driven tendency of biblical scholars to privilege the canonical texts above apocryphal texts as worthy of scholarly interest, as witnesses for the development of Christianity in variegated ways, and even, potentially, as relevant for our understanding of the historical Jesus. As Helmut Koester characterized it in the conclusion to his and James Robinson's *Trajectories through Early Christianity*, "The distinctions between canonical and noncanonical, orthodox and heretical are obsolete. The classical 'Introduction to the New Testament' has lost its scientific justification. One can only speak of a 'History of Early Christian Literature.'"[1]

---

1. Koester, "Conclusion," 270.

But in the framing of its detractors, the Harvard School approach to the study of early Christian literature, largely due to shifting social, cultural, and religious mores, unjustly valorizes apocryphal texts above canonical texts, consistently regarding them as witnesses to a very early stage of Christianity before it was corrupted by the canonical writings and their proto-orthodox enablers. Luke Timothy Johnson's characterization of the scholarship of John Dominic Crossan—who did not study or teach at Harvard, and yet represents the perspective of the Harvard scholarship perhaps even more than Koester himself—can serve here as a more general representation of the way that the detractors assess the Harvard School:

> [T]he game is fixed. Crossan's remarkably early dating for virtually all apocryphal materials, and his correspondingly late dating for virtually all canonical materials, together with his frequent assertion that the extracanonical sources are unaffected by the canonical sources and therefore have independent evidenciary value, rests on little more than his assertions and those of the like-minded colleagues he cites.[2]

Obviously, these definitions of the Harvard School diverge quite markedly; nevertheless, they do agree that the chief concern of this approach is how to evaluate the much less-studied CA in comparison with the familiar and cherished NT gospels. The Harvard School approach does not attempt to study the CA in isolation from canonical writings—and as we shall see, some approaches to the study of the CA have indeed done just that—but insists on confrontation, comparison, and, at least in its earliest incarnation under Helmut Koester, on making a choice between whether a given CA text has preserved a more archaic tradition than found in a comparable NT writing.

In its insistence on giving these historically-maligned writings a fair hearing alongside of traditional Scripture, the Harvard School of CA Studies in fact replicates some of the characteristics of the broader study of religion at Harvard. In an essay entitled "The Harvard Way in the Study of Religion," William Darrow identifies a number of traits that have recurred at this institution, many of which are directly pertinent to the Harvard School of CA Studies:

> the celebration of religious diversity and variety; a focus on the individual as the locus for the construction of religious meaning; ... a fundamentally historicist stance toward human religiousness; an eschewal of systematic theological construction...; and

---

2. Johnson, *Real Jesus*, 47.

finally a deep sensitivity to the problems posed by modernity to religiosity.³

In short, the study of religion at Harvard, long before the arrival of the Harvard School on the scene in the late 1950s, had situated itself largely in opposition to normative and traditional modes of religiosity.

If we were to search for the ultimate origin of this distinctively Harvardian approach to the study of religion that eventually gives birth to the Harvard School, a very appropriate starting point would be an event that took place at Harvard Divinity School 175 years ago. On July 15, 1838, the essayist and poet Ralph Waldo Emerson, himself a graduate of both Harvard College and the Divinity School, presented the so-called "Divinity School Address" to Harvard seminarians during graduation ceremonies. As Jeffrey Kripal describes, it was by no means a typical, staid commencement address:

> ... Emerson simultaneously denied the unique divinity of Christ and affirmed the divinity of the 'infinite soul' as he celebrated the personal revelations of contemporary religious experience ... He called on his listeners to 'live with the privilege of the immeasurable mind' and to refuse the temptation of traditional authority. He encouraged them to move beyond 'historical Christianity,' an institution whose singular divinization of Jesus as the only divine human being and whose idolatrous reliance on the Bible as somehow final and complete he found particularly odious.⁴

Emerson's understanding of Jesus' significance had nothing to do with Jesus' death and resurrection and everything to do with his teachings. As he stated in the Divinity School address:

> Jesus belonged to the true race of prophets. He saw with open eye the mystery of the soul. Drawn by its severe harmony, ravished by its beauty, he lived in it, and had his being there. One man was true to what is in you and me. Alone in all history he estimated the greatness of man. He saw that God incarnates himself in man ... He said in this jubilee of sublime emotion "I am divine. Through me God acts, through me God speaks."⁵

Yet 1838 was not 2013, even at Harvard Divinity School. Emerson's address provoked outrage in Boston and charges of both atheism and

3. Darrow, "Harvard Way," 233–34.
4. Kripal, *Comparing Religion*, 62.
5. See Emerson, *Annotated Emerson*, 105–7.

blasphemy were leveled at him. He was effectively banned from Harvard for 25 years thereafter. But the parallels between Emerson's thought and apocryphal Christian writings were not lost on Helmut Koester, who observed in a 2006 lecture that "Emerson would have found an affinity of ideas exactly in those mystic sayings of the *Gospel of Thomas*."[6]

Of course, Emerson was not aware of the *Gospel of Thomas*, and even the earliest discoveries of Gnostic writings like the Askew and Bruce codices had not yet been disseminated. The earliest instance that I have found of a scholar at Harvard discussing the CA in any detail, and indeed the only example prior to Koester's arrival, is James Hardy Ropes, who taught at Harvard from 1895 to 1933. In the two years prior to his appointment at Harvard, he studied in Berlin under the direction of Adolf von Harnack. The fruit of this labor was Ropes's study of the agrapha, published in German in 1896.[7] Ropes's book was in large part a critique of the conclusions that Alfred Resch drew from his own monumental study of the agrapha.[8] It is, of course, common knowledge in the field of CA Studies that Resch assembled the first major compilation of the sayings of Jesus preserved outside the canonical gospels. But what is less well-known is that Resch believed that many of these sayings derived from a single primitive Hebrew gospel. Ropes strongly criticized this thesis, and he also reduced Resch's estimation of the number of agrapha that could plausibly go back to the historical Jesus. However, Ropes's monograph was never translated into English, and so, predictably, it did not lead to any sort of groundswell of interest in the CA among other scholars at Harvard, nor did he undertake any further substantial study of the CA.

PART TWO: HELMUT KOESTER AND THE BIRTH OF THE HARVARD SCHOOL

In the fall of 1958, Helmut Koester joined the faculty of Harvard Divinity School, which at that time already included Arthur Darby Nock, Krister Stendahl, and Amos Wilder.[9] He was one of the final students of the great Rudolf Bultmann, and his dissertation at the University of Marburg was on Synoptic tradition in the Apostolic Fathers.[10] What was it that led to

6. Koester, "Thomas Jefferson," 200.
7. Ropes, *Sprüche Jesu*.
8. Resch, *Agrapha*.
9. For the situation at Harvard at the time of Koester's arrival, see Wilder, "New Testament Study."
10. Published as Koester, *Synoptische Überlieferung*.

Koester's interest in the CA? To some degree, it emerged organically out of his dissertation research.

> My study of the gospel traditions in the Apostolic Fathers brought me to the conclusion that gospel materials that were not dependent upon the canonical writings might have survived well into the second century. But I was also aware of the prevailing opinion, which saw all apocryphal gospels as works that came into existence after the completion of the canonical writings. Attempts to discover in apocryphal materials pre-canonical traditions regularly met with severe criticism.[11]

Although Bultmann himself never devoted much writing exclusively to the CA, certainly he did refer to these texts quite frequently throughout his *History of the Synoptic Tradition*, and his interpretation of the Gospel of John, as is well known, relied heavily on extracanonical texts, particularly the recently-discovered Mandaean writings. But it was Bultmann's pioneering work on form criticism that provided Koester with a method for placing apocryphal Christian gospels on an equal playing field with the canonical gospels. Koester did not have to demonstrate that the apocryphal gospels contained much material that could be traced back to the historical Jesus, but only that they, like the canonical gospels, were the products of the life of the earliest Christian communities. In his 1968 essay, "One Jesus and Four Primitive Gospels," Koester writes:

> To be sure, form criticism may very well, as a by-product, demonstrate that only a little of the apocryphal material can qualify as "historical" or "genuine." But this is not its primary function. Its foremost task is to determine the original *Sitz im Leben* of the material which is now available in the apocryphal gospel tradition, however inauthentic it may be with regard to the historical Jesus, and however secondary and derivative may be the use made of it in the contexts in which it is now preserved. The stage at which both the apocryphal and canonical traditions can be compared is their original *Sitz im Leben* in the early Christian church.[12]

Once Koester's methodological starting point is clearly recognized as form criticism, it is impressive to observe how consistently he maintained this orientation in his later scholarship. In contrast to other scholars of the Harvard School who have used and privileged apocryphal texts for

---

11. Koester, *Ancient Christian Gospels*, xxix.
12. Koester, "One Jesus and Four Primitive Gospels," 160.

reconstructing the historical Jesus, Koester has generally remained, like his mentor, largely skeptical of the Quest. It is true that he does not deny that some share of these materials does go back to Jesus himself, and sometimes he goes even further and names specific sayings or ideas from the CA as representative of Jesus' thought.[13] Even so, he has never attempted a full-scale reconstruction of Jesus' life in which apocryphal writings play a central role, unlike, say, John Dominic Crossan.

Although Koester's work on the CA was truly groundbreaking, it must be remembered that there were several major external influences that clearly informed his decision to devote his efforts to this corpus of material. First, although the Nag Hammadi library had been discovered in the late 1940s, the first publication of the *Gospel of Thomas* only took place in 1959, just as Koester was beginning his career at Harvard. This text offered a wealth of additional evidence for the argument that Koester had made in his dissertation about the existence of early gospel traditions independent of the four NT gospels. Second, in 1964, the second German edition of Walter Bauer's 1934 monograph *Orthodoxy and Heresy in Earliest Christianity* was published by Georg Strecker,[14] an event that reacquainted German scholars with Bauer's radical thesis about the secondary nature of Christian orthodoxy—and would soon lead to the work's explosive introduction to American scholarship. No doubt Koester was familiar with Bauer's work prior to the release of the second edition; yet, the fact that he characterizes Bauer as "well known as a lexicographer but unfortunately little known as a historian of the ancient church"[15] in the opening of his 1965 article "*GNOMAI DIAPHORAI*: The Origin and Nature of Diversification in the History of Early Christianity," suggests that Koester had already presaged the profound influence that this book would have for American scholars, well prior to its translation into English in 1971. In most serendipitous fashion, it was also in 1971 that Koester's and James Robinson's path-breaking collection of essays, *Trajectories through Early Christianity*, appeared; together, Koester and Robinson's research and mentoring shaped more than a generation's worth of scholars in the NT and the CA.[16]

---

13. Consider, for example, this statement from "One Jesus and Four Primitive Gospels": "Jesus radicalized the traditional apocalyptic expectation of the kingdom; his message demands that the mysterious presence of the kingdom in his words be recognized. The Gnosticism of the *Gospel of Thomas* appears to be a direct continuation of the eschatological sayings of Jesus" (175).

14. Bauer, *Rechtgläubikeit und Ketzerei*.

15. Koester, "GNOMAI DIAPHORAI," 114.

16. See also Koester's reflections on his friendship and scholarly partnership with Robinson in his "Intellectual Biography of James M. Robinson."

Although Bauer says relatively little about CA texts in his monograph, Koester clearly applied Bauer's theory about heresy often preceding orthodoxy to the study of early Christian gospel traditions. In so doing, it is important to recognize that he was charting a very new course, even among—indeed, especially among—specialists in the CA at that time. In his 1980 article, "Apocryphal and Canonical Gospels," Koester singles out for criticism Wilhelm Schneemelcher's characterization of the CA in the first English translation of *New Testament Apocrypha* (published in 1963–1965), in which Schneemelcher wrote, "Apocrypha are writings ... which from the point of view of Form Criticism further develop and mold the kinds of style created and received in the NT, whilst foreign elements certainly intrude."[17] Accordingly, Koester faults Schneemelcher for maintaining "a distinction in principle between canonical and apocryphal"[18] and deems that, despite being the first new English-language anthology of the CA in 40 years, "Schneemelcher's evaluation of the apocryphal literature by no means signals a new era in the appreciation of these writings."[19]

Space does not permit here a full cataloguing of Koester's scholarship on the CA. Instead, I will present and evaluate two different kinds of arguments he has made about either the priority or contemporaneity of apocryphal and canonical gospels. The first kind of argument looks generally at the manuscript and citational evidence of apocryphal gospels compared with canonical gospels ("external evidence,"[20] in his words). The second kind of argument involves making form-critical and redaction-critical arguments for the priority of certain apocryphal gospels over and against canonical gospels ("internal evidence,"[21] in his words). I will limit myself to a very brief discussion of four such texts: the *Gospel of Thomas*, *Papyrus Egerton 2*, the *Gospel of Peter*, and the *Secret Gospel of Mark*.

In "Apocryphal and Canonical Gospels," Koester begins his discussion by comparing the papyrus manuscripts of NT and apocryphal Christian writings from the second and third centuries. He notes that of the only two papyrus fragments that had been dated to the first quarter of the second century, one was canonical—𝔓52, from the Gospel of John—and the other was apocryphal—*Egerton 2*.[22] Since the writing of that article, *Egerton 2* has

---

17. Hennecke and Schneemelcher, eds., *New Testament Apocrypha*, 1:61.
18. Koester, "Apocryphal and Canonical Gospels," 105.
19. Ibid., 106.
20. Ibid., 107.
21. Ibid.
22. Ibid., 108.

been re-dated to ca. 200, a re-assessment with which Koester has agreed.[23] Although this re-dating means that *Egerton 2* is less likely to be the earliest extant Christian manuscript, it is important to bear in mind two considerations. First, even if *Egerton 2* dates from ca. 200, it is still highly impressive evidence of an early date for this intriguing apocryphal gospel (about which I will have more to say below). Second, the usual dating of 𝔓52 to the year 125 has been questioned recently by Brent Nongbri,[24] and more scholars are expressing hesitation about whether any extant Christian manuscripts can reasonably be dated prior to 150.[25] So, even though the assessment of the evidence has changed since Koester's 1980 article, it is fair to characterize the contest for the earliest dateable Christian literary evidence between *Egerton 2* and 𝔓52 as a stalemate at this point. In the rest of the papyrus remains from the second and third centuries, the apocryphal gospels lag behind the canonical gospels: by my tally Koester mentions a total of 21 manuscripts—16 canonical and 5 apocryphal, a score that would be categorized as a blowout in baseball. Yet, the *Gospel of Thomas* performs rather well in this contest, accounting for a total of three "runs" (P. Oxy. 1, 654, and 655). John is the big winner, with a total of 10 "runs," then Matthew at 6, and Luke at 4—Mark was hitless in this one. Although *Thomas* holds its own, the CA does not fare particularly well overall in a comparison of papyrological evidence—something that Koester does not address explicitly in the analysis that follows.[26]

A much more favorable comparison comes next, in which early Christian writings are mined for quotations of gospel texts. Here the evidence not only demonstrates a much higher frequency with which CA texts are cited, but also, in complementary fashion, underscores the extreme fluidity of Jesus traditions in the earliest of Christian writings: "free sayings" of Jesus (agrapha, in other words) appear in Paul, the Deutero-Paulines, *1 Clement*,

---

23. Koester, *Ancient Christian Gospels*, 206.

24. Nongbri, "Use and Abuse of 𝔓52."

25. See the discussion in Bagnall, *Early Christian Books in Egypt*, 1–49.

26. Koester offers no comments directly following his chart of manuscript dates in "Apocryphal and Canonical Gospels," 108. Following his chart of quotations of gospel materials in early Christian writings (in which the CA fares much better), he seems to summarize both sets of data together as follows: "This survey shows clearly that about a dozen gospels were known in the second century and that the evidence for the apocryphal writings compares quite well with the evidence for the canonical gospels. The attestations do not support a distinction between canonical and apocryphal gospels" (110). This summary is very accurate as far as the quotations of gospel materials is concerned, but less so for the number of manuscripts of apocryphal gospels compared with canonical gospels.

Ignatius, Papias, *2 Clement*, Justin Martyr, and the *Epistula Apostolorum*.[27] If nothing more, Koester has succeeded in showing in these two sets of comparisons that, on the basis of external evidence, there is absolutely no reason to regard all of the CA gospels (or more broadly, noncanonical Jesus traditions) as obviously secondary in their date of origin to their canonical counterparts. And while the comparison of papyrus fragments would certainly seem to show a greater popularity for canonical gospels, the reconstruction of early Christian gospel traditions cannot be simply a popularity contest. Popularity may matter for what ends up in the canon, but Koester's presentation of the external evidence validates his earlier insistence from the conclusion of *Trajectories* that the anachronistic "Introduction to the New Testament" must be abandoned in favor of a "History of Early Christian Literature" if a historically accurate picture of the development of the Jesus tradition is the goal.

Koester's second approach is the attempt to demonstrate, in terms of form and redaction criticism, evidence for the priority of certain CA gospels—most importantly the *Gospel of Thomas*, *Papyrus Egerton 2*, the *Gospel of Peter*, and the *Secret Gospel of Mark*. There is insufficient space here to examine in detail his theories regarding each of these texts. For now, it will suffice to say the following. Koester regards the *Gospel of Thomas*, with its non-eschatological wisdom focus, to be approximately as old as the earliest layer of Q.[28] He regards *Egerton 2* as evidence for a very early stage in the gospel tradition, before the differences between the Synoptic and Johannine traditions had become so divergent.[29] To my mind, this is the most intriguing of his theories, and I will simply say that in that parlor game scholars sometimes play where they are asked which fragmentary or lost text do you wish was available today, I always choose *Egerton 2*. The *Gospel of Peter* is considered by Koester a witness to the earliest stage of composition for the narrative of Jesus' death, a stage in which the presence of scriptural allusions to the Hebrew Scriptures were built into the narrative itself, rather than explicitly marked out by formal citations.[30] Although in "Apocryphal and Canonical Gospels," Koester seemed to regard *Peter* as having preserved the archaic pre-Markan passion narrative itself, by the time his *Ancient Christian Gospels* monograph was published in 1990, after Crossan's articulation

---

27. Ibid., 108–111.

28. See his discussions in "One Jesus and Four Primitive Gospels," 166–87; "Apocryphal and Canonical Gospels," 112–19; and *Ancient Christian Gospels*, 75–128.

29. See "Apocryphal and Canonical Gospels," 119–23; and *Ancient Christian Gospels*, 205–16.

30. See "Apocryphal and Canonical Gospels," 126–30; and *Ancient Christian Gospels*, 216–40.

of his "Cross Gospel" theory,[31] Koester was much more reticent about whether there was a fully-formed written passion narrative prior to Mark. Finally, and perhaps most daringly, he out-Morton-Smiths Morton Smith with his argument that *Secret Mark* was not simply a different ancient recension of Mark, but was actually a form of Mark more archaic than canonical Mark.[32]

Suffice it to say that Koester's theories have not commanded universal assent; indeed there are even many scholars who I would associate with the Harvard School who have serious misgivings about one or more of these theories. As such, Ulrich Luz, in his review of Koester's *Ancient Christian Gospels* said, with an obvious mix of admiration and disagreement, that the book "is not so much an introduction into the Gospels as it is an introduction to Koester, and as such, it definitely has its great merits."[33] I would frame it slightly differently: even if Koester is ultimately proven wrong in many of his theories, he is brilliantly, spectacularly wrong.

PART THREE: FRANÇOIS BOVON, KAREN KING, AND BEYOND: THE POST-KOESTER DEVELOPMENT OF THE HARVARD SCHOOL

In some ways, it is not entirely appropriate to refer to the decades from the 1990s until the present as the "post-Koester era." After all, Koester only retired from Harvard Divinity School in 1998, last taught a course at HDS in the fall of 2013 (his 55th year at Harvard!), and has published as recently as 2011. Nevertheless, the adjective "post-Koester" is a fitting descriptor for developments in the Harvard School that have taken place in the past two and a half decades. For during this time, two scholars at HDS, François Bovon and Karen King, have sought to nuance some of the excesses of Koester's viewpoints and to analyze specific corpora of CA in more detail than was typical of Koester.

The first of these two scholars to arrive at Harvard was my *Doktorvater*, François Bovon, who joined the HDS faculty in 1993 from the University of Geneva. Discussing the legacy of Bovon is bittersweet: he died shortly after the 2013 York Symposium was held, from a cancer that robbed him—and us—of an untold number of productive years and edifying exchanges. Bovon was one of the founders of L'Association pour l'étude de la littérature

---

31. See Crossan, *Cross That Spoke*.

32. See Koester, "History and Development of Mark's Gospel"; and *Ancient Christian Gospels*, 293–303.

33. Luz, review of Koester, *Ancient Christian Gospels*, 88.

apocryphe chrétienne (AELAC), the scholarly organization of primarily French and Swiss scholars devoted to the study of the CA.[34] AELAC remains, without a doubt, the true center of gravity in CA scholarship, recent developments on the North American front notwithstanding. Its annual meeting is held in late June (historically in Dole, but in Strasbourg for 2014), with smaller meetings around specific textual corpora taking place during the winter months. Its members have contributed to a number of series published by Brepols, but the flagship publication is certainly the Corpus Christianorum Series Apocryphorum, a series of critical editions of CA. With Bovon's arrival at Harvard in 1993, there was now a bridge linking the mostly European scholars of AELAC with CA specialists in North America, and Bovon was truly the driving force behind this union. The co-organizer of this symposium, Tony Burke, published his critical study of the *Infancy Gospel of Thomas* in the CCSA,[35] and I hope soon to publish my study of the *Revelation of the Magi* in the series as well. For both of us, François Bovon has been instrumental in our journeys from doctoral students to published authors in a prestigious series produced by world-class CA scholars.

So, one major contribution of Bovon to the Harvard School has been organizational, in helping to forge more substantial connections between North American and European scholarship on the CA. There are several other distinctive elements that Bovon brought to the Harvard School, each of which, in its own way, refines Koester's viewpoints. I will discuss three of these here: first, a dedication to bringing attention to the interpretation of more-neglected CA; second, an encouragement to undertake difficult but essential manuscript research; and third, a multifaceted blurring of the lines between the categories of "canonical" and "apocryphal."

First, Bovon devoted much of his scholarly attention to the interpretation of CA texts that are far less prominent and sensational than the texts—the *Gospel of Thomas*, the *Gospel of Peter*, and so forth—favored by Koester. Bovon focused much of his energies on the apocryphal acts of the apostles, a corpus of texts that make no strong claim to existing prior to the canonical writings and are decidedly secondary from a chronological perspective. Yet, Bovon insisted that such writings deserved to be studied with as much care as the earliest apocryphal gospels. He made an especially telling remark in this regard with his reasoning for choosing to study the traditions associated with the apostle Philip—namely, that he studied Philip because he was particularly unknown: "My personal curiosity and interests

---

34. See Bovon's own recounting of AELAC's inception and development in his essay "Corpus Christianorum Series Apocryphorum."

35. Burke, *De infantia Iesu*.

have tended to push me to investigate neglected figures; almost arbitrarily, I chose the apostle Philip."[36] This curiosity ultimately led Bovon to discover a previously-unknown but more archaic version of the *Acts of Philip* in a monastery on Mount Athos.[37] Bovon's interest was broader than the apocryphal acts; he directed his attention also toward other apocryphal writings that had suffered similar neglect. He produced an illuminating study of the neglected gospel fragment P. Oxy. 840 that shifted the discussion away from its relevance for the study of the historical Jesus and toward a more likely context of early Christian debates around baptism.[38] He also subjected the curious incident of the suspension of time at the moment of Jesus' birth in the *Protevangelium of James* to a penetrating exegesis, such as one might find if a substantial commentary on this text—extremely influential in ancient and medieval Christian piety—were ever to be written.[39]

As a second distinctive contribution, Bovon emphasized the need for scholars of the CA to develop familiarity with the bewildering world of manuscript studies. One of the key features of many of the CCSA volumes that makes them so valuable is that they incorporate new manuscript witnesses that were unknown at the time of the nineteenth-century critical editions of Lipsius-Bonnet and Tischendorf. As mentioned above, this was the case with Bovon's own CCSA volume on the *Acts of Philip*,[40] but it is also true of the volumes on the *Acts of John*,[41] the *Acts of Andrew*,[42] the Irish infancy gospels,[43] and the *Infancy Gospel of Thomas*[44]—and in many of these cases, it was the editors themselves who discovered these new manuscripts. In Bovon's viewpoint, it was wholly inadequate that a specialist in the CA should have little or no first-hand contact with manuscripts. Because of this, Bovon made it a priority to train his students in the arts of manuscript research and paleography, utilizing Harvard's rich library and faculty resources in these areas. One of Bovon's lesser-known works is an immensely valuable "how to" guide to manuscript studies, walking the reader, step by

---

36. Bovon, "Editing the Apocryphal Acts," 4.

37. See the critical edition by Bovon, Bouvier, and Amsler, *Acta Philippi*, and the recent English translation by Bovon and Matthews, *Acts of Philip*.

38. See his "*Fragment Oxyrhynchus 840.*"

39. See his "Suspension of Time."

40. Bovon, Bouvier, and Amsler, *Acta Philippi*.

41. Junod and Kaestli, *Acta Iohannis*.

42. Prieur, *Acta Andreae*.

43. McNamara et al., *Apocrypha Hiberniae*.

44. Burke, *De infantia Iesu*.

step, through the practical aspects of producing a critical edition based on first-hand manuscript consultation.[45]

This emphasis on the physical evidence of CA texts is quite relevant to the third of Bovon's distinctive contributions: his troubling of the line between "canonical" and "apocryphal" literature. For it is often the manuscripts themselves that betray evidence of uncertain boundaries between these categories: consider, for example, that some of the most important manuscripts of the NT, like Codex Sinaiticus and Codex Alexandrinus, contain extracanonical early Christian writings, such as the *Epistle of Barnabas*, *1 Clement*, *2 Clement*, and the *Shepherd* of Hermas.[46] Recall that Koester also wanted to delegitimize the distinction between "canonical" and "apocryphal," but he did so in a way that almost always tended to place gospel traditions from the CA chronologically prior to their canonical counterparts—a tendency that has been the most enduring and damaging criticism of the Harvard School. Bovon approached the matter differently, making at least two cogent observations. First, although the vast majority of the CA are certainly later than the writings of the NT, their usefulness in reconstructing the history of early Christian literature does not necessarily require them to be as early as the NT writings. One reason that texts like the apocryphal acts of the apostles are especially valuable, Bovon argued, is that the peculiar and often haphazard circumstances of their preservation as noncanonical texts provide us with a window onto how the canonical gospels were preserved and edited *prior to* the more rigid form imposed upon them as canonical, authoritative texts. In essence, the apocryphal acts are a "time machine" that allow us to see how fluid and unbounded the state of the NT gospels was before their canonization.[47] In making such an argument, Bovon was no doubt influenced by his enormous body of work on the Gospel of Luke, written by an author who showed no compunction about editing, deleting, and rearranging the source material (including the now-canonical Gospel of Mark) that he had at his disposal. Bovon's ultimate conclusion in this article is, arguably, just as radical as any of Koester's theories, and has the extra advantage of being far less speculative:

> If the conditions under which the Synoptic Gospels were circulating before 180 CE are comparable to that of the later apocrypha, if Matthew and Luke used the same editorial methods

---

45. Bovon, "Editing the Apocryphal Acts."

46. Whether any of these writings can be described convincingly as "Christian Apocrypha" is less important than the fact that they occur alongside writings that came to be included in our present-day NT.

47. Explored particularly in Bovon, "Synoptic Gospels."

as the authors of the apocrypha, and if the first scribes who copied the Synoptic Gospels at that time had the same liberty that we have observed among those who copied apocryphal or hagiographic works, the question of the integrity of the Synopotic [sic] Gospels deserves renewed explanation.[48]

Bovon's second key observation about the division between the "canonical" and "apocryphal" was that this sort of binary opposition, this sort of "either/or," "in or out" assumption about the way early Christians treated their writings is a gross mischaracterization of what our sources actually say. In one of his last major articles, Bovon addressed the notion found in many ancient Christian texts of a third category that is neither "canonical" or "apocryphal," but instead "useful for the soul."[49] In calling attention to this third category, Bovon reminds us that the most noticeable result of a book being "canonical" was that it was permissible to be read aloud in church services, preached from, and so forth, whereas the "texts of the apocrypha, on the contrary, should not reach the ears of the people of God."[50] But alongside of public, liturgically-centered reading, there was also the possibility, for those having the requisite skills of literacy, of private devotional reading by individuals or of use within a closed monastic setting. The books used in these latter settings were sometimes called *antilegomena* ("disputed") and sometimes called *psychophele* ("useful for the soul"), and would frequently contain books from the canonical NT, the CA, and the Apostolic Fathers, all side-by-side. Such tripartite divisions appear long after Athananius "settled" the 27-book NT canon in 367, for in the ninth-century *Stichometry* by Nicephorus, Patriarch of Constantinople, the *antilegomena* include the (canonical) Book of Revelation, the *Apocalypse of Peter*, the *Epistle of Barnabas*, and the *Gospel of the Hebrews*.[51]

In such sophisticated and nuanced ways, then, François Bovon refined the perspective of the Harvard School on the relationship between canonical and apocryphal writings. His approach profitably might be called the "Reformed" Harvard School (after all, Bovon *did* spend most of his academic career in John Calvin's Geneva), since it does not follow Koester in the daring move of leapfrogging the CA over the NT writings chronologically. Instead, Bovon's approach maintains that the ways in which canonical and apocryphal writings were *treated* in early Christian circles were not as simple as might have been assumed. I would tend to associate myself more

---

48. Ibid., 32.
49. Bovon, "Beyond Canonical and Apocryphal."
50. Ibid., 134.
51. Ibid., 127.

closely with Bovon's "Reformed" School, while not wanting to reject out of hand the possibility that a select number of noncanonical writings—the *Gospel of Thomas, Papyrus Egerton 2*, and, *de facto,* Q—do indeed predate the gospels of the NT. Nevertheless, it is the more radical Koesterian approach that has tended to attract the most attention, certainly within scholarly circles, but especially within popular culture. This has been the perspective of John Dominic Crossan, perhaps the most visible historical Jesus scholar in the world.[52] The Koesterian Harvard School position has also informed some of the recent, highly spectacular discoveries of lost Christian writings. For example, in the case of the *Gospel of Judas*, the media immediately trumpeted this text as possibly containing the "true story" behind Judas's betrayal of Jesus—despite the fact that no scholars working on this text had actually made such a claim. Nevertheless, the sensationalizing approach of the media was not entirely invented out of whole cloth, but was instead cultivated, at least in part, through the very public advocacy of the Koesterian approach by Crossan and other members of the Jesus Seminar. As we shall see momentarily, the Koesterian approach has also played a significant role in the controversy surrounding another highly spectacular but hotly-debated CA discovery—this time, enveloping one of the other reformers of the Koesterian approach, Karen King.

Karen King came to Harvard Divinity School in 1997 from Occidental College in California, where she had taught since receiving her doctorate in 1984; she has been, since 2009, the Hollis Professor of Divinity, the oldest endowed chair in the United States (1721). Although she received her PhD at Brown University, she spent a significant portion of her time as a doctoral student studying with Hans-Martin Schenke at the Humboldt University of Berlin. Schenke was, until his death in 2002, one of the leading scholars of the Nag Hammadi library and the founder of the Berliner Arbeitskreis für koptisch-gnostische Schriften, the group tasked with translating the Nag Hammadi writings into German. The subject of her dissertation and her first publication was the Nag Hammadi text known as *Allogenes*, a revelatory discourse with virtually no references to NT writings.[53]

The (inter)relationship between the Nag Hammadi library and the CA is a complex problem, since many specialists in the former corpus tend to know little of the latter, and vice versa.[54] When can a text legitimately count

---

52. Even if, as Stephen Patterson notes elsewhere in this volume, for all of the scholarly consternation over Crossan's remarkably early dating for noncanonical texts, Crossan's Jesus is, overall, a Jesus based on the Synoptics.

53. King, *Revelation of the Unknowable God.*

54. For a discussion of this problem, see Nicola Denzey Lewis's piece elsewhere in this volume.

as belonging to both entities? If some texts from the NHL would count as CA based upon consensus definitions of the CA,[55] does the fact that at least some of these texts are far more "gnostic" (whatever that means)[56] than most other examples of the CA have any bearing upon their membership in the CA? Leaving such troublesome questions unresolved for the time being, it is clear that Karen King has done substantial editorial and exegetical work on two CA texts typically associated with the study of the Nag Hammadi library. She has written book-length studies of both the *Gospel of Mary*[57] and the *Apocryphon of John*,[58] and, as such, she shares the same concern for the production of thorough textual analyses of the CA as did Bovon—a key feature of the post-Koesterian Harvard School.

King would also share Bovon's insistence on the slipperiness of the categories of "canonical" and "apocryphal" in early Christianity. The difference, however, is that King argues her case with specific reference instead to discourses of "orthodoxy" and "heresy," and is strongly influenced by post-structuralist insights about the impossibility of objectively determining meaning and truth. What this means, according to King, is that "orthodoxy" or "heresy" (and presumably, by extension, "canonical" and "apocryphal") look different depending upon who is using said terms and to what rhetorical ends. King sums up her approach as follows:

> In practice, early Christian discourses of difference operated by treating differences differently: some are emphasized or even created; others are harmonized to make them disappear; others are simply ignored, never rising to the level of discursive employment. Constructing the impression of unity out of all this multiformity required emphasizing or even manufacturing similarities (often through harmonization) while ignoring differences. In contrast, excluding heretics meant emphasizing or even manufacturing differences while overlooking similarities. The result is that it becomes difficult for us to see the immense common territory that those who are labeled heretics shared

---

55. See, for example, the definition put forth in Burke, *Secret Scriptures Revealed*, 6: "The term 'Christian Apocrypha' designates non-biblical Christian literature that features tales of Jesus, his family and his immediate followers. They are similar in content and genre to texts included in the New Testament; the essential difference is that they were not selected for inclusion in the Bible, either because those who decided on the Bible's contents did not approve of them, or because they were composed after the time of this selection process."

56. For King's magisterial analysis of this complex problem, see her *What Is Gnosticism?*

57. King, *Gospel of Mary of Magdala*.

58. King, *Secret Revelation of John*.

with other Christians; where the real differences between them lie and what is at stake; and where there is (perhaps mutual) incomprehension, either because they simply had different theological interests or because they sidestepped, ignored, or simply failed to be cognizant of the interests of the other....[59]

Overall, then, the perspectives of Bovon and King are more similar than they are different: both exemplify the emphases of the post-Koesterian Harvard School on detailed exegetical work and a move beyond basic discussions of chronological priority to a more complex understanding of the ways in which "canonical" and "apocryphal" writings have much more in common than such binary labels might imply. In my opinion, both of these emphases are very worthwhile endeavors, and are bringing the study of the CA in North America into the twenty-first century, each in their own way.

CONCLUSION: AN UNCERTAIN TEXT AND AN UNCERTAIN FUTURE

In September of 2012, Karen King revealed to the world a small manuscript fragment, owned by an anonymous collector, containing the following Coptic phrase: "Jesus said to them, 'My wife...'"[60] Based upon this phrase, King christened the document the *Gospel of Jesus' Wife*. Despite King's insistence that the document, if it were authentic, would tell us nothing about the marital status of the historical Jesus, the reputation of the Harvard School served to shape the subsequent, entirely predictable media firestorm in much the same way as with the *Gospel of Judas* several years earlier. Accusations, first of sensationalism, and then, very shortly thereafter, of forgery came fast and furiously. Due to concerns around the authenticity of the document, King's promised article on the fragment for *Harvard Theological Review* was delayed until further testing could be done. Then, in April of 2014, a Harvard press release trumpeted that carbon-14 dating had determined the manuscript to be an authentic ancient manuscript and not a forgery.[61] Shortly thereafter, Coptic specialist Christian Askeland observed that a manuscript fragment of the Gospel of John from the same batch as the *Gospel of Jesus' Wife* not only had very similar handwriting and ink, but also was almost certainly a forgery of an existing Coptic manuscript of John. Therefore, if Askeland is correct, the *Gospel of Jesus' Wife* surfaced with and

---

59. King, "Which Early Christianity?," 79–80.
60. See King, "'Jesus said to them, "My wife...'"
61. See the Harvard press release by Beasley, "Testing Indicates."

bears striking resemblances to an obvious forgery, and is very likely to be a forgery itself. The strange case of the *Gospel of Jesus' Wife* has had so many twists and turns that it is very unwise to pronounce the matter settled; yet at the time that this essay is being finalized, the odds are not in the *Gospel of Jesus' Wife*'s favor.[62]

My point in mentioning this episode is not to criticize King; indeed, she has been an absolute model of professionalism throughout the entire controversy. Rather, such an episode serves as a portent for the present state of the Harvard School, and by extension, CA Studies in North America more generally. The Harvard School, no matter how much it refines and nuances its perspectives on the relationship between "canonical" and "apocryphal," will always shape the media narratives surrounding any well-publicized future discoveries of CA. No, we do not possess a manuscript telling Judas's side of the story; no, we do not have evidence that Jesus was married; but we as CA specialists now live in a post-*Da Vinci Code* world, and that world was made possible in part by Helmut Koester and others who claimed that the canonical gospels had been "sanitized" of information that is now found only in the CA. This metanarrative will not only impact how any future discoveries (and let us hope there are many!) will be represented in popular culture, but, more importantly for our day-to-day operations, it will also continue to color the perceptions of (at least some) other biblical scholars about what we are up to.[63] But our task must remain the same: to devote more and more detailed attention to CA both familiar and unfamiliar, and to raise challenging questions and offer more sophisticated arguments about what, if anything, the terms "apocryphal" and "canonical" actually signify.

The *Gospel of Jesus' Wife* incident also occasions reflection on the uncertain future of the Harvard School, both as an institution and as a way of training future scholars to think about the CA. At present, the only current faculty member at Harvard Divinity School with expertise in the CA is Karen King, and—as she would certainly admit—her interest focuses primarily on the Coptic material of Nag Hammadi, not in other corpora of CA. Despite the faculty line opened by Bovon's retirement, Harvard chose not to hire a junior scholar specializing in the CA. As a result, the institution that was, for many decades, the obvious place to go for doctoral students with an interest in the CA, is no longer that place. Nor (with apologies to Claremont, which

---

62. At the time of this paper's completion, the best overview of the current state of the debate can be found in Goodstein, "Fresh Doubts." But see also Mroczek, "'Gospel of Jesus' Wife,'" for an important discussion of the misogynistic dimensions of Askeland's presentation of his forgery thesis.

63. See the thoughtful analysis of the reaction of conservative scholars to developments in CA Studies in Burke, "Heresy Hunting."

is undergoing a similar dwindling of its resources without any indication of replenishment) has any other top-tier doctoral program become the "new Harvard" for CA Studies. As the 2013 York Symposium indicates, there is no shortage of mid-career and younger scholars in North America working in CA Studies, but I do wonder whether a program will emerge as a center for training new specialists—a question made even more difficult by the serious pressures that liberal arts departments in the US and Canada are presently experiencing.

— 4 —

Excavating Museums
From Bible Thumping to Fishing in the Stream of Western Civilization

— Charles W. Hedrick —

INTRODUCTION

I was given the task of writing "a scholar's autobiography" and commenting on my experiences with "some of the most interesting and controversial issues in the field of Christian apocrypha," as it was put in the charge. It is true that I have been involved in varying degrees, Forest-Gump-like, with a number of interesting discoveries beginning with my time in graduate school, but I did not begin with the critical study of religion as a career goal. I was much more interested in the practical confessional aspects of religion, and spent more time than I care to admit "Bible thumping" for lost souls.

Perhaps "Bible thumping" is not exactly correct as a description of my activities, but several times in my life I did make my living as a Southern Baptist minister in Mississippi and California, and once served as interim minister of a Congregational Church in New York City. I was commissioned as a U.S. Army reserve chaplain at Needles, California, serving some 30 years, and retiring with the rank of Colonel. I was called up for active duty as a Southern Baptist chaplain during Operation Desert Storm (Iraq), serving for the duration at the Pentagon. But at the very least I do admit "thumping" a few Bibles while fishing for converts on the back roads of Issaquena County, Mississippi, and preaching Baptist revivals in the backwoods of North Carolina and even on the streets of San Francisco.

THE CHURCH AND THE BIBLE

My youth was nourished by the Mississippi Delta of the 1940s and 1950s, and my life from earliest memory was shaped by traditional Southern Baptist preaching. One thing I learned as a youth, indeed perhaps the most important thing, was that the Bible was the Word of God. My memory is that young people growing up in the church took that teaching seriously, since we were taught to treat the Bible as a holy book. In a Baptist church we were taught nothing about the history of the texts or the culture that produced them; instead, we were taught to revere the texts, to memorize passages (from the King James Version), and to practice the teachings of the Bible in our lives.

While still in high school (Greenville, Mississippi) I decided to become a minister, and after graduation, entered Mississippi College, a Southern Baptist educational institution. My undergraduate education was interrupted by three years of military service. Later, I graduated with a Bible major (Latin and History minors), having studied Koine Greek for two semesters, and serving two years as student minister in a Baptist church in the tiny village of Mayersville in Issaquena County, Mississippi. After graduation, I moved to California and enrolled in Golden Gate Southern Baptist Theological Seminary. My wife, an Army Baptist chaplain's daughter, considered California as her home; so the move brought her nearer family and I was anxious to get out of Mississippi. I recall that the seminary curriculum did not have a course in the text and canon of the New Testament. One of my New Testament professors (Clayton K. Harrop), who had written a dissertation on that topic at Southern Baptist Theological Seminary, offered to teach such a course if I could draft enough students to make the class viable. I did, and as a result I had one course in seminary on the textual history of the New Testament. I also had two semesters each of Greek and Hebrew. During seminary, and while working full time as a chemist for the Colgate Palmolive Company in Berkeley, California, I started a church on a vacant lot in Woodacre, California, in Marin County, and served it as pastor for one year.

Up to this point in my education the closest I came to apocryphal literature (henceforth, noncanonical literature)[1] was in a course on Archaeology. The professor (Kyle M. Yates, Jr.) had students read a few selections in translation of the literature of the ancient Mediterranean world. Meanwhile, in the text and canon course I read selections from the Apostolic Fathers (the *Didache* and the *Epistle of Barnabas*). But no attempt was made in the seminary curriculum to familiarize ministerial students with noncanonical literature. Such study was not in the purview of Southern Baptist theological education at Golden Gate Seminary. A brief survey course on Church History (with William A. Carleton) certainly informed me that there was a vast body of other literature written in the early Christian period, but the ancients who produced such literature were presented in the texts we used as illegitimate competitors to the genuine Christian tradition, which was only to be found in the Biblical canon and subsequent orthodox Church leaders. After seminary, I became pastor of a Southern Baptist church in Needles, California. My sermons, commensurate with my training, were, for the most part, traditional Southern Baptist sermons. While at Needles (1962–1965), however, I purchased a set of *The Interpreter's Dictionary of the Bible*,[2] and actually used it here and there as a resource in sermon preparation. More than anything, however, it served to make me aware of how intellectually superficial and narrow my seminary training had been.

GRADUATE STUDY

Looking back today, I was not satisfied then with either the depth or the breadth of my training, and hence felt the need to continue my education. After three years I resigned as pastor of the Needles church to begin a Masters program in Religion at the University of Southern California, and at the same time I began work as a Deputy Probation Officer in the Los Angeles County Probation Department, Juvenile Probation (1965–1978) to support my family. My reason for enrolling at USC is that I wanted to continue my education but I wanted to do it outside of a Baptist framework. This was a deliberate decision. I wanted to do independent work on the biblical materials. By now I had become quite aware of the confessional constraints that today

---

1. The term "apocryphal," applied to works of doubtful authorship and authenticity, can also be applied to many of the texts in the New Testament. In the minds of many the term means not-as-reliable as canonical texts. I find the term noncanonical to be more neutral, for each of these texts has a place in writing the history of the early Christian period.

2. Buttrick, et al., eds., *Interpreter's Dictionary of the Bible*.

continue to plague the education Baptist institutions provide. I wanted to examine the Christian tradition from different perspectives. Continuing my education was the only way I could, in short term, satisfy my curiosity. My years at Golden Gate (1959–1962) overlapped with the Ralph Elliott controversy in Southern Baptist life. Elliott was a professor of Hebrew and Old Testament at Midwestern Southern Baptist Theological Seminary in Kansas City, Missouri. In 1961 he published a small book entitled *The Message of Genesis* with the Baptist Press (Broadman).[3] The book contained nothing that was not being said in mainstream colleges, seminaries, and graduate schools around the world, although Elliott's study tended toward the conservative side of issues. Nevertheless, vigorous protests erupted among the rank and file throughout the Southern Baptist Convention. Elliott was asked to withdraw the book; he refused. As a result, Broadman Press recalled all copies of the book, and in 1962 Elliott was terminated from Midwestern Seminary. Academic freedom and independent critical thinking have never been an essential part of the educational experience in Baptist academic institutions, and that is no less true of many other private academic institutions that have significant ties with religious denominations.[4]

My Masters level work at the University of Southern California (USC) included surveys in the backgrounds of both the New Testament and Old Testament (so designated). I have no doubt that my teachers at USC (Gene Tucker and Eldon Epp) appreciated both the literature of the ancient Mediterranean world and early Christian noncanonical literature, but the focus of my classes was still the study of the Bible. We read very little in noncanonical literature and no courses, or individual classes, were devoted to a careful analysis of particular noncanonical texts. It was not until my PhD work at Claremont Graduate University (then Claremont Graduate School) that I began the intensive study of individual noncanonical texts of the New Testament period as a subject worthy of interest, as opposed to studying them simply as background material for understanding the New Testament literature. I went to Claremont intending to study apocalyptic literature, an out-growth of my Master's thesis, "Eschatological Existence: The Meaning of Eschatology. A Study of Rudolf Bultmann's Understanding of Eschatology in the New Testament." At Claremont I immediately stumbled into the study of Coptic, Gnosticism, and the Nag Hammadi library. Virtually one-half of the courses I took at Claremont were on the Nag Hammadi texts and related literature; it was the hot topic of the day. In addition to my course work and my full-time employment as a Deputy Probation Officer, I became the

---

3. Elliott, *Message of Genesis*.
4. This is how I described the situation in my 1984 essay "On Wearing Two Hats."

unpaid office manager for the Coptic Project at the Institute for Antiquity and Christianity at Claremont, which in part necessitated correspondence around the world regarding the Nag Hammadi texts.

I do not recall a flash of insight at some particular moment suggesting that noncanonical texts had inherent value for study in themselves as well as for the history of early Christianity in particular and Western civilization in general, a determination that led me to conclude they should be studied as carefully as the New Testament literature is studied. I do recall, however, a conversation with my first Claremont advisor, Robert Hamerton-Kelly, in which he asked me at one point, "what is your goal in this program? Do you see yourself as a servant of the church or a servant of the discipline?" I thought it was an odd question at the time (I am not sure, but I think that because of my background there may have been suspicions that I was a "fundamentalist"), but that conversation helped clear up any ambiguity in what I wanted out of my training at Claremont. I immediately answered "a servant of the discipline."

At the time I did not see any serious conflict between the two options he offered me, but after a 24-year career teaching Religious Studies in a university partially supported by the state of Missouri, where I did research and published without ideological constraints and at the same time maintained active membership in the religious denomination of my youth, I have been forced to revise my opinion. In historical scholarship it is not possible, in the final analysis, to be a servant of the church and the discipline at the same time. Eventually, the outcomes conflict,[5] and at that point, whether consciously or unconsciously, confessional constraints are ignored and research disturbing the confessional status quo proceeds, or else a scholar will be guided by confessional constraints and find research subjects fitting safely within confessional boundaries. Noncanonical literature has always been perceived as a threat to the church, and its designation as "apocryphal," or spurious, is designed to render the church impervious to any new ideas for constructing Christian origins that such literature might bring to the table. It was simply the culture of Claremont at the time of my matriculation that all texts from the ancient world should be studied for themselves with an eye toward how they fitted into their own historical clime, and we students, almost without being aware of the change in focus, forged ahead studying the assigned noncanonical texts in photographs, and provisional Coptic transcriptions and translations. There were no default "school solutions"; what carried the day was logical argument. Our teachers were not formally trained in the subject matter, and secondary literature on the Nag Hammadi

---

5. As I argued a decade ago in the essay "Religion and Public Education."

texts was virtually non-existent. We all learned together in seminars—it was a very heady time! Claremont was one of the few places in the country where the Coptic language could be studied, but there were not many resources available to us. I was introduced to the basics of Coptic grammar by Ernie Tune, the librarian of the Southern California School of Theology at Claremont, using an unpublished mimeographed Coptic grammar (by Orval Wintermute from Duke University) keyed to the *Gospel of Thomas*, and eventually graduated to the excellent small grammar by Walter Till, *Koptische Grammatik*. Later, I became the teacher of a new group of Coptologists in an unofficial class at the university. Enrolled in that class were R. Scott Birdsall, Walter F. Taylor, Jr., Caurie Beaver, and Marvin W. Meyer.

While still a graduate student at Claremont I learned that the University of Mississippi had a complete Coptic codex—then referred to as the Crosby Codex, after the husband of the donor, Margaret Reed Crosby, who provided the funds for its purchase. On one visit to my parents' home in Greenville, Mississippi in 1971, I took the family car and travelled to Oxford to examine the Crosby Codex. I asked for and was granted permission from the Director of Libraries, John Sykes Hartin, to take photographs of the codex to Claremont to prepare a single modern pagination system for the codex, since each text in the codex had its own separate numbering system. In 1988, the codex was sold and became known henceforth as Crosby-Schøyen Codex MS 193. In 1990 it was published in the CSCO series, and I provided the critical edition of one of the texts, *Jonah the Prophet*.[6]

Due to the efforts of James M. Robinson, Claremont was the only place in the country with a complete set of the UNESCO photographs of the manuscripts in the Nag Hammadi library. From 1971 to 1975, while still a graduate student, I made annual trips to Cairo as a part of Jim Robinson's team along with the UNESCO International Committee for the Nag Hammadi Codices, of which Robinson was permanent secretary. My role was to reconstruct the original sequence of the Coptic pages of the manuscripts, place fragments and in some cases to reconstruct the papyrus leaves, and then take new photographs of the reassembled pages for Robinson's *Facsimile Edition of the Nag Hammadi Codices*. During the work of reconstructing the manuscripts, I prepared and eventually published a short essay on techniques for placing papyrus fragments.[7] When it came time to select a dissertation topic at Claremont, I expanded a seminar paper on one of the Nag Hammadi texts, the *Apocalypse of Adam*,[8] into a two-volume dissertation:

---

6. Goehring, ed., *Crosby-Schøyen Codex MS 193*; Hedrick, "Jonah."
7. Hedrick, "Some Techniques."
8. The paper was expanded and published as "Apocalypse of Adam" in 1972.

"The Apocalypse of Adam. A Literary and Source Analysis," completed in 1977. The thesis was published as a Society of Biblical Literature monograph in the Dissertation Series.⁹

While I was working as Office Manager of the Coptic Project of the Institute for Antiquity and Christianity at Claremont, one of our translators, William R. Murdock, abruptly resigned his academic post for personal reasons, gave up one of his assignments for the Coptic Project, and moved out of the country. I was asked to assume responsibility for his assignment of the *Second Apocalypse of James*, which was published in 1977 in popular form and later in the critical edition.¹⁰ When one of the volume editors of the critical edition, John D. Turner, was assigned to other responsibilities on the project, I assumed responsibility for editing and seeing through the press three of the most fragmentary Nag Hammadi Codices: XI, XII, and XIII.¹¹

ACADEMIA AND THE DISCIPLINE

I graduated from Claremont in 1977 and resigned from the L. A. County Probation Department (as Deputy Probation Officer III, while awaiting appointment as Supervising Deputy Probation Officer) in order to take a tenure track Assistant Professor position at Wagner College, Staten Island, New York, a private liberal arts college with roots in the Lutheran Church tradition. I was one of three graduates of the New Testament program at Claremont that year and the only one that managed to find an academic post—academic posts were very tight in 1978. The Head of the Religious Studies Department at Wagner, Carlyle Holland, privately and candidly told me on one occasion that the reason they hired me was not the excellence of my training at Claremont, in which they had confidence, but what tipped the scales in my favor was the fact that I had been a juvenile probation officer and the search committee felt that I should be able to handle in class what they referred to as the "street-wise" kids from New York City that matriculated at Wagner in large numbers. For the two years I taught at Wagner, I had four new preparations each semester in addition to tutoring one Master's student. With such a tight schedule, I accomplished very little in the scholarship of discovery, though I did manage to continue work editing (in

---

9. It was first published in the Dissertation Series in 1977 and reprinted by Wipf and Stock in 2005.

10. "Second Apocalypse of James (V, 4)," in *The Nag Hammadi Library in English* and "(Second) Apocalypse of James (V, 4) 44,11—63,32," in *Nag Hammadi Codices V, 2-5 and VI*.

11. Hedrick, ed., *Nag Hammadi Codices XI, XII, XIII*.

my basement on Staten Island) Nag Hammadi Codices XI, XII, XIII, which finally saw publication in 1990. At the end of 1979 I was terminated by Wagner College, along with 20% of the teaching faculty of the college, because of a financial exigency crisis—since I was the last person hired in the Religious Studies department, I was one of those selected for termination![12]

In 1980 I was hired by Missouri State University (then Southwest Missouri State University) in Springfield, Missouri to teach in the Religious Studies department. I was told by Gerrit tenZythoff, Chair of the department, that one of the reasons my packet rose to the top of the stack of the many job applications received at Missouri State was that I included my pastoral experience in my vita—go figure! My tenure at Missouri State (1980–2004), with congenial and supportive colleagues, allowed me to follow my curiosity—this was particularly true during two five-year appointments (1991–2000) as Distinguished Scholar, which came with a reduced teaching load of six hours per semester. Later (2001–2004) I was "promoted" to Distinguished Professor with a small increase in pay, but alas no reduction in teaching load.

I have never thought of myself as focusing on a particular problem in New Testament Studies, although I have thought of myself as a student of the New Testament, but always broadly conceived in terms of the literature of the early Christian period—a historian of Christian origins, if you will. I have simply pursued my interests allowing my curiosity to lead me, and for that reason, if one thinks about it at all, I suspect I might be imagined as something of a dilettante. Writing this essay, however, has made me see certain patterns in my work, which hopefully may save me from the dilettante charge—at least it does in my own mind. Looking back over my publication record, I discovered I have worked in several areas: New Testament literature, New Testament world, noncanonical literature, and the nexus between them.[13] Significant nuances between what is regarded as historical narrative, fictional narrative, and forged narrative may not be as great as we currently suppose in that all three add considerably to our historical knowledge of the ancient past. This realization led me to explore in a series of articles the fine line that exists between ancient fiction and early Christian gospel literature; in particular, the affinity between the narrative conventions of early gospel literature and the narrative techniques of ancient fiction tend to undermine

---

12. I was called in to the office of the President the day before pink slips went out to the faculty and was offered an administrative position, which I declined. Several years later, after the settlement of the court case, I was offered my old job back by order of the court. I declined.

13. For example, the following articles I consider as early Christian world: "Conceiving the Narrative"; "Representing Prayer in Mark"; and "Gnostic Proclivities."

confidence in the former as historical sources.[14] Occasionally I have moved completely out of the study of antiquity—the historical stream of Western civilization is both broad and long.[15]

I particularly enjoy reading ancient texts that have not been read since antiquity, and I have had a bit of luck in stumbling across a few of them. On one occasion during my regular travels to Egypt in the early 70s, I asked the Curator of Manuscripts of the Coptic Museum in Old Cairo, Samiha Abd El Shaheed Abd El Nour, if she had any manuscript "trash"—that is, fragments of papyrus or vellum leaves on which no one else was working. It turned out that she did, and she showed me five glass plates, which the photographer of the museum, Makram Girgis Gattas, photographed for me. The fragments were not discovered in a controlled excavation, but had been found by locals around Antinoë in Upper Egypt and sold to an antiquities dealer, who made a gift of them to the Coptic Museum in 1909. There were some biblical texts found among the fragments: Matthew, Acts, Revelation, and Hebrews,[16] which I was unable to publish until years later. But the most interesting of these disassociated fragments were the Christian noncanonical texts, all of which were unknown to modern scholarship before they were published. Two fragments provided a small window into the diversity of the early Christian period in Egypt. One fragment was a monastic exorcism text (4th to 6th centuries), likely a Coptic translation from a Greek original.[17] The second was a fragment of a revelation discourse of Jesus, which tied into early christological controversies; the text represented a Monophysite view of Christ.[18] But the most interesting fragments fitted together to form a substantial part of an early Christian codex with excerpts of two texts: a Psalms testimony text and a gospel homily.[19] The Psalms testimony "handbook" was the larger and more important since it confirmed J. Rendell Harris's thesis that early Christians collected testimonies to Jesus from the old covenant writings and published them as written texts.

In 1983 my colleague in New Testament Studies at Missouri State, Robert Hodgson, Jr., and I conducted an international conference at Springfield, Missouri focusing on the relationship between Gnosticism and Early Christianity. It was Bob's idea but we both worked on the project together,

---

14. For example, "Narrator and Story in the Gospel of Mark," and "Conceiving the Narrative."

15. Hedrick, "Emergence of the Chaplaincy"; and "On Foreign Soil."

16. See Hedrick, "Unpublished Coptic Fragment"; "Newly Identified Fragments"; and "New Coptic Fragment of the Book of Hebrews."

17. Hedrick, "Monastic Exorcism Text."

18. Hedrick, "Revelation Discourse of Jesus."

19. Hedrick, "Vestiges of an Ancient Codex."

securing a National Endowment for the Humanities Conference Grant. Thirteen scholars, recognized for their work in Gnosticism and Church History, were brought to Springfield for the discussions of their papers. The sessions were audio and video-taped and all made a part of the Meyer Library at Missouri State University. The papers were later published.[20]

THE *GOSPEL OF THOMAS*

Through the years I have maintained an interest in the Nag Hammadi literature, publishing on texts that suited my interest in the nexus between noncanonical literature and New Testament.[21] The most promising Nag Hammadi text for studying this nexus is the *Gospel of Thomas*. All of the Nag Hammadi texts have something to contribute to the study of early Christianity, since early Christianity was not a monolithic movement but a phenomenon of varying shades and facets. In my judgment, however, *Thomas* still remains the most promising. One of the areas for my doctoral exams focused on the *Gospel of Thomas*. And in later years, consequently, I have published a number of topical studies attempting to rehabilitate *Thomas* as a reliable source for clarifying early Christian history.[22] Recently I published a full-length monograph on the text, *Unlocking the Secrets of the Gospel according to Thomas*, in which I argued that *Thomas* was an early Christian text that radicalized the early Jesus traditions. As a collection of collections of Jesus traditions, *Thomas* drew eclectically from Hellenistic traditions throughout its viable life to make sense of faith—not unlike the canonical writers did.

THE *GOSPEL OF THE SAVIOR*

In 1991 I went to Berlin on a National Endowment for the Humanities Summer Stipend to work on the codicology of Codex Berolinensis P20915, a fourth- or fifth-century Coptic (Sahidic) papyrus codex in fragmentary condition mounted in 70 glass plates.[23] While working in the storage area of the Berlin Egyptian Museum, I ran across several leaves of a fragmentary Coptic codex of rather beautiful vellum lying on a light table. I asked the curator of manuscripts, Bill Brashear, if anyone was working on it; he replied

20. Hedrick and Hodgson, eds., *Nag Hammadi, Gnosticism, and Early Christianity*.
21. See Hedrick, "Kingdom Sayings"; and "Christian Motifs."
22. Hedrick, "Thomas and the Synoptics"; "Treasure Parable"; "An Anecdotal Argument"; "Parables and the Synoptic Problem"; and "Flawed Heroes."
23. See Robinson, "Codex Berolinensis P20915."

that no one was, although he had tried to get people interested in the text. So I began coming to the museum early at 6 am to work on these fragments (three fragmentary sheets, three fragmentary leaves, and twenty-nine fragments constituted the remains of a codex), which I supposed to have been at one time a complete codex (P22220). Later in the morning I would return to work on P20915. I reported on P22220 at the sixth international Coptic Congress in 1996,[24] and later published the fragmentary codex, christening its text the *Gospel of the Savior*, in a joint effort with Paul A. Mirecki, who, as it turned out, had begun preliminary work on the fragments some years before.[25]

Except for a challenge to the codicological reconstruction of the fragments by Stephen Emmel,[26] who argued for a reordering of pages and events in the codex, the text seems to have survived scholarly scrutiny as an ancient gospel text. However, I found reason to question Emmel's reordering of the codex; in my opinion, Emmel reversed physical data that should not have been reversed.[27] Recently the dating of the *Gospel of the Savior* has been called into question at a Christian Apocrypha Section of the Society of Biblical Literature in 2011. Mirecki and I had argued that the *Gospel of the Savior* likely dated to the late second century, but attempts were made in 2011 to place its composition in the fifth/sixth century. I argued in a 2013 article that the earlier date seems more appropriate.[28]

THE *GOSPEL OF JUDAS*

In a 2002 article, I commented that I had seen photographs of a *Gospel of Judas*.[29] A year later, I mentioned in another article that the *Gospel of Judas* had been on the market for a number of years.[30] Aside from these comments, I have never published anything of substance on the text. However, I was drawn into the web of intrigue surrounding this rather spectacular Coptic text by my association with Bruce Ferrini.[31] Mr. Ferrini was a dealer in antiquities from Akron, Ohio. I never met him personally, but I had been

24. Hedrick, "Preliminary Report."
25. Hedrick and Mirecki, *Gospel of the Savior*.
26. Emmel, "Recently Published *Gospel of the Savior*."
27. Hedrick, "Caveats to a 'Righted Order.'"
28. Hedrick, "Dating the *Gospel of the Savior*."
29. Hedrick, "34 Gospels," 26.
30. Hedrick, "Secret Gospel of Mark," 138.
31. James M. Robinson has chronicled my minimal involvement in *Secrets of Judas*, 129–57.

recommended to him as someone who could give competent judgments on ancient texts and objects. From time to time he would send me photographs of such items and I would identify and/or translate them for him. I accepted no pay for this service; being allowed to see, read, and identify the texts and objects, to me was compensation enough. In 2001 he sent me several sets of low-quality photographs of a hopeless jumble of papyrus pages taken with a digital camera and ten professionally-made photographs. I transcribed and translated the professionally-made photographs consisting of three leaves (six pages), which I took as belonging to the *Gospel of Judas*, since one page contained a subscript title of the text. I circulated my transcriptions and translations in 2004 to colleagues with whom I had worked in the Nag Hammadi project at Claremont.

In 2005 Mr. Ferrini requested that I send what material I had to someone he described as a reporter (Michel van Rijn) working on a story about the *Gospel of Judas*. I sent him copies of my provisional translations to assist him in his article. Mr. van Rijn, without my permission, immediately (around March of 2005) published my translation of the pages and photographs of the pages (which did not come from me) on his blog. It turned out that van Rijn was not a reporter in the traditional sense at all, but a blogger of whatever is spectacular and sure to make a splash.

Later that same year I received telephone calls and two letters from lawyers in Cleveland, Ohio subtly threatening legal action if I did not, among other things, turn over the photographs, which had been loaned to me by Mr. Ferrini, to the Maecenas Foundation (Switzerland). They thought that I was in a race to publish the codex before the National Geographic Society, who had purchased rights to the text's publication, because van Rijn had said so much on his blog. I did not conceive of myself in a race with the National Geographic Society. What I did say is that I would publish what I had if the publication of the codex was unnecessarily delayed. I ignored the lawyers' demands on the advice of my counsel (my wife, Peggy S. Hedrick, is an attorney). However, when I received emails in 2005 from Rodolphe Kasser, a Swiss colleague in Coptic Studies, who asked if he could have access to the Ferrini photographs for the National Geographic Society publication of the *Gospel of Judas*, I agreed, provided that he could secure funding for reproducing the photographs and the cost of mailing the material to him. I could not send him what was in my possession because I considered that they belonged to Ferrini. Kasser secured the funding from the Maecenas Foundation, and the cost of reproduction and mailing were paid up front by Mario J. Robarty of the Maecenas Foundation before I mailed the material to Kasser. It seems that the photographs in my possession had been taken of the manuscript at an earlier point in time in the life of this poor unfortunate codex, hence they may be expected to preserve text now missing from the actual manuscript—and indeed they do.³²

While I regard the *Gospel of Judas* as of great historical significance for the history of early Christianity, particularly early Christianity in Egypt, and the study of the Coptic language, its theological significance for the contemporary Christian church will be found to be nil. In 2005 I was interviewed for an article in a German newsmagazine and was asked if the *Gospel of Judas* was really significant theologically. I am quoted as replying: "'Ich bezweifle,' sagt Charles Hedrick, 'dass die Führer der organnisierten Christenheit einen zweiten Gedanken daran verschwenden werden, wenn die Aufregung über seine Endeckung einmal vorbei ist.'"³³ And that still remains my view. Too many discoveries that do have theological significance for the church have been bypassed for the most part in theological education and by the pulpit, for this particular noncanonical text to hold a continuing interest for the church. Nevertheless, hopefully the theological diversity in the *Gospel of Judas* will challenge the church to do its modern theology with a wary eye on the religious pluralism that existed in "early Christianity" in the first three centuries of the Christian era.³⁴

THE *SECRET GOSPEL OF MARK*

I unintentionally became involved in the *Secret Mark* affair because I happened to be in the right place at the right time. Color photographs of Clement's letter *To Theodore*, which contains the *Secret Mark* fragments, taken by the former librarian of the Greek Orthodox Patriarchate Library in Jerusalem, Kallistos Dourvas, were made available to me through a Greek colleague, Nikolaos Olympiou. The article that was subsequently published with these photographs aimed only to describe how I came by the photographs and to describe the state of the *Secret Mark* affair as I understood it at the time.³⁵ Three years later, I deliberately involved myself in the turbulence

---

32. Kasser and Wurst, eds., *Gospel of Judas*, see pp. 182 and 258. The photographs I sent Kasser revealed more text than the originals in some cases. Note that they could not call them the "Ferrini photographs" because of a previous court case, so they used my name instead.

33. Pöhner, "Judas, der Held," 79; translation in Robinson, *Secrets of Judas*, 176: "I doubt," says Charles Hedrick, "that the leaders of organized Christianity will waste a second thought on it, once the excitement about its discovery has passed."

34. As I tried to signal in a brief article in 2011 about one of the prime tenets of Christianity: "Is belief in the divinity of Jesus essential to being Christian?"

35. Hedrick and Olympiou, "Secret Mark: New Photographs." Almost ten years later in 2009 I was asked to set out the neutral data on *Secret Mark* for a series of articles

in the guild[36] over Clement's letter and *Secret Mark*, not because I had an opinion on the authenticity of the fragments but because I was shocked by the venomous *ad hominem* attacks on Morton Smith, and because I was embarrassed by the careless logic and circumstantial proof supporting what had become a popular idea in the guild that the Secret Gospel was a modern forgery. I thought scholarship had lost its way by trying to pin a modern forgery on Smith using evidence that only served to convince those who were already "true believers" in Smith's culpability. I felt at the time that a better approach for dealing with the *Secret Mark* fragments contained in the letter would have been to leave the question of authenticity open until more-definitive evidence turned up; but modern forgery theorists aimed at discrediting the text because of who discovered it—guilt by association, so to speak, or so it seemed to me. My hope was that what had become a stalemate in the guild over Clement's letter and the Secret Gospel could be set aside and scholars would give Clement's letter a fair hearing apart from its discoverer.[37] But it did not happen; if anything, more voices were raised against Smith and his "modern forgery." The guild as a whole remained silent on the issue, and except for a few critics the guild largely seemed to have lost interest in the manuscript.

Almost a decade later, at the 2008 National Meeting of the Society of Biblical Literature, the Synoptic Gospels Section held a session titled "Secret Mark after Fifty Years." I participated in the session, offering responses to papers by Birger A. Pearson, Stephen C. Carlson, and Allan J. Pantuck. My comments focused on Stephen Carlson's book, *The Gospel Hoax*, which I described as the "most complete form of a hoax theory," laying out the argument that convicted Morton Smith of perpetrating a hoax on the guild. I took up each of the elements of Carlson's argument under the rubrics of motive, opportunity, and means, aiming to show that Carlson's purported evidence was "less-than-circumstantial."[38]

I still did not have an opinion one way or the other on the authenticity of *Secret Mark*, but in April 2011 for the York University Christian Apocrypha Symposium meeting in Toronto, Canada, I was asked to prepare a paper arguing for the gospel's authenticity, a task that at the time I considered impossible—and still do. My conclusion in the paper was that there are two

---

on the text, without taking a position on its authenticity; see "Amazing Discovery."

36. By the "guild" I refer to those involved in the historical critical study of Christian origins.

37. Hedrick, "Secret Gospel of Mark."

38. These three rubrics were employed by Carlson to press his argument: *Gospel Hoax*, 74–78. My address was later published in revised form as "Evaluating Morton Smith."

equally-plausible options for explaining the previously unknown pericopae from a secret Gospel of Mark cited in Clement's letter: either they are first-century additions to the Gospel of Mark by its original author or excellent second-/third-century additions to the Gospel of Mark by an editor who was completely familiar with Mark's language, syntax, style, and narrative.[39]

A PERSONAL THEORY OF CHRISTIAN ORIGINS

Some may be curious about the theoretical rationale that took me from a professional pastoral ministry bounded by canonical texts and traditional Southern Baptist theology into an academic career that treasures even the minute noncanonical manuscript debris of Christian antiquity. Originally I had worked out no such theory; as I noted earlier, I enjoyed reading and identifying the bits of papyrus and vellum trash that archaeologists abandoned in the dust bins of libraries and museums. I recall one of the earliest bits of vellum that I transcribed and translated; it turned out to be a fragment from the Letter to the Hebrews (1:1–13). I sent photocopies of the fragment to Robert A. Kraft at the University of Pennsylvania and he identified the text by typing a sequential string of Coptic letters in its sequence from my fragment into his computer program of collected Coptic texts. His identification of the fragment as coming from the Letter to the Hebrews made it possible for me to restore the probable text lost in the lacuna of a fragment that was split down the center and having half of the text lost.[40]

Looking back, however, it is obvious to me now that a number of ideas, which have evolved through the years, gradually changed the course of my scholarship and allowed my career to go in the direction it did. For example, when I started teaching at Missouri State I changed the basic course in New Testament from "Introduction to the New Testament" to "The Literature and World of the New Testament." The change of title was more than cosmetic. The syllabus description mandated that we spend as much time with the culture, context, and religious ideas of the New Testament period as with the New Testament itself. Approaching the course in this way meant that all of the New Testament literature could not be covered, but it enabled the students to study the texts in their historical context—a much more wholistic approach.

The New Testament canon is an artificial arrangement of texts produced within the social world of the early Roman Empire. Before these texts were assembled into a collection and unilaterally designated the holy

---

39. Hedrick, "*Secret Mark*: Moving on from Stalemate," esp. 59.
40. Hedrick, "New Coptic Fragment of the Book of Hebrews."

writings of the church, they belonged to the common heritage of Western civilization, and constituted only a part of the literary residue of a broad and diverse series of religious movements inspired by different ideas about Jesus of Nazareth. What remains to scholarship of the rich heritage of these diverse movements can only be described as a residue of literary debris—so, every new text or related fragment that is found in an archaeological excavation, discovered lying forgotten on a shelf in a museum or library, is made available by a private collector, or is purchased in a Middle East market becomes an unparalleled treasure, and has at least the potential of shedding light on the past.

Originally the individual texts in the canon were never authoritative or special; they had to compete for readers without any advantage in the world of the religious ideas of late antiquity. By designating them "canonical," and thereby giving them a special status, the framers of the canon separated them from their natural historical context in which they were competitors and dialogue partners. At the same time they slandered other early Christian texts as "apocryphal" (false or spurious). These noncanonical Christian texts were also part of the competitive dialogue taking place in the stream of Western civilization, and have value for reconstructing the literary history of Western civilization in general and the early Christian movements in particular. Hence, all texts in late antiquity whose origin is stimulated in some way by ideas about Jesus of Nazareth are primary basic data for historians to use in reconstructing early Christian history. No matter how tenuously they may be connected to one another, they are nevertheless related as a part of the response of the ancient world to ideas about Jesus, which makes them a legitimate part of early Christian history. A construct that myopically prefers canonical texts over the so-called "apocryphal" texts in the reconstruction of early Christian history is biased, and historical reconstruction should first and foremost be unbiased description—that is to say, historians chronicle what actually happened.

Every historical narrative is a construct made from the point of view of a certain historian. However, the raw data of history consists of millions of billions of planned and unplanned, recorded and unnoted occurrences that have taken place in the past all over the universe. Each event/occurrence is a complete part of its historical matrix, and is a serious part of its own immediate social cause and effect pattern, but together these raw data are our common heritage. Out of this incoherent and unsorted mass of data historians plot out a literary narrative of what they regard as significant events on the basis of a cause and effect process as accurate and unbiased as they can, treating events as complete in themselves and as a serious part of the social context in which they occurred. History, therefore, is a historian's imagined construct (a plot, if you will) of selected aspects of the raw data of human life. In short, historians invent the narrative, which comes to be regarded as history and their historical constructs last until a better model comes along

These two observations (canon is an artificial construct, and historical narrative is a historian's invention) have led me to two conclusions: there can never be a monolithic narrative of early Christian history, such as the framers of the canon wanted to provide by selecting "legitimate Christian texts" and discarding all others, and every ancient Christian text, or fragment, is legitimate and deserves a place at the table in reconstructing early Christian origins and history.

CONCLUSION

Many scholars of Christianity are able to ignore the Christian Apocrypha, no doubt for a variety of reasons—not the least of which is that they bear the disreputable classification "apocrypha." These writings, as our traditional designation for them suggests, are regarded as spurious—that is, not genuine, not true. Such an evaluation is both biased and shortsighted. It can only be used about these writings from the perspective of a canonical bias, and it overlooks the fact that these texts at the very least are historical witnesses to other ways of viewing what it meant to be Christian. Nevertheless, the individuals or groups that produced such diverse texts trace their roots to Jesus of Nazareth, and hence are varieties of "Christianity" that did not fit the theological attitudes of the framers of the canon. They are part of the raw data of Christian history in that they reflect the ideas of some ancient writer about Jesus, or some aspect of Christian faith and praxis. Even if they turn out to be ancient forgeries or are found to be completely fictional narratives, they still give us brief glimpses into early Christianity at the time of their composition.

— 5 —

Scriptural Trajectories Through Early Christianity, Late Antiquity, and Beyond

Christian Memorial Traditions
in the *longue durée*[1]

— Pierluigi Piovanelli —

EARLY CHRISTIAN OR LATE ANTIQUE APOCRYPHAL TEXTS?

A FEW YEARS AGO, at an international colloquium on "The Reception and Interpretation of the Bible in Late Antiquity" organized in 2006 in Montreal by Lorenzo DiTommaso and Lucian Turcescu, I made a first attempt to address the question of the nature and value of late-antique apocryphal literature in contemporary research.[2] On the one hand, I noticed that the new perspectives opened by specialists engaged with the Association pour

---

1. It is, as usual, a great pleasure to thank the colleagues and friends who offered suggestions or comments on earlier drafts of this essay: Alessandro Bausi, Rajiv Bhola, Tony Burke, Lorenzo DiTommaso, Robert M. Edwards, Jean-Michel Roessli, Witold Witakowski, and Claudio Zamagni.
2. Piovanelli, "Reception of Early Christian Texts."

l'étude de la littérature apocryphe chrétienne (AELAC)—in particular Éric Junod, Jean-Daniel Kaestli, and Jean-Claude Picard—had led to renewed interest in a series of late-antique texts written between the fourth and the sixth century CE, such as, the *Questions of Bartholomew*, the *Acts of Philip*, the *Gospel of Nicodemus*, and the *Book of the Rooster*.[3] On the other hand, I wondered whether the inclusion of these apparently secondary and tertiary texts in the field of Christian apocryphal literature might create some troubles for those—the specialists of Early Christianity and/or the general public—who still believe that after the end of the third century CE there are no more "New Testament Apocrypha" or, more precisely, that no text written after that time can make a positive contribution to the study of the first two centuries of Christian history.

A review of the scholarly literature enabled me to identify three main arguments used to increase the value of late-antique texts or, rather, those discovered in relatively late manuscripts and/or anthologies, in order to "market" them to contemporary audiences.

1. According to the first argument, late texts are invaluable because, in spite of their relatively young age, they appear to faithfully preserve some portions of earlier *written* sources/documents. This is clearly the case for the Pseudo-Clementine *Homilies* and *Recognitions*, in which interest lies not only in their fourth-century final editions, as the recent studies of Dominique Côté,[4] Nicole Kelley,[5] and Annette Yoshiko Reed[6] abundantly demonstrate, but also in their second- or third-century Jewish Christian *Urtexten*, brilliantly reconstructed by F. Stanley Jones.[7]

2. The second argument is that late texts deserve special attention because, in spite of some superficial updates, they preserve much older *oral* traditions. This could be the case, for example, with the *Questions of Bartholomew* and the closely-related Coptic *Book of the Resurrection of Jesus Christ by Bartholomew the Apostle*, at least according to a specialist as competent as Jean-Daniel Kaestli.[8]

---

3. On the key question of apocryphicity, or apocryphal hermeneutics, see Piovanelli, "What Is a Christian Apocryphal Text"; and Piovanelli, "Qu'est-ce qu'un 'écrit apocryphe chrétien'?" (revised and expanded French translation of the previous essay).

4. See now Côté, "Les procédés rhétoriques"; and Côté, "La forme de Dieu."

5. See now Kelley, "Theological Significance"; Kelley, "Astrology"; Kelley, "What is the Value of Sense Perception?"; and Kelley, "On Recycling Texts and Traditions."

6. See now Reed, "Heresiology"; Reed, "'Jewish Christianity' as Counter-history?"; Reed, "From Judaism and Hellenism"; and Boustan and Reed, "Blood and Atonement."

7. See now the collected studies in Jones, *Pseudoclementina Elchasaiticaque*.

8. See especially Kaestli, "Où en est l'étude de l'*Évangile de Barthélemy*?"; Kaestli and Cherix, *L'évangile de Barthélemy*. On the complex question of dating the *Questions*

3. As for the third argument, a few texts copied in late antique or even medieval manuscripts might not be late at all, but as old as, for instance, the Greek originals of the texts belonging to the Nag Hammadi library or discovered in the Al-Minya Codex.[9] This was the claim made by the editors of two Coptic fragmentary texts: the so-called *Gospel of the Savior*, published in 1999 by Charles Hedrick and Paul Mirecki,[10] and an apparently archaic version of the *Transitus Mariae*, published by Hans Förster in 2006.[11]

Concerning the first and the second arguments, I must confess that I tend to now consider the case of the *Pseudo-Clementines* as more the exception than the rule, and that there exists an inverse relationship between the possibility to retrieve older traditions and the literary talent displayed by late-antique narrators.[12] In other words, those who utilized preexisting tales and traditions in order to produce the *Questions of Bartholomew*, the dormition story of the *Liber Requiei*, the "orthodox" *Apocalypse of Paul*

---

of *Bartholomew*, see now Markschies, "Fragen des Bartholomaeus," 708–709.

9. It is certainly fascinating to study Nag Hammadi and related texts—as Jenott ("Clergy, Clairvoyance, and Conflict," and "Recovering Adam's Lost Glory") and a few others do—in the framework of the fourth-century Coptic monastic milieus that probably held and almost certainly read them. One should not forget, however, that their primary interest lies in the fact that they are translations of second- or third-century Greek "gnostic" texts of the highest importance for the reconstruction of early Christian history. Actually, this should be envisioned as a two-way dynamic process: better knowledge of how translations of early Christian writings worked in the late antique and even medieval cultural milieus that inherited them cannot but improve our ability to read through the actual texts back towards their original models, a point that I emphasize in Piovanelli, "L'Enoch Seminar," concerning the Ethiopic version, from a Greek *Vorlage*, of *1 Enoch* copied exclusively in medieval and modern manuscripts.

10. On this poorly-preserved "Passion gospel," to be more probably identified with a late antique homily on the Passion, see the bibliographic references given below, nn. 19–22.

11. Förster, *Transitus Mariae*. Förster's proposal has been criticized by Norelli, *Marie des apocryphes*, 140–42, and especially Shoemaker, "Mary the Apostle." This has not prevented Förster from translating the Coptic fragment P.Vindob. K. 7589 that he had previously published, together with the relatively late Greek *Transitus* attributed to John the Evangelist, in Markschies and Schröter, *Antike christliche Apokryphen*, 1:299–307. Those who are really interested in the earliest dormition narratives—i.e., the mid to late fourth-century *Liber Requiei*, which survives in an Ethiopic version and a series of Syriac, Coptic, and Georgian fragments—are advised to consult Shoemaker, "Epiphanius of Salamis"; Shoemaker, "New Syriac Dormition Fragments," 260–63 and 267; Tedros Abraha, "Some Philological Notes"; as well as the collected studies of Mimouni, *Les traditions anciennes sur la Dormition*.

12. An even clearer exception is represented by the *Apostolic Constitutions*, a late fourth-century, slightly-edited compilation of the *Didascalia Apostolorum* (books 1–6), the *Didache* (book 7), and the *Apostolic Tradition* (book 8), on which see now Ehrman, *Forgery and Counterforgery*, 14–19 and 390–96. The majority of cases, however, are far from being as simple.

(originally written in Greek around 400 CE), or the *Book of the Rooster*, did not act simply as redactors, but conspicuously adapted and creatively reworked their apocryphal heritage, be it of "gnostic," "Jewish Christian," or other origins.[13] It would be vain to scrutinize the actual text of these works in order to isolate sources that certainly existed but are presently impossible to retrieve and, frankly speaking, out of scope.

Instead of looking for the citations of lost documents or the remains of previous editions, what I tried to do in the case of, for example, the *Apocalypse of Paul* and the *Book of the Rooster* was to read each of them as a coherent narrative, and then recontextualize each of them in what I supposed were their original environments—in both cases, Palestinian monastic communities. Only later, when it came to the question of the origins of some of their most curious traditions—such as, for instance, the extremely negative characterization of Judas Iscariot in the *Book of the Rooster*—did I do my best to locate them within a series of trajectories that go from the beginnings of Christianity to the fifth century and beyond. Thus, the interplay between early Christian (the newly rediscovered *Gospel of Judas*, the speeches Celsus attributes to a Jewish informant, the testimonies of Tertullian and Commodian) and late antique traditions and texts (the *Book of the Rooster*, the *Toledot Yeshu*,[14] the *Book of the Resurrection of Jesus-Christ by Bartholomew the Apostle*) tends to show that already in the second half of the second century different groups—Jewish, "Jewish Christian," "gnostic," etc.—were able to use the figure of the "wayward" disciple as a narrative straw man at the service of intergroup polemics.[15] As for the identity of the confidant of Jesus in charge of transmitting his revelations to the apostles, the line of evolution from early Christian (*Gos. Thom.* 114; *Gos. Phil.* 32 and 55; the *Gospel of Mary*, and other "gnostic" revelation dialogues) to late antique apocryphal texts (the *Liber Requiei* and other dormition narratives, the various *Apocalypses of the Virgin*, the *Questions of Bartholomew*, the *Book of the Resurrection of Jesus Christ by Bartholomew the Apostle*) clearly demonstrates that the prerogatives of Mary (of Magdala) the *koinōnos*, or "companion," were progressively passed on to Mary the mother.[16] This kind

---

13. See Piovanelli, "Le recyclage des textes apocryphes."

14. A fifth-century date and a Syro-Palestinian location for its original kernel can be inferred also from a number of observations made by Stökl Ben Ezra, "Ancient List of Christian Festivals," 490–92 ("between the late-fourth and mid-fifth centuries"), and Gribetz, "Hanged and Crucified," 171–73 (on anti-Christian attitudes at the occasion of Purim).

15. See Piovanelli, "Rabbi Yehuda"; Piovanelli, "Toledot Yeshu"; and Piovanelli, "De l'usage polémique," 133–40.

16. See Piovanelli, "Le recyclage des textes apocryphes," 280–87; and Piovanelli,

of approach—namely, one that takes into account the evolution of scriptural traditions in the *longue durée* of Christian history[17]—is in my opinion the most apt for explaining a good number of what at first sight appear to be perplexing phenomena in the never-ending production of our apocryphal texts.

But it is the third option that I find the most risky and, in many cases, difficult to follow without discussion. In 2006 I had already expressed some doubts about an early dating for the *Gospel of the Savior*. Since then, the publication in 2009 by Peter Hubai, of two similar (but not identical!)[18] Coptic texts—the *Discourse of the Savior about the Cross* and the *Dance of the Savior around the Cross*—discovered in much better condition in a tenth-century devotional codex at Qasr el-Wizz (Central Nubia),[19] has confirmed that such a cluster of texts is the result of a long trip away from the second century. Thus, both the *Gospel of the Savior* and the *Dance of the Savior around the Cross* can be, partially or entirely, interpreted as late, more "orthodox" rewritings of the pre-passion episode of Jesus' public dance and hymn in *Acts of John* 94–96 and the esoteric revelation of the mystery of the Cross of Light that follows it in *Acts of John* 97–102, originally intended to provide memorial justification for a liturgical celebration of a "Johannine gnostic" or, perhaps, "Valentinian" group or community.[20] Moreover, as Joost Hagen[21] and Alin Suciu[22] have independently and convincingly shown, the best literary parallels to the *Gospel of the Savior* are to be found in a group of Coptic homiletic texts that claim to draw upon memoirs of the apostles discovered in Jerusalem, but actually are replete with apocryphal traditions, such as the sermon *On the Life and the Passion of Christ* attributed to Cyril of Jerusalem, recently published by Roelof van den Broek.[23]

"Rewriting," 100–106.

17. A phenomenon that—as I argue in Piovanelli, "*Rewritten Bible* ou *Bible in progress?*"—is deeply rooted in Second Temple Judaism.

18. To the best of my knowledge, no serious attempt has been made so far to demonstrate that the *Discourse of the Savior about the Cross* and/or the *Dance of the Savior around the Cross* are "genetically" derived from the *Gospel of the Savior*. In my opinion, it is more probable that they form a cluster of three closely-related, yet independent, texts.

19. Hubai, *Koptische Apokryphen aus Nubien*.

20. See Piovanelli, "Thursday Night Fever," 241–48. Compare the reaction of Hedrick, "Dating the *Gospel of the Savior*," as well as the contributions of Dilley, "*Christus Saltans*," and Yingling, "Singing with the Savior."

21. Hagen, "Ein anderer Kontext."

22. Suciu, "Apocryphon Berolinense/Argentoratense."

23. Van den Broek, *Pseudo-Cyril of Jerusalem*.

If a late dating of this *Apocryphon Berolinense/Argentoratense* (a revised title proposed by Suciu to rebaptize the *Gospel of the Savior*) seems to be established, other candidates to an older, more venerable, yet equally improbable, age have been more recently proposed. I am thinking here of the *Revelation of the Magi*, a beautiful apocryphal story inserted in the Syriac *Chronicle of Zuqnin* in the last quarter of the eighth century. Brent Landau,[24] who recently rediscovered and reevaluated it, suggests that, because its contents were already known and summarized by the author of the so-called *Opus imperfectum in Matthaeum* in the fifth or sixth century,[25] the *Revelation of the Magi* should be older, possibly a late second- or early third-century text.[26] One should note, however, that the Adamic traditions deployed in the *Revelation of the Magi*, especially the motif of the preservation

---

24. Landau, "Sages and the Star-Child"; Landau, "*Revelation of the Magi* in the *Chronicle of Zuqnin*"; Landau, *Revelation of the Magi*; and Landau, "'One Drop of Salvation.'"

25. Under the eloquent title of *Liber apocryphus nomine Seth. Mons Victorialis*, "The Mountain of Victories, an apocryphal book on the name of Seth," which seems to me the only meaningful way of translating the beginning of the notice in the *Opus imperfectum in Matthaeum* (English translations are provided by Landau, *Revelation of the Magi*, 103–105, and Toepel, "Apocryphon of Seth"). If the reference to the "Mountain of Victories"—mentioned in the *Revelation of the Magi* (4:1–2, 7; 5:2; 11:3; 12:1; 14:9; 17:4; 27:4), on whose heights is located "the Cave of the Treasures of the hidden mysteries" in which were placed "the Books of Seth," i.e., "the Books of Commandments" inherited by the magi—seems an appropriate title for this text, from a narrative point of view its Sethian attribution is unjustified; only the "excerpts" inserted between chapters 5 and 11 are actually taken from the Books of Seth.

26. On the parallels that the *Revelation of the Magi* shares with the "Third Source" (in addition to the *Protevangelium of James* and the *Gospel of Pseudo-Matthew*) of the Latin and Irish *Liber de Nativitate Salvatoris*, see Landau, "Sages and the Star-Child," 202–18; and Landau, *Revelation of the Magi*, 18–25 and 111–13. The perspective of a relationship between the two texts has been developed further by Kaestli, "Mapping," 526–33. According to Landau, "if we assume that the *Revelation of the Magi* came into being sometime after *Infancy Gospel X* [i.e., the 'Third Source'] of the *Liber de Nativitate Salvatoris*], then it was probably written in the late second or early third century. It was then 'corrected' in the late third or early fourth century by adding the concluding narrative about the Apostle Thomas's visit to the Magi" (*Revelation of the Magi*, 25). Without entering into too-technical details, it is noteworthy that a certain number of the parallels identified by Landau and Kaestli are shared also by the *Armenian Infancy Gospel* (see especially 11:9–23 in the new translation of Terian, *Armenian Gospel of the Infancy*, 51–58). This would point to the existence, in the fifth or the sixth century, of Greek or Syriac infancy compilations structurally similar to those found in the *Liber de Nativitate Salvatoris* and in the *Armenian Infancy Gospel*. As for the second-century date of the hypothetical "*Infancy Gospel X*," advocated especially by Kaestli, "Recherches nouvelles," it is simply too speculative to be of any use for the dating of the equally hypothetical *Urtext* of the *Revelation of the Magi*.

of antediluvian teachings and books,[27] seem to depend on those found in the second-century (?) *Life of Adam and Eve*, the third-century (or later) *Testament of Adam*, and/or the fifth- or sixth-century *Cave of Treasures*. All of these texts specify that Adam's body was placed in a cave alongside the gold, myrrh, and incense he had brought with him from the Garden of Eden until, the narrator of the *Testament of Adam* adds, "the sons of kings, the magi, will come and get them, and they will take them to the son of God, to Bethlehem of Judea, to the cave" (3:6).[28] As for the *Opus imperfectum in Matthaeum*, if Gustavo Piemonte's proposal to attribute all, or at least part, of it to the Irish theologian and polymath Johannes Scotus Eriugena (ca. 815–876/7) is to be accepted,[29] its use of the *Revelation of the Magi* would only demonstrate that at least a Latin summary of such a text was known in the West in the ninth century. In the end, one is left with the impression that in the *Revelation of the Magi*, at least in its final form, Adam and Seth's traditions of old[30] were probably recycled in the second half of the fourth or at the beginning of the fifth century[31] and connected with Matthew's story of the magi in order to provide Syriac Christianity with an even stronger biblical lineage.

27. On which see Piovanelli, "From Enoch to Seth," 101–10.

28. Trans. Stephen E. Robinson in Charlesworth, ed., *Old Testament Pseudepigrapha*, 2:994. See Klijn, *Seth in Jewish, Gnostic and Christian Literature*, 44–47; Tubach, "Seth and the Sethites," 193–201.

29. Piemonte, "Recherches sur les *Tractatus in Matheum*."

30. Together with "Zoroastrian" motifs (on which see, most recently, Witakowski, "Magi in Syriac Tradition," 837–38) and "docetic" images of Jesus—notably his polymorphism in 14:3–8; 28:1–3, reminiscent of *Acts John* 88–94; *Acts Thom.* 143; *Acts Pet.* 20–21 (as noticed by Landau, *Revelation of the Magi*, 132 n. 125)—that undoubtedly contribute to make the *Revelation of the Magi* appear, at first sight, so archaic. However, as the presence of analogous polymorphic traditions in Pseudo-Cyril's homily *On the Life and the Passion of Christ* (§§73, 75, 78–79 and 137, on which see van den Broek, *Pseudo-Cyril of Jerusalem*, 50–56) demonstrates, archaic features do not necessarily betray the antiquity of a given text.

31. A mid fourth-century date is suggested by Witakowski, "Magi in Syriac Tradition," 813–14, while Reed, "Beyond the Land of Nod," 77–82, prefers "to posit a later date for the present form of the work—or, more specifically, for its reference to Šir as the homeland of the Magi . . . perhaps closer in time to Cosmas [Indicopleustes, who wrote his *Christian Topography* around 550]" (ibid., 80). As Kristian Heal puts it, "serious consideration needs to be given to the dating of the text. Careful analysis of a variety of linguistic, thematic and text critical issues need to temper the natural desire to date a text as early as possible" (review of Landau, *Revelation of the Magi*, 298; similar concerns are also expressed in Annette Y. Reed's review, especially 46–49). On the number and the names of the magi in Syriac tradition, see also Witakowski, "Magi in Ethiopic Tradition," 83–87 (on an Ethiopic version of Ibn aṭ-Ṭayyib's *Commentary on the Gospel of Matthew*); Debié, "Suivre l'étoile à Oxford"; Haelewyck, "Le nombre des Rois Mages."

THE STRANGE CASE OF
A NEW ETHIOPIC APOCRYPHAL TEXT

In 2010 I had the chance to discover a new, previously unknown Ethiopic apocryphal text, the *Zena ḥəmamatihu lä-Krəstos*, or *Story of the Passion of Christ* (literally, "Story of the Sufferings of Christ"), an extremely short revelation about the pains that Jesus endured during his passion. The text was copied generally at the end of a number of modern manuscripts of the *Ləfafä ṣədq*, or *Bandlet of Righteousness* (or *Justification*), the devotional booklet or parchment scroll containing the secret and "magical" names that Jesus disclosed to his mother and his apostles in order to enable them, as well as the faithful who own, bear, and are buried with it, to "be saved from the consuming fire" of Gehenna.[32] In Tesfa Gebre Selassie's popular edition of the *Bandlet of Righteousness*, published in 1961 EC (= 1969–1970 CE), the *Story of the Passion of Christ* runs as follows.

> In the name of the Father, the Son, and the Holy Spirit, one God. Let us write the story of the passion of our Lord Jesus Christ, which he revealed to three women, who are Mary, Salome, and Mary of Magdala: they are those who wrapped him with the fingers folded up. 22 (are) the times that they dragged him with a rope and kicked him with (their) feet. 22 (are) the times that they slapped his face with (their) hands. 22 (are) the times that they spat on him unclean spittles on his face. 22 (are) the times that they hit him on the head with a reed. 22 (are) the times that they struck him with a rod to the point that it was possible to count his bones. 22 (are) the times that they laughed at him. As for me, I do not laugh every time that I see your holy linen cloth in which your body was shrouded by Joseph and Nicodemus! O Lord be benevolent in your compassion for the sake of your death and your burial, you who reign forever and ever.[33]

---

32. On the *Bandlet of Righteousness*, see Chernetsov, "Ethiopian Magic Texts," 196–97; Burtea, "Ləfafä ṣədəq"; Wion, "Onction des malades," 48–50. To date, I have been able to identify sixteen manuscripts of the *Bandlet of Righteousness*, the large majority being quite recent (twentieth century), that contain also the *Story of the Passion of Christ*. I was able to procure a diplomatic edition of four Parisian manuscripts, three of the *Story of the Passion of Christ* (Bibliothèque nationale de France, Éth. 546 [Griaule 238], last 28 lines; Éth. 591 [Griaule 283], fol. 20^v; Éth. 671 [Griaule 363], pp. 118–24) and one of the related *Revelation about the Passion of Christ* (Éth. 86 [*olim* 62], fol. 120^v, on which see below); see further Piovanelli, "The *Story of the Passion of Christ*: A New Ethiopic Apocryphon Attributed to Salome, Elizabeth, and Mary of Magdala," to be published in a volume in memory of the great Italian specialist of Ethiopian Studies Paolo Marrassini (1942–2013).

33. Tesfa Gebre Selassie, *Ṣalot bä'əntä Ləfafä ṣədq*, 83–84. One should note that

The structure of the text is relatively simple: after the usual Trinitarian invocation comes the identification of the holy women under whose authority the revelation is placed; then, the main body of the text provides a detailed list of each abuse inflicted on Jesus following the same repetitive pattern, "a certain number of times (in this case, 22) they did such-and-such evil thing to him"; finally, the narrator dissociates himself/herself from the behavior of the persecutors—"they laughed at him . . . I do not laugh"—and implores Jesus' intercession.

Without surprise, each section of the *Story of the Passion of Christ* differs from one manuscript to the next.[34] Notably, in the majority of the manuscripts the three receivers of the revelation are designated as being Sarah, Salome, and Mary of Magdala, or, in a different order, Mary of Magdala, Sarah, and Salome. A few other manuscripts have the mysterious Sarah replaced with Elizabeth—likely to be identified with the mother of John the Baptist and, according to Luke 1:36, Mary's *syngenēs*, or "relative"—to produce the sequence Salome, Elizabeth, and Mary of Magdala; others simply omit the names of the three holy women. As for the enigmatic identification that "(they are) those who wrapped him with the fingers folded up (literally, 'by the wrapping up of the fingers')," this seems to be a reference to the women's role in the preparation of Jesus' body for the burial,[35] especially in placing Jesus' hands together on his chest or across his groin.

---

the scholarly editions of the *Bandlet of Righteousness*—Budge, *Bandlet of Righteousness*, and Euringer, "Binde der Rechtfertigung," as well as the translations of Turaiev, *Lefâfa-Sedeq*, and Fusella, "*Maṣḥafa heywat* et *Mangada samāy*"—do not include the *Story of the Passion of Christ*.

34. If we take Tesfa Gebre Selassie's printed text as a point of comparison, the second section, with the list of the various torments inflicted on Jesus, is shorter in manuscripts Éth. 546 (three items) and 671 (five), but longer in Éth. 591 (nine); also, Éth. 671 has a relatively long and elaborate final invocation, while Éth. 591 seems to have drastically abridged the last two sections.

35. Their close association with Jesus' death and entombment is confirmed by both canonical and apocryphal traditions. Thus, in the Gospel of Mark, Mary of Magdala, Salome, and Mary the mother of James the younger and Joses are among the women who observe Jesus' crucifixion from a distance (15:40), and two days later bring spices to the tomb in order to anoint his body (16:1). Sarah too is mentioned—albeit in a single text, the *Epistle of the Apostles* (9–10), also translated into Ethiopic—as one of the three women, together with Martha and Mary of Magdala, who bring aromatic unguents to Jesus' tomb. Salome, who is completely absent from the rest of the New Testament writings, reappears in the company of Mary of Magdala as Jesus' sister and/or disciple in early Christian and late antique apocryphal literature. On the question of the two Salomes, see especially Bauckham, *Gospel Women*, 225–56. As for Mary of Magdala, the historical person and the literary character, the relevant bibliography can be found in Piovanelli, "Rewriting," 101 nn. 40–42.

The special emphasis that the narrator of the *Story of the Passion of Christ* puts on Jesus' sufferings seems to point to a great concern, shared by his or her original audience, for the crude reality of the torments inflicted on the man of Nazareth and their salvific effects for the faithful—a theological preoccupation that, since its first narrative epiphany in fourth or fifth-century apocryphal passion gospels,[36] has never ceased to permeate Christian retellings of Jesus' death, even in modern times.[37] Therefore, in the absence of more specific clues, I would have tentatively suggested that the *Story of the Passion of Christ* is either a late antique apocryphal text—perhaps the "orthodox" rewriting of a revelation dialogue of the risen Jesus with the women disciples[38]—or an apocryphal byproduct of medieval or even early modern popular devotion. However, the discovery of its subtext allowed me to be more precise and, contrary to my initial, overly optimistic expectations of "great antiquity," to envision a date of composition as late as (depending on the age of its oldest manuscript copies) the eighteenth or the nineteenth century.

The origins of the *Story of the Passion of Christ* are to be found in another Ethiopic text under the title of *Revelation about the Passion of Christ*, which was inserted at the end (on fol. 120^v) of the Parisian manuscript Bibliothèque nationale de France, Éth. 86 (*olim* 62), a seventeenth-century codex containing a collection of miscellaneous prayers and hymns. In this text, however, the most significant novelty is that the source of the revelation is no longer attributed to three holy women in Jesus' entourage, but to three European saints well-known for their visionary experiences: St. Brigit of Sweden (1303–1373), St. Mathilde of Hackeborn (1241–1299), and St. Elisabeth, Queen of Hungary (1207–1231). An English translation of the text runs as follows.

36. See, for example, the remarks about the *Gospel of the Savior* and the *Book of the Rooster* in Piovanelli, "Thursday Night Fever," 245 n. 57.

37. Mel Gibson's highly controversial movie, *The Passion of the Christ* (New York and Los Angeles: Newmarket Films, 2004), being a contemporary example of such a trend.

38. One should not forget the significant role that Mary of Magdala and Salome play in early Christian "gnostic" dialogues. Thus, Jesus recommends both women as exemplary figures in the new Coptic version of the *First Apocalypse of James* from the recently published Al-Minya Codex: "Let yourself be persuaded by this other (circumstance), which is that of Salome, Mariahmme, and Arsinoe, whom I shall introduce to you because [they] are worthy of the One Who Is" (27.25–28.2, trans. Marvin Meyer and François Gaudard in Kasser and Wurst, eds., *Gospel of Judas*, 155 and 157). See also *Gos. Thom.* 61, where Salome asks Jesus, "Who are you, mister? You have climbed onto my couch and eaten from my table as if you are from someone," and finally enthusiastically proclaims, "I am your disciple" (trans. Marvin Meyer in Meyer, ed., *Nag Hammadi Scriptures*, 147).

Revelation about the passion of our Lord Jesus Christ, the Savior of the world, which he revealed to the three holy women called St. Brigit (*Bräzeda*), St. Mathilde (*Metelda*) and St. Elizabeth (*Eləsabeṭ*). These are <...>. How they struck his face 20 times with (their) fingers folded up. How they slapped his cheek 120 times. How they struck his mouth 30 times with (their) fingers folded up when they tied him up. How he fell to the ground 7 times when he was taken from the garden to Anna's house. How they kicked him with their feet 140 times on the back and on the front. How they struck his shoulder 62 times. How they struck his chest and his belly 20 times. How they struck his feet 37 times. How they struck his legs 80 times. How they dragged and caused him to rise from the ground by a rope and by the hair of his head 305 times. The strokes that he received on his flesh, each of them almost killing him, were 190. They treated him violently against a pillar 1 time. Having tied (him) up to the pillar, they scourged him 6,666 (times). The beatings and the wounds inflicted on him, to the point that his bones became visible, were 666. The large wounds of his head were 72. The holes in his head (made) by the crown of thorns were 1,000. How he fell in the street under the cross 5 times, and how they treated him violently 3 times until they crucified him. How they spat on his face 73 times. The wounds that became blue and black were 1,190. The soldiers who were there with their weapons were 580, and the other people who were there were 230. Those who were dragging (him) with ropes were 3. The drops of blood that were poured from him were 1,925. A faithful man should neither rejoice at all nor laugh every time he reflects assiduously upon these sufferings with righteousness all the time.

Even more intriguingly, this *Revelation about the Passion of Christ*, which provided the textual basis for the rewriting of the *Story of the Passion of Christ*, is not even an Ethiopic production, but the translation into Ethiopic of a Birgittine devotional apocryphon: the *Revelation of Christ's Wounds*. Derived from the famous prayers attributed to St. Brigit known as the *Fifteen Oes*,[39] the *Revelation of Christ's Wounds* probably was writ-

---

39. "Alongside the gradual development of a Birgittine canon, a number of apocryphal texts came to be associated with the Swedish saint, such as the work known as the 'Fifteen Oes,' a sequence of 15 prayers on Christ's sufferings at his passion, each beginning with 'O.' It was one of the most popular devotions in the fifteenth and sixteenth centuries, available in as many as ten European languages, and was particularly popular in England and the Low Countries. It was falsely associated with Birgitta in the fifteenth century and has been attributed to her in numerous editions and translations ever since: a testimony, if one were needed, of the enormous following she left behind

ten originally in Latin, perhaps towards the end of the sixteenth century. It survives in a seventeenth-century Irish version, a translation into English,[40] a German abridgement,[41] and a series of nineteenth- and twentieth-century Italian manuscripts, prints, and popular oral versions.[42] For the purpose of comparison, I give here the English version copied by an Irish soldier named Thomas Crewe in 1686, maintaining the orthography of the original.

> In the name of God, Jesus, Maria, Joseph, being my light in my Way. Amen.
>
> This Revelation was made by the Mouth of our Saviour Jesus X to the Sts. St. Elizabeth, St. Malachias (*sic*), St. Bridgitt, desiring to have something in particular of the Blessed Passion of our Ld. J.X.: at last, & after much Prayer done unto God X. answered & revealed as here followeth.
>
> 1. I received 200 Blows with a Whip.
>
> 2. I recd 30 Cuffs when I was apprehended in the Garden.
>
> 3. I recd 7 Blowes when I was comming from Annanias (*sic*) his house.
>
> 4. I recd 100 Cuffs upon my head.
>
> 5. I recd 81 Cuffs upon my Shoulders—from the Ground.
>
> 6. They gave me 232 Cuffes & 3 Times on the Teeth.
>
> 7. I breathed out 8000 Sighs.
>
> 8. They drew me by the Beard 8 times.
>
> 9. I recd 3 mortall Wounds by the Foot of the Cross.
>
> 10. I recd 6666 Blowes of a Whip when I was bound to the Pillar.
>
> 11. I was 100 Times wounded in my Head.
>
> 12. When I was hanged on the X I recd 5 mortall Wounds.
>
> 13. They spitted in my Faces 65 Times.
>
> 14. The Soldiers gave me 8182 Blowes of a Whip.

---

her, not only in terms of her prophetic voice and her orthodox upholding of traditional doctrine but also of her influence on private devotion" (Searby and Morris, *Revelations of St. Birgitta of Sweden*, 25).

40. Published by Flower, "Revelation of Christ's Wounds."

41. Translated into English by Henderson, *Notes on the Folk Lore*, 137.

42. See Piazzesi, *Acta Sanctae Sedis*, 740–42 (reproducing a long version of the *Revelation of Christ's Wounds* originally published in 1893), and more recently, Galizzi, "Orazioni ed Epistole ad uso salvifico."

(. . .) This Revelation was found in a certain Tombe in Jerusalem, & approved by Holy Mistimus (*sic*) & Pursetonor (*sic*) & other superior officers.

This practice was begun by me about Michaelmas (i.e., October 10 or 11) 1686.

Tho: Crewe.⁴³

The discovery of the *Revelation about the Passion of Christ* allows us to solve a few textual problems of the *Story of the Passion of Christ* and to reconstruct some aspects of its genesis. Thus, concerning the original meaning of the expression "with the fingers folded up" mentioned above, two passages of manuscript Éth. 86—"How they struck his face 20 times with (their) fingers folded up. (. . .) How they struck his mouth 30 times with (their) fingers folded up"—clearly show that such an expression is simply an attempt to convey the idea that Jesus was actually *punched*, as we read in the Italian version ("i pugni"), or *slapped* as it is incessantly repeated in the English version ("Cuff[e]s").⁴⁴ Moreover, at the very end of the initial section of the *Revelation about the Passion of Christ*, something is missing from the Ethiopic text of manuscript Éth. 86 after "these (masculine) are. . ." Apparently, the Ethiopian scholar who felt the need to rewrite this text, when confronted with the difficulties of its first lines, preferred to identify the three unfamiliar receivers of the revelation with three well-known followers of Jesus and, having interpreted the expression "with the fingers folded up" as a reference not to throwing punches or slaps at Jesus, but to preparing his body for entombment, completed the last defective sentence of the introduction as "(they are) those who wrapped him with the fingers folded up."

The most plausible conclusion to this state of affairs is that the Ethiopic *Revelation about the Passion of Christ* derives from a now-lost Latin text brought to Ethiopia by Catholic missionaries and translated some time before their expulsion from the country in 1632.⁴⁵ As for the *Story of the Passion of Christ*, it is an inner-Ethiopic rewriting of the *Revelation about the Passion of Christ*, now a brand-new apocryphal text attributed to

---

43. Taken from Flower, "Revelation of Christ's Wounds," 40. The substitution of "St. Mathilde" with "St. Malachias" is a special feature of the Irish version of the *Revelation of Christ's Wounds*, from which this English translation was made.

44. Then, "with the fingers folded up" seems to be an awkward rendering of the Latin *digitis convolutis* or the like.

45. See, in general, Pennec, *Des jésuites au royaume du Prêtre Jean (Éthiopie)*; Cohen, *Missionary Strategies*, esp. 98–100 (on the translations from Latin or Portuguese to Ethiopic).

Salome, Elizabeth, and Mary of Magdala, three women among Jesus' closest disciples, produced at a date as late as the eighteenth or nineteenth century.

THE BEST CRITIC OF APOCRYPHAL TEXTS TRANSMITTED THROUGH LATE TRADITIONS

In the end, if it was still possible just two or three centuries ago for a Christian culture as traditional as the Ethiopian one to recycle an early modern pseudo-revelation in order to create an entirely new apocryphal narrative which quickly became one of the most popular apotropaic writings employed by Ethiopian faithful, one legitimately may wonder about the number of other apocryphal texts that have been crafted throughout the history of a variety of Christianities for an array of reasons and purposes.[46] Even if it is perfectly understandable that specialists of early Christianity are interested primarily in apocryphal texts written before the end of the third century CE, only a minority of those transmitted through late traditions are as old (and meaningful for Early Christian Studies) as, for example, the *Gospel of Thomas* or the *Gospel of Judas*. And even if it is true that every discoverer of an unknown text is always filled with excitement and great expectations, in some cases manuscript hunters end up with unexpected surprises that can have, perhaps, the same relevance for the study of epochs and cultural areas other than the origins of Christianity.[47]

The true question is how contemporary critics can distinguish what is really ancient from what is late antique, medieval, or even later. In this regard, I think that the best piece of advice is still the one given by the great Italian philologist Giorgio Pasquali (1885–1952) in his much-celebrated *History of Tradition and Textual Criticism* of classical texts.

> A judgment concerning the facility or the difficulty of a reading will be that much surer if the one judging knows the habits of language and of thought of the age that has transmitted the reading, and that may have created it. The best critic of a Greek text transmitted through the Byzantine tradition will be the one who, besides being a perfect Greek scholar, is also a perfect Byzantinist. The best editor of a Latin author transmitted in medieval or postmedieval codices will be the one who, along with

---

46. An impressive number of analogous cases concerning the prophecies of Daniel in the *longue durée* in various cultures have been reported by DiTommaso, *Book of Daniel*.

47. For another telling example, see the complementary articles of Bouvier and Bovon, "*Prière et Apocalypse de Paul*," and Piovanelli, "*Prière et Apocalypse de Paul*."

his author and his author's language and times, will know just as well the Middle Ages or (Renaissance) humanism. Such a critic is an ideal that no one can incarnate perfectly in himself, but which each has the obligation to try to approach.[48]

In other words, competent editors and commentators of Thucydides and Plato's works should also be excellent connoisseurs of Byzantine culture, while the specialists of Cicero and Tacitus should also be conversant in medieval and early modern philology, in order to properly appreciate the influence of later cultures on the transmission of ancient writings.[49] This still is (or should be) the ideal profile for a classical philologist, but in the case of the study of apocryphal literature transmitted in Coptic, Syriac, Ethiopian, Armenian, Georgian, Slavonic, and other late antique and medieval Christian cultures, this kind of double competence was, until recently, much rarer, limited to a few scholars as illustrious as August Dillmann (1823–1894), in the field of Biblical and Ethiopian Studies, François Bovon (1938–2013), in Early Christian and Byzantine Studies, or Michael E. Stone (born 1938), in Second Temple Judaism and Armenian Studies.[50]

If multi- and interdisciplinary approaches can, hopefully, save us from making embarrassing mistakes of appreciation and/or interpretation,[51] there still is, in my opinion, an increasingly urgent need for modifying the perception of both colleagues indirectly involved in the study of apocryphal texts and the general public: it should be made clear enough that, on the one hand, the boundaries between Jewish and Christian apocryphal texts are not so well defined and some of the so-called "Old Testament Pseudepigrapha" are actually Christian rewritings of Jewish subtexts;[52] on the other

---

48. Karla Mallette's translation (slightly modified), taken from her monograph, *European Modernity*, 1–2. The Italian original can be found in Pasquali, *Storia della tradizione*, 123.

49. See the remarks on Nag Hammadi texts and *1 Enoch* I made above, n. 9.

50. Happily enough, double specializations have become more frequent among the scholars belonging to the last two generations, such as Lorenzo DiTommaso (Second Temple Judaism and Byzantine Studies), Ted Erho (Second Temple Judaism and Ethiopian Studies), Cornelia Horn and Stephen Shoemaker (Late Antiquity and Syriac Studies), or Annette Y. Reed (Second Temple Judaism and Late Antiquity), to name just a few.

51. Such as mistaking the long recension of the so-called *Slavonic Enoch*, with its medieval Christian developments, for an authentic Second Temple Jewish text. On the philological aspects of this question, see the decisive arguments of Navtanovich, "Second Enoch"; Navtanovich, "Provenance of 2 Enoch."

52. As convincingly argued by Davila, *Provenance of the Pseudepigrapha*, and confirmed by Piovanelli, "In Praise of 'The Default Position.'" On the artificial nature of this category, see Reed, "Modern Invention."

hand, some of them, both Jewish and Christian, are manifestly late and have been, in some cases, written long after the institutionalization of rabbinic Judaism and orthodox Christianity. I am glad to see that the pioneering initiatives taken some 30 years ago by the founding members of the AELAC[53] are now going to be implemented, on behalf of English-speaking audiences, by the editors of the new and forthcoming *More Noncanonical Scriptures* anthologies,[54] a series of volumes in which Jewish and Christian apocryphal texts from both antiquity and late antiquity finally will be available in translation together.

---

53. Materialized, at a more general level, in the form of a highly inclusive anthology: Bovon, Geoltrain, and Kaestli, eds., *Écrits apocryphes chrétiens*.

54. Bauckham, Davila, and Panayotov, eds., *Old Testament Pseudepigrapha*; Burke and Landau, eds., *New Testament Apocrypha*.

— 6 —

Jesus at School among Christians, Jews, and Muslims

— Cornelia Horn[1] —

THE TALE OF JESUS going to school constitutes the core of the ancient Christian apocryphal *Infancy Gospel of Thomas*. That story, comprising *Inf. Gos. Thom.* 6–7 and retold in 14, likely was the initial narrative around which additional material was gathered to form an account of Jesus' childhood endeavors, including his educational adventures. Scholarship has already expended much energy trying to reconstruct the early form of the apocryphal episode of Jesus at school, the text's original context, and purpose.[2] Some attention has been paid to the story's afterlife as well[3]; yet in that realm in particular there is room for further exploration and expansion.

This essay advances the study of the famous episode of Jesus engaging his teacher in the course of studying the alphabet by examining elements of its reception history across different language traditions as well as in interreligious perspective. Focusing on the reception of the story in Irenaeus of Lyons, the *Armenian Infancy Gospel*, the Jewish *Toledot Yeshu*, and the Islamic *Umm al-kitāb*, it highlights the role of the episode of Jesus at school

---

1 The research and writing of this article for publication was supported through a Heisenberg Fellowship (GZ HO 5221/1–1), for which the author wishes to express her gratitude to the Deutsche Forschungsgemeinschaft.

2. For example in the monographs Aasgaard, *Childhood of Jesus*; Burke, *De infantia Iesu*; and Davis, *Christ Child*. Particular attention is paid to the schoolroom story in Frilingos, "No Child Left Behind"; and Paulissen, "Jésus à l'école."

3. For example, Gero, "Stern Master"; and Anthony, "Legend of 'Abdallāh ibn Saba'."

as an element of interreligious interactions, perhaps even polemic, in the realm of theological inquiry concerning Christology. This area of research into Christian apocrypha across dividing lines of religions constitutes one of the new or renewed frontiers of apocrypha research.

JESUS AT SCHOOL IN IRENAEUS OF LYONS' *AGAINST HERESIES*

The story of Jesus at school frustrating his teachers' efforts at instructing him in the basics of the alphabet constitutes the earliest component of *Inf. Gos. Thom.*, for which evidence in ancient sources is available. In his second-century treatise *Against Heresies*, Irenaeus of Lyons raised criticism against the Marcosians, a Valentinian group that was active in Gaul.[4] Irenaeus spoke of "an untold multitude of apocryphal and spurious writings," which had been composed by heretical groups and which were circulating and confusing those without sufficient understanding.[5] One such misleading story, a "falsification" [τὸ ῥᾳδιούργημα], told that,

> When the Lord was a child and was learning the letters (of the alphabet) [τὰ γράμματα], his teacher said (to him), as is customary: "Say, 'alpha.'" He responded, "Alpha." Again, the teacher demanded (from him) to say "beta." The Lord responded, "You tell me first, what 'alpha' is, and then I will tell you what 'beta' is."

Irenaeus comments that his adversaries interpreted this story as an indication that "he alone [i.e., the Lord Jesus as a child] knew the unknown which he revealed in the form of the alpha [ὡς αὐτοῦ μόνου τὸ ἄγνωστον ἐπισταμένου, ὃ ἐφανέρωσεν ἐν τῷ τύπῳ τοῦ ἄλφα]." For the Marcosians, the story's comment pertaining to the letter alpha, or rather, the lack of explicit comment by the child Jesus on the letter alpha, carried meaning since it granted the reader an opportunity to gain insight into the depths of the knowledge Jesus was thought to have possessed. Whether or not the apocryphal Jesus-episode had gnostic origins, it is relevant that Irenaeus seemed to have thought that the story was important in the context of religious controversy between Marcosians and mainline Christians. One notes, moreover, that Irenaeus employed the story in order to reveal to his readers

---

4. On the Marcosians and their founder, see Förster, *Marcus Magus*, and for a discussion that points to the sophistication of the Marcosians' rituals, see Denzey Lewis, "Apolytrosis."

5. For this and the following quotations see Irenaeus of Lyons, *Haer.* 1.20.1 (ed. and French trans. Rousseau et al.; English trans. Horn).

that for the Marcosians, it provided special insights into Jesus' extraordinary nature. At the hands of the earliest witness who preserved this story for posterity, the narrative of Jesus' exposure to the alphabet in a dialogue with the child's teacher at school either continued to be, or was transformed into, a story that illustrated a particular theological perspective regarding Jesus' special knowledge, control, and power.

Other evidence for the possible second-century circulation of the episode of Jesus learning the alphabet from a teacher is offered in the apocryphal text known as the *Epistula Apostolorum*, which is preserved in Ethiopic, Coptic, and in a Latin palimpsest fragment.[6] This text places the episode of Jesus as an extraordinary student in a wider context of demonstrating his powers of creation as well as his abilities to work miracles (see *Ep. Apos.* 4). Both Irenaeus' witness and the *Epistula Apostolorum* demonstrate quite clearly that already in the second century, the story played a role in Christological discussions.

In the later history of the reception of the episode, the aspect of the story that concentrated on the student turning into a teacher either of his own teacher or of others developed into a significant feature of the tradition as it went across religious boundaries. The theological concern in featuring Jesus as a teacher of wisdom expanded into showing how Jesus was the unique guide into the depth of the mysteries of God's being. Given that the three monotheistic religions of the ancient world disagreed with regard to the precise nature of Jesus' identity, the reception of the motif of Jesus as a student and teacher developed also along the lines of interreligious polemic.

JESUS AT SCHOOL IN THE *ARMENIAN INFANCY GOSPEL* INTERSECTING WITH JEWISH TRADITIONS REFLECTED IN THE *TOLEDOT YESHU*

The Armenian tradition preserves a narrative of Jesus' infancy that is marked by a high degree of literary development. This Armenian apocryphal text is of particular value for the study of traditions about Jesus in the Syriac, Aramaic, and Arabic linguistic milieus. In 2008, Abraham Terian published an English translation of one of the three recensions of the longer version of *Arm. Gos. Inf.* based on the earliest witness to the complete text: Matenadaran 7574, a manuscript kept at the library of the Matenadaran in Yerevan in Armenia dated to 1239 CE.[7] Matenadaran 7574 refers to

---

6. Hills, *Tradition*, 3. Indispensible for the study of this text is Schmidt, *Gespräche Jesu*.

7. Terian, *Armenian Gospel of the Infancy*. See vii and xxvi–xxxiii for details of

the work it presents as a "document" (Arm. *gir*) and as a "history" (Arm. *patmut'iwn*), and thus reveals how the translator or a later copyist preferred to categorize the story.⁸

Distinct syntactical features in the Armenian text speak to the Syriac background of the work. These consist primarily of the presence of the combined usage of participles together with verbs of synonymous meaning, of the monotonous repetition of the verb "said" in communications without employing variant forms like "asked" or "answered" in interrogative dialogue situations, and of the usage of combinations of two nouns in which the second one, consisting of an abstract noun in the genitive case, functions in a way that is similar to an adjective expressing a quality of the more concrete, preceding noun.⁹ Moreover, even a cursory reading of the text will bring to the mind of a reader familiar with Syriac literary traditions the memory of Syriac dialogue poetry, with its numerous examples of lively conversations of biblical characters or personified abstract qualities engaging in extended conversations with one another. Quite a few of the rich dialogues of *Arm. Gos. Inf.*—for example the conversation between Joseph and Mary, in which Joseph expresses his concerns about the origins of Mary's pregnancy (*Arm. Gos. Inf.* 6), or the dialogue between Eve and Salome (*Arm. Gos. Inf.* 9:3–4)—are strongly reminiscent of the form of such dialogues in Syriac compositions.¹⁰ On the level of details within individual episodes one can discern further evidence for the likelihood of a Syriac text underlying *Arm. Gos. Inf.* In the story of Jesus at school, for example, the letters of the alphabet which Jesus is supposed to study are identified as "alaph" and "beth" (*Arm. Gos. Inf.* 20:3) revealing the greater probability that the *Vorlage* for the story of this Armenian text was written in Syriac. Such additional observations only add to the evidence identified by Terian and confirm the strong impression that *Arm. Gos. Inf.* has its roots in a Syriac *Vorlage*, which, however, has not yet been recovered.¹¹

External evidence points to the sixth century as the date at which an extra-biblical writing on Jesus' infancy was translated from Syriac into Armenian. The historian Samuel of Ani in the twelfth-century, followed by Kirakos of Gandzak and Mkhit'ar of Ani in the thirteenth century, reported

the manuscript.

8. Ibid., xii n. 3.

9. Ibid., xxii–xxiii.

10. For some early examples of Syriac dialogue poems, see the five dialogue poems between Mary and the Angel, Mary and Joseph, Mary and the Magi, and the two versions of the dialogue poem between Mary and the Gardener translated in Brock, *Bride of Light*, 135–60.

11. Terian, *Armenian Gospel of the Infancy*, xi.

from one or several sources that missionaries of the Church of the East who had come to Armenia from Syria in ca. 590 CE, had brought along several apocryphal texts, one of which carried the title the "Infancy of the Lord."[12] The date of this translation is confirmed indirectly given that several authors, reaching back to the seventh-century writer Ananias of Shirak and the ninth-century exegete Hamam Arewelts'i (the Easterner), used such an apocryphal infancy-of-Jesus text in their own works.[13] *Arm. Gos. Inf.* then, in the form in which it is available at present, likely has its roots in a sixth-century translation of an earlier Syriac text; thus it has a place in the network of oriental Christian apocryphal texts that have their origins in infancy traditions about Jesus that reach back into the Syriac/Aramaic realm. It is not decisive for the present examination of aspects of the reception history of scenes of Jesus at school, to decide whether or not *Inf. Gos. Thom.* as a literary composition was originally composed in Greek or in Syriac.[14] As far as the available evidence is concerned, *Arm. Gos. Inf.* constitutes the point of access for the reception of *Inf. Gos. Thom.* and related traditions into Armenian. That reception seems to have been via Syriac traditions.

As *Arm. Gos. Inf.* unfolds its rich narrative, it tells of Joseph entering the public arena in pursuit of educational opportunities for Jesus. While the boy was six years old and his family dwelled in Israel in "a city called Bodoroson" (19:1),[15] Joseph meets the local Hebrew king and offers his services as "a master carpenter" (19:3). Next Joseph asks for protection against any discrimination against him "as a foreigner" (19:3). Having brought along Jesus and telling the king (in version C) that he was "a very clever boy," Joseph finally requests that the king might "grant . . . that [Joseph's] child be educated" (19:4). The king commands that a teacher be called "whose name was Gamaliel." Two of the three teachers in *Inf. Gos. Thom.* are nameless; the other is called Zakkai or Zacchaeus, who as Neusner argued might have been the first-century Rabbi Yohanan ben Zakkai, who lived in Galilee and

12. Ibid., xix. According to Kirakos of Gandzak, the missionaries of the Church of the East came to Armenia in 588. Other apocryphal books which they translated into Armenian include the *Vision of Paul* and the *Repentence of Adam*. See Melik'-Ōhanjanyan and Aghabeki, *Patmut'yun Hayots'*, 51, and Bedrosian, *Kirakos Gandzakets'i's History*, 45.

13. See Conybeare, "Discourse of Ananias," 333; for the Armenian text, see Abrahamyan et al., eds., *Anania Shirakats'u matenagrut'yune*, 289. For comments on Ananias of Shirak's and Hamam Arewelts'i's familiarity with *Arm. Gos. Inf.*, see Terian, *Armenian Gospel of the Infancy*, xix, with n. 3, 29, and 111.

14. For some discussion of the relevance of the Syriac material, see Burke, *De infantia Iesu*, 56–68; and Burke, "Infancy Gospel of Thomas," esp. 241–47.

15. The quotations of *Arm. Gos. Inf.* are drawn from Terian's English translation (*Armenian Gospel of the Infancy*, 3–149).

founded the academy at Yavneh. In *Arm. Gos. Inf.* the teacher carries the same name as the Pharisee Gamaliel, Paul's teacher known from Acts 22:3 and 5:34.[16] Introducing the child to Gamaliel, the king presents Jesus as "the son of a wealthy man, from a royal dynasty" and as being under Joseph's guardianship, but not as Joseph's biological son.

A full account of the specific details of all the parallels between the story of Jesus' schooling with one or several teachers in *Arm. Gos. Inf.* and the various other versions in *Inf. Gos. Thom.* would be highly valuable, but is not the goal here. Examined instead are a few noteworthy distinct characteristics of the Armenian story that illustrate the possibility that *Arm. Gos. Inf.* may have played a role in mediating the reception of the story between the Christian realm and Jewish and Islamic texts. One notes, for instance, that *Arm. Gos. Inf.* places a strong emphasis on the great respect with which Jesus as a student acts towards his teacher Gamaliel. Jesus shows appropriate humility as "he bowed down humbly to him [i.e., to Gamaliel]" upon meeting his teacher on Jesus' first day at school (20:1). When Gamaliel finished writing letters on the child's writing board, "the child bowed down humbly to him and took the board from him" (20:2). Moreover, at the end of the lesson, Jesus "took the board" from his teacher, "bowed down to him" and asked that "the Lord God [would] recompense [the teacher] for [his] good labor," although Jesus expresses to his mother at home later on that what he had learned at school was, in essence, "that the teacher could not answer [him]" (20:6).

Arm. Gos. Inf. did not invent the *topos* that a student needed to show appropriate behavior towards his teacher.[17] *Inf. Gos. Thom.* had already introduced the expectation that a student should study letters with a teacher and learn "to honor old age and revere elders," so that he or she may pursue as her or his ultimate goal to "acquire a desire for children" and be "teaching [those children] in return" (6:2).[18] Yet *Inf. Gos. Thom.* presents its audience with the idea that it was the correct behavior of a student to strive to honor elders and parents and learn to teach her or his own children in the future as the result of a teacher's instruction that the student received. The description of Jesus' humble behavior towards his teacher in *Arm. Gos. Inf.*, on the

---

16. See also Terian, *Armenian Gospel of the Infancy*, 91 n. 392.

17. For the discussion of a set of stories that feature a teacher/master putting his student(s)/disciple(s) to the test and excluding, in some instances only temporarily, the one who through his failure displays wrong behavior, see Gero, "Stern Master." Also this story travelled across the boundaries between ancient religions, here those of Judaism and Christianity.

18. Quotations from *Inf. Gos. Thom.* are from the English translation of the Greek S form of the text in Burke, *De infantia Iesu*, 302–37.

other hand, places on display that the child Jesus already possessed such proper behavior before receiving any lessons to that effect. There may have circulated, at the time of the production of *Arm. Gos. Inf.*, or of its Syriac *Vorlage*, accusations against Jesus acting irreverently towards his teachers; if so, the author or redactor of *Arm. Gos. Inf.* worked hard to counteract such claims.

The appropriateness of Jesus' attitude towards his teacher at school came to be a relevant topic in non-Christian writings, including texts that played a role in interreligious polemics. The characterization of Jesus as a student at school interacting with his Jewish teacher was relevant, for instance, in a polemic about Christology that can be observed, on the one side, in the apocryphal Syro-Armenian infancy-of-Jesus tradition and, on the other side, in the Jewish tradition concerning Jesus.

Elements of the Jewish side of this polemical interaction can be found in the development of the *Toledot Yeshu*, a Jewish text which one might identify as an apocryphal anti-gospel. Starting with an account of Yeshu's illegitimate beginnings as the son of Mary through an adulterous relationship with a neighbor, the *Toledot Yeshu* characterizes Yeshu first as a rebellious youth and later on as a magician, working miracles. After several incidents of conflict and competition with his Jewish opponents, the latter are finally shown to have overcome Yeshu through their acts of magic and Yeshu is put to death. The story of the afterlife of Yeshu's community turns on the increasingly clear-cut separation between Yeshu's followers and the Jewish community. In the past, scholarship has long decried the *Toledot Yeshu* as a Jewish work of hatred against Christianity; yet more recently the text has begun to be appreciated as a Jewish attempt to set clearer boundaries between Judaism and the Christian other.[19]

The date of origin and the geographical and cultural provenance of the *Toledot Yeshu* have received renewed and refined attention in recent scholarly discussions. The initial layers of the text appear to have been produced and transmitted orally. The earliest textual evidence consists of tenth-century manuscript fragments in Aramaic found in the Cairo Geniza.[20] Studying the Aramaic dialect that is in evidence in these fragments, both Willem Smelik and Michael Sokoloff have placed the fragments in the first half of the first

---

19. A clear witness to this increased interest in the text is Schäfer, Meerson, and Deutsch, eds., *Toledot Yeshu*; Meerson, Schäfer, et al., eds., *Toledot Yeshu*.

20. For publications of the Aramaic evidence, see Harkavy, "Leben Jesus"; Adler, "Un fragment araméen"; Krauss, "Fragments araméens"; Krauss, *Leben Jesu*, 143–44; Ginzberg, ed., *Genizah Studies*, 1:329–38; Horbury, "Trial of Jesus," 116–21; Falk, "New Fragment"; Boyarin, "Revised Version"; Niclós, ed., *Šem Ṭob ibn Šapruṭ*; Deutsch, "New Evidence"; and vol. 2 of Meerson, Schäfer, et al., eds., *Toledot Yeshu*.

millennium, with Smelik opting for a third- to fourth century Jewish Palestinian context and Sokoloff arguing for a Jewish Babylonian provenance, dating "towards the middle of the first millennium CE."[21] On the basis of the much more recent Hebrew sources for the text (in this case the so-called Strasbourg manuscript dating to the eighteenth century), William Horbury followed observations by Daniel Stökl Ben Ezra and concluded from a detailed observation of isolated, smaller episodes or micro elements of the narrative that the composition of at least some elements of the *Toledot Yeshu* could be located in "Palestine or Syria in the fourth or early fifth century."[22] The evidence for the text that is preserved in Latin, Judaeo-Arabic, Yiddish, and other languages speaks to the *Toledot Yeshu*'s wide circulation and, at the same time, illustrates how it reflects significant polemical concerns in the course of the reception history of the work.[23]

For our purposes, one scene in the *Toledot Yeshu* is of particular interest.[24] Once the son, to whom Miriam had given birth and whom she had named Jehoshua, had grown a few years, she presents him to a teacher named Elchanan for instruction. At school, the boy proves to be a good student. One day, young Jehoshua passes by a gathering of the Sanhedrin in Jerusalem. The *Toledot Yeshu* states that it was customary for anyone passing the members of the Sanhedrin to cover their head, bend over, and bow down in reverence in front of them. Yet, contrary to such expected behavior, Miriam's son keeps his head uncovered, looks them straight in the eye, and passes them by with his body kept straight up, not offering any signs of reverence. One manuscript tradition of the text, the one represented in the edition of Johannes Christophorus Wagenseil, reports the incident differently. In this version, Jesus passes by the members of the Sanhedrin with his head uncovered, his glance directed straight at them, but bowing down only in front of his own teacher Elchanan.[25] Then the story continues with the rabbis concluding from the boy's irreverent behavior that he must be a bastard. Reflections and inquiries into Jehoshua's illegitimate origins follow, as well as the resolution to rename him and call him henceforth Yeshu, from the Hebrew phrase ימח שמו וזכרונו (*yimach shemo uzikrono*), "his name and his memory shall be extinguished."[26]

21. Smelik, "Aramaic Dialect(s)"; and Sokoloff, "Date and Provenance," 25.
22. Horbury, "Strasbourg Text," 56; and Stökl Ben Ezra, "Ancient List."
23. See, for example, Goldstein, "Judeo-Arabic Versions"; Stanislawski, "Preliminary Study"; and Karras, "Aerial Battle."
24. See Krupp, *Vom Leben und Sterben*, 34–37.
25. Ibid., 34–35; and Wagenseil, *Tela Ignea Satanae*, 5.
26. Wagenseil, *Tela Ignea Satanae*, 6.

The text's emphasis on the expected behavior of bowing down in front of the rabbis is relevant for the present discussion. Though the *Toledot Yeshu* evidence varies with regard to whether or not Jesus bowed down to his own teacher in the scene, the very fact that this is a practice with regard to which the Jewish tradition itself was in flux supports the observation that both *Arm. Gos. Inf.*, possibly in conjunction with its Syriac *Vorlage*, on the one hand, and the variant traditions contained in the different recensions of the *Toledot Yeshu*, on the other, participated in a wider conversation concerning the behavior which was appropriate for Jesus when engaging his teacher(s). This evidence reflects at the least some concern—possibly also an exchange or controversy between varying traditions, conversations, or even disputations across the divide between Jewish and Christian communities—about whether or not Jesus as a student at school, as narrated in *Inf. Gos. Thom.*, showed any reverence for his own teacher; or if he did, how much and of what quality. As *Arm. Gos. Inf.* depicts a respectful student, it may have been witnessing to an on-going, but then also transformed, reception of Jewish teaching within the Syro-Armenian tradition. The *Toledot Yeshu*, for its part, places greater emphasis on the break with the Christian tradition and considers that break to have been a radical one.

JESUS AT SCHOOL IN THE *ARMENIAN INFANCY GOSPEL* INTERSECTING WITH ISLAMIC TRADITIONS REFLECTED IN *UMM AL-KITĀB*

A second characteristic element of *Arm. Gos. Inf.*'s story of Jesus at school pertains to the set of interpretations that are offered for the meaning of the letters of the alphabet, which Jesus is supposed to study. When Gamaliel embarks upon his lesson by writing down twelve letters on the child's writing board, the teacher orders the boy to "name the first letter," though the teacher did not first pronounce it for his student (20:3). Only when Jesus resists and states that he does not see any point in doing so, does Gamaliel teach him, saying "The name of the letter is *alaph*." In the ensuing dialogue between them, Jesus requests to be told the significance of the letter, the existence of the meaning of which Gamaliel denies. Prompted by Jesus' comments that the first two letters differ from one another with regard to visual form, shape, or semblance, Gamaliel in turn now requests to learn "the significance of the letters" from Jesus. Version C offers a more extended conversation in which Jesus indicates that he has knowledge "that the mystery of the meaning unfolds as one moves from one letter to the other"; in response, Gamaliel defends his ignorance by taking recourse to the fact that "[n]one of the ancient teachers, the wise, or the scribes were able to say one more word on the letters." Both version C and Terian's main text, version A, in which Gamaliel excuses his ignorance by stating that the extent of his knowledge coincides with what he had "learned from the forefathers," set the scene well for the child Jesus, now functioning in effect as the teacher for his own ignorant teacher, to reveal the depth of his knowledge. Thus *Arm. Gos. Inf.* features Jesus as instructing Gamaliel that, "The *alaph* signifies the Name, God; and the *beth*, the Word to be born, the Word of God becoming embodied." Versions B and C of the Armenian text present Jesus as offering a theologically fuller and more developed explanation of the alphabet that also accounts for the Holy Spirit and the concept of the Trinity. Yet in those versions, Jesus' comments do not take the names of the individual letters as explicit reference points, but begin more generically with the concept of the letter. The more fully-developed theological argumentation of versions B and C suggests that the relevant material in B and C is secondary. The fourth and final recension, recension D, tends to amplify the text when compared to what is available in recension A; but here version D omits the entire discussion between Gamaliel and Jesus. It is possible then that D's omission of the explanation of the letters *alaph* and *beth* witnesses to the original form of the text, while recension A's explanation might mark the beginning of the insertion of this discussion.

Recension D is represented by Matenadaran 5599, dated to 1347 CE—a manuscript that is just about 100 years younger than the oldest and best manuscript evidence for the text, which presents Jesus' explanations of the letters *alaph* and *beth* as referring to God and the Word of God. If Matenadaran 5599 indeed witnesses to the oldest form of the text, then the theological explanation of the meaning of the letters *alaph* and *beth* entered the tradition at a point prior to or coinciding with the date of recension A, which is represented by and preserved in Matenadaran 7574, dated to 1239 CE. Possible reasons for the insertion of this material at this point in time may become clearer on the basis of considering the non-Christian line of reception of the story of Jesus at school.

If, instead, Matenadaran 7574 witnesses to the oldest text form of *Arm. Gos. Inf.*, then the child Jesus' theological explanation of the letters *alaph* and *beth* could have been part of the text from its composition, perhaps even in the gospel's Syriac *Vorlage*. Terian has already commented on how the first two letters of the alphabet in both Armenian and Syriac correspond to the content of the child Jesus' theological explanation. Both in Armenian and Syriac, the word for "God," *astowats* in Armenian and *aloho* in Syriac, begins with the letter "a"—that is, the letter *ayb* in Armenian and *alaph* in Syriac. The child's explanation, "The *alaph* signifies the Name, God" (20:3), then makes good sense in either Armenian or Syriac. With regard to the explanation of the meaning of the letter *beth*, the situation is more complicated. The text has Jesus say: "the *beth* [signifies] the Word to be born, the Word of God becoming embodied" (20:3).[27] In Syriac, the letter *beth* begins the word *bro*, "son," but it does not constitute the initial letter of the word for "Word," which is *meltho*. In Armenian, however, the letter "b" (*ben* in Armenian), begins the word *ban*, the term used for "logos" or "word." The specific formulation of the second part of the theological explanation, therefore, seems to point to an Armenian milieu, in which at least parts of the statements may have had their origins. An additional observation, however, may allow one to argue that the statement that the child Jesus offers here also could have made sense in a Syriac-speaking context. One notes, with Terian, that the Syriac word for "father," *abo*, likewise starts with *alaph*. If the child Jesus had said: "The *alaph* signifies the Name, Father (*abo*); and the *beth*, the Son (*bro*) to be born, the Word of God becoming embodied," the names of letters and their referents would have lined up well in Syriac too. A Syriac-speaker also would have been able to make good sense of the statement: "The *alaph* signifies the Name, God (*aloho*); and the *beth*, the Son (*bro*) to be born, the Word of God becoming embodied." One could easily understand that a translator from Syriac into Armenian would have been inclined to accept a stylistically inferior move—here the repetition of the word *ban* (for the letter and for "the Word") in the same sentence—in order to be able to represent also in Armenian that the letter *beth* functioned as the initial letter of a meaningful term in the sentence. If the Syriac *Vorlage*, as mentioned above, derived indeed from the milieu of the Church of the East, then the Armenian translator's replacing of "son" with "word" may also reflect the translator's theological preferences, as he could have been (but did not have to have been) a member of the anti-Chalcedonian branch of the Armenian church. Although there is no ancient Syriac text extant that would decide the question, the second one of the two constructions suggested above may be the most likely formulation, which the Armenian translator could have had in front of her or his eyes. Without positive evidence from a Syriac *Vorlage*, moreover, the primacy of version D over version A also cannot be decided. Given the active revisionary work that is in evidence in recension D, mostly in the form of amplifications, at the present instance recension D may simply have employed a different method of revision, having excised text instead of amplifying it. Without a

27. The present discussion considers Terian's translation as well as the reading found in MS Matenadaran 7574, fol. 95ʳ. I am most grateful to Abraham Terian for supplying me with images of the manuscript pages for chapter 20 of the text of the *Armenian Infancy Gospel*.

fuller study of the characteristic procedures that D employed in its editorial work, no definitive decision concerning the probability of such a move can be made. As far as the evidence for the reception of the scene of Jesus at school is concerned, *Arm. Gos. Inf.* emerges as the earliest apocryphal Christian text in which the interpretation of the meaning of the letters of the alphabet is presented as carrying theological, and here both Christological and Trinitarian meaning.

Relating letters to names and their meanings is not an exercise confined to the Christian realm. It is not the task of this article to explore exhaustively the development of speculations on the meaning of the divine name or names. It would be a fruitful exercise to explore this topic on the basis of bringing into dialogue with one another the material in *Arm. Gos. Inf.* and Jewish apocryphal traditions. Interactions between the Christian apocryphal reception of the story of Jesus at school interpreting the letters of the alphabet and developments within the world of Islam can be examined as well. While the first task has to remain for future work, one way of approaching at least some elements of the second task is by considering a seemingly circumstantial element in the story: Jesus' writing board.

In *Arm. Gos. Inf.* one encounters, seemingly for the first time in the reception history of this story, references to a writing board that Jesus was said to have brought along with him to class and that he took home with him after school. According to the text, Joseph picks up "a (writing) board" (*takhtak*) when he comes with Jesus to Gamaliel (20:1). On the way, Jesus may have carried the board himself, given that after initial exchanges of welcome and identifications at Gamaliel's house, "the teacher took the board from the child's hand" (20:2). Then, "holding it [i.e., the board] he [i.e., Gamaliel] began to write twelve letters" (20:2). Terian has noted already that the number twelve here conveniently amounts to about half of the number of the letters of the Hebrew alphabet. As Gamaliel writes the letters on the board, Jesus observes "first the meaning of the (written) word and then the letters themselves." After he finishes writing, Gamaliel "gave (the board) to the child, and the child bowed down humbly to him and took the board from him" (20:2). Following the exchanges between Gamaliel and Jesus concerning the letters and their meaning, in the course of which Gamaliel perceives and acknowledges Jesus' superior knowledge, Gamaliel first calls in Joseph and eventually dismisses Jesus in peace. While Joseph remains behind in order to consult Gamaliel for further advice on what to do regarding Jesus' education, Jesus "took the board, bowed down to him [i.e., Gamaliel]" and expressing his wish that God might recompense the teacher for his "good labor," goes home to his mother Mary. When Joseph joins them at home later on, having been instructed by Gamaliel to teach Jesus the "trade of carpentry," he sees Jesus "sitting with the board on his hand" (20:7).

The references to the presence of a writing board in this scene are unique to *Arm. Gos. Inf.* and serve a range of different purposes. They support the characterization of Jesus as a well-disciplined, well-prepared, orderly student, who brought his materials with him to class, used them appropriately, and took good care of them when leaving the classroom and going home for further study. The motif of the writing board, which Jesus still held in hand when Joseph came home to begin teaching him carpentry, also serves well as a literary detail that connects the two scenes of instruction, one at school and one in Joseph's workshop, with one another, because Jesus' first lesson in carpentry requires working with two boards to make a "bed for the king" (20:8). One could be satisfied with an explanation of the motif of the writing board as simply constituting a narrative element that supports the literary depiction of work at a school. Yet it may be possible to consider additional functions, or developments, of this writing board, or what it stood for, in the tradition of Jesus at school as told in *Arm. Gos. Inf.* and subsequent texts. The reference to the writing board in *Arm. Gos. Inf.* allows one to discern some traces of specific avenues by which the story of Jesus at school may have travelled from the Christian tradition into religious traditions outside of Christianity. One of these avenues to external traditions can be recovered from among the religious texts of Shī'ī Islam.

One text, which is preserved into modern times in a translation into archaic Persian and which is central to the sacred literature of the Shī'ī Islamic group known as the Ismā'īlī, represents a rather intriguing moment in the reception history of the narrative of Jesus at school, transformed into a new context. The text in question carries the title *Umm al-kitāb*. This title may be translated literally as "Mother of the Book," but perhaps also as "essence of the book" or "essence of the scripture."[28] The Qur'ān employs the phrase *umm al-kitāb* in *sūrat al-ra'd* (the Thunder) 13:39, stating that "Allah eliminates what he wills and confirms [what he wills], and with him [is] the Mother of the Book (*umm al-kitāb*)." One may see a connection of this verse and expression with two other verses that occur in *sūrat al-burūj* (the Big Star) 85:21–22, which speak of "a glorious Qur'ān (*qur'ān^{un} majīd^{un}*), in a guarded/preserved tablet (*fī lawḥ^{in} maḥfūẓ^{in}*)."[29] Speculation concerning this tablet as a form of medium for the revelation and/or transmission of the Qur'ān arises from here.

28. Ivanow, "Notes sur l'*Ummu'l-kitāb*," 421.

29. For reflections on the tablet from heaven see, for example, the eighth-century Islamic traditionist Muqātil b. Sulaymān, who originated from the regions of modern-day Afghanistan (McAuliffe, "Text and Textuality," 60).

Although it is now available in ancient Persian, *Umm al-kitāb* appears to have been translated from an Arabic original.[30] The book only entered the purview of Western scholarly study when a manuscript came into the hands of a Russian functionary, Alexander Alexandrovich Polovtsev, at the occasion of his travels in Central Asia at the beginning of the nineteenth century. In 1936, a Russian scholar of Oriental Studies, Vladimir Alexeyevich Ivanov (or Wladimir Alekseevich Ivanow), published a preliminary edition of the Persian text on the basis of Polovtsev's manuscript and additional copies that had come to light in subsequent decades.[31] In his study of Islamic Gnosticism that clearly identified distinct sections of the *Umm al-kitāb* and succeeded in demonstrating the work's composite character, Heinz Halm, specialist in Ismā'īlī Studies, dated the earliest layers of the text to the second/eighth centuries.[32] In his recent examination of the text, Sean W. Anthony places the work in reference to developments within Shī'ī heresiology and historiography and argues for a later date of the earliest strata, suggesting instead the fourth/tenth centuries for the oldest material.[33] Studies by Wilferd Madelung, supported by Anthony's recent research, argue for the sixth/twelfth centuries as the date for the integral text.[34] One observes here that the redaction of the Shī'ī or Ismā'īlī *Umm al-kitāb* that integrated its present material appears to have predated the earliest manuscript evidence for *Arm. Gos. Inf.* by about a century. The earliest layers of *Umm al-kitāb*, however, post-date by two centuries the likely point in time when a Syriac *Vorlage* of an infancy-of-Jesus narrative was translated into Armenian and developed into *Arm. Gos. Inf.*

For the most part, especially in its oldest portion, *Umm al-kitāb* consists of discourses concerning cosmology and soteriology. They are presented as having been offered by the fifth of the twelve Shī'ī *imām*s, Muḥammad al-Bāqir (d. 114/732[?]), who delivered them in response to questions posed by his disciples.[35] Introductory material to the text as a whole situates these discourses with reference to the context in which they took place. Immediately relevant for our purposes is that the narrative presents *imām* Bāqir

---

30. For a discussion of the characteristic features of the archaic Persian language as it is used in *Umm al-kitāb*, see Ivanow, "Ummu'l kitāb," 9–15.

31. Ivanow, "Ummu'l kitāb." See also Ivanow, "Исмаилитские рукописи," 362–65; and Ross, "Summary and Review."

32. Halm, *Die islamische Gnosis*, 120–21.

33. Anthony, "Legend of 'Abdallāh ibn Saba'."

34. Madelung, review of Filippani-Ronconi, "*Ummu'l kitāb*," 355; and Anthony, "Legend of 'Abdallāh ibn Saba'." 9.

35. Ivanow, "Notes sur l'*Ummu'l-kitāb*," 421; see also Halm, *Die islamische Gnosis*, 85.

from the outset as a boy of only five years of age. This characterization of the fifth *imām* occurs in the so-called "School Anecdote," which directly precedes the *Apocalypse of Jābir*, the oldest part of the text. Whether the "School Anecdote" may also belong to this early stratum of *Umm al-kitāb*, or whether it was instead a part of the redaction that integrated the other sections in the sixth/twelfth centuries, or sometime in between, is open for debate.

Sean Anthony examined the "School Anecdote" as an Islamic transformation of the story of Jesus at school that is offered in *Inf. Gos. Thom.* and several of its stages of reception in later centuries, including the *Gospel of Pseudo-Matthew* and the *Arabic Infancy Gospel*.[36] He placed the "School Anecdote" in *Umm al-kitāb* in some relation to the reception of episodes concerning Jesus at school in the Islamic *Lives of the Prophets*, a connection which contextualizes that reception to the period around the sixth/twelfth centuries.[37] Yet it is necessary to differentiate more carefully between different lines of recension of the story of Jesus at school, which appear to have materialized in the Islamic tradition. Greater precision here may allow one to discern more clearly any theological profiles of authors or redactors in the process, thereby allowing one to recognize polemical elements in the reception of at least some of the material.

Within Shī'ite tradition, *imām* Bāqir is featured as having been intimately familiar with the tradition and experience of Jesus at school as a child. Several Shī'ī authors report that Bāqir transmitted the story of Jesus explaining the letters of the alphabet as revelations of distinct attributes of God. The *isnād* for this transmission reaches back from Bāqir to Muḥammad b. Ibrāhīm b. Isḥāq. In this tradition, Mary is said to have brought Jesus to school when he was merely seven months old. He receives oral instruction from a teacher, first of a religious nature and then concerning the alphabet. When threatened by the teacher with the whip to say and then explain the alphabet, the child Jesus responds by stating:

> "As for the *alif*, it is the blessings [*ālā'*] of God; the *bā'* the splendor [*bahja*] of God; the *jīm* the beauty [*jamāl*] of God; the *dāl* the religion [*dīn*] of God. Now, *hawwaz*: the *hā'* is the terror [*hawl*] of God, the *wāw* the woe [*wayl*] of the inhabitants of hell, the *zā'* the moans [*zafīr*] of Gehenna. *Ḥuṭṭī*: the sins of the penitent have been absolved [*ḥaṭṭat khaṭāyā al-mustaghfirīn*]. *Kalman*: the word [*kalām*] of God, there is no altering his words. *Saʿfaṣ*: measure for measure, and portion for portion [*ṣāʿun*

---

36. Anthony, "Legend of 'Abdallāh ibn Sabaʾ," 15 and 17.
37. Ibid., 16–17.

bi-ṣāʿin wa-l-juzāʾ bi-l-juzāʾ]. Qurshut: the (souls') collecting and assembling [*qashruhum wa-ḥashruhum*]."[38]

This one-by-one explanation of eleven letters of the alphabet details specific qualities of God and God's actions. With regard to this aspect, the present passage is similar to the reception of Jesus' explanation of the alphabet that can be found in the literature pertinent to the *Lives of the Prophets*, the so-called *qiṣaṣ al-anbiyāʾ* literature. With Anthony, one notes that the underlying alphabet belongs to the realm of Semitic languages.[39] This serves at least as one indication of the likelihood of a Syriac *Vorlage* for the story, potentially transmitted through one or several Arabic intermediaries. It is less likely that the *Vorlage* was based on a Greek version of the story of Jesus at school.

This material concerning *imām* Bāqir's reported acquaintance with the story of Jesus at school is instructive for our understanding of the reception of *Inf. Gos. Thom.* into the milieu of Islam. It documents the presumed familiarity of the *imām* with the tradition concerning Jesus. But in Shīʿī, or Ismāʿīlī, tradition represented by *Umm al-kitāb*, the literary adoption of the story of Jesus at school went a step further by transforming the *imām* Bāqir himself, on the literary level, into a wise and omniscient child at school, just as in the story the Christian tradition had developed about Jesus. The relevant episode in the text reads:

> Then Imām al-Bāqir was sent to school [*kuttāb*]. To him was revealed divine glory and divinely inspired wisdom and knowledge unknown to any schoolmaster. Jābir b. ʿAbdallāh al-Anṣārī narrated that at this time the Discloser of Knowledge [*bāqir al-ʿilm*] was still yet a five-year-old child when he was sent to the school of ʿAbdallāh-i Sabaʾ. As [13] is the custom of schoolmasters, he wrote the twenty-nine letters of the alphabet on his tablet—a tablet of pure silver—and placed it in the hands of Bāqir al-ʿIlm. 'Say *alif*,' he commanded. Bāqir al-ʿIlm said, '*Alif*.' 'Say *bey*,' ʿAbdallāh said. Bāqir said, 'I won't until you say the meaning of *alif*!' 'O delight of the eyes of believers! *Say alif, O Bāqir!*' Then he said, '*Alif* is God [*Allāh*]; there is no god but he, the living, the enduring.' This He said: 'O ʿAbdallāh, *alif* is the Lord [*khodāvand*]. The *lām* above that (*alif*) is Muḥammad. The meaning of *alif* is the spirit of Muḥammad. *Alif* is three letters and one [14] diacritic: the *alif*, *lām*, *fāʾ*, and the diacritic of the *alif* are Muḥammad. The *lām* is ʿAlī, and the *fāʾ* is Fāṭima. *Nūn*

---

38. Ibid., 16–17.
39. Ibid., 17.

is Ḥasan and Ḥusayn; for a *nūn* is at the end of Ḥasan and Ḥusayn, and at the end of *alif* is a diacritic [*nuqṭa*].'

'Abdallāh was in awe and said: 'O Light to the believers' eyes! What a wondrous thing, this uncreated book you speak of in describing the properties of *alif*!' (*Umm al-kitāb*, 12–14)[40]

Subsequent to this passage, the text develops several further sets of explanations of the meaning of the letters *alif* and *bā'*, primarily, as well as of other letters, with a view to how they point to characteristics of 'Alī, Muḥammad, and the cosmos. The detailed consideration of the latter interpretive material could be used in the study of Ismā'īlī mysticism.

The passage that features Bāqir as a five-year-old boy sent to school provides one with the opportunity to comment on the identity of 'Abdallāh-i Saba', the presence of the tablet, and the content of the identification of the letters of the alphabet. The ancient reader of *Umm al-kitāb* may have been aware that the schoolmaster 'Abdallāh-i Saba' was to be identified with a certain 'Abdallāh-i Saba', whom Shī'ī tradition elsewhere represented as a Jew who had converted to Islam merely nominally and who was said to have introduced heretical ideas into Islam.[41] The teacher Zakkai or Zacchaeus in *Inf. Gos. Thom.* represents quite clearly a Jewish teacher.[42] When he was renamed Gamaliel in *Arm. Gos. Inf.*, however, one is confronted with the image of a Jewish teacher who, in the Christian tradition, instructed Paul, whose figure, in turn, stood for a Jew who converted and, from the perspective of the Jews, radically distorted the ideas of his religion of origins. In Christian apocryphal writings that derive from the Jewish-Christian milieu, moreover, more specifically in the *Pseudo-Clementine Romance*, Paul the apostle appears behind the figure of Simon Magus as the heretic or enemy.[43] One discerns then, in both *Arm. Gos. Inf.* and *Umm al-kitāb*, a tendency to suggest to the reader that the respective schoolmaster might have been the originator of challenging, even radical ideas that some in turn may have perceived as heretical.

Additional comments are required concerning the role of the tablet in the "School Anecdote" in *Umm al-kitāb*. In the story of Jesus at school which Shī'ī tradition ascribes to *imām* Bāqir and which presents Jesus explaining

40. For the Persian text, see Ivanow, "Ummu'l kitāb," 105; the quotation of the English translation is from Anthony, "Legend of 'Abdallāh ibn Saba'," 21–22.

41. Anthony, "Legend of 'Abdallāh ibn Saba'," 1, 4, 13, and 19.

42. See Neusner, "Zaccheus/Zakkai."

43. For different perspectives concerning the interpretation of the characterization of Simon Magus as a representative of Paul in the *Pseudo-Clementines*, see Bockmuehl, *Remembered Peter*, 101–12; Côté, *Le theme de l'opposition*; and Côté, "La function littéraire de Simon."

eleven letters of the alphabet as indicators of some of the attributes of God, no references appear to any writing utensils used by either the schoolmaster or the child Jesus. Yet in contrast to this, the relevant passage in *Umm al-kitāb* features the schoolmaster ʿAbdallāh-i Sabaʾ as following "the custom of schoolmasters" and writing "the twenty-nine letters of the alphabet on his tablet" (*Umm al-kitāb* 13). The text further specifies that said tablet was "of pure silver" and that the teacher then "placed it in the hands of Bāqir al-ʿIlm." Scholarly comments on the Persian text pertinent to the phrase "a tablet of pure silver" consider it to be a later gloss.[44] One also notes that the tablet in question appears to have been the teacher's tablet, not one that the child Bāqir had brought along to the school. Nevertheless, the tablet takes on a central role in the episode as the carrier of the letters that are written upon it and that give rise to Bāqir's subsequent revelatory explanation of their meaning in reference to God, Muḥammad, and eventually also ʿAlī. The writing board, that appears in *Arm. Gos. Inf.* as the tool the child Jesus brought along to the classroom and upon which his teacher Gamaliel wrote the letters, plays the very same role. In addition, one notices that in both texts the teacher is said to have placed the tablet or writing board in the child's hand. To the extent that the Islamic tradition that can be grasped in *Umm al-kitāb* transformed the story of Jesus at school into one of *imām* Bāqir at school, it may have had access either to *Arm. Gos. Inf.* or to that text's Syriac *Vorlage* when it developed the details of the mechanics of how the teacher instructed the child.

Considerations of the role of a special tablet function internal to, as well as outside of, the "School Anecdote" in *Umm al-kitāb*. In its introductory remarks, for instance, the text announces that it is making known "the realities of the creative powers of God," which include "the tablet" (*Umm al-kitāb* 10).[45] When offering details concerning the system of spirits that were to be differentiated, *Umm al-kitāb* presents a "spirit of memory" or "spirit of preservation" (*rūḥ al-ḥifẓ*) as being represented by "the Tablet Preserved (*lawḥ-i maḥfūẓ*) of the Most High King" (*Umm al-kitāb* 21 and 32).[46] Yet the text manifested already in the way in which *Umm al-kitāb* positioned and framed its recounting of the "School Anecdote," that it followed the line of exegetes of the Qurʾān that connected Q 3:7 with Q 85:22. It built upon the Qurʾān's idea that the *umm al-kitāb*, or "essence of the book" which was

44. Halm, *Die islamische Gnosis*, 370 n. 251; and Tijdens, "Der mythologisch-gnostische Hintergrund," 279.

45. *Umm al-kitāb* 10 (ed. Ivanow, "Umm'l kitāb," 106; tr. Anthony, "Legend of ʿAbdallāh ibn Sabaʾ," 21).

46. *Umm al-kitāb* 21 and 32 (ed. Ivanow, "Umm'l kitāb," 103 and 101; tr. Anthony, "Legend of ʿAbdallāh ibn Sabaʾ," 24 and 26).

transmitted in the Qur'ān, was understood to have been conveyed via the means of a special tablet, spoken of as the Preserved Tablet (*lawḥ-i maḥfūẓ*) in Q 85:22. In the Shī'ī *Umm al-kitāb* it is presented as the tablet on which the schoolmaster wrote the alphabet for *imām* Bāqir. In the sentences immediately leading up to the "School Anecdote," *Umm al-kitāb* twice explicitly cites relevant phrases from Q 3:7, both times speaking of "verses made clear, these are the *umm al-kitāb*." At the second instance, Bāqir is presented as a newborn child, who seemingly right after birth spoke to his mother, Āmīna, in revelatory discourse concerning this *umm al-kitāb*. Any Islamic reader not only would note the paralleling of Bāqir to Muḥammad through the ahistorical naming of Bāqir's mother as Āmīna, but she or he also would recognize the parallel that is established here between Bāqir speaking at his birth and Jesus speaking in the cradle or as a newborn child in *sūrat al-'Im'rān* (the Family of Imrān) Q 3:46, *sūrat al-māidah* (the Table spread with Food) Q 5:110, and *sūrat Maryam* (Maryam) Q 19:29. In the logic of the narrative of *Umm al-kitāb* then, what *imām* Bāqir already knew as a child concerning *umm al-kitāb* informs his explanation of what he reads on the tablet in the "School Anecdote" that immediately follows. In that passage, the gloss, if it is one, of "a tablet of pure silver" emphasizes the exceptional preciousness of the tablet in question. Such unusual material as a utensil for writing or reading highlights the exceptional depth of the knowledge that was revealed through it. Of course, one may wonder how it would have been possible for a schoolmaster, acting "[a]s is the custom of schoolmasters" (*Umm al-kitāb* 13) to write on a silver tablet. The reference to silver, instead of wax or clay, could have suggested that writing on the tablet had to occur not through ordinary means but through incising the letters on a more durable, precious material, and thus giving them permanence. It may also have given rise to the idea that the tablet, for the most part, already contained incised writing upon it that the teacher could use as the basis for his instruction. Such a reading might fit with ideas conveyed in other Shī'ī accounts. For example, in *Umm al-kitāb*'s "School Anecdote" Jābir merely figures as a later transmitter in the chain in the *isnad* connected with the story of Bāqir at school. Yet in some Shī'ī accounts he is said to have produced a copy from a special green tablet. Gabriel had handed over that tablet to Fāṭima, Muḥammad's daughter, who in the Shī'ī tradition among Ismā'īlīs is considered to have been one of the five manifestations of Allah.[47]

One may detect yet another parallel between the "School Anecdote" in *Umm al-kitāb* and the story of Jesus at school in *Arm. Gos. Inf.*, a parallel

---

47. See also Kohlberg, "Authoritative Scriptures," 304; and Anthony, "Legend of 'Abdallāh ibn Saba'," 13 n. 50. In other accounts, Fāṭima is featured as the recipient of yet other tablets. See Kohlberg, "Unusual Shī'ī *isnād*," 144 n. 10.

that strengthens the likelihood that the Islamic tradition reflected in the Shīʿī text may have been acquainted with the Christian apocryphal narrative through contact either directly with the Armenian milieu or with the Syriac-speaking milieu in which the Syriac *Vorlage* originated, possibly the Church of the East. The discussion of the child Jesus' explanation of the letters *alaph* and *beth* in *Arm. Gos. Inf.* offered above details the text's strongly theological, and specifically Christological and Trinitarian interpretation of the alphabet. In the Shīʿī tradition that is external to *Umm al-kitāb* and that features Jesus explaining about half of the letters of the Semitic alphabet as representing God's attributes and actions, a God-focused line of interpretation is in evidence as well. Yet that line of interpretation, which also might originate in a Syriac *Vorlage*, as Anthony has argued,[48] differs from the God-focused interpretation of the alphabet that is provided in the "School Anecdote" in *Umm al-kitāb*. The first one concentrates on having the letters of the alphabet spell out distinct aspects of God; the second, on the other hand, concentrates its interpretation on how the letter *alif* at once signifies the one God, "the Lord" (*khodāvand*), and how it manifests God equally in the five persons that were most central to Shīʿī belief: Muḥammad, ʿAlī, Fāṭima, Ḥasan, and Ḥusayn.[49] Quite similar in some regard to the Christian conception of the one God manifested in a Trinity of persons, in this extremist Shīʿī or Ismāʿīlī (so-called pentadist) understanding, each one of the five persons mentioned is regarded as manifesting God.[50] Such an interpretation of *alif* as the signifier or mystical representative of God is different from the Islamic traditions that spell out how individual letters of the alphabet represent aspects of God. Yet it has at least one significant feature in common with the interpretation of the letter *alaph* as the name of God that one encounters in *Arm. Gos. Inf.*, in which the initial letters of the alphabet are applied to spelling out the Trinitarian vision of God. In the pentadist interpretation of the *alif* one likewise encounters the same signifier, the letter "a" as the starting point for mapping an interpretation onto individual persons representing God as that which is signified. This is not to say that there is a perfect overlap between the Syro-Armenian and the extremist Shīʿī tradition here, but the combination of the presence of the tablet as a unique element in *Arm. Gos. Inf.*, the Islamic reception of the story of Jesus at school in the "School Anecdote" in *Umm al-kitāb* with the noteworthy parallel between the Trinitarian-oriented interpretation of the alphabet in *Arm. Gos. Inf.* on the one hand and the pentadist interpretation of the letter *alif* in that same

---

48. Anthony, "Legend of ʿAbdallāh ibn Sabaʾ," 16–17.
49. Ibid., 18.
50. Ibid., 14.

"School Anecdote" on the other hand, speak to a distinct possibility that the traditions underlying *Umm al-kitāb* and *Arm. Gos. Inf.*, or the Syriac *Vorlage* to which it witnesses, were in some contact with one another. At least one task of further research is to investigate whether more can be said about the geographical and/or historical context in which such a contact may have occurred. Mesopotamia seems to be a reasonable assumption.[51]

CONCLUSIONS

Working at the intersection not only of multiple language traditions and various interpretations of the Christian message within the wider framework of Christianity and what insiders might call deviations, but also at the intersection of different religions that share quite clearly identifiable apocryphal narratives with one another, offers numerous challenges. The limitations of this discussion render these challenges all too obvious. One of the great opportunities, however, that emerges from working at this new or (re)new(ed) frontier in Christian Apocryphal Studies is that the discovery of intersections between these texts and literatures has an enormous potential to highlight the relevance of studying Christian apocrypha for vastly new audiences and their understanding and appreciation of the historical formation and development of their own traditions and cultural contexts. At the same time, often it is not clear in which direction changes to a given tradition developed. Here the more detailed knowledge of the reception history of a given Christian apocryphal text beyond the classical borders of Christian, or even Christian and Jewish literature, may allow one to discover the origins of elements that were subsequently received into Christian texts. It is beyond doubt that more work on contextualizing such tracings historically is necessary.

---

51. Wasserstrom, "Moving Finger," 4–5 and 16; and Anthony, "Legend of 'Abdallāh ibn Saba'," 22 n. 96.

— 7 —

Nag Hammadi, Gnosticism, Apocrypha
Bridging Disciplinary Divides

— Nicola Denzey Lewis[1] —

The fields of apocryphal Studies and Gnostic Studies were birthed just over a century ago, with key figures such as Constantin von Tischendorf in the nineteenth century defining the apocrypha and, a century later, Hans Jonas elaborating on the work and attitudes of his predecessors (primarily in Philosophy) in forging a new definition of "Gnosticism" and, consequently, concepts such as a "Gnostic religion" or a "Gnostic worldview"[2]—oversimplifications from which the apocrypha managed to escape. From the nineteenth century forward, Christian apocrypha and our so-called gnostic texts have become the ugly, wicked stepsisters in the fairy tale of New Testament Studies—one silly, the other dangerous. The apocrypha do occasionally teeter on the uncomfortable edge of Christian belief, tumbling toward a childish naiveté which is sometimes charming but often unseemly. One of the first English editors of a collection of Christian apocrypha, M. R.

---

1. I wish to thank Dr. Tony Burke for his generous assistance in preparing this talk for publication in the present volume. It would not have seen the light of day without his care and rigorous work. Of course, any omissions or errors that remain are fully my own responsibility.

2. Jonas, *Gnostic Religion*.

James, termed them both "theatrical" and "jejune."[3] Upholders of Christian orthodoxy—of whatever particular stripe—could cast supercilious smiles over apocryphal texts with their flying contests, obedient bedbugs, and talking dogs. The folkloric charm of such texts, however, posed no real danger to the more sober world of the New Testament where roosters simply crow when and as they are supposed to, and apostles never resort to flying around the forum to prove the truth and value of their message. The gnostic texts, by contrast, provide potentially an insidious and compelling wicked stepsister to our New Testament Cinderella; they possess the power of seductive words and the promise of autonomous self-divination, bypassing theologies of redemption, grace, and universal salvation that later came to shape Christianity.

The apocrypha and the so-called gnostic corpus are also linked by their implicit categorization as "low" literature. The gnostic texts, with their scandalously misguided interpretations of Plato and their high intellectual pretensions, reflect the sub-elitist mental phantasms of Romans too self-absorbed with their own cleverness to really understand the true (and humble) message of orthodox (read: populist) Christianity.[4] The apocrypha, by contrast, are the tales of the vulgar: entertaining stories for garrulous women and bored monks. As M. R. James writes, "they do not achieve either of the two principal purposes for which they were written, the instilling of true religion and the conveyance of true history."[5] In either case, interpreters have traditionally considered both the apocrypha and the so-called gnostic writings as beyond contempt, and of no use in helping us to reconstruct the history of Christianity. Of course, these are broad generalizations, assuming classifications—apocryphal and gnostic—in a way that does a disservice to both.

But classification is an imperfect science. Let us start with simple terminology. In the case of the apocrypha and gnostic writings, the issue is not simple at all. The literal translation of *apocryphon*, "hidden," applies perhaps more fittingly to some supposedly gnostic texts, like the *Gospel of Thomas*, with its "hidden or secret sayings which the living Jesus spoke to Thomas Judas Didymus" (*Gos. Thom.* Prol.). In our work parsing out these ancient sources, neither content nor form affects how they have traditionally been classified. But then is "tradition" to blame for vexatious acts of categorization? Patristic sources tell us of the existence of apocryphal books of Adam

---

3. James, *Apocryphal New Testament*, xii.

4. On negative assessments of Gnosticism, see Denzey Lewis, "'Enslavement to Fate.'"

5. James, *Apocryphal New Testament*, xii.

and of Moses, but only two texts still extant from Christian antiquity are titled "apocrypha," namely the *Apocryphon of John* and the *Apocryphon of James*, both from the Nag Hammadi library. These are considered "gnostic" texts rather than apocryphal texts. A closer look at the classificatory term "gnostic" is warranted at this point.

The term "gnostic," whether applied to texts or to people, has undergone significant revision in the past 20 years, such that many North American scholars of Gnosticism feel comfortable speaking of it only with scare quotations or the helpful adjective "so-called." The pioneering work of Karen King and Michael Williams has rightfully trained us to be wary of the term.[6] Unlike the term *apocryphon*, which at least was used in Christian antiquity, albeit (though crucially) differently than we use it today, the term "gnostic" (as in "gnostic gospel") appears nowhere in antiquity as part of a title or self-description—at least certainly not of the texts in that classification. Although some scholars hold on to the term "gnostic" to describe some of these texts, the past two decades has seen concerted efforts to be agnostic, if you will, about them. Scholars are now alternately deconstructionist and precise in their approaches, excising, for example, a Valentinian Christianity from a fictive "Gnostic Christianity" as a whole, and then continuing to push hard on even that subcategory to interrogate its accuracy and usefulness.[7] We are on the cusp, it seems, not only of the mainstreaming of "so-called" Gnosticism but also "so-called Valentinianism" and "so-called Sethianism."

All of this heuristic self-reflection and revisionism is good for our discipline. But it leads to a number of problems of categorization. Where do we put ancient texts? How do we categorize them? *Do* we categorize them? What happens to them when we do? (As we invariably do). Let us consider a few "case studies" of texts that do yeoman's duty as both apocryphal and gnostic, and sometimes not usefully so.

THE *HYMN OF THE PEARL* FROM THE *ACTS OF THOMAS*

The *Hymn of the Pearl*, appearing as part of the *Acts of Thomas* in only one of the text's six Syriac manuscripts (British Library, Add. 14645; dated to 936 CE) and one of the Greek (Rome, Biblioteca Vallicelliana, B35; 11th cent.),

---

6. King, *What Is Gnosticism?*; Williams, *Rethinking "Gnosticism."* See also, more recently, Brakke, *Gnostics*.

7. For reassessments of Valentinus and Valentinianism, see primarily Dunderberg, *Beyond Gnosticism*; Markschies, *Valentinus Gnosticus?*

is a wandering piece of hymn or song that seems to have drifted around. It was not native to the *Acts of Thomas*, but was at some point embedded into it.[8] Attempts to place it, in terms of genre, are fairly imprecise. The theosophist scholar G. R. S. Mead, long ago, called it "indubitably Gnostic"—a label which has perdured.[9] But what makes it "gnostic," precisely? Mead suggested that the answer could be found in the hymn's core myth, in which an individual's deeper, truer "self" (also described here as the spirit, soul, or living element) has come from a kingdom in the East. In other words, the core spiritual part of each individual originates in the spiritual world. But that self has come to reside in a state of alienation, described variously as sleep or drunkenness. The self is kept imprisoned in that state by malevolent beings. But the "king" or "father," by an act of his will, sends a message to awaken the self from its spiritual stupor. Upon that awakening or illumination, the self learns to discriminate between light and darkness, and to return to its proper state of spiritual recognition. So far, this comports well with what previous generations of Gnosticism scholars such as Hans Jonas called "the Gnostic myth." The *Hymn of the Pearl*'s myth comports very well, in fact, with the famous 1966 Messina Definition of Gnosticism:

> A coherent series of characteristics that can be summarized in the idea of a divine spark in man, deriving from the divine realm, fallen into this world, of fate, birth, and death, and needing to be awakened by the divine counterpart of the self in order to be finally re-integrated.[10]

This is no surprise, since in fact the assumption that the *Hymn of the Pearl* was gnostic drove the composition of the Messina Definition in the first place.

The real question, I suggest, is how to interpret the hymn. Is it an allegory? If so, what is it really about? The soul's journey after death? The spiritual journey of a seeker? Or is it about Jesus and a hidden spiritual journey? How does our own assumption that it is a religious text color our allegorical interpretation of it? Could it not just be a journey narrative? Does it have to be religious? In a journey narrative, the hero goes to another compelling but dangerous land. While he is there, he forgets who he is and what his task is. To give some modern but familiar examples from the world of Hollywood, this is the theme behind Dorothy in the *Wizard of Oz*, Neo in *The Matrix*, and Bud in *Pleasantville*, all of which express journey narratives in their

---

8. For a detailed discussion of the hymn see Drijvers, "*Acts of Thomas*," 330–33; Poirier, *L'Hymne de la perle*.

9. Mead, *Hymn of the Robe*, 10.

10. Bianchi, *Le Origini*, xxvi.

most modern form. In all of these movies, the hero enters a strange land and becomes captivated by its charms, but eventually he regains the knowledge of who he really is and seeks to return home.

The embeddedness of the hymn in the *Acts of Thomas* also affects how we read the story. What if it were found, for example, in the middle of Ephraem's hymns? Would it still have been singled out as gnostic? The *Hymn of the Pearl*'s early characterization as gnostic effectively orphaned it from a proper placement in Syriac literature and Syriac Christianity, its native setting where it is seldom studied today. It is, at the same time, orphaned also from Gnosticism, where, since the discovery of the Nag Hammadi library and the subsequent rethinking of the category of Gnosticism, it is no longer taken seriously as a "gnostic" text.

The *Hymn of the Pearl*, then, presents considerable hermeneutical and classificatory challenges. It defies categorization. As interpreters, we become caught in a recursive loop, unable to bring to the text anything apart from our own frames of meaning which shift with our own training and inclination as exegetes. The hymn is gnostic if you believe that Gnosticism exists as a viable analytic category and if you adhere to a particular hermeneutical positioning that gives space for this writing. For those who define Gnosticism differently (as, for example, the historian David Brakke) or who reject the category completely (Williams, King), there is little commitment either to the category or to any emplacement of this text within this category. But the *Hymn of the Pearl* is hardly alone in having been orphaned, so to speak, from our constructed analytical categories. Next we turn to another categorically vexing text: the *Round Dance of the Cross*.

ROUND DANCE OF THE CROSS FROM THE *ACTS OF JOHN*

Like the *Hymn of the Pearl*, the *Round Dance of the Cross* (*Acts John* 94–95) was early on identified as a gnostic hymn. It shows up as such in modern collections of gnostic literature.[11] In Willis Barnstone's *The Gnostic Bible*, for example, it is not explicitly called "gnostic" in the short introduction that precedes it (although supposed Valentinian elements are briefly highlighted), but of course, it is included apparently unproblematically in *The Gnostic Bible* in the first place. The text is charming, and conjures up happy images of peasants circle-dancing in harmless pagan ways as peasants were wont to do, at least in our imaginations. There is nothing particularly "gnostic"

---

11. Layton, *Gnostic Scriptures*, 366–75; Barnstone, *Gnostic Bible*, 386–94; Cameron, *Other Gospels*, 87–96.

about it—that is to say, it does not fit the Messina Definition. There is no demiurgical figure, no internal divine spark for the dancers to discover, no elaborate cosmology or mythopoesis.

Like the *Hymn of the Pearl*, the *Round Dance* has become a classificatory orphan. Although the *Acts of John* is counted among the extant corpus of Christian apocrypha, the *Round Dance of the Cross* (like the *Hymn of the Pearl*) is often drawn out from the text in which it was emplaced in antiquity and published separately or considered apart from it. As such, it has become alienated from the broader corpus of apocrypha where it resided, for a time, as a "gnostic" fragment in an otherwise non-gnostic text. The re-classification emerged from the erroneous association of docetism with Gnosticism. Once docetism is challenged as a theological attribute or characteristic of Gnosticism, arguments for the *Round Dance*'s so-called gnostic qualities have no foundation. Again, however, the consequence of interrogating our basic categories is the marginalization of ancient texts that we simply do not know how to re-categorize and which therefore fall between our own subdisciplinary purviews.[12]

THE PROBLEM OF THE NAG HAMMADI LIBRARY

The discovery of the Nag Hammadi library in 1945 and the subsequent eruption of these texts into the scholarly world beginning in earnest in 1972 irrevocably changed our understanding of Gnosticism.[13] Virtually no so called gnostic text discovered prior to the Nag Hammadi library is now studied as evidence for Gnosticism.[14]

---

12. For a detailed commentary on the *Round Dance*, see Junod and Kaestli, eds., *Acta Iohannis*, 2: 621–27 and 642–55; for a discussion of similarities between the *Round Dance* and material in the *Gospel of the Savior*, see Piovanelli, "Thursday Night Fever."

13. The *Facsimile Edition of the Nag Hammadi Codices* began publication in 1972, followed by Robinson, *Nag Hammadi Library*, in 1977 as the first scholarly translation of the Nag Hammadi corpus.

14. The exceptions are the texts found in the Askew Codex (containing the *Pistis Sophia* and two untitled fragmentary treatises), the Bruce Codex (the two *Books of Jeu* and several untitled texts), and the Berlin Codex (with the *Gospel of Mary*, the *Apocryphon of John*, the *Act of Peter*, and the *Sophia of Jesus Christ*). Note, however, that the Bruce Codex was not published until 1955 (see Till, *Die gnostischen Schriften*), years after the Nag Hammadi discovery, and two of the texts in the codex, the *Apocryphon of John* and the *Sophia of Jesus Christ*, are found also among the Nag Hammadi codices. One other exception is the *Gospel of Thomas*, though its earlier remains discovered at Oxyrhynchus, published in 1897 and 1904 (see Grenfell and Hunt, *Logia Iesou*; Grenfell and Hunt, *New Sayings of Jesus*), are very fragmentary. In short scholarship on non-Nag Hammadi writings, although discovered prior to 1945, receive far less scholarly attention in light of the Nag Hammadi discovery.

Since a number of the writings contained in the Nag Hammadi library are technically apocryphal texts, their discovery led to some reclassification and even renaming of previously-known apocrypha. When fewer manuscripts were available to scholars, efforts were made to identify the various "gnostic" texts mentioned by the early church writers with the evidence that was at hand. Any text not included in the New Testament was assumed to have been excluded because it was gnostic. A case in point: before Nag Hammadi, the name of the Greek fragments of the *Gospel of Thomas* was unknown; often they were simply referred to as the "Oxyrhynchus Sayings." The name "Gospel of Thomas" belonged to another text: the *Infancy Gospel of Thomas*. The identification of the infancy gospel with the "Gospel of Thomas" mentioned by church fathers into the eleventh century began with its first publication in the seventeenth century.[15] The absence of gnostic features in the infancy gospel led to the creation of an "expurgation" theory explaining its development—the gnostic content must have been removed from the text. It never occurred to the pre-Nag Hammadi scholars that there could be another gospel ascribed to Thomas. This confusion of the two Thomas apocrypha continues to influence scholarship on the texts.

Surprisingly, only a few of the new Nag Hammadi apocrypha regularly appear in Christian apocrypha collections. The update of M. R. James by J. K. Elliott, for example, includes only the *Gospel of Thomas* and the *Apocryphon of James*.[16] The Nag Hammadi apocrypha fare better in the fifth edition of Hennecke-Schneemelcher, which includes seven texts: the *Gospel of Thomas*, the *Book of Thomas*, the *Apocryphon of James*, the *Dialogue of the Savior*, *1 Apocalypse of James*, *2 Apocalypse of James*, and the *Letter of Peter to Philip*.[17] Even the otherwise-expansive *Écrits apocryphes chrétiens* volumes published in the Pléiade series have only the *Gospel of Thomas*, though the gnostic texts are included in a separate Pléiade volume (*Écrits gnostiques*).[18] This separation between the two bodies of literature is reflected also in the creation of a Nag Hammadi Section, separate from the Christian Apocrypha, for the annual meetings of the Society of Biblical

---

15. See the history of scholarship on the text in Burke, *De infantia Iesu*, 45–126.

16. Elliott, *Apocryphal New Testament*.

17. Translated into English from the corrected sixth edition: Schneemelcher, ed., *New Testament Apocrypha*.

18. The Italian collection by Erbetta, *Gli Apocrifi del Nuovo Testamento*, is a notable exception to this separation of gnostic and non-gnostic apocrypha. The second volume features a large section dedicated to "Vangeli gnostici e testi affini," which includes Nag Hammadi texts rarely featured in apocrypha collections, such as the *Apocryphon of John*, the *Hypostasis of the Archons*, the *Three Steles of Seth*, as well as other gnostic texts, such as the *Pistis Sophia*, and the two *Books of Jeu*.

Literature. Henceforth, scholars specialized, and conversation between the two sections became, if not strained, then perhaps attenuated. Nevertheless, there is an argument to be made for the Nag Hammadi library's reintegration into the field of apocrypha. But if the Christian apocrypha collections are any indication, this is slow coming.

Two texts within the Nag Hammadi library present particular problems for categorization: the *Acts of Peter and the Twelve Apostles* and the *Gospel of Thomas*. The *Acts of Peter and the Twelve Apostles* is an allegorical text found in Codex VI, and it is safe to say that it wins the "which one of these things is not like the others" game easily. An apocryphal act—but different from our other apocryphal *Acts of Peter*—it tells of the apostles' sea journey to a city named "Abide-in-Endurance" where they encounter a man named Lithargoel—an angelic name meaning "shining stone"—who calls out "Pearls! Pearls!" The rich people of the city ignore him but the poor and beggars want to see this pearl, which is intended in the text as a symbol for spiritual salvation. He says he will give them the pearl if they come to his city, but to do so they must abandon all of their possessions. The apostles accept Lithargoel's invitation. When they reach the city, they see Lithargoel dressed now as a physician. Soon he stands revealed as the risen Christ, who sends the apostles back to "Abide-in-Endurance" with his medicine bag to bring physical and spiritual health to the people.

Acts Pet. 12 Apos. shares the genre of romance literature with our other apocryphal acts; however, it is more explicitly allegorical than those texts. Still, this does not make it more gnostic. Only one other so-called gnostic text, the *Hymn of the Pearl* is (potentially) allegorical, and, as noted above, that text is not gnostic either. What is particularly striking, however, is that the truth of the allegory in *Acts Pet. 12 Apos.* points to something very ungnostic: the Pearl Merchant is revealed to be Jesus, not *gnosis* itself. By contrast, in the *Hymn of the Pearl*, the pearl is self-knowledge. In other words, those foolish people in the village who do not recognize the pearl in their midst are simply bad Christians in the sense that they do not have the proper belief: the capacity to recognize that their savior had arrived. This is a fairly normative Christian message, but here it is sitting in the middle of a corpus of so-called heretical, so-called gnostic texts, without further elaboration or explanation. In my opinion, *Acts Pet. 12 Apos.* should be re-classified formally as an apocryphal, not gnostic, text, if only so that more work could be done on it, and that it might enter conversations among those who work primarily on Christian apocrypha, because its positioning within the Nag Hammadi library effectively has sidelined it from work in both fields.

This brings us to the problem of the *Gospel of Thomas*. Disciplinarily, the problem of *Thomas*'s status as gnostic/apocryphal was solved, on one level, by its excision from both SBL groups and the creation of a group all its own: the Thomasine group. But such a strategy is problematic, since it results in significant disciplinary fragmentation: the creation of a third group with little conversational overlap with the others.

Is *Thomas* apocryphal? It certainly presumes to be "hidden." Is it gnostic? I would say so, because *gnosis* is valued as a form of salvation (see esp. *Gos. Thom.* 2, 3, 5, 18, 19, 31, 67, 69, 80, 91). Other specialists disagree, because it contains no Demiurge and no elaborate cosmology.[19] A third option is possible also: the *Gospel of Thomas* is not a "full-blown" gnostic text, but it can be (indeed, was) valued by gnostic Christians, just as other, nongnostic texts were, such as the Gospel of Mark, the Gospel of John, and even the letters of Paul. In the end, it might be best to remain "agnostic" about how to categorize this puzzling text, and let it continue to be considered both gnostic and apocryphal, as reflected in its inclusion in both collections of gnostic scriptures and apocryphal gospels. If a bridge is sought between the two categories, the *Gospel of Thomas* certainly fits the bill.

RETHINKING "NONCANONICAL"

We can all agree that the Christian apocrypha and the so-called gnostic corpus comprise noncanonical texts. But the confessional underpinnings of the category "noncanonical" itself (as juxtaposed with, and consequently devalued in contrast with, canonical writings) are troubling to some of us. In my estimation, the category has heuristic or perhaps even sentimental value to some Christians who have a vested interest in tracing things back, if not to Jesus, then at least to the apostolic age. For others, however, "noncanonical" carries only negative value; texts in this category are perceived as corrupted and derivative, unworthy of the attention awarded to canonical writings.

Once one delves into codicology and textual criticism, "noncanonical" gets particularly troubling as a category. The Codex Alexandrinus contains, along with the writings of our modern New Testament, and virtually a complete translation of the Septuagint, the *Epistle to Marcellinus* ascribed to Athanasius, inserted before the Book of Psalms. In the New Testament section we find *1* and *2 Clement*, and an index in the codex indicates that the *Psalms of Solomon* originally followed *2 Clement*, but the pages are no longer extant. Codex Sinaiticus from the mid-fourth century follows the New Testament books with the *Epistle of Barnabas* and the *Shepherd of Hermas*. Earlier still, the third/fourth-century 𝔓72 contains Jude, 1–2 Peter, the

---

19. See, e.g., the discussions in Marjanen, "Is *Thomas* a Gnostic Gospel?"; Wilson, "Gospel of Thomas"; and Patterson, *Gospel of Thomas and Jesus*.

Protevangelium of James, the Corinthian correspondence (including *3 Corinthians*), the eleventh *Ode of Solomon*, and several other texts.[20] Obviously canonicity in late antiquity simply was not the concern that it has been for us today. It is, frankly, also a way of marginalizing the status of non-Western churches, since the "standard" "measuring rod" that determines the canon is Western. As we know, the canons of the Ethiopian Church, the Coptic Church, the Syriac Church, and other ancient divisions of Christianity hold different canons that draw rather different lines around those texts they considered canonical or apocryphal.[21]

In holding on to these categories, "apocrypha" and "gnostic"—with their ensuing evaluative and rigid assumptions that traditionally lie behind their construction—are we inadvertently continuing the work of the church rather than the Academy? And if so, which church? These are, after all, categories of our own making. The science of classification was a particular preoccupation of the nineteenth century. What is needed, I believe, is a more up-to-date, polythetic system. But what might that look like? One solution is to call for the abandonment of established disciplinary boundaries, to call all this what it is: early Christian literature, and then to focus on sub-genres, such as "apocalyptic," or "romance," or even "gospel." We also know that these sub-categories themselves are slippery enough. In what sense, for instance, is the *Gospel of Thomas* a gospel? What has it to do with the *Gospel of Philip*? What does either have to do with the Gospel of Mark? It may be that the very grandest categories—apocrypha or gnostic writings—are simply too broad to be meaningful and too laden with erroneous assumptions or ideological bias to be of much use.

Another approach would be to allow all these texts to stand together as an undifferentiated group ("early Christian literature") but then to consider the work that such texts did, individually considered, in antiquity. In his foreword to a volume of studies on the apocryphal acts, Lawrence Sullivan touches on the issues these texts raise:

> [These studies] raise a number of important questions and hypotheses concerning the formation of texts, the transformation of religious experience into oral and narrative expression, and the meaning and interpretation of specific symbolic complexes and practices. Indeed, the volume makes the case that understanding how these apocryphal texts originated and developed

---

20. For a more detailed description of these manuscripts, along with a survey of other New Testament manuscripts with curious contents, see Epp, "Issues in the Interrelation."

21. See the descriptions in Metzger, *Bible in Translation*, 25–51.

offers a model for understanding the formation of canonical Christian scripture.[22]

I do not agree that the primary purpose of apocryphal texts ought to be what they teach us about canonical texts, but Sullivan still raises significant points. The canonical scriptures themselves simply cannot, and will not (however massaged) teach us all we need to know about the formation of early Christian texts or canons, or about the relationship between religious experience and its oral and written expression. The proposed approach considers not the classification of a text, but how it was read in antiquity. Was it read in the same way as a canonical text? Were gnostic and apocryphal texts read the same way as one another? Sullivan, again, suggests that the apocryphal acts were read as, for instance,

> allegories of the changes that occur within the soul, as inspirational material for sermons, as devotional reading for private piety, as librettos for dramatic spectacles and visual art, as enchantments during the liturgy, and as sources for doctrinal debate.[23]

The same could be said for so-called "gnostic" texts. In their practical use within communities, then, there is much work still left to be done in thinking across categories.

A third proposed way forward in bridging the disciplinary divide between Gnostic and Christian Apocrypha Studies is to spend more time thinking about how texts were bundled together into collections. It has been our training and inclination, due to the drive in New Testament Studies to find the earliest and best, most "authentic" Christian documents, to become obsessed with origins, and to always seek to uncover the most original form of a text. In Gnostic Studies, for instance, we have classically been drawn to claiming a second-century Greek milieu for the Nag Hammadi texts, even though this is a) only presumed and b) the only forms in which we have virtually all these texts are in late fourth-century versions in Coptic. Although it puts us in the world of the fourth century and beyond, examining how texts were bundled together provides a clue into how people in late antiquity read texts. Bookbinding was uncommon and expensive, thus the choice of books within a particular codex was presumably more than what happened to be on hand. If we consider some famous codices, we immediately see that the people who assembled them worked with a different idea of what was "apocryphal" and what was "gnostic" and what, even, was

---

22. Sullivan, Foreword to Bovon, Brock, and Matthews, *Apocryphal Acts*, xi.
23. Ibid.

"canonical." The fifth-century Berlin Codex, for example, contains the *Act of Peter*, the *Gospel of Mary*, the *Apocryphon of John*, and the *Sophia of Jesus Christ*. While the first, if originally a portion of the *Acts of Peter*, is generally classified under "apocrypha," the others are generally seen as "gnostic." But what linked them in the mind of whoever bound them together? The sixth-century Codex Panopolitanus contains portions of *1 Enoch*, the *Apocalypse of Peter*, the *Gospel of Peter*, and the *Martyrdom of St. Julian*.[24] Why? What ties these texts together? These examples could be multiplied, but my point is the same: what use are our categories when we consider the way in which these diverse texts were bundled?

CONCLUSION

What ties together scholars of Christian apocrypha and Gnosticism is the love and enthusiasm which we feel for our texts and our fields of study. But to move forward constructively, we must divest ourselves of the terminology we conventionally use that serves only to divide us. In so doing, we risk losing at least part of our audience—those who are captivated by the idea that we possess "hidden" or "secret" or "heretical" texts from early Christianity. Would anyone buy books like Willis Barnstone's *The Other Bible*, or Ehman's *Lost Scriptures*, or Layton's *The Gnostic Scriptures* if they were just called *Early Christian Literature*? At the same time, such re-branding also may break the stranglehold that terms like "canon" and "normativity" and "orthodoxy" or "proto-orthodoxy" have—terms that cause so many of us to parse out these texts into, implicitly, valuable or merely quaint, doctrinally-sound or eye-raisingly dangerous.

What we are doing with this approach would be akin to allowing late antique Christians the opportunity to genre-build themselves, without our own interpretations of what ancient text was orthodox and what heretical, or what was "low" literature and what "high." It moves us that much farther away from value-laden categories: profane myths and old wives' tales (1 Tim 4:7), endless genealogies (1 Tim 1:4), and "the profane chatter and contradictions of what is falsely called knowledge" (1 Tim 6:20). Never mind that these texts were differently valued in various Christian communities: sometimes made canonical, widely translated, and wildly popular. In the

---

24. The proposed date of the codex ranges from the sixth to the eighth century; for a summary, see Ehrman and Pleše, *Apocryphal Gospels*, 373. The spirit of this inquiry into the contents of codices and their meaning lies behind also the re-examination of origin of the Nag Hammadi codices in Denzey Lewis and Blount, "Rethinking the Origins."

end, then, it becomes clear that these categories do not serve us; rather they prohibit conversation and scholarly exchange.

– 8 –

Canon Formation
Why and Where Scholars Disagree

— Lee Martin McDonald —

UNTIL THE REFORMATION ERA, few Christians showed much interest in the scope of their biblical canons. That was especially true for the earliest Christians. In recent years there has been a renewed interest in the notion of canon and the formation of the Old and New Testaments. While there were occasional and substantial examinations of canon formation in the late nineteenth and early twentieth centuries (indeed, only a handful[1]), this began to change in the latter part of the twentieth century and subsequently many important studies have emerged on various aspects of canon formation. Research in canon formation has become something of a "cottage industry" and has been accompanied also by significant interest in research into so-called apocryphal and pseudepigraphal texts. Considerable attention has been focused also on the origin and notion of canon as well as on the criteria employed by the ancient Christians to define the scope of their

---

1. This small group of scholars of the canon includes Theodore Zahn, Herbert E. Ryle, Gerrit Wildeboer, Henry Barclay Swete, Moses A. Stuart, Max L. Margolis, Adolf von Harnack, Edgar J. Goodspeed, and more recently, Hans von Campenhausen. Their contributions formed the major treatments of canon formation until relatively recent times. The last 30 years has seen a wealth of scholarly advances in this field of inquiry and also a much greater focus on the so-called noncanonical literature.

sacred scripture. Why were some well-known ancient books eventually rejected from those collections? When was agreement reached on which books were accepted or rejected? The process led to placing the texts into the categories that are now commonly used but widely acknowledged as anachronistic—namely, canonical, noncanonical, apocryphal, pseudepigraphal, biblical, or non-biblical texts. Most, if not all, of this literature was welcomed as sacred scripture in some ancient churches—that is, they were allowed to be read in worship and as catechetical instruction by *some* early and later Christians.

It is well known that some rejected books continued to be cited and read as scripture in congregations long after some church councils had rejected them (*1 Enoch, Didache, Shepherd of Hermas*, etc.). Regularly, and for obvious reasons, many books ceased being copied and distributed in churches because they were widely rejected. Therefore, it is understandable that they were no longer copied or circulated in churches and in many cases were lost or even thrown away. While many of those disenfranchised books were lost, some have been recovered and scholars often find in them considerable insight into the historical context of Judaism of late antiquity and early Christianity.

Biblical scholars often disagree over the formation of the Jewish and Christian biblical canons. An obvious reason for this has to do with the shortage of primary literature from antiquity that informs us about the origins, formation, and canonization of the biblical literature. If we are talking about process, we may all agree that the processes of canon formation began with the production of the texts in question and their early reception in ancient churches. In the case of the Gospels, for instance, there are several examples of their use, especially Matthew, in the second-century churches and possibly also at the end of the first century CE. But the final and universal agreement on the shape of the biblical canon took centuries longer and in the case of the Old Testament or Hebrew Bible, there has never been complete agreement in the churches. As we will see below, the notion of a fixed canon of New Testament writings has been welcomed more eagerly in Western than in Eastern churches. This fluidity is observable in the listing of books in the Old and New Testaments over a lengthy span of time, a practice more common in the East than in the West. Ancient texts focusing on the formation of the Bible fall considerably short of providing clear answers to questions related to the scope of the biblical canon. In what follows I will focus on some of the more controversial issues and offer a few suggestions on how some of them might be resolved, or at least better understood.

THE NOTION OF SCRIPTURE

The belief that God speaks through messengers or prophets who communicate their message orally is found in the stories of the pre-literary prophets (e.g., Elijah and Elisha) in the OT/HB. The notion of a *written* message from God, namely "scripture," refers to the belief that a divinely-inspired message was revealed to a prophet who subsequently communicated that message to others; some of these prophets put that message in writing and circulated it within their religious communities. This belief appears quite early among the Jews, beginning when Jewish prophets wrote down what they believed were oracles from God. In such cases, the concept of authoritative religious writings was clearly operative and we have early instances of the notion of scripture, though without the familiar special terms for its description (*ketubim* or *graphai*). In Jewish tradition, written authoritative texts come directly from God, who not only inspired the prophets, but even wrote the Ten Commandments on stone and gave them to Moses. The story of God's activity among the Jews in their exodus from Egypt and the story of God's preservation of the Jews eventually became the core of the Jewish authoritative written traditions. However, the notion of a *written* prophetic oracle clearly has earlier antecedents than those in ancient Jewish scripture. Armin Lange, for example, has shown that both oral and written prophecies were common in the Middle East as early as the ninth century BCE and also later among the Greeks, especially in the prophetic oracles that took place at Delphi.[2] The notion of sacred scripture, or sacred writing, derives ultimately from a belief that God has communicated a message to a prophetic figure who wrote it down and shared it with others.[3]

WHAT IS A BIBLICAL CANON?

Scholars seeking the origins of biblical canons in antiquity generally look for several identifying features. According to Vardi, these include:

> (a) a list (b) of selected literary works, (c) which are regarded as sharing a special value (being the only ones extant, the best, the most representative, or the most suitable for a special purpose); in addition such a list should also be (d) more or less standard and generally known, as well as (e) authoritative, in the sense

---

2. See a useful discussion of this practice in Lange, "Oral Collection and Canon"; and also Miller Parmenter, "Bible as Icon." She depends here on Widengren, *Ascension of the Apostle*.

3. This matter is discussed at length in McDonald, *Biblical Canon*, 20–37.

that it is generally accepted or at least acknowledged when it is rejected.[4]

For some time, I have followed Eugene Ulrich on the definition of canon as the "established and exclusive list of books that hold supreme authoritative status for a community."[5] He focuses mostly on the end of the canonical process and brings much-needed clarity to the question of the formation of the Bible, but he is aware that some texts functioned authoritatively in churches and synagogues for various periods of time before they were rejected.

Biblical scholars often talk past one another when discussing canon formation and I suspect that in no small measure this is due not only to the scarcity of ancient artifacts that reflect on such investigations, but also because it appears in some cases that we view those investigations from different historical and theological perspectives. There are many challenging questions related to canon formation, especially about how canon scholars consider the many historical, textual, and theological questions related to the process.

Scholars have long been divided over the meaning of "canon" itself and so we begin our focus here. The modern application of the term "canon" is, of course, anachronistic when applied to the earliest stages of the church's scripture development. If we are referring to a fixed biblical canon, there is no evidence that the term was used to distinguish a list of sacred religious literature in the time of Jesus or before. It was not used of a fixed collection of sacred books in the church before the fourth century CE, when Athanasius composed his famous 39th *Festal Letter* (in the year 367). In the first century CE, there were no *fixed* biblical canons of Jewish or Christian sacred books, and because there are no *known* early traditions that tell the story of how and why Christians selected the sacred writings that eventually comprised their canon of sacred scriptures, some confusion in this area invariably will continue.

But again, what do we mean by canon? Scholars generally use this term in two important and often overlapping ways, though there are some important distinctions. As is generally known, "canon" originally referred to measuring instruments, but eventually it came to refer to models or guides that were followed, such as we see in the various architectural models that survive antiquity, as well as in philosophy, music, and even grammatical norms; it is especially used to describe literary collections.[6] Although the

---

4. Vardi, "Canons of Literary Texts at Rome," 131.

5. See Ulrich, "Canonical Process," 269–76; and also Ulrich, "Notion and Definition of Canon."

6. I have discussed this matter at length in previous publications, especially in

term "canon" is found in the New Testament, it is not used in reference to a list of books; rather, it identifies the limits of Paul's ministry (2 Cor 10:13, 15, 16) and is once used as the standard or norm of true Christian faith (Gal. 6:16). Similarly, Josephus uses the term to refer to Josiah's ascension to the "throne [= rulership]" (as we see in 2 Kgs 22:1; 2 Chron 34:1) and also to indicate that King David was a model upon "whom he [Josiah] made the pattern and rule [*kanoni*] of his whole manner of life" (*Ant.* 10.49). Later, Clement of Rome speaks about "the venerable rule [*kanona*] of our tradition" (*1 Clem.* 7.2). In the second century the term is regularly used of the "rule" of faith or truth and includes the core beliefs that identified Christian faith (see Irenaeus, *Haer.* 1.10.1; cf. 3.4.2).[7]

While it is likely that the term "canon" was not used before the fourth century *in churches* to identify a fixed collection of sacred writings (Origen being the possible exception), the notion of an authoritative written guide used in multiple ways in religious communities was clearly present from the church's beginnings. This can be seen in early Christian acceptance and use of Jewish scripture in worship and their use of Christian writings alongside of and often instead of the Jewish scriptures in church worship assemblies (Justin, *1 Apol.* 67). However, the notion of an authoritative collection of sacred writings clearly can be seen at the end of the first century CE in Josephus (*Ag. Ap.* 1:37–43), though he does not identify the specific writings he has in mind, but only the categories (five books of Moses, 13 books of the prophets, and four books of hymns) and the number of books in Jewish scripture (22). There is no doubt that all Jewish sects in the time of Jesus recognized the authority of sacred books, but which books they recognized or rejected at that time is unclear.

I regularly distinguish the recognition of authoritative sacred texts in religious community as "Canon 1"—that is, the *first* phase of canon formation when the authority of a religious text is acknowledged well before the usual designation "scripture" is attributed to it. I also use "Canon 2" to describe a fixed collection of canonical writings that appear considerably later. I have adapted these designations from Gerald Sheppard, but I use them somewhat differently.[8] Canon 1 recognizes the authoritative function of a sacred text *before* there is a term or category that encompasses or comprehends the practice. Eusebius, for instance, does not use *kanon* as it is commonly used today; rather, he claimed that the church's "encovenanted" (*endiatheke*) writings were those that were undisputed (*anantirreta*) and

---

McDonald, *Biblical Canon*, 38–48; and *Forgotten Scriptures*, 14–23.

7. For further discussion here, see McDonald, *Biblical Canon*, 294–300.

8. See Sheppard, "Canon," 64–67.

widely-recognized (*homolegoumena*) in the churches (*Hist. eccl.* 6.25.3–14; see also 3.25.1–7).

Some contemporary scholars use "canon" to refer either to texts or stories that function with religious authority in believing communities (what Sanders calls *norma normans*; my "Canon 1"), or to an authoritative collection of religious writings (what Sanders calls *norma normata*, and I call "Canon 2").[9] Thomassen uses "rule" to describe the former of these distinctions and "list" or "catalog" to describe the latter. Canon, in the sense of "rule" or authority, appears quite early in the church, but canon as "list" or "catalog" comes into use considerably later.[10] Aichele more recently defines canon essentially as a fixed collection of religious texts to which nothing can be added or taken away, and adds that "canon defines the identity of the group of people by drawing a line around a group of texts that is in some way associated with the people's beliefs and values."[11] If scholars choose this definition—namely, canon as that which functions authoritatively in a religious community—they also need to find an appropriate way to identify those texts that functioned temporarily as scripture (*1 Enoch*, *Odes of Solomon*, and others), often for centuries, in various churches, but eventually were not included in the final fixed sacred collections. By the end of the fourth century CE, considerable agreement was reached on most of the 27 books that comprise the New Testament; nevertheless, other contenders continued to have widespread circulation and use in churches for several centuries (*3 Corinthians*, *Shepherd of Hermas*, *Epistle of Barnabas*, *Didache*, and *1 Clement*, but also others).

If canon refers to a select collection of religious texts or books that cannot be changed and are placed in a collection or list of generically similar sacred texts, then that notion of canon is a later development among Jews and Christians. As noted, the first to use *kanon* in reference to a limited select collection of sacred books is Athanasius in 367 CE in his famous 39th *Festal Letter*. Such collections are more common in the fourth century, beginning especially with Eusebius, though there *may* have been earlier antecedents such as Victorinus of Pettau (see the discussion of the Muratorian Fragment below) and possibly earlier in the case of Origen who knew of the "twenty-two canonical books, according to the Hebrew tradition" (Eusebius, *Hist. eccl.* 6.25.1, but also see 6.25.2–14). Eusebius describes Origen's awareness of the Jewish collection of sacred books, and also mentions his listing of the

---

9. See Sanders, *Torah and Canon*, 1–9; and Sanders, "Canon, Hebrew Bible," 839 and 847.

10. Thomassen, "Some Notes," 9–10. Thomassen reflects Sanders's earlier comments on these two notions of canon.

11. See Aichele, "Canon," 58.

Christian scripture as including the four Gospels, the letters of Paul (not identified), Peter (one letter and another that is doubted = 2 Peter), John (the Gospel, Revelation, one epistle and possibly two more = 2 and 3 John), and Hebrews (written by one close to Paul, but not by Paul). Such lists were in vogue in the last half of the fourth century and later, due in large part, perhaps, to Constantine, who was anxious to bring unity to the churches and, like his predecessors, also in the rest of his empire. His calling on Eusebius to produce 50 volumes containing the church's scripture may well have been an incentive for the church to determine the scope of their collection of sacred texts.

Surveys of the various lists or catalogs of sacred scripture that survive antiquity[12] show that these catalogs varied often considerably, even though the core books seldom changed. Most include one or more of the canonical Gospels and *most* include several of the letters attributed to Paul. Some of the books whose canonicity were disputed for a longer period of time, often dubbed "fringe books" in canon formation, were included in the later stabilized biblical canons, but some were not (often Revelation). Some of those books took longer than others to be recognized, as in the cases of Hebrews, James, 2 Peter, 2 and 3 John, Jude, and Revelation, but also the Pastoral Epistles that are missing in $\mathfrak{P}46$ (ca. 200 CE) and Codex Vaticanus (ca. 350 CE). The Pastorals are included, however, in Codex Sinaiticus (ca. 375 CE). Revelation was finally included in the canon of the Eastern Orthodox churches, but it is rejected for placement in their lectionaries.[13] Some books that had received widespread recognition earlier eventually were rejected by the majority of churches, as in the cases of the *Didache*, *Epistle of Barnabas*, *Apocalypse of Peter*, *Shepherd of Hermas*, and others. By the middle of the third century, there were growing doubts about the status of *1 Enoch*, as well as other books such as the *Testaments of the Twelve Patriarchs*. Origen was openly accepting of *1 Enoch* in his earlier writings, but later seems to have reversed his thinking.[14] The presence of authoritative

---

12. Many of these are listed in McDonald, *Biblical Canon*, 439–51; McDonald, *Formation of the Bible*, 82–86 and 152–58; and in www.biblicalstudies.mcdonald.continuumbooks.com; but also in Ryle, *Canon of the Old Testament*, 221–49; Swete, *Introduction to the Old Testament*, 197–214; and Souter, *Text and Canon*, 188–220.

13. See Constantinou, "Banned from the Lectionary."

14. Origen defends a theological position citing the "scriptures" of Ps 139:16 and *1 Enoch* 17, following up with "For it is written in the same book of Enoch, 'I beheld the whole matter'" (*Princ.* 1.3; 4.35 cf. 4.1.31), but seems to ignore it after that and there are no further comments on its scriptural status either by Origen or *most* of those who followed him (see Rufinus, *Orig. Hom. Num.* 28.2 and *Orig. Hom. Jon.* 6.42). The primary exceptions are, of course, Lactantius and Eusebius in the fourth century, but it is difficult to find any references to *1 Enoch* outside of the Abyssinian churches that

Christian writings that informed the faith of the early followers of Jesus and were used in several of the early apologies of the churches is well established in the Apostolic Fathers and by some later writers, but no one in the first or second centuries spoke about a fixed or limited collection of sacred writings—that is, a Canon 2 development—with the one exception of Irenaeus, who limited the Gospels that were to be read in the churches to four and no more (*Haer.* 3.21.3–4; see also 3.3.3; 3.11.8; 3.12.15; 3.14.1–15). Melito of Sardis spoke of a sacred collection of Old Testament books (Eusebius, *Hist. eccl.* 4.26.13–14), but he did not produce a list of Christian books.

It is often overlooked that Christian biblical catalogs or canons appear to have flourished longer in the Western churches than in churches of the East where there was greater fluidity for centuries. Vahan S. Hovhanessian's recent collection of essays on this topic reflects a more fluid biblical canon in both the Old and New Testament collections. He also claims that no councils of the East made a final decision on the scope of the biblical canons similar to the decisions of the Council of Trent in 1546. Eastern churches appear to have welcomed what was commonly-accepted from tradition rather than legislated by council decisions.[15]

If by canon we are simply referring to the recognition of the sacredness and authority of ancient texts, then of course the notion of canon as an authoritative list of texts exists quite early. Many of the writings of the Old Testament were welcomed in an authoritative manner well before such writings were called inviolable scripture. See, for example, references to Moses' writings in Ezra 3:2; 7:6, 10, 12; 9:10; 10:3 and in Neh 1:5–9; 8:9–15, 18; 9:3, 13–14, 16, etc., and even to Haggai and Zechariah in Ezra 5:1–2. The influence of Mosaic and other prophetic writings is clear in 2 Kings 17:13, but there was no reference to a fixed list of scripture at that time even though the notion is clearly present without the familiar designations. This can be seen also in Sirach 44–49 where several references to influential authors can be detected, but again there is no widespread terminology for such literature or even the notion of a fixed list of sacred books *at that time*, despite the reference to the "Twelve Prophets" (likely the "Minor Prophets,"

---

recognized its sacredness.

15. See Hovhanessian, ed., *Canon of the Bible*. Examples of this fluidity can be seen in the continuing presence of the *Prayer of Manasseh, Testament of Solomon, Repose of the Evangelist John, Petition of Euthalius,* and *3 Corinthians* in Eastern manuscripts. Several so-called "noncanonical" writings were still cited as scripture as late as the 1800s. It is clear that the Western biblical canons were not as common or popular in the East. See McDonald, Review of Hovhanessian, ed., *Canon of the Bible*. The current biblical canons are more Western than Eastern. Canon scholars are also aware of the considerable difference in the Ethiopian biblical OT and NT canons. See Cowley, "Biblical Canon"; and McDonald, *Forgotten Scriptures*, 95–96.

Sir 49:10). There are a number of early precedents for recognizing sacred authoritative writings, as in the case of the Christians' acceptance of the OT/HB books.[16] Christians obtained their notion of sacred scripture from their Jewish siblings, although the Christians emphasized more of a Christological and eschatological focus in their use of the same sacred books. This focus has parallels in some segments of the Jewish community, as in the Bar Cochba rebellion that was largely a messianic movement among the Jews (132–135 CE). Like their Jewish siblings, Christians welcomed and read sacred religious texts in their worship and catechetical meetings (Justin, *1 Apol.* 67). Public reading of sacred texts in worship was a primary function of sacred writings in Judaism and this practice continued in the early Christian churches. But, only in the late fourth century did church councils begin to list those writings that were deemed worthy of being read in worship;[17] only then do we begin to encounter the second meaning of canon—namely, that of a selected and fixed collection of sacred books that informed Christian faith.

Note, however, that the two functions of canon—i.e., norm or authoritative function, and list or shape—are not mutually exclusive but sometimes overlap. Thomassen rightly observes that lists can function authoritatively.[18] Fixed lists or catalogs of sacred scripture may have emerged to a limited extent in the second century CE, as in the case of Irenaeus's fixed four-gospel canon, but their widespread emergence generally took place in the middle of the fourth century and later when canon formation was *largely* finished, especially in the West in most *but not all* orthodox churches. The books that were eventually accepted as sacred scripture in various religious communities had earlier functioned as scripture in some churches. Such acceptance occurs *before* books are placed in lists or catalogs of sacred, authoritative scripture. If canon refers only to the recognition of the sacredness of ancient Jewish or Christian religious texts and their authoritative use in Jewish and/or Christian communities, then, of course, canon formation is clearly much earlier than the final formation of the Jewish or Christian Bibles. If canon formation is limited to *only* a fixed collection of biblical books that comprise the Jewish and Christian sacred scripture, then of course canon formation occurs in the fourth century and later. Scholars debating this matter regularly talk past one another, not infrequently criticizing those whose conclusions differ from their own without adequate understanding of the

---

16. See numerous examples listed in Lim, *Formation of the Jewish Canon*.
17. Thomassen, "Some Notes," 19–22.
18. Ibid., 9–10.

other positions.[19] Seldom are all scholars on the same page in the important points of reference.

John Barton has ably shown that definition is one of the critically important places where scholars seldom communicate adequately and, I might add, where they often ignore the realities that other scholars seek to establish in the complex discussion that we call canon formation.[20] This communication problem is not insurmountable if all who tell the story of the formation of the Bible are consistent in their definition of canon and make clear to their readers what they have in mind. All of us, nonetheless, have difficulties articulating consistently the implications of what the surviving artifacts of history have to tell us about the story of canon formation. Again, what hinders the telling of this story most is that the *ancients* never adequately articulated their understanding of canon formation!

Long ago Theodore Zahn argued that the New Testament canon emerged in the first century CE, but he based his argument on the circulation of Christian texts that had influenced the early followers of Jesus. He saw this influence especially in regard to the Gospels and to some extent in some of the letters of Paul; consequently, he concluded that the biblical canon began for the Christians at that time. It is true that some of the stories about Jesus' teaching and deeds were circulating among his followers even before his death and subsequently in the early churches before they were put in writing.[21] They were welcomed as authoritative traditions from their early oral stages of development, but this does not mean, as Zahn claimed, that there was an emergence of something like a biblical canon by the end of the first century, even though the *process* of canonization had already begun with the circulation and use of early Christian documents, as we see in the apparent familiarity of the author of Revelation with the Gospels (Rev 2:7, 17, 29; 3:6, 13, 22, drawing upon Mark 4:9; Luke 14:35; Matt 13:16–17).

Adolf von Harnack argued subsequently that Marcion had invented the notion of a biblical canon by rejecting Jewish scripture altogether and limiting his sacred writings to a truncated Gospel of Luke and selected writings of Paul. Subsequently, he claimed, the churches responded to Marcion's challenge by including both the OT/HB and even more Christian writings than Marcion had included in his canon. Von Campenhausen

---

19. See e.g., Seitz, *Goodly Fellowship*. See also McDonald, Review of Seitz, *Goodly Fellowship*.

20. Barton (*Holy Writings, Sacred Text*, 1–34) clarifies the three competing notions of canon current today.

21. This is made especially clear in Dunn, *Jesus Remembered*, 173–336, in which he stresses the importance of the oral tradition about Jesus, whose actions and teachings before his death were remembered by his disciples after his death.

later extended Harnack's conclusion and claimed that the early churches largely determined their New Testament canon in response to the so-called second-century heresies, especially those of the Marcionites, Gnostics, and Montanists. Following Eusebius, he argued that the Montanists produced a plethora of so-called inspired writings and the orthodox churches responded by eliminating those writings and by identifying the writings that had wider circulation in churches. That collection was believed to be sacred scripture and the only books that could be read in the churches. The problem with this popular notion is that there is no second-century evidence for it and the challenges of the so-called second-century heretical movements were not addressed by establishing a canon of scripture, but by adopting and promoting a proto-Nicene orthodox canon of faith (*regula fidei*). The notion of *Christian* Scripture is clearly present by the end of the second century, especially in the writings of Irenaeus, and Christian scriptures were regularly used by the early church fathers to identify their canon of faith.

I underscore here again that the problem of definition need not be as daunting as it has become if scholars who use the term *kanon* also clarify what they mean by it. Some scholars are beginning to distinguish between the two realities in antiquity: the authoritative use of a text and subsequently its placement or lack of placement into a fixed collection of sacred texts.

POSSIBLE ORIGINS OF THE NOTION OF A BIBLICAL CANON

Are there antecedents to the Jewish and Christian biblical canons? While there are no exact parallels, there appear to be some similarities between Jewish and Christian biblical canons and literary canons in the Greco-Roman world. The latter were not fixed, nor, of course, did they form a supreme basis for determining the identity of God, how one related to God, or how believers ought to live. Further, it does not seem that there was a problem in criticizing them. However, there are some parallels with Jewish and Christian canon formation that may suggest dependence.

The famed poet and Alexandrian librarian, Callimachus (b. in Cyrene ca. 305 and d. 240 BCE), produced a classification system of the volumes in the Alexandrian library. Callimachus's classifications were followed by two other well-known Alexandrian librarians named Zenodotos of Ephesus (ca. early third century BCE) and later Aristarchus of Samothrace (ca. 217–145 BCE). There were some 120 volumes of classifications or catalogs that Callimachus called *pinakes* (sing. *pinax*) or "lists" that grouped the various lyric and epic poets as well as their fields of writing. Among the volumes collected at Alexandria were works—such as Homer's *Iliad* and *Odyssey*, the Three Attic Writers, the Nine Lyric Poets, and the *Lives of Ten Orators*[22]—that demonstrated to poets who came after them the standards or models that they had to follow in order to have their works considered for inclusion in subsequent model collections that would also be recognized by others. The lists or catalogs were not closed or fixed, but contemporary works generally were not considered for inclusion until after the author had died. In this sense, the Alexandrian literary canons were open, but nevertheless formed authoritative models or guides for others to follow.

The similarities between Jewish and Christian collections of sacred writings and literary collections of classical writings have long been known, but are often ignored in canon formation discussions. This is due in part to the nomenclature—namely, Callimachus used the term *"pinakes"* instead of *"kanon,"* but those terms are not mutually exclusive. The Alexandrian lists have *some* similarities with early Jewish and Christian biblical canons, namely *some* of the *pinakes* literature was limited to a select collection of model literature. What appears similar to the Canon 1 definition mentioned earlier is that there were few *fixed* lists in the literary canons. Callimachus, for instance, could not add himself to the list of poets (he was still living), but several of his works were widely quoted and highly prized in antiquity. Also, special numbers—namely 3, 5, 7, and 10—were assigned to the most esteemed writings; it is not altogether clear what those numbers originally meant, but their presence suggests an authoritative status in the classical period and later.[23] Other canon parallels in antiquity can be seen in Aristotle's guidelines for rhetoric. He gave, as it were, canons or models to follow in producing writings.[24] Homer, of course, was the standard of all standards in Greek literary models and in the education of Greek citizens.[25] Many

22. For a useful discussion of Greek literary canons, see Hägg, "Canon Formation"; and also Vardi, "Canons of Literary Texts," 135–42, who observes that canon lists were not confined in Alexandria to Quintilian and Dionysius but were more widespread.

23. I have discussed these parallels at greater length in McDonald, "Hellenism and the Biblical Canons."

24. See his *Categories* and *Interpretation* that speak of ten categories (*kategoria*) for interpreting given subjects, or his guidelines on what comprises appropriate rhetoric in his *Rhetorica* that are still valuable reminders of appropriate communication. For instance, his example of what goes into an Epilogue is instructive: "The epilogue is composed of four parts: to dispose the hearer favorably to oneself and unfavorably toward the adversary; to amplify and depreciate; to excite the emotions of the hearer; to recapitulate" (*Rhet.* 3.19.1).

25. See Marrou, *History of Education*, 3–13; Morgan, *Literate Education*, 67–73, 97–115, 165–66; Hägg, "Canon Formation," 111–13. Josephus (*Ag. Ap.* 1.10–13) and the subsequent rabbis were quite familiar with Homer and there are several parallels to Homer even in the New Testament, despite Jewish and Christian rejection of much

Greeks believed that Homer was not only wise, but he was also all-knowing. Homer's priority among the Greeks can be seen also in the actions of Alexander the Great, who started a cult of Homer in Alexandria.

Because the Homeric writings were lost or destroyed early on and subsequently passed on orally by others who reportedly took considerable liberties in changing them, a legendary tradition circulated among the Greeks in three known traditions that Homer's writings were restored at the instigation of Peisistratus (565–525 BCE), the so-called "tyrant of Athens."[26] He reportedly asked some "72 grammarians" to produce a "perfect" edition of Homer's *Iliad* and the *Odyssey*. The legend of the 72 grammarians is the same as the number of translators of the Pentateuch in the *Letter of Aristeas*.[27] Is the Peisistratus tradition what lies behind the *Letter of Aristeas*, or could the story of the 72 grammarians at work on restoring Homer depend on the legend of Aristeas? The number of these grammarians is admittedly late in origin and is told in a context of apologetic, so the story is likely legendary. But the well-known editorial work of the Alexandrian librarians on the works of Homer is not considered legend or myth.

Unlike other ancient Greek writings, each book or chapter in Homer's *Iliad* and *Odyssey* was identified in sequence by one of the 24 letters of the Greek alphabet. The significance of this may be reflected in Revelation 1:8 and 22:13 in which God and the risen Christ are identified as the "alpha and the omega"—the first and last letters of the Greek alphabet. Could the

---

of the mythology and legends conveyed in his writings (Sandnes, *Challenge of Homer*, 44–49). See also MacDonald's *Homeric Epics*, and his earlier *Does the New Testament Imitate Homer?*; and *Christianizing Homer*.

26. The Peisistratus recension is described in three *scholia* to Dionysius Thrax (ca. 170–90 BCE), likely coming from his student, Asclepiades of Myrlea (1st cent. BCE). These are: Scholiorum collectio Vaticana, Scholiorum collectio Marciana, and Scholiorum collectio Londinensis. The second of these has language that reflects the number (72) and isolation of experts or grammarians (*grammatikoi*) as they performed their task. Further, the experts "all decided, in common and unanimously, that the compilation and correction of Aristarchus and Zenodotus had prevailed." The *scholia* are, of course, historically unreliable, but they reflect views from the late second century to the first century BCE. They wrongly make Peisistratus (ca. 565–526 BCE) contemporary with Aristarchus (2nd century BCE) and try to show the superiority of the Aristarchus translation. This data is reported in Wyrick, *Ascension of Authorship*, 205–20.

27. See Veltri, *Libraries*, 79–89, for an interesting discussion of these parallels, including the later addition to the story of the editing of 72 grammarians. See Isodore of Seville's reference to Peisistratos and the creation of the libraries in Athens and Alexandria (especially *Orig.* 6.3.3–4; see Veltri, *Libraries and Canon*, 82–83). Bishop Isodore, like Epiphanius of Salamis, was known for his preservation of otherwise unknown or lost sources. Here Isodore refers to the Aristeas tradition about the origin of 70 translators of the Hebrew scriptures into Greek and how they were placed in the library at Alexandria.

notion of 24 elders in Revelation also have some parallels here? It is interesting that Josephus in the last decades of the first century, like many early church fathers, identified the number of the Jewish scriptures as 22 (*Ag. Ap.* 1.37–43), which is also the number of letters in the Hebrew alphabet, but the author of *4 Ezra* (ca. 90–95 CE) spoke of 24 books along with 70 others in which is "the spring of understanding, the fountain of wisdom, and the river of knowledge" (14:45–47; trans. Metzger). The church fathers generally refer to the 22 sacred books of the Jews, but during the rabbinic period the number 24 prevailed. These are most likely the same books as the 22, but grouped differently, as we see in *b. Baba Bathra* 14b, the first text to list the specific books of Hebrew scripture. This number, the same as the letters of the Greek alphabet, stuck and continues now in the Hebrew Bible. Is this coincidence or further evidence of the influence of Homer among Jews and Christians in the first and second centuries?[28] The change from 22 to 24 raises questions about why this unusual change from one alphabet number to another took place without changing the books included.

The interpreters of the Jewish[29] and Christian Scriptures[30] who listed their sacred scripture in limited collections may have found their model in the Alexandrian library. In an unpublished paper delivered to the SBL/SE Regional Annual Meeting, March 1984, John Van Seters noted that:

> The scholarly tradition of the Alexandrian library was likewise concerned with the listing and classification of its works. In this regard it established tables, i.e., lists (pinakes) of writers and classical works from the past, and excluded spurious works whose creation was very common in the Hellenistic period. These tables are the ancestors of the canons of writers that one

---

28. It is well known that several of the Psalms (e.g., Psalm 119) are acrostics, arranged using the 22 letters of the Hebrew alphabet, but did this practice originate with Homer? A late edition of *Jubilees* offers a 22 book collection of Jewish scriptures (see Epiphanius's citation of *Jub.* 2:23–24 in *De mens. et pond.* 22–23), but there is nothing mentioned of 22 books in the earliest edition of *Jubilees* discovered at Qumran.

29. As in the case of Philo's interpretation of Sarah and Hagar in his *On the Preliminary Studies* (*Congr.* 74–78 and *Legat.* 3.244–45) where Abraham's intercourse with Hagar is interpreted as preliminary education, and his sojourn with Sarah is virtue. Sarah encourages Abraham to participate in preliminary studies when virtue is not contradicted! See Sandnes, *Challenge of Homer*, 68–71; and the useful discussion of rabbinic use of allegory in Stern, "On Canonization," 237–40.

30. See Sandnes's discussion (*Challenge of Homer*, 84–87) of Justin who shows that he was quite familiar with the best of the Greek philosophers and showed their *occasional* compatibility with the Christian proclamation in *1 Apol.* 10.1–8; 20.5, but he clearly rejected Homer and the poets (*1 Apol.* 54.1–2). Clement of Alexandria did the same and was known for his familiarity with classical literature. See the discussion of Clement in McDonald, *Biblical Canon*, 301–3.

encounters in the Roman and Byzantine periods. I think it is obvious that the concern to establish a canon of scripture in Judaism and Christianity draws directly upon this scholarly tradition.³¹

Van Seter's view is seconded by James VanderKam who adds: "Perhaps further study of πίνακες will cast much needed light on the obscure process through which the canon of the Hebrew Scriptures were formed."³² Jews and Christians seem to have been influenced also by the text-critical techniques of the Alexandrian scribes. Origen, for example, used an apparatus of critical signs for reconstructing original texts that was created by Zenodotos and Aristarchus for their editions of Homer.³³ Note also that the Greek translation of the Jewish Scripture, the Septuagint, is believed to be a product of Alexandria, and the first church father to use the term *kanon* in reference to a list or catalog of sacred Christian Scripture was Athanasius *from Alexandria*, the primary place where such lists (or *pinakes*) circulated in antiquity, though not the first or only place.

The parallels between the Greco-Roman literary canons and biblical canons are not insignificant. Literary canons were well-known in the ancient world and it should not be surprising that the term was eventually employed by the Christians to identify their sacred collections of scripture. While it is true that lists alone are not equivalent to a canon, some lists of selected works are, and that is also what we find in the scripture lists created in the patristic period. At that point, the Christian lists or catalogs are canon, that is, authoritative Christian scripture. Similarly, biblical canons, like the Greek *pinakes*, function as models for their readers. They reflect a particular perspective about God and, in the case of the New Testament books, God's divine activity in Jesus. The books that did not follow this (proto-orthodox?) pattern or perspective were not included in the final collections of sacred books. What was said about Jesus had to fit with traditions already well-established and passed on in the churches (Irenaeus's *regula fidei*). As noted above, significant differences between biblical and Greco-Roman literary canons remain, but the similarities are not negligible.

---

31. This quotation from Van Seters is cited with approval in VanderKam, *From Revelation to Canon*, 30.

32. VanderKam, *From Revelation to Canon*, 30.

33. Hull, *Story of the New Testament Text*, 31–35, describes Origen's considerable familiarity and method of dealing with New Testament textual variants. On Origen and the formation of the biblical canon, see also Armstrong, *Role of the Rule of Faith*, esp. ch. 2; and Gallagher, *Hebrew Scripture*, 30–49.

BOOKS IN THE ANCIENT SCRIPTURE MANUSCRIPTS

What books and texts are actually in the ancient manuscripts and which ones are not? Most canon studies have only focused on the New Testament books in those manuscripts and largely ignore both the other books also contained in them and the New Testament books that are *not* in them. An example of this is 𝔓72 (3rd cent.), which contains not only Jude and 1–2 Peter (in that sequence) but several other books as well. The full list of contents, in order, is: *Protevangelium of James*, the Corinthian Correspondence, *Ode* 11 from the *Odes of Solomon*, Jude, Melito's *Homily on the Passover*, a hymn fragment, *Apology of Phileas*, Psalms 33 and 34, and 1 and 2 Peter. There is nothing in this codex that distinguishes the biblical books from the non-biblical books, but it does show that the selection of books here was unlike the contents of later New Testament collections.[34]

Similarly, if the scope of the New Testament had been settled for all Christians by the fourth or fifth centuries, why does the late fourth-century Codex Sinaiticus include the *Epistle of Barnabas* and the *Shepherd of Hermas*? Also, the miniscule Gregory 1505 (ca. 12th cent.) discovered at the Laura monastery on Mt. Athos, ends its New Testament collection with Hebrews followed by non-biblical psalms and odes; there is no Revelation. Those who produced this manuscript were clearly not in *full* agreement with other Christians on the scope of their New Testament scripture. Even after the fourth century, some of the so-called apocryphal and pseudepigraphal writings continued to be used and cited in various churches. For almost a thousand years Latin and Armenian churches continued to include *3 Corinthians* in their collections of scripture. Of the 127 (or 128, and growing in number) papyrus manuscripts, only 14 are sufficiently well-preserved to indicate they contained more than one book; this raises a further question regarding which books actually informed the faith of the earliest Christians. Further, how important is it that, of the 310 uncial manuscripts that currently exist, only a handful of them include *most* of the New Testament books?[35] This is especially important in the fourth century when the technology of the codex advanced to the point where it was possible to include some 1600 pages of parchment—i.e., the whole Christian Bible. The contents of these ancient manuscripts enable scholars to discern the status and views of the Christian biblical canons at various stages of church history.

---

34. Several of these manuscripts are identified in van Haelst, *Catalogue des papyrus*, and also Comfort and Barrett, *Text of the Earliest New Testament Greek Manuscripts*.

35. The first manuscripts to contain all of the New Testament books, and only those, date to around 1000 CE! See Schmidt, "Greek New Testament as a Codex."

Along with the continuous text biblical manuscripts, the ancient lectionaries also allow us to see what texts actually informed the faith of the early Christian communities. Little research into the full contents of these lectionaries has been done thus far, as a quick look at the textual apparatus in the major editions of the Greek New Testament demonstrates. Scholars seldom consult the lectionaries when seeking to establish the earliest text of the New Testament books, but these texts often tell another very important story—namely, which scriptures informed the faith of the early Christians and were more familiar to them. The surviving ancient translations also let us know what books Christians were reading in the non-Greek speaking churches.[36] Most of the ancient translations of the biblical books do not contain *all* of the biblical books and often not *only* the biblical books. Furthermore, from the manuscript evidence, it appears that few churches possessed all of the biblical books and only those books. One is tempted to ask what the faith of the earliest Christian churches might have looked like if they had all of the books that are in the current Christian Bibles!

TEXTUAL FLUIDITY AND CANONICITY

Fixed biblical canons began to appear in the fourth century, though some of them may have been produced in the last half of the third century. Those canons did not focus on the text of the sacred books, but only on identifying books that could be read in churches and which could not. Some of the early church fathers recognized the disparity between the various manuscripts that were circulating in the churches, especially Irenaeus and Origen. Later, Augustine acknowledged that inferior scribes and translators often made clumsy errors and even intentional changes in the text of the books that they copied or translated.[37] However, very little was done to stabilize the text of the church's Scripture before modern times and, given the expense of producing manuscripts, the church was largely but not completely dependent on untrained literate "amateurs" to produce them.[38] There are some exceptions to this, as in the case of the copyist of $\mathfrak{P}$75, but there were not many expert scribes in churches before the fourth and fifth centuries. Text critics today are well aware of the more than 200,000 (conservatively speaking) to 400,000 (maximal number) variants in the existing New Testament

---

36. For a catalogue of these, see Metzger, *Bible in Translation*.

37. See a discussion of this in Hull, *Story of the New Testament Text*, 23–34, and observe that Augustine, *Doctr. chr.* 2.32–72, speaks at length about why variants emerge in translations and copies of the Church's scriptures.

38. Metzger and Ehrman, *Text of the New Testament*, 275.

manuscripts. Of the surviving Old Testament manuscripts (some 9000) and New Testament manuscripts (some 5740), no two are exactly alike![39] I might note that even in textual criticism, the ever-growing number of editions of the Greek text witnesses the difficulty of establishing a final fixed text of the biblical books today. The church has never fully agreed on the text of the New Testament books, though the task of establishing the earliest and most reliable text is still an ongoing process. We are doubtless closer to the original text now than ever before due to the dedicated efforts of a small community of text-critical scholars (probably no more than 40–50 in the world!), but no one claims that we have arrived at the originals yet! So which text of the New Testament books are canon for churches today and provide an authoritative text for preaching and teaching in churches? That is an open question!

Scholars today are well aware of the textual fluidity of all ancient literary productions. Because of fluidity, Socrates was especially skeptical of written documents since, according to him, once they left the hand of the author, they were no longer under the author's control (Plato, *Phaedrus* 275). He opined that no written text could simulate an author's oral text. This is not unlike Paul's comment in 2 Cor 3:3–6 when he appeals not to the written law on tablets of stone, but the law written upon the heart. Unlike an oral text, a written text cannot provide its own explanation.[40] Written texts were often changed in various recensions after they left the hand of the author, as we see in the case of Homer. Authors of ancient plays and songs felt quite free to introduce changes into Homer's works. As noted above, Josephus drew considerable attention to the fluidity of the written text of Homer, as contrasted with the much more stable and carefully transmitted Jewish Scripture (*Ag. Ap.* 1.37–43). Speaking of the inconsistencies in Homeric writings, Josephus observes that Homer himself, according to the Greeks, did not leave his poems in writing, but that at first they were "transmitted by memory" and "the scattered songs were not united until later; to which circumstance the numerous inconsistencies of the work are attributable" (*Ag. Ap.* 1:12, LCL).

Making changes in the text of sacred scripture took place regularly both among the Jews and subsequently among the Christians. We now know how scriptures were often modified and reinterpreted over time by various scribes. Examples of this are already in Hebrew scripture as we see

---

39. See Aichele, "Canon, 49–50. After mentioning the large number of variants in the New Testament manuscripts in a paper I presented at Acadia University, Emanuel Tov commented to me that there were some 900,000 such textual variants in the surviving manuscripts of the Hebrew Bible.

40. See Aichele, "Canon," 49.

in Chronicles and likely also in Deuteronomy. Scholars are aware also of several books found among the Dead Sea Scrolls that can be identified as "Rewritten Bible" or "Rewritten Scriptures," a term that generally refers especially to *Jubilees*, the *Temple Scroll*, the *Genesis Apocryphon*, and 4QRP (Rewritten Pentateuch).[41] In the New Testament, Matthew and Luke took considerable liberties in rewriting and even correcting Mark as they also attempted to tell their story of Jesus (see Luke 1:1–3). The act of rewriting sacred texts often points to the priority of antecedent texts, especially if their reception and authority were recognized within the community for whom the newer rewritten texts were prepared. That appears to be the case in the examples from Qumran, but likely also in the case of the Synoptic Gospels. By the middle of the second century the Gospels, especially Matthew, were widely viewed as reliable witnesses to the Christ event and were welcomed as authoritative religious texts possibly shortly after the time they were produced, perhaps as catechetical instruction material in churches and to aid the church's mission. They were circulated in churches early on and gained priority among the various gospels circulating in the second-century churches.[42] Subsequently, many changes were made to those texts and, although the changes were fewer in number by the seventh or eighth centuries with the use of more professional scribes, nevertheless changes continued to be made until the invention of moveable type and the printing press. Indeed, all ancient writings, whether sacred or not, were somewhat fluid and not infrequently modified to address contemporary needs of congregations (e.g., 1 John 5:7–8).

So, what can we say about which *canonical text* of the scriptures we should use for reading in the synagogues and churches today? I am aware of the significant shift by several influential text critics away from the search for the *original* text, as if that could be established with any certainty. They have chosen instead to pursue more the study of the surviving ancient texts with the goal of arriving at a greater understanding of the narrative social context of the early manuscripts and the churches that produced them, especially by looking more carefully at the intentional changes in the biblical texts.[43] That, of course, is an excellent focus that needs to be examined more carefully than earlier scholars have been able to do. Nevertheless, we still need to answer the question of which text to read in churches or synagogues today.

---

41. See the recent discussion of this topic in Molly Zahn, "Rewritten Scripture"; and Lange, "Textual Plurality of Jewish Scriptures," esp. 66–88 where he cites two primary examples of rewritten text, namely Jer 29 and Deut 5.

42. See Bauckham, *Jesus and the Eyewitnesses*, 1–66.

43. See the important arguments for this position presented by Epp, "It's All about Variants," esp. 282–98.

For example, what text of 1 Sam 10:27 should be read in Jewish and Christian centers of worship and instruction? The Masoretic Text is currently reflected in the text of the famed Leningrad Codex that also depends on the slightly earlier Aleppo text (ca. 975 CE). But should scholars follow the Proto-Masoretic Text of the earlier Dead Sea Scrolls manuscripts with some of the variants, or should they seek to establish the reconstructed antecedent text used by the translators of the Septuagint? Recently, biblical translators added four more unnumbered sentences after 1 Sam 10:27 (NRSV) or at the beginning of 11:1 (NIV). Should readers accept the shorter MT text or the newly-constructed longer one which makes better sense because it identifies Nahash? Similarly, should readers follow the Masoretic Text of Jeremiah or recognize the shorter and probably more-original version of the text reflected in the LXX that likely depends on an earlier antecedent of the Hebrew text than the longer Proto-Masoretic Text? Should Christians read Mark 16:9–20 in their worship services when it is absent from all of the earliest manuscripts of Mark? Which form of Mark 1:1 should clergy read to their parishioners—the shorter text in Codex Vaticanus or the longer one in Codex Sinaiticus that adds "the Son of God" (*huiou theou*)?

Today, as George Aichele has observed, the digitized transmission of the Bible on the internet and various other computerized venues has reintroduced fluidity into the transmission of the biblical text. Authors and preachers often change the biblical text to "in other words" kinds of readings and interpretations and often these "other words" are read in the churches that honor their sacred texts.[44] I suspect that most members of such congregations do not know when texts have been changed to something that supposedly clarifies its original meaning.

THE MURATORIAN FRAGMENT

One of the more controversial issues in New Testament canon studies for more than a generation is what I have occasionally dubbed the "Achilles' heel" of canon studies—namely, establishing the date and provenance of the Muratorian Fragment (MF), a canon list apparently translated from Greek into poorly-constructed Latin. Ludovico Antonio Muratori discovered the Fragment at the Ambrosian Library in Milan and it was subsequently published in 1740. Over the last century scholars have assigned its composition to several authors at various times, though the most popular theory until recently was to assign it to the end of the second century CE and assume that it was produced in Rome. Albert Sundberg, Geoffrey Hahneman, and

---

44. Aichele, "Canon," 63–65.

I have argued at length, however, that there are too many anomalies and oddities in the text to assign it a late second-century date. I have posited that if it is a late second-century document, it has no parallels in primary literature on the canon for at least another 150 years. If it was a second-century document, it had no *discernible* influence on the development of the New Testament canon until the mid-to-late fourth century where several similar (not exact) parallels do exist. And, if it reflected widespread views even in the fourth century, Eusebius and other church fathers clearly were not aware of them.[45]

More recently, Jonathan J. Armstrong has advanced an alternative position that may solve much of the controversy and, if correct, could well change much of the debate over of the origins of the MF. He contends that Victorinus, bishop of Pettau (or Petovium, in Pannonia Superior in modern Slovenia) produced this catalog in poor Latin in the middle of the third century (ca. 258 CE).[46] Armstrong presents several parallels between Victorinus's known writings and the MF and points to his well-known weakness in Latin translation (Jerome noted that Victorinus was known for writing good Greek, but very poor Latin—see *Vir. ill.* 74.1 and *Epist.* 58.10). Armstrong's treatment is certainly the best case presented since Hahneman's earlier work and his reasoning has plausibility, but his parallels require more study. If Victorinus produced the MF, then it is more likely that he produced it shortly before his martyrdom in 307 CE. If Armstrong is correct, I favor a new date for the MF sometime between 290 and 307 CE during the peak time of his literary productivity. This date also has closer historical and contextual parallels with other canon lists in the fourth century and following.

The anomalies in the MF are more strange if the text is given a second-century date, such as placing the Wisdom of Solomon in a New Testament list, a practice that has no parallel in catalogs until the fourth century. Likewise, the MF accepts that John wrote more than one epistle, though not

---

45. See Hahneman, *Muratorian Fragment and the Development of the Canon*, and his "Muratorian Fragment and the Origins of the New Testament Canon"; see also McDonald, *Biblical Canon*, 369–78.

46. Armstrong, "Victorinus of Pettau." I think it is more likely that if Victorinus constructed the list, it took place shortly before his martyrdom in the early fourth century during the Diocletian persecutions. His list is closer to that of Eusebius in the first third of the fourth century than to the later, more-developed lists that include books the MF does not have. Armstrong's position is intriguing and he makes a good case for a plausible re-dating of this mysterious document. The forthcoming publication of Armstrong's doctoral dissertation (*Role of the Rule of Faith*) promises to have more substantial arguments to suggest that Origen may well be the father of the notion of a Christian biblical canon and his ideas were passed on in Victorinus's *Commentary on Matthew*. I should note here that Origen also led a school in Alexandria where many literary canons were well-known in his day.

three. This is unlike anything else known from the second century and it is also unlike Eusebius in the early fourth century who questions the authenticity of both 2 and 3 John (see *Hist. eccl.* 3.25.2–3).

SCRIPTURAL CITATION FORMULAE

Much has been made of the use of familiar scriptural formulae in the New Testament for determining whether a book is cited as scripture or simply as illustrative material. If, for example, a text was introduced with the familiar formulae ("it is written," "as the Scripture says," and such like), most scholars agree that the cited text was recognized as sacred scripture; however, if those formulae are not used, could the texts still have been considered scripture, as some scholars claim? For example, Jude 14 appears to cite *1 Enoch* 1:9 in a scriptural manner and if the author had instead cited any biblical text, no question would have been made about Jude citing the text as scripture.[47] Seldom do scholars deny that Jesus cited Dan 7:13 as scripture in Mark 14:62, but few notice that he used no scriptural formulae to do so! Likewise, the author of Hebrews cites or quotes proportionately more Old Testament texts than any other writer of the New Testament, but only once does so using the formula "it is written" (Heb 10:7), even then the formula is already contained in the LXX citation that the author uses. The author of Hebrews also cites Wis 7:25–26 in Heb 1:3 in the same way he cites other scriptures, though without the scriptural formulae.

It is true that the use of scriptural formulae clearly identifies texts that were viewed as scripture, but such formulae are also later used sometimes in reference to both apocryphal and pseudepigraphal literature in the early church fathers.[48] The explanations for early church fathers citing "non-biblical books" have ranged from how they somehow lost the biblical canon that Jesus gave to the apostles to other, even stranger explanations. The formulae are useful, but their use does not account for all of the New Testament's scriptural citations from both biblical and non-biblical sources. Since a considerable number of early church fathers' scriptural citations are also of Jewish and Christian noncanonical writings, often using the scriptural

---

47. Beckwith (*Old Testament Canon*, 402) denies that Jude cites *1 Enoch* as scripture but only as illustrative material. However, his view appears theologically motivated and lacks awareness of how Jewish scriptures were cited in the New Testament and early Christianity.

48. See Penner, "Citation Formulae." Penner's careful exposition of the formulae and how they were used establishes a *minimum* of texts cited as scripture, but not a *maximum* or complete reflection of what was considered sacred scripture in the early churches.

formulae to cite them, the presence or absence of formulae alone cannot be determinative.

THEOLOGICAL FORMULATION AND CANON FORMATION

The recognition and function of some Christian writings *as scripture* is present in a few early church fathers from the mid-to-late second century, though, as noted earlier, their recognition and use as scripture in the church's preaching and teaching mission most likely began in several cases soon after the writings were produced and read in churches in the first century. In the second century, there is only one known example of an interest in a fixed collection of Christian scriptures: Irenaeus's four-gospel canon. Several church fathers, for instance, spoke against certain teachings that did not measure up to the acceptable standards of truth in their day, and though they often cited writings in their arguments that later formed the New Testament, they did not respond to those teachings by producing a biblical canon; rather, they appealed to a canon of faith (*regula fidei*) that they claimed was circulating in churches from early times and was handed on to the churches through the bishops. Irenaeus, especially, argued against gnostic writings and was the first known church father to attack the *Gospel of Judas* (*Haer.* 1.31.1; see also Epiphanius, *Pan.* 39), but he did not promote the adoption of a biblical canon to make his case.

The absence of a universally-acknowledged New Testament canon at the end of the second or early third century CE can be seen in Eusebius's story of bishop Serapion, who initially allowed his churches to read the *Gospel of Peter* in worship services. This took place some 20 to 30 years *after* Irenaeus had argued for the authority of only the four canonical Gospels. Later, Serapion reversed his position, not because the *Gospel of Peter* was not included in a fixed collection of gospels, but because he believed that it was contrary to the *rule of faith* or theological foundation of the churches (Eusebius, *Hist. eccl.* 6.12.3–6). This development illustrates that there was no universal agreement about Irenaeus's earlier arguments for the acceptance of the four Gospels and those gospels alone. Irenaeus's position certainly was widespread by the fourth century—see, for example, Eusebius's "holy tetrad" of the four canonical gospels (*Hist. eccl.* 3.25.1; based likely on the views of both Irenaeus and Origen, see *Hist. eccl.* 6.25.3–6) and the Muratorian Fragment's mention of Luke and John as the *third* and *fourth* gospels (the names of the first two are lost due to manuscript damage, but likely Matthew and Mark were listed).

The ancient Christians adopted the writings that they believed best reflected who Jesus was and they taught this tradition as it had been handed down to them through their church leaders. In time, the selection process was essentially one of recognizing the loyalty of various Christian texts to the canon of faith that had been passed on in the churches. Irenaeus is the first to make this argument (*Haer.* 1.10.1; 3.4.2), and it is critically important in the process of canon formation. In the second century, there were no *fixed* lists identifying which books were true and faithful to the "apostolic deposit" or tradition that had been handed down to them, though it was clear even then that some books measured up (the canonical Gospels and Paul) and some did not (those of the Gnostics and Montanists). Early Christians believed that they lived in the age of the Spirit and the Spirit had been poured out on the whole church (Acts 2:17–21); so, there is no evidence that Christians of the first or second centuries believed that inspired writings had ceased in their time.[49] The Montanists, supported by Tertullian, demonstrate the contrary and they evidently produced many texts that they believed were inspired by God (see Hippolytus, *Haer.* 8.12; Eusebius, *Hist. eccl.* 5.16.3–4). There is no biblical or theological argument in early Christianity that limited the number of sacred books to any fixed collection.

By the fourth century, however, a historical argument emerged, namely that only the books that were closest to the church's primary authority, Jesus and the apostles, should be read in the churches. The author of the Muratorian Fragment, for instance, rejects the *Shepherd of Hermas* because it was written not in the times of the apostles, but in the post-apostolic era. It was widely agreed upon in antiquity that those closest to Jesus, that is, the apostolic community, left behind an authoritative tradition about Jesus that gave the church its identity and core beliefs. This authoritative tradition reflected a "proto-orthodoxy" that was certainly present in the second century in the writings of the Apostolic Fathers and in Justin, Irenaeus, and others, but became the dominant church theology in the third and fourth centuries. The widespread reception of this tradition in churches, along with the scriptures that reflected them, and their continuing adaptability in each new generation of Christians apparently all weighed heavily in the canon selection process. Notions of inspiration were present, but they reflected more what the churches believed was true about Jesus than criteria for accepting sacred texts as scripture.

I stress here the importance of the development of the church's theology as a significant criterion for their acceptance and rejection of various books by the early churches. This is seldom considered in the canonical

---

49. See Kalin, "Argument from Inspiration"; and Kalin, "Inspired Community."

processes, but how could the majority of churches have established a widespread biblical canon before they had widespread agreement on their beliefs about Jesus and the major tenets of their faith? How could there be any agreement on the scope of the New Testament canon before the Council of Nicea (ca. 325 CE) clarified the identity of Jesus?

One of the strengths of Robert Jenson's recent *Canon and Creed* volume is that he rightly sees a relationship between the church's episcopate, creed, and canon—*in that order*.[50] The death of the Apostles, the failure of Jesus to return by the end of the first century, the emergence of various heresies (*docetism* especially) in the churches, and the sporadic persecutions of Christians at the end of the first and early second centuries all brought significant challenges to the early Christians. They addressed them by the emergence of a stronger episcopate (especially seen in Ignatius's writings) with a greater emphasis on the teaching arm of the church, especially in the development of creeds that reflected the faith of early Christian churches. The subsequent selection of sacred writings for a Christian canon reflected the faith of early Christian communities. The later biblical canons could hardly have emerged without the development of a strong episcopate in early Christianity (in the late first and second century) and a clear understanding of the church's *regula fidei* or creed that reflected what was believed to be the earliest and most reliable beliefs circulating in the churches. However, the relationship between the episcopate, creeds, and canon formation needs far more exploration than Jenson has addressed thus far. He calls for all biblical interpretation to emerge from the episcopate and the ancient creeds; doing so, he believes, leads to a more careful interpretation of Scripture. However, Biblical scholars today generally recognize that appropriate biblical research and interpretation must be free from ecclesiastical constraints if it is to arrive at plausible interpretations of biblical texts. Biblical scholars in all church denominations would surely challenge the notion that the church's bishops are the only ones—or even the best ones—to interpret Scripture.

It is clear that all three developments—episcopate, creeds, and canon formation—played a part in helping the churches deal with the major challenges facing them at the end of the first century and thereafter. A study of the church's theological development clarifies my two notions of canon in antiquity, namely Canon 1 and Canon 2, even though there was little or no consciousness of such distinctions in antiquity. Some books functioned as Canon 1 for a while, but in time were no longer perceived to reflect the church's most cherished beliefs, so they did not find a place in the Canon 2

---

50. See Jenson, *Canon and Creed*, and my review of both the strengths and weaknesses of his approach to the formation of the biblical canon in McDonald, Review of Jenson, *Canon and Creed*.

collections. Others did, however; indeed, for several books there was never any serious doubt about their value, as in the cases of Matthew, John, and most of the letters attributed to Paul. For others, the church struggled for centuries over their acceptance or rejection. An awareness of the important contributions that the episcopate and the creeds played in the formative stages of canon formation cannot be overestimated.

FINAL REFLECTIONS

The above topics are at the heart of several recent scholarly debates over the formation of biblical canons in antiquity. There is little historical evidence that anyone in early Christianity was remotely interested in the notion of a *fixed* biblical canon before the fourth century CE. The interest initially was to make sure that "heretical" teaching in the churches was eliminated and this was responded to by a canon or "rule" of faith, not a canon or "fixed list" of scriptures. In time, lists of books considered acceptable for reading in the churches were drawn up and in time these lists eventually became fixed. There was no initial agreement among the churches on which books accurately reflected the sacred teachings handed down to them, first orally and then in writing.

There certainly appears to have been a gradation of acceptance of the Christian writings as sacred scripture. There is no doubt that the Gospels, especially Matthew, received widespread acceptance and were among the earliest Christian writings identified as Scripture. Writings attributed to Paul were also welcomed widely in churches and they were among the earliest writings cited as scripture in the early churches. Widespread acceptance of all the 27 books did not take place much before the mid-to-late fourth century by most churches, but still there was considerable variance on the so-called fringe areas of the New Testament canon (Hebrews, James, 2 Peter, 2 and 3 John, Jude, Revelation) and in some cases the Pastoral Epistles. But as has been pointed out, it is clear that the end of the process of canonization was more one of rejection of older and often familiar writings than the inclusion of new ones. This process of rejection, or "de-canonization" as some have called it, appears to be similar in both the rejection of Christian apocrypha and of Old Testament pseudepigrapha. The processes of both Old and New Testament canonization took centuries and without initial or even later complete agreement in the churches.

There are several other important areas that affect our understanding of the formation of the biblical canons. These include:

(1) The Social Context. The biblical canon emerged in a multi-layered social context that included not only literary canons circulating in the Greco-Roman world, but also a number of historical conditions and influences. Surely Constantine's role in seeking unity in churches and calling the first ecumenical council of the churches at Nicea to discuss the identity of Jesus was influential in framing the context for later canon discussions. As noted above, it would be difficult indeed to establish a biblical canon without considerable agreement on the theology of the churches. Scholars have long known the significant divisions that existed among early followers of Jesus over theology, behavior, and practice. After the apostles were gone and Jesus had not returned, much of the earlier apocalyptic focus in churches began to subside. At the same time, various pockets of persecution of Christians broke out as Christians lost their *religio licita* status as a Jewish sect. Christians responded to this persecution by creating new apocalyptic texts. Such circumstances led to a vacuum of authority in the early churches and a wide variety of differences in Christian beliefs and Christian sects began to emerge in the late first century and following.[51] When empire-wide persecutions of Christians took place in the mid-third century and early fourth centuries, with the consequent confiscation and burning of the Christians' sacred scriptures, many Christians had to determine what sacred texts they should hide from the Roman authorities and which ones they could turn over to them—presumably they handed over those that were not deemed as important or as useful in the churches as those they considered sacred scripture. Several divisions among Christians emerged in churches before, during and after these events and, after his conversion to the Christian faith, Constantine, like all previous Roman emperors, sought unity in the empire and also in the churches. Since the identity of Jesus was central among the divisions in churches, this was the heart of the discussions at Nicea. Only after such issues were dealt with could there be any significant agreement, even if not universal, on the scope of the churches' scriptures.

(2) Temporary Canonicity. Scholars have not sufficiently considered the implications of temporary canonicity—namely, what do we call those books (*1 Enoch, Shepherd of Hermas,* and others) that were initially welcomed in a Canon 1 fashion, functioned in an authoritative or scriptural manner in the churches for a time, and were even called "scripture," but later no longer functioned that way?

(3) Catalogs of Scriptures. Lists or catalogs of the books that comprised the church's scriptures continued well into the sixteenth century and the

---

51. For a helpful discussion of this variety of Christian expressions in second-century Christianity, see Robinson and Koester, *Trajectories*; and Bauer, *Orthodoxy and Heresy.*

later catalogs list not only the acceptable books that comprised the biblical canons, but also those books that were rejected or disputed. Listing rejected or doubted books *centuries* after the earlier councils had rejected them suggests their continued acceptance in some churches. Rejected books were listed as late as Pseudo-Athanasius (ca. 500–550 CE) and the *Synopsis of Nicephorus* (ca. 850 CE). We have to ask why churches would list books as apocryphal (rejected) or *antilegomena* (writing spoken against) if no-one was still using them.

(4) *The Council of Trent.* Finally, biblical scholars seldom reflect on the significance of the continuing doubts about the scope of the biblical canon as late as the time of the Reformation. Why would the Roman Catholic Church see the need for the Council of Trent in 1546, which met in part to identify the books of the Bible, if all churches had already agreed on the shape of the biblical canon? And how could Martin Luther have felt free to marginalize several books of the New Testament canon (Hebrews, James, Jude, and Revelation), which he placed at the end of his translation after making disparaging remarks about them, if the current New Testament canon had been universally-accepted in his generation? It may seem strange to us that Martin Luther, who was so given to *sola scriptura,* also questioned the authority of some Old and New Testament books.

The questions related to canon formation cannot be fully explored until the issues discussed above are addressed and the debates over *why* a biblical canon emerged, *when* it emerged, even *where* it emerged (in the East or West), and specifically *what* books comprised the biblical canons are all given more complete discussion.

Scholars can learn a great deal about the New Testament and the early church by studying the so-called noncanonical books that eventually lost favor in the majority of churches. The ancient biblical manuscripts reflect the growth and development of early Christianity as well as the growth and also rejection of books in the formation of a biblical canon. Biblical scholars of all persuasions have increasingly discovered important treasures in the ancient literature once accepted by many Christians, but then marginalized and subsequently dismissed. There is nothing that should prevent all Christians from being informed by the same religious texts that informed their ancient predecessors. We are hardly able to understand fully the biblical text or the history of the early developing churches unless we are familiar with all of the literature that initially informed their faith.

— 9 —

Apocryphal Gospels and Historical Jesus Research

A Reassessment

— Stephen J. Patterson —

THE SYMPOSIUM ORGANIZERS, Tony Burke and Brent Landau, have asked me to assess the impact of the apocryphal gospels on the historical study of Jesus in North America. If truth be told, this could be a very brief presentation: the apocryphal gospels have had virtually no impact on the historical study of Jesus in North America.[1] If we were to expand our topic to include the rest of the scholarly world, this talk might go on just long enough to state that neither have the apocryphal gospels made any impact on the historical study of Jesus in Europe, Asia, Africa, India, Australia, or South America. So far as I know, no one studies these things in Antarctica.

Perhaps exceptions come to mind.

One, perhaps, is the Jesus Seminar, whose efforts famously included an assessment of everything in all of the gospels written in the first three centuries. But of all the gospels considered in its study, only one, the *Gospel of Thomas*, contributed anything to the eventual database of things Jesus

---

1. For an overview of the situation, see Patterson, "Gospel of Thomas and Christian Beginnings"; reprinted in Patterson, *Gospel of Thomas and Christian Origins*, 261–77.

might have said or done. This was the "fifth gospel" in *The Five Gospels*, the initial report of the Jesus Seminar published in 1993.[2] Much has been made of the statistical fact that, in *The Five Gospels*, *Thomas*, of all the gospels, ended up with the highest percentage of red or pink sayings (approximately 38%). Indeed, this is perhaps important, but more telling is the fact that out of 44 sayings in *Thomas* considered either red or pink, only two do not have close parallels in the Synoptic Gospels: logion 97 (the Parable of the Woman with the Jar) and logion 98 (the Parable of the Assassin).[3] One should note, however, that initially both were voted "gray"; only on later consideration were they voted into the "pink" category. The vote on a third saying, logion 42, was a statistical tie, and so by rule was printed "gray."[4] Every one of the other 41 red or pink sayings in the *Gospel of Thomas* have close Synoptic parallels. So, what the Jesus Seminar data on *Thomas* really shows is a preference in that body for a certain kind of Synoptic saying that happens also to turn up in *Thomas* with considerable frequency. If I may characterize the type formally, it runs to the simple aphorism, proverb, or prophetic saying (that is, social criticism), and the unembellished parable. Anyone who has read the *Gospel of Thomas* will see immediately that this is not the voice of Jesus that is distinctive of the *Gospel of Thomas*. This tendency to see Jesus as a simple, if clever, intellect—long-standing in North American scholarship—perhaps explains in some measure why the apocryphal gospels have only rarely come into the discussion of the historical Jesus, and never in a way that seriously challenges the direction of the conversation.

Again, perhaps exceptions come to mind.

One is the remarkable work of John Dominic Crossan, whose 1991 book, *The Historical Jesus*, is the most creative new proposal to emerge in historical Jesus studies for many years.[5] Crossan's method, which included the principle that canonical boundaries are not relevant to the historian, prompted him to consider apocryphal gospels, but in practice only *Thomas* and the *Gospel of Peter* come in for serious consideration. Of these, again, it is *Thomas* that has the most impact on his work, but this is because of the importance he places on multiple independent attestation. This meant that, for Crossan, the distinctive voice of Jesus would be determined by the dozens of *Thomas*/Synoptic overlaps, among which are found so many of those simple aphorisms, prophetic sayings, and parables. Crossan's close tradition-historical work with these multiply-attested sayings was also im-

2. Funk and Hoover, eds., *Five Gospels*.
3. For logion 97, see ibid., 523–24; for logion 98, ibid., 524–25.
4. Ibid., 496.
5. Crossan, *Historical Jesus*.

portant, however. Crossan's work tended to show that the apocalypticism of the Synoptic side of these parallels was distinctive of the Synoptic sayings, and often manifestly secondary—as in the case of allegorically-dressed-out parables—so that one may rightly wash this trait out of the commonly-held, earliest layer of the tradition. By this same method, of course, the distinctive voice of *Thomas* was also washed out—what Crossan would later call the "ascetical eschatology"[6] of this tradition. The result was the hypothesis that Jesus advocated a new Kingdom of God, a concept that should be understood "sapientially" rather than "apocalyptically"—that is, a Kingdom of God "described by his parables and aphorisms as a here and now Kingdom of nobodies and the destitute, of mustard, darnel, and leaven."[7] Crossan's Jesus is to be discerned primarily in the simple but clever voice of the aphorisms, prophetic sayings, and parables.

The critics of this approach were many. Laying aside the dozens of American scholars, especially, whose prior confessional commitments to the Bible predisposed them to a biblical Jesus untainted by non-biblical, heretical gospels, we might cite just one critical scholar, whose objections were both typical and well-stated. Dale Allison argued that the use of *Thomas* to check the apocalypticism of the Synoptic tradition overlooked the fact that *Thomas* may itself reflect the views of an author who had rejected the apocalypticism of the Jesus tradition, which the Synoptic Gospels reflect with historical accuracy.[8] In other words, *Thomas* had "de-apocalypticized" the tradition. I have since argued against Allison's view,[9] so I will not belabor this discussion further, except to note that critical scholars can arrive at very different conclusions. This also goes without saying for the presupposition of Crossan's view, that *Thomas* is indeed a more or less independent witness to the Jesus tradition, a question to which one of the respondents to this paper recently has devoted an entire monograph—another discussion that could easily occupy us for hours.[10]

But the relevant point I would like to stress now about Crossan is that *Thomas* was not the only, nor even the primary evidence driving him toward a sapiential, non-apocalyptic Jesus. Crossan's view of the parables and aphorisms as central to Jesus' message was more important. Also key was

6. Crossan, *Birth of Christianity*, 265–71.

7. Crossan, *Historical Jesus*, 292.

8. Allison, *Jesus of Nazareth*, 122–28. Also see ibid., 10–33 for Allison's critique of Crossan's method on a number of different points.

9. Patterson, "Apocalypticism or Prophecy"; earlier see also the exchange of views on this and other matters between Dale Allison, Marcus Borg, John Dominic Crossan, and Stephen J. Patterson in Miller, ed., *Apocalyptic Jesus*.

10. Goodacre, *Thomas and the Gospels*.

his acceptance of John Kloppenborg's theory about an early, sapiential edition of Q (Q1).[11] *Thomas* and other apocryphal gospels were not necessarily determinative of this shift to a non-apocalyptic Jesus. This was also true of the work of Norman Perrin, perhaps the first North American scholar to incorporate the *Gospel of Thomas* into a full-blown treatment of the historical Jesus. In his 1967 book, *Rediscovering the Teaching of Jesus*, Perrin used evidence from *Thomas* to argue for a less apocalyptic Jesus.[12] But he had already argued his basic hypothesis about the Kingdom of God in his dissertation, published in 1963 as *The Kingdom of God in the Teaching of Jesus*, in which *Thomas* plays no role.[13] Perrin's teacher, Joachim Jeremias, began using *Thomas* to do tradition-historical analysis of the parables very similar to that of Crossan in the 1962 edition of his classic work, *Die Gleichnisse Jesu*, but nonetheless retained his more "eschatological" view of Jesus. And on the other side, one should note that the originator of the most recent protest against an apocalyptic interpretation of Jesus, Marcus Borg, made his "Temperate Case for a Non-Eschatological Jesus" without reference to the *Gospel of Thomas*.[14] Therefore, if one of the most striking recent trends in historical Jesus scholarship is the questioning of the apocalyptic hypothesis, this is not due primarily to the *Gospel of Thomas*.[15]

So, there are exceptions and qualifications and protests one might register to my fundamental thesis, but no real argument against it: the apocryphal gospels have played virtually no role in the latest phase of the quest for the historical Jesus, in North America, or on any other continent for that matter. For the most part, the Synoptic Jesus is still the focus of this work, and the resulting portraits are either a straight-up repristinization of the Synoptic view, or a simpler, critically-derived Jesus who spoke in aphorism and parable. Since my own Jesus work fits snugly into this characterization,[16] might I be forgiven if I raise a few critical questions about it—questions I have raised with myself? Might not a skeptic observe our discipline from afar and conclude that the canonical status of gospels apparently does mat-

---

11. Kloppenborg, *Formation of Q*.

12. For comments on the status of *Thomas*, see esp. Perrin, *Rediscovering the Teaching of Jesus*, 37.

13. To illustrate, compare Perrin's analysis of Luke 17:20–21 in *Kingdom of God* (174–78) and the later work, *Rediscovering the Teaching of Jesus* (68–74).

14. Borg, "Temperate Case"; reprinted in Borg, *Jesus in Contemporary Scholarship*, 47–67.

15. In my 1995 essay, "End of Apocalypse," I cited the discovery of the *Gospel of Thomas* as one reason for the collapsing consensus around an apocalyptic interpretation of Jesus. That was clearly wrong, with few exceptions.

16. Patterson, *God of Jesus*.

ter, even to a body like the Jesus Seminar, which explicitly renounced it? Might a critic point out that the trend toward a simpler, plain-spoken Jesus avoids not just the embarrassment of apocalypticism (a critique often heard of Crossan and others who share his view), but also the mysticism, asceticism, and Platonism of the apocryphal gospels? North American Jesus scholarship has a long history of preferring the simple, plain-spoken Jesus. When cutting and pasting together his "Philosophy of Jesus of Nazareth" in 1804, Thomas Jefferson's aim was not simply to eliminate all the miracle stories, but also the equally-suspect work of "the Platonists and Plotinists, the Stagyrites and Gamalielites, the Eclectics, (and) the Gnostics."[17]

Here is an example of this trend from Crossan, whose work, let me repeat, represents in my view the best that this generation has to offer. On p. 295 of *The Historical Jesus*, Crossan takes what can only be described as a surprising turn, veering off into a cluster of sayings having to do with primordial androgyny, including logion 22 of the *Gospel of Thomas* ("When you make the two one ... in order to make the male and the female into a single one, so that the male will not be male and the female will not be female..."[18])—words that are not likely to make it into anyone's database of authentic sayings of Jesus. But Crossan wades in. He likes the fact that Paul has something like this in Galatians 3:28 ("there is neither male nor female")—though most would hesitate to call this a "version" of the *Thomas* saying. But it is a parallel showing at least that very early nascent Christians could think this way; what is more, 1 Corinthians 11:2–16 shows that men and women in a Pauline community might even go so far as to enact this primordial androgyny. But then, on the question of whether this idea could have come from Jesus, he demurs, following Dennis MacDonald's learned opinion: "The anthropology and Genesis speculation implied by the saying were foreign to Jesus, but were quite at home in Alexandrian Judaism...."[19] My instincts, too, have inclined me against the view that Jesus was interested in androgyny. But the author of the *Gospel of the Egyptians* thought he was;[20] so did the author of *2 Clement* (12.2). In fact, the idea is fairly common in the apocryphal gospels. So, do our instincts tell us that it was too sophisticated

---

17. From a letter from Jefferson to John Adams, 13 October 1813 (see *Writings of Thomas Jefferson*, 6:218). The quotation from this letter turns up in the Wikipedia entry on the Jefferson Bible, which must be where I first encountered it—with thanks to the savant who anonymously entered it there.

18. All quotations from the *Gospel of Thomas* are based on the author's own translation from the Coptic.

19. Crossan, *Historical Jesus*, 298; quoting MacDonald, *There is No Male and Female*, 128.

20. As this lost work is cited by Clement of Alexandria (*Strom.* 3.13.92).

an idea for Jesus? The "not-well-born" rustics Paul had recruited into the Corinthian community seem to have taken to it well enough—if indeed the Corinthian prophets Paul engages in 1 Corinthians 11:2–16 had developed a liturgical expression of "neither male nor female" in their worship practices.[21] Was it just too odd for Jesus—is that what our instincts are telling us? Is it odder, really, than the notion that a divine-human warrior will come from the sky and destroy one's enemies with earthquake and fire? I don't think it is. There are many odd things in the canonical gospels with which we have become comfortable through repeated exposure, and many scholars just assume Jesus said or did these things. In the end, Crossan settles for the idea that the sayings relating to primordial androgyny, though not authentic, are an interpretation of something that was authentic: radical egalitarianism.[22] I recall reading this at one time with a sense of relief and satisfaction. But now I wonder if I shouldn't have been a little disappointed.

For the sake of argument, I want to suggest the *possibility* that our lack of interest in the apocryphal gospels as a source of information about what Jesus said, did, or thought reflects a certain lack of imagination. If the apocryphal gospels strike us as more speculative, mystical, ascetical, enigmatic, or just downright confusing, should this necessarily disqualify them completely from the discussion? Is it unthinkable that Jesus could have been speculative, mystical, ascetical, enigmatic, or just downright confusing? If so, let me attempt to convince you, and myself, that it is not unthinkable.

To do this I want to begin, not with Jesus, but before Jesus—with the teacher of Jesus: John the Baptist. What did John teach Jesus? Now, in the Synoptic Gospels John appears like Jesus—a prophetic figure with an apocalyptic message. If the Synoptic Jesus is the historical Jesus, this could be the historical John as well. But in the Fourth Gospel, John the Baptist is not like this at all. It is supposed, rather, that he was someone about whom the Johannine Prologue could have been composed—that is why the Fourth Evangelist inserts vv. 6–8 into the Prologue, as Bultmann argued many years ago.[23] In other words, in the Fourth Gospel, the Johannine Baptist is like the Johannine Jesus. So, the Synoptic John is like the Synoptic Jesus, and the

---

21. That 1 Cor 11:2–16 reflects a Corinthian interpretation of Gal 3:28 ("there is no male and female") was first argued by Wayne Meeks in "Image of the Androgyne," esp. 200–203; later MacDonald argued similarly (*There is No Male and Female*, 72–110). Both assume that the passage has to do principally with women (not women *and* men), and think of their ritual in terms of women becoming like men. But vv. 4, 7, 11–12, and 14 indicate that the passage concerns the practice of both men and women. Men with long, flowing hair (v. 14) would have represented a compromise of the masculine ideal as much as women with hair unbound (v. 15), a compromise of the feminine ideal.

22. Crossan, *Historical Jesus*, 298.

23. Bultmann, *Gospel of John*, 48–49.

Johannine John is like the Johannine Jesus. I am skeptical of this strategic alignment: is the precursor simply being made to match the successor? Are there other, less strategic witnesses to what John the Baptist might have taught? Indeed, there are other followers of John the Baptist to whom we might appeal. The followers of Simon Magus held Simon to be the chief disciple of John the Baptist, as was also Dositheus, who is said to have led the Baptist sect after John's death.[24] Dositheus also turns up as the source of the Sethian text, the *Three Steles of Seth*, from Nag Hammadi Codex VII. The Mandaeans, of course, also claimed descent from John the Baptist.[25] That is all very interesting to note, but having seen that canonical boundaries might matter after all, at least sub-consciously, I would prefer another canonical witness to John the Baptist. Is there one? What about Apollos?

Apollos, of course, was Paul's rival in Corinth (see 1 Cor 1–4). Remember how he is described in Acts 18:25: "He had been instructed in the Way of the Lord... and taught accurately the things concerning Jesus, though he knew only the baptism of John." Acts goes on to state that Priscilla and Aquila went about setting him straight, presumably on the issue of Jesus' preeminence over John. But then in chapter 19, our account goes on to state that when Paul came later to Ephesus, he encountered disciples who had been baptized "into John's baptism" (Acts 19:3)—presumably by the hand of Apollos or others whom Apollos had instructed. Paul, by this account, sets them straight—now explicitly—on the issue of Jesus' preeminence over John (Acts 19:4). If this odd little episode in Acts may be counted upon to provide at least a faded memory of Apollos, we might infer that, 1) Apollos was a follower of John the Baptist, as well as Jesus; 2) that he baptized in the manner of John the Baptist; and 3) that he did not teach that John was merely Jesus' precursor. In other words, Apollos was not just a Jesus follower. He was also a Baptist follower. And when he came to Ephesus, and later to Corinth, he was still a Baptist follower. If, then, we can discover what Apollos taught, we will perhaps also discover what John the Baptist taught—not only to Apollos, but also to his more famous pupil, Jesus of Nazareth. Let us proceed, then, with two questions: 1) what did Apollos teach? and 2) is there any evidence in the Jesus tradition that Jesus might also have learned similar ideas from John the Baptist, and promulgated them?

So, what did Apollos teach? I will answer the question with the assumption, undefended in this very brief frame, that many of the ideas against

---

24. In the Pseudo-Clementine writings, *Hom.* 2 (see Irmscher and Strecker, "Pseudo-Clementines," 512–13).

25. In the *Haran Gawaita* scroll (see Rudolph, *Gnosis*, 363).

which Paul argues in 1 Corinthians 1–4 will have come from Apollos—a premise that is not undisputed, and yet, widely held.[26]

Let us begin with the most certain of things based on this assumption: Apollos was a baptizer. The factionalism running through the Corinthian communities was apparently based on partisan notions of baptism (1;12–17). Since Apollos was a follower of John the Baptist, and he apparently baptized in the Johannine manner, let us assume that the dust-up over baptism in Corinth was due in part to the presence of Apollos the baptizer.

Did John's other famous pupil, Jesus, also baptize? Curiously, the Synoptic Gospels do not say that he did . . . nor that he didn't (although, the passages Clement associates with the *Secret Gospel of Mark* depict the young man who comes to Jesus by night as prepared for baptism). The Gospel of John does say that Jesus baptized people (3:22, 26; 4:1), but then, in an editorial aside—perhaps from the ecclesiastical redactor—denies it (4:2). I assume, then, that John 3:22, 26, and 4:1 represents the earlier tradition and constitutes evidence that Jesus, too, *may* have learned to baptize people in the way John had baptized. If he did, what did it mean to him? What did it mean to Apollos?

Returning to 1 Corinthians 1–4 we may infer that Apollos's baptism was part of a tradition in which wisdom in the form of words, or sayings, was conveyed. This is clear from 1:17, 18–25; 2:1 (etc.) and is, moreover, consistent with the commonplace that initiation would be accompanied by specialized teaching. It should be noted, too, that what Paul opposes in Corinth is described as a "secret" (*mysterion*—1 Cor 2:1), a term he uses to describe his own counter-wisdom teaching in 2:7. Secret teaching would also have been a commonplace in such cultic settings. Since, in 2:14—3:4, the apostle goes on to wrangle over who is to be considered truly "spiritual," who has truly received "the things of the spirit," and who is worthy of being addressed as "*pneumatikos*," we may further infer that, in addition to special, secret teaching, those who received Apollos's baptism were thought also to receive the "spirit" and thereby to join the ranks of the "spiritual." Did Apollos get any of this from John the Baptist?

We know John the Baptist mostly as a baptizer, but we should also assume that he taught his initiates something as well. In Q he is identified, alongside Jesus, as one of "Wisdom's (Sophia's) children" (Q 7:35), and the Prologue to the Fourth Gospel presupposes an audience who might have been inclined to see John as the descending/ascending Logos figure, instead of Jesus (John 1:6–8). So John had wisdom credentials—and not just in later Mandaean and Sethian circles. Moreover, his baptism was also thought to

---

26. See Fee, *First Epistle to the Corinthians*, 56–57.

impart the "holy spirit," as the scenes of Jesus' own baptism in Q, Mark, and John all attest. John is not depicted in the Synoptics or the Gospel of John as offering secret wisdom teachings, but among the Mandaeans he was, of course, known primarily for this.[27]

And is there evidence that when Jesus baptized people he also conveyed to them wisdom teaching, even secret wisdom teaching, accompanied by the imparting of the "spirit?" That Jesus' baptism was accompanied by the imparting of the spirit is claimed by the Synoptic accounts of John's preaching *about* Jesus: "I have baptized you with water; but he will baptize you with the Holy Spirit" (Mark 1:8). Q contains nearly identical wording to this, save the addition of "fire": "he will baptize you in a holy spirit and fire" (Q 3:16). In the Fourth Gospel John the Baptist says something similar about Jesus: "He on whom you see the Spirit descend and remain is the one who baptizes with the Holy Spirit" (John 1:33). Since these claims play virtually no role in the canonical accounts of Jesus' unfolding career, I am inclined to credit them as an obscure historical memory that, for whatever reason, was later denied (as, specifically, in John 4:2).

Did Jesus, like Apollos, have secret wisdom teachings that were imparted only to an inner circle of initiates? There is, perhaps surprisingly, widespread agreement about this among the sources. The apocryphal gospel Q claims it explicitly:

> 21 Then (Jesus) said, "I bless you, Father, Lord of heaven and earth, for you have hidden these things from sages and scholars and revealed them to babes. Yes, Father, for this is what seemed right to you. 22 All things have been entrusted me by my Father. And no one knows the son except the Father, and none the Father except the son, and anyone to whom the son wishes to reveal (him)." (Q 10:21–22[28])

The *Gospel of Thomas* is a collection of just such sayings ("These are the secret sayings that the Living Jesus spoke . . ." [Prologue]), and the Gospel of Mark—if a canonical witness is preferable—claims this secret status for Jesus' teaching about the kingdom of God: "To you has been given the secret (*mysterion*) of the kingdom of God, but for those outside everything is in parables" (Mark 4:11). Elsewhere in Mark we hear about this secret

---

27. See, e.g., *Right Ginza*, Books 7 and 8 (see Lidzbarski, *Ginza*; an English translation of the *Ginza* may now be found in Barnstone and Meyer, eds., *Gnostic Bible*, with relevant passages on John the Baptist on pp. 549–51).

28. All quotations from Q are the author's own translation based on the reconstructed Greek text of Q created by the International Q Project: Robinson et al., *Sayings Gospel Q*.

teaching only in the fragments Clement assigns to *Secret Mark*. This occurs (in fragment 1 of *Secret Mark*) when Jesus raises a young man from the dead in Bethany. "Six days later" this same young man comes to Jesus by night, "dressed only in a linen cloth"—a clear reference to baptism—and Jesus teaches him "the secret (*mysterion*, again) of the kingdom of God."[29] This is the only tradition in which baptism and secret teaching are linked in connection with Jesus.

This is all very interesting. But is any of it *historical*? Let me remind you that I have not been charged here with a discussion of the historical Jesus, but with *how* we have talked about the historical Jesus. Is it not surprising how easily noncanonical sources fit into a discussion about the historical Jesus, even when that discussion begins and is guided by some of the earliest texts and traditions at our disposal—Paul's letters and Q? And the results—that Jesus might have baptized people, imparting to them the spirit, and initiating them into secret wisdom teachings—are perhaps as strange as anything you have ever heard from a respectable scholar (respectable, that is, until now). And yet, are they really all that far-fetched? My point is this: how we have read these early sources and the possibilities we see in them has been guided and limited by certain constraints imposed by the Synoptic portrait. Does this not indeed indicate a certain lack of imagination? How far could a reasonable, yet imaginative, inquiry along theses line continue?

I proceed, then—even if I have gone too far already.

Let us begin again with baptism and an early tradition indicating its meaning among nascent Christians. This tradition is, in fact, the earliest baptismal tradition we have in early Christian literature:

> As many of you as were baptized into Christ have clothed yourselves with. There is no longer Jew or Greek, there is no longer slave or free; there is no longer male and female; for you are all one in Christ Jesus. (Gal 3:27–28)

Again, in this limited frame I will not delve into the reasons why so many scholars regard this as a pre-Pauline formula, nor into an exegesis of it vis-à-vis Paul's own interests in Galatians.[30] I am only interested in what it might tell us about how very early followers of Jesus understood the practice of baptism. In this vein it is rather remarkable: in baptism the basic distinctions by which human beings order themselves—ethnicity, class, and gender—are all overcome. And perhaps the most remarkable of these three distinctions

---

29. For references to *Secret Mark*, see Smith, *Clement of Alexandria*. The translation used here is that of Helmut Koester in Miller, ed., *Complete Gospels*, 415.

30. See, for example, Meeks, "Image of the Androgyne," 180–82. The idea, however, is very old in scholarship—see MacDonald, *There is No Male and Female*, 4 n. 7.

is the third: "there is no longer male and female." Many have called attention to the slightly distinct wording of this member of the formula ("male and female" rather than "neither man nor woman") designed to reflect more precisely the language of Genesis 1:27. The earliest, nascent Christian understanding of baptism apparently included the notion that redemption finally must involve a return to the beginning, before Adam's fall, when he still retained the image of God in which he was created: androgynous, at once both male and female.[31] This was the part of the formula that perhaps made Paul uncomfortable—or so one might infer from his choice to omit it when he repeats the formula in 1 Corinthians (12:13). Perhaps the reason for this is revealed in chapter 11 of that letter, where Paul tries to dissuade people in Corinth from praying and prophesying in a manner of dress and coiffeur that blurs the distinction between male and female. I am convinced by Meeks and others that this was indeed an attempt by the Corinthian prophets to enact in ritual the baptismal claim that in Christ there is no longer male and female. Where did this idea come from? Not from Paul, who claims not to have baptized anyone in Corinth—except Crispus and Gaius, the household of Stephanas ... and maybe a few others (1 Cor 1:14–16). They must have gotten it from the other baptizer in Corinth, Apollos. Could this also have been something Apollos learned from his baptizer, John? Let us consult John's other, more famous pupil, to see if he too held such a view of baptism.

Could Jesus have understood baptism in this way—as signaling a return to Adam's pre-lapsarian state of androgynous perfection? The canonical gospels, which are largely silent on the issue of Jesus' baptizing activity, also say nothing about how Jesus might have understood baptism. But the apocryphal gospels do. Of the apocryphal gospels, the *Gospel of Philip* is the most expansive on the subject. But *Philip* is probably too late to be of any real help. The *Gospel of Thomas*, however, contains at least one saying purporting to offer Jesus' view of baptism, logion 37:

> 1His disciples said, "When will you appear to us and when will we see you?" 2 Jesus said, "When you undress without being ashamed and take your clothes (and) put them under your feet like little children and trample them, 3then [you] will see the son of the Living One, and you will not be afraid."

As Jonathan Z. Smith has shown,[32] the valences of this odd saying are two. On the one hand, it references the Jewish and early Christian baptismal

---

31. Meeks, "Image of the Androgyne," 183–97.
32. Smith, "Garments of Shame."

practice of disrobing—the only kind of cultic nudity tolerated by Jews and Christians in antiquity. On the other hand, disrobing *without shame* refers to the primordial nakedness of Adam, before the fall—a theme that also accompanies later Christian baptismal practice. In other words, here is an interpretation of baptism that involves a return to Adam's primordial state before the fall. Now, this is quite in keeping with soteriology in the *Gospel of Thomas*, generally speaking, where the end is said to be like the beginning (logion 18). Logion 22, which is not a baptismal saying, clarifies the meaning of this protological idea further:

> ⁴ Jesus said to them, "When you make the two one and when you make the inside like the outside and the outside like the inside and the above like the below—⁵ that is, in order to make the male and the female into a single one, so that the male will not be male and the female will not be female—⁶ when you make eyes in place of an eye and a hand in place of a hand and a foot in place of a foot, an image in place of an image, ⁷ then you will enter the Kingdom."

Thomas credits Jesus with a protological soteriology, in which the image of God, which Adam lost when he sinned, is regained through baptism and enlightenment through the secret sayings of Jesus.[33] And so we arrive at that point where Crossan turned back in 1991 and opted for a slightly less speculative Jesus, who promoted the general principle of egalitarianism, rather than ritual androgyny. Perhaps his reserve yields a more plausible historical Jesus. But another, stranger Jesus, is not really so far from our sources than one might think.

Just to complete this thought experiment, I want to return to the Jesus Seminar. It did not contemplate putting *Thomas* 22 into the database of historical Jesus sayings. But it did include one very odd saying from the Gospel of Matthew:[34]

> For there are eunuchs who have been so from birth, and there are eunuchs who have been made eunuchs by others, and there are eunuchs who have made themselves eunuchs for the sake of the kingdom of heaven. Let anyone accept this who can. (Matt 19:12)

I take it that the history of religions context for this saying is relatively clear. Some in the Jesus movement had adopted the practice of ritual self-castration, much like the *galli* of the Great Mother cult. The *galli* were thought to

---

33. See esp. Pagels, "Exegesis of Genesis 1"; also Davies, "Christology and Protology."
34. Funk and Hoover, eds., *Five Gospels*, 220.

be neither male nor female, but something like androgynous servants of their androgynous god. I recall voting against this saying in the Seminar, ostensibly because it was attested only once, and late; but really it was because it was just too strange for my Jesus. But Arthur Dewey made a strong case for authenticity based on dissimilarity and general embarrassment.[35] On that count he had us, and the saying was voted in. On that day the historical Jesus became just as daring as the author of Matthew thought he was: a promoter of self-castration for the sake of the kingdom of heaven. To the ancient way of thinking, this goes beyond *ritual* androgyny to the real thing.

North American New Testament scholarship has more or less absorbed the insights of Walter Bauer and begun to see the unfolding of early Christianity as a widely diverse phenomenon where many interpretations of Jesus are possible.[36] But his insight has not been brought to bear on historical Jesus scholarship. Generally speaking, the Synoptic Jesus still reigns supreme. But what if Jesus himself was part of a more diverse and interesting religious event, one in which John participated as well, which spawned strange hybrids like Apollos, devoted to them both? What if the Synoptic Gospels represent only a limited band-width of this event, only a part of what could have emanated from it with authenticity? If so, in order to gain a fuller sense of what Jesus and his companions were up to, what they were thinking and doing, we might need to listen to more than just the Synoptic representation of him. Conservative scholars have long admonished us not to overlook the Fourth Gospel nor the Pauline epistles. We have looked at them here. But is there a reason not to cast our net wider still, beyond the artificial boundaries of the Christian canon, to include apocryphal gospels and their traditions as well? The question is not, after all, which of the gospels best represents the historical Jesus. The question for critical scholarship is how to imagine a historical figure from which could emanate all of the various traditions and interpretations that appear in the first century or so of nascent Christian development. If we frame the question in this way, I am convinced that we still have much more to talk about before we close the door on the quest for the historical Jesus.

---

35. Dewey, "Unkindest Cut."
36. Bauer, *Orthodoxy and Heresy*.

– 10 –

Apocryphal Gospels and Historical Jesus Research

A Response to Stephen Patterson

— John S. Kloppenborg —

A FEW YEARS AGO Mark Goodacre, Tony Burke, and I participated in a conference at the University of Toronto on "Erasure History." The premise of the conference was counterfactual: what would the study of Greek Literature, ancient Christianity, and Roman history look like if certain data had not survived—Homer, the Gospel of Mark, Codex Sinaiticus, the *Martyrdom of Perpetua*, Tacitus, and so forth. Giovanni Bazzana was asked to write on "If Egypt Weren't So Dry: The Erasure of Documentary Papyri and the Earliest Christian Literature."

Bazzana's answer to the question, "what would the study of early Christianity look like if no papyri had survived?" is quite similar to Patterson's answer to the question put to him on the impact of Christian apocrypha on the study of the Historical Jesus: not much different. This is because for all the papyrological discoveries that have occurred since the expeditions of Grenfell and Hunt—9274 Greek, Demotic, and Coptic documentary papyri published to date and many thousands still awaiting publication—there has been only a very small impact on our understanding of the social, economic, and literary contexts of the early Jesus movement.

Some of the reasons for this neglect can be surmised: the study of papyri is limited, even in departments of Classics; the Greek of the papyri is usually sub-literary; scribal conventions are not very easy to master; and the many farm accounts, leases, loan documents, police reports, private letters, and so forth are probably considered too remote from the genres and conceptual interests of the documents of the Jesus movement to be of much interest or pertinence. These sentiments are most unfortunate, but I will leave the defense of a study of papyri to another paper.

Stephen Patterson's paper raises some important questions about the degree to which the plain-talking Synoptic Jesus—ignoring a few odd bits like the saying on eunuchs for the kingdom of heaven (Matt 19:12)—has become canonical even for those scholars who eschew the canon as a historiographic principle. Patterson presents an interesting case for imagining a Jesus who was a bit stranger than we sometimes like to imagine. As he points out, there are already some very strange bits that have become part of the canonical portrait: for example, the Jesus who will reappear as a fiery apocalyptic deliverer, which found its way into the now-canonical portrait of Jesus—not because, as Schweitzer thought, it was so strange, but because the representation of a Jesus who spoke of the definitive transformation of human existence by a deity and a Jesus who himself effected that definitive transformation were so congenial to the project of the articulation of a Christology that pronounced Jesus to be unique and unsurpassed.[1] The Jesus who praised those who castrated themselves evidently had a more limited appeal.

Should the apocryphal gospels have had a greater impact? Undoubtedly yes. But their impact has been limited by at least two factors: the way the criteria of authenticity are applied, and the immense gravitational pull of the Synoptic Jesus.

1. *Criteria*. Patterson notes that John Dominic Crossan considered *Gos. Thom.* 22 ("When you make the two one . . .") as belonging to a sayings cluster that was among the most strongly attested by the criterion of multiple attestation. Although Crossan did not conclude that the saying stems from the historical Jesus, true to his method, he could argue that it was "an interpretation of something that does,"[2] and settled on the suggestion that it reflected an authentic commitment to "radical egalitarianism." There is even a hint that he thought it would pass the criterion of dissimilarity:

> Jesus' Kingdom of nobodies and undesirables in the here and now of this world was surely a radically egalitarian one, and, as

1. See Kloppenborg, ed., *Apocalypticism*.
2. Crossan, *Historical Jesus*, 298.

such, it rendered sexual and social, political and religious distinctions completely irrelevant and anachronistic.[3]

There are two respects in which Crossan's method and its inclusion of noncanonical gospels might legitimately inform constructions of the historical Jesus. One is the way in which Crossan uses it: starting his reconstruction with those sayings and anecdotes that express multiple independent attestations. Here it is important to note that apocryphal gospels play a key part for Crossan, since they raise the baptism of Jesus from singly attested (Mark = John) to triply attested. "All sins are forgiven" (Mark 3:28; Q 12:10; *Didache* 11.7) receives another attestation in Thomas (*Gos. Thom.* 44), and "Children and the Kingdom" (Mark 10:15; Matt 18:3; John 3:3) has four attestations with *Gos. Thom.* 22.

The significance of multiple attestation can be seen not only in the fact that Crossan considers these sayings as salient for reconstructing the historical Jesus but in the prominence he assigns to them. While Sanders, for example, does not mention the "Children and the Kingdom" saying at all in order to characterize Jesus' view of the kingdom, the sayings cluster is central to Crossan's first main chapter on the message of Jesus ("Kingdom and Wisdom").[4] Almost as well attested is "blessed are the poor," found in Q, Thomas, and James. Hence, multiple attestation does not simply get sayings into the inventory; the stronger the attestation, the more centrally the saying or anecdote should be used in a reconstruction of the historical Jesus. Thus, if we were to take multiple attestation seriously, *Gos. Thom.* 22 on androgyny or some saying expressing some kind of mitigation of sexual difference should be prominent in reconstructions of the historical Jesus.[5]

This position might receive additional support from another saying attested, according to Crossan, four times: the divorce saying (Mark 10:11–12; Q 16:18; 1 Cor 7:10–11; *Herm. Mand.* 4.1.6). The odd formulation of the saying—"whoever divorces his wife and marries another commits adultery against her"—makes adultery a charge that can be leveled, not against an interloper who interferes with another man's wife by "stealing" the husband's honor, but against the husband who steals his wife's honor. That is, the saying makes honor gynaikocentric as well as androcentric.[6]

---

3. Ibid.
4. Sanders, *Jesus and Judaism*.
5. I note that Theissen and Merz (*Historical Jesus*, 117) mention *Gos. Thom.* 22 in connection with the criterion of multiple attestation, but only in relation to the appearance of the term "kingdom."
6. On this see Kloppenborg, "Alms, Debt and Divorce."

Multiple attestation is potentially important in a second respect. The effect of the ignoring of Mark 10:13–16 ("Children and the Kingdom") by Sanders, Wright, Gnilka, and others is noteworthy. Although Q 6:20b, "blessed are the poor," is given some attention by Sanders, Gnilka, Witherington, and Wright, it is hardly central to their reconstructions. Meier gives it considerable attention, and reads it as an expression of the expectation that God will intervene in the near future on behalf of the poor and oppressed.[7]

But when Q 6:20b is interpreted alongside Mark 10:13–16, what becomes more visible is the contrast between statuses: the rich (who are usually thought to be blessed) *versus* the poor, and adults and other persons with status *versus* insignificant, non-statused persons. Thus, the kingdom as characterized by Q 6:20b and Mark 10:13–16 is not just about God's eventual elevation of the poor and lowly, but an implicit *threat* in the present to the customary valuations of hierarchy, age, wealth, and power.[8] Crossan's "Kingdom of Nobodies" includes a critical nuance that is lacking in the more usual constructions of the Kingdom based on Q 6:20b. Moreover, against Meier it can be observed that *none* of the texualizations of the poverty beatitude construes it as future talk. In Q it appears in a cluster describing one's (present) conduct in light of the conviction that one belongs to the kingdom; in James it concerns conduct in relation to wealth; and there is no reason to suppose that Thomas's version (which lacks much context), is futuristic. Without using noncanonical gospels to import *new* sayings, Crossan's procedure allows him to lift up authentic *intracanonical* sayings which, because of their radical character, are in danger of being ignored by those who base their portraits solely on the intracanonical gospels. And, as I have suggested, it should also assist us in interpreting sayings attributed to Jesus by paying attention to the ways in which the saying has subsequently been textualized.

Of course, Crossan's procedure is vulnerable if one challenges his view that the Gospels of *Thomas*, the *Hebrews*, or the *Egyptians* are independent of the Synoptics, for in that case one has lost one or two independent attestations. This is not an issue that is solved by Meier's wholesale dismissal of the import of apocryphal gospels, or by a naive inclusion of everything in the noncanonical gospels, a charge to which Crossan is vulnerable. Reviewing both the works of Meier and Crossan, David Aune sagely remarks,

---

7. Meier, *Marginal Jew*, 2:317–36.
8. This point is developed further in Kloppenborg, "Sources."

> John Meier does not come off nearly so well [as Jens Schröter],[9] for I think that it would be incredible if a document like Thomas, containing nearly 150 sayings of Jesus, and compiled ca. 140 CE (while oral tradition still retained some measure of vitality) did not contain at least some happy vestiges of original historical Jesus traditions. Crossan does not comport himself very well either, for it would be incredible if a document like Thomas did not contain at least a smidgen of Jesus traditions which were dependent on the Synoptic Gospels.[10]

Meier's mantra that even if the *agrapha* and a few sayings from noncanonical gospels were authentic, "nothing new would be added to our picture" is surely wrong.[11] Aune rightly observes that Meier "has temporarily lost sight of the value of the criterion of multiple attestation in valuing 'what is new' and 'different' in Jesus traditions."[12]

2. My second comment has to do with what I have called the immense gravitational pull of the Synoptics, and their depictions of Jesus that are comfortable and seem to belong within the bounds of *our* imaginations of piety.

Patterson suggests that the Synoptic Gospels have a "limited bandwidth" and that protological speculations might have been within Jesus' purview. I can, I think, guarantee that this suggestion will get little traction, not because of the limited bandwidth of the Synoptics, but because of the limited bandwidth of our imaginations of what is possible.

Several years ago I surveyed the reaction to the so-called Cynic hypothesis—the suggestion that either Jesus or Q might profitably be seen as adopting a cynic-like posture towards Galilean society.[13] The reaction to this suggestion was instructive, insofar as the opponents of the thesis adopted argumentative strategies that were internally incoherent. It was asserted, for example, that there were no Cynics in the Galilee (even though the Cynic hypothesis, since it used "Cynic" typologically rather than genealogically, did not require followers of Diogenes of Sinope to be there). But simultaneously, opponents argued that Q's mission instructions, which forbade the carrying of a *pera*, were anti-Cynic. Either Cynics were in the Galilee or nearby, such that their behavior could be rejected, or they were not present, in which case Q 10 is not anti-Cynic. One cannot have it both ways.

9. The reference is to Schröter, *Erinnerung an Jesu Worte*.
10. Aune, "Assessing," 269.
11. Meier, *Marginal Jew*, 1:114.
12. Aune, "Assessing," 247.
13. Kloppenborg, "Dog among the Pigeons."

Once Cynics had been banished from Galilee, the road was open to proclaim that Jesus was not a Cynic, but a prophet. It was scarcely even noticed that Josephus, our one source for information about the Galilee in the time of Antipas and Agrippa, *never* locates a prophet there. They are all Judaean. What was stunning about the opposition's argument was that, having applied strictures to the Cynic hypothesis, those strictures were immediately relaxed once one's more comfortable thesis came up for consideration. Nor was it noticed that τάδε λέγει κύριος, the standard marker of prophetic speech, never appears on Jesus' lips.

I mention this, not because it involves noncanonical gospels, but because it points to a deep anxiety in the guild when it comes to suggestions that Jesus was something other than "man's best friend" and might have had a bark and a bite. Or Patterson's suggestion that Jesus might have thought about androgyny or castration, or a host of other practices and beliefs that might sound to us as just a little too weird.

The problem of the ideological setting of the interpreter of ancient history having a measurable effect on the way that history is constructed is not unique to historical Jesus studies. Gibbon's hostility to organized religion and his optimism about rational progress led to an estimate of the Roman Empire that was sharply different from Mikael Rostovtzeff's account, which was influenced by the fact that Rostovtzeff was a refugee from the Russian revolution. Our problems are perhaps exacerbated by the fact that the Jesus who is the subject of historical inquiry is also the object of weekly praise, petition, and sermon-making in congregations that, for the most part, do not embrace monastic ideals of celibacy, still less ideals of androgyny, or that engage in anti-social behavior such as eating with disreputables or loud and brash lampooning of authorities—I'm not talking about Diogenes of Sinope, but about the Woes in Q 11:39–52. The gravitational pull of a respectable, plain-spoken Synoptic Jesus is still very strong.

– 11 –

Apocryphal Gospels and Historical Jesus Research

A Response to Stephen Patterson

— Mark Goodacre —

STEPHEN PATTERSON'S IMAGINATIVE PAPER provides a stimulating proposal about how apocryphal gospels might interact with reflections on the canonical gospels to produce a different picture of the historical Jesus, one that takes seriously ascetic and protological traditions. Yet, his paper is surprisingly downbeat about recent scholarship and the extent to which apocryphal gospels have played a role in the historical study of Jesus. In this response, I would like to suggest that Patterson is unduly pessimistic about the advances in scholarship over the last generation or so, and that the failure to take apocryphal gospels seriously is related to the conservative nature of the guild. I will go on to suggest that there are, nevertheless, intractable difficulties with the use of many apocryphal writings for studying the historical Jesus, difficulties that relate to their date and distance from the early Jesus movement. I will conclude by proposing that our obsession with the historical Jesus frequently acts as a serious barrier to our taking noncanonical materials seriously and it is only when we re-invest in the study of the full range of early Christian materials that we will be able to embrace what they have to teach us.

Patterson argues that "the apocryphal gospels have had virtually no impact on the historical study of Jesus in North America" (p. 173), but this may underestimate the extent to which they have influenced the field. We could, for one thing, take "the historical study of Jesus" in its broadest sense as covering not only the quest of the historical Jesus, but also the study of how Jesus is represented in early Christian writings. But even if we take it in the narrower sense as referring solely to historical-Jesus research, there are clear signs of major influence. It is not right to say that they "have played virtually no role" (p. 176).

Patterson's pessimism is surprising in the light of his own work in this area. Since he is too modest to mention it, I will underline here that his *Gospel of Thomas and Jesus*[1] played a major role in persuading scholars that the *Gospel of Thomas* should be taken seriously in research on the historical Jesus and Christian origins, not least because it was the first clear exposition of the case that the *Gospel of Thomas* was independent—or, more accurately "autonomous"—of the Synoptic Gospels and John. Patterson examined every parallel and argued against direct contact between these works. If Patterson is right, and there are many scholars who think that he is, then the *Gospel of Thomas* has to be a key player in the discussion of the earliest traditions about Jesus. Although some have argued against Patterson,[2] there is no doubt about the importance of his work in establishing the case for *Thomas*'s autonomy, a case that has had a particularly marked influence in North American scholarship, though its effects have been felt in Europe too.

Although playing down his own role, Patterson rightly affirms John Dominic Crossan's seminal contribution in this area.[3] No one has done more than Crossan to break down canonical walls in Jesus scholarship, at all times asking the question about the possibility that noncanonical writings might tell us as much as or more about Jesus than the Synoptics and John. Patterson mentions the role played in this regard by the gospels of *Thomas* and *Peter*, but one might add also *P. Egerton 2*, the *Gospel of Hebrews*, and several others.[4] It is a sign of Crossan's success that Gerd Theissen

---

1. Patterson, *Gospel of Thomas and Jesus*.

2. Most recently see Gathercole, *Composition*; and Goodacre, *Thomas and the Gospels*.

3. Although Crossan was committed to Thomas's independence of the Synoptics and John before Patterson's monograph was published, he nevertheless endorsed its approach to the problem on the basis of his Claremont PhD dissertation (Patterson, "Gospel of Thomas") in Crossan, *Historical Jesus*, esp. 427; see also Crossan, *Birth of Christianity*, esp. 117–18.

4. See in particular Crossan, *Four Other Gospels*, for a study of how four noncanonical gospels can inform serious historical discussion.

and Annette Merz's textbook on the historical Jesus treats "attention to non-canonical sources" as one of the major characteristics of the third quest of the historical Jesus.[5] It is a move that probably has more to do with Helmut Koester than anyone else, and if there is one key character missing from Patterson's paper, it is surely Koester. His *Ancient Christian Gospels*,[6] while not focused narrowly on the historical Jesus, established the importance of reading and critically engaging with the many early gospels if one is to understand the development of trajectories in early Christianity.

The value of Koester's approach is straightforward to understand when one compares Fitzmyer's condescending comments about Elaine Pagels's *The Gnostic Gospels* in 1980 with Koester's response the same year. For Fitzmyer, what Pagels was studying was "gibberish" and "schlock."[7] For Koester, this was an unacceptable value judgment[8] on writings that should be taken seriously as witnesses to the differing strands of early Christian thought. Value judgments and sweeping statements from senior scholars have not gone away. When John Meier says of Crossan's approach, "In the face of this uncritical romping through the apocrypha, I would urge a return to sobriety," one cannot help hearing the echo of the pastor chastising the aberrant drunken heretic.[9] This is not so much a historical judgment as a theological reaction, and a pretty unsophisticated reaction at that.

There may be other factors at work in the failure to take noncanonical writings seriously in historical-Jesus scholarship. Patterson draws attention to the work of the Jesus Seminar as an honorable exception to the rule that historical-Jesus scholars generally ignore noncanonical writings, and his further discussion helpfully illustrates the problem. He notices that even the Jesus Seminar, which takes *Thomas* seriously, tends to favor "the simple aphorism, proverb, or prophetic saying (that is, social criticism), and the unembellished parable" (p. 174). Given these tendencies, wedded as they remain to the form-critical perspective from which they derive, it is hardly surprising that so few other apocryphal gospels find their way into the

5. Theissen and Merz, *Historical Jesus*, 11.

6. Koester, *Ancient Christian Gospels*.

7. Fitzmyer, "Gnostic Gospels," 123: "That there were Christians with protognostic tendencies at the end of the first century is undeniable . . . But that they were of the ilk responsible for the schlock that is supposed to pass as 'literature' in the Nag Hammadi library is another question." For "gibberish," see 123–24.

8. Koester, "Apocryphal and Canonical Gospels," 106.

9. Meier, "Present State," 464. Note also his remark that "In my view, if we can use the *Infancy Gospel of Thomas*, we can use *Alice in Wonderland* just as well" (464). It is arguable that Meier marginalizes the *Gospel of Thomas* by characterizing it repeatedly as "the Coptic *Gospel of Thomas*," thus confusing the literary work with one of its textual witnesses.

inventory of historical-Jesus sayings. The *Gospel of Thomas* is special in providing such terse versions of Jesus' sayings and in an approach that prefers simplicity it is natural that *Thomas* gets particular notice. *Thomas*'s version of the Parable of the Lost Sheep, for example, is less than half the length of Matthew's and Luke's versions (Matt 18:10–14//Luke 15:3–7).[10] The version of the parable in the *Gospel of Truth* (31,35–32,16), with its embellishments about the left hand and the right hand, by contrast, is even longer than Matthew's and Luke's. It is hardly surprising that the *Gospel of Truth* version seldom gets a look-in in historical-Jesus work; it is not even listed in Crossan's itinerary of sayings.[11]

Furthermore, as Patterson points out, the Thomasine sayings that find their way into the Jesus Seminar's red/pink category are almost all sayings with parallels in the Synoptic Gospels. This may witness simply to the fact that of all the noncanonical gospels, *Thomas* is the one with the most parallels to Synoptic sayings material. And in a method that prejudices multiple attestation, it is inevitable that *Thomas* gets this kind of special treatment. While other early gospels—such as the *Gospel of Mary*, the *Dialogue of the Savior*, the *Gospel of Philip*—have occasional Synoptic parallels, they are a tiny proportion of the number found in *Thomas*, and they are rarely of the nature that would cause historical-Jesus scholars to sit up and take notice, even if they had read these works.

However, considerations like these only take us part of the way in understanding the issues in the scholarship. Patterson's paper is in some respects a lament about the lack of serious discussion of noncanonical writings in Jesus research, and it is a lament with which it is easy to sympathize. Scholars of Christian origins work in a deeply conservative guild, conservative not so much in the sense of being influenced by confessional Christian perspectives, though that is present too, but in the sense of adherence to the status quo. The wheels of scholarship turn slowly. Scholars repeat what they heard in graduate school and they find comfort in what is familiar. The introductory textbooks are often a generation or more behind the newer trends in scholarship, and our teaching inevitably retards the development of the discipline and the introduction of new ideas as well as new texts.[12]

---

10. Matthew's version is 113 words of English translation, Luke's 175, and Thomas's 52. See further my *Thomas and the Gospels*, 148. The *Gospel of Truth* version is 198 words of English translation.

11. For Crossan (*Historical Jesus*, 351, 440), the Lost Sheep is 1/2 (first stratum, attested twice).

12. See Koester's complaint in "Apocryphal and Canonical Gospels," 106, about introductory textbooks that barely mention noncanonical gospels.

Moreover, the North American universities and colleges still configure their teaching in largely canonical terms. There are many courses that provide an "Introduction to the Bible," or an "Introduction to the New Testament." While many will attempt the kind of historical perspective championed in a textbook like Bart Ehrman's *Historical Introduction*, there are few courses that will introduce much more than the *Gospel of Thomas* into their survey, and our academics therefore reinforce the canonical bias that runs through the field.

For many interpreters, though, the strange, unfamiliar nature of the noncanonical writings renders them undesirable. Thus Patterson asks, "If the apocryphal gospels strike us as more speculative, mystical, ascetical, enigmatic, or just downright confusing, should this necessarily disqualify them completely from the discussion?" (p. 178 above). The question is a good one because it reaches into the heart of the guild's canonical bias. Of course these things should not disqualify noncanonical gospels from the discussion, yet it is likely that they often do. "Enigma" is in the eye of the beholder, "confusion" in the mind of the interpreter. How can we be sure that it is not just tired scholarly habits and the lethargic attachment to the familiar that make noncanonical texts appear so strange?

Patterson's discussion of asceticism, protology and androgyny suggests a helpful remedy to this state of affairs. As he points out, "There are many odd things in the canonical gospels with which we have become comfortable through repeated exposure" (p. 178 above). Consideration of noncanonical writings alongside canonical ones can help us not so much to make the noncanonical gospels familiar as to make the canonical gospels strange to us again. One of the values of studying noncanonical gospels is that they can remind us of our distance from the ancient world, but this should not be at the expense of privileging, domesticating, and sanitizing canonical gospels. Rather, the strangeness of apocryphal gospels helps us to wake up to the strangeness of the canonical gospels that we thought we knew.

Patterson's admittedly speculative discussion of protology and androgyny provides an excellent illustration of this general point. New students confronted with the Thomasine sayings about protology (*Gos. Thom.* 18, 22, 37) might well balk at the unfamiliar until they notice the utter oddity of Matthew's saying about eunuchs (Matt 19:12, p. 184) or Paul's discussion of gender relations in his churches (Gal 3:27–28, p. 182; 1 Corinthians 11, p. 183). Whatever the origins and background of this material, Paul and Matthew, like *Thomas*, all witness to an ancient mindset about the construction of gender that we find foreign. But is this kind of primal androgyny also likely to have been an element in the historical Jesus' thought? The idea should certainly not be excluded on the grounds that it is too strange for Jesus. The historical Jesus surely thought and taught all sorts of strange things. The difficulty, however, with historical-Jesus research is that we have so little certain access to his teaching, and we never have access to original contexts and nuances. To the extent that we can judge by well-attested early traditions, the saying about divorce and remarriage reported by both Paul and Mark (1 Cor 7:10–11; Mark 10:1–10) and paralleled in Matthew and Luke (Matt 5:31–32; Matt 19:1–9; Luke 16:18) suggests a certain radicalism about marriage relationships. In the longer Marcan version paralleled in Matthew, there are reflections on the "male and female" of Genesis 1, but the saying is not configured in terms of primal androgyny but in terms of the Torah and what "Moses commanded" (Mark 10:3), the very things that are conspicuously and typically absent in *Thomas*,[13] factors that may tell us more about *Thomas*'s characteristic emphases than about the historical Jesus.

Patterson's discussion reminds us that sources do matter. For the historian, the source's character and date are paramount. Canonicity in and of itself is irrelevant. Apollos is indeed a case in point. The reason that Paul's witness in 1 Corinthians is so useful is that it is contemporary—he actually knows Apollos. It is the same reason that we prejudice Paul's witness in historical-Jesus traditions. Though Paul did not know Jesus, he knew people who did, and he sometimes puts us directly in touch with those earliest tradents, especially—again—in 1 Corinthians.

Insofar as issues of canonicity impinge on the discussion, it is simply that the Synoptic Gospels and Paul happen to be among our earliest sources for historical-Jesus material. The *Gospel of Philip*—and one could name many other apocryphal gospels—is simply not so early or so useful for understanding the historical Jesus as are the Synoptics and Paul. Although Patterson does not make this point explicitly, he broadly agrees with this question of the quality of sources, and with the issues of date and dependence. Historical-Jesus research simply has no option but to work with the best source material. It is why Patterson appeals extensively to Q, even if in this context he attempts to give it some added frisson by labeling it an "apocryphal gospel."[14] It is why he takes seriously the *Gospel of Thomas* in this context—it has a claim to antiquity. Even though I disagree with Patterson

---

13. For Thomas's attitude to the Hebrew Scriptures, see Goodacre, *Thomas and the Gospels*, 187–91.

14. The idea of Q as a noncanonical or "extracanonical" gospel owes a lot to the work of Crossan, e.g. "Q was quite acceptable as long as it was nothing more than a source to be found within the safe intracanonical confines of Matthew and Luke. But now the Q *Gospel* is starting to look a little like a Trojan horse, an extracanonical gospel hidden within two intracanonical gospels" (*Birth of Christianity*, 111).

on the specifics, accepting neither the existence of Q nor the autonomy of *Thomas*,[15] I quite agree with his instinct to work with older, more reliable sources in historical-Jesus research.

In other words, it is important to question the assumption that those who apparently privilege canonical sources always do so because they are canonical. The reason that no one seriously studies the *Protevangelium of James* as a major source for the historical Jesus, the historical Mary or the historical Joseph is that it is clearly dependent on and secondary to the Gospels of Matthew and Luke. Examples of the same thing could be multiplied. In some respects, this is what is so unfortunate about Fitzmyer's and Meier's negative remarks about apocrypha. By framing the issue as a question of canon and orthodoxy, they detract attention from the issues of sources and dates, the issues that really matter—or really should matter—for the historical-Jesus scholar.

To be clear, this is not to say that apocryphal gospels do not matter or that intellectual historians should value them less than their canonical counterparts. The point is that historical-Jesus scholarship simply has no choice but to prejudice the best source material for the quest in which it is engaged. Thus Patterson's paper is in the end informative and imaginative in aiding reflection on the broader and—some might say—more interesting topic of the emergence of the early Christian movement, a topic about which the study of the gospels of *Thomas* and *Philip*, as well as Matthew, Paul, and Acts, have a great deal to say.

I would like to conclude this response by suggesting that one of the difficulties with the topic is its starting point. There is an assumption at work in a lot of scholarship on Christian origins that what truly matters is the historical Jesus. Gospels only have value if we can locate them in the first century, and the traditions they contain have added value if we can somehow link them to the historical Jesus. But it is unnecessary to buy into this way of thinking as a means of defining value. The fact is that we will never come to a definitive statement about the historical Jesus, however much we continue to sift, stare at, and parse every tradition. Apocryphal writings are not interesting or important because of what they can tell us about the historical Jesus, which is in any case negligible, but because of what they tell us about the authors who wrote them, the communities to which they belong, and the people who read them, copied them, and saved them. We do not need the historical Jesus to legitimize our interest in these writings. We do not need to apologize for their failure to tell us about a character who

---

15. My argument for the former is in Goodacre, *Case against Q*; my argument for the latter is in Goodacre, *Thomas and the Gospels*.

is in any case a scholarly enigma. What we need is to celebrate what these writings reveal about what they can tell us about, and so to enrich our study of early Christian writers and the worlds from which they came.

– 12 –

The Distinctive Sayings of Jesus Shared by Justin and the *Pseudo-Clementines*

— F. Stanley Jones —

SINCE 1832, SCHOLARS HAVE been aware of a striking agreement between Justin Martyr and the *Pseudo-Clementines* in several sayings of Jesus at variance with the canonical Gospels.[1] This distinctive correspondence has played a central role in judgments about the origin of the sayings of Jesus in both Justin and the *Pseudo-Clementines*, respectively and collectively.

Historical scholarship of the nineteenth century dealt intensively with the question of the origin of the sayings of Jesus in the *Pseudo-Clementines*. Three positions developed in the debate:

(1) The *Pseudo-Clementines* quote freely from the canonical Gospels and either employ oral tradition or freely create quotations (J. K. Orelli, K. Semisch).

(2) The *Pseudo-Clementines* quote from one or more of the canonical Gospels and from one or more noncanonical gospels (J. Mill, A. Neander, K. A. Credner, A. Hilgenfeld, G. Salmon, H. M. van Nes).

(3) The *Pseudo-Clementines* quote freely from the canonical Gospels and another source that derived from the canonical

---

1. Credner, *Evangelien der Petriner*, 211, 301, 330.

Gospels, such as a harmonized gospel (G. F. Frank, G. Uhlhorn, W. Sanday).[2]

In the twentieth century, source criticism came to the fore. In particular, the concept established itself of a Basic Writing used independently by the creators of the two preserved recensions of the *Pseudo-Clementines*—namely, the *Recognition* and the *Klementia* (often called the *Recognitions* and the *Homilies*).[3] But source criticism did not stop with this insight. It dominated research in the further postulation of a source of the Basic Writing, entitled Kerygmata Petrou ("Preachings of Peter"). Much research of the twentieth century was focused on the reconstruction of this supposed source.

In the twenty-first century, the abandonment of the postulation of a Kerygmata Petrou has become more mainstream; simultaneously, appreciation of the Basic Writer as a creative author has increased. The Basic Writer's concern to refute Marcionism, in particular, has become more evident.[4] Furthermore, it is becoming increasingly apparent that the time is ripe for the investigation of the redactional profiles of the Recognitionist and the Klementinist.

With regard to the sayings of Jesus in the *Pseudo-Clementines*,[5] the distinctive agreements with Justin Martyr have maintained central and

2. For bibliographical and further details for this and the following, see Jones, "Pseudo-Clementines: A History of Research," 63–69 (=Jones, *Pseudoclementina Elchasaiticaque*, 81–86).

3. I am using here what I believe to have been the original titles of these works, though they differ from contemporary convention; for reasoning, discussion, and the history of confusion regarding the titles, see Jones "Photius's Witness." In brief, the currently conventional titles (*Recognitions* and *Homilies*) are, in my progressing judgment, not only incorrect but also so academically and intellectually misleading that they, unfortunately perhaps, need to be abandoned. The study of the *Pseudo-Clementines* is complex enough without having these stumbling-blocks at every turn.

4. Identification of the anti-Marcionite tendency in modern research began with F. C. Baur and was extended variously by scholars such as A. D. Loman, A. Hilgenfeld, H. Waitz, A. Harnack, H. J. Schoeps, and H. J. W. Drijvers. See the history of research and further development in Jones, "Marcionism in the *Pseudo-Clementines*."

5. The various collections of these sayings in past research are reviewed in the indicated section of Jones, "Pseudo-Clementines: A History of Research." For the sake of initial orientation and handy reference, the collection in Waitz, *Pseudoklementinen*, 271–360, can perhaps be recommended because of its generally comprehensive presentation of the texts in Greek and Latin; the Syriac is missing, however, and other studies and collections ultimately must be drawn upon to round out and update Waitz's presentation. Following the suggested procedure of the current study, one should start with the sayings witnessed for the Basic Writing—i.e., those saying that Waitz documents both in Greek (the *Klementia*) and in Latin (the *Recognition*). A fairly recent study and catalogue is Amsler, "Les citations évangéliques."

critical importance. A widespread, though not unchallenged,[6] modern view is that Justin and the *Pseudo-Clementines* used the same harmony of the canonical gospels.[7] The current study examines the central material again (the distinctive agreements between Justin Martyr and the *Pseudo-Clementines*) and tries to apply the achievements of source criticism (particularly the establishment of a Basic Writing) to advance the discussion. This procedure seems promising especially since a preponderance of the distinctive agreements between Justin and the *Pseudo-Clementines* in the sayings of Jesus is found in material witnessed by both the *Recognition* and the *Klementia*—thus, clearly these sayings were present in the Basic Writing. The question accordingly seems to have advanced to the stage of asking about the origin of the agreements in the sayings in Justin and in the Basic Writing, rather than agreements between Justin and the *Klementia*.[8] In any event, the place to start in the evaluation of the sayings of Jesus in the *Pseudo-Clementines* is the Basic Writing—i.e., those sayings found in both the *Recognition* and the *Klementia*.

The advances in historical studies and source criticism with regard to Justin Martyr will also guide this investigation. In particular, attention will be directed to Justin's (now lost) work against Marcion. Justin expressly refers to this previous work in *1 Apol.* 26.8, where he calls it the *Syntagma*; thus, the *Syntagma* was composed before the *Apology* and the *Dialogue with Trypho*.[9] Fragments from this lost work will be cited below.

As an initial example, compare the combination of Luke 6:35b–36 and Matt 5:45 in both *R* and *KlH* as well as in Justin:[10]

6. Strecker, "Evangelienharmonie."

7. The theory that Justin employed a harmony of the gospels was promoted in recent times especially by Bellinzoni, *Sayings of Jesus*; this theory was then applied to explain in further detail the correspondences with the *Pseudo-Clementines* by Kline, *Sayings of Jesus*.

8. The title of Kline's useful work clearly betrays this limitation.

9. For a fairly recent discussion of the *Syntagma*, see, for example, Norelli, "Que pouvons-nous reconstituer du *Syntagma*." At root is a discussion between Harnack and Lipsius that encompassed, e.g., Lipsius, *Zur Quellenkritik des Epiphanios*; Harnack, *Zur Quellenkritik der Geschichte des Gnosticismus*; and Lipsius, *Quellen der ältesten Ketzergeschichte*, and was joined by Hilgenfeld, *Ketzergeschichte des Urchristentums*. The question of whether the *Syntagma* "against all heresies" (mentioned by Justin, *1 Apol.* 26.8) is the same as the *Syntagma* "against Marcion" (mentioned by Irenaeus, *Haer.* 4.6.2) is not of absolutely critical importance for the present study, though the identity of the two seems likely (so also, e.g., Norelli, "Que pouvons-nous reconstituer du *Syntagma*," 168).

10. Translations are my own, unless otherwise indicated. Collection of parallels: Resch, *Aussercanonische Paralleltexte*, 3:85–92; Kline, *Sayings of Jesus*, 42. Minor differences in the Syriac text (pointing and punctuation) from Frankenberg, *Die syrischen*

KlH 3.57	R 5.13.2	Justin, 1 Apol. 15.13	Justin, Dial. 96.3	Luke 6:35b–36	Matt 5:45
Γίνεσθε ἀγαθοὶ καὶ οἰκτίρμονες ὡς ὁ πατὴρ ὁ ἐν τοῖς οὐρανοῖς, ὃς ἀνατέλλει τὸν ἥλιον ἐπ' ἀγαθοῖς καὶ πονηροῖς καὶ φέρει τὸν ὑετὸν ἐπὶ δικαίοις καὶ ἀδίκοις.	Estote boni et misericordes sicut et pater vester caelestis misericors est, qui oriri facit solem suum super bonos et malos et pluit super iustos et iniustos.	Γίνεσθε δὲ χρηστοὶ καὶ οἰκτίρμονες ὡς καὶ ὁ πατὴρ ὑμῶν χρηστός ἐστι καὶ οἰκτίρμων, καὶ τὸν ἥλιον αὐτοῦ ἀνατέλλει ἐπὶ ἁμαρτωλοὺς καὶ δικαίους καὶ πονηρούς.	Γίνεσθε χρηστοὶ καὶ οἰκτίρμονες, ὡς καὶ ὁ πατὴρ ὑμῶν ὁ οὐράνιος. καὶ γὰρ τὸν παντοκράτορα θεὸν χρηστὸν καὶ οἰκτίρμονα ὁρῶμεν, τὸν ἥλιον αὐτοῦ ἀνατέλλοντα ἐπὶ ἀχαρίστους καὶ δικαίους, καὶ βρέχοντα ἐπὶ ὁσίους καὶ πονηρούς.	Ἔσεσθε υἱοὶ ὑψίστου, ὅτι αὐτὸς χρηστός ἐστιν ἐπὶ τοὺς ἀχαρίστους καὶ πονηρούς. Γίνεσθε οἰκτίρμονες καθὼς [καὶ] ὁ πατὴρ ὑμῶν οἰκτίρμων ἐστίν.	ὅπως γένησθε υἱοὶ τοῦ πατρὸς ὑμῶν τοῦ ἐν οὐρανοῖς, ὅτι τὸν ἥλιον αὐτοῦ ἀνατέλλει ἐπὶ πονηροὺς καὶ ἀγαθοὺς καὶ βρέχει ἐπὶ δικαίους καὶ ἀδίκους.
Be good and merciful as the Father who is in the heavens, who raises the sun on the good and evil and brings the rain on the righteous and the unrighteous.	Be good and merciful just as also your heavenly Father is merciful, who makes his sun rise over the good and bad and rains over the just and unjust.	Be good and merciful as also your Father is good and merciful, and he raises his sun over the sinners and righteous and the evil.	Be good and merciful as also your heavenly Father. For we see even the all-powerful God good and merciful, raising his sun over the ungrateful and the righteous and raining on the holy and the evil.	Be sons of the most high because he is good toward the ungrateful and the evil. Be merciful, just as your Father is merciful.	Thus, be sons of your Father in the heavens, because he raises his sun over evil and good and rains on righteous and unrighteous.

One finds here distinctive agreements between the Basic Writing and Justin in their presentation of a combined citation: both have the adjective "merciful," which is witnessed only in Luke, while both also have the "Father in the heavens," the reference to the sun, and the object "righteous," which are witnessed only in Matthew. Are there any hints as to the original context of this combined citation?

Remarkably, Tertullian writes in his refutation of Marcion (*Marc.* 4.17.6):

> *Because*, he continues, *he is kind unto the unthankful and evil.* Well done, Marcion. Cleverly enough you have deprived him of rain and sunshine, that he might not be taken for the Creator.[11]

Tertullian's statement is notable because he, too, mentally connects the statements of Luke 6:35b–36 (kind to the unthankful) with Matt 5:45 (rain and sunshine) and objects to Marcion's dissociation of the two. The original context of the saying in the Pseudo-Clementine Basic Writer is best witnessed at *R* 3.38, which runs parallel to *KlH* 18.1–2. Here, the question is how one-and-the-same can be good and just (a classic Marcionite question),[12] and both versions respond with "giving the sun to the good and the bad and the rain to the righteous and unjust" (*KlH* 18.2.2) // "it is of the good one to give his sun and rain equally to the just and unjust" (*R* 3.38.2). In other words, the context of this combined citation in both Tertullian and the Pseudo-Clementine Basic Writer is an anti-Marcionite discussion. This coincidence raises the question of whether this setting might also lie in the background of the combined citation in Justin. While there is no such indication in the context of *1 Apology* and the *Dialogue*, nevertheless it may be asked if this citation was in Justin's prior work against Marcion, the *Syntagma*, particularly because a branch of scholarship believes Tertullian employed this work by Justin in his own *Adversus Marcionem*[13] and because a branch of scholar-

---

Clementinen, derive from my own reading of the manuscripts for my projected new edition of the Syriac *Pseudo-Clementines* in the Corpus Christianorum Series Apocryphorum. The English translation of the preliminary edition has been published as Jones, Syriac *"Pseudo-Clementines."*

11. Translation by Evans, *Tertullian: Adversus Marcionem*, 349.

12. See, e.g., Harnack, *Marcion*, 111–13 (76–77 in the English translation), for discussion, texts, and nuances.

13. Harnack, *Zur Quellenkritik der Geschichte des Gnosticismus*, 66. This was doubted by Lipsius, *Quellen der ältesten Ketzergeschichte*, 70–71. Quispel, *De bronnen van Tertullianus' Adversus Marcionem*, 30–31, rejected the theory for book one of *Adversus Marcionem* and then argued (pp. 56–59) that Tertullian used Justin's *Dialogue* in book three of *Adversus Marcionem*. More recently, Norelli, "Que pouvons-nous reconstituer du *Syntagma*," 180, proposes use of Justin's *Syntagma* by Tertullian in his

ship on the *Pseudo-Clementines* has suggested all along that Justin's treatise was used in the *Pseudo-Clementines*.[14] The evidence seems all reconcilable with the view that Justin used or first formulated this combined saying in his treatise against Marcion (and repeated it in 1 *Apology*) and that it was picked up from there by the Basic Writer and similarly known from Justin by Tertullian.[15]

A similar instance is found in *KlH* 18.4.2 // *R* 2.47.3:

		2		
KlH 18.4.2 = 17.4.3	*R* 2.47.3 Latin	*R* 2.47.3 Syriac	Justin, 1 *Apol*. 63.3	Matt 11:27
Οὐδεὶς ἔγνω τὸν πατέρα εἰ μὴ ὁ υἱός, ὡς οὐδὲ τὸν υἱόν τις οἶδεν εἰ μὴ ὁ πατὴρ καὶ οἷς ἂν βούληται ὁ υἱὸς ἀποκαλύψαι.	Nemo novit filium nisi pater, neque patrem quis novit nisi filius et cui voluerit filius revelare.	ܐܠܐ ܐܒܐ ܠܐ ܐܢܫ ܝܕܥ ܠܒܪܐ. ܘܠܒܪܐ ܐܦ ܠܐ ܐܢܫ ܝܕܥ ܐܠܐ ܐܒܐ. ܘܠܐܝܠܝܢ ܕܨܒܐ ܐܠܗܐ ܕܢܓܠܐ.	Οὐδεὶς ἔγνω τὸν πατέρα εἰ μὴ ὁ υἱός, οὐδὲ τὸν υἱὸν εἰ μὴ ὁ πατὴρ καὶ οἷς ἂν ἀποκαλύψῃ ὁ υἱός.	Οὐδεὶς ἐπιγινώσκει τὸν υἱὸν εἰ μὴ ὁ πατήρ, οὐδὲ τὸν πατέρα τις ἐπιγινώσκει εἰ μὴ ὁ υἱὸς καὶ ᾧ ἐὰν βούληται ὁ υἱὸς ἀποκαλύψαι.
No one knew the Father except the Son, and no one knows the Son but the Father and those to whom the Son wishes to reveal.	No one knew the Son except the Father and no one knew the Father except the Son and to whom the Son should wish to reveal.	No one knew the Father except the Son, and neither does anyone know the Son except the Father and those to whom God wishes to reveal.	No one knew the Father except the Son, and not the Son except the Father and those to whom the Son reveals.	No one knows the Son except the Father, and no one knows the Father except the Son and whoever to whom the Son should wish to reveal.

Distinctive here (in the Basic Writing and Justin) against Matt 11:27 are not just the reverse order of the Son and the Father (altered back by Rufinus in his Latin translation) but also the past tense of the first verb.[16] Irenaeus,

---

Adversus Marcionem.

14. Documentation and more on this, below.

15. Epiphanius, *Pan*. 33.10.5 and 66.22.4, uses a similar form of the saying against the anti-cosmic Ptolemaeans and Manichaeans and doubtless drew this saying from the heresiologists he had read. The suggestion that Epiphanius drew this saying directly from "a harmony in wide circulation in the early church" (Bellinzoni, *Sayings of Jesus*, 13) is far-fetched. The scattered witnesses to this saying more correctly led G. Strecker to speak "von einer unkanonischen, gegenüber der synoptischen Tradition selbständigen Tendenz" ("Evangelienharmonie," 313). The exact history of this "tendency" cannot currently be traced in all instances.

16. Luke 10:22 is not of direct relevance here: οὐδεὶς γινώσκει τίς ἐστιν ὁ υἱὸς εἰ μὴ ὁ πατήρ, καὶ τίς ἐστιν ὁ πατὴρ εἰ μὴ ὁ υἱὸς καὶ ᾧ ἐὰν βούληται ὁ υἱὸς ἀποκαλύψαι. The most extensive collection of parallels is evidently Winter, "Matthew xi 27," esp. 112–27; see also Resch, *Aussercanonische Paralleltexte*, 3:200–205.

Haer. 4.6.1, knows that "those who would be wiser than the Apostles" write the statement in precisely this form. The reverse order is known also to Tertullian, *Marc.* 4.25.10, and the reverse order plus the past tense in the initial verb is found on the lips of a Marcionite in Adamantius, *Dialogue on the Orthodox Faith* 1.23: οὐδεὶς ἔγνω τὸν πατέρα εἰ μὴ ὁ υἱός, οὐδὲ τὸν υἱόν τις γινώσκει εἰ μὴ ὁ πατήρ. It seems that this was the form of the saying in Marcion's gospel. Alongside the Marcionite character in Adamantius's *Dialogue*, Tertullian provides some indication as to how the Marcionites interpreted this special form of the saying: "And so Christ proclaimed an unknown god" (*Marc.* 4.25.10).[17]

It is remarkable that Justin would cite this form of the saying in *1 Apology*, but it seems to be yet another indication that Justin relied on his earlier work for sayings of Jesus,[18] though some scholars have suggested that Justin used a harmony of the gospel sayings.

The view that the *Pseudo-Clementines* are dependent on Justin's treatise against Marcion is indeed known and was initially promoted, not least on the basis of this last saying of Jesus and its similar context in Irenaeus and the *Pseudo-Clementines*, by J. Quarry in 1890.[19] Hans Waitz presented a more extensive argument in 1904.[20] While Quarry spoke of the "Clementine Homilies," Waitz assigned usage of Justin to his supposed anti-Marcionite redaction of the Kerygmata Petrou. W. Bousset commented briefly that the dependency on Justin is instead on the part of the Basic Writer,[21] and later B. Rehm affirmed categorically and without further elaboration that "Justin ist jedenfalls vorausgesetzt" by the Basic Writer.[22] G. Strecker only briefly cast doubt on Waitz's case for dependency on Justin and urged instead that the Basic Writer used another unspecified anti-Marcionite source.[23] Ascription of the anti-Marcionite polemic to the Basic Writer was promoted more recently by H. J. W. Drijvers, who saw further expression of it in the Basic Writer's usage of Bardaisan, another critic of Marcionism.[24]

---

17. Evidence that Tertullian got this form of the saying here from a Marcionite or anti-Marcionite context is found in *Praescr.* 21.2, where he cites the saying in its canonical order.

18. Skarsaune, *Proof from Prophecy*, 212, agrees that *1 Apol.* 63 is likely to have been excerpted from the *Syntagma*.

19. Quarry, "Notes," 248–49.

20. Waitz, *Pseudoklementinen*, 163–67.

21. Bousset, Review of Waitz, *Pseudoklementinen*, 439.

22. Rehm, "Zur Entstehung der pseudoclementinischen Schriften," 157.

23. Strecker, *Judenchristentum*, 131 n. 1, 168–69, 255.

24. Drijvers, "Adam and the True Prophet," 318–23. For more history of research into anti-Marcionism in the *Pseudo-Clementines*, see my "Marcionism in the

The drift of research is thus clearly toward an acknowledgment of the Basic Writer's anti-Marcionite stance. The most striking instance of agreement between Justin's anti-Marcionite tractate and the *Pseudo-Clementines* is found in the only preserved certain citation from Justin's treatise (in Irenaeus, with the Greek excerpted by Eusebius):

Irenaeus, *Haer.* 4.6.2 (Eusebius, *Hist. eccl.* 4.18.9)	*R* 2.45.5 Syriac	*R* 2.45.5 Latin	*KlH* 16.15.1
Καὶ καλῶς ὁ Ἰουστῖνος ἐν τῷ πρὸς Μαρκίωνα συντάγματί φησιν ὅτι αὐτῷ τῷ Κυρίῳ οὐκ ἂν ἐπείσθην ἄλλον Θεὸν καταγγέλλοντι παρὰ τὸν Δημιουργόν.	ܘܐܦ ܠܐ ܐܠܘ ܒܫܪܪܐ ܢܒܝܐ ܕܐܠܗܐ ܐܬܚܙܝ ܘܐܬܘܬܐ ܘܬܕܡܪܬܐ ܝܗܒ ܡܛܠ ܕܢܗܝܡܢ ܘܐܡܪ ܠܢ ܕܢܦܠܘܚ. ܠܐܠܗܐ ܐܚܪܢܐ ܠܒܪ ܡܢ ܗܘ ܐܠܗܐ ܕܝܗܘܕܝܐ. ܘܐܦܠܐ ܠܗ ܠܗܘ ܡܗܝܡܢܝܢ ܗܘܝܢ.	etiamsi verus aliquis surgeret propheta, qui signa et prodigia faceret, suadere autem vellet, ut coleremus deos alios praeter Iudaeorum deum, numquam ei credere possemus.	Ἐπειδὴ καὶ τῷ τὰ σημεῖα καὶ τέρατα διδόντι προφήτῃ, ἄλλον δὲ θεὸν λέγοντι φῂς μὴ δεῖν πιστεύειν . . .
And Justin states well in the Syntagma against Marcion: "I would not believe even the Lord himself should he proclaim a god other than the Creator."	Not even if truly a prophet of God appeared and gave signs and wonders in order that we might believe, but said to us that we should worship gods other than the God of the Jews, will we believe him.	Even if a true prophet should arise who should make signs and wonders, but should wish to persuade us to worship gods other than the God of the Jews, we would never be able to believe him.	Since you say that one should not believe even the prophet who gives signs and wonders but says there is another god . . .

Irenaeus preferred to cite Justin here probably because he did not want to make this somewhat irreverent statement himself (about not believing the Lord). The Pseudo-Clementine Basic Writer could take over the thought only by toning it down with a reference to Deut 13:1–2; nevertheless, the *Recognition* seems to have preserved the essential element of radicality (found in Justin) when it applies the notion to a "true prophet": according to *R* 1.16.5–6 // *KlH* 1.19.5–6, once it is determined that someone is a true prophet, one should believe him in whatever henceforth he says.

Strecker's brief comments against Waitz's case for dependency on Justin in this passage fail to address the evidence (he does not even mention or list the parallel passages from the *Pseudo-Clementines* given by Waitz and printed above).[25] Waitz noted further that, in both Irenaeus and the *Pseu-*

Pseudo-Clementines," 152–55.

25. Strecker, *Judenchristentum*, 133 n. 1, lists only other Pseudo-Clementine

do-Clementines, the citation and discussion of the distinctive saying of Jesus that corresponds roughly to Matt 11:27 (just documented and discussed above as no. 2) occurs in the immediate context (*Haer.* 4.6.1, 3; *R* 2.47.3). Thus, not only does Justin's remarkable assertion agree with the *Pseudo-Clementines*, but the context also agrees, including a distinctive form of a saying of Jesus.

The one saying that even Strecker[26] acknowledged to be in exceptionally strong agreement with Justin is *KlH* 19.2.5:[27]

3			
KlH 19.2.5	Justin, *Dial.* 76.5	Matt 25:30	Matt 25:41
Ὑπάγετε εἰς τὸ σκότος τὸ ἐξώτερον, ὃ ἡτοίμασεν ὁ πατὴρ τῷ διαβόλῳ καὶ τοῖς ἀγγέλοις αὐτοῦ.	Ὑπάγετε εἰς τὸ σκότος τὸ ἐξώτερον, ὃ ἡτοίμασεν ὁ πατὴρ τῷ σατανᾷ καὶ τοῖς ἀγγέλοις αὐτοῦ.	καὶ τὸν ἀχρεῖον δοῦλον ἐκβάλετε εἰς τὸ σκότος τὸ ἐξώτερον.	Πορεύεσθε ἀπ' ἐμοῦ [οἱ] κατηραμένοι εἰς τὸ πῦρ τὸ αἰώνιον τὸ ἡτοιμασμένον τῷ διαβόλῳ καὶ τοῖς ἀγγέλοις αὐτοῦ.
Go to the outer darkness that the Father prepared for the devil and his angels.	Go to the outer darkness that the Father prepared for Satan and his angels.	And cast the useless slave into the outer darkness.	Go away from me, condemned ones, into the eternal fire prepared for the devil and his angels.

This saying appears verbatim in the *Pseudo-Clementines* and Justin[28] (with the exception of "the devil" instead of "Satan")[29] and appears to be a conflation of the two Matthean passages. Since the context in the *Pseudo-Clementines* is the question of the origin of evil and since this is known to

---

passages, which are not mentioned by Waitz and which have essentially nothing to do with the fragment from Justin, and correctly concludes that *this* evidence is weak. The uniqueness of the correspondence seems to be verified by Irenaeus, who cites the passage from Justin apparently because he himself would not dare to take over this assertion in his own name.

26. Strecker, "Evangelienharmonie," 313–14.

27. For parallels, see Resch, *Aussercanonische Paralleltexte*, 2:313–16.

28. "Go to the outer darkness" is witnessed *only* in Justin and the *Pseudo-Clementines*.

29. This difference does not necessarily indicate that the *Pseudo-Clementines* cannot be dependent on Justin, contra Kline, *Sayings of Jesus*, 15, and Bellinzoni, *Sayings of Jesus*, 116, along with Strecker, "Evangelienharmonie," 314. The insertion of "devil" instead of "Satan" may be attributed not just to a tendency to conform more with the text of Matthew but especially also to the tendency of the *Pseudo-Clementines* to avoid the word "Satan," as can now be determined with the concordance (the word is found only once [*KlH* 19.2.3 in a citation of Matt 12:26 and apparently is to be attributed to the author of the *Klementia*]; the word is avoided in references where the gospels have "Satan," e.g., in the reception of the temptations at *R* 4.34 // *KlH* 8.21; 11.35.3).

have been a central issue in Marcionite thought (see, e.g., Tertullian, *Marc.* 1.2.2), it must be considered a distinct possibility that Justin used this saying of Jesus in his case against Marcion. Something of the original argument seems likely to have been preserved in Irenaeus, *Haer.* 2.23.3, which insists that the place of condemnation originally was not intended for humans but for the devil and his angels. Likely connected with this context is another citation from Justin in Irenaeus, *Haer.* 5.26.3 (Greek preserved via the catena and partially in Eusebius, *Hist. eccl.* 4.18.9):

> πρὸ μὲν τῆς τοῦ Κυρίου παρουσίας οὐδέποτε ἐτόλμησεν ὁ Σατανᾶς βλασφημῆσαι τὸν Θεόν, ἅτε μηδέπω εἰδὼς τὴν ἑαυτοῦ κατάκρισιν, διὰ τὸ ἐν παραβολαῖς καὶ ἀλληγορίαις κεῖσθαι, μετὰ δὲ τὴν παρουσίαν τοῦ Κυρίου ἐκ τῶν λόγων αὐτοῦ καὶ τῶν ἀποστόλων μαθὼν ἀναφανδὸν ὅτι πῦρ αἰώνιον αὐτῷ ἡτοίμασται κατ' ἰδίαν γνώμην ἀποστάντι τοῦ Θεοῦ καὶ πᾶσι τοῖς ἀμετανοήτως παραμείνασιν ἐν τῇ ἀποστασίᾳ, διὰ τῶν τοιούτων ἀνθρώπων βλασφημεῖ τὸν τὴν κρίσιν ἐπάγοντα Κύριον, ὡς ἤδη κατακεκριμένος, καὶ τὴν ἁμαρτίαν τῆς ἰδίας ἀποστασίας τῷ ἐκτικότι αὐτὸν ἀποκαλεῖ, ἀλλ' οὐ τῇ ἰδίᾳ αὐθαιρέτῳ γνώμῃ, ὡς καὶ οἱ παραβαίνοντες τοὺς νόμους, ἔπειτα δίκας διδόντες, αἰτιῶνται τοὺς νομοθέτας, ἀλλ' οὐχ ἑαυτούς. (ed. Rousseau, et al.)

> Before the coming of the Lord, Satan never dared to blaspheme God, since he did not yet know of his condemnation, because it was indicated in parables and allegories. But after the coming of the Lord, once he has learned clearly from the sayings of him and of the apostles that eternal fire had been prepared for him, who of his own decision abandoned God, and for all those who remained unrepentant in the rebellion, he blasphemes through such people the Lord who is bringing judgment, as already condemned, and he attributes the sin of his own apostasy to the one who made him, not to his own independent decision, just as also those who break laws, when they are brought to trial, blame the lawgivers but not themselves.

Along similar lines is the following distinctive saying of Justin and the Pseudo-Clementine Basic Writer:[30]

---

30. See the display of the parallels in Kline, *Sayings of Jesus*, 27–28, which, however, omits the Syriac of *R* 3.4.6. Kline also fails to note a number of other parallels found elsewhere; see, e.g., Resch, *Aussercanonische Paralleltexte*, 3:298–301.

Justin, 1 Apol. 19.7	KlH 17.5.2	R 3.4.6 Syriac	R 3.4.6 Latin	Matt 10:28	Luke 12:4–5
Μὴ φοβεῖσθε τοὺς ἀναιροῦντας ὑμᾶς καὶ μετὰ ταῦτα μὴ δυναμένους τι ποιῆσαι, φοβήθητε δὲ τὸν μετὰ τὸ ἀποθανεῖν δυνάμενον καὶ ψυχὴν καὶ σῶμα εἰς γέενναν ἐμβαλεῖν.	Μὴ φοβηθῆτε ἀπὸ τοῦ ἀποκτέννοντος τὸ σῶμα, τῇ δὲ ψυχῇ μὴ δυναμένου τι ποιῆσαι. φοβήθητε δὲ τὸν δυνάμενον καὶ σῶμα καὶ ψυχὴν εἰς τὴν γέενναν τοῦ πυρὸς βαλεῖν.	ܡܢ ܐܝܠܝܢ ܕܩܛܠܝܢ ܦܓܪܐ ܘܢܦܫܐ ܠܐ ܡܫܟܚܝܢ ܠܡܩܛܠ ܐܠܐ ܕܚܠܘ ܡܢ ܗܘ ܕܡܫܟܚ ܕܐܦ ܦܓܪܐ ܘܐܦ ܢܦܫܐ ܢܘܒܕ ܒܓܗܢܐ	Nolite timere eos qui occidunt corpus, animam autem non possunt occidere; timete autem eum qui potest et corpus et animam perdere in gehennam.	μὴ φοβεῖσθε ἀπὸ τῶν ἀποκτεννόντων τὸ σῶμα, τὴν δὲ ψυχὴν μὴ δυναμένων ἀποκτεῖναι· φοβεῖσθε δὲ μᾶλλον τὸν δυνάμενον καὶ ψυχὴν καὶ σῶμα ἀπολέσαι ἐν γεέννῃ.	μὴ φοβηθῆτε ἀπὸ τῶν ἀποκτεινόντων τὸ σῶμα καὶ μετὰ ταῦτα μὴ ἐχόντων περισσότερόν τι ποιῆσαι. ὑποδείξω δὲ ὑμῖν τίνα φοβηθῆτε· φοβήθητε τὸν μετὰ τὸ ἀποκτεῖναι ἔχοντα ἐξουσίαν ἐμβαλεῖν εἰς τὴν γέενναν.
Do not fear those who kill you but are not able to do anything after that. Fear the one who after death is able to cast both the soul and the body into gehenna.	Do not fear the one who kills the body but is not able to do anything to the soul. Fear the one who is able to cast the body and the soul into the gehenna of fire.	Do not fear those who kill the body and are not able to kill the soul. But fear the one who is able to destroy both the body and the soul in gehenna.	Do not fear those who kill the body but are not able to kill the soul; but fear the one who is able to make away with both the body and the soul into gehenna.	Do not fear those who kill the body but are unable to kill the soul. Fear rather the one who is able to destroy both the soul and the body in gehenna.	Do not fear those who kill the body and after that are not able to do anything further. I will show you who you should fear: Fear the one who has the authority, after the killing, to cast into gehenna.

What distinctively connects Justin and the Basic Writing is the mention of both the soul (found only in Matthew) and the notion of *casting* into gehenna (found only in Luke).

For Marcion, this verse means that one should fear only the lower god and his devil; the higher god should never be a cause of fear.[31] The anti-Marcionite argument is that this verse proves that God is indeed to be feared and that he is the one who will condemn. This anti-Marcionite interpretation is visibly preserved in *KlH* 17.4–5 (the context of the saying), where it is argued (by Simon in standard Marcionite style) that a just and avenging God cannot be good.[32]

A saying of Jesus that occurs several times in the *Klementia*, though not in the *Recognition*, is:

5				
KlH 18.3.4	Matt 19:17	Luke 18:19	Mark 10:18	Justin, *Dial.* 101.2
Μή με λέγε ἀγαθόν· ὁ γὰρ ἀγαθὸς εἷς ἐστιν, ὁ πατὴρ ὁ ἐν τοῖς οὐρανοῖς.	Τί με ἐρωτᾷς περὶ τοῦ ἀγαθοῦ; εἷς ἐστιν ὁ ἀγαθός.	Τί με λέγεις ἀγαθόν; οὐδεὶς ἀγαθός εἰ μὴ εἷς ὁ θεός.	Τί με λέγεις ἀγαθόν; οὐδεὶς ἀγαθός εἰ μὴ εἷς ὁ θεός.	Τί με λέγεις ἀγαθόν; εἷς ἐστιν ἀγαθός, ὁ πατήρ μου ὁ ἐν τοῖς οὐρανοῖς.
Do not call me good, for one is good, the Father in the heavens.	Why do you ask me about the good. The good is one.	Why do you call me good? No one is good except one, God.	Why do you call me good? No one is good except one, God.	Why do you call me good? One is good, my Father in the heavens.

This distinctive form of Jesus' saying (in the *Klementia* and Justin) combines Luke's element of Jesus objecting to being called good with Matthew's simple assertion that one is good. This same combination is

---

31. Cf., e.g., Tertullian, *Marc.* 4.8.7: Marcion deum suum timeri negat ("Marcion denies that his god is to be feared").

32. 2 *Clem.* 5.4 (καὶ ὑμεῖς μὴ φοβεῖσθε τοὺς ἀποκτέννοντας ὑμᾶς καὶ μηδὲν ὑμῖν δυναμένους ποιεῖν, ἀλλὰ φοβεῖσθε τὸν μετὰ τὸ ἀποθανεῖν ὑμᾶς ἔχοντα ἐξουσίαν ψυχῆς καὶ σώματος τοῦ βαλεῖν εἰς γέενναν πυρός [ed. Bihlmeyer]) agrees with the reading of *KlH* 17.5.2 ("into the gehenna of fire") against Justin. This expression "gehenna of fire" is witnessed elsewhere in the gospel tradition (Matt 5:22; 18:9) and the words "of fire" are a popular addition to the saying currently under consideration (see the Latin [Cyprian, Augustine] and Syriac witnesses listed in Vööbus, "Oldest Extant Traces," esp. 201). This agreement thus cannot be used to argue the case that the *Pseudo-Clementines* are dependent not on Justin but on a source shared with 2 *Clement*. A new addition to the discussion is P.Oxy. 4009, but its attribution to the *Gospel of Peter* by Lührmann, *Die apokryph gewordenen Evangelien*, 73–86, is uncertain and thus its potential to clarify the history of this saying is quite limited. Justin and 2 *Clement* distinctively share the phrase "after death," a type of paraphrase also found in Theodotus (Clement of Alexandria, *Exc.* 14.3).

witnessed for Marcion (Hippolytus, *Haer.* 7.31.6: Τί με λέγετε ἀγαθόν; εἷς ἐστιν ἀγαθός; Epiphanius, *Pan.* 42.11.17, Scholion 50: Μή με λέγε ἀγαθόν· εἷς ἐστιν ἀγαθός ὁ θεός). Epiphanius also comments explicitly on the Marcionite "addition" of "Father," which is found in neither Matthew nor Luke, though in both Justin and the *Klementia*. This combination is witnessed for Marcosians by Irenaeus (*Haer.* 1.20.2) and Epiphanius (*Pan.* 34.18.10–11) and for the Naasenes by Hippolytus (*Haer.* 5.7.26). Even if the saying was known elsewhere, its occurrence in Justin and the *Klementia* is readily explainable on the theory that the *Pseudo-Clementines* acquired it from Justin. The Marcionite interpretation of the passage is clear in *KlH* 18.1.3, where Simon introduces the saying with the words, "Jesus preached a different one [sc. god] when he said . . ." This is the same interpretation—not an evident one—that Irenaeus attributes to the Marcosians. The Marcionite context of the saying in the *Klementia* is again evidenced in another occurrence of the saying in *KlH* 17.4.2–3:

> For when he says to someone, as I learn, "Do not call me good, for the good one is one," he no longer calls good that righteous one whom the scriptures preach, who kills and makes alive: while he kills the sinners, he makes alive those who live according to his opinion. For truly he did not call the creator good, which is apparent to one who is able to understand.

It is quite possible that the *Klementia* here has preserved the essence of an argument in Justin's *Syntagma*.

The instances of stronger agreement between Justin and the *Pseudo-Clementines* in sayings of Jesus have now been reviewed, and all display a Marcionite or anti-Marcionite profile. In my judgment, the conclusion seems to lie at hand that the Pseudo-Clementine Basic Writer used Justin's lost tractate against Marcion, all the more since the one certain surviving fragment of Justin's *Syntagma* also finds a parallel in the Basic Writing. This is the solution to the old riddle posed by the agreements. No decision has yet been made about where Justin got these sayings of Jesus. While he might or seems to have taken over some from Marcion (nos. 2, 5), such adoption does not seem to be the case for all of the sayings (some are anti-Marcionite: nos. 1, 3, and perhaps 4). Justin may have used a harmony, but the apparent anti-Marcionite slant of several of the sayings would seem to make this unlikely—possibly he created (or adopted from Marcion) the harmonistic sayings on a case-by-case basis in his argument against Marcion. The result of this study to this point is that the *Pseudo-Clementines* can lend no independent support for Justin's use of a pre-existing harmony. This conclusion is significant because the correspondences with the *Pseudo-Clementines* have, in recent research, been a main support for the postulation of a harmony used by Justin.³³ In the preserved *Apologies* and *Dialogue*, Justin seems to have cited the sayings in largely the same form as he presented them in the *Syntagma*; perhaps he just used his previous tractate (or notes made for this tractate) as a reference for his new works.

This result would seem to be also the best explanation for less striking instances of agreement between Justin and the *Pseudo-Clementines* in sayings of Jesus. For example, the saying in *KlH* 17.7.1 has a correspondence with Justin, *1 Apol.* 16.6, in the definition of the greatest commandment:

6		
KlH 17.7.1	Justin, *1 Apol.* 16.6	Matt 22:37–38
ἀφ' ὧν ἐντολῶν αὕτη πρώτη καὶ μεγάλη τυγχάνει, τὸ φοβηθῆναι κύριον τὸν θεὸν καὶ αὐτῷ μόνῳ λατρεύειν.	Μεγίστη ἐντολή ἐστι· Κύριον τὸν θεόν σου προσκυνήσεις καὶ αὐτῷ μόνῳ λατρεύσεις ἐξ ὅλης τῆς καρδίας σου καὶ ἐξ ὅλης τῆς ἰσχύος σου, κύριον τὸν θεὸν τὸν ποιήσαντά σε.	ἀγαπήσεις κύριον τὸν θεόν σου ἐν ὅλῃ τῇ καρδίᾳ σου καὶ ἐν ὅλῃ τῇ ψυχῇ σου καὶ ἐν ὅλῃ τῇ διανοίᾳ σου· αὕτη ἐστὶν ἡ μεγάλη καὶ πρώτη ἐντολή.
Of these commandments, the first and greatest is to fear the Lord God and to serve him alone.	The greatest commandment is: You shall worship the Lord God and serve him alone from all your heart and from all your strength, the Lord God who made you.	You shall love the Lord your God in all your heart and in all your soul and in all your mind. This is the greatest and first commandment.

The distinctive points of agreement between Justin and the *Pseudo-Clementines* against Matthew are the preliminary position given to the words "(first and) greatest commandment" and also the substitution of "fear/worship" of God and "serving" God for the Matthean "love" of God. The anti-Marcionite slant of the saying in the *Pseudo-Clementines* is apparent in the use of the verb "fear" with respect to God. Tertullian, too, used this expression to argue against the Marcionite understanding of God (*Marc.* 2.13.5). It is at least possible that Justin used this saying (with the verb "fear") in his *Syntagma*.³⁴

---

33. See Kline, *Sayings of Jesus*, 198, Bellinzoni, *Sayings of Jesus*, 12–13, 140–42.

34. *KlH* 15.5.5 with Justin, *1 Apol.* 16.1–2, may present a similar instance; see the data on Marcion's gospel (and Marcionite usage) in Harnack, *Marcion*, 193*, who concludes that the evidence would indicate that Marcion followed a text already mixed with elements from both Luke and Matthew. See also important parallels from Clement of Alexandria in Resch, *Aussercanonische Paralleltexte*, 3:75–77. A further similar case may lie behind *KlH* 8.4.1 // R 4.4.3 with Justin, *Dial.* 76.4; 120.6.

214　Forbidden Texts on the Western Frontier

Given the result achieved above, it may be asked also if it is possible to move beyond the sayings preserved in Justin's *Dialogue* and *Apologies* to postulate that certain other sayings in the *Pseudo-Clementines* likely derive from Justin's *Syntagma*. One instance is *KlH* 18.15.1, which has a close parallel in Tertullian, where Marcion is quoted:

7				
KlH 18.15.1 (Simon)	Tertullian, *Marc.* 4.25.1	Epiphanius, *Pan.* 42.11.6, Scholion 22 (Marcion)	Luke 10:21	Matt 11:25
ἐξομολογοῦμαί σοι, κύριε τοῦ οὐρανοῦ καὶ τῆς γῆς, ὅτι, ἅπερ ἦν κρυπτὰ σοφοῖς, ἀπεκάλυψας αὐτὰ νηπίοις θηλάζουσιν.	gratias enim, inquit, ago, et confiteor, domine caeli, quod ea quae erant abscondita sapientibus et prudentibus, revelaveris parvulis.	"εὐχαριστῶ σοι, κύριε τοῦ οὐρανοῦ." οὐκ εἶχεν δὲ "καὶ τῆς γῆς", οὔτε "πάτερ" εἶχεν.	ἐξομολογοῦμαί σοι, πάτερ, κύριε τοῦ οὐρανοῦ καὶ τῆς γῆς, ὅτι ἀπέκρυψας ταῦτα ἀπὸ σοφῶν καὶ συνετῶν καὶ ἀπεκάλυψας αὐτὰ νηπίοις.	ἐξομολογοῦμαί σοι, πάτερ, κύριε τοῦ οὐρανοῦ καὶ τῆς γῆς, ὅτι ἔκρυψας ταῦτα ἀπὸ σοφῶν καὶ συνετῶν καὶ ἀπεκάλυψας αὐτὰ νηπίοις.
I praise you, Lord of heaven and of earth, because the things that were hidden from the wise you have revealed to suckling babes.	For he says, "I thank and praise, Lord of heaven, because the things that were hidden from the wise and prudent, you have revealed to babes."	"I give thanks to you, Lord of heaven." He did not have "and of earth" nor did he have "Father."	I praise you, Father, Lord of heaven and earth, because you have hidden these things from the wise and intelligent and have revealed them to babes.	I praise you, Father, Lord of heaven and earth, because you have hidden these things from the wise and intelligent and have revealed them to babes.

The Marcionite interpretation of this passage as pointing to their Unknown God is found in the discussion at *KlH* 18.14–15 and is apparent also in Tertullian's exposition. It must be considered possible that both the Basic Writer and Tertullian drew this saying from Justin. The Basic Writer was particularly bothered by the Marcionite interpretation of this saying and seems to have developed his own further refutation on the basis of the following saying of Jesus:[35]

35. Further Pseudo-Clementine parallels are *R* 1.54.7 (Syriac: "the key to the kingdom of heaven, which they received from Moses in order to hide it"; Latin: "the key to the kingdom of heaven, they hid it from the ears of the people"), *R* 2.46.3 (Syriac: "the scribes received from the tradition of Moses and hid as the key that fits the house of the kingdom"; Latin: "the scribes and Pharisees, having received the key of knowledge, had not shut in but shut out"), *KlH* 18.15.7 ("with whom the key of the kingdom of heaven

8				
R 2.30.1 Latin	R 2.30.1 Syriac	Justin, *Dial.* 17.4	Matt 23:13	Luke 11:52
Similiter quoque etiam erga scribas et Pharisaeos ultimo doctrinae suae tempore gerit, arguens . . . quod clavem scientiae quam a Moyse traditam susceperant, occultarent, per quam posset ianua regni caelestis aperiri.	ܐܟܣܢܐ ܘܐܟܣܢܐ . . . ܣܦܖ̈ܐ ܠܐ ܗܘܐ ܠܟܠܗܘܢ ܕܠܐ ܗܘ ܕܠܗܘܢ ܡܢ ܡܘܫܐ ܐܬܝܗܒܬ ܘܐܢ ܠܗܘܢ ܛܫܝܘܗܝ ܐܝܟ ܕܠܐܪܟܘܢܬܐ ܕܒܝܬ ܡܠܟܘܬܐ.	Οὐαὶ ὑμῖν, γραμματεῖς, ὅτι τὰς κλεῖς ἔχετε, καὶ αὐτοὶ οὐκ εἰσέρχεσθε καὶ τοὺς εἰσερχομένους κωλύετε·	Οὐαὶ δὲ ὑμῖν, γραμματεῖς καὶ Φαρισαῖοι ὑποκριταί, ὅτι κλείετε τὴν βασιλείαν τῶν οὐρανῶν ἔμπροσθεν τῶν ἀνθρώπων· ὑμεῖς γὰρ οὐκ εἰσέρχεσθε οὐδὲ τοὺς εἰσερχομένους ἀφίετε εἰσελθεῖν.	Οὐαὶ ὑμῖν τοῖς νομικοῖς, ὅτι ἤρατε ["Western": ἐκρύψατε] τὴν κλεῖδα τῆς γνώσεως· αὐτοὶ οὐκ εἰσήλθατε καὶ τοὺς εἰσερχομένους ἐκωλύσατε.
Similarly, then, during the last time of his teaching, he charged the scribes and the Pharisees as he argued that they had hidden the key of knowledge that they had received, passed down from Moses, by which the gate of the heavenly kingdom might be opened.	He reproved both the scribes and the Pharisees, . . . though in truth it was not all of them but rather the ones by whom the teaching from Moses was received and who hid it like the key that is fitting for the royal palace.	Woe to you, scribes, because you have the keys and you yourselves do not enter and you hinder those who enter.	Woe to you, scribes and Pharisees, hypocrites, because you lock the kingdom of heaven before humans. For you do not enter nor do you allow those entering to enter.	Woe to you lawyers because you took ["Western": hid] the key of knowledge. Your yourself did not enter and you hindered those entering.

Even though Tertullian also discusses this saying (*Marc.* 4.27–28), there is not enough evidence (such as distinctive agreements with Justin's form of the saying) to make the conclusion probable that this saying was used in an anti-Marcionite manner in Justin's *Syntagma*. In fact, it seems to

was laid, that is, knowledge of the secrets"), *KlH* 18.16.2 ("since they hid the knowledge of the kingdom and neither themselves entered nor allowed those who wished to enter"), *KlH* 3.18.3 ("them he said [to hear], as they were entrusted with the key of the kingdom, which is knowledge . . . They hold the key but they do not allow those who wish to enter"). Further parallels in Resch, *Ausscanonische Paralleltexte*, 3:290, and Strecker, *Judenchristentum*, 126. See also *Gos. Thom.* 39 with the study and additional parallels in van Amersfoort, "Evangelie van Thomas," 171–79.

be unlikely since Justin did not count the Pharisees among the legitimate Jews (*Dial.* 80.4). Instead, this saying of Jesus seems to have been developed as part of the anti-Marcionite argument after Justin, most likely by the Basic Writer personally. The Basic Writer repeatedly appeals to this saying to prove that the Jews knew God before Jesus' proclamation (R 2.46.3–4 // KlH 18.15).

In sum, it has been seen that the distinctive sayings of Jesus shared by Justin and the *Pseudo-Clementines* display Marcionite or anti-Marcionite features. Justin must have used and/or formulated these sayings in his *Syntagma* and then repeated them in similar form in his later writings. The Pseudo-Clementine Basic Writer utilized several sources for the anti-Marcionite arguments and is likely to have employed Justin's writings, too. The sayings of Jesus that the *Pseudo-Clementines* share with Justin apparently derive from employment of Justin's *Syntagma*, not from some lost gospel or harmony. This is the solution to the old riddle posed by the correspondences between Justin and the *Pseudo-Clementines* in sayings of Jesus; this solution must be the cornerstone for studying Justin's evangelical sayings as well as for the study of the sayings of Jesus in the *Pseudo-Clementines*. As the last example demonstrated, the Basic Writer apparently also added to the body of "anti-Marcionite" sayings of Jesus, in partial imitation of Justin.

If the results of this study raise the desire to investigate Justin's sayings of Jesus in greater detail and as a whole, it is surprising that the old mystery of the sayings of Jesus in the *Pseudo-Clementines* consequently seems largely resolved. While I have argued elsewhere that the *Recognition*-1 source (R 1.27–71) is dependent on the *Gospel of the Ebionites*, the relevant sayings-material of the *Gospel of the Ebionites* is not cited as sayings of Jesus but reformulated into narrative material in *Recognition*-1.[36] The author of the *Klementia*, in contrast, did introduce one undeniable agraphon, "Become wise money-changers" (KlH 2.51.1; 3.50.2; 18.20.4), in support of the theory of false pericopes. This author can readily be credited with free alterations (even creations) of sayings to support this theory[37] and with free altera-

---

36. See Jones, *Ancient Jewish Christian Source*, 148–49. Note particularly the reformulation of the saying of Jesus, "I have come to abolish sacrifices, and unless you desist from sacrificing, wrath will not desist from you" (preserved in Epiphanius, *Pan.* 30.16.5) into the summary of Jesus's mission in R 1.39.1, "He would admonish them first to cease with sacrifices."

37. E.g., KlH 2.51.2 = 3.50.1 = 18.20.3 ("Therefore you are deceived, not knowing the true things of the scriptures, on account of which you are unaware [also] of the power of God"); KlH 3.50.2b ("Why do you not understand the reasonable of scriptures?"), in which case even Kline, *Sayings of Jesus*, 166, admits that the words "appear to be the *ad hoc* creation of the writer to fit his immediate context and argument on the false pericopes of scripture."

tions/creations of other gospel accounts and sayings, such as one finds in the story of Justa in *KlH* 2.19–20. Indeed, this author seems to display a penchant for known noncanonical variants and sayings.[38] Otherwise, the remaining sayings of Jesus in the *Pseudo-Clementines*, particularly those witnessed for the Basic Writing, do not evidence remarkable agreements with external witnesses and/or tendencies that extend beyond a somewhat loose dependency on the canonical gospels (especially Matthew, as well as Luke, though evidently not Mark and perhaps not John). At most, one might want to say that such a loose employment of the gospels at the time of the Basic Writing (ca. 220 CE) is indeed unusual and calls for further investigation into the context of possible Jewish Christian distance from the evolving Gentile Christian canon. The Basic Writer never acknowledges the gospels themselves as authoritative and thus never cites them as "scripture," in contrast to the treatment of the Hebrew Bible (LXX). However, the Basic Writer does possess an image of the historical Jesus and holds as authoritative both this image as well as accompanying sayings, known from Matthew and Luke but also from Justin's valued tract against Marcion, as this study has argued. Generally, this procedure (an image of Jesus that guides the selection and precise formulation of sayings of Jesus) parallels Justin's, though well after the time of Justin and thus seemingly anachronistic in the context of the evolving Great Church and its incipient canon.

---

38. E.g., *KlH* 12.29.1 ("The good must come; blessed is the one through whom it comes"), which is also found in Aphrahat, *Dem.* 5.1, and the *Manichaean Psalm-Book* 39.27; *KlH* 19.20.1 ("Guard the mysteries for me and the sons of my house"). In this category belongs perhaps the saying in *KlH* 3.19.3; 12.32.1, which displays some similarities with the saying in the *Didache* 1:3 and Justin, *1 Apol.* 15.9.

– 13 –

The *Tiburtine Sibyl*, the Last Emperor, and the Early Byzantine Apocalyptic Tradition

— Stephen J. Shoemaker —

ALTHOUGH IT NOW STANDS largely forgotten, the *Tiburtine Sibyl* (*Tib. Sib.*) was once one of the most influential and widely read texts in Western Christendom. Ranking high on any list of medieval best sellers, this oracle survives in over 130 known Latin manuscripts, as well as in a Greek version and in an as-yet-unknown number of Arabic, Ethiopic, and Slavonic manuscripts.[1] And while this Sibylline apocalypse is fairly obscure today—even among scholars of late antiquity and Christian apocrypha—for much of the Middle Ages its influence on Christian eschatology easily surpassed that of the canonical Apocalypse, and its broader impact on medieval Christianity was seemingly exceeded only by the Bible and the writings of the church fathers.[2] But now, most scholars of Christian apocrypha have scarcely even

---

1. Concerning the Latin manuscripts, see Verhelst, "La préhistoire des conceptions d'Adson," 99, and now Holdenried, *Sibyl and her Scribes*, 173–221, which includes an inventory of the known manuscripts. The Greek version has been edited in Alexander, *Oracle of Baalbek*. Regarding the other traditions, see Basset, *La sagesse de Sibylle*; Schleifer, *Erzählung der Sibylle*; Ebied and Young, "Newly Discovered Version"; Ebied and Young, "Unrecorded Arabic Version"; and Gaster, "Sibyl and the Dream." Concerning possible evidence of an Armenian tradition, see Basset, *La sagesse de Sibylle*, 8; and Schleifer, *Erzählung der Sibylle*, 75.

2. Cohn, *Pursuit of the Millennium*, 32–33. See also McGinn, "Teste David cum

heard of the text. Such dramatic reversals of fortune are of course not uncommon in the history of apocryphal literature, particularly inasmuch as medieval readers valued these extrabiblical traditions for very different reasons than modern scholars. Like *Tib. Sib.*, other such wildly popular apocrypha as the *Apocalypse of the Virgin* and the *Letter from Heaven* spoke powerfully and directly to the hopes and expectations of a medieval audience in a way that often does not translate well for more recent readers.[3] Modern scholars, by contrast, tend to favor apocryphal traditions that are both early and express pronounced dissonances—rather than harmony—with the received tradition. Accordingly, like so many other apocrypha whose fame has now faded, *Tib. Sib.* remains banished from the modern canons of apocryphal writings, not even meriting so much as a marginal reference in the major compendia, except only for its appearance as an appendix in the admirably inclusive compilation by Mario Erbetta.[4] To be sure, Western medievalists have paid this text considerable attention, inasmuch as it deeply influenced medieval religious culture, but in the study of Christian late antiquity and apocryphal literature, it remains largely unknown and unexplored. Yet, for scholars of apocrypha, surely a text that was once as widely influential as this late ancient Sibylline oracle merits far more attention than it has thus far received. Insofar as the study of Christian apocrypha professes to be concerned with the broader phenomenon of apocryphicity, and not just Christian origins, texts such as *Tib. Sib.* and others sharing a similar fate would seem to merit broader inclusion in collections and discussions of Christian apocryphal literature.

Moreover, it is certainly not without note that there was a revival of interest in *Tib. Sib.* and other related texts as recently as the later nineteenth century, in conjunction with the emergence of the Prussian Empire, which some then saw as a successor to the Holy Roman Empire. As Paul Alexander

---

Sibylla," 24, 28–29; McGinn, "Oracular Transformations," 603–605; Olster, "Byzantine Apocalypses," 51–52; Magdalino, "History of the Future," 20. Holdenried, *Sibyl and her Scribes* is especially invaluable for its demonstration of *Tib. Sib.*'s influence and popularity in the Middle Ages, particularly for the attention it draws to the importance of traditions beyond just the figure of the Last Emperor. Nevertheless, in making this much needed argument, Holdenried goes a bit too far in seeking to diminish the importance of the Sibyl's eschatological traditions. While its traditions concerning the life of Christ were certainly more important to medieval Christians than some scholars have recognized, the Sibyl's prophecies concerning the end times and the Last Emperor were indeed paramount in their influence on medieval eschatology.

3. Concerning the popularity of these two frequently-overlooked traditions, see Bauckham, "Virgin"; Bauckham, "Four Apocalypses," 332–38; Mimouni, "Apocalypses de la Vierge"; and van Esbroeck, "La lettre sur dimache."

4. Erbetta, *Gli Apocrifi del Nuovo Testamento*, 3:527–35.

notes, there was in this context renewed interest especially in the figure of the apocalyptic Last Emperor, who features prominently in *Tib. Sib.*'s eschatological conclusion.[5] In what was to become a centerpiece of medieval Christian eschatology (both East and West), the Last Emperor was imagined as a ruler who would appear in the end times to restore the Christian Empire's greatness just prior to the Second Coming of Christ. This future emperor, it was believed, will subdue or convert all of the Christian faith's enemies and opponents and establish righteousness on the earth. Then he will travel to Jerusalem, where he will lay down his crown and imperial garments, yielding sovereignty to God, and thus bringing an end to the Christian Roman Empire and setting in motion the events of the *eschaton*. The conclusion of *Tib. Sib.* preserves the earliest known version of this apocalyptic legend, dating most likely to the later fourth century. Obviously then, this apocryphon is of the utmost importance for understanding the early development of this cornerstone of medieval Christian apocalypticism, and it is largely in this context that *Tib. Sib.* has been studied. Nevertheless, it has yet to be fully appreciated how much this particular text and the broader tradition of early Byzantine imperial eschatology (of which *Tib. Sib.* is a foundational document), have to offer for understanding the origins of Islam. Indeed, the fusion of imperial ambition and eschatological urgency that seem to have defined earliest Islam come into much clearer perspective when understood in light of the apocalyptic fervor that had taken hold of the Byzantine world in the sixth and seventh centuries, all the more so in light of the Byzantine expectation that the *eschaton* would be inaugurated through the military triumph of their divinely-favored empire.

THE *TIBURTINE SIBYL*: A LATE ANCIENT APOCRYPHAL APOCALYPSE

Of course, before proceeding any further, one might wish to raise the question of whether or not *Tib. Sib.* should rightly be considered as a Christian apocryphon, particularly in light of its overtly "pagan" framework. Certainly if one adheres to the older definition of Christian apocrypha advanced by the Hennecke-Schneemelcher collection of "New Testament Apocrypha," it is not entirely clear that this text would qualify as an apocryphon. In addition to the differences in literary style and the problem of its late fourth-century date, it is rather difficult to envision *Tib. Sib.*, as Schneemelcher's definition requires, as a text "which by title and other statements lay claim

---

5. Alexander, "Byzantium," esp. 48–53.

to be of equal status to the writings of the canon."[6] Nevertheless, despite similar issues regarding genre and canonical intent, a selection of earlier "Christian Sibyllines" appears not only in the Hennecke-Schneemelcher collection but in the other major collections as well. Likewise, many of these same texts have been published also as part of a larger collection of "Sibylline Oracles" in collections of the "Old Testament Pseudepigrapha."[7] On the basis of these precedents then, only the relatively late composition of this particular Sibylline oracle could possibly stand in the way of its inclusion in the corpus of Christian apocrypha.

Nevertheless, now that scholars are largely agreed in removing this chronological limitation, it seems clear that *Tib. Sib.* is rightly regarded as a late ancient apocryphon that continues in the well-established tradition of Jewish and Christian Sibylline apocrypha. Moreover, despite the pagan trappings of this Christian apocalypse, its contents focus squarely on events and characters from the biblical writings.[8] In addition to its passing mention of the life and teachings of Jesus and the ministry of the apostles, the bulk of this vision concerns, among other key elements of biblical eschatology, the peoples of Gog and Magog, the appearance of the Antichrist, and the Second Coming of Christ. Yet, leaving behind the formalities and abstractions of defining the limits of apocryphal literature, the function and status of this text in the Middle Ages unmistakably reveal its parallel authority to the biblical traditions. Perhaps there is no more famous example of this than the opening stanza of the "Dies irae" hymn from the Latin Requiem Mass, where we find the lines, "Dies irae! Dies illa! Solvet sæclum in favilla: teste David cum Sibylla!" Here the Sibyl's authority regarding the end times is placed on par with the biblical tradition, which is hardly a surprise given that, as already noted, *Tib. Sib.* was more influential on medieval eschatology than the canonical Apocalypse.[9] *Tib. Sib.*, then, was more than just a supplement to the canonical texts but was also considered an authoritative source of Christian doctrine. And the fact that its authority could on some topics equal and even surpass the authority of the biblical tradition certainly

---

6. Schneemelcher, *Neutestamentliche Apokryphen*, 1:6; English trans., Schneemelcher, *New Testament Apocrypha*, 1:27.

7. E.g., Collins, "Sibylline Oracles," in Charlesworth's *Old Testament Pseudepigrapha* .

8. Following here especially the influential definition of apocrypha proposed in Junod, "Apocryphes du Nouveau Testament ou apocryphes chrétiens anciens?" 412. For further discussion, see Shoemaker, "Early Christian Apocryphal Literature," esp. 528–32.

9. See, e.g., McGinn, "*Teste David cum Sibylla*," 19.

raises some intriguing questions about the function and significance of the canon in the Middle Ages.

The Textual Tradition and Its Date of Composition

At present *Tib. Sib.* is best known from the Latin edition by Ernst Sackur. Sackur was able to identify several different Latin recensions of the text, of which his edition published the oldest on the basis of the manuscripts then known to him.[10] Nevertheless, despite Sackur's remarkable achievement, it is clear that a more comprehensive critical edition is needed, not only in light of the abundance of the manuscript tradition,[11] but also because the later Latin recensions were not dependent on the version edited by Sackur, and thus they occasionally preserve some elements of the ancient text that were for some reason left out from the oldest recension. The potential value of these later versions has been demonstrated in part by the discovery and publication of a Greek version of *Tib. Sib.*, which contains some parallels to these other Latin versions, indicating that the passages in question must have once stood in their common Greek source.[12] Even though Greek was the original language of *Tib. Sib.*'s composition, it is widely agreed that the Latin translation preserves an earlier version than we have in the extant Greek. The Greek version's editor, Paul Alexander, has convincingly demonstrated that this version was redacted at the very beginning of the sixth century, judging from the historical events and individuals to which it refers.[13] Like so many other apocalyptic texts, the prophecies of the Greek *Tib. Sib.* juxtapose a rehearsal of recent historical events with what amount to genuine predictions of events to come that will soon usher in the *eschaton*. Not surprisingly, as the text transitions from its historical section to forecasts of the future, the seer's prognostic powers suddenly depart, and in this seam we can identify a fairly reliable date for the text's composition. As Alexander accordingly observes, "every apocalypse must have been written not long after the latest event to which it alludes," and so in the case of the Greek

---

10. Sackur, *Sibyllinische Texte und Forschungen*, 126–37; see also Alexander, *Oracle of Baalbek*, 3–5 and 60–62.

11. Holdenried, *Sibyl and her Scribes* has laid important groundwork for a new edition in this regard.

12. See, e.g., Alexander, *Oracle of Baalbek*, 53–55 and 63–64, examples that are also noted below.

13. Alexander, *Oracle of Baalbek*, 41–47 and also 75–105. Concerning the original language, see Alexander, *Oracle of Baalbek*, 60–65.

Tib. Sib., this locates its production—or rather, its redaction—sometime between 502 and 506.[14]

Despite some minor complications, the same principles convincingly date the Latin version over a century earlier, to the end of the fourth century. The main issue is that this earliest Latin version, as preserved in its oldest manuscripts, includes an editorial update designed to refresh its prophecies for more recent generations by inserting a list of Lombard and German rulers from the sixth through the eleventh centuries near the end of its historical section.[15] Nevertheless, these medieval interpolations are rather obvious and easy to isolate from the much earlier text in which they are embedded, so that there is solid consensus that *Tib. Sib.* as preserved in this Latin translation is indeed a late antique text. Leaving then these medieval insertions to the side (they are italicized in Sackur's edition), Sackur's painstaking analysis of the text demonstrates that the latest historical events to which the original Latin *Tib. Sib.* refers are from the later fourth century, a point on which there also has been broad scholarly agreement.[16] Except for the medieval interlopers, the latest figures to which Sackur's edition of *Tib. Sib.* refers are Constantine and his sons, and the text likewise shows a fairly detailed knowledge of events in the eastern provinces at the end of Constantius II's reign.[17] Through comparison of the Latin versions with the Greek, Alexander has demonstrated also that a passage found in certain Latin manuscripts referring to the death of the emperor Valens (d. 378) likely appeared in the original Latin translation, thus postponing the date of composition to a little later.[18] In view of this fact one might wish to reconsider

14. Alexander, "Medieval Apocalypses," 998–99, 1009.

15. Sackur, *Sibyllinische Texte*, 129–37, 181–84; Alexander, *Oracle of Baalbek*, 60–62.

16. See, e.g., Bousset, *Antichrist Legend*, 45–49, 62–65; Bousset, "Antichrist"; Kampers, *Die deutsche Kaiseridee*, 18–19; Sackur, *Sibyllinische Texte*, 162–63; Konrad, *De ortu et tempore Antichristi*, 43–53; Alexander, *Oracle of Baalbek*, 49–65; Alexander, "Byzantium," 67 n. 35; Alexander, "Medieval Legend," 14–15; Alexander, "Diffusion of Byzantine Apocalypses," 56–57; Alexander, *Byzantine Apocalyptic Tradition*, 171–72 esp. n. 74; Podskalsky, *Byzantinische Reichseschatologie*, 55 n. 333; Rangheri, "La «Epistola ad Gerbergam»," 708–709 n. 79; Wortley, "Literature of Catastrophe," 16–17; McGinn, *Visions of the End*, 43–44; McGinn, "Teste David cum Sibylla," 26–28; McGinn, "Oracular Transformations," 612–13; Brandes, "Die apokalyptische Literatur," 309; Möhring, *Weltkaiser der Endzeit*, 49. Note that, while some of these scholars have on occasion expressed some doubt as to whether the Last Emperor tradition was a part of this late fourth-century *Tib. Sib.* (a point discussed in some detail below), they are agreed that the text otherwise—except for the medieval king lists—dates to this time.

17. Sackur, *Sibyllinische Texte*, 157–62; see also Alexander, *Oracle of Baalbek*, 49–65.

18. Alexander, *Oracle of Baalbek*, 63–64; for the text see ibid., 14. See also McGinn,

Sackur's conclusion that *Tib. Sib.* shows no knowledge of Julian's apostasy to paganism. While there is no unmistakable reference to this dramatic turn of events, perhaps *Tib. Sib.*'s persistent concern to confront paganism should be understood in this light, and likewise its notice that, "another ... king will arise, a mighty man and a warrior, and many neighbors and relatives will become indignant with him," may refer to Julian's apostasy.[19]

Alexander's careful analysis of the Greek and Latin versions likewise identifies another passage from the later Latin versions that also seems to have been part of the original text: a prediction that he names the "Constantinopolitan Oracle." In the Greek version, the account of Constantine's reign concludes with a reference to Byzantium's elevation as a new imperial capital named Constantinople, followed by a forecast that warns, "Do not boast, city of Byzantium, thou shalt not hold imperial sway for thrice sixty of thy years!"[20] As Alexander notes, this amounts to 180 years, an interval of time consistent with the Greek version's redaction sometime between 502 and 506. According to such reckoning, the Greek *Tib. Sib.* expects Constantinople's downfall roughly in 510, soon after its composition, presumably with the end of the world not far thereafter. Although Sackur's edition contains no equivalent passage, several of the later Latin versions preserve a strikingly similar prediction, albeit one that is well suited to the earlier date of the Latin translation. In these manuscripts, following the description of Constantine and a reference to his new city, the Sibyl warns, "Do not rejoice with joy: they will not rule from Byzantium within 60 years."[21] As with the Greek version, the interval again fits perfectly with the date of the text as determined on the basis of its most recent historical references. The fall of Constantinople is thus forecast for the year 390, and since this prophecy did not in fact come true, it would appear that the Latin version of *Tib. Sib.*, or more precisely, its Greek source, must have been composed sometime between 378 and 390. Indeed, even in the absence of the Greek parallel, there is good reason to suppose that this prophecy belonged to the original text. The fact that it was not fulfilled makes it very unlikely that some medieval redactor would have added the prophecy to the text centuries later, while its evident falsification presents a powerful motive for its elimination by a later editor. The Greek version simply reflects a different strategy for overcoming this difficulty: its reviser has extended the deadline by just over a century in

---

"Oracular Transformations," 640.

    19. Sackur, *Sibyllinische Texte*, 183; see also 160–62.

    20. Alexander, *Oracle of Baalbek*, 14; trans. 25.

    21. Ibid., 53–55; for the Latin text see Sackur, *Sibyllinische Texte*, 128 n. 4; and Alexander, *Oracle of Baalbek*, 14. See also McGinn, "Oracular Transformations," 640.

order to place the fall of Constantinople again on the immediate horizon. Thus, Alexander's recovery of this prophecy, which has been excised from the version edited by Sackur, adds important confirmation of *Tib. Sib.*'s composition in the later fourth century, after which time this prophecy would have been falsified.

At a more general level, structural comparison of Sackur's Latin version with the Greek also demonstrates the former's relative antiquity, revealing that the Greek version has revised an earlier source that now largely survives in the Latin translation. There are to be sure some significant differences between the Greek and the Latin, but as Alexander notes, they "tell essentially the same story," one which the Greek has adapted to meet the circumstances of elapsed time.[22] In essence, the Greek version updates the events of the Latin version's historical section, leaving out some elements entirely, in order to make room for more than a century of new events that had elapsed by the time of its redaction. By compressing the time between the Sibyl's prognostications and the appearance of Constantine and also by eliminating much of the Latin version's detail concerning the later fourth century, the Greek editor opens up space in the prophetic vision to introduce the history of the fifth century before the events of the *eschaton* are unleashed.

The Sybil's Vision

Tib. Sib. begins sometime back in the mists of early Roman history, during the reign of the "Trojan" emperor, a reference, as Sackur rightly concludes, to Rome's legendary foundation by Aeneas and other Trojan refugees.[23] When the leading citizens of Rome learn of this woman's great prophecies, they persuade the emperor to bring her to Rome with great honor. We then learn that in one night 100 men from the Roman senate had the same dream. It was a vision of nine different suns, each one having specific qualities that distinguished it from the others. The men approach the Sibyl, seeking the meaning of their dream, and she explains to them that "the nine suns that

---

22. Alexander, *Oracle of Baalbek*, 48–55, 63–64.

23. Although some manuscripts read instead "Traiani," it does not seem possible to identify this figure with Trajan, since the Sibyl subsequently explains that the nine suns represent "all future generations," with the fourth generation witnessing the birth of Christ. Accordingly, some manuscripts read here instead "of their king Romulus" or "of the consul, whose name was Trojanus" or "of the senators." Sackur explains, however, that "Troiani" is in fact the correct reading, and is a reflection of the traditions that the Romans were descended from the Trojans, and so their ancestral king here is here named Trojanus: see Sackur, *Sibyllinische Texte*, 172–73.

you saw prefigure all future generations. Truly the differences that you see among them will also be a different life for humankind" (6).[24] The Sibyl then begins to reveal the future, describing each of the nine generations to come. The first two ages will be idyllic; but things begin to take a turn for the worse in the third, when "nation will rise up against nation, and there will be many battles in Rome" (6). The fourth generation will witness the birth of Christ, and here the Sibyl accordingly relates what Alexander calls the "Sibylline Gospel." This brief account of the birth, crucifixion, and resurrection of Christ draws the ire of some of "the priests of the Hebrews," whom the Sibyl is quick to silence (6–7).[25] The fifth generation will witness the spread of the gospel by the apostles, and the sixth, seventh, and eighth generations will see continued turmoil in the Roman Empire. Then in the ninth generation, after the rule of four kings (i.e., the Tetrarchy), there "will arise another king, with the name C [Constantine], mighty in battle, who will reign for 30 years and will build a temple to God and will fulfill the law and establish justice on the earth for God's sake" (8). The "Constantinopolitan Oracle" then seemingly follows as does the reference to Valens.

At this point a lengthy insertion concerning the Lombard and German kings intrudes, eventually yielding to a forecast of war, famine, and natural disasters, as well as political corruption and religious persecution, although this section itself is also briefly interrupted twice with notices concerning later medieval kings (8–9). These calamities are the events that Sackur correlates convincingly with the reign of Constantius II, but in *Tib. Sib.* they clearly appear also as portents of the impending end of the world. Then, as things reach a fever pitch, with "afflictions such as there have not been since the beginning of the world" and the world completely abandoned to the wicked and unjust (9), the figure of the Last Emperor makes his dramatic appearance: "And then will arise a king of the Greeks, whose name is Constans, and he will be king of the Romans and the Greeks. He will be tall in stature, handsome in appearance, shining in countenance, and well put together in all of his bodily features. And his reign will end after 112 years." His reign will witness great wealth and abundance, and this king will have before him a "scripture" that says, "The king of the Romans will claim the entire kingdom of the Christians for himself." Then he will "devastate

---

24. Translations and section numbers correspond with my forthcoming translation of this text (based on Sackur, *Sibyllinische Texte*) in Burke and Landau, eds., *New Testament Apocrypha*.

25. Alexander considers the peculiarities of this "Sibylline Gospel" in *Oracle of Baalbek*, 67–74. David Flusser ("Early Jewish-Christian Document," esp. 168–69, 176–78) has proposed on the basis of this Sibylline gospel that the core of *Tib. Sib.* goes back to the late first century CE, although I do not find the argument very persuasive.

all the islands and cities of the pagans and destroy all the temples of idols. He will call all the pagans to baptism, and the Cross of Jesus Christ will be erected in all the temples," and "the Jews will be converted to the Lord." At this time the Antichrist will arise and lead many astray, and "the most unclean nations that Alexander the Indian king enclosed, God and Magog, will arise from the north." After the Last Emperor annihilates the peoples of God and Magog, "then he will come to Jerusalem, and there having laid down the diadem from his head and all his royal garb, he will hand over the kingdom of the Christians to God the Father and Jesus Christ his Son." With the Roman Empire now having come to an end, "the Antichrist will be openly revealed." The apocalypse then concludes with his defeat "by the power of the Lord by the Archangel Michael on the Mount of Olives" (10).

This figure of the apocalyptic Last Emperor, who appears here seemingly for the first time, quickly became one of the cornerstones of medieval Christian eschatology. The Roman Empire and its emperor were imagined as agents of Christian deliverance that would emerge resurgent at the end of time. The roots of this idea were developed in the context of Constantine's conversion and the Christianization of the Roman Empire during the fourth century, from which emerged a political ideology that envisioned the Empire and its ruler as divinely appointed to rule on God's behalf and to defend and advance the Christian faith on Earth.[26] The Roman Empire was identified as the fourth kingdom of Daniel 2, the kingdom of iron, which was to be the last world empire, after which would follow the Kingdom of God.[27] Even Christians living beyond the Empire's borders were quick to embrace this idea of Rome's divine election and commission. For instance, Aphrahat, the Persian Sage, also identified Rome with the fourth Danielic kingdom and believed that it would remain unvanquished until the return of Christ. God, as he explains, had given over his rule to the Romans ("the children of Esau"), and accordingly God will preserve Rome until the end of time, when "He should come Whose it is" and the Romans "will deliver up the deposit to the Giver."[28] Thus, from the fourth century onward, Christians increasingly looked to the Roman Empire and its emperor as having been divinely appointed to subdue and defeat the enemies of Christ in order to prepare for his Second Coming.

---

26. See, e.g, Podskalsky, *Byzantinische Reichseschatologie*, 11–12.

27. Eusebius of Caesarea, *Dem. ev.* 15, frag. 1 (Heikel, ed., *Eusebius Werke*, 493–94).

28. Aphrahat, *Dem. 5: On Wars* 13–14, 24 (Graffin et al., eds., *Patrologia syriaca*, 1:207–12; 233–34; trans. Schaff and Wace, *Select Library*, 13:361).

THE LAST EMPEROR IN THE LATER MEDIEVAL TRADITION: THE *APOCALYPSE OF PS.-METHODIUS*

In *Tib. Sib.* the enemies of Christ are the pagans and the Jews, as one would certainly expect from a late fourth-century composition. Nevertheless, as this legend of the Last Emperor transitioned into the Middle Ages, the face of the Empire's enemies predictably would change, particularly with the effective elimination of "paganism" from the Mediterranean world. Perhaps even more important, however, was the emergence of Islam during the seventh century as a new and formidable threat to the Christian Empire's position in the world. Indeed, with the Islamic conquest of the Roman Near East, North Africa, and the Sasanian Empire, the majority of the world's Christians suddenly found themselves living not under the protection of the Christian Empire and its emperor but instead under the rule of Muslim infidels.[29] In this new geopolitical and religious order, Islam and the Arabs quickly emerged as the primary foes of Christ and his chosen Empire. This animosity reconfigured Christian imperial eschatology almost immediately, as we see in the Syriac *Homily on the End* attributed to Ephrem and most especially in the *Apocalypse of Ps.-Methodius* (=*Apoc. Ps.-Meth.*). In these two apocalypses from the mid-seventh century, the "Hagarenes" or the "Ishmaelites" have now become the ultimate enemies whom the Christian Empire must defeat before Christ returns to reign.[30] Moreover, like *Tib. Sib.*, *Apoc. Ps.-Meth.* draws its focus on a final "emperor of the Greeks" who will fulfill this task, thus offering a rather distinctive version of the Last Emperor myth that differs significantly from *Tib. Sib.* but also has some important points of contact.[31]

Apoc. Ps.-Meth. was written in Syriac in northern Mesopotamia sometime between 644 and 670. Although certain specialists on Syriac literature, most notably Sebastian Brock and Gerrit Reinink, recently proposed a date for the text toward the end of the seventh century, the internal evidence

---

29. See, e.g., Griffith, *Church in the Shadow*, 11.

30. Ps.-Ephrem, *Homily on the End* 8 (Suermann, *Die geschichtstheologische Reaktion*, 25). There has been some debate as to whether the bulk of Ps.-Ephrem's *Homily* may in fact be even earlier, and some scholars have proposed that the section concerning Islam was later inserted into an apocalyptic homily from the later fourth century. Nevertheless, there is a fairly broad consensus that the work as it presently stands was produced ca. 640. The main exception to this consensus would seem to be Reinink (and Hoyland?), who considers 640 a *terminus post quem*, finding a *terminus ante quem* in 683. See Reinink, "Pseudo-Ephraems 'Rede über das Ende,'" esp. 439–41, 455–63; and Hoyland, *Seeing Islam*, 261–63.

31. *Apoc. Ps.-Meth.* 13.11–14.6 (Reinink, ed., *Syrische Apokalypse*, 38–45 [Syr] & 63–74 [German]; English trans. Palmer, *Seventh Century*, 237–40).

provided by the textual tradition itself clearly favors an earlier dating, as Alexander and Harald Suermann both recognized.[32] Brock and Reinink base their determination on the reading of a single manuscript that predicts that the Muslims will rule for ten weeks of years,[33] which they take to mean that almost seventy years had elapsed from the beginnings of Islam until the time of *Apoc. Ps.-Meth.*'s composition. Thus they conclude that the text was written just prior to 692.[34] Nevertheless, with the exception of this one Syriac manuscript, all of the other witnesses to this text instead forecast that Muslim rule will last for seven weeks of years, which, following the same principles, would place the anticipated turn of events in 671. This would seem to exclude the possibility of *Apoc. Ps.-Meth.*'s composition after 670. Brock and Reinink give no clear reasons for adopting the unique reading of this single manuscript (which was long the only known Syriac manuscript), and in fact, Brock, in his own translation of the final sections of *Apoc. Ps.-Meth.*, actually translates "seven" weeks of years and notes "ten" as a variant that occurs only in this single manuscript.[35] Robert Hoyland proposes that the "substitution" of seven weeks instead of ten "is easily explained as the preference for a more charismatic number and symmetry with the seventh millennium."[36] Yet such charisma and symmetry seem just as likely to have influenced the original author to set a deadline of 49 years; moreover, one must not overlook the fact that 70 (ten weeks) is itself a pretty charismatic and symmetrical number whose charms also could have easily swayed a later editor. To the contrary then, it seems more likely that "ten" has been substituted here by someone not long after the text's composition but after the 49th year had passed, in order to extend the deadline. The single Syriac manuscript preserving this variant likely reflects changes of this sort in its earliest antecedent. It certainly makes more sense to suppose that this one manuscript reflects a change made to the original text, rather than assuming that the other Syriac manuscripts and both the Greek and Latin translations

---

32. Alexander, *Byzantine Apocalyptic Tradition*, 24–8; Suermann, *Die geschichtstheologische Reaktion*, 159–61

33. *Apoc. Ps.-Meth.* 5.9; 10.6; 13.2 (Reinink, ed., *Syrische Apokalypse*, 11, 23, 35 [Syr] & 15, 39, 57 [Germ]), although according to the edition the manuscripts read in the third instance "in the last week" rather than "in the tenth." The Greek and Latin persistently have seven weeks of years in all three instances, and the edition indicates that the other Syriac manuscripts either read seven weeks or are lacking the passage in question (as the apparatus seems to indicate in 5.9).

34. E.g., Brock, "Syriac Views," 19; Palmer, *Seventh Century*, 225; Reinink, "Ps.-Methodius," 150, 178–84; cf. Hoyland, *Seeing Islam*, 264 n. 17.

35. Palmer, *Seventh Century*, 230, 236, although Brock translates "seventh" in the second instance instead of "last," presumably for consistency with the first passage.

36. Hoyland, *Seeing Islam*, 264 n 17.

(which also have seven weeks of years) have all somehow uniformly deviated from the original.[37] Alexander recognized this even before the Syriac manuscripts reading seven weeks had been discovered, and it is not at all clear to me why these other scholars have ignored his compelling reasoning, particularly in light of the new evidence confirming it.[38]

Apoc. Ps.-Meth. was quickly translated into Greek and Latin, and through these translations it made a deep and lasting impact on medieval Christian eschatology. The Latin translation was made from the Greek, and since we have a Latin manuscript dating to the early eighth century, both translations must have been realized quite rapidly. The recent editors of both versions estimate a date of 710–720 for the Latin translation and 700–710 for the Greek, although they are prevented from proposing an earlier date by Reinink's late dating for the Syriac original.[39] Yet in light of the very short interval between the Syriac original's composition and the first Latin manuscript, it would seem that a slightly earlier date for the Syriac also would fit much better with such rapid transmission into Greek and Latin. And so possibly these translations may have been produced a little earlier than the editors suggest. In any case, as it passed into these new cultural contexts, *Apoc. Ps.-Meth.* met with enormous popularity. In Byzantium it circulated widely, and its profound influence is evident in all of the subsequent Byzantine apocalyptic tradition.[40] In the Latin West, the text was even more enthusiastically received. Over 200 Latin manuscripts are presently known, in addition to even more copies surviving in vernacular

---

37. *Apoc. Ps.-Meth.* 10.6; 13.2 (Reinink, ed., *Die Syrische Apokalypse*, 23, 35 [Syr] & 39, 57 [German]; Aerts and Kortekaas, *Apokalypse des Pseudo-Methodius*, 1:134–35, 164–65)

38. Alexander, "Medieval Apocalypses," 1001; Alexander, *Byzantine Apocalyptic Tradition*, 52–53. See also Martinez, "Apocalyptic Genre in Syriac," 337–52, 340–41 n. 9. Brock and Reinink also point to eschatological fervor, the threat of apostasy, and tax increases as motives for *Apoc. Ps.-Meth.*'s composition. Yet eschatological fervor and the threat of apostasy seem just as relevant to the middle of the seventh century as the end, and the suggestion of a response to 'Abd al-Malik's tax increases, while not impossible, is highly speculative. It is perhaps worth noting, however, that taxation is a theme seemingly common to the Last Emperor traditions, as evidenced in the Greek version of *Tib. Sib.* and the *Apocalypse of Elijah*, a text that seems to have strongly influenced *Tib. Sib.* and the Last Emperor tradition, as noted further below. See Alexander, *Oracle of Baalbek*, 21, 29; and Steindorff, *Apokalypse des Elias*, 86; English trans. in Frankfurter, *Elijah in Upper Egypt*, 312.

39. Aerts and Kortekaas, *Apokalypse des Pseudo-Methodius*, 16, 30, 57.

40. See, e.g., Alexander, *Byzantine Apocalyptic Tradition*, 13–14; Podskalsky, *Byzantinische Reichseschatologie*, 53–6; Aerts and Kortekaas, *Apokalypse des Pseudo-Methodius*, 16–18; Garstad, *Apocalypse Pseudo-Methodius*, ix–x.

translations.⁴¹ Indeed, its impact on medieval culture was such that one can equally say of *Apoc. Ps.-Meth.*, as was similarly noted concerning *Tib. Sib.* above, that "scarcely any other text of the Middle Ages had such universal influence, excepting the canonical Scriptures and the Church Fathers."⁴² Perhaps nowhere is this influence more evident than with respect to the Last Emperor. Ps.-Methodius's vision of the Last Emperor's triumph over the sons of Ishmael and his final surrender of authority to God at Jerusalem largely determined the shape of these traditions in the Christian East, and in the West its distinctive account of these events rivaled the parallel version offered by *Tib. Sib.*⁴³ Eventually, even *Tib. Sib.* itself would come partly under Ps.-Methodius's influence, so that in a later version the Last Emperor—perhaps also for obvious historical reasons—defeats not the Jews and pagans but the Saracens instead.⁴⁴

In light of the substantial influence that *Apoc. Ps.-Meth.* had on medieval eschatology in the Christian West, some scholars have even gone so far as to suggest that the myth of the Last Emperor is in fact the genius of its author. The most aggressive of these hypotheses argue that the legend of the Last Emperor was not actually present in the original fourth-century version of *Tib. Sib.*, but instead it is a medieval interpolation that has been introduced on the basis of *Apoc. Ps.-Meth.*, which is credited with the legend's invention.⁴⁵ Moreover, certain specialists of Syriac and *Apoc. Ps.-Meth.* have for whatever reason seemingly ignored *Tib. Sib.* altogether, without affording it any consideration, simply assuming that the legend originates with Ps.-Methodius. The reason for this oversight is not entirely clear: one suspects that they may have similarly assumed that the Last Emperor tradition is a medieval insertion into the late ancient text of *Tib. Sib.*; accordingly it does not merit consideration, although this is never stated.⁴⁶

It certainly is not entirely out of the question that *Tib. Sib.*'s Last Emperor tradition may be a later interpolation, and comparison of the Latin

41. Aerts and Kortekaas, *Apokalypse des Pseudo-Methodius*, 19.

42. Sackur, *Sibyllinische Texte*, 6.

43. See, e.g., Alexander, *Byzantine Apocalyptic Tradition*, 152–84; Alexander, "Byzantium," esp. 53–62; Alexander, "Diffusion of Byzantine Apocalypses"; McGinn, "Oracular Transformations," 604–12; Kraft, "Last Roman Emperor Topos."

44. McGinn, "Oracular Transformations," 631, 642.

45. Alexander, "Byzantium," 67 n. 35; Wortley, "Literature of Catastrophe," 16–17; McGinn, *Visions of the End*, 44; McGinn, "*Teste David cum Sibylla*," 26–27; McGinn, "Oracular Transformations," 607, 609, 613.

46. E.g., Reinink, "Die syrischen Wurzeln," 195–209; Reinink, "Pseudo-Methodius und die Legende," esp. 82–83; Reinink, "Ps.-Methodius," esp. 153–55, 165–78; Suermann, *Die geschichtstheologische Reaktion*, 208; Suermann, "Der byzantinische Endkaiser," esp. 144–5; Kraft, "Last Roman Emperor," although see 217 n. 18.

with the Greek version possibly could suggest this. Nevertheless, the evidence afforded by the account itself seems to secure its antiquity as well as its presence in the original late fourth-century version of this influential apocalypse. And even if by some odd chance the Last Emperor legend was not a part of this earliest version, there can be little question that *Tib. Sib.*'s account of the Last Emperor myth belongs to late antiquity, antedating significantly both *Apoc. Ps.-Meth.* and the Islamic conquests. Admittedly, one of the most puzzling aspects of *Tib. Sib.*'s transmission history is the Last Emperor's near absence from the early sixth-century Greek version, and the same is similarly true of the much later Arabic, Karshuni, and Ethiopic versions that have been published to date, all of which seem to derive from this Greek redaction. It is largely on this basis that some scholars have raised doubts regarding the textual status of the Last Emperor tradition; the silence of the Greek especially has invited suspicion of an interpolation. There are, however, some apparent vestiges of the Last Emperor myth in these more recent versions, as others have also noted. For instance, in the Greek, just before the Antichrist's appearance, a final emperor is identified who will arise and defeat the king of the East. Then, like the Last Emperor of the Latin version, his reign will be marked by abundance and prosperity, until his defeat and murder by the Antichrist.[47] The same is also true of the Arabic, Karshuni, and Ethiopic versions, which similarly describe an era of great prosperity under the final emperor before the Antichrist's appearance.[48] Although many important elements of the Latin version are clearly lacking, René Basset concludes that these texts preserve here an abridged version of the same Last Emperor tradition.[49] Indeed this does seem to be the case, but it is certainly a little curious that the Greek editor would have redacted the legend so dramatically.

Nevertheless, despite the significant differences between the Latin *Tib. Sib.*'s legend of the Last Emperor and these more recent versions, the internal evidence of the legend itself offers compelling evidence of its late antique origin and its independence from *Apoc. Ps.-Meth.* The most decisive feature in this regard is the complete absence of any mention of the Muslims or the Islamic conquests, which are defining features of *Apoc. Ps.-Meth.* and the rest of the post-Islamic apocalyptic tradition.[50] Instead, we find the Last

47. Alexander, *Oracle of Baalbek*, 21, 29.

48. Schleifer, *Erzählung der Sibylle*, 38–41, 66–67. This similarity in particular suggests the dependence of these versions on the Greek version edited by Alexander, although as he notes, they have been subjected to a tremendous amount of editing during their subsequent transmission: see Alexander, *Oracle of Baalbek*, 5–6 n. 9.

49. Basset, *La sagesse de Sibylle*, 19.

50. Alexander, *Byzantine Apocalyptic Tradition*, 156. Sackur's edition does refer

Emperor confronting pagans and Jews, who here constitute the main rivals of the Christian faith. Pagans in particular figure very prominently in the Last Emperor's actions; he will devastate their "islands and cities," call them to baptism, establish the cross in all of their temples, so that they will be eradicated or converted to Christianity. The Sibyl additionally cites a slight variation on Ps 68:31, "Egypt and Ethiopia will hasten to offer their hand to God," as affording biblical proof of the Last Emperor's anticipated success against the pagans. It is quite difficult to imagine such pronounced concern with subduing the pagans—and none whatsoever for the Muslims—in a text composed only after the Islamic conquests. All the more so it is hard to imagine that a medieval interpolator would have eliminated the Muslims from an existing tradition in order to replace them with pagans and Jews, as dependence on *Apoc. Ps.-Meth.* would require.

Other specific features of *Tib. Sib.*'s Last Emperor similarly fit much better with a late fourth-century context than with a medieval interpolation. For instance, the reference to Ps 68:31 appears to be a reference to the recent conversion of Egypt and especially Ethiopia from paganism to Christianity in the fourth century. Eusebius of Caesarea offers a roughly contemporary witness to the interpretation of this passage as a prophecy of pagan conversion (*Hist. eccl.* 2.1.13). Moreover, Sackur and others after him have noted that in *Tib. Sib.* the Last Emperor is said to lay down the "diadem of his head" in Jerusalem rather than a "crown." This detail seemingly reflects the custom of the late ancient emperors who wore on their heads a diadem, an adorned headband, as opposed to the medieval Latin kings who instead favored crowns.[51] Judged on the whole, then, *Tib. Sib.*'s account of the Last Emperor appears to be solidly late antique in its content. Comparison with the Last Emperor traditions of *Apoc. Ps.-Meth.* only strengthens this conclusion.

PS.-METHODIUS'S ADAPTATION OF THE TIBURTINE SIBYL'S LAST EMPEROR TRADITIONS

Careful comparison of *Tib. Sib.* with the Last Emperor traditions of *Apoc. Ps.-Meth.* reveals that there is almost no chance that the former depends on the latter while also confirming that the traditions of *Tib. Sib.* are almost

---

twice to the Hagarenes, but these are clearly medieval interpolations of the late antique text related to the medieval kings who have been added.

51. Sackur, *Sibyllinische Texte*, 167–68. See also Konrad, *De ortu et tempore Antichristi*, 46–47; and Möhring, *Weltkaiser der Endzeit*, 42; cf. McGinn, *Visions of the End*, 295 n. 9.

certainly older. These two versions of the Last Emperor myth are so strikingly different from one another that, as Alexander concludes, the Sibyl's Last Emperor simply "cannot be interpolated from Pseudo-Methodius where the details given differ on a number of points." There is in fact nothing at all to indicate that *Tib. Sib.*'s account has borrowed anything from *Apoc. Ps.-Meth.*[52] Yet influence in the opposite direction not only seems possible but in fact highly likely. In several instances it would appear that Ps.-Methodius has developed earlier traditions about the Last Emperor that appear in *Tib. Sib.* and adapted them to his Syriac cultural milieu and to the circumstances of Islamic hegemony. This is particularly true of Ps.-Methodius's account of the Last Emperor's person and his actions, his (re)interpretation of Ps. 68:31, and his description of Gog and Magog, all of which seem to reflect the use of earlier traditions about the Last Emperor found in *Tib. Sib.*

The Figure of the Last Emperor and His Abdication

One important difference between *Tib. Sib.*'s Last Emperor and his appearance in *Apoc. Ps.-Meth.* and the later apocalyptic tradition is that the Sibyl assigns him multiple tasks. He brings prosperity and defeats paganism by force, calling the pagans to conversion so that Egypt and Ethiopia will offer their hand to God. He also converts the Jews and then defeats Gog and Magog before finally surrendering power to God at Jerusalem. By contrast, in *Apoc. Ps.-Meth.* and other later texts, Alexander states, "the Last Emperor is severely specialized and limits himself to the defeat of the unbelievers (Moslems) and the surrender of his rule."[53] *Tib. Sib.*'s Last Emperor stands out against this later tendency toward narrowing his role.[54] Moreover, *Tib. Sib.* is the only text to assign the Last Emperor the task of defeating Gog and Magog, which in the later apocalypses instead falls to an angel. In *Apoc. Ps.-Meth.* and the subsequent tradition, the Emperor's victory over Gog and Magog has been displaced by his triumph over the Muslims, leaving this eschatological conquest instead to supernatural forces.[55]

The later tradition also mythologizes the figure of the Last Emperor in comparison with *Tib. Sib.* Whereas the Sibyl knows this emperor's name and

---

52. Alexander, "Diffusion of Byzantine Apocalypses," 58, 63–64, and esp. 93–94 n. 9; so also Sackur, *Sibyllinische Texte*, 170; and Rangheri, "'Epistola ad Gerbergami'," 708–9 n. 79.

53. Alexander, "Diffusion of Byzantine Apocalypses," 58.

54. Ibid., 63–64.

55. Alexander, *Byzantine Apocalyptic Tradition*, 156, 158, 163, 166; Alexander, "Diffusion of Byzantine Apocalypses," 63–64.

describes his personal appearance, the later apocalyptic tradition has lost these elements. In *Apoc. Ps.-Meth.* and other more recent texts, the Last Emperor appears less as an actual historical figure "comparable to the Roman emperors of the past and present" and instead more as a shadowy, mythological figure who stands on the margins of history.[56] His rise to power is also cast in more mythic and even supernatural terms. According to *Tib. Sib.*, this Last Emperor, like others before him, will simply "arise" (*surget*), a verb applied routinely to the many kings and emperors mentioned in her vision (10). Nevertheless, *Apoc. Ps.-Meth.* adds considerable mystique and moment to the Last Emperor's appearance: not only will he go forth against the Arabs, but "he will be awakened against them like 'a man who has shaken off his wine'—someone who had been considered by them as though dead."[57] Here Ps.-Methodius associates the Last Emperor with the Lord by invoking Ps 78:65, which reads in the Peshitto, "The Lord was aroused like a sleeper and like a man who shakes off his wine."[58] This same reference also resounds in the Byzantine apocalyptic tradition, and as it passed into Greek through the translation of *Apoc. Ps.-Meth.*, misunderstandings of the Syriac original only "served to intensify the aura of paradox and mystery created by the citation of the Psalm," as Alexander notes.[59]

Other differences between *Tib. Sib.* and *Apoc. Ps.-Meth.* seem to reflect the latter's efforts to adapt earlier traditions concerning the Last Emperor to the contours of its Syriac cultural milieu. For instance, according to the Sibyl, the Last Emperor "will come to Jerusalem, and there having laid down the diadem of his head and all his royal garb, he will hand over the kingdom."[60] Ps.-Methodius relates these same events much more elaborately, with greater drama and specificity. In *Apoc. Ps.-Meth.*, the Emperor will finally "go up and stand on Golgotha and the holy Cross shall be placed on that spot where it had been fixed when it bore Christ. The king of the Greeks shall place his crown on the top of the holy Cross, stretch out his two hands towards heaven, and hand over the kingdom to God the Father. And the holy Cross upon which Christ was crucified will be raised up to heaven, together with the royal crown."[61] As Sackur noted over a century

56. Alexander, *Byzantine Apocalyptic Tradition*, 152–53, 166–67.

57. Reinink, ed., *Syrische Apokalypse*, 38 (Syr); English trans. Palmer, *Seventh Century*, 237.

58. Trans. in Alexander, *Byzantine Apocalyptic Tradition*, 166.

59. Ibid., 167.

60. Reinink, ed., *Die Syrische Apokalypse*, 44 (Syr); English trans. Palmer, *Seventh Century*, 240.

61. Reinink, ed., *Die Syrische Apokalypse*, 44 (Syr); English trans. Palmer, *Seventh Century*, 240.

ago, this scene seems to depend on a similar narrative from the late fifth or early sixth-century Syriac Julian Romance. There, following Julian's death, the imperial crown is placed atop the army's standard Cross, from which it miraculously descends to rest upon Jovian's head. In similar fashion, the sixth-century Syriac *Cave of Treasures* relates that the world's first king, Nimrod, received his crown through its miraculous descent from heaven. Thus the specific details concerning the crown's placement on the Cross and its ascent into heaven seem to have been added to the Last Emperor legend by Ps.-Methodius on the basis of these traditions specific to his Syriac cultural context.[62] Moreover, in conjunction with this new focus on the Cross, the *Cave of Treasures* also seems to have inspired the location of these events at Golgotha. While *Tib. Sib.* merely notes that this Last Emperor will hand over power in Jerusalem, Ps.-Methodius has further developed this tradition by specifying Golgotha as the site of the Emperor's abdication. As Reinink and others have noted, "In locating the abdication of the Last Emperor on Golgotha, Ps.-Methodius depends on traditions related to the Cross and Golgotha in the *Cave of Treasures*."[63] And so this addition too seems to derive from the author's Syriac cultural heritage.

Psalm 68:31 and Ethiopia

As Ps.-Methodius continues, he begins to expound the significance of the Cross and its ascent to heaven with the crown, and before long he introduces a reference to Ps 68:31, cited in a slightly different context from *Tib. Sib.* and also according to certain nuances that are present only in the Syriac version of this passage. Here, once again comparison of the references to this Psalm in *Tib. Sib.* and *Apoc. Ps.-Meth.* indicates that the latter has seemingly adapted an earlier tradition to fit its Syriac cultural context.[64] *Tib. Sib.* introduces this passage immediately after the Last Emperor's conversion of the pagans, so that it stands as a prophecy of their conversion, as repre-

---

62. Sackur, *Sibyllinische Texte*, 44. See also Konrad, *De ortu et tempore Antichristi*, 48; Reinink, "Die syrischen Wurzeln," 202; Reinink, "Ps.-Methodius," 170–74; Reinink, "Romance of Julian the Apostate," 75–86; Martinez, "Apocalyptic Genre in Syriac," 349–50. For the passage from the Syriac Julian Romance, see Hoffmann, *Iulianos der Abtruennige*, 200–201. For the Syriac *Cave of Treasures*, see *Cave of Treasures* 24:24–26 (Su-Min Ri, ed., *La caverne des trésors*, 192–95 [Syr] and 74–75 [Fr]).

63. Reinink, "Ps.-Methodius," 176–77. See also Konrad, *De ortu et tempore Antichristi*, 47–48; Reinink, "Die syrischen Wurzeln," 201; Martinez, "Apocalyptic Genre," 351.

64. In addition to the following discussion, see also Sackur, *Sibyllinische Texte*, 170–71; and Alexander, *Byzantine Apocalyptic Tradition*, 167–69.

sented by Egypt and Ethiopia. When the Sibyl predicts the conversion of the Jews immediately thereafter, she invokes Jeremiah 23:6 ("In those days Judah will be saved and Israel will dwell in confidence"), thus making the meaning of the Psalm even more clear through the parallel structure (*Tib. Sib.* 10). Ps.-Methodius, however, takes this passage in a decidedly different direction, which is governed largely by his elaborate speculations concerning the Ethiopian lineage of the Greek kings in combination with certain ambiguities present in the Syriac version of the Psalm that are absent from the Greek. For Ps.-Methodius this verse stands not as a prophecy of the pagans' conversion but as a forecast of the Last Emperor's abdication, which will fulfill the Psalmist's prediction (in 68:31) that "'Kush [Ethiopia] will hand over power to God,' . . . for a son of Kushyat, daughter of Pil, king of the Kushites [Ethiopians], is the person [i.e., the Last Emperor] who will 'hand over power to God.'"[65]

In offering this interpretation, Ps.-Methodius explicitly rejects an already-established tradition of interpreting this verse as a reference to the kingdom of Ethiopia and its conversion, and he insists instead that this prophecy concerns the kingdom of the Greeks (i.e., Byzantium).[66] In order to justify this interpretation, *Apoc. Ps.-Meth.* devotes much of its "historical" section to demonstrating the Ethiopian lineage of the Byzantine emperors through Alexander the Great, in an effort to underscore, according to Reinink, the unity of the Greek-Roman-Byzantine Empire as the fourth and final empire predicted by Daniel.[67] The end result, as Alexander observes, is that the author "dedicates the entire first half of the work to proof of the proposition that the 'Ethiopia' of the Psalmist was not, as some earlier members of the clergy had believed, the historical and contemporary kingdom of Ethiopia but the Roman (i.e., Byzantine) Empire."[68] Yet the interpretation is so awkward, so forced, that one would imagine that the author had inherited a tradition already linking this verse with the Last Emperor's appearance, thus requiring him to rethink the verse's eschatological meaning. Of course, by the mid-seventh century it no longer made much sense to understand this verse as a prophecy forecasting the conversion of Ethiopia just before the end of time. That event had already taken place in the mid-fourth century, and so it made much better sense as a portent of the *eschaton* for *Tib.*

65. Reinink, ed., *Syrische Apokalypse*, 44–45 (Syr). My translation, although see also Reinink, ed., *Syrische Apokalypse*, 73–74 (Germ); Reinink, "Ps.-Methodius: A Concept of History," 161–62; and Palmer, *Seventh Century*, 240.

66. Reinink, ed., *Syrische Apokalypse*, 19–20 (Syr) and 29–34 (German).

67. See e.g., Reinink, "Ps.-Methodius," 161–68; Reinink, "Alexander the Great," 175–76.

68. Alexander, *Byzantine Apocalyptic Tradition*, 168.

Sib.'s author. Yet identifying Ethiopia with the Byzantine Empire likewise would not make much sense if by "hastening to offer its hand to God" one envisioned the Empire's conversion: this too had already taken place long ago. Ultimately, Ps.-Methodius's reinterpretation of Ethiopia as Rome only becomes intelligible on the basis of an ambivalence specific to the Syriac version of this Psalm that is absent from the Greek.

The Syriac expression that translates the phrase "offer its hand" has a significant range of meaning beyond the Greek version: in Syriac the expression *tashlem ido* can also mean "will hand over power," and this is the sense with which the author of *Apoc. Ps.-Meth.* has determined to understand the passage.[69] Accordingly, the Psalm predicts not Ethiopia's conversion, as *Tib. Sib.* and other sources have understood it; instead this verse portends the surrender of power to God by "Ethiopia," which is here the Roman Empire, through the Last Emperor's deposition of his crown and robe at Golgotha. The fact that Ps.-Methodius not only deliberately rejects an earlier interpretation of this verse that is present in *Tib. Sib.* but also reinterprets this verse in a manner specific to the nuances of the Syriac translation again seems to indicate that he has developed an earlier tradition in some new directions. In this instance as well then, *Apoc. Ps.-Meth.* seems to have adapted earlier traditions about the Last Emperor that are witnessed in *Tib. Sib.* in order to adjust them to a seventh-century Syriac milieu.

Gog and Magog

Tib. Sib. and *Apoc. Ps.-Meth.* also share a tradition concerning Alexander the Great's enclosure of the 22 peoples of Gog and Magog, and here again Ps.-Methodius's description of Gog and Magog and their role in the events of the *eschaton* appears to be much more developed and recent in comparison with the Sibyl's. Sackur seemingly was the first to notice this relationship, and he considered it one of the clearest indications of *Tib. Sib.*'s independence from *Apoc. Ps.-Meth.* and other later apocalyptic texts. The key difference, according to Sackur, is that *Tib. Sib.* names only Gog and Magog, whereas Ps.-Methodius provides a list identifying each of the 22 peoples that Alexander enclosed. On the basis of this difference as well as the Last Emperor's removal from Gog and Magog's defeat, Sackur concludes that Ps.-Methodius has adapted here an earlier tradition from *Tib. Sib.*[70] Yet in other ways also, Ps.-Methodius shows evidence of having expanded the

---

69. Martinez, "Apocalyptic Genre," 347–48; Greisiger, "Ein nubischer Erlöser-König," 195.

70. Sackur, *Sibyllinische Texte*, 171–72.

significance of Gog and Magog in this eschatological narrative. For instance, the account of their enclosure by Alexander behind a bronze gate occupies a significant portion of *Apoc. Ps.-Meth.*'s historical section—essentially all of book eight. By contrast *Tib. Sib.*, which mentions no gate, merely notes their enclosure, their appearance at the end of time, and their defeat by the Last Emperor, all in just a few lines.[71] Likewise, *Apoc. Ps.-Meth.* and other later traditions describe the savagery and cruelty of these peoples in some detail, as well as the terror and plight of their victims. *Tib. Sib.* has none of this, noting only that these nations are "unclean" (*spurcissime*),[72] and as Reinink has demonstrated, Ps.-Methodius had drawn all of this additional information concerning Gog and Magog primarily from the *Syriac Alexander Legend*.[73] Once again it would appear that here also Ps.-Methodius has developed earlier traditions present in *Tib. Sib.* by expanding them and adapting them to his Syriac cultural context.

Nevertheless Paul Alexander, in a marginal note added to his posthumously published book, remarks that "the combination of Gog and Alexander is not attested before the seventh century." On this basis he suggests there that the Last Emperor's abdication in *Tib. Sib.* is an interpolation, which "if not derived from Pseudo-Methodius, is contemporary with it, or possibly may have a common source."[74] Yet, even if it were true that Alexander (the Great) is not linked with Gog and Magog prior to the seventh century, this small point hardly seems sufficient to justify eliminating the entire Last Emperor episode from *Tib. Sib.*, particularly in light of all of the evidence considered above. And as Paul Alexander himself notes elsewhere with unmistakable clarity, in light of the differences between the two traditions, it simply does not seem possible that *Tib. Sib.* could depend on *Apoc. Ps.-Meth.*[75] Much more importantly, it is clear that the tradition of Alexander's enclosure of Gog and Magog in the north is indeed earlier than the seventh century and even earlier than the late fourth century, the time of *Tib. Sib.*'s composition.[76]

Already at the beginning of the Christian era, Hellenized Jews in Alexandria had begun to merge the biblical traditions of Gog and Magog

---

71. Reinink, ed., *Syrische Apokalypse*, 13–17 (Syr) and 19–26 (German); Sackur, *Sibyllinische Texte*, 186, lines 2–5.

72. See Alexander, *Byzantine Apocalyptic Tradition*, 187.

73. See Reinink, ed., *Syrische Apokalypse*, 21–26 and 67–68 (Germ), esp. 21 n. 4 and 67 n. 2.

74. Alexander, *Byzantine Apocalyptic Tradition*, 163 n. 44.

75. Alexander, "Diffusion of Byzantine Apocalypses," 58, 63–64, & esp. 93–94 n. 9; cf. Alexander, "Medieval Legend," 15; Sackur, *Sibyllinische Texte*, 170.

76. Möhring, *Weltkaiser der Endzeit*, 44.

"with stories of how, during his military campaigns, Alexander the Great built enormous iron gates in order to prevent barbarous incursions from the north."[77] Josephus is an early witness to this emergent tradition. In his *Jewish War* he refers to the "Scythians" as enclosed behind "the pass which king Alexander had closed with iron gates" (*J.W.* 7.7.4, trans. Thackeray), while elsewhere, in the *Antiquities*, he equates the Scythians with Gog and Magog (*Ant.* 1.6.1). Jerome also seems to know a similar tradition concerning a place in the north "where the gates of Alexander keep back the wild peoples behind the Caucasus" (*Epist.* 77.8, trans. Hilberg). And even the Gog and Magog traditions of the *Syriac Alexander Legend* and the homily on Alexander attributed to Jacob of Serug are not as securely dated to the early seventh century as Paul Alexander seems to presume. Despite Reinink's arguments to the contrary, it seems quite possible that both texts draw on an earlier common source, and some specialists even remain convinced that Jacob's homily is in fact authentic.[78] Sackur for his part does admit some concern regarding the mention of 22 peoples in *Tib. Sib.*, inasmuch as Josephus and Jerome do not indicate any particular number, and accordingly he allows for the possibility that the sentence specifying their number may be an interpolation.[79] Nevertheless, the earliest version of the *Alexander Romance*, from the third century if not perhaps even earlier, concludes with the notice that Alexander "overcame twenty-two barbarian peoples."[80] Undoubtedly this tradition is the source of the number 22 in *Tib. Sib.* and in later apocalyptic texts as well.

TIBURTINE SYBIL AND LATE ROMAN POLITICAL ESCHATOLOGY

Comparison of the Last Emperor traditions from *Tib. Sib.* and *Apoc. Ps.-Meth.* thus shows not only that the former is not dependent on the latter, but

---

77. Van Donzel, Schmidt, and Ott, *Gog and Magog*, 9; see also Pfister, *Alexander der Grosse*, 319–27.

78. See the discussion of the various hypotheses in Reinink, *Das syrische Alexanderlied*, 1–15. On the authenticity of the homily attributed to Jacob of Sarug (d. 521), see Zuwiyya, ed., *Companion to Alexander Literature*, 42–45.

79. Sackur, *Sibyllinische Texte*, 172.

80. Kroll, *Historia Alexandri Magni*, 146; trans. Stoneman, *Greek Alexander Romance*, 159. This passage is also confirmed by the Latin and Armenian translations, both of which were realized very early: Kübler, *Iuli Valeri Alexandri*, 168; Wolohojian, *Romance of Alexander the Great*, 158 (trans. of the Armenian). Concerning the date and these versions, see Zuwiyya, ed., *Companion to Alexander Literature* 2–3, 5–6; Stoneman, *Greek Alexander Romance*, 8–14.

to the contrary, if anything, Ps.-Methodius seems to have further developed earlier traditions that are found in the Sibyl's prophecies. No part of the Sibyl's predictions concerning the Last Emperor requires *Apoc. Ps.-Meth.* to explain its presence, and other, much earlier sources provide strong precedent for most of the legend's content. The basic building blocks of the Last Emperor tradition had in fact already found expression in the late third-century *Apocalypse of Elijah*, as David Frankfurter and others have noted. Here one finds, among other parallels with *Tib. Sib.*, a king from the "City of the Sun," whose striking similarities to the Latin Sibyl's Last Emperor suggest that we have here "one of the 'last emperor's' ideological roots."[81] As Frankfurter writes, "This penultimate savior in the Apocalypse of Elijah no doubt forms one of the major sources of the 'Last Emperor' tradition in Byzantine apocalypticism: a human ruler whose beneficent accession and dominion would paradoxically usher in the period of the Antichrist."[82] Moreover, as noted already above, the ideology of the Roman Empire as a divinely-elected polity was well-established by the late fourth century, as was the notion that, as the last of Daniel's four kingdoms, Rome was destined to be the last world empire, after which would follow the Kingdom of God. It certainly is no great leap to combine this ideology with the idea of a final eschatological king such as we find in the *Apocalypse of Elijah* to yield the myth of the Last Roman Emperor.

The idea of a Last Emperor thus was already implicit in the eschatology and political ideology of fourth-century Christianity; all *Tib. Sib.*'s author had to do was pull these two related themes together. Only the means by which this Last Emperor would relinquish authority remained to be imagined. That Jerusalem would be the site is certainly to be expected, given the Holy City's paramount importance in Jewish and Christian eschatology.[83] As for the Emperor laying down his diadem, the symbolism of this deed is fairly obvious, and its inclusion does not require much imagination. Yet this act too is not without precedent; as Sackur notes, the tradition of hanging "crowns" in holy places is an ancient custom, and Constantine himself had his diadem hung in Hagia Sophia.[84] There was also a late-antique practice of sending royal headgear to Jerusalem, as witnessed by the Piacenza Pilgrim,

---

81. Frankfurter, *Elijah in Upper Egypt*, 24, 202; Alexander, *Oracle of Baalbek*, 60, 137.

82. See *Apoc. Elijah* 2.46—3.1 (Steindorff, *Apokalypse des Elias*, 84–87; trans. Frankfurter, *Elijah in Upper Egypt*, 311–13). On the relation between the *Apocalypse of Elijah* and *Tib. Sib.*, see Frankfurter, *Elijah in Upper Egypt*, 24, 202; Alexander, *Oracle of Baalbek*, 60, 137.

83. See, e.g., Alexander, "Medieval Legend," 5–7.

84. Sackur, *Sibyllinische Texte*, 165.

who saw imperial crowns hanging from the Holy Sepulchre in the later sixth century.[85] King Kaleb of Ethiopia affords a specific example of this practice: after defeating the Himyarites in Yemen at the beginning of the sixth century, Kaleb abdicated his rule in order to enter a monastery, sending his crown to Jerusalem to hang before the door of the Holy Sepulchre.[86] Thus the basic elements of *Tib. Sib.*'s Last Emperor traditions all seem to have been well in place long before *Apoc. Ps.-Meth.* was translated into Greek and Latin.

Nevertheless, the question still remains as to why this Last Emperor legend is largely absent from the Greek version of *Tib. Sib.*, and the answer admittedly is not entirely clear. As noted above, some of the most basic elements of the Last Emperor tradition do in fact appear, reflected in the reign of prosperity that is promised under the final emperor, just prior to the Antichrist's manifestation. But much more is lacking, including the description of the Last Emperor's physical appearance and his name, his subjugation and conversion of the pagans and Jews, his defeat of Gog and Magog, and his deposition of his diadem and royal garb at Jerusalem. If these themes belong to the earliest layer of the textual tradition, why then are they missing from the Greek? It certainly is possible that for some reason these traditions were absent from the particular version of *Tib. Sib.* that this Greek redactor used; perhaps it was a slightly older redaction that did not yet have the Last Emperor traditions included. Alternatively, these elements may have been deliberately left out by the Greek redactor, as Rangheri and Möhring have proposed.[87] Possibly the legend's specific links to the fourth century, and especially the Last Emperor's name "Constans" and its focus on converting the pagans, seemed less relevant to the sixth-century editor. Rangheri and Möhring both additionally suggest a possiblity that the legend may have been a separate early tradition that was added to the Latin version of *Tib. Sib.* at the time of its translation from Greek during the later fourth century.[88]

There certainly is no way to exclude entirely the possibility that the Last Emperor tradition may have been interpolated into the Latin *Tib. Sib.*, perhaps even sometime after its translation from Greek into Latin. Yet there are no obvious textual signs of an interpolation, and the legend seems to fit its context rather well. And if it is an interpolation, it does not depend

---

85. Antonius of Piacenza, *Itinerarium* 18 (Geyer, ed., *Itineraria et alia Geographica*, 138).

86. *Martyrdom of St. Arethas and His Companions* 39 (Detoraki, ed., *Le martyre de Saint Aréthas*, 284–85)

87. Rangheri, "'Epistola ad Gerbergami,'" 708–9 n. 79; Möhring, *Weltkaiser der Endzeit*, 43.

88. Rangheri, "'Epistola ad Gerbergami,'" 708–9 n. 79; Möhring, *Weltkaiser der Endzeit*, 43–44. Cf. Alexander, *Oracle of Baalbek*, 63–65.

on *Apoc. Ps.-Meth.*, which it clearly predates. Not only are there too many differences between the accounts to imagine that *Tib. Sib.*'s version could possibly derive from Ps.-Methodius, but the content of the Sibyl's prophecies concerning the Last Emperor clearly marks them as late-antique and pre-Islamic. Moreover, it would seem that despite their preservation now only in Latin, these early traditions of the Last Emperor were circulating broadly in the eastern Mediterranean world prior to the advent of Islam. Their adaptation by Ps.-Methodius itself offers compelling evidence of this fact. Equally important is the appearance of the Last Emperor in *5 Baruch*, an Ethiopic apocalypse that seemingly dates to the early seventh century[89] and significant echoes of this myth that register in Jewish apocalyptic literature from the same era,[90] both of which appear to confirm the legend's broader cultural currency. Consequently there can be little doubt that the final triumph and abdication of the Last Emperor had entered into the Christian eschatological imagination sometime before the Islamic conquests, and already in late antiquity this myth formed an important part of the Byzantine apocalyptic tradition.

Yet the emergence of this legend prior to the rise of Islam holds significance beyond merely refining our knowledge of early Byzantine apocalypticism and imperial eschatology. The circulation of the Last Emperor myth in late antiquity is equally important, as noted above, for understanding the broader religious milieu that gave rise to the Islamic tradition. In particular, the Last Emperor tradition can help to illuminate the apocalyptic political ideology that seems to have fueled formative Islam.[91] In contrast to the somewhat different memories of Islamic origins that were canonized by the classical Islamic tradition during the later eighth and ninth centuries, earliest Islam appears to have been an eschatological movement focused on Jerusalem. There, it would seem, Muhammad and his followers expected their righteous polity to triumph over the infidels and liberate the Promised Land, thus ushering in the Final Judgment of the Hour and the eschato-

---

89. For the text of *5 Baruch* see Halévy, *Tĕëzâza sanbat*, 95–96; trans. in Leslau, *Falasha Anthology*, 75–76. Regarding the date, Pierluigi Piovanelli recently presented his arguments in a paper entitled "The Visions of Baruch and Gorgorios: Two 'Moral' Apocalypses in Late Antique Ethiopia," at the 2012 Annual Meeting of the Society for Biblical Literature in Chicago (19 November 2012). The foundation of the argument is the text's failure to make any mention of the Islamic conquests or any other event beyond the end of the sixth century.

90. See, e.g., Van Bekkum, "Jewish Messianic Expectations," 95–112, 107–8; Reeves, *Trajectories*, 20, 31–39, 58–66; Stoyanov, *Defenders and Enemies*, 53–54; Himmelfarb, "*Sefer Eliyyahu*," 229–30. See also Suermann, "Der byzantinische Endkaiser," 148–55.

91. For more on this topic, see Shoemaker, "Reign of God."

logical reign of God.[92] Although the sixth and early seventh centuries were generally an age of intense and intensifying eschatological expectation in Byzantium,[93] the legend of the Last Emperor in particular offers important precedent for early Islam's vision of an eschatological imperial triumph that would be fulfilled in Jerusalem. Other sources from the period, especially Jewish sources, similarly envision the *eschaton*'s arrival through victory over the enemies of God in the Holy Land. But *Tib. Sib.* indicates that such ideas were equally current among the Christians of late antiquity. The myth of the Last Emperor then was not something new that first emerged only in the wake of the Islamic conquests, as some studies of this tradition in Syriac especially seem to suggest. Rather, it reflects an already-established apocalyptic political ideology that was an important facet of early Byzantine imperial eschatology. The Last Emperor's appearance in *Apoc. Ps.-Meth.* and other related texts thus reflects the reinvigoration of an already-established tradition in reaction to the ascendancy of Islam. Consequently, we should understand this influential theme from the Byzantine apocalyptic tradition not merely as a response to Islamic dominion, but also as an important element of the immediate religious context that gave birth to the Islamic tradition itself.

92. See, e.g., Shoemaker, *Death of a Prophet*.

93. Mango, *Byzantium*, 203–204; Magdalino, "History of the Future," 4–5; Alexander, *Oracle of Baalbek*, 118–20; Brandes, "Anastasios ὁ δίκορος," 26–32, 39–40, 53–63; Ashbrook Harvey, "Remembering Pain," 298–302; Nicholson, "Golden Age," 11–18; Brandes, "Die apokalyptische Literatur," 308; Stoyanov, *Defenders and Enemies*, 55, 62. In a forthcoming article, however, Averil Cameron raises a challenge to this consensus of a spike in apocalypticism in the sixth and seventh centuries: "Late antique apocalyptic: a context for the Qur'an?" I thank Prof. Cameron for sharing the text of this article in advance of its publication.

— 14 —

Confused Traditions?
Peter and Paul in the Apocryphal Acts

— David L. Eastman —

IN THE BOOK OF Acts, Luke's account of the post-Jesus period, Peter and Paul play the lead roles. The impulsive fisherman from Galilee and the erstwhile persecutor of the followers of Jesus become the primary mouthpieces for this new movement among both Jews and Gentiles. Yet for all of Luke's descriptions of the apostles' travels and their deeds, he leaves large gaps in the overall narratives of their lives. For later Christians these biographical gaps, particularly as they pertain to the ends of the apostles' lives, needed to be filled. This gave rise to a robust corpus of literary, artistic, and liturgical traditions that drew inspiration from, and then expanded freely upon, both the Acts of the Apostles and the Pauline and Petrine epistles. But these later expansions were not uniform in content or scope. The evidence reflects multiple, even conflicting traditions about elements of the apostolic biographies. I have demonstrated elsewhere, for example, that there were two different sites in Rome identified as the place of Paul's death,[1] and my forthcoming volume on the accounts of the martyrdoms of Peter and Paul will show how varied these stories are in many details.[2] Given the

---

1. Eastman, *Paul the Martyr*, 62–69.
2. Eastman, *Ancient Martyrdom Accounts*. This volume will include new translations

variety of sources and the variety within those sources, it is not surprising that some peculiar dynamics entered the tradition. In this essay I will focus on one of these dynamics, namely the tendency to conflate and/or confuse Paul and Peter with one another.

Peter and Paul stood as the two primary pillars upon which Christianity was built. They were the dual apostles—Peter being the apostle to the Jews,[3] and Paul being the apostle to everyone else. The pairing of Peter and Paul thus represented all of Christianity. The Roman church laid particular claim to these apostles as the founders of their community, and this was the basis of Rome's claim to authority, a claim that would rival or even surpass those of other cities such as Antioch and Alexandria. While the pairing of these apostles was not unique to the Roman context, the overwhelming majority of surviving artistic evidence comes from Rome. Here the theme of the *concordia apostolorum* ("harmony of the apostles") is featured prominently as the image of church unity and apostolic foundation.[4]

Yet even the pairing of these apostles in Rome and elsewhere was not necessarily an easy task, for the canonical record suggests that the relationship between Paul and Peter was at times strained. In Galatians 2:11–14 Paul reports the famous "Antioch incident," in which he confronts Peter and accuses him of hypocrisy; so there is no doubt that tensions existed at least on this occasion. Paul's report of a peaceful meeting with Peter/Cephas in Jerusalem in Gal 1:18 confirms that they were not at odds on every occasion; so we would be wise to avoid repeating the mistake of constructing a metanarrative of early Christianity based on Galatians 2, while ignoring Galatians 1, to say nothing of Acts. Some read tension in the apostolic relationship into the late second-century *Acts of Peter*, where Peter does not arrive to counter Simon the sorcerer (Simon Magus) until after Paul has left for Spain.[5] Yet the author of the *Acts of Peter* also makes clear that Peter has come to protect the church Paul has built, rather than to alter or destroy it. Indeed, Paul had told a certain Ariston to be on the lookout for Peter's arrival (*Acts Pet.* 6), so the friction of Galatians 2 is not really on display

---

of 15 texts (or at least parts thereof), some of which have not yet appeared in English translation. All translations of primary texts in this essay are my own unless otherwise noted.

3. The debate over translating the Greek Ἰουδαῖος as *Jew* or *Judean* is well documented (see, e.g., Reinhartz, "*Vanishing Jews of Antiquity*"; Daniel Schwartz, "'Judaean' or 'Jew'?"; and Seth Schwartz, "How Many Judaisms Were There?"). Due to the concerns raised by Jewish scholars about the elimination of Jews from ancient texts by the use of the term *Judean*, I have opted for the term *Jew* here.

4. See, e.g., Huskinson, *Concordia Apostolorum*.

5. Cartlidge and Elliott, *Art and the Christian Apocrypha*, 135.

here. Beginning at least as early as the eighteenth century, some scholars have read the Pseudo-Clementine *Homilies* and *Recognitions* (composed probably in the third or fourth century) as an indication of apostolic rivalry. Johann Salomo Semler was the first to make this explicit connection, although his ideas were probably influenced by the arguments that John Toland had earlier put forward in his *Nazarenus*. Semler agreed with Toland that primitive Christianity was strongly Judean and anti-Pauline, and he saw the *Pseudo-Clementines* as vestiges of this earliest layer of the tradition.[6] These ideas were reworked by scholars such as J. K. L. Gieseler and later F. C. Baur, who is popularly but incorrectly credited with their genesis.[7] Because Baur's name is most often connected to these ideas, his work has been the object of the most criticism. Strong points in opposition to Baur's anti-Pauline reading of the *Homilies* and *Recognitions* have been raised,[8] so these texts may ultimately complicate, rather than clarify, early Christian perceptions of the apostolic relationship.

To this point, then, we have already seen several complexities in the presentations of Peter and Paul. Even taken separately, they are figures that sparked the creation of various traditions and images, not all of which were in concert with one another. Together they are often portrayed as the apostolic pair *par excellence*, the pillars of the church in Rome and elsewhere, even if their relationship was complicated by different perspectives on key issues such as legal observance or by different bases for their claims to authority. These complexities warrant and have received considerable scholarly attention, yet in this paper I want to muddy the waters even further concerning the later reception of the apostolic traditions. Even in cases where authors and artists seem to take for granted a harmonious apostolic history, they sometimes conflate and/or confuse Paul and Peter with one another.

---

6. Semler, *Abhandlung von freier Untersuchung des Canon*, 4:Vorrede b8; Toland, *Nazarenus*.

7. Baur, "Christuspartei in der korinthischen Gemeinde." On the complicated but likely flow of influence from Toland through Semler and Gieseler to Baur, see Jones, "From Toland to Baur." Jones specifies that Baur probably never read Toland directly. David Lincicum agrees concerning Toland's indirect influence on Baur and also suggests possible influence from another English deist, Thomas Morgan. See Lincicum, "F.C. Baur's Place." These essays are important for their contributions in correcting the prevalent myth in New Testament scholarship that Baur was the originator of these ideas.

8. See, e.g., the substantial critique by Bockmuehl, *Remembered Peter*, 102–12, esp. 102, n. 36 for further bibliography.

CONFUSION IN CHRISTIAN LITERATURE

I will turn my attention first to the textual traditions. The apocryphal acts represent one of the primary means by which later authors sought to fill in the missing details in the apostolic biographies. Second-century texts like the *Acts of Peter* and the *Acts of Paul* were reappropriated, altered, and expanded upon in the apostolic acts of the fourth, fifth, and sixth centuries and beyond. The acts of Pseudo-Linus, Pseudo-Marcellus, and Pseudo-Abdias, along with the epistle of Pseudo-Dionysius the Areopagite to Timothy, are among more than a dozen late antique accounts of the later adventures and eventual martyrdoms of these two apostles. In these texts Paul and Peter speak at length, particularly on the issues of legal observance and suffering. But the authors here face a fundamental problem: Paul has much more to say on these and other questions than Peter does in the canonical sources. The 13 letters of the traditional Pauline corpus, combined with the majority of the book of Acts, provide much more material from which one might draw than do the two brief Petrine epistles and the sermons in Acts ascribed to Peter. Apparently, it was challenging to present Peter and Paul as equals, or even Peter as Paul's superior, when Paul had provided so much of the best teaching on the topics at hand. The apocryphal texts present two solutions to this problem.

One solution was simply to take the words of Paul and place them in Peter's mouth. In the Pseudo-Linus *Martyrdom of Blessed Peter the Apostle* (=*Mart. Pet.*; composed probably in the fourth century), for example, this happens on multiple occasions as the text reaches its climax. In one scene, Peter agrees, at the behest of the Christians in Rome, to leave the city in order to preserve his life. However, he is met at the gate of the city by Christ, who says that he is going to Rome to be crucified again (this is the famous "Quo vadis?" scene). Peter understands that this is the Lord's directive for his own death and returns to Rome determined to face his fate. Now back in the city, he begins to give his final directives and words of encouragement:

> "It is easy for the Lord to strengthen the hearts of his servants even without my humble admonition. Those whom he planted he will make grow to the point that they may be able to plant others. But I, as a servant, must follow the will of the Lord to the end. Therefore, if he sends me back to linger in the flesh for your sake, then I will not resist. But if he has decided that I should suffer for his name and sees fit to receive me through my passion, then I exult and rejoice in his grace." (*Mart. Pet.* 7)

Here Peter is presented as alluding to two separate Pauline passages. In the first instance he reminds his audience that the Lord is the one who makes the faith of believers grow to the point that they can tell others. This is reminiscent of 1 Cor 3:5–9, where Paul uses the same imagery to address divisions within the Corinthian community. Paul has heard that the Corinthians are split into factions associated with Peter/Cephas, Paul, and Apollos. Part of his response to this situation is to strip the apostles of any credit by giving to God all the glory for the growth among them: "I planted, Apollos watered, but God gave the growth. So neither the one who plants nor the one who waters is anything, but only God who gives the growth" (1 Cor 3:6–7). In this text "Peter" alters the emphasis, but his point is the same. God ultimately grows the church, so the believers in Rome do not need Peter with them to ensure that they will survive and flourish.

In the second part of this passage, Peter wrestles with the same quandary that vexes Paul in Philippians. Paul writes, "For to me, living is Christ and dying is gain. If I am to live in the flesh, that means fruitful labor for me; and I do not know which I prefer. I am hard pressed between the two: my desire is to depart and be with Christ, for that is far better; but to remain in the flesh is more necessary for you" (Phil 1:21–24). In *Mart. Pet.*, Peter, like Paul in Philippians, desires to depart and be with the Lord, yet he understands that he may need to remain in the flesh for the sake of other Christians. Although Paul decides that he will linger in the flesh for the sake of the Philippians (Phil 1:25–26), Peter seems uncertain of the outcome. From a narrative perspective, Peter's ambiguity is perplexing, because he had just returned from his meeting with Christ at the gates of Rome. Peter knows perfectly well what must happen to him, but the author paints him with a Pauline brush, because Paul provides the example of an apostle who struggles within himself over the issues of death, life, and the fate of his disciples after his departure. In this story Peter mimics, and for the Roman context supplants, Paul in this role. Replacing Paul with Peter thus makes the Romans decidedly *Peter's* spiritual children in the way that the Philippians had been Paul's.

The Pauline citations do not stop here, however. When he faces the Roman prefect Agrippa, Peter declares, "I have no glory except the cross of my Lord Jesus Christ, whose servant I am" (*Mart. Pet.* 8). This is clearly taken from Gal 6:14, where Paul writes, "May I never boast of anything except the cross of our Lord Jesus Christ, by which the world has been crucified to me, and I to the world." The appeal to Paul is logical, for in Galatians Paul links this declaration to a sense of his own symbolic crucifixion. In *Mart. Pet.* Peter is facing his real crucifixion; so the author places in his mouth this Pauline quotation, which draws attention to Peter's sacrifice as a follower of Christ while still elevating Christ's crucifixion to a higher level of importance. Indeed, this elevation is clarified in the lines that follow:

> And Agrippa said, "Do you wish, therefore, to be crucified just as your God was crucified?" Peter responded, "I am not worthy to make the testimony of my passion to the world on an upright cross, but through whatever kinds of entreaties are necessary, I wish and desire to follow in the footsteps of his passion" (*Mart. Pet.* 8).

Peter wants to die by crucifixion so that Christ might be "crucified again" through him, but he does not feel worthy to die in the same position. This leads to his famous request for inverted crucifixion—a request based in the Pauline conception of Christ's cross as a source of boasting, rather than shame.

In the sections that follow, Peter continues to pepper his prose with Pauline passages. When he stands before a mob and tries to dissuade them from revolting against Agrippa because he had sentenced Peter to death, the apostle encourages the crowd, saying, "Remain calm, therefore, rejoicing and happy that I may offer my sacrifice to the Lord with gladness, for God loves a cheerful giver" (*Mart. Pet.* 9). Paul had written to the Corinthians that "God loves a cheerful giver," but this was to remind them to fulfill their promise of a financial gift for the believers suffering in Jerusalem (2 Cor 9:7). Pseudo-Linus reappropriates the line for a different context, and thus Paul's statement about money is reinterpreted as a declaration of God's desire for believers to offer their lives as martyrs. Later, at the close of what seems to be Peter's final speech—although it turns out that he has much, much more to say—the apostle tells his listeners, "Farewell, brothers. Be steadfast, and preserve the things that you have heard" (*Mart. Pet.* 10). Peter's admonition invokes 2 Thess 2:15, where Paul (or "Paul") instructs, "So then, brothers and sisters, stand firm and hold fast to the traditions that you were taught by us, either by word of mouth or by our letter." The Romans, like the Thessalonians, should preserve especially what they have heard directly from the apostles. Here again, Peter thus becomes the primary apostolic voice for the Roman church, as Paul had been for the Thessalonians.[9] Furthermore, when Peter is instructing his executioners on how to crucify him, he identifies

---

9. The fact that Peter does not also appeal to the authority of a letter, as Paul does, may be explained by the fact that neither of the Petrine epistles is addressed to Rome. However, there is a tradition that both were written *from* Rome; so, by the fourth century, the Roman community likely would have had access to "Peter's" teachings through these letters. I will return below to the peculiar lack of Petrine allusions to 1 and 2 Peter in the apocryphal texts.

himself as the "least of all servants" (*Mart. Pet.* 12), echoing Paul's claim to be the "least of all" (1 Cor 15:9; Eph 3:8).

Once on the cross, Peter returns to preaching and sets out to explain—to those who can understand it—"the mystery of all nature and the beginning of everything that has been made" (*Mart. Pet.* 14). He is concerned with the connection between his inverted crucifixion position and the inverted position of children at birth, with the reversal of things that are left and right, with the symbolism of the cross as fallen human nature, and with the discrepancy between the material and the spiritual. This section of the text is quite convoluted and therefore difficult to translate. What is clear, however, is a dichotomy between the situation of the "first man" and the "Progenitor" of the new race of Christians. The "first man" was essentially born dead, with his head dropped as a sign of his fallen state. Through him human nature "suffered the error of alteration" and was doomed to destruction. But Christ reversed the situation:

> However, drawn by his own mercy, the Progenitor came into the world through a corporeal being to the very one whom he had cast to the earth by a just sentence. Suspended on a cross, he restored the first man through the appearance of the calling that must be honored—namely the cross—and he established for us the things that formerly had been altered by the regrettable error of men.... Through God and man, however, that [human] nature has recovered its true understanding. (*Mart. Pet.* 14)

The incarnate Christ, who was fully both God and human, reversed the curse brought upon humanity by Adam's sin. The dichotomy that Peter presents is taken directly from 1 Cor 15:20–23 and Rom 5:12–21, where Paul argues that just as death came through the one man Adam, so does resurrection come through the one man Jesus Christ. Paul explains this reversal as a manifestation of the contrast between that which is earthly (or natural) and that which is spiritual (1 Cor 15:45–49), a theme that Pseudo-Linus picks up in Peter's sermon as well. Peter's mystical presentation of human history and Christ's redemptive work, therefore, is constructed on a Pauline theological framework and employs Pauline language, even if the Peter of this text applies the reversal metaphor in ways that Paul had not.

Finally, as Peter praises Christ just before dying, he proclaims,

> "In you we live, move, and exist. Therefore, we ought to have you as our everything, so that you may give to us those things that you have promised, things which neither eye has seen nor ear has heard nor have entered into the heart of man, things which you have prepared for those who love you." (*Mart. Pet.* 15)

As with our first example above, we find here a double Pauline reference. The first is a direct citation from Paul's Areopagus speech in Acts 17:28: "In him we live and move and have our being."[10] Then Peter shifts suddenly and cites Paul's claim that no one can conceive of the rewards awaiting the faithful: "What no eye has seen, nor ear heard, nor the human heart conceived, what God has prepared for those who love him" (1 Cor 2:9). There is no doubt that Pseudo-Linus is quoting Paul because, while modern translations tend to identify 1 Cor 2:9 as a citation from Isaiah (and perhaps the Psalms), in fact it is not. No other known text presents this litany in its Pauline form;[11] so Pseudo-Linus's Peter is certainly again citing Paul, not a passage from the Hebrew Bible. Thus, when the author of the Pseudo-Linus *Martyrdom of Blessed Peter the Apostle* sets out to present Peter as a learned teacher of divine mysteries, he cannot do so without references to Paul. Peter does not have his own words to speak. He can find expression of the eternal truths revealed to him only through the language of the apostle whose knowledge of the gospel came first and foremost through divine revelation.

Pseudo-Linus is not the only author who places Paul's words in the mouth of Peter, although no other text includes Pauline citations in such quantity or density. The author of the sixth-century Latin *Passion of the Holy Apostles Peter and Paul* (=*Pass. Holy*)[12] likewise draws from Paul's epistles in giving voice to Peter. The text opens with a chaotic scenario in which the Judean leaders seek Paul's assistance in silencing Peter, and the Judean and Gentile Christians are in open conflict with one another. Both apostles address the crowds in an attempt to restore peace, and when Peter turns his attention to speaking to the Judean leaders, he offers this explanation and justification for the foundation of the church:

> "In order that [Christ] might fulfill the necessary redemption for the world, he allowed himself to undergo all these things, so that just as Eve was formed from the rib of Adam (Gen 2:21–22), so too from the side of Christ—who was placed on the cross—the church may be formed, which has neither stain nor wrinkle." (*Pass. Holy* 8)

---

10. The main alteration from the Vulgate of Acts 17:28 is the change of the pronoun from "him" to "you." Vulgate Acts 17:28: *in ipso enim vivimus et movemur et sumus*. Cf. *Mart. Pet.* 15: *in te vivimus movemur et sumus*.

11. On the possible sources for 1 Cor 2:9 see Conzelmann, *1 Corinthians*, 63–64.

12. From this point forward I will refer to this text as the Latin *Passion*. It is traditionally ascribed to a certain Marcellus, who is mentioned in the story as a nobleman who had been following Simon the sorcerer but was converted by the teaching of Peter.

Peter appeals to the Genesis creation story as the model for the birth of the church and then punctuates his statement with a reference to Eph 5:27: "... so as to present the church to himself in splendor, without a spot or wrinkle or anything of the kind." Peter's church is spotless, as it was for the writer of Ephesians, and Peter is even more Pauline in that his commentary expands on the Pauline model of the church as Christ's bride, articulated most explicitly in Eph 5:22–23.[13] Just as Eve was born from Adam's side and then became his wife, so was the church born from Christ and is now his bride. Peter's teaching, therefore, may be read as a kind of midrash on Eph 5:22–27, although Peter applies this imagery to the church rather than to the household.[14]

That Peter so often parrots Paul is significant, but it is all the more striking when we take into account the lack of Petrine allusions to "his own" letters. In fact, in the later apocryphal acts, I know of not a single case in which Peter quotes 1 or 2 Peter. It is not as if the Petrine epistles would offer no relevant material. In 1 Pet 2:11–17, 3:13–4:2, 4:12–19, and 5:9–10, the author addresses the issues of persecution and the Christian's proper conduct toward the government authorities. Surely something of this would have been useful for an author constructing a narrative of Peter before Nero. In 2 Pet 1:13–14, the author predicts his imminent demise and refers to his clear sense of what he must do while he remains in the body. Why would Peter not use "his own" words in the later texts to speak of his death? And why would a Peter struggling (in Pauline fashion) with whether life or death is preferable for him (see above) not refer back to this same issue in 2 Peter?[15]

The only explicit reference to a Petrine epistle in the apocryphal texts comes from the Latin *Passion* and is actually placed in the mouths of misguided Judean Christians. As part of their polemic against the Gentile believers, they proclaim, "We are the elect, royal race of the friends of God: Abraham, Isaac, Jacob, and all the prophets" (*Pass. Holy* 5). This is an allusion to 1 Pet 2:9: "But you are a chosen race, a royal priesthood, a holy

---

13. See also 2 Cor 11:2–4 and Rom 7:7, which were no doubt the source of Eph 5:22–23. The imagery of God and the people being married has deep roots in the Hebrew Bible, e.g., Isa 54:4–6, 62:4–5; Ezek 16:8; Hosea.

14. When the Pseudo-Marcellus text was translated into Greek (known as the *Acts of the Holy Apostles Peter and Paul*, hereafter referred to as the Greek *Acts*), the translator maintained this Pauline connection (*Acts Pet. Paul* 29).

15. Scholars generally deny Pauline influence on 2 Peter, but it may be that the Pauline description of the church as having no σπίλον (Eph 5:27) has influenced the Petrine admonition to the believers to remain ἄσπιλοι (2 Pet 3:14), which notably comes just prior to the reference to Paul and his epistles. In any event, perhaps the apocryphal author's choice not to cite 2 Peter is evidence of the early church's hesitation to acknowledge its authorship as apostolic.

nation." The Greek version of these acts (the *Acts of the Holy Apostles Peter and Paul*; =*Acts Pet. Paul*) makes the connection to 1 Peter even stronger by employing terminology identical to 1 Peter: "We are a chosen race, a royal priesthood, of the tribe of Abraham, Isaac, Jacob, and all the prophets" (*Acts Pet. Paul* 26).[10] Both Paul and Peter subsequently speak out against this sense of superiority and entitlement among the Judean believers. Thus, the only explicit reference to the Petrine epistles in these early acts provokes not apostolic support, but apostolic rebuke. The words of Peter seem to pale in comparison to those of Paul in terms of their relevance and authority; so these authors simply have Peter speak with Paul's words.

The other solution to the relative lack of usable Petrine language was to present the words of each apostle as the words of both apostles, although here again Paul enjoys pride of place. In both the Latin *Passion* and the closely-related Greek *Acts*, Peter and Paul engage in a lengthy debate with Simon the sorcerer in the presence of Nero. Initially, Peter and Simon are the primary verbal combatants, but then Nero turns to Paul and asks what teaching he had learned from his master (Jesus) and then spread through his own preaching. Paul gives a lengthy response, in the midst of which he explains to Nero:

> "Concerning the teaching of my master, however, about which you asked me, no one can understand it except those who accept faith with a pure heart (1 Tim 1:5; 2 Tim 2:22). For whatever things concern peace and love, I have taught them. Throughout my journey from Jerusalem as far as Illyricum (Rom 15:19), I have spread the word of peace. I have taught men to love one another. I have taught them to outdo one another in showing honor (Rom 12:10). I have taught the lofty and the rich not to elevate themselves and hope in the uncertainty of riches, but to place their hope in God (1 Tim 6:17). I have taught those with ordinary food and clothing to be content (1 Tim 6:8). I have taught the poor to rejoice in their poverty (cf. 2 Cor 6:10). I have taught fathers to teach their sons the discipline of the fear of God (cf. Eph 6:4). I have taught sons to obey their parents and the salvific admonitions (Col 3:20; Eph 6:1). I have taught those who have possessions to pay tribute out of duty. I have taught merchants to pay taxes to the servants of the republic (Rom 13:5–7). I have taught wives to love their husbands and fear them as their masters.[17] I have taught husbands to be faith-

---

16. *Acts Pet. Paul* 26: ἡμεῖς γένος ἐσμὲν ἐκλεκτὸν βασίλειον ἱεράτευμα. Cf. 1 Pet 2:9: ὑμεῖς δὲ γένος ἐκλεκτὸν βασίλειον ἱεράτευμα.

17. No such command is given even among the disputed Pauline epistles.

ful to their wives, just as they wish to keep themselves blameless in every way (Col 3:18–19; Eph 5:22–28). That which a husband punishes in an adulterous wife, the Father and maker of all things, God himself, punishes in an adulterous husband. I have taught masters to deal mildly with their servants (Phlm; Col 4:1; Eph 6:9). I have taught servants to serve their masters faithfully and as if working for God (Col 3:22–24; Eph 6:5–6). I have taught assemblies[18] of believers to worship the one omnipotent, invisible (Col 1:15; 1 Tim 1:17), incomprehensible God. This teaching was given to me not by men, nor through another man, but through Jesus Christ and the Father of glory, who spoke to me from heaven (Gal 1:1, 11–12)." (*Pass. Holy* 36–38; parallel to *Acts Pet. Paul* 57–59)

This is a remarkably dense series of allusions to the Pauline epistles, but it is not a summary of any particular letter. Rather, the author has pulled teachings from a wide variety of sources, for seven of the 13 Pauline letters are cited in this one passage. When Paul finally finishes his monologue, Nero turns back to Peter to see if he has anything to add. Peter responds, "All the things that Paul said are true" (*Pass. Holy* 39; parallel to *Acts Pet. Paul* 60). He then recounts the story of Paul's background and conversion, ending with the summary statement, "He abandoned what he was defending and began to defend that which he was persecuting—that is the path of Christ, which is the way for those walking in purity, the truth for those who are not deceivers, and the life eternal for those who believe (John 14:6)" (*Pass. Holy* 39; parallel to *Acts Pet. Paul* 60). Peter, therefore, testifies that all of Paul's teachings are true and implicitly affirms that they were given to him directly by Christ. This Petrine confirmation is in effect a recapitulation of Paul's central claims in Galatians 1–2, namely that he received his gospel from Christ alone and not from any person (Gal 1:11–12), and that neither Peter nor anyone else had anything to add to his gospel (Gal 2:6–9). Peter's relative silence at the end of Paul's speech before Nero shows that even at the end of their lives, Peter still had nothing to add to Paul's teaching. He simply accepted it as his own, thus making Paul's gospel his, as well.

In the scene that follows, Peter condemns Simon the sorcerer once more, saying, "There is no truth in you, but everything you say and do comes from only falsehood" (*Pass. Holy* 40; *Acts Pet. Paul* 61). Nero then turns back to Paul to ask what he might say. The process is now reversed, for Paul retorts, "Consider that the things you heard from Peter were also said by me. We feel the same way, because we have one Lord, Jesus Christ"

---

18. Or "churches."

(*Pass. Holy* 41).[19] When one apostle speaks, both speak, for they have the same Lord and therefore will supposedly teach exactly the same message. It is notable, however, that in this exchange of apostolic affirmations, Paul still maintains the privileged position. As we have seen, Peter gives his approval to an extended litany of Paul's teachings drawn from seven letters. All that Paul is agreeing with in the text is a single statement of Peter condemning Simon the sorcerer. Paul does not assent to Petrine teaching in general, and certainly not to any material taken from the Petrine epistles. Thus, it is still Peter who primarily benefits from this apostolic univocality.

Peter's perceived lack of authoritative teachings created a problem for authors desiring to present the apostles as equals, and even more so for those for whom Peter ought to represent some kind of primacy. Robbing Paul to pay Peter was the solution, whether this took the form of ascribing Paul's words to Peter or declaring their words indistinguishable from each other. The goal seems to have been the same, namely to obfuscate any qualitative differentiation between the apostle with great theological gravitas and the one who (it would seem) had made little contribution through his two meager epistles. This robbing, I would suggest, may have had a marked impact on later reception history. Phrases and concepts that we identify as distinctly Pauline, because we are familiar with them through our study of the scriptural texts, might have sounded Petrine to later audiences, if their primary exposure to these ideas had come through the very popular stories of the martyrdoms of Peter and Paul. In such contexts, Peter would become not only one of Jesus' closest disciples and a worker of miracles, but also a theologian on par with Paul himself.

Paul and Peter are confused in some of these texts also through the presentations of what they did and how certain people reacted to them. From reading texts such as Galatians, Romans, and Acts, for example, we learn that Paul's missionary preaching was more successful among Gentiles than among Jews, in large part because his teachings about Torah observance often provoked the ire of devout Jews. In fact, Luke tells us that Paul's position on the law was the primary factor in his arrest in Jerusalem and even prompted a death squad to seek his life (Acts 21:27–33; 23:12–15). Peter accepts Gentiles based on the Cornelius story but still seems to support legal observance, which caused him to fall afoul of Paul at Antioch (Gal 2:11–14). Thus, we would expect the animosity between Paul and other Jews, and the close connection between Peter and Torah-observant Jews, to carry over into the apocryphal acts. However, many of these texts are

---

19. This section is missing from the text of the Greek *Acts*.

silent on any controversy between Paul and the Jews.[20] A debate between the apostles and some Judean leaders is featured at the opening of the Latin *Passion*, but notably the traditional apostolic roles are reversed:

> When Paul had come to Rome, all the Jews came together to him, saying, "Protect our faith in which you were born. It is not right that you, who are a Hebrew of Hebrews, should consider yourself a teacher of the Gentiles; or that you, who are circumcised, have become a defender of the uncircumcised and nullify the faith of the circumcision.[21] Therefore, when you see Peter, stand against his teaching, because he has nullified all observance of our law, has eliminated our Sabbath and new moons, and has decimated our lawful feasts." Paul responded to them, "From this you will be able to prove that I am a Judean, and a true Judean, namely that you will truly be able to observe the Sabbath and pay heed to circumcision. For on the Sabbath day God rested from all his works. We have the fathers and the patriarchs and the law. What sort of thing is Peter preaching in the kingdom of the Gentiles? But if by chance he wants to introduce any new teaching, then without any disturbance or animosity or troublemaking tell him that we should see him, and in your presence I will refute him. And if by chance his teaching is supported by true testimony and the books of the Hebrews, then it is proper that we all obey him." (*Pass. Holy* 1–2)

Paul's arrival in Rome brings not a hostile reception by the Judean leaders, nor even the initially ambivalent reception of Acts 28:17–29 by leaders who claim to have heard nothing about him. Rather, he is welcomed with great enthusiasm. The Jews of Rome have heard rumors about him and ask him to prove his fidelity to the traditions of the elders by confronting a known enemy of the law in Rome (Peter), who "has nullified all observance of our law, has eliminated our Sabbath and new moons, and has decimated our lawful feasts." Paul begins his answer by assuaging their fears, assuring them that he does observe the law and respect the patriarchs. Thus, Paul is the traditionalist, while Peter is the one accused of subverting the law. Paul even offers a thinly-veiled threat directed at Peter: if Peter is indeed teaching something new to the Gentiles, then the Jews should bring him quietly to Paul, and Paul will correct him in their presence. This scenario would be the Antioch incident in reverse, for here Paul would be rebuking Peter for *not* observing the law, instead of for observing it too rigorously.

20. These texts credit Paul's legal issues to the fact that he ascribes true kingship to Jesus, not Nero, or that he is involved in the showdown with Simon the sorcerer.

21. Or, "faith in circumcision."

Paul adds the final condition that if "the books of the Hebrews" (presumably the Hebrew Bible) support Peter's teaching, then all should obey him. The author of this text must want the reader to assume that Paul finds this to be the case, because in the text there is never any hint of theological debate between the apostles.

The Greek version of this text (the Greek *Acts*) tells a story that is similar in many ways but features a few notable changes. While Paul's arrival in Rome marks the beginning of the Latin *Passion*, in the Greek *Acts* this occurs in chapter 22. The first 21 chapters of the Greek *Acts* contain a detailed account of Paul's journey from Malta to Rome. Most scholars agree that this section is a later addition, and it contains some important details. The account opens with Paul's departure from Malta, and the news reaches Rome of his impending arrival there. The response of the Jews is quite different from that in the Latin *Passion*:

> Therefore, falling into great distress and losing heart, they said to themselves, "It does not suffice that he alone afflicted all our brothers and fathers in Judea and Samaria and all of Palestine. He was not satisfied by these things, but behold, he even comes here, having appealed to Caesar so that through an attack he may destroy us." Therefore, after all the Jews had turned the Senate against Paul and had contrived many things, it seemed good to them to go to Nero, the king who was ruling in those days, so that he would not permit Paul to come to Rome. Therefore, after they had prepared many gifts and had deliberated among themselves, they went to him with their petition, saying, "We beg you, noble king, to send out orders to all the provinces under control of your piety that Paul should not come near to these regions. We ask this because this man Paul, who has afflicted the entire race of our people, has asked to come here so that he may also destroy us. And the distress that we have from Peter, most pious king, is already sufficient for us." Having heard these things, the emperor Nero answered them, "It is done according to your will, and we are writing to all our provinces, so that he may certainly not drop anchor in the regions of Italy." And they informed even Simon the sorcerer, having summoned him so that, as has been said, Paul may not at all set foot in the regions of Italy. (*Acts Pet. Paul* 2–4)

Rather than waiting to welcome Paul, the Jews of Rome secure an order from Nero that Paul is to be killed on sight. Some Gentile converts hear of this and send a warning; so Paul remains hidden for a week after his arrival in Puteoli.

Then follows an almost-comical scene in which the captain of Paul's ship, a recent convert named Dioscorus, goes into Puteoli declaring the gospel. Because he is preaching Christ and is bald,[22] the local authorities assume that he is Paul, decapitate him, and send his head to Caesar (*Acts Pet. Paul* 5–10).

> Then Caesar summoned the leaders of the Jews and reported to them, saying, "Rejoice greatly,[23] because your enemy Paul is dead." And he even showed them his head. Therefore, after they had held a great celebration on that day, which was the fourteenth day of the month of June, each of the Jews was fully satisfied. (*Acts Pet. Paul* 10).

Paul's eventual arrival in Rome, therefore, is not met at all with enthusiasm, but with trepidation:

> But it became know in the city of Rome that Paul, the brother of Peter, was coming. Those who had come to believe in God were rejoicing greatly.[24] But there was a great disturbance among the Jews, and they went to Simon the sorcerer and begged him, saying, "Report to the king that Paul did not die, but is alive and has come." But Simon said to the Jews, "Whose, then, is the head that came to Caesar from Puteoli? Was this not also the head of a bald man?" And after Paul had come to Rome, a great fear fell upon the Jews. (*Acts Pet. Paul* 21–22)

The authorities in Puteoli had killed the wrong bald man. Then, as now, bald guys just can't get a break.

When the Greek *Acts* joins the narrative of the Latin *Passion*, the leaders of the Jews, despite their fear, still come to Paul and beg him to defend the traditions of the elders and to confront Peter's new teaching. But their charge against Peter is more general, for they say only that "he has undermined every observance of our Law" (*Acts Pet. Paul* 22), failing to specify his infractions against the Sabbath and their feasts, as they do in the Latin version. Paul's response is also noticeably shorter: "If his teaching is true, confirmed by the witness of the Hebrew books, then it is fitting that all of us obey him" (*Acts Pet. Paul* 23). Paul here repeats only the final condition from the Latin text, namely that the "Hebrew books" will be the standard of his assessment of Peter's teaching. The Greek translator has redacted the text

---

22. Paul's traditional identification as a bald man is based on *Acts Paul* 1.7.

23. Literally, "Rejoice a great joy." This is one of several Semiticisms in this section of the text.

24. Literally, "rejoicing a great joy."

by omitting two elements. First, Paul does not claim that he will confirm his "Judeanness" by his actions. He makes no promises about observing the Sabbath or circumcision, and he is silent on following the patriarchs and the law. This seems to be a more *canonical* Paul. He is not necessarily opposed to such observance among Jews, but he also will not yield in the face of pressure from his Judean brothers.[25] He feels no compulsion to show that he is truly a "Hebrew of Hebrews" by outward demonstrations of legal piety. Instead, his focus is only on what can be shown by the "Hebrew books." A second difference is that Paul does not offer a potential confrontation with Peter—the would-be Roman inversion of the Antioch incident. This could be another gesture toward the canonical texts, in which Peter is typically the more scrupulous one on legal matters. Yet it could also be a result of the Greek redactor's desire to present a united apostolic front, perhaps taking his cue from texts such as Acts, 2 Pet 3:15–16, and later authors like Irenaeus. Indeed, the next passage in the Greek *Acts* (now again following the Latin *Passion*) is the account of the apostles' joyful and tearful reunion (*Pass. Holy* 3; *Acts Pet. Paul* 24). No suggestion of potential apostolic disagreement is discernible.

The Latin *Passion* and the Greek *Acts* provide an interesting case study in apostolic description and ambiguity. The earlier Latin text reverses the dominant traditions about Paul and Peter on the issue of legal observance. It is Peter whom the Judean authorities in Rome fear most, for he, not Paul, has been offering "new teachings" among the Gentiles. The Jews seek Paul as their ally, and he seems willing to play this role, confirming that he is legally observant and will rebuke Peter if his teachings do not conform to the Hebrew scriptures. The translator-redactor of the Greek *Acts* corrects this confusion of Peter and Paul. His added prelude specifies early on that the Jews in Rome fear Paul because he had "afflicted all our brothers and fathers in Judea and Samaria and all of Palestine" (*Acts Pet. Paul* 2). They secure an execution order on Paul, in order to finish the task that the Jerusalem-based death squad had failed to complete. Paul's apparent death is an occasion for rejoicing, but fear and confusion grip them once again when the apostle arrives. They do seek Paul's help in thwarting Peter, but Paul is much less conciliatory in his response and omits any mention of a possible *tête-à-tête*

---

25. According to Acts 16:1–3, Paul did have Timothy circumcised, because he was known by the Jews of Lystra to have a Greek father. But Timothy also had a Jewish mother, so there was some possible cause for him to be circumcised. The case of Titus in Jerusalem is a better indication of Paul's resolve (Gal 2:3–5). There Paul refused to have Titus circumcised, despite intense pressure from "false brothers," because Titus was a Greek. For Paul the central message of the gospel was at stake: "We did not submit to them even for a moment, so that the truth of the gospel might always remain with you" (Gal 2:5).

with Peter. The redactor of the Greek text, therefore, seeks to set the record straight on his notion of Paul's *real* relationship to the law to Jews pushing for traditional legal observance, and to Peter.

Another source of confusion in later texts is the attribution of events to the wrong apostle. One notable example is found in the *Teaching of the Apostles* (also known in scholarship as the *Didascalia Apostolorum*) a text produced in Syriac somewhere in the Christian East prior to the sixth century.[26] It states that following the miraculous events of Pentecost, the apostles set down regulations concerning worship, the church calendar, the roles and qualifications of church leaders, and various other ethical issues. The second half of the text specifies which apostles allegedly established the priesthood in regions of the Christian world from Britain to India. The author closes with the following lines:

> Timothy and Erastus of Lystra and Menaeus, the first disciples of the apostles, accompanied Paul until he was taken to the city of Rome after he stood against the orator Tertullus.[27] And Nero Caesar killed Shimeon Kepha[28] with a sword in the city of Rome.[29]

The author of this text obviously is not confined by the traditional details of the accounts of the apostles' deaths. The *Acts of Peter* and the apocryphal texts that depend upon it state that Peter died in Rome by inverted

---

26. The exact dating is difficult. It survives in three manuscripts in the British Library collection, with the earliest dating from the fifth or sixth century: *Add. 14644* (5th/6th cent.), *Add. 14531* (7th/8th cent.), and *Add. 17193* (dated 874). William Cureton had done extensive study on this and some other closely related texts and planned to publish a lengthy introduction to accompany his edition and translation of them (*Ancient Syriac Documents*, 24–35 [English], 24–35 [in Syriac numbering]). However, his untimely death in 1864 left this work undone. Pratten, extrapolating from some notes left by Cureton on the origins of the *Teaching of the Apostles*, included this text in his *Syriac Documents Attributed to the First Three Centuries*, but such an early date for this text is far from established. Note that Pratten, following Cureton (*Ancient Syriac Documents*, 166–67), incorrectly lists *Add. 17193* as *Add. 14173* (*Syriac Documents*, 36).

27. Timothy and Erastus are mentioned together in Acts 19:22, and Tertullus is the orator (ῥήτωρ) employed by the high priest Ananias to bring charges against Paul in Acts 24:1–9. Menaeus is not known from the New Testament and should not be confused with Paul's alleged opponent, Hymenaeus, mentioned in 1 Tim 1:20 and 2 Tim 2:17.

28. It is notable that the Syriac text prefers Peter's Semitic names Shimeon and Kepha. In Syriac the form Shimeon (initial Šin) was frequently used for Peter, so that he would not be confused with Simon (initial Semkath) the sorcerer. Greek and Latin lack the ability to distinguish between these initial *Sh* and *S* sounds.

29. Cureton, *Ancient Syriac Documents*, 35.

crucifixion,[30] while the *Acts of Paul* and others say that Paul died at the edge of the sword by decapitation. Traditionally, it is believed that Nero killed them both. Here, however, the author of the *Teaching of the Apostles* brings Paul to Rome to face Nero but then leaves him there, while Peter dies by the sword. On one level it is not surprising that the death of Peter, not of Paul, is the one explicitly described in Rome, for earlier in the text the author had stated,

> The city of Rome and all of Italy, Spain, Britain, and Gaul, along with the rest of the countries around them, received the apostles' ordination to the priesthood from Shimeon Kepha, who went there from Antioch. He was the ruler and leader in the church that he built there and in the regions around it.[31]

Shimeon Kepha, not Paul, was the primary figure associated with the Roman church; so the retelling of his martyrdom there would be most important.

This divergence from the tradition caught the attention of at least one of the scribes who transmitted the text and felt the need to make a correction. In British Library *Add. 17193*, the scribe added the phrase "crucifying him on a cross," thus recasting the final line: "And Nero Caesar killed him [i.e. Paul] with a sword and Shimeon Kepha, crucifying him on a cross in the city of Rome." This alteration also requires the insertion of an implied *waw* ("and"), which is not actually in the text. The addition creates a differentiation between the methods of death for Paul and Peter and brings the text in line with the dominant tradition. A subtler but equally telling addition occurs in the English translation by William Cureton. Cureton correctly left off the reference to the crucifixion but did insert the implied *waw*, yielding, "And Nero the Emperor slew him [Paul] with the sword, and Shimeon Kepha, in the city of Rome."[32] The addition of a comma followed by "and" suggests that the reference to death by the sword should apply to what came before (i.e., the reference to Paul), while the mention of Shimeon Kepha is a new topic. Cureton's version states that Shimeon Kepha also died in Rome at the hands of Nero, but the sword that laid Paul low does not carry over to the other apostle. Cureton does not explain the reasons for his

30. Timothy D. Barnes has claimed with baffling certainty that Peter was burned alive based on John 21:18–19, but the evidence he offers is far from sufficient to support his enigmatic argument. See *Early Christian Hagiography*, 5–31. He restated this theory at the 2013 Peter in Early Christianity conference at the University of Edinburgh. Barnes's title, "'Another shall gird thee'—Ancient Evidence vs. New Testament 'Scholarship,'" is indicative of his dismissive treatment of any theory about the end of Peter's life other than his own.

31. Cureton, *Ancient Syriac Documents*, 33.

32. Ibid., 35.

alteration to the text, but I would interpret it a result of his reading the text through the lens of tradition.

Although the *Teaching of the Apostles* takes us into a later period, I would note that the ambiguity in this Syriac text is a foreshadowing of even greater confusion among later chroniclers in Arabic, who were heavily dependent upon Syriac sources. For example, the tenth-century Islamic chronicler Abū Ja'far Muhammad b. Jarīr al-Tabarī records the following: "Nero ruled for fourteen years. He slew Peter and crucified Paul head down."[33] Here the fate of the apostles under Nero is completely reversed, with Peter being slain (the sword is implied) and Paul being crucified upside down. Another tenth-century Arabic chronicler, the Christian bishop Agapius of Menbidj,[34] was equally perplexed and noted that others were, as well:

> Then Nero cut off the heads of Shimeon Kepha and Paul. As for Shimeon, there are some who claim that his head was not cut off, but that his beard was cut off, and that he was crucified with his head down. Paul had his head cut off at the same time that Shimeon, who is the same as Peter, was crucified with his head down, in the thirteenth year of his [Nero's] reign.[35]

Agapius himself seems a bit uncertain about the details, for his statement that both apostles were decapitated is quickly followed by a caveat that others tell a different story. It is interesting that he does not simply state the tradition that Shimeon/Peter died by inverted crucifixion. Those who support this crucifixion account apparently must respond to a well-known account that *something* on Peter was cut off by Nero. They argue that it was his beard, not his head, but Agapius's comments indicate that the story of Peter's decapitation was known in Syriac (the language from which the bishop takes nearly all of his material), for some felt the need to counter this version. As if this first citation from Agapius were not problematic enough, Agapius introduces further confusion when he returns just a few lines later to the apostolic martyrdoms: "Then madness seized Nero, and his reason was disturbed. He killed his mother, his aunt, and many of his relatives. He killed Peter and Paul by crucifying them head down, as we have related."[36]

33. *Ta'rīkh al-rusul wa'l-mulūk* 741 (trans. Perlmann, 126).

34. This city in Syria was known as Hierapolis in Greek.

35. *Kitab Al-'Unvan / Histoire universelle* 2.1 (adapted from Vasiliev's translation, 493). On the debates over whether or not the apostles died on the same day, see Eastman, *Paul the Martyr*, 23 n. 19. Traditions concerning the exact year of the apostolic deaths present their own problems and are the subject of a publication currently in process.

36. *Kitab Al-'Unvan / Histoire universelle* 2.1 (adapted from Vasiliev's translation, 494).

But Agapius had not related that story. Rather, he had just stated that Paul died by decapitation and Peter by either decapitation or crucifixion. How might we explain this discrepancy? The modern editor of this chronicle gives no indication of any textual problems or evidence of scribal emendation here; so the text seems secure. It might simply be the case that Agapius himself is confused by the various traditions at his disposal and chooses to transmit them all, even if they do not agree with one another. The reasons for Agapius's enigmatic text ultimately remain unknown, but at some point the blurring of the lines between the Petrine and Pauline traditions must have played a role.

If we return from the Medieval period to late antiquity, we find yet another example of confusion about apostolic traditions in the anti-Christian polemical text known as the *Toledot Yeshu* (*Life of Jesus*). This tractate is a mélange of defaming stories (most of them seemingly of rabbinical origin[37]) about Jesus and his followers. Parts of the text could date to the third or fourth century, although the work is first attested as a whole in the ninth century.[38] Of particular interest to us is the end of the text, where the Judean sages appeal for help in separating the followers of Jesus from the other Jews:

> The Sages desired to separate from Israel those who continued to claim Yeshu as the Messiah, and they called upon a greatly learned man, Simeon Kepha (*sic*), for help. Simeon went to Antioch, main city of the Nazarenes and proclaimed to them: "I am the disciple of Yeshu. He has sent me to show you the way. I will give you a sign as Yeshu has done." Simeon, having gained the secret of the Ineffable Name, healed a leper and a lame man by means of it and thus found acceptance as a true disciple. He told them that Yeshu was in heaven, at the right hand of his Father, in fulfillment of Psalm 110:1. He added that Yeshu desired that they separate themselves from the Jews and no longer follow their practices, as Isaiah had said, "Your new moons and your feasts my soul abhorreth." They were now to observe the first day of the week instead of the seventh, the Resurrection instead

---

37. See, e.g., Tosefta *Chullin* 2:22–24, where Jesus is identified as the illegitimate son of a Roman soldier named Pantera.

38. Even after this date the text is not static, for it survives in more than one form. Advocates for an early date for this material include Horbury ("Critical Examination"), who argues for a possible third-century date; and Schonfield (*According to the Hebrews*, 214–27), who suggests a date as early as the fourth century for the original version of the text. Most scholars assume the text took shape later, e.g. Gero, "Stern Master"; Newman, "Death of Jesus"; Rubenstein, *Stories of the Babylonian Talmud*, esp. 147 n. 94; Schäfer, *Jesus in the Talmud*, 2–3.

of the Passover, the Ascension into Heaven instead of the Feast of Weeks, the finding of the Cross[39] instead of the New Year, the Feast of the Circumcision instead of the Day of Atonement, the New Year[40] instead of Chanukah; they were to be indifferent with regard to circumcision and the dietary laws. Also they were to follow the teaching of turning the right if smitten on the left and the meek acceptance of suffering. All these new ordinances which Simeon Kepha (or Paul, as he was known to the Nazarenes) taught them were really meant to separate these Nazarenes from the people of Israel and to bring the internal strife to an end.[41]

When we come upon this reference to "Simeon Kepha," we certainly expect to hear about Simon/Cephas/Peter. The name is quite specific, even if the description of him as "a greatly learned man" does not necessarily fit the canonical presentation of Peter as a fisherman.[42] The claim that he was a disciple of Jesus also points toward Peter, who reportedly performed healings and did travel to Antioch (Acts 3:1–10; Gal 2:11–14). Even the fact that Simeon Kepha supposedly told the Nazarenes to "separate themselves from the Jews and no longer follow their practices" need not necessarily surprise us, for we have already seen that in several texts Peter is presented as undermining Torah observance.

The surprise comes when this figure is identified as "Paul, as he was known to the Nazarenes." Indeed, the characteristics fit Paul well: very learned, went to Antioch, performed miracles (e.g., Acts 14:8–10), and taught against strict legal observance. Yet how does the name Simeon Kepha become attached to these traits? Is Peter being confused with Paul here, or is Paul being confused with Peter? The author of this part of the text has eliminated the distinction between Simon/Cephas/Peter and Paul and seems to think that the members of the early Nazarene sect also held them to be one and the same person. Although the Nazarenes are obviously viewed

---

39. This is an obvious anachronism, for the True Cross was not allegedly found by Helena, Constantine's mother, until sometime between 326 and 328 (Socrates Scholasticus, *Hist. eccl.* 1.17).

40. This seems to be a textual problem, because the New Year that had just been supplanted by the discovery of the True Cross is now reinstated in place of Chanukah.

41. Trans. Goldstein, in *Jesus in the Jewish Tradition*, 153–54. Goldstein does not assign section numbers in his translation.

42. Cf. *Toledot Yeshu* 8.1–20 (trans. Schonfield, *According to the Hebrews*, 59–61). Schonfield translates a different version of the text, in which Simeon Kepha is also very learned and is in fact the leader of the Sanhedrin before he is forced to join the Nazarenes in order to prevent violence against other Jews. This version knows nothing of the connection to Paul, however.

negatively by the author, this Peter-Paul conflation actually serves a positive purpose, "to separate these Nazarenes from the people of Israel and to bring the internal strife to an end." In other words, this figure solves the internal strife over issues of Torah observance by convincing the followers of Jesus to split voluntarily from the rest of the Judean community and go their own way. This description would fit neither the canonical nor the apocryphal Peter or Paul, who sought to broker a peaceful détente between Judean and Gentile believers. In the *Toledot Yeshu*, however, the problem of Jesus is finally resolved by this Peter-Paul figure, who effects a "parting of the ways" between Jesus' followers and the rest of Israel.

CONFUSION IN CHRISTIAN ART

Literature is not the only medium in which we find apostolic confusion. It also occurs in early Christian art on late Roman gold glass. In the Christian burial grounds around Rome, archaeologists have discovered the decorated bottoms of over 500 glass drinking vessels. Many of these preserve the images of martyrs, and the breakage pattern suggests that the glasses were fractured in a way that intentionally preserved the images. Scholars date these glasses to the fourth and perhaps early fifth centuries CE. They may have been used in commemorative banquets honoring the apostles, taken home as pilgrim tokens, or given as gifts—or all of these, as I have argued elsewhere.[43] Of the numerous representations of Paul and Peter, many reflect the standard iconography for these apostles. Paul is bald (or at least balding) based on the description in *Acts Paul* 3.3 and has a pointed beard. Peter has a full head of hair and beard. We see these typical presentations in Figure 1.

Figure 1: The standard iconography of Peter (left) and bald Paul (right). Vatican Museums inv. 60768. Photograph by David Eastman.

Paul, on our right, is quite bald and has a beard that comes to a point. Peter has hair and a full but neatly trimmed beard. These images match the iconography of numerous other apostolic images, including those on late antique sarcophagi representing the apostolic martyrdoms, on the fifth-century arch mosaic in Santa Maria Maggiore, and in

43. Eastman, *Paul the Martyr*, 79–81.

a fourth-century fresco of Christ flanked by the apostles in the Catacomb of Marcellinus and Peter (not the apostle) on the Via Labicana. Indeed, the vast majority of apostolic iconography throughout history follows this ancient pattern.

Among the gold glass, however, we see two other phenomena. First, the two apostles may be visually indistinguishable from each other, as we see in Figures 2 and 3.

Figure 2: Peter and Paul presented as the nearly-indistinguishable apostolic twins.
Vatican Museums inv. 60798.
Photograph by David Eastman.

Figure 3: Peter and Paul as mirror images of each other.
Vatican Museums inv. 60762.
Photograph by David Eastman.

In Figure 2 both apostles have the same amount of hair and effectively the same hairstyle. There seems to be some hair on the face, punctuated by prominent beards that look almost like goatees. They wear identical clothing, even down to the brooch on the front of their garments. Only the inclusion of their names allows us to distinguish them. In Figure 3 the apostles are virtually mirror images as they look at each other. Their hair and clothing are again the same, and here both don the pointed beard that typically was associated with Paul. Such images were probably meant to emphasize the *concordia apostolorum* and the reception of Paul and Peter as the twin apostles of Rome. Prudentius even fashioned them the new Romulus and Remus, who had re-established the city of Rome as a Christian capital on the banks of the Tiber.[44] The apostolic twins replaced the mythological twins, and in these gold vessels their "twindom" is accentuated by their

---

44. Prudentius, *Perist.* 12.7–58. See Eastman, *Paul the Martyr*, 29–35.

identical physical appearance.⁴⁵ In some sense this is the visual equivalent of the literary device discussed above, in which the words of one are presented as the words of both, but here the distinction between Paul and Peter is eradicated iconographically.

Figure 4: Traditional apostolic iconography but with Peter and Paul reversed.

Vatican Museums inv. 60717.
Photograph by David Eastman.

The second phenomenon goes beyond this blending into outright inversion. Figure 4 presents an image very similar to Figure 1. On our left is a figure with a full head of hair, while on the right is a bald apostle, both being crowned by Christ. Both also wear tunics fastened by brooches, yet there is an important distinction. The fully-locked figure on the left is identified as *PAULUS*, while the balding figure on the right is *PETRUS*. The artist has confused the apostles and switched the names attached to each figure. The bald man is on the viewer's right, and this should be Paul, for in every other example of Roman gold glass known to me on which Peter and Paul are shown side-by-side, Paul is always on the viewer's right. This is because Christ is often shown between them, and the apostle on the viewer's left (Peter) is actually at Christ's right hand, thus reinforcing Petrine primacy in the Roman church.⁴⁶ However, in Figure 4 Peter is the bald one, while Paul is on the viewer's left and at Christ's right hand. The artist has the iconography "correct" and has aptly shown one apostle as bald and the other as amply coiffed, but the identification of these figures is reversed. The artist must have known the artistic tradition very well, for this image is a near copy of scenes like the one in Figure 1.

How, then, might we explain this reversal? I do not think we should read this as a subversive statement against Petrine and Roman primacy, as some have argued for certain images in Ravenna that seem to favor Paul over

45. It is not possible to determine if Romulus and Remus were similarly presented as identical in appearance, because Remus appears so seldom in Roman art. Apart from the image of the twins with the Lupa Romana and a few images of the boys as babies, no other known representation of Remus survives. See Small, "Romulus et Remus," 644 and figs. 15, 20, 24, 25.

46. Vatican Museums inv. 60619 is a gold glass fragment imbedded in plaster and at first glance seems to be an exception, for Paul is on the left. However, closer inspection shows that the names are backwards, revealing that the piece was stuck into the plaster with the side meant to be viewed (with Peter on the left) facing the plaster, not the viewer.

Peter. There a cluster of *traditio legis* scenes show Paul standing at Christ's right hand receiving the law: on the Sarcophagus of the Twelve Apostles (5th cent.) in the Church of S. Apollinare in Classe, on the Pietro Peccatore Sarcophagus (5th/6th cent.) in the Church of Santa Maria in Porta fuori le Mura, and on the Sarcophagus Barbatianus (5th/6th cent.).[47] Scholars have read these images as propaganda reflecting Ravenna's orientation toward Constantinople to the detriment of Rome. Here in Figure 4, however, it seems that we simply have a case of apostolic confusion. Peter and Paul were so closely linked in the Roman ecclesiastical and artistic traditions that at points it is difficult to tell them apart. This artist has unwittingly taken the next step of complete inversion, in the same way that the authors of texts discussed above reverse the traditions concerning the apostolic deaths.

CONCLUSION

Peter and Paul were inextricably linked from the early decades of Christianity. Taking their cue from the accounts in the canonical literature, apocryphal authors and artists paired the apostle to the Jews and the apostle to the Gentiles as the two primary pillars upon which the church rested. Tensions within their relationship were deemphasized in favor of the *concordia apostolorum*, particularly in the Roman context, where appeals to dual apostolic foundation functioned as the justification for claims of ecclesiastical authority. Paul and Peter were so closely linked in some cases, however, that the distinction between them was lost. Authors borrowed Paul's words to put them into the mouth of Peter, or the words of one were taken as the words of both. Traditions about their deaths were inverted, as were their iconographical representations. In the *Toledot Yeshu* this process reaches its most radical expression in the total conflation of the two apostles into a Peter-Paul hybrid, yet even this literary twist in many ways follows the trajectory of earlier literature and art. The unity of the apostles was paramount, and in some traditions the expression of this unity seems to have led to outright confusion.

---

47. Sullivan, "Saints Peter and Paul," esp. 67–68; Cartlidge and Elliott, *Art and the Christian Apocrypha*, 135, 169; Bovini, *Ravenna*, 178 and figs. 107, 108, 110; Weis-Liebersdorf, *Christus- und Apostelbilder*, 69–70; Klauser and Deichmann, *Frühchristliche Sarkophage*, fig. 35.2.

— 15 —

Digital Humanities and the Study of Christian Apocrypha

Resources, Prospects and Problems

— Kristian S. Heal —

"I WOULD LIKE TO invite you to join me on a journey." So begins François Bovon's engaging description of "Editing the Apocryphal Acts of the Apostles."[1] Bovon invites the reader to retrace his steps through the libraries, critical editions, manuscripts, and reference works that he used in preparing his exemplary edition of the Greek text of the *Acts of Philip*, offering as he does so not only the kind of compelling details on manuscript research only given by an expert guide, but also answering the vital questions that every scholar should be asking of their texts and tools at each stage of this process. The purpose of this chapter is to once again describe the journey of selecting, locating, and editing an apocryphal text, but this time with reference to the various digital humanities research tools that are now, or soon will be available to help with this process.[2] This, then, is not a nostalgic jour-

1. Bovon, "Editing the Apocryphal Acts," 1.
2. For two useful points of entry into the world of digital humanities and digital text studies, see *A Companion to Digital Humanities* (Online: http://www.digitalhumanities.org/companion/), and *A Companion to Digital Literary Studies* (Online: http://www.digitalhumanities.org/companionDLS/).

ney, seeking to recreate a glorious past. Things have changed. Instead of the encyclopedias and dictionaries, bibliographies, manuscript catalogues, text collections, and critical editions encountered by Bovon on his journey—what we could call the print infrastructure supporting research on Christian apocrypha—this chapter describes new sights—the increasing number of digital tools that do and will constitute the digital infrastructure for the future study of Christian apocrypha.[3] To avoid getting lost in this emerging landscape, I will follow Bovon's lead and narrate a personal journey about one text and the tools that help in the production of its edition, translation, and commentary.

This journey involves the preparation of a critical edition, translation and commentary of the Syriac version of the *History of Joseph* for the Corpus Christianorum Series Apocryphorum. Thus, whereas Bovon described journeying in the world of Greek manuscripts and texts, this article is focused rather on the world of Syriac texts, which is an increasingly important source for apocryphal literature. Even though the first milestone on this journey has already been reached,[4] we shall go back to the beginning and reimagine you, the reader, undertaking this work in the context of current and future tools.

FINDING A TEXT

Apocryphal texts often cast a long shadow in Syriac literature, and many scholars discover these texts by following that shadow rather than focusing their research on this particular genre. For example, the homilies on the apostle Thomas by Jacob of Sarug (d. 521) draw from and thus point scholars back to the apocryphal *Acts of Thomas* written in Syriac in the early third century. Others will come to the Syriac sources in search of versional witnesses. However, despite the fact that certain texts are very well studied, a focus on Christian apocrypha among Syriac scholars is rare enough that it did not even warrant a separate entry in the recent *Gorgias Encyclopedia*

---

3. The print infrastructure for Syriac Studies has been expertly delineated (with links to available online resources) by Scott Johnson, Jack Tannous and Sebastian Brock on the Dumbarton Oaks page, "Resources for Syriac Studies." Online: http://www.doaks.org/research/byzantine/resources/syriac. A general treatment of the emerging digital infrastructure for Syriac Studies is found in Heal, "Corpora, eLibraries and Databases."

4. Heal, "Syriac History of Joseph." The full journey is being traversed in the fine company of Joseph Witztum, Aaron Butts, and Geoffrey Moseley, who are respectively responsible for the Arabic, Ethiopic, and Latin recensions of this text.

of the Syriac Heritage—more dispiriting is the fact that it did not even make it into the index.[5]

However, if you were to search BYU's *Variorum History of Syriac Literature* (in preparation)[6] then you would find the extended section in Ruben Duval's *History of Syriac Literature* devoted to Old and New Testament apocrypha.[7] This is useful, but to find more recent material you must turn to the *Comprehensive Bibliography on Syriac Literature*.[8] This well-thought-out and extensively-tagged bibliographical database was assembled by Sergey Minov, in large part from existing printed bibliographies.[9] You can browse the bibliography by author, keyword, date of publication, or by one of four eras of Syriac literature. The keyword and other search options add enormous value, enabling the researcher to combine keywords, or limit the search by author or date, or both. A keyword search for OT Apocrypha and NT Apocrypha yields a splendid 1210 references.

Let us say that your entry point into the world of early Syriac texts on Joseph begins with reading the cycle of four homilies on Joseph attributed to Narsai, the fifth-century head of the school of Edessa.[10] When you look up the edition of this text in the *Comprehensive Bibliography on Syriac Literature* you see that it is tagged with "Genesis," and "Joseph." A new search using these two keywords gives a list of 31 bibliographical items, including the *editio princeps* of the *Syriac History of Joseph* published in two parts.[11] You are intrigued and search for these out-of-copyright volumes in Google books, but only find the first part. Archive.org does not have both parts either, nor are they included in the BYU-CUA Syriac Studies Reference Library, so you are back in the analogue world for a while, until you can find a copy, scan it, and load it up into archive.org yourself.[12]

---

5. Brock, Butts, Kiraz and Van Rompay, eds., *Gorgias Encyclopedic Dictionary*.

6. When available, it will be accessible via http://cpart.maxwellinstitute.byu.edu/home/resources/.

7. Duval, *La litteratur Syriaque*, 79–111. However, she would have to look elsewhere in the volume (p. 319) to find a reference to what was then the recently-published *editio princeps* of the *Syriac History of Joseph*.

8. Online: http://csc.org.il/db/db.aspx?db=SB

9. Listed online here: http://csc.org.il/template/default.aspx?PageId=8

10. Bedjan, *Liber superiorum*.

11. Weinberg, *Geschichte Josefs* (vol. 1); Link, *Geschichte Josefs* (vol. 2).

12. Online: http://books.google.com/; https://archive.org/; http://lib.byu.edu/collections/syriac-studies-reference-library/.

LOCATING THE MANUSCRIPTS

Reading Weinberg and Link's edition of the *Geschichte Josefs*, you learn that it is based on a single manuscript: Berlin, Sachau 9. A visit to the website of the Berlin State Library reveals that many of their manuscripts have been digitized and are available in their digital repository.[13] When you perform a general search for Sachau 9, you discover that this manuscript is online.[14] Your own inspection of the manuscript confirms the presence of a major lacuna—a missing leaf that falls in the middle of the most interesting narrative expansion in the entire text. So, more manuscripts are definitely necessary if you want to complete the text and produce a critical edition.

An increasing number of manuscripts are now available online. You may start your search by looking at some collections that are familiar to you. Perhaps you first search among the digitized manuscripts of the BYU Oriental Christian Microfilm collection, only to learn that of the 1800 manuscripts in this collection, just a few are in Syriac—the collection is predominately comprised of Arabic manuscripts from the Coptic Museum and the Coptic Orthodox Patriarchate.[15] Nor is the *Syriac History of Joseph* found among the Vatican Library's collection of digitized manuscripts, which include 80 Syriac manuscripts digitized for a BYU-Vatican Library project.[16] A search among the digititized manuscripts from the library of the St. Thomas Syrian Catholic Church in Mosul similarly yields no results.[17]

Searching through familiar online collections is not really paying dividends. Fortunately there are three major resources for discovering manuscripts containing Syriac Christian apocrypha. The most exciting is the Hill Museum and Manuscript Library's repository of over 125,000 microfilmed and digitized manuscripts. Over the past decades this collection has been enriched by 1000s of manuscripts from the Middle East, principally from Lebanon, Turkey, Syria, and Iraq. These collections have been frustratingly-inaccessible for a long time, often only tantalizingly and briefly described in catalogues made by the few lucky European and Middle Eastern scholars able to gain access, or in hard-to-obtain Syriac or Arabic catalogues. All this has been changed by the monumental project led by Fr. Columba Stewart.

---

13. Library site online: http://staatsbibliothek-berlin.de/; digital collections online: http://digital.staatsbibliothek-berlin.de/

14. Links to all of the online Syriac manuscripts from this collection can be found here online: http://cpart.maxwellinstitute.byu.edu/home/syriac-studies/libraries/sbb/

15. Online: http://cpart.maxwellinstitute.byu.edu/home/resources/manuscripts/.

16. Online: http://www.mss.vatlib.it/guii/scan/link.jsp.

17. Online: http://cpart.maxwellinstitute.byu.edu/home/resources/manuscripts/st-thomas-mosul/.

The value of the work of the Hill Museum and Manuscript Library is found in the combination of an ambitious field effort, a commitment to cataloguing, and a powerful online catalogue (in progress).[18] In utilizing this catalog you can opt for the simple Keyword Search, using the string, "History of Joseph," or use the advanced search, which allows you to specify that you want to search for a particular title and language. A search of the HMML catalogue yields one additional manuscript, Kerkuk Ms 1. You order the manuscript and it is put up online within days.

The second resource is the hagiographical database compiled over the past two decades by Fr. Ugo Zanetti. This content-rich database is currently being converted into a state-of-the-art digital resource by the Syriaca.org team in a project led by Jean-Nicole Saint-Laurent (in preparation). This resource substantially improves on the print tools of Peeters and Fiey, dramatically increasing the number of known saints and hagiographical texts.[19] Not least among the additions to this resource are details of the manuscript witnesses for each work cited. Several Joseph texts are included in the database, including the *Syriac History of Joseph*. Three more manuscripts are identified in this database, one each from Oxford, Paris, and London. Two of these you can order on microfilm; the third, in Oxford, can be photographed on site (if you happen to be passing through).

The third resource may prove to be the most useful to you, as it aspires to comprise a union catalogue of all Syriac manuscripts. This is the ambitious French-based e-Ktobe project.[20] Several researchers are contributing to the database, and descriptions are currently being added of manuscripts in Paris and other French collections, as well as Charfet, Florence, Berlin, Damascus, London, Cambridge, Tehran, Trichur, and the Vatican Library. The power of e-Ktobe is in the detailed cataloguing schema, which facilitates searches over a number of fields, including content type—where you can simply select all manuscripts containing apocryphal texts, for example, and then limit the search by collection—or other criteria. Though it will take several years to populate this database, it will be an enormously valuable tool for a wide variety of researchers, but especially those working with apocryphal texts.

A search for "*Histoire de Joseph*" in the general search box gives you results in several manuscripts, two of which (Sachau 9 and Bibliothèque nationale de France, Syriaque 309) you know already from previous searches.

18. Online: http://www.hmml.org/oliver.html. Requests can also be made for copies of manuscripts from more than 100 other collections that have been scanned but not catalogued.

19. Peeters, *Bibliotheca hagiographica orientalis*; Fiey, *Saint syriaques*.

20. Online: http://www.mss-syriaques.org/.

If you wish, your search can be further refined by using the advanced search options, such as searching for "*Histoire de Joseph*" in the "Scope" content box, limiting the search to results in Syriac, and items tagged as "Apocryphes." This search yields a further witness to the text in Tehran, Fonds Issayi Syr. 18.[21]

LITERARY CONTEXT AND RECEPTION

When examining the manuscript witnesses of the *Syriac History of Joseph* you might find yourself interested in the company that the text keeps. In Oxford, Syr. F. 12, for example you see that the *Syriac History* is found with other hagiographical texts and three apocryphal acts, including the *Acts of Thomas*. Tehran, Fonds Issayi 18 similarly is a miscellaneous collection of hagiographical and apocryphal texts, including the *Acts of Matthew and Andrew*, the *Life of the Man of God*, and the *Apocalypse of Paul*. E-Ktobe allows you to quickly assess the manuscript witnesses of these adjacent texts, helping to build up a more nuanced picture of the codicological profile of the *Syriac History of Joseph*.

You came to the *Syriac History of Joseph* from within the shadow this text cast over the Syriac homiletic tradition. The vast and rich corpus of Syriac homilies dating from between the fourth and sixth centuries is a rich repository for the study of the reception history of apocryphal texts and traditions. *The Repertorium of Late Antique Syriac Sermons* (in preparation) will enable you to more easily identify other relevant Syriac homilies.[22] From the Repertorium you learn that there are more than ten individual homilies or cycles on Joseph in the Syriac tradition, and each one has a clear relationship to the *Syriac History of Joseph*. These texts will provide rich material for your commentary.

DIGITAL TEXT AND TEXT ANALYSIS

Having gathered the manuscripts of the *Syriac History* and identified related texts in the Syriac tradition you are ready to begin preparing the edition. The first step is to acquire an electronic text. This is often a time-consuming project, involving many hours of typing and proofing by scholars who should be spending their time more usefully. Fortunately, the *Syriac History of Joseph* and many of the related *memre* are found among the hundreds

---

21. Described in Desreumaux, "Un manuscrit syriaque."
22. Online: http://cpart.maxwellinstitute.byu.edu/home/resources/.

of texts transcribed for the *Oxford-BYU Syriac Electronic Corpus* (in progress). The Syriac corpus is a lemmatized database of texts linked to a digital dictionary.

In order to facilitate maximum functionality, each element in the corpus has a Unique Resource Identifier (URI), which means it is possible to link to a particular author, text, or individual token (i.e., a text word, which may comprise prefixes and a suffix attached to a stem), or to a particular lexeme within the lexicon. Authors in the corpus are linked out to external reference resources. This expanding resource is currently focused in the short-term on creating a concordance to the works of Ephrem the Syrian, and in the long-term on building a comprehensive lemmatized and annotated corpus of classical Syriac texts (of the second to seventh centuries) that will be used to build a better Syriac lexicon.

Tools prepared by the Syriac corpus team allow you to lemmatize and grammatically tag your own corpus and use that data to prepare concordances of various sorts, or to search the analyzed corpus using BYU's "WordCruncher" software. This software package works comfortably with texts in any Unicode script and in multiple languages, and can be freely downloaded for scholarly use.[23] In addition to a browser, you can also download the "Publisher Toolkit," that easily converts any Microsoft Word XML or RTF document into a WordCruncher text. Once in WordCruncher, you can undertake complex searches and comparisons between texts. This will greatly facilitate the process of preparing detailed philological notes and assessing the relationships between texts.

Texts from the Syriac Corpus are already available for download from within the software.[24] New texts will be added over the coming months and years. As texts are improved, upgraded versions of texts will be added to replace previous, inferior versions. All texts compiled as WordCruncher documents are automatically indexed, and every token appears on the WordWheel, which is visible when one performs any search. Simple and Boolean searches enable you to locate both key terms and phrases. The wildcard character "*" enables complex searches even in unlemmatized texts. Search results give the equivalent of a Key-Word-in-Context concordance, enabling you to quickly find relevant passages.

More complex searches are possible with annotated and grammatically-analyzed texts. However, even with plain texts you can readily use one of the new features of WordCruncher to compare texts to quickly identify

---

23. Online: http://wordcruncher.com/. Select "Downloads" and "WordCruncher," and follow the installation instructions.

24. Select "File," then "WordCruncher bookstore."

overlapping vocabulary and phrases.[25] For example, a comparison between the *Syriac History of Joseph* and the Pseudo-Narsai memre on Joseph yields a list of 53 phrases of between three and nine tokens in length that appear in both texts. Similar comparisons easily can be made between other related texts, such as, for example, between the New Testament and the *Acts of Thomas*.

THE EDITION

The actual process of preparing editions with complex apparatuses and annotated translations can be readily done by using Classical Text Editor (CTE), a powerful and flexible software package developed by the Austrian Academy of Sciences.[26] CTE provides you with all the functionality you need to create a full critical edition of your text. You can set up your page as you wish; with line or paragraph numbers, marginal notes, a single apparatus or several, and a linked, facing translation if you wish. However, because CTE is a full-featured software package for preparing the most complex of editions, you may find the initial learning curve to be quite steep. There are benefits to persevering though. For example, CTE also allows scholars to export their texts in TEI-XML format or html format, greatly facilitating web publication of editions. Given that certain funding agencies now require edition projects to have a web component, this is a very important addition to the CTE platform. It would be thoroughly desirable for the major publications series to prepare CTE templates to enable scholars to take charge of the editorial process and limit the often-frustrating problem of a scholar carefully preparing an edition only to have mistakes introduced in the process of re-typesetting the work.

The difficult parts of editing texts are still difficult. Judgments need to be made. Methodological decisions have to be taken. Variants need to be carefully weighed. Stemmata need to be established and so on. Moreover, the careful work of relating one's text to the broader corpus of related apocryphal and other literature, though facilitated by digital humanities tools, still requires thorough familiarity with a variety of literatures and traditions in order to be done successfully. It is this set of activities that are still at the heart of the textual critic's work. Digital humanities projects certainly

---

25. Found in the menu: Book/Book Reports/Phrase Compare Report.

26. Online: http://cte.oeaw.ac.at/. The software can be freely downloaded and tested, but a license needs to be purchased in order to print a document and enjoy full functionality.

can help you in your text critical labors.[27] However, if you are seduced into undertaking your own digital humanities project in connection with your edition, you may find yourself fatally distracted and falling terribly behind with your deadlines.

CONCLUSION

This journey with the *Syriac History of Joseph* has highlighted some of the exciting digital humanities resources now available and currently in preparation. These resources certainly do and will enrich and facilitate the study of Syriac Christian apocrypha, better enabling scholars in this field to work with Syriac texts in the context of the broader corpus of Syriac literature. Similar resources are being created in other relevant fields, and these resources need to be similarly enumerated.[28] Much remains to be done, especially with the conversion of the more important print resources for the study of Christian apocrypha into digital tools. Until then, it will still be necessary to read this description together with Bovon's.

---

27. See, for example, the Digital Mishnah project. Online: http://www.digitalmishnah.org/. A list of other digital critical editions can be found here online: http://wiki.digitalclassicist.org/Digital_Critical_Editions_of_Texts_in_Greek_and_Latin, and here online: http://www.digitale-edition.de/.

28. See, for example, the projects enumerated in Clivaz, Gregory, and Hamidović ed., *Digital Humanities*.

– Appendix –

Select Digital Humanities Resources

ONLINE MANUSCRIPT COLLECTIONS

a. Hill Museum and Manuscript Library (http://www.hmml.org/)

   Holdings: More than 125,000 manuscripts (access online by request).

b. BYU Oriental Microfilm Collection (http://cpart.byu.edu/)

   Holdings: Over 2,000 manuscripts, mostly from Egypt (access online and by request).

c. Sinai Manuscripts (http://www.e-corpus.org/fre/notices/96558-Microfilms-manuscrits-Mt-Sinai.html)

   Holdings: 1,474 manuscripts originally microfilmed by the Library of Congress.

d. E-Corpus (http://www.e-corpus.org/)

   Holdings: Over 14,000 manuscripts.

e. Virtual Manuscript Library of Switzerland (http://www.e-codices.unifr.ch/en/)

   Holdings: Over 1,000 medieval manuscripts from 47 Swiss Libraries.

f. French National Library (http://gallica.bnf.fr/)

   Holdings: 45,490 manuscripts.

g. Berlin State Library (http://digital.staatsbibliothek-berlin.de/dms/suche/)

Holdings: Catalogue, electronic texts, and other tools (subscription required).

h. Vatican Library (http://www.vatlib.it/guii/scan/link.jsp)
Holdings: Currently over 2,000 manuscripts.

ONLINE MANUSCRIPT CATALOGUES

a. Fihrist (http://www.fihrist.org.uk/)
Description: Towards a union catalogue for manuscripts in Arabic script.

b. E-Ktobe (http://www.mss-syriaques.org/)
Description: Towards a union catalogue of Syriac manuscripts. Advance search by genre.

c. Corpus of Coptic Literary Manuscripts (http://www.cmcl.it/)
Description: Towards a union catalogue of Coptic manuscripts and literature.

DIGITAL TEXTS & TOOLS

a. Oxford-BYU Syriac Digital Corpus (http://cpart.byu.edu/)

b. BYU's WordCruncher: Electronic Text Viewer (http://wordcruncher.com/)

c. Coptic Scriptorium (http://www.carrieschroeder.com/scriptorium/)

d. Classical Text Editor (http://cte.oeaw.ac.at/)

e. Christian Apocrypha in translation (http://www.earlychristianwritings.com/apocrypha.html)

REFERENCE COLLECTIONS

a. Comprehensive Bibliography on Syriac Christianity (http://csc.org.il/db/db.aspx?db=SB)

b. Dumbarton Oaks Resources for Syriac Studies (http://www.doaks.org/research/byzantine/resources/syriac)

c. Syriac Reference Portal (http://syriaca.org/)

d. Clavis Patrum Copticorum (http://cmcl.aai.uni-hamburg.de/chiam_clavis.html)

e. Armenian Reference Materials (http://rbedrosian.com/patristics.html)

f. Pleiades—Gazetteer of Ancient Places (http://pleiades.stoa.org/)

DIGITAL HUMANITIES

a. Companion to Digital Humanities (http://www.digitalhumanities.org/companion/)

b. Companion to Digital Literary Studies (http://www.digitalhumanities.org/companionDLS/)

DIGITAL HUMANITIES TOOLS AND MODELS

a. Timelines
   i. Simile Timeline (http://www.simile-widgets.org/timeline/)
   ii. Timeglider (http://timeglider.com/)

b. Maps
   i. Google Maps (https://developers.google.com/maps/)
   ii. Harvard World Map (http://worldmap.harvard.edu/)

c. Text Annotation & Analysis
   i. BRAT rapid annotation tool (http://brat.nlplab.org/index.html)
   ii. Many Eyes (http://www-958.ibm.com/software/data/cognos/manyeyes/)
   iii. Voyant (http://voyant-tools.org/)

d. Digital Editions
   i. CollateX (http://www.interedition.eu/)
   ii. Classical Text Editor (http://cte.oeaw.ac.at/)

e. Digital Clavis
   i. Perseus Catalogue (http://catalog.perseus.org/)
   ii. Classical Works Knowledge Base (http://cwkb.org/home)

— 16 —

Conversions of Paul
Comparing Acts and *Acts of Paul*

— Glenn E. Snyder —

MANY EARLY TRADITIONS DESCRIBE Paul's conversion,[1] including the stories collected in the canonical Acts and the noncanonical *Acts of Paul*. These stories constitute a set of "parallels" between Acts and the *Acts of Paul*, and one of the tasks of scholarship is to compare such "parallels" historically and critically. Scholarship on the comparison of Acts and the *Acts of Paul* has assumed that Acts—a single, coherent whole text—was composed prior to the *Acts of Paul*. The question debated, therefore, has been: Was the *Acts of Paul* dependent on Acts, and if so, how? Various answers have

---

1. In this article, I am using the term "conversion" loosely to refer to the events and/or process(es) allegedly related to Paul's proclamation of Jesus. In addition to the stories preserved in Acts and the *Acts of Paul*, other traditions were composed: see for example *Ep. Apos.* 29–34 ("Saul" and "Paul"); *Letter of Peter to James* ("the enemy"; incorporated into *Kerygmata Petrou*); Ps.-Clem., *Rec.* 1.71–72 (also as "the enemy"); if Paul is to be identified as "Simon," then also Ps.-Clem., *Hom.* 2.16–17; 11.35–56; 17.13–19; *Toledot Yeshu* 10 ("Eliahu"); and Epiphanius, *Pan.* 30.16.6–9 (concerning *Ascents of James*). Some of these traditions are related to the allegedly autobiographical narrative in Gal 1:11–24 (cp. 2 Cor 11:32–33). Among the "undisputed" letters, other autobiographical details do or may occur in Rom 9:3–5; 11:1–2a; 1 Cor 9:1; 15:1–11; 2 Cor 4:6; 11:21b–23(ff.); 12:1–10; Gal 2:1–10, 11–21; Phil 3:4b–6.

been proposed, from literary dependence[2] to independence,[3] and occasionally, appeal has been made to common antecedents ("sources," "intertexts," "traditions," etc.).[4] But what if Acts was *not* written before the *Acts of Paul*? What if Acts and the *Acts of Paul* were works in progress when their stories were composed?

In this article, I use the conversion stories as a case study for how to rethink the relations between Acts and the *Acts of Paul*. Both Acts[5] and one of the traditions in the *Acts of Paul* called the *Ephesus Act* (= *Acts Paul* 9)[6] have recently been redated around the reign of Hadrian (117–138 CE), and according to these revised datings the conversion stories in Acts and *Acts of Paul* were contemporaneous productions. Rather than assuming the priority of Acts (chronologically, historically, etc.), I propose therefore to study the traditions and redactions of the conversion stories in Acts and the *Acts of Paul*, in order to reflect more historically and critically on the compositional practices that produced various πράξεις about Paul.

THE CONVERSION STORIES IN ACTS

Acts offers at least three accounts of "the" conversion of Paul.[7] The first is presented as a narrator's description of the event (Acts 9:1–21); the second is styled as Paul's speech before an angry mob in Jerusalem (22:3–21); and the third is portrayed as an ἀπολογία in Caesarea Maritima before Herod Agrippa II, his wife Bernice, and other Galilean notables, as well as Roman

2. Literary dependence: Schmidt, *Acta Pauli*; Schmidt and Schubart, *ΠΡΑΞΕΙΣ ΠΑΥΛΟΥ*; Vouaux, *Actes de Paul*; Pervo, "Hard Act to Follow"; Hills, "Acts of the Apostles"; Hills, "*Acts of Paul*"; Bauckham, "*Acts of Paul* as a Sequel"; Bauckham, "*Acts of Paul*: Replacement"; Marguerat, "*Acts of Paul*"; Czachesz, "*Acts of Paul*."

3. Literary independence: Rordorf, "Im welchem Verhältnis" (repr. in Rordorf, *Lex Orandi*, 449–74); and Rordorf, "Paul's Conversion."

4. Common antecedents: Schneemelcher and Kasser, "*Acts of Paul*," 233. See also Schneemelcher, "Apostelgeschichte des Lukas" (repr. in Schneemelcher, *Gesammelte Aufsätze*, 204–22); MacDonald, *Legend and the Apostle*.

5. For example, Pervo, *Dating Acts*, esp. "Appendix II: Scholarly Estimates of the Date of Acts," 359–63; Tyson, *Marcion and Luke-Acts*; Townsend, "Date of Luke-Acts."

6. Snyder, *Acts of Paul*, esp. 66–99, 191–95, 225–32, 254–56.

7. For broader literary contexts, see Acts 9:1–30 (with 7:58; 8:1, 3); 21:17—22:29; 25:13—26:32. Particularly useful secondary sources in English include Cadbury, *Making of Luke-Acts*; Cadbury, *Book of Acts in History*; Czachesz, *Commission Narratives*; Dibelius, *Book of Acts: Form, Style, and Theology*; Dupont, *Sources of the Acts*; Gasque, *History*; Haenchen, *Acts of the Apostles*; Hedrick, "Paul's Conversion/Call"; Lohfink, *Conversion of St. Paul*; Lüdemann, *Early Christianity*, Parsons and Pervo, *Rethinking*; Pervo, *Profit with Delight*; Pervo, *Acts: A Commentary*; Talbert, *Reading Luke-Acts*; Tannehill, *Narrative Unity*; Trocmé, *Le livre des Acts*.

procurator Porcius Festus (26:2–23). A fourth account occurs at Acts 9:27, where the narrator describes what Barnabas reported to "the apostles"; but this account is an epitome of the report in Acts 26:12–20a.[8] None of these descriptions is within the "we" materials of Acts (16:9–20; 20:5—21:18; 27:1—28:16); and practically all of the descriptions are unattested in the "D" text type.[9] But all of the conversion stories, including the speeches, were produced in their final form(s) by the scribe—or set of scribes—known as "Luke." The contents and sequence of these are charted in Table 1.

Table 1. Conversion Stories in Acts

	Acts 9:1–30	Acts 22:3–21	Acts 26:2–20/23
addressed auditors	—	Roman chiliarch; angry mob in Jerusalem	ruler of Galilee (etc.); governor of Judea
credentials	— (see 7:58; 8:1, 3)	22:3 [H1]	26:2–8 [H2]
διώκω ("chase, pursue; persecute; prosecute")	9:1–2 (A1; A2) ←	22:4–5 [A1] ←	26:9–11 [A2]
vision of ΦΩΣ on the way	9:3–5 (B) ←	22:6–8 [B] →	26:12–15 (B)
—commission	—	—	26:16–18 [C2]
—command	9:6–8/9 (C1) ←	22:9–11 [C1]	—
Ananias	9:9/10–19a [D] →	22:12–16 (D)	—
preaching in "Damascus"	9:19b–21 (A2; E2)	—	—

8. Acts 9:27 states the description: πῶς ἐν τῇ ὁδῷ εἶδεν τὸν κύριον (cp. Acts 26:12–14a) καὶ ὅτι ἐλάλησεν αὐτῷ (cp. 26:14b–18) καὶ πῶς ἐν Δαμασκῷ ἐπαρρησιάσατο ἐν τῷ ὀνόματι τοῦ Ἰησοῦ (cp. 26:19–20a). The source of the broader subsection (9:26–28/30), which I have labeled "F1/F1'" in Table 1, may imply Barnabas had captured Paul.

9. Codex Bezae (D05), one of the primary witnesses to the "Western" or "D" form of Acts, does *not* include Acts 8:29—10:14; 11:2–10; 22:10–20; 22:29—end. Therefore, only part of one of the four conversion stories in Acts is attested within the extant parts of Codex Bezae (D05): Acts 21:37—22:9, 21. Technically, the Greek text of Bezae includes the first four words from 22:10 (fol. 508ᵇ) and the final seven words from 22:20 (fol. 510ᵇ). Between these fol. 509 is absent, but according to its Latin equivalent on 510ᵃ, the Greek on fol. 509ᵇ must have included the remainder of Acts 22:10–20. My thanks to Richard I. Pervo and especially Eldon J. Epp for personal correspondence about these details, which are based on the critical edition of Scrivener, *Bezae Codex Cantabrigiensis*. Other "D-text" parallels *may* occur in manuscripts such as 𝔓29 and 614, but it is improbable that either should be considered representative of "the D text" as such.

preaching in "Damascus"	9:22–25 [**E1**]	→	—	26:19–20a [**E2**]
preaching in Jerusalem/Judea	9:26–28 [**F1**]	→	[22:17?]	26:20b [**F2**]
vision in Temple	—		22:17–21 [**G**]	—
preaching to ἔθνη	[9:29–30?] [**F1′?**]	→	[22:21?]	26:20c [**F2′**]

Table 1 is a representation of the contents and sources for the conversion stories in Acts. Abstract(ed) subsections are aligned by rows, and within each row the location of distinct sources has been marked with a bold capital letter in brackets (e.g., "[**B**]" at Acts 22:6–8)—with the caveat that, in Table 1, a "source" of material may include Lukan productions *de novo*. If an abstract subsection includes two or more sources, these have been further delimited with numbers (e.g., "[**A1**]" at 22:4–5 and "[**A2**]" at 26:9–11 designate competing stories about Paul's preconversion activity). Lukan rewriting of these sources is indicated by solid arrows and *italics* in parentheses: for example, in the subsection on διώκω, Acts 9:1–2 includes the Lukan reworking of materials from sources **A1** (short arrow, plus "(*A1*)") and **A2** (long arrow, plus "(*A2*)"). Dotted arrows indicate possible reproductions of source material (e.g., within the subsection on preaching in Damascus [**E**], the short summary in 26:19–20a [**E2**] may be a Lukan reworking of source material from 9:22–25 [**E1**]). The designation **F2′** (26:20b) demarks the continuation of **F2** (26:20c), which abstractly bookends or is at odds with the events in **G** (22:17–21); similarly, Acts 9:29–30 [**F1′**] may continue 9:26–28 [**F1**]. Prefaced materials are sequenced last (**H1** and **H2**), and Lukan introductions and conclusions are unmarked.

As indicated in Table 1, the conversion stories in Acts are sequenced similarly, and there are at least three "big picture" similarities among the accounts: (1) that the character in question—who is not explicitly identified as Παῦλος within any of the conversion stories but whom I shall call "Paul" anyway[10]—was an adherent of Israelite Temple religion in Judea; (2) that Paul, with authorization from the Temple's aristocracy, was pursuing followers of Jesus on the way to Damascus; and (3) that en route, ΦΩΣ—a light and/or man from heaven—arrested (i.e., stopped) Paul. When addressed by the transliterated Hebrew name Σαούλ,[11] Paul asks who this κύριος is,

---

10. Acts 13:9 is commonly understood to equate Σαῦλος ("Saul") and Παῦλος ("Paul"). I am intentionally reinscribing this interpretive tradition, because it was apparently promoted by the scribe(s) known as "Luke."

11. Senselessly, the name "Saul" is used in English translations to represent both the transliterated Hebrew name Σαούλ and the Greek adjective σαῦλος. See further n. 17 below.

and the Lord reveals that he is "Jesus, whom you are διώκω-ing"—pursuing, persecuting, or even prosecuting. Following these three "parallels," each of the stories adds further instruction for Paul.

But there are also dissimilarities among the conversion stories. Several of these differences may be explained simply as Lukan redaction and/or composition, based on stylistic, contextual, and other factors. For example, based on the editorial principles of the scribe(s) called "Luke," the different stories of ΦΩΣ arresting Paul (9:3–5; 22:6–8 [B]; 26:12–15) do not require more than one origin, Lukan or otherwise.[12] However, some non-paralleled materials, as well as discrepancies among the "parallels," probably imply the use of pre-Lukan materials ("sources," "intertexts," "traditions," etc.). Many of these instances are well known and often discussed: most conspicuous are the backstories for Paul pursuing Jesus' followers (see A1 and A2: 22:4–5; 26:9–11); the aural or visual means by which the ΦΩΣ is perceived (9:6–9; 22:9–11); ΦΩΣ's direct commission (C2: 26:16–18) versus the command to receive instruction later in Damascus (C1: 22:9–11; cp. 9:6–9); and the relevance of Ananias and baptism for that instruction (D: parts of 9:10–21). Discrepancies such as these have led scholars to hypothesize various source materials behind the stories.[13]

---

12. The source of material for the arrest by ΦΩΣ is best represented in 22:6–8. Whether this source of material was Lukan or pre-Lukan (and hence a "source" or "tradition" proper), I have labeled it as "**B**" in Table 1. The solid arrows and *italicized "B"*s indicate that "**B**" was (further) rewritten at 9:3–5 and 26:12–15 by the scribe(s) known as "Luke."

13. Five questions summarize most of the relevant issues and options: Did "Luke" use any traditions when composing the conversion stories in Acts 9, 22, and 26? If so, were one or more traditions used throughout those stories? In particular, what are the redactions versus the tradition(s), and in which verses do these occur? Moreover, what motivated the redactions by the scribe(s) known as "Luke"? And how should the tradition(s) and redaction be evaluated historically? (The latter question is normally answered by comparison with Gal 1–2.) Scholars such as the ones listed in nn. 2 and 4 above have debated these questions, hypothesizing various oral to written sources. A common option has been to hypothesize only one source of tradition (oral and/or written) and to interpret all three (or four) stories as redacting that single source. Within that approach, differences occur not only on how and where to isolate the tradition from its redaction but also on how to understand the source identified: was it a conversion story, a punishment story, a call story, etc.? (See Talbert, *Reading Acts*, 95–103.) Surprisingly few scholars have hypothesized multiple oral and/or written sources for the conversion stories, preferring to explain differences entirely (and hence exclusively) in terms of Lukan redaction of one source—perhaps on the historical maxim of "the simpler, the better."

In my current opinion,[14] discrepancies among the conversion stories in Acts are based on the Lukan use of three distinct blocks of material.[15] At least two and perhaps all three blocks of material are pre-Lukan traditions, but one is the most representative of Luke's ideology of "Paul." The first, most "Lukan" block of material[16] is about a prosecutor from the Jerusalem Temple named Σαούλ—a Greek transliteration of the Hebrew name.[17] The source of this material, if it is pre-Lukan, is best preserved in Acts 22 (see A1: 22:4–5; B: 22:6–8; and C1: 22:9–11), and Acts 9 includes a Lukan reproduction of that material (9:1–2; 3–5; 6–8/9; so also 26:12–15).[18] Within

14. For the 2013 York Symposium on Christian Apocrypha, I worked through the discrepancies in detail, in order to adduce a theory for reconstructing sources for the materials used in the conversion stories of Acts. In this article, I simply state the results of my work and illustrate the method I used by discussing the "parallels" that are most important for comparing Acts and the *Acts of Paul*: the stories in Acts 9:9/10–19a and 22:12–16.

15. In this article, I am not discussing separately extant sources. For example, Acts 9:22/23–25 may have been composed on the basis of 2 Cor 11:32–33; Acts 21:37–38 may have been based on Josephus (see *J.W.* 2.254–63; *Ant.* 20.161–71); Acts 26:4–5 may be inspired by Gal 1–2; and Acts 26:16–18 may be inspired by deutero-Pauline materials (esp. Ephesians). For such matters, see especially Pervo, *Acts: A Commentary*.

16. Occasionally "parallels" are adduced to this block of material from 2 Macc 3:1—4:6 (allegedly based on the earlier work of Jason of Cyrene); *Jos. Asen.* 1–21 (see Pervo, *Acts*, 235 for a parallel presentation); and/or Apuleius, *Metamorphoses* 11.1–30. Others have included the *Coptic Act of Peter*; *Genesis Apocryphon* 20; Xenophon, *An Ephesian Tale*; and *Testament of Job* 3. Also, 4 Macc 3:19—4:14 imitates 2 Macc (Pervo, *Acts: A Commentary*, 234 n. 17).

17. The transliterated Hebrew name Σαούλ is always and only used within Acts' conversion stories (Cadbury, *Making of Luke-Acts*, 226), in particular when he is addressed directly (and indeclinably) by Jesus or Ananias: Acts 9:4 *bis*, 17; 22:7 *bis*, 13; and 26:14 *bis*. (Acts 13:21 is a reference to the first king of Israel, Σαοὺλ υἱὸν Κίς, "Saul son of Kish," the Benjaminite.) Within Acts, this functions among other ways to bolster Paul's status as a speaker of "the Hebrew dialect" (τῇ Ἑβραΐδι διαλέκτῳ: 21:40; 22:2; 26:14), whether such refers to Aramaic (versus Greek), Hebrew (apparently used in contemporary Jerusalemite liturgy, versus more vernacular Aramaic), or a particular dialect or diction of Hebrew. All other occurrences translated as "Saul" are based on the Greek adjective σαῦλος, "straddling; waddling; toddering": Acts 7:58 (νεανίου καλουμένου Σαύλου); 8:1, 3; 9:1, 8, 11, 22, 24; 11:25, 30; 12:25; 13:1, 2, 7, and 9.

18. For example, Acts 9:1–2 may be explained as a Lukan simplification of the first-person story of 22:4–5 into the third person, plus harmonization with 26:9–11. (Note also that the only occurrence of the term σαῦλος in this block of material is in 9:1.) Moreover, the discrepancy between "seeing" or "hearing" may be explained most simply by "Luke" (in 9:7) emending the source (in 22:9) in order to harmonize with the third block of material, since the blinding in Acts 22 is a different kind of blindness than in Acts 9. Moreover, Acts 22:10a includes a second question that precedes the reply by ΦΩΣ, which was excised in Acts 9. Evidence for continuing scribal harmonizations occurs with the variants at Acts 9:7 (adding from 22:8 are E gig vg^mss sy^hmg) and 22:7 (adding from 26:14 are A C E 104 h p t vg^mss sy^p, h**).

this block of material, emphases are on "the Way," the high priest (and Sanhedrin), letters for Damascus, binding people, and imprisoning them in Jerusalem. Remarkable in this block of material is the blindness that Σαούλ receives from seeing ΦΩΣ, and it is probable that the blindness received by Σαούλ was a punishment from the Lord.[19] This is especially so if Acts 22 represents a more original form of this material, for in Acts 22, all of the travelers see ΦΩΣ (22:9) but only Σαούλ is blinded (22:11).[20]

A second block of material[21] also concerns a prosecutor who is aligned with the Temple, perhaps as some kind of official, but in this material the character is anonymous (A2: Acts 26:9–11), for the name Σαούλ appears only in Acts 26:12–15, which includes the Lukan rewriting of [B] (22:6–8; par. 9:3–5).[22] But after an event equivalent to block one's ΦΩΣ-revelation,[23] the "conversion" of this official is a figurative enlightenment that is acquired through direct revelation (C2: 26:16–20, 23 [parts]).[24] Emphases in this block of material include references to prosecution on the basis of the authority (ἐξουσία) of "the chief priests" in Jerusalem, Jesus as a "Nazorean" (Ναζωραῖος), his followers as "saints," and the defendant's irrational passion

---

19. Compare Zechariah's punishment of loss of speech (Luke 1:20) and its restoration (1:64).

20. The story in Acts 22 reads as if Σαούλ is later healed by Ananias (ἀναβλέψα εἰς αὐτόν, 22:13). But even assuming that this is the proper reading of "looked up," it should be noted that Acts 22:12, 16 is not part of the same source material; rather, it is Lukan rewriting of block three material (see below). Therefore, it is unclear, within the source for block two material, whether the blindness Σαούλ received was intended to be temporary or permanent. Compared to Greek mythology, two observations may be pertinent: a prophet or seer is often a blind person or someone blinded; and one god or goddess cannot undo what another has done. For example, the prophet Teiresias of Thebes was blinded by Hera; and to compensate Teiresias, Zeus provided Teresias with prophetic abilities and with life for seven generations. See further n. 27 below.

21. Acts 26:2–8, the "uprising" or "resurrection" speech, is a distinct block of material. In a proto-form of Acts (or one of its sources), this block of material may have been related to the material preserved at Acts 22:30—23:11, which only partly recounts a story of Paul defending himself before high priest Ananias's council in Jerusalem. The imagined timeframe of that story is the day after Paul's speech to the angry mob in Jerusalem (Acts 21:17—22:29), during which Paul called on the high priest and council as witnesses to his prior life (22:5).

22. Interesting is also the Lukan addition σκληρόν σοι πρὸς κέντρα λακτίζειν (26:14b). Apparently an inspiration for many visual representations of Paul's conversion, the phrase is understood often to portray Paul as a beast of burden who stubbornly kicks against its master's prodding; another interpretation is that Paul is harshly spurring on his own ride, in his zeal to chase after Jesus and his followers.

23. Acts 26:12–15 is Lukan reproduction of block one material (including its use of Σαούλ), but a functionally equivalent event must have occurred at this location in block two's source material.

24. Compare Paul's vision of the Lord in the Temple at Acts 22:17–21.

not only to imprison the "saints" but even to pursue, beat, and kill them in "the outer cities." Assuming a philosophical dichotomy between the irrational passions and rational mind, this character's conversion from "dark" to "light" is not a bodily healing from blindness to sight; it is a change from the darkness of passions to rational enlightenment, which is correlated with a different ideology of Χρίστος and God's people and a turn from ethnic and/or geopolitical exclusivity (Ιουδαῖοι) to some kind of inclusion (ἔθνη). As a protreptic speech, the source for Acts 26:9–11, 16–20, 23 portrays its protagonist as a model for repentance and turning to the light.[25]

The third block of material is the most critical for comparing with the *Ephesus Act*, since all of the "parallels" between Acts and the *Acts of Paul* occur in Acts 9:9/10–19a and 22:12–16. Often cited by its reference to the character Ananias, this block of material tells the story of a blind man who was healed in Damascus in the house of a certain Judas. The "parallels" to the *Ephesus Act* that occur within this block of material do not occur within the parts that were composed by Luke *de novo* ("redaction"); rather, parallel materials occur within a pre-Lukan source that was partly incorporated in Acts 9:9/10–19a ("tradition"), which was also epitomized in Acts 22:12–16 (esp. vv. 12–13, 16). Precisely how and where to delimit this tradition versus its Lukan redaction is difficult to determine, so a number of hypotheses have been offered.[26] Moreover, matters may be complicated if other parts of Acts preserve fragments of the pre-Lukan source in question.[27] But a selec-

---

25. Note that the first block of material (Acts 22:4–11) is situated within a speech that allegedly occurs "in the Hebrew dialect" before the angry mob of Jerusalemites, whereas the second block of material (Acts 26:9–11, 16–20, 23) is situated within a Greek *apologia* to Herod Agrippa II, etc. With comparison to other Greek novels (esp. two speeches in Chariton 5.6–8), Pervo (*Profit with Delight*, 76) has argued that it was an intentional matter of Lukan style to compose two distinct Greek *apologiai* for Paul—one more "barbarian" (Acts 22), another more lettered (Acts 26). But such differences may be explained also by the use of different sources, which "Luke" artfully (re)situated in appropriate rhetorical contexts.

26. Pervo (*Acts: A Commentary*, 239) distinguishes three layers within Acts 9:9–19a, which for him is part of a broader unit that includes 7:58; 8:1, 3; and 9:1–8. According to Pervo, the first layer is a miraculous tale of Paul's punishment and healing (9:9–10, 11 through "Σαούλ," and parts of 15, 17, 18, 19); the second layer is a pre-Lukan stage of redaction that changes the first source into a story of Paul's conversion (9:11 after "Σαούλ," 12, and parts of 16 and 18); and the third layer is Lukan redaction (9:13–14, and parts of 15, 16, and 17). Pervo dates the immediate source for Lukan redaction (i.e., the second stage, where the tradition has acquired another layer of redaction) to ca. 85–90 CE and proposes a provenance similar to Ephesus (*Acts: A Commentary*, 240).

27. For example, prior to its extant form(s), Acts 13:4–12 may have told the story of someone who was punished with blindness, perhaps for promoting νόμος and περιτομή. Was such a story related to one of the characters who later "saw the light"? Beneath the

tive comparison of the stories in Acts 9:9/10–19a and 22:12–16 illustrates some of the issues and options; see Table 2.

Table 2. The House of Judas in Damascus

9:9 καὶ ἦν ἡμέρας τρεῖς μὴ βλέπων καὶ οὐκ ἔφαγεν οὐδὲ ἔπιεν.	[—]
9:10a Ἦν δέ τις μαθητὴς <u>ἐν Δαμασκῷ</u> ὀνόματι Ἀνανίας,	22:12 Ἀνανίας δέ τις, ἀνὴρ εὐλαβὴς κατὰ τὸν νόμον, μαρτυρούμενος ὑπὸ πάντων τῶν κατοικούντων Ἰουδαίων, ...
9:10b καὶ εἶπεν πρὸς αὐτὸν ἐν ὁράματι ὁ κύριος· Ἀνανία. ὁ δὲ εἶπεν· ἰδοὺ ἐγώ, κύριε. 11 ὁ δὲ κύριος πρὸς αὐτόν· ἀναστὰς[a] πορεύθητι ἐπὶ τὴν ῥύμην τὴν καλουμένην Εὐθεῖαν καὶ ζήτησον ἐν οἰκίᾳ Ἰούδα Σαῦλον ὀνόματι Ταρσέα.[b] ἰδοὺ γὰρ προσεύχεται 12 καὶ εἶδεν ἄνδρα [<u>ἐν ὁράματι</u>][c] <u>Ἀνανίαν ὀνόματι</u> εἰσελθόντα καὶ ἐπιθέντα αὐτῷ [τὰς] χεῖρας[d] ὅπως ἀναβλέψῃ.	[—]
[omission of 9:13–16, which is Lukan composition]	[rough "parallels" at 22:14–15]
9:17 Ἀπῆλθεν δὲ Ἀνανίας καὶ εἰσῆλθεν εἰς τὴν οἰκίαν καὶ ἐπιθεὶς ἐπ' αὐτὸν τὰς χεῖρας εἶπεν· <u>Σαοὺλ</u> ἀδελφέ, ὁ κύριος ἀπέσταλκέν με, <u>Ἰησοῦς ὁ ὀφθείς σοι ἐν τῇ ὁδῷ ᾗ ἤρχου</u>, ὅπως ἀναβλέψῃς καὶ πλησθῇς πνεύματος ἁγίου. 18a–b καὶ εὐθέως ἀπέπεσαν αὐτοῦ[e] ἀπὸ τῶν ὀφθαλμῶν ὡς λεπίδες, ἀνέβλεψέν τε ...[f]	22:13 ἐλθὼν πρός με καὶ ἐπιστὰς εἶπέν μοι· <u>Σαοὺλ</u> ἀδελφέ, ἀνάβλεψον. κἀγὼ αὐτῇ τῇ ὥρᾳ ἀνέβλεψα εἰς αὐτόν.
[rough "parallels" at 9:13–16]	[omission of 22:14–15, which may be Lukan rewriting of 26:16c]
9:18c ... καὶ ἀναστὰς ἐβαπτίσθη 19a καὶ λαβὼν τροφὴν ἐνίσχυσεν.	22:16 καὶ νῦν τί μέλλεις; ἀναστὰς βάπτισαι καὶ ἀπόλουσαι τὰς ἁμαρτίας σου ἐπικαλεσάμενος τὸ ὄνομα αὐτοῦ.

---

material in Acts 13:4–12 may lie a more infamous but related story, about a "σαῦλος" who opposed "the Lord's" ideals and was blinded for such, yet rewarded with the gift of prophecy. Intriguingly, it is in this pericope that Sergios Paulos is introduced (13:7), and that a "σαῦλος" is identified (apparently in contrast to Sergios) as "the one who's also Παῦλος" (13:9). There is an odd coincidence of straight paths, blinding (with comparison to seeing sun), and being led by the hand. See further the discussions of Σαοὺλ and σαῦλος at n. 17.

a. Only B reads ἀνάστα
b. Compare Acts 21:39; see n. 35 below.
c. B ἄνδρα ἐν ὁράματι; 614 (which is late and harmonizes various types) ἐν ὁράματι ἄνδρα; others, ἄνδρα.
d. Varied are uses of the article; also attested is χείρᾳ (614, with L, Ψ, 33, 323, 1175, 1241, 𝔐, it, vg^{mss}, sy), which in this case may indicate an earlier form where Ananias placed something [in the accusative] upon Tarseus "by hand"; if so, it may indicate oil, water, mud, saliva, or a host of other media for healing. Compare 9:17, where "hands" is definitely attested, according to a more Lukan procedure.
e. Some manuscripts, including 614, locate αὐτοῦ after the prepositional phrase ἀπὸ τῶν ὀφθαλμῶν.
f. Many manuscripts use ὡσεί rather than ὡς; many of the same also add παραχρῆμα at the end of the quoted material.

The account in Acts 9:9/10-19a was epitomized in Acts 22:12-16, in order to harmonize with the preceding "block one" material (22:4-11) and with the themes in Acts 26:16-18 (part of the "block two" material). Compared to Acts 9:9/10-12, 17-19a, the conversion story in Acts 22:12-16 provides a more Lukan description of Ananias ("a man acceptable according to the law, attested by all the resident Judeans," 22:12); it cuts the dialogue with Ananias (9:10b-12 [as well as the Lukan addition at 9:13-16], 17; cp. 22:14-15); it excises where and by what means Ananias came into contact with Paul (cp. 9:11-12, 17); it deletes references to things falling from the eyes of Paul (9:18a), to him being filled "with (a) spirit that is holy" (anarthrous, 9:17), and to him taking nourishment afterward (9:19a; cp. 9:9 on three days of neither eating nor drinking); it highlights the immediacy with which Paul was given sight (22:13b); and it adds Lukan emphases on being "washed from sins" and "calling on his name" (22:16).[28] Shorter, strikingly Lukan, and/or harmonizing in its additions, the "parallels" in Acts 22:12-16 are thus a Lukan reproduction of material in Acts 9:9/10-19a.

But was the material in Acts 9:9/10-19a also Lukan in origin, or does it originate from a pre-Lukan source? First of all, the block of material in 9:9/10-21 is not without Lukan additions. Acts 9:13-16 is entirely Lukan, produced in order to harmonize with 26:9-11;[29] so also is Acts 9:19b-21, which harmonizes with 26:9-11 and 26:19-20a. In Table 2, I have underlined several additional phrases that are <u>possible Lukan additions</u> to the source material: these include the transliterated Hebrew name Σαούλ (9:17; see 22:7), reference to seeing the Lord Jesus "on the way" (9:17; see 22:6-10),

28. According to Lüdemann (*Early Christianity*, 112), Conzelmann should receive credit for noting the Lukan theme of "the name" (see Acts 3:16; 4:12; 8:12; etc.). Odd remains the aorist middle imperative: βάπτισαι, "immerse" (Acts 22:16).

29. In Ananias's rebuttal (Acts 9:13-14), note the shared references to Jerusalem, "saints," "chief priests," and "authority" (26:9-11). Further similarities occur with references to ἔθνη, etc., in 9:15-16. Similar valuation with different explanations is common (e.g., Hedrick, "Paul's Conversion/Call," 419-21; Lüdemann, *Early Christianity*, 111-12; Haenchen, *Acts of the Apostles*, 324-25).

and location in the city of Damascus (9:10a; see 22:6, 10, 11; cp. 26:12). Secondly, the material that remains is *not* characteristically Lukan: "double" visions are not commonplace in Acts,[30] several of the phrases are atypical or unattested,[31] the main character is Ananias rather than Luke's hero Paul, and—in contrast to the stories in Acts 22 and 26—the plot is a simple healing story.

For the tradition behind Acts 9:10-19a, this healing occurs in order to give sight to someone who was blind(ed). Whether the man was completely or partially blind, and for how long and why, we do not know once we separate this tradition from the preceding "block one" materials—unless 9:9's reference to three days is part of the source material. What we do know is that the healing occurs on a "street called Straight" in the house of Judas with the hands of Ananias;[32] and once Ananias speaks to the man, undescribed entities fall from the man's eyes "like flakes." Thereafter, the man looks up, rises, and is immersed, as though being purified after a spell of "leprosy" (9:18; cp. Lev 13-14). Moreover, like someone who had ritually fasted before a healing (cp. 9:9), the man subsequently receives nourishment and is strengthened (9:19a).

So who was healed? Rather than calling him by the transliterated Hebrew name Σαούλ (assuming that Acts 9:17 is Lukan reproduction of 22:7), the source describes the man as σαῦλον ὀνόματι Ταρσέα. As with the introduction of Ananias in 9:10a (τις μαθητὴς . . . ὀνόματι Ἀνανίας, "a certain disciple . . . by the name Ananias"), the word order implies that this is "*saulos* by the name Tarseus."[33] But who or what is σαῦλος? It is not the

---

30. Like an Israelite prophet, Ananias is summoned and commissioned in a vision (ὅραμα), and he is told that the man praying has seen (in a vision) what will occur (Acts 9:10-12). Within Acts, parallels occur with Peter and Cornelius in Acts 10 and partially with Philip and the Ethiopian eunuch in Acts 8. Some (e.g., Lüdemann, *Early Christianity*, 111, 113) understand these "parallels" to be Lukan production, but others (e.g., Pervo, *Acts*, 239) do not. For discussion, see Pervo, *Profit with Delight*, 73; Pervo, *Acts: A Commentary*, esp. 236 n. 31 and 238 n. 44.

31. Lüdemann, *Early Christianity*, 111-12; Pervo, *Acts: A Commentary*, 242-44.

32. Probably this is neither the Ananias of Acts 5, nor the high priest Ananias of Acts 23-24. But as a healing story, it should be noted that the various procedures in Leviticus 13-14 require a high priest, bodily inspection, ritual cleansing (sometimes including animal slaughter, touching with blood, anointing with oil, etc.), and ritual bathing, normally following a seven-day period of impurity. Textual variants in Acts 9:10-19a indicate scribal uncertainties about its source material.

33. Within Acts, 17 of 21 occurrences definitely occur with this pattern (so also all 5 occurrences in Luke). The only definite exceptions are Acts 5:1 (also, interestingly, Ἀνὴρ δέ τις Ἀνανίας ὀνόματι) and 9:12 (ἄνδρα [ἐν ὁράματι] Ἀνανίαν ὀνόματι), where some scribes have duplicated a preceding phrase. Other exceptions probably include the appositional clauses introducing Apollos (18:24) and may include Demetrios the

person's name; rather, it is a restrictive use of a Greek adjective, followed by the further specification of the person's name: "a stumbling man[34] by the name Tarseus." The man in question is both σαῦλος, "stumbling," and named Ταρσεύς, which—if it should be etymologized—means either "Tarsian" (one from Ταρσός)[35] or "basket-weaver" (artisan or caretaker of ταρσός, "basket; matting; flattening").[36] The third block of material, whose source is partially preserved in Acts 9:9/10–12, 17–19a, is a story therefore about a stumbling blind man named "Tarseus" who was healed—if not ritually purified from leprosy—at the house of Judas.

The scribe or set of scribes whom we call "Luke" used these three distinct blocks of material to produce the conversion stories in Acts 9, 22, and 26. The Lukan portrait of Paul is based therefore not on a single reliable source for a historical individual; rather, it is based on the artful cutting and piecing together of several blocks of material, for, as a patchwork superhero, the Paul of Acts is ascribed a conversion that is temporary punishment (block one), enlightenment (block two), healing/purification (block three), and commission all in one. This ÜberPaul was made to play a part in the broader Lukan story, which explains how the Spirit spread God's kingdom from Jerusalem to Rome. Within this story, Paul is a dynamic and charismatic character, whose dramatic way of life and conversion are used to

"silver-striker" (19:24). But none of these examples are definitely Lukan production; all may derive from source materials, and 9:12 may even be a later scribal addition.

34. LSJ indicates that sexual entendre may accompany the term's reference to a gait and carriage; so in addition to "straddling, waddling," the term may also refer to sauntering, prancing, and so forth—walking provocatively. The latter was used to describe prostitutes, Bacchae, Dionysus, etc. Based on what may be known of the literary context, I have preferred a translation that may imply the unsteady walk of a blind(ed) person. But other options are possible, including the cute description of Paul as ἀγκύλον ταῖς κνήμαις in the *Acts of Paul and Thecla* 3.3.

35. Among the canonized writings, the only other occurrence of Ταρσεύς is Acts 21:39. There it is commonly (mis)understood to mean "Tarsian," a citizen of Tarsus (see Acts 9:30; 11:25; 22:3). But must the occurrence in 21:39 mean "Tarsian"? Not necessarily, *pace* many commentators. Syntactically, it is just as likely that Ταρσεύς is a proper name ("Tarseus of Cilicia"), as it is a city of origin ("a Tarsian of Cilicia"), for the rhetorical context requires Paul to persuade the chiliarch why he should be able to address the citizens of Jerusalem. The Lukan dialogue, which probably depends on Josephus for its imagined context (see n. 15 above), includes Paul's reply to whether he is "the Egyptian." I retranslate Acts 21:39: ἐγὼ ἄνθρωπος μέν εἰμι Ἰουδαῖος, Ταρσεὺς τῆς Κιλικίας, οὐκ ἀσήμου πόλεως πολίτης · δέομαι δέ σου, ἐπίτρεψόν μοι λαλῆσαι πρὸς τὸν λαόν, as: "I, a human, am in fact a *Judean* [= resident of Judea], Tarseus of Cilicia, a citizen of no insignificant *polis* [= Jerusalem]. So I beg of you: permit me to speak to the people [of Judea]." References to the *polis* Ταρσός occur only at Acts 9:30; 11:25; 22:3. The first two are Lukan narrations; the last may be the product of Lukan harmonization.

36. On baskets, see Acts 9:22/23–25 and 2 Cor 11:32–33.

catalyze the diaspora from beginning to end. Nonetheless, this "Paul" is a Lukan collage, assembled to represent the artistic vision of "Luke."

Therefore, it is important to rethink how to compare the conversion story in the *Acts of Paul* with the conversion stories in Acts, for Acts does not speak with a unified voice; or, if it does so, it does not speak only or simply with the final voice of "Luke" but also with the voices of the traditions that were used as sources and redacted by the scribe(s) of Acts. To consider the relations, possible and actual, between Acts and the *Acts of Paul*, it is necessary therefore to study the various stages of composition within and behind both sets of stories. So, just as we have considered the discrete traditions and redactions of the conversion stories in Acts, let us now turn to a "part" of the hypothetical whole "*Acts of Paul*," to consider how Paul's conversion was constructed in the *Ephesus Act*.

THE CONVERSION STORY IN THE EPHESUS ACT

The *Ephesus Act*, which is abstractly labeled *Acts Paul* 9 according to the forthcoming critical edition of the Corpus Christianorum Series Apocryphorum,[37] is attested independently in the late fourth-century Coptic manuscript *Papyrus Bodmer* 41 (*P. Bodm.* 41)[38] and in the early fourth-century Greek collection of "*Acts of Paul*" at Hamburg (*P. Hamb.*).[39] The Coptic manuscript *P. Bodm.* 41 has preserved only the beginning of the *Ephesus Act*, and the Greek manuscript *P. Hamb.* has preserved only its end. But the manuscripts overlap in their contents, and a critical comparison of the two indicates that the Coptic of *P. Bodm.* 41 is a translation of basically the same text-type as the Greek preserved in *P. Hamb.* Therefore, the later Coptic manuscript may attest to a form of the *Ephesus Act* that is at least as early as *P. Hamb.* (ca. 300 CE), and the two together may preserve an early form of the *Ephesus Act* in its entirety. In any case, the conversion story of the *Ephesus Act* is extant only in the Bodmer manuscript, which is a "(demi?)-cahier" written in the Lyco-diospolitan (or Subakhmimic) dialect of Coptic. In this late fourth-century translation, the story of Paul's conversion is narrated in the first person, as part of a sermon that is preached to an assembly at the house of Aquila and Priscilla in Ephesus.

Paul's sermon at the house of Aquila and Priscilla is about entering into and/or progressing in one's faith (*Acts Paul* 9.5–10; *P. Bodm.* 41 ^{e}b–^{e}e),

---

37. A penultimate translation for the CCSA edition has been prepared by Willy Rordorf, with Pierre Cherix and Rodolph Kasser, "Actes de Paul."

38. Kasser and Luisier, "Papyrus Bodmer XLI."

39. Schmidt and Schubart, ΠΡΑΞΕΙΣ ΠΑΥΛΟΥ.

and the occasion of the speech is the festival of Pentecost. Paul's "hearers," who have "faith in Christ," include both "catechumens" and "the faithful." The speech begins with the *Ephesus Act*'s story of Paul's conversion (9.5–6). It continues with the story of Paul traveling with a certain widow Lemma and her daughter Ammia on the road to Jericho,[40] when he baptizes the lion (9.7–9).[41] Paul's speech ends with a direct address to the hosts Aquila and Priscilla (9.10), and the story ends with the statement that many were "added to the faith" (9.11).

The conversion story in the *Ephesus Act* begins with the geographic setting *hn tamaskos* ("in Damascus")[42] and a description that Paul was *ᵉr diōke ᵉntpistis ᵉmpnoute* ("pursuing the faith of God"). Within Acts, the verb διώκω is used variously to refer to Paul chasing, persecuting, or even prosecuting followers of Jesus; and as readers who are acquainted with Acts, it is tempting for us to "upload" such ideas into the *Ephesus Act* (especially if presupposing its literary dependence on Acts). But there are no descriptions of Paul pursuing such activities within the *Ephesus Act* (or within "Acts of Paul" more broadly), nor is there an account of Paul traveling *on the way* to Damascus. Rather, according to the *Ephesus Act*, Paul's "pursuit" of "the faith of God" occurs *within* Damascus, and it is not explicitly described as negative. Paul's "pursuit" may even be a positive search, like the journey of a catechumen.

---

40. Coptic *eeinabōk hᵉn ašierikhō ᵉnte phunikē*, "As I was about to go into Jericho of Phoenicia." Scholars who assume that "Damascus" is Damascus (in Syria) and that "Jericho" is Jericho (in Judea) often claim that the scribe or a predecessor introduced an error for *phoinikōn* and hence "Jericho of the Palms" (cp. Deut 34:3; and on Jericho in other Pauline tradition, see the [Coptic] *Apocalypse of Paul*, NHC V,2). See Kasser and Luisier, "Papyrus Bodmer XLI," 319 n. 7; and on the scribal inadequacies of *P. Bodm.* 41, see ibid., 285–88, 306–7 et passim. My own opinion is that the scribe of *P. Bodm.* 41 was copying an earlier Coptic version rather than functioning as a translator.

41. For a figurative reading of the story, as would have been done later in ascetic venues, see Rordorf, "Quelques jalons." I am undecided whether there is intertextual allusion to the story of Samson's affair with a Philistine (Judges 14). Kasser and Luisier ("Papyrus Bodmer XLI," 321 n. 8) have also proposed Ezek 37:1 for the valley of (dry) bones. For a discussion of the diverse attestation to this particular story, see Schmidt and Schubart, ΠΡΑΞΕΙΣ ΠΑΥΛΟΥ, 85–98.

42. Rordorf, "Paul's Conversion." The voiced delta (*d*) was apparently "absorbed" into the unvoiced tau (*t*): *tdamaskos > tamaskos*.

When Paul is pursuing the faith in Damascus, it is "the Mercy"[43] who descends from the Father and proclaims the good news about God's Son.[44] Thereafter, Paul enters into a large *ekklēsia*,[45] referring to a particular assembly in Damascus. Only it is not explained what this "entry" (*bōk ahoun a-*) was: Was Paul accepted fully, for example through a baptism of initiation and with admission to the Eucharist? Or did Paul simply begin to affiliate with a church, starting a catechetical process? Often it is assumed that Paul simply and quickly converted.[46] But in the *Ephesus Act*, the details are unclear.

Once Paul "enters" the large church in Damascus, he advances in stages. Initially, at least *within* Paul's speech (*Acts Paul* 9.5), it is said that Paul receives *tagapē etjase ᵉnte tpistis*, meaning either "the exalted love of the faith"[47] or perhaps "the love that is above the faith" (cp. 1 Corinthians 13). But the first stage of Paul's development is being a hearer of the Lord's words—glossed as "the revelation of Christ." Apparently, after an examination in which Paul proves "strong enough" to be "worthy of the word," he is then promoted (*protrepe*, 9.6), so that he is also able to speak (*seje*). Not surprisingly, Paul is beloved by those who hear him (9.6). Formally speaking, this is where Paul's conversion story seems to end, implying the use of earlier source material by the author of the *Ephesus Act*, who produced the remainder of Paul's speech (9.7ff.).

But there is more to say about the tradition that was redacted by the author of the *Ephesus Act*. Just as the Mercy was used as a medium for announcing the Son, another was instrumental in Paul's development: a

---

43. The critical edition (Kasser and Luisier, "Papyrus Bodmer XLI," 317 n. 5) explains that "the copyist" of *P. Bodm.* 41 added a superlinear stroke over *pna*, apparently misunderstanding *pnae* ("the Mercy") as the *nomen sacrum* for πνεῦμα; as indicated by Kasser's earlier English translation (Schneemelcher and Kasser, "*Acts of Paul*," 264), even a critical scholar can duplicate such mistakes. That mistake in particular has been used by Bauckham ("*Acts of Paul*: Replacement") to argue for compatibility with Acts 9, as well as the alleged tendency of *Acts of Paul* to "harmonize" Acts and Galatians. Whether *pnae*'s revelation was external or internal is unclear, as is its identity: the Mercy that preaches to Paul in the *Ephesus Act* may be a divine being or one of the sacraments of the church (its masculine gender in Coptic is irrelevant, but its Greek original was probably ὁ ἔλεος, which is also masculine).

44. Mercy was issued from the Father to produce new life in Paul (see *Acts Paul* 9.5: *eeinaōnh hrēi ᵉnhētᵉf*, "so that I might live in him," and *pōnh ethᵉn peᵉkhrs*, "the life in Christ"; Kasser and Luisier, "Papyrus Bodmer XLI," 316–18). Compare Gal 2:19–20; 2 Cor 4:10–11; 2 Tim 1:1.

45. The church is large but local; it is a particular assembly in Damascus, not a proto-catholic reference to "the Great Church."

46. Compare Acts 9:26, 28–30, where such an event is distrusted.

47. As translated by Kasser in Schneemelcher and Kasser, "*Acts of Paul*," 264.

certain Judas. This "Judas" is a resident of Damascus, who is twice called "blessed" and is also described as "the brother of the Lord" and a "prophet." Like Elijah with Elisha or John with Jesus, Judas is remembered as training Paul: it was Judas who from the beginning gave Paul "the love that is above the faith," who helped Paul "enter a large *ekklēsia*" in Damascus, who helped Paul to be nourished with the Lord's words, and who—once Paul had become strong enough to be worthy—promoted him to speaker of the word.

The conversion story in the *Ephesus Act* thus portrays Paul as a disciple of the brother of Jesus, whose early development and preaching occurred in Damascus. Within this "conversion story," it is difficult to know whether Paul converted first (e.g., via baptism) and only later developed into a preacher, or whether Paul entered into a process of conversion that continued through the promotion to speaker of the word. Nor is it clear whether the "large church" in Damascus was a house-church or some other kind of assembly (e.g., a gravesite gathering). Nonetheless, it is certain that Judas was a prophet—perhaps *the* prophet—at the *ekklēsia* in question, and that it was under his authority that Paul progressed in the faith on a path familiar to many catechumens of the second century.

Subsequent to this "conversion story" (*Acts Paul* 9.5–6), the author of the *Ephesus Act* produced the remainder of Paul's speech at the house of Aquila and Priscilla in Ephesus (9.7–10). Regardless of whatever the tradition of Paul's conversion story may have originally claimed (9.5–6), the author of the *Ephesus Act* reframed that material with a subsequent story (9.7–9) and exhortation (9.10) in order to present Paul's development in Damascus as the beginning of a conversion process. The story is Paul's famous baptism of the lion (9.7–9). As told by the author of the *Ephesus Act*, the story begins one evening, prior to the *agapē*, when fully-initiated Christians would participate in Eucharist. Paul—with a widow Lemma and her daughter Ammia—departs from the church in Damascus and travels the dark and lonely path to Jericho. Having survived the night, a crisis occurs when a terrible lion arises from the valley of bones. But evil is averted when Paul subordinates the beast with baptism, conquering its dangerous passions. In other words: Paul masters his own beastly passions through immersion, either as a second, "encratic" baptism or an "eastern" form of baptism that preceded sexual continence.[48] (Lest we not catch the double entendre, the author throws us a bone: thereafter the beast is enabled not to submit to a lioness.)

---

48. See Rordorf, "Quelques jalons." Also, the promotion of a second baptism in Acts 19:1–7, when read in context of the preceding verses about Aquila and Priscilla (Acts 18:1–3; 18:18–21; and esp. 18:24–28), may offer another useful "parallel" between Acts and the *Ephesus Act*. See my discussion in Snyder, *Acts of Paul*, 89–90 (§2.3.2). For critical comparison with Thecla's baptism, see my discussion in Snyder, *Acts of Paul*,

After the stories of Paul's development in Damascus (9.5–6) and baptism of the lion on the way to Jericho (9.7–9), Paul's speech ends with a direct, protreptic address to the hosts of the house-church, Aquila and Priscilla (9.10). Sadly, the Coptic is poorly preserved at this point (*P. Bodm.* 41 *ᶜc* lines 27–28), but in my opinion Paul first addresses the couple, then he describes their becoming faithful to God (*ᵉr pisteue apnoute*) and their subsequent teaching (*tsebo*) and preaching (*taše*), and finally he calls upon them to *tahe* themselves and/or their "hearers." Immediately after this exhortation to *tahe* ("stand up," "establish," or even "graduate"), the author narrates what happens next: *au{ou}nač ᵉmmēše ouōh atpistis* (9.11). Because "catechumens" and "the faithful" were Paul's audience for the speech, it is difficult to know how this "large crowd" was "added to" or "increased" its faith. But it is clear that the story of Paul's development in Damascus (9.5–6) was used by the author of the *Ephesus Act* to exhort believers of one kind or another to progress in the faith. Like the scribe(s) of Acts, the author of the *Ephesus Act* selectively redacted earlier tradition in order to produce a particular portrait of Paul.

COMPARING THE CONVERSION STORIES

So how shall we compare the stories of Paul's conversion in Acts and the *Acts of Paul*? Should we assume that Acts is earlier than and/or more reliable than the *Ephesus Act*? The difficulty with this common tactic is that there is no single conversion story in Acts; rather, its conversion stories were produced by artfully cutting apart, reproducing, and piecing together at least three blocks of material. One block, best preserved in Acts 22, describes the persecutor named Σαούλ who was blinded for opposing the Way; the second block of material, mainly in Acts 26, is the story of a Jerusalemite prosecutor who "sees the light" about Χρίστος and the ἔθνη; and the third block, whose source is partly preserved in Acts 9, is the story of the blind man "σαῦλος named Ταρσεύς," who was healed and perhaps purified from leprosy. Should any of these conversion stories be considered earlier or more reliable than the story of Paul's catechesis in the *Ephesus Act*? If so, which one(s), and why?

Too often it has been presupposed that Acts was composed as a single coherent whole text (normally, in its "B" or "Alexandrian" form) prior to

---

146–47 (part of §3.5) and 225–32 (§6.1.3). In its earliest extant form, the *Acts of Paul and Thecla* was composed by someone familiar with the *Ephesus Act*; and by the era of Jerome, the stories were apparently circulating together, perhaps as part of a broader cycle.

the composition of the *Acts of Paul*—allegedly another coherent whole text. Working on these presuppositions, the goal has been to determine whether, where, how, and why the *Acts of Paul* may have depended upon Acts literarily, historically, and otherwise. Therefore, "parallels" have been discussed exclusively in terms of the motives, themes, etc., of the imagined author of "*Acts of Paul*." For example, it has been commonplace to allege that the references to "Judas" and "Damascus" in the *Ephesus Act* depend knowingly, if not literarily, on the account in Acts 9, and that these traditions were artistically enhanced by the imagined author of "*Acts of Paul*."[49] Not only is such a claim anachronistic (especially based on recent redatings of Acts and the *Ephesus Act* in particular), it is also mereologically fallacious[50]: even if *Acts Paul* 9.5–6 were dependent upon a source for its references to Judas and Damascus, its dependence would not necessarily be upon Acts, for its "parallels" are not with any of the Lukan redactions in Acts 9 but with the pre-Lukan tradition that was "Luke's" third block of source material (9:9/10–12, 17–18a). Indeed, if *Acts Paul* 9.5–6 *were* dependent upon a written source, its source would probably be the same source that "Luke" used. "Luke," as we know, reproduced that story of the blind man selectively, weaving it together with at least two other stories, as part of his grand artistic vision for Acts. How or why would it be different for the author of the *Ephesus Act* to take the same source and stitch (parts of) it into a story of Paul's gradual enlightenment through a large church in Damascus (cp. also Acts 9:19b, 22)?

As implied by my rhetoric, a more critical and historical method for comparing Acts and the *Acts of Paul* would be to analyze the compositional practices used by both (sets of) scribes who produced these stories, including the distinction of tradition(s) and redaction(s). Such a method would not be based on the presupposition that each text is a coherent final whole, nor on a correlative prejudgment that one story preceded another. While continuing to ask how "*Acts of Paul*" may have redacted traditions otherwise attested in Acts, it would also consider how the scribe(s) of Acts may have redacted traditions attested in "*Acts of Paul*," as well as how the scribes of both corpora (if and when such are distinct) used other sources—from Pauline letters, to the Gospels, Septuagint, apocrypha, and beyond.

---

49. See the works listed in n. 2.

50. Another, more basic mereological fallacy is assuming that the variety of traditions abstractly ascribed to "*Acts of Paul*" represent parts of an early coherent whole text (see Snyder, *Acts of Paul*). Just as the traditions in Acts should be considered individually, so should the traditions ascribed to "*Acts of Paul*." For, at least three—and perhaps four or more—distinct compositional strands occur among those traditions, each of which has its own provenance, intertexts, ideology, etc.

In the case of Paul's conversion, I have illustrated one way to study the compositional practices that resulted in the conversion stories of Acts and in the *Ephesus Act*. Working on the presupposition that the *Ephesus Act* was composed separately from other "*Acts of Paul*," I studied each of the stories using redaction and literary criticism, in order to separate their traditions and redactions. Within and among the stories in Acts, I identified three distinct sources, at least two of which must have been pre-Lukan. The first (Acts 22:4–11) and second (26:9–11, 16–18) blocks of material used by "Luke" tell a similar basic story: both explain how an aristocrat from Jerusalem, with legitimation from the Temple, was pursuing followers of Jesus until he "saw the light." But beyond that simple story, each block of material has so many of its own highlights, themes, etc., that it is debatable whether these stories were discussing the same person, however historical or imagined.

The third block of material used by "Luke" (Acts 9:9/10–12, 17–18b) is even more distinct, as it tells the story of how a stumbling blind man named Tarseus was healed by a certain Ananias. This "enlightenment" occurred in the house of Judas on "Straight Street" in Damascus. Like the other blocks, the source of this pre-Lukan tradition does not explicitly call the blind man Παῦλος, a Hellenized form of the Latin *Paulus*, "little one" (cp. Greek μίκρος). But it is interesting to note that some of its details are paralleled in the conversion story of the *Ephesus Act*. In that story, a certain *paulos* is pursuing the faith; and at a large church in Damascus, Judas, the "brother of the Lord," is the one who oversees Paul's development in the faith. Indeed, from the perspective of a historian who does not privilege Acts *a priori*, it may even be argued that, to the extent that the conversion stories behind Acts 22 and 26 are similar, the conversion stories behind Acts 9 and the *Ephesus Act* are as well, for both pre-redacted traditions may tell the story of an individual who acquires "eyes to see" and a "mouth to speak" at the house-church of a certain Judas in Damascus. Granted, each of the stories has its own highlights, themes, etc. But are the differences in the traditions behind Acts 9 and the *Ephesus Act* any more marked than the ones between Acts 22 and 26? Might it not be the case that both Acts 9 and the *Ephesus Act* are alternate receptions of a tradition local to Damascus—one redacting the story of a blind man's healing in order to produce the "Paul" of Acts, and another interpreting the tradition figuratively to refer to Paul's conversion (for example, as mediated through an intertext like Isa 35:5–6)? To this day there is a site in Damascus (oddly called "the house of Ananias" rather than "the house of Judas") that claims to commemorate Paul's illumination.

In any case, a comparison of the conversion stories collected in Acts and the "*Acts of Paul*" illumines the fact that, regardless of which text preserves a story, the historical issues of priority and reliability should be determined not on the basis of whole texts but at the level of traditions and redactions, for the scribes of Acts and "*Acts of Paul*" were participating in the same compositional practices. Each received various traditions, oral and/or written; based on certain criteria, each preserved some or all of those traditions; and then, in order to tell a broader story (or set of stories) with a character named "Paul," each reproduced parts of the traditions preserved—while adding, deleting, and changing as necessary—in order to reform those traditions to their artistic model(s). Canonized or noncanonized, orthodox or heretical, historical and/or otherwise, such are the conversions of Paul.

Bibliography

PRIMARY SOURCES

2 Clement. In *Die apostolischen Väter*. Vol. 1. Edited by Karl Bihlmeyer. 3rd ed. Tübingen: Mohr/Siebeck, 1970.
Acts of Andrew. Acta Andreae. Edited and translated by Jean-Marc Prieur. CCSA 5–6. Turnhout: Brepols, 1989.
Acts of John. Acta Iohannis. Edited and translated by Éric Junod and Jean-Daniel Kaestli. CCSA 1–2. Turnhout: Brepols, 1983.
Acts of Philip. Acta Philippi. Edited and translated by François Bovon et al. 2 vols. CCSA 11–12. Turnhout: Brepols, 1999.
Adamantius. *Dialogue on the Orthodox Faith. Der Dialog des Adamantius*. Edited by W. Hendrik van de Sande Bakhuyzen. GCS 4. Leipzig: Hinrichs, 1901.
Agapius of Menbidj. *Kitab Al-'Unvan / Histoire universelle*. Translated by Alexander Vasiliev. PO 7.4. Paris: Firmin Didot, 1911.
Alexander Romance. The Greek Alexander Romance. Translated by Richard Stoneman. Penguin Classics. New York: Penguin, 1991.
———. *Historia Alexandri Magni (Pseudo-Callisthenes)*. Vol. 1, *Recensio vetusta*. Edited and translated by Wilhelm Kroll. Berlin: Weidmann, 1926.
———. *Iuli Valeri Alexandri Polemi Res gestae Alexandri Macedonis translatae ex Aesopo graeco. Accedunt Collatio Alexandri cum Dindimo, rege Bragmanorum, per litteras facta et Epistola Alexandri ad Aristotelem magistrum suum, de itinere suo et de situ Indiae*. Edited by Bernhard Gustav Adolf Kübler. Leipzig: Teubner, 1888.
———. *The Romance of Alexander the Great*. Translated by Albert Mugrdich Wolohojian. Records of Civilization: Sources and Studies 82. New York: Columbia University Press, 1969.
———. *Das Syrische Alexanderlied: die drei Rezensionen*. Edited by Gerrit J. Reinink. 2 vols. CSCO 454–455. Leuven: Peeters, 1983.
Ananias of Shirak. *Anania Shirakats'u matenagrut'yune: usumnasirut'yun (The Writings of Ananias of Shirak)*. Edited by Ashot G. Abrahamyan et al. Yerevan: HSSR Matenadarani Hratarakch'ut'yun, 1944.
Apocalypse of Elijah. Die Apokalypse des Elias: Eine unbekannte Apokalypse und Bruchstücke der Sophonias-Apokalypse. Edited by Georg Steindorff. TUGAL 17.39 (Neue Folge, 2.3a). Leipzig: Hinrichs, 1899.

Apocalypse of Pseudo-Methodius. Die Apokalypse des Pseudo Methodius: die ältesten griechischen und lateinischen Übersetzungen. Edited by Willem J. Aerts and Georgius A. A. Kortekaas. 2 vols. CSCO 569–570. Leuven: Peeters, 1998.

———. *Die Syrische Apokalypse des Pseudo-Methodius.* Edited by Gerrit J. Reinink. 2 vols. CSCO 540–541, Scriptores Syri 220–221. Leuven: Peeters, 1993.

Apocryphon of Seth. "Apocryphon of Seth." Translated by Alexander Toepel. In *Old Testament Pseudepigapha: More Noncanonical Scriptures.* Vol. 1, edited by Richard Bauckham, James Davila, and Alexander Panayotov, 33–39. Grand Rapids: Eerdmans, 2013.

Armenian Infancy Gospel. The Armenian Gospel of the Infancy with Three Early Versions of the Protevangelium of James. Edited by Abraham Terian. Oxford: Oxford University Press, 2008.

Bandlet of Righteousness. The Bandlet of Righteousness: An Ethiopian Book of the Dead. The Ethiopic Text of the Ləfafä ṣədq in Facsimile from Two Manuscripts in the British Museum. Edited and translated by E. A. Wallis Budge. Luzac Semitic Text and Translation Series 19. London: Luzac, 1929.

———. "Die Binde der Rechtfertigung (Lefâfa ṣedek̲)." Translated by Sebastian Euringer. *Or* 9 (1940) 76–99 and 244–59.

———. *Lefàfa-Sedeq. Svitok opravdanija.* Translated by Boris A. Turaiev. Pamjatniki efiopskoj pis'mennosti 7. St. Petersburg: Kershbauma, 1908.

———. "*Maṣhafa heywat* et *Mangada samāy* d'après onze manuscrits inédits." Translated by Luigi Fusella in *Études éthiopiennes. Actes de la Xe Conférence internationale des études éthiopiennes (Paris, 24-28 août 1988),* edited by Claude Lepage et al., 363–67. Paris: Société française pour les études éthiopiennes, 1994.

———. *Ṣalot bä'əntä Ləfafä ṣədq, wä-Mängädä sämay, wä-Zena ḥəmamatihu lä-Krəstos.* Translated by Tesfa Gebre Selassie. Addis Abäba: Tesfa Printing Press, 1969–1970.

Brock, Sebastian. *Bride of Light: Hymns on Mary from the Syriac Churches.* Mōrān 'Ethō 6. Baker Hill, Kottayam and Kerala, India: St. Ephrem Ecumenical Research Institute [SEERI], 1994.

Cave of Treasures. La caverne des trésors: les deux recensions syriaques. Edited by Su-Min Ri. 2 vols. CSCO 486–487, Scriptores Syri 207–208. Leuven: Peeters, 1987.

Dhorme, Édouard, Antoine Guillaumont, and Franck Michaéli, translators. *La Bible. L'Ancien Testament.* Bibliothèque de la Pléiade 120. Paris: Gallimard, 1956.

Dupont-Sommer, André, and Marc Philonenko, eds. *La Bible. Écrits intertestamentaires.* Bibliothèque de la Pléiade 337. Paris: Gallimard, 1987.

Emerson, Ralph Waldo. *The Annotated Emerson.* Edited by David Mikics. Cambridge: Harvard University Press, 2012.

Epiphanius. *Ancoratus und Panarion.* Edited by Karl Holl. 2nd ed., rev. Edited by Jürgen Dummer, et al. 3 vols. GCS 25, 31, 37. Berlin: Akademie, 1980–2013.

Eusebius. *Die Demonstratio evangelica.* Vol. 6. of *Eusebius Werke.* Edited by Ivar A. Heikel. GCS 23. Leipzig: Hinrichs, 1913.

———. *Sancti Eusebii Hieronymi Epistulae.* 2nd ed. 3 vols. Edited by Isidor Hilberg. CSEL 54–56. 1910–1918. Reprinted, Vienna: Österreichische Akademie der Wissenschaften, 1996.

Funk, Wolf-Peter. *Kephalaia (I): Zweite Hälfte [Lieferung 13–14].* Stuttgart: Kohlhammer, 1999.

———. *Kephalaia (I): Zweite Hälfte [Lieferung 15–16].* Stuttgart: Kohlhammer, 2000.

Geyer, Paul, ed. *Itineraria et alia Geographica*. CCSL 175. Turnhout: Brepols, 1965.
Goehring, James E., ed. *The Crosby-Schøyen Codex MS 193 in the Schøyen Collection*. CSCO 521, Subsidia 85. Leuven: Peeters, 1990.
Graffin, René, Jean Parisot, François Nau, and Mihály Kmoskó, eds. *Patrologia syriaca*. 3 vols. Paris: Firmin-Didot et socii, 1894.
Gros, Paul, Jean Grosjean, and Michel Léturmy, translators. *La Bible. Le Nouveau Testament*. Bibliothèque de la Pléiade 226. Paris: Gallimard, 1971.
Hippolytus. *Refutation of All Heresies. Refutatio omnium haeresium*. Edited by Paul Wendland. Vol. 3 of *Hippolytus: Werke*. GCS 26. Leipzig: Hinrichs, 1916.
History of Joseph. Die Geschichte Josefs angeblich verfasst von Basilius dem Grossen aus Cäsarea nach einer syrischen Handschrift der Berliner kgl. Bibliothek mit Einleitung, Uebersetzung und Anmerkungen herausgegeben. Vol. 1 edited by Magnus Weinberg. Halle: H. Itzkowski, 1893. Vol. 2 edited by Samuel Wolf Link. Berlin: Itzkowski, 1895.
———. "The Syriac History of Joseph: A New Translation and Introduction." Translated by Kristian S. Heal. In *Old Testament Pseudepigrapha: More Noncanonical Scriptures*, Vol. 1, edited by Richard Bauckham, James R. Davila and Alexander Panayatov, 85–120. Grand Rapids: Eerdmans, 2013.
Infancy Gospel of Thomas. De infantia Iesu euangelium Thomae graece. Edited and translated by Tony Burke. CCSA 17. Turnhout: Brepols, 2010.
Irenaeus. *Against Heresies. Contre les herésies*. Edited and translated by Adelin Rousseau, et al. 10 vols. SC 263–64, 293–94, 210–11, 100, 152–53. Paris: Cerf, 1965–1982.
Jarīr al-Tabarī. *The History of al-Tabarī*. Vol. 4, *The Ancient Kingdoms*. Translated by Moshe Perlmann. Albany: SUNY Press, 1987.
Jefferson, Thomas. *The Writings of Thomas Jefferson*. Edited by Henry Augustine Washington. 9 vols. New York: Riker, Thorne, 1853–1854.
Josephus. *Jewish Antiquities*. Edited and translated by Henry St. John Thackeray, Ralph Marcus, Allen Paul Wikgren, and Louis H. Feldman. 9 vols. LCL. Cambridge: Harvard University Press, 1998.
———. *The Jewish War*. Edited and translated by Henry St. John Thackeray. 3 vols. LCL. Cambridge: Harvard University Press, 1927–1928.
Julian the Apostate. *Iulianos der Abtruennige. Syrische Erzählungen*. Edited by Johann Georg Ernst Hoffmann. Leiden: Brill, 1880.
Kirakos of Gandzak. *Kirakos Gandzakets'i's History of the Armenians*. Translated by Robert Bedrosian. New York: Sources of the Armenian Tradition, 1986.
Justin Martyr. *1 and 2 Apologies* and *Dialogue with Trypho. Die ältesten Apologeten*. Edited by Edgar J. Goodspeed. Göttingen: Vandenhoeck & Ruprecht, 1914.
Mahé, Jean-Pierre and Paul-Hubert Poirier, eds. *Écrits gnostiques*. Bibliothèque de la Pléiade 538. Paris: Gallimard, 2007.
Martyrdom of St. Arethas and His Companions. Le martyre de Saint Aréthas et de ses compagnons (BHG 166). Edited by Marina Detoraki. Travaux et mémoires du Centre de recherche d'histoire et civilisation de Byzance Monographies 27. Paris: Association des amis du Centre d'histoire et civilisation de Byzance, 2007.
McNamara, Martin et al., eds. *Apocrypha Hiberniae 1: Evangelia infantiae*. 2 vols. CCSA 13–14. Turnhout: Brepols, 2001.
Patmut'yun Hayots'. Edited by K. A. Melik'-Ōhanjanyan and Karapet Aghabeki. Erevan: Haykakan SSR Gitut'yunneri Akademiayi Hratarkch'ut'yun, 1961.

Pseudo-Abdias. *Apostolic History. Anonymi Pilalethi Eusebiani in vitas, miracula passionesque Apostolorum Rhapsodiae.* Edited by Friedrich Nausea. Cologne: Peter Quentel, 1531.

———. *Abdiae Babyloniae episcopi et apostolorum discipuli de historia certaminis apostolici libri decem.* Edited by Wolfgang Lazius. Basel: Ioannis Oporini, 1552.

Pseudo-Clementine Homilies and Recognitions. Die Pseudoklementinen I: Homilien. Edited by Bernhard Rehm. 3rd ed., rev. GCS 42. Berlin: Akademie, 1992.

———. *Die Pseudoklementinen II: Rekognitionen in Rufins Übersetzung.* Edited by Bernhard Rehm. 2nd ed., rev. GCS 51. Berlin: Akademie, 1994.

———. *Die syrischen Clementinen mit griechischem Paralleltext: Eine Vorarbeit zu dem literargeschichtlichen Problem der Sammlung.* Edited by Wilhelm Frankenberg. TUGAL 48.3. Leipzig: Hinrichs, 1937.

Pseudo-Cyril of Jerusalem. *On the Life and the Passion of Christ: A Coptic Apocryphon.* Edited by Roelof van den Broek. VCSup 118. Leiden: Brill, 2013.

Sackur, Ernst, ed. *Sibyllinische Texte und Forschungen: Pseudomethodius, Adso und die tiburtinische Sibylle.* Halle: Niemeyer, 1898.

Schaff, Philip and Henry Wace, eds. *A Select Library of Nicene and Post-Nicene Fathers of the Christian Church.* Second Series. 14 vols. New York: Christian Literature Co., 1890.

Tertullian. *Adversus Marcionem.* Edited and translated by Ernest Evans. 2 vols. OECT. Oxford: Clarendon, 1972.

Tiburtine Sibyl. "The Tiburtine Sibyl (Greek)." Translated by Rieuwerd Buitenwerf. In *Old Testament Pseudepigrapha: More Noncanonical Scriptures.* Vol. 1, edited by Richard Bauckham, James Davila, and Alexander Panayotov, 176–88. Grand Rapids: Eerdmans, 2013.

Toledot Yeshu: The Life Story of Jesus. 2 vols. Edited and translated by Michael Meerson and Peter Schäfer with the collaboration of Yaacov Deutsch, David Grossberg, Avigail Manekin, and Adina Yoffie. TSAJ 159. Tübingen: Mohr/Siebeck, 2014.

———. *Das Leben Jesu nach jüdischen Quellen.* Edited by Samuel Krauss. Berlin: Calvary, 1902.

———. *Vom Leben und Sterben des Juden Jeschu. Und wie die Rabbanim wieder Frieden zwischen Christen und Juden stifteten. Eine jüdische Erzählung. Sefer Toldos Jeschu. Faksimile-Ausgabe des Erstdrucks Altdorf 1681.* Edited by Michael Krupp. Ein Karem and Jerusalem: Lee Achim Sefarim, 2001.

———. *Šem Ṭob ibn Šapruṭ, "La piedra de toque": Una obra de controversia judeo-cristiana: introduccion, edición critica, traducción y notas al libro I.* Edited by José-Vicente Niclós. Madrid: Consejo Superior de Investigaciones Cientificas, 1997.

———. *Tela Ignea Satanae. Hoc est: Arcani et horribiles Judaeorum adversus Christum Deum, et Christianam Religionem Libri ANEKΔOTOI.* Edited by Johannes Christophorus Wagenseil. Altdorfi Noricorum: Excudit Joh. Henricus Schönnerstaedt, Academiae Typographus, 1681.

SECONDARY SOURCES

Aasgaard, Reidar. *The Childhood of Jesus: Decoding the Apocryphal Infancy Gospel of Thomas.* Eugene, OR: Cascade Books, 2009.

Adler, Elkan N. "Un fragment araméen de Toldot Yéschou." *REJ* 61 (1910) 126–30.

Aichele, George. "Canon, Ideology, and the Emergence of an Imperial Church." In *Canon and Canonicity: The Formation and Use of Scripture*, edited by Einar Thomassen, 45–65. Copenhagen: Museum Tusculanum Press, 2010.

Alexander, Paul J. *The Byzantine Apocalyptic Tradition*. Edited with an introduction by Dorothy deF. Abrahamse. Berkeley: University of California Press, 1985.

———. "Byzantium and the Migration of Literary Works and Motifs: The Legend of the Last Emperor." *Medievalia et Humanistica* n.s. 2 (1971) 47–68.

———. "The Diffusion of Byzantine Apocalypses in the Medieval West and the Beginnings of Joachimism." In *Prophecy and Millenarianism: Essays in Honour of Marjorie Reeves*, edited by Ann Williams, 53–106. New York: Longman, 1980.

———. "Medieval Apocalypses as Historical Sources." *AHR* 73 (1968) 997–1018.

———. "The Medieval Legend of the Last Roman Emperor and Its Messianic Origin." *Journal of the Warburg and Courtauld Institutes* 41 (1978) 1–15.

———. *The Oracle of Baalbek: The Tiburtine Sibyl in Greek Dress*. Dumbarton Oaks Studies 10. Washington, DC: Dumbarton Oaks Center for Byzantine Studies, 1967.

Allison, Dale C. *Jesus of Nazareth, Millenarian Prophet*. Minneapolis: Fortress, 1998.

Amersfoort, Jacobus van. "Het Evangelie van Thomas en de Pseudo-Clementinen: Een studie van de Woorden van Jezus in het Evangelie van Thomas en hun parallellen in de evangeliecitaten in de Pseudo-Clementijnse *Homiliae* en *Recognitiones*." ThD diss., Rijksuniversiteit te Utrecht, 1984.

Amiot, François, ed. *La Bible Apocryphe*. 2 vols. Textes pour l'histoire sacrée 5. Paris: Fayard, 1952–1953.

Amsler, Frédéric. "Les citations évangéliques dans le roman pseudo-clémentin: Une tradition indépendante du Nouveau Testament?" In *Le canon du Nouveau Testament: Regards nouveaux sur l'histoire de sa formation*, edited by Gabriella Aragione et al., 141–67. Le monde de la Bible 54. Geneva: Labor et Fides, 2005.

Andrist, Patrick. Review of *De infantia Iesu euangelium Thomae graece*. *Apocrypha* 24 (2013) 298–304.

Anthony, Sean W. "The Legend of 'Abdallāh ibn Sabaʾ and the Date of *Umm al-Kitāb*." *JRAS* (3rd ser.) 21/1 (2011) 1–30.

Armstrong, Jonathan J. *The Role of the Rule of Faith in the Formation of the New Testament Canon*. Lewiston, NY: Mellen, 2014.

———. "Victorinus of Pettau as the Author of the Canon Muratori." *VC* 62 (2008) 1–34.

Ashbrook Harvey, Susan. "Remembering Pain: Syriac Historiography and the Separation of the Churches." *Byzantion* 58 (1988) 295–308.

Aune, David E. "Assessing the Historical Value of the Apocryphal Jesus Tradition: A Critique of Conflicting Methodologies." In *Der historische Jesus: Tendenzen und Perspektiven der gegenwärtigen Forschung*, edited by Jens Schröter and Ralph Brucker, 243–72. BZNW 114. Berlin: de Gruyter, 2002.

———. *Jesus, Gospel Tradition and Paul in the Context of Jewish and Greco-Roman Antiquity. Collected Essays II*. WUNT 309. Tübingen: Mohr/Siebeck, 2013.

———. "Reconceptualizing the Phenomenon of Ancient Pseudepigraphy." In *Pseudepigraphie und Verfasserfiktion in frühchristlichen Briefen*, edited by Jörg Frey et al., 789–824. WUNT 1/246. Tübingen: Mohr/Siebeck, 2009.

Backus, Irena Dorota. "Les apocryphes néo-testamentaires et la pédagogie luthérienne des XVIe-XVIIe siècles: les recueils de Michael Neander (1564, 1567) et Nicolas

Glaser (1614)." In *Apocryphité. Histoire d'un concept transversal aux religions du livre. En hommage à Pierre Geoltrain*, edited by Simon Claude Mimouni, 263–76. Bibliothèque de l'École des Hautes Études. Sciences religieuses, 113. Turnhout: Brepols, 2002.

———. "Early Christianity in Michael Neander's Greek-Latin Edition of Luther's Catechism." In *History of Scholarship. A Selection of Papers from the Seminar on the History of Scholarship held Annually at the Warburg Institute*, edited by Christopher Ligota and Jean-Louis Quantin, 197–230. Oxford: Oxford University Press, 2006.

———. *Historical Method and Confessional Identity in the Era of Reformation (1378–1615)*. Studies in Medieval and Reformation Thought 94. Leiden: Brill, 2003.

———. "Jacques Lefèvre d'Etaples. A Humanist or a Reformist View of Paul and His Theology." In *A Companion to Paul in the Reformation*, edited by R. Ward Holder, 61–90. Brill's Companions to the Christian Tradition 15. Leiden: Brill, 2009.

———. "Renaissance Attitudes towards New Testament Apocrypha. Jacques Lefèvre d'Étaples and His Epigones." *Renaissance Quarterly* 51 (1998) 1169–97.

Bagnall, Roger S. *Early Christian Books in Egypt*. Princeton: Princeton University Press, 2009.

Barnes, Timothy D. *Early Christian Hagiography and Roman History*. Tria corda 5. Tübingen: Mohr/Siebeck, 2010.

Barnstone, Willis, and Marvin Meyer, eds. *The Gnostic Bible*. Boston: Shambhala, 2003.

Barton, John. *Holy Writings, Sacred Text: The Canon in Early Christianity*. Louisville: Westminster John Knox, 1997.

Basset, René. *La sagesse de Sibylle*. Les Apocryphes Éthiopiens 10. Paris: Bibliothèque de la Haute Science, 1900.

Bauckham, Richard. "The *Acts of Paul* as a Sequel to Acts." In *The Book of Acts in Its Ancient Literary Setting*, edited by Bruce W. Winter and Andrew D. Clarke, 105–52. The Book of Acts in Its First Century Setting 1. Grand Rapids: Eerdmans, 1993.

———. "The *Acts of Paul*: Replacement of Acts or Sequel to Acts?" *Semeia* 80 (1997) 159–68.

———. "The Four Apocalypses of the Virgin Mary." In *The Fate of the Dead: Studies on Jewish and Christian Apocalypses*, 332–62. NovTSup 93. Leiden: Brill, 1998.

———. *Gospel Women: Studies of the Named Women in the Gospels*. Grand Rapids: Eerdmans, 2002.

———. *Jesus and the Eyewitnesses: The Gospels as Eyewitness Testimony*. Grand Rapids: Eerdmans, 2006.

———. "The Study of Gospel Traditions Outside the Canonical Gospels: Problems and Prospects." In *The Jesus Tradition Outside the Gospels*, edited by David Wenham, 369–403. Gospel Perspectives 5. Sheffield: JSOT Press, 1985.

———. "Virgin, Apocalypses of the." In *ABD* 1:854–56.

Bauckham, Richard et al., eds. *Old Testament Pseudepigrapha: More Noncanonical Scriptures*. Vol. 1. Grand Rapids: Eerdmans, 2013.

Baudoin, Anne-Catherine. Review of *Jesus, Gospel Tradition and Paul in the Context of Jewish and Greco-Roman Antiquity: Collected Essays II*, by David E. Aune. *Apocrypha* 25 (2014) 267–70.

Bauer, Walter. *Das Leben Jesu im Zeitalter der Neutestamentlichen Apokryphen*. Tübingen: Mohr/Siebeck, 1909. Reprint, Darmstadt: Wissenschaftliche Buchgesellschaft, 1967.

———. *Orthodoxy and Heresy in Earliest Christianity*. Translated by the Philadelphia Seminar on Christian Origins. Philadelphia: Fortress, 1971. Originally published as *Rechtgläubigkeit und Ketzerei im ältesten Christentum*. 2nd ed. Edited by Georg Strecker. Tübingen: Mohr/Siebeck, 1964 (1934).

Baum, Armin Daniel. *Pseudepigraphie und literarische Fälschung im frühen Christentum*. WUNT 2/138. Tübingen: Mohr/Siebeck, 2001.

Baur, Ferdinand Christian. "Die Christuspartei in der korinthischen Gemeinde, der Gegensatz des petrinischen und paulinischen Christenthums in der ältesten Kirche, der Apostel Petrus in Rom." *Tübinger Zeitschrift für Theologie* 5 (1831) 61–206.

Beasley, Jonathan. "Testing Indicates 'Gospel of Jesus's Wife' Papyrus Fragment to be Ancient." *Gospel of Jesus' Wife*. Posted 14 April 2014. http://gospelofjesusswife.hds.harvard.edu/testing-indicates-gospel-jesuss-wife-papyrus-fragment-be-ancient.

Becker, Adam H., and Annette Yoshiko Reed, eds. *The Ways That Never Parted. Jews and Christians in Late Antiquity and the Early Middles Ages*. TSAJ 95. Tübingen: Mohr/ Siebeck, 2003.

Beckwith, Roger T. *The Old Testament Canon of the New Testament Church*. Grand Rapids: Eerdmans, 1985.

Bédier, Joseph. "La tradition manuscrite du Lai de l'Ombre: réflexions sur l'art d'éditer les anciens textes." *Romania* 54 (1928) 161–96 and 321–56.

Bedjan, Paul, ed. *Liber superiorum, seu Historia Monastica, auctore Thoma, Episcopo Margensi. Liber Fundatorum Monasteriorum in regno Persarum et Arabum. Homiliae Mar-Narsetis in Joseph. Documenta Patrum de quibusdam verae fidei dogmatibus*. Leipzig: Harrassowitz, 1901.

Bekkum, Wout Jac van. "Jewish Messianic Expectations in the Age of Heraclius." In *The Reign of Heraclius (610–41): Crisis and Confrontation*, edited by Gerrit J. Reinink and Bernard H. Stolte, 95–112. Groningen Studies in Cultural Change 2. Leuven: Peeters, 2002.

Bellinzoni, Arthur J. *The Sayings of Jesus in the Writings of Justin Martyr*. NovTSup 17. Leiden: Brill, 1967.

Bianchi, Ugo, ed. *Le Origini dello Gnosticismo: Colloquio di Messina, 13–18 Aprile 1966*. SHR 12. Leiden: Brill, 1970.

Bickerman, Elias. "Faux littéraires dans l'Antiquité classique. En marge d'un livre récent." *Rivista di filologia e di istruzione classica* 101 (1973) 22–41. Reprinted in Elias Bickerman, *Studies in Jewish and Christian History*. Vol. 3, 196–211. Arbeiten zur Geschichte des antiken Judentums und des Urchristentums 9/1. Leiden: Brill, 1986.

Bisson, Gisèle et al. "Vengeance du Sauveur." In *Écrits apocryphes chrétiens*, vol. 2, edited by Pierre Geoltrain and Jean-Daniel Kaestli, 371–98. Bibliothèque de la Pléiade 516. Paris: Gallimard, 2005.

Bock, Darrell L. *The Missing Gospels: Unearthing the Truth behind Alternative Christianities*. Nashville: Nelson, 2006.

Bockmuehl, Marcus. *The Remembered Peter in Ancient Reception and Modern Debate*. WUNT 1/262. Tübingen: Mohr/Siebeck, 2010.

Borg, Marcus. *Jesus in Contemporary Scholarship*. Valley Forge, PA: Trinity, 1994.

———. "A Temperate Case for a Non-Eschatological Jesus." *Forum* 2 (1986) 81–102.

Böttrich, Christfried. Review of *Antike christliche Apokryphen in deutscher Übersetzung*, edited by Christoph Markschies and Jens Schröter. *Plekos* 15 (2013) 69–75.

Bousset, Wilhelm. "Antichrist." In *Encyclopedia of Religion and Ethics*, edited by James Hastings, 1:578–87. 13 vols. New York: Scribner, 1908–1927.

———. *The Antichrist Legend: A Chapter in Christian and Jewish Folklore*. London: Hutchinson, 1896.

———. Review of *Die Pseudoklementinen, Homilien und Rekognitionen: Eine quellenkritische Untersuchung*, by Hans Waitz. *Göttingische gelehrte Anzeigen* 6/ (1905) 425–47.

Boustan, Ra'anan S. and Annette Y. Reed. "Blood and Atonement in the Pseudo-Clementines and *The Story of the Ten Martyrs*: The Problem of Selectivity in the Study of 'Judaism' and 'Christianity.'" *Henoch* 30 (2008) 333–64.

Bouvier, Bertrand, and François Bovon. "*Prière et Apocalypse de Paul*. Un fragment grec inédit conservé au Sinaï. Introduction, texte, traduction et notes." *Apocrypha* 15 (2004) 9–30. Reprinted in François Bovon, *Dans l'atelier de l'exégète. Du canon aux apocryphes*, 297–315. Christianismes antiques 4. Geneva: Labor et Fides, 2012.

Bovini, Giuseppe. *Ravenna*. Translated by Robert Erich Wolf. New York: Abrams, 1969.

Bovon, François. "Beyond the Canonical and the Apocryphal Books, the Presence of a Third Category: The Books Useful for the Soul." *HTR* 105 (2012) 125–37. Reprinted in François Bovon. *The Emergence of Christianity: Collected Studies III*, edited by Luke Drake, 147–60. WUNT 319. Tübingen: Mohr/Siebeck, 2013.

———. "The Corpus Christianorum Series Apocryphorum and the Assocation pour l'étude de la littérature apocryphe chrétienne." *Early Christianity* 3 (2012) 137–43.

———. "The *Dossier* on *Stephen*, the First Martyr." *HTR* 96 (2003) 279–315.

———. "Editing the Apocryphal Acts of the Apostles." In *Apocryphal Acts of the Apostles: Harvard Divinity School Studies*, edited by François Bovon et al., 1–35. Religions of the World. Cambridge: Harvard University Center for the Study of World Religions, 1999.

———. "*Fragment Oxyrhynchus 840*, Fragment of a Lost Gospel, Witness of an Early Christian Controversy over Purity." *JBL* 119 (2000) 705–28.

———. "The Suspension of Time in Chapter 18 of *Protevangelium Jacobi*." In *The Future of Early Christianity: Essays in Honor of Helmut Koester*, edited by Birger A. Pearson, 393–405. Minneapolis: Fortress, 1991.

———. "The Synoptic Gospels and the Noncanonical Acts of the Apostles." *HTR* 81 (1988) 19–36.

———. "Vers une nouvelle édition de la littérature apocryphe chrétienne: la *Series Apocryphorum* du *Corpus christianorum*." *Aug* 23 (1983) 373–78.

Bovon, François et al., eds. *Les Actes apocryphes des Apôtres. Christianisme et monde païen*. Publications de la faculté de théologie de l'Université de Genève 4. Geneva: Labor et Fides, 1981.

Bovon, François et al. *The Apocryphal Acts of the Apostles: Harvard Divinity School Studies*. Religions of the World. Cambridge: Harvard University Center for the Study of World Religions, 1999.

Bovon, François et al., eds. *Écrits apocryphes chrétiens*. 2 vols. Bibliothèque de la Pléiade 442 and 516. Paris: Gallimard, 1997–2005.

Bovon, François, and Bertrand Bouvier. "La translation des reliques de saint Étienne le premier martyr." *AnBoll* 131 (2013) 5–50.

Bovon, François, and Christopher R. Matthews. *The Acts of Philip: A New Translation*. Waco, TX: Baylor University Press, 2012.

Boyarin, Daniel. *Border Lines: The Partition of Judaeo-Christianity*. Philadelphia: University of Pennsylvania Press, 2004.

———. "A Revised Version and Translation of the 'Toledot Yeshu' Fragment." *Tarbiz* 47 (1978) 249–52 [in Hebrew].

Brakke, David. *The Gnostics: Myth, Ritual, and Diversity in Early Christianity*. Cambridge: Harvard University Press, 2010.

Brandes, Wolfram. "Anastasios ὁ δίχορος: Endzeiterwartung und Kaiserkritik." *ByzZ* 90 (1997) 24–63.

———. "Die apokalyptische Literatur." In *Quellen zur Geschichte des frühen Byzanz (4.–9. Jahrhundert)*, edited by Friedhelm Winkelmann and Wolfram Brandes, 305–22. Amsterdam: J. C. Gieben Verlag, 1990.

Brock, Ann Graham. "Genre of the Acts of Paul: One Tradition Enhancing Another." *Apocrypha* 5 (1994) 119–36.

Brock, Sebastian. *Bride of Light: Hymns on Mary from the Syriac Churches*. Mōrān 'Ethō 6. Baker Hill, Kottayam and Kerala, India: St. Ephrem Ecumenical Research Institute [SEERI], 1994.

———. "Syriac Views of Emergent Islam." In *Studies on the First Century of Islam*, edited by G. H. A. Juynboll, pages 9–21, 199–203. Carbondale and Edwardsville: Southern Illinois University Press, 1982.

Brock, Sebastian P., Aaron Butts, George A. Kiraz and Lucas Van Rompay, eds. *Gorgias Encyclopedic Dictionary of the Syriac Heritage*. Piscataway, NJ: Gorgias, 2011.

Brown, Scott G. *Mark's Other Gospel: Rethinking Morton Smith's Controversial Discovery*. ESCJ 15. Waterloo, ON: Wilfrid Laurier University Press, 2005.

Bujanda, Jesús Martinez, ed. *Index des livres interdits*. Vol. 2. *Index de l'Université de Louvain 1546, 1550, 1558*. Sherbrooke: Centre d'études de la Renaissance Sherbrooke, 1986.

Bultmann, Rudolf. *Die Geschichte der synoptischen Tradition*. FRLANT 29. Göttingen: Vandenhoeck & Ruprecht, 1921.

———. *The Gospel of John: A Commentary*. Translated by G. R. Beasley-Murray. Philadelphia: Westminster, 1971.

———. *Theologie als Kritik. Ausgewählte Rezensionen und Forschungsberichte*. Edited by Matthias Dreher and Klaus W. Müller. Tübingen: Mohr/Siebeck, 2002.

Burke, Tony, ed. *Ancient Gospel or Modern Forgery? The Secret Gospel of Mark in Debate*. Proceedings of 2011 York University Christian Apocrypha Symposium. Eugene, OR: Cascade Books, 2013.

———. "Entering the Mainstream: Twenty-Five Years of Research on the Christian Apocrypha." In *Rediscovering the Apocryphal Continent: New Perspectives on Early Christian and Late Antique Apocryphal Texts and Traditions*, edited by Pierluigi Piovanelli et al., 19–48. WUNT 1/349. Tübingen: Mohr/Siebeck, 2015.

———. "Heresy Hunting in the New Millennium." *SR* 39 (2010) 405–20.

———. "The *Infancy Gospel of Thomas* from an Unpublished Syriac Manuscript. Introduction, Text, Translation, and Notes." *Hugoye* 16.2 (2013) 225–99.

———. *Secret Scriptures Revealed: A New Introduction to the Christian Apocrypha*. Grand Rapids: Eerdmans, 2013.

Burke, Tony, and Brent Landau, eds. *New Testament Apocrypha: More Noncanonical Scriptures*. Vol. 1. Grand Rapids: Eerdmans, forthcoming.

Burnet, Régis. Review of *Ancient Gospel or Modern Forgery? The Secret Gospel of Mark in Debate*, edited by Tony Burke. *Apocrypha* 24 (2013) 290–93.

312 Bibliography

Burtea, Bogdan. "Ləfafä ṣədəq." In *Encyclopaedia Aethiopica*. Vol. 3. Edited by Siegbert Uhlig, 542–43. Wiesbaden: Harrassowitz, 2007.

Buttrick, George Arthur, et al., eds. *The Interpreter's Dictionary of the Bible: An Illustrated Encyclopedia*. 4 vols. New York: Abingdon, 1962.

Cadbury, Henry J. *The Book of Acts in History*. London: Black, 1955.

———. *The Making of Luke-Acts*. New York: Macmillan, 1927. Repr., London: SPCK, 1961.

Cameron, Ron, ed. *The Other Gospels: Non-Canonical Gospel Texts*. Philadelphia: Westminster, 1982.

Carlson, Stephen C. *The Gospel Hoax: Morton Smith's Invention of Secret Mark*. Waco, TX: Baylor University Press, 2005.

Cartlidge, David R., and J. Keith Elliott. *Art and the Christian Apocrypha*. New York: Routledge, 2001.

Cerquiglini, Bernard. *Éloge de la variante: Histoire critique de la philologie*. Paris: Le Seuil, 1989.

Charlesworth, James H. *Authentic Apocrypha: False and Genuine Christian Apocrypha*. The Dead Sea Scrolls & Christian Origins Library 2. North Richland Hills, TX: BIBAL, 1998.

———, ed. *The Old Testament Pseudepigrapha*. 2 vols. Garden City, NY: Doubleday, 1983–1985.

———. "Research on the New Testament Apocrypha and Pseudepigrapha." In *ANRW* II.25.2 (1988) 3919–68.

Charlesworth, James H. and James R. Mueller. *The New Testament Apocrypha and Pseudepigrapha: A Guide to Publications, with Excurses on Apocalypses*. ATLA Bibliography Series 17. Metuchen, NJ: Scarecrow, 1987.

Chernetsov, Sevir. "Ethiopian Magic Texts." *Forum for Anthropology and Culture* 2 (2006) 188–200.

Cirillo, Luigi, and Michel Frémaux. *Évangile de Barnabé*. Paris: Beauchesne, 1977.

Clark, Elizabeth A. *Founding the Fathers: Early Church History and Protestant Professors in Nineteenth-Century America*. Divinations: Rereading Late Ancient Religion. Philadelphia: University of Pennsylvania Press, 2011.

Clivaz, Claire et al., eds. *Digital Humanities in Biblical, Early Jewish and Early Christian Studies*. Scholarly Communication 2. Leiden: Brill, 2013.

Cobb, James Harrel and Louis B. Jennings. *A Biography and Bibliography of Edgar Johnson Goodspeed*. Chicago: University of Chicago Press, 1948.

Cohen, Leonardo. *The Missionary Strategies of the Jesuits in Ethiopia (1555–1632)*. Äthiopistische Forschungen 70. Wiesbaden: Harrassowitz, 2009.

Cohn, Norman. *The Pursuit of the Millennium: Revolutionary Millenarians and Mystical Anarchists of the Middle Ages*. Rev. and expanded ed. New York: Oxford University Press, 1970.

Collins, John. J. "Sibylline Oracles." In *The Old Testament Pseudepigrapha*, edited by James H. Charlesworth, 1:317–472. 2 vols. Garden City, NY: Doubleday, 1983.

Comfort, Philip W., and David P. Barrett, eds. *The Text of the Earliest New Testament Greek Manuscripts: A Corrected, Enlarged Edition of The Complete Text of the Earliest New Testament Manuscripts*. Wheaton, IL: Tyndale, 2001.

Constantinou, Eugenia Scarvelis. "Banned from the Lectionary: Excluding the Apocalypse of John from the Orthodox New Testament Canon." In *The Canon of the Bible and the Apocrypha in the Churches of the East*, edited by Vahan S.

Hovhanessian, 51–61. The Bible in the Christian Orthodox Tradition 2. New York: Lang, 2012.
Conybeare, Frederick C. "The Discourse of Ananias, Called the Counter upon the Epiphany of our Lord and Saviour." *Expositor* V 4 (1896) 321–37.
Conzelmann, Hans. *1 Corinthians*. Translated by James W. Leitch. Hermeneia. Philadelphia: Fortress, 1975.
Côté, Dominique. "La forme de Dieu dans les *Homélies pseudo-clémentines* et la notion de Shiur Qomah." In *"Soyez des changeurs avisés." Controverses exégétiques dans la littérature apocryphe chrétienne*, edited by Gabriella Aragione and Rémi Gounelle, 69–94. Cahiers de Biblia Patristica 12. Strasbourg: Université de Strasbourg, 2012.
———. "La function littéraire de Simon le Magicien dans les Pseudo-Clémentines." *LTP* 57 (2001) 513–23.
———. "Les procédés rhétoriques dans les *Pseudo-Clémentines*. L'éloge de l'adultère du grammairien Apion." In *Nouvelles intrigues pseudo-clémentines—Plots in the Pseudo-Clementine Romance: Actes du deuxième colloque international sur la littérature apocryphe chrétienne, Lausanne—Genève, 30 août—2 septembre 2006*, edited by Frédéric Amsler et al., 189–210. Publications de l'Institut romand des sciences bibliques 6. Lausanne: Zèbre, 2008.
———. *Le théme de l'opposition entre Pierre et Simon dans les Pseudo-Clémentines*. Paris: Institut d'Études Augustiniennes, 2001.
Cowley, Roger W. "The Biblical Canon of the Ethiopian Church Today." *Ostkirche Studien* 23 (1974) 318–23.
Credner, Karl August. *Die Evangelien der Petriner oder Judenchristen*. Vol. 1 of *Beiträge zur Einleitung in die biblischen Schriften*. Halle: Waisenhauses, 1832.
Crossan, John Dominic. *The Birth of Christianity: Discovering What Happened in the Years Immediately after the Execution of Jesus*. San Francisco: HarperSanFrancisco, 1998.
———. *The Cross That Spoke: The Origins of the Passion Narrative*. 1988. Reprinted, Eugene, OR: Wipf & Stock, 2008.
———. *Four Other Gospels: Shadows on the Contours of Canon*. 1985. Reprinted, Eugene, OR: Wipf & Stock, 2008.
———. *The Historical Jesus: The Life of a Mediterranean Jewish Peasant*. San Francisco: HarperSanFrancisco, 1991.
Cureton, William. *Ancient Syriac Documents Relative to the Earliest Establishment of Christianity in Edessa and the Neighboring Countries*. 1864. Reprinted, Eugene, OR: Wipf & Stock, 2004.
Czachesz, Istaván. "The *Acts of Paul* and the Western Text of Luke's Acts: Paul between Canon and Apocrypha." In *The Apocryphal Acts of Paul and Thecla*, edited by Jan N. Bremmer, 107–25. Kampen: Kok Pharos, 1996.
———. *Commission Narratives: A Comparative Study of the Canonical and Apocryphal Acts*. Studies on Early Christian Apocrypha 8. Leuven: Peeters, 2007.
Daniel-Rops, Henri. *Histoire de l'Église du Christ*. 12 vols. Paris: Fayard, 1948–1965.
Darrow, William R. "The Harvard Way in the Study of Religion." *HTR* 81 (1988) 215–34.
Davies, Stevan L. "The Christology and Protology of the Gospel of Thomas." *JBL* 111 (1992) 663–82.
Davila, James R. *The Provenance of the Pseudepigrapha: Jewish, Christian or Other?* Journal for the Study of Judaism Supplements 105. Leiden: Brill, 2005.

Davis, Stephen J. *Christ Child: Cultural Memories of a Young Jesus*. New Haven: Yale University Press, 2014.

Debié, Muriel. "Suivre l'étoile à Oxford, inédits sur la venue des Mages." In *Malphono w-Rabo d-Malphone: Studies in Honor of Sebastian P. Brock*, edited by George A. Kiraz, 111–33. Gorgias Eastern Christian Studies 3. Piscataway, NJ: Gorgias, 2008.

Denis, Albert-Marie et al. *Introduction à la littérature religieuse judéo-hellénistique (Pseudépigraphes de l'Ancien Testament)*. 2 vols. Turnhout: Brepols, 2000.

Denzey Lewis, Nicola. "*Apolytrosis* as Ritual and Sacrament: Determining a Ritual Context for Death in Second-Century Marcosian Valentinianism." *JECS* 17 (2009) 525–61.

———. "'Enslavement to Fate,' 'Cosmic Pessimism' and Other Explorations of the Late Roman Psyche: A Brief History of a Historiographical Trend." *SR* 33 (2005) 277–99.

———. *Introduction to "Gnosticism": Ancient Voices, Christian Worlds*. Oxford: Oxford University Press, 2013.

Denzey Lewis, Nicola, and Justine Ariel Blount. "Rethinking the Origins of the Nag Hammadi Codices." *JBL* 133 (2014) 399–419.

Desreumaux, Alain. "Un manuscrit syriaque de Téhéran contenant des apocryphes." *Apocrypha* 5 (1994) 137–64.

Deutsch, Yaacov. "New Evidence of Early Versions of *Toledot Yeshu*." *Tarbiz* 69 (2000) 177–97 [in Hebrew].

Dewey, Arthur J. "The Unkindest Cut of All: Matt 19:11–12." *Forum* 8.1-2 (1992) 113–21.

Dibelius, Martin. *The Book of Acts: Form, Style, and Theology*. Edited by K. C. Hanson. Translated by Mary Ling with Paul Schubert. Fortress Classics in Biblical Studies. Minneapolis: Fortress, 2004.

Dilley, Paul. "*Christus Saltans* as Dionysos and David: The *Dance of the Savior* in Its Late-antique Cultural Context." *Apocrypha* 24 (2013) 237–53.

DiTommaso, Lorenzo. *The Book of Daniel and the Apocryphal Daniel Literature*. SVTP 20. Leiden: Brill, 2005.

Donzel, Emeri J. van, Andrea B. Schmidt, and Claudia Ott. *Gog and Magog in Early Eastern Christian and Islamic Sources: Sallam's Quest for Alexander's Wall*. Brill's Inner Asian Library 22. Leiden: Brill, 2010.

Drijvers, Han J. W. "*Acts of Thomas*." In *The New Testament Apocrypha*. Vol. 2, *Writings Relating to the Apostles, Apocalypses, and Related Writings*, edited by Wilhelm Schneemelcher, 322–411. Rev. ed. Translated by Robert McL. Wilson. Louisville: Westminster John Knox, 1991.

———. "Adam and the True Prophet in the Pseudo-Clementines." In *Loyalitätskonflikte in der Religionsgeschichte: Festschrift für Carsten Colpe*, edited by Christoph Elsas and Hans G. Kippenberg, 314–23. Würzburg: Königshausen & Neumann, 1990.

Dubois, Jean-Daniel. "L'AELAC, vingt ans après, ou remarques sur l'étude des littératures apocryphes." *Bulletin de l'AELAC* 11 (2001) 24–30.

———. "L'apport des chrétiens au langage symbolique dans l'Antiquité: l'exemple de la littérature apocryphe chrétienne." In *Les Pères de l'Église au XXe siècle: histoire, littérature, théologie: l'aventure des Sources chrétiennes*, edited by Étienne Fouilloux et al., 237–49. Patrimoines et christianismes, 1997. Paris: Cerf, 1997.

———. *Jésus apocryphe*. Jésus et Jésus Christ 99. Paris: Mame Desclée, 2011.

———. "The New 'Series Apocryphorum' of the 'Corpus Christianorum.'" *SecCent* 4 (1984) 29–36.
Dunderberg, Ismo. *Beyond Gnosticism: Myth, Lifestyle, and Society in the School of Valentinus*. New York: Columbia University Press, 2008.
Dunn, James D. G. *Jesus Remembered*. Vol. 1 of *Christianity in the Making*. Grand Rapids: Eerdmans, 2003.
Dupont, Jacques. *The Sources of Acts*. Translated by Kathleen Pond. New York: Herder & Herder, 1964. Originally published as *Les Sources du Livre des Acts*. Bruges: de Brouwer, 1964.
Duval, Rubens. *La littérature Syriaque*. 3rd ed. Paris: Lecoffre, 1903.
Dzon, Mary, and Theresa M. Kenney, eds. *The Christ Child in Medieval Culture: A es et O!* Toronto: University of Toronto Press, 2012.
Eastman, David L. *The Ancient Martyrdom Accounts of Peter and Paul*. WGRW 39. Atlanta: SBL Press, 2015.
———. *Paul the Martyr: The Cult of the Apostle in the Latin West*. WGRWSup 4. Atlanta: Society of Biblical Literature, 2015.
Ebied, Rifaat Y., and Michael J. L. Young. "A Newly Discovered Version of the Arabic Sibylline Prophecy." *OrChr* 60 (1976) 83–94.
———. "An Unrecorded Arabic Version of the Sibylline Prophecy." *OLP* 43 (1977) 279–307.
Ehrman, Bart D. "Christianity Turned on Its Head: The Alternative Vision of the Gospel of Judas." In *The Gospel of Judas*, edited by Rudolphe Kasser, Marvin Meyer, and Gregor Wurst, 77–120. Washington, DC: National Geographic Society, 2006.
———. *Forgery and Counterforgery: The Use of Literary Deceit in Early Christian Polemics*. Oxford: Oxford University Press, 2013.
———. *Lost Christianities: The Battles for Scripture and the Faiths We Never Knew*. Oxford: Oxford University Press, 2003.
———. *The Lost Gospel of Judas Iscariot: A New Look at Betrayer and Betrayed*. Oxford: Oxford University Press, 2006.
———. *Lost Scriptures: Books That Did Not Make It into the New Testament*. Oxford: Oxford University Press, 2003.
———. *The New Testament: A Historical Introduction to the Early Christian Writings*. 5th ed. Oxford: Oxford University Press, 2012.
Ehrman, Bart, and Zlatko Pleše, eds. and trans. *The Apocryphal Gospels: Texts and Translations*. Oxford: Oxford University Press, 2011.
———. *The Other Gospels: Accounts of Jesus from Outside the New Testament*. Oxford: Oxford University Press, 2014.
Elliott, J. K., ed. and trans. *The Apocryphal New Testament: A Collection of Apocryphal Christian Literature in an English Translation*. Oxford: Clarendon, 1993. Updated paperback ed., 2005.
———. "The 'New' Hennecke." *JSNT* 35 (2013) 285–300.
———. Review of *The New Testament Apocrypha and Pseudepigrapha: A Guide to Publications, with Excurses on Apocalypses*, by James H. Charlesworth and James R. Mueller. *NovT* 31 (1989) 182–85.
Elliott, Ralph H. *The Message of Genesis*. Nashville: Broadman, 1961. Reprinted, Abbot Books for the Bethany Press, 1962.

Emmel, Stephen. "The Recently Published *Gospel of the Savior*. A New Ancient Gospel ("Unbekanntes Berliner Evangelium"): Righting the Order of Pages and Events." *HTR* 95 (2002) 45–72.

Epp, Eldon Jay. "Issues in the Interrelation of New Testament Textual Criticism and Canon." In *The Canon Debate*, edited by Lee Martin McDonald and James A. Sanders, 485–515. Peabody, MA: Hendrickson, 2002.

———. "It's All about Variants: A Variant-Conscious Approach to New Testament Textual Criticism." *HTR* 100 (2007) 275–308.

Erbetta, Mario. *Gli Apocrifi del Nuovo Testamento*. 3 vols. Torino: Marietti, 1966–1981.

Esbroeck, Michel van. "La lettre sur le dimanche descendue du ciel." *AnBoll* 107 (1989) 267–84.

Evans, Craig A. Review of *The Revelation of the Magi. The Lost Tale of the Wise Men's Journey to Bethlehem*, by Brent Landau. *RBL*. Posted June 2012. No pages. http://www.bookreviews.org/pdf/7944_8683.pdf.

Fabricius, Johann Albertus. *Bibliotheca Graeca sive notitia scriptorum veterum Graecorum, quorumcumque monumenta integra aut fragmenta edita exstant tum plerorumque e mss. ac deperditis. Editio secunda ab auctore recognita et plurimis locis aucta*. 14 vols. Hamburg: Liebezeit, 1705–1728.

———. *Codex apocryphus Novi Testamenti: Collectus, Castigatus, Testimoniisque, Censuris & Animadversionibus illustratus*. Vol. 1. Hamburg: Schiller & Kisner, 1705. Rev. ed. in 3 vols. Hamburg: Schiller & Kisner, 1719.

———. *Codex pseudepigraphus Veteris Testamenti, collectus castigatus testimoniisque, censuris et animadversionibus illustratus*. Hamburg: Liebezeit, 1713.

Falk, Ze'ev W. "A New Fragment of the Jewish 'Life of Jesus.'" *Tarbiz* 46 (1977) 319–22 [in Hebrew].

Fee, Gordon D. *The First Epistle to the Corinthians*. NICNT. Grand Rapids: Eerdmans, 1987.

Fiey, Jean Maurice. *Saints syriaques*. Studies in Late Antiquity and Early Islam 6. Princeton: Darwin, 2004.

Fitzmyer, Joseph A. "The Gnostic Gospels according to Pagels." *America* 123 (16 February 1980) 122–24.

Flower, Robin. "The Revelation of Christ's Wounds." *Béaloideas: The Journal of the Folklore of Ireland Society* 1 (1927–1928) 38–45.

Flusser, David. "An Early Jewish-Christian Document in the Tiburtine Sibyl." In *Paganisme, judaïsme, christianisme: influences et affrontements dans le monde antique: mélanges offerts à Marcel Simon*, edited by André Benoit, Marc Philonenko, and Cyrille Vogel, 153–83. Paris: de Boccard, 1978.

Förster, Hans. *Transitus Mariae: Beiträge zur koptischen Überlieferung. Mit einer Edition von P. Vindob. K. 7589, Cambridge Add 1876 8 und Paris BN Copte 12917 ff. 28 und 29*. Die griechischen christlichen Schriftsteller der ersten Jahrhunderte, N.F. 14. Berlin: de Gruyter, 2006.

Förster, Niclas. *Marcus Magus: Kult, Lehre und Gemeindeleben einer valentinianischen Gnostikergruppe. Sammlung der Quellen und Kommentare*. WUNT 114. Tübingen: Mohr/Siebeck, 1999.

Foster, Paul. *The Apocryphal Gospels: A Very Short Introduction*. Oxford: Oxford University Press, 2009.

———. *The Gospel of Peter. Introduction, Critical Edition, and Commentary*. TENTS 4. Oxford, 2010.

Frankfurter, David. *Elijah in Upper Egypt: The Apocalypse of Elijah and Early Egyptian Christianity*. SAC. Minneapolis: Fortress, 1993.
Frilingos, Chris. "No Child Left Behind: Knowledge and Violence in the *Infancy Gospel of Thomas*." *JECS* 17 (2009) 27–54.
Fritz, Kurt von, ed. *Pseudepigrapha I. Pseudopythagorica. Lettres de Platon. Littérature pseudépigraphique juive*. Entretiens sur l'antiquité classique 18. Geneva: Fondation Hardt, 1972.
Funk, Robert W., and Roy W. Hoover, eds. *The Five Gospels: The Search for the Authentic Words of Jesus—New Translation and Commentary*. New York: Macmillan, 1993.
Gagné, André, and Jean-François Racine, eds. *En marge du canon: Études sur les textes apocryphes juifs et chrétiens. 65e congrès de l'Association catholique des études bibliques au Canada*. L'Écriture de la Bible 2. Paris: Cerf, 2012.
Galizzi, Flavio. "Orazioni ed Epistole ad uso salvifico." *Quaderni brembani* 3 (2004–2005) 4–7.
Gallagher, Edmon L. *Hebrew Scripture in Patristic Biblical Theory: Canon, Language, Text*. VCSup 114. Leiden: Brill, 2012.
Garstad, Benjamin. *Apocalypse of Pseudo-Methodius. An Alexandrian World Chronicle*. Dumbarton Oaks Medieval Library 14. Cambridge: Harvard University Press, 2012.
Gasque, W. Ward. *A History of the Interpretation of the Acts of the Apostles*. Peabody, MA: Hendrickson Publishers, 1989. Originally published as *A History of the Criticism of the Acts of the Apostles*. BGBE 17. Tübingen: Mohr/Siebeck, 1975.
Gaster, Moses. "The Sibyl and the Dream of One Hundred Suns: An Old Apocryphon." *JRAS* 42 (1910) 609–23.
Gathercole, Simon. *The Composition of the Gospel of Thomas: Original Language and Influences*. SNTSMS 151. Cambridge: Cambridge University Press, 2012.
Gero, Stephen. "The Stern Master and His Wayward Disciple: A 'Jesus' Story in the Talmud and in Christian Hagiography." *JSJ* 25 (1994) 287–311.
Ginzberg, Louis, ed. *Genizah Studies in Memory of Doctor Solomon Schechter (Ginze Schechter)*. 3 vols. Texts and Studies of the Jewish Theological Seminary of America 7–9. New York: Jewish Theological Seminary of America, 1928.
Goldstein, Miriam. "Judeo-Arabic Versions of Toledot Yeshu." *Ginzei Qedem* 6 (2010) 9–42.
Goldstein, Morris. *Jesus in the Jewish Tradition*. New York: Macmillan, 1950.
Goodacre, Mark. *The Case against Q: Studies in Markan Priority and the Synoptic Problem*. Harrisburg, PA: Trinity, 2002.
———. *Thomas and the Gospels: The Case for Thomas's Familiarity with the Synoptics*. Grand Rapids: Eerdmans, 2012.
Goodspeed, Edgar J. *Strange New Gospels*. Chicago: Chicago University Press, 1931. Expanded as *Modern Apocrypha and Famous "Biblical" Hoaxes*. Grand Rapids: Baker, 1956.
Goodstein, Laurie. "Fresh Doubts Raised about Papyrus Scrap Known as 'Gospel of Jesus' Wife.'" *New York Times*, 4 May 2014. http://www.nytimes.com/2014/05/05/us/fresh-doubts-raised-about-papyrus-scrap-known-as-gospel-of-jesuss-wife.html?_r=1.
Gounelle, Rémi. Review of *En marge du canon. Études sur les textes apocryphes juifs et chrétiens. 65e congrès de l'Association catholique des études bibliques au Canada*, edited by André Gagné and Jean-François Racine. *RHPR* 93 (2013) 598–99.

———. "Sens et usage d'*apocryphus* dans la *Légende dorée*." *Apocrypha* 5 (1994) 189–210.

Grafton, Anthony. "Higher Criticism Ancient and Modern: The Lamentable Deaths of Hermes and the Sibyls." In *The Uses of Greek and Latin. Historical Essays*, edited by A. C. Dionisotti, Anthony Grafton, and Jill Kraye, 155–70. Warburg Institute Surveys and Texts 16. London: Warburg Institute, University of London, 1988. Reprinted as "The Strange Deaths of Hermes and the Sibyls." In Anthony Grafton, *Defenders of the Text. The Traditions of Scholarship in an Age of Science, 1450–1800*, 162–77 and 297–304. Cambridge: Harvard University Press, 1991.

Greisiger, Lutz. "Ein nubischer Erlöser-König: Kūš in syrischen Apocalypsen des 7. Jahrhunderts: Gesammelte Studien zu Ehren Jürgen Tubachs anläßlich seines 60. Geburtstages." In *Der christliche Orient und seine Umwelt*, edited by Sophia G. Vashalomidze and Lutz Greisiger, 189–213. StOR 56. Wiesbaden: Harrassowitz, 2007.

Grenfell, Bernard P., and Arthur S. Hunt, eds. and trans. *New Sayings of Jesus and Fragment of a Lost Gospel from Oxyrhynchus*. London: Oxford University Press, 1904.

———. *Logia Iesou: Sayings of Our Lord from an Early Greek Papyrus*. London: Frowde, 1897.

Gribetz, Sarit K. "Hanged and Crucified: The Book of Esther and *Toledot Yeshu*." In *Toledot Yeshu ("The Life Story of Jesus") Revisited: A Princeton Conference*, edited by Peter Schäfer et al., 159–80. TSAJ 143. Tübingen: Mohr/Siebeck, 2011.

Griffith, Sidney H. *The Church in the Shadow of the Mosque: Christians and Muslims in the World of Islam*. Jews, Christians, and Muslims from the Ancient to the Modern World. Princeton: Princeton University Press, 2008.

Grynaeus, Johann J. *Monumenta sanctorum Patrum orthodoxographa, etc.* Basel: Ex officina Henricpetriana, 1569.

Guignard, Christophe. "Tradition horizontale et tradition verticale: réflexions ecdotiques à partir de l'introduction de Schwartz à son édition de l'Histoire ecclésiastique d'Eusèbe." *Bulletin de l'AELAC* 18–19 (2008–2009) 21–31.

Haelewyck, Jean-Claude. "Le nombre des Rois Mages. Les hésitations de la tradition syriaque." *Graphè* 20 (2011) 25–37.

Haelst, Joseph van. *Catalogue des papyrus littéraires juifs et chrétiens*. Université de Paris IV, Paris-Sorbonne, série "Papyrologie" 1. Paris: Publications de la Sorbonne, 1976.

Haenchen, Ernst. *The Acts of the Apostles: A Commentary*. Translated by Robert McLachlan Wilson et al. Philadelphia: Westminster, 1971. Originally published as *Die Apostelgeschichte*. 14th ed. Göttingen: Vandenhoeck & Ruprecht, 1965.

Hagen, Joost L. "Ein anderer Kontext für die Berliner und Strassburger 'Evangelienfragmente.' Das 'Evangelium der Erlösers' und andere 'Apostelevangelien' in der koptischen Literatur." In *Jesus in apokryphen Evangelienüberlieferungen. Beiträge zu ausserkanonischen Jesusüberlieferungen aus verschiedenen Sprach- und Kulturtraditionen*, edited by Jörg Frey and Jens Schröter, 339–71. WUNT 1/254. Tübingen: Mohr/Siebeck, 2010.

Hägg, Tomas. "Canon Formation in Greek Literary Culture." In *Canon and Canonicity: The Formation and Use of Scripture*, edited by Einar Thomassen, 109–28. Copenhagen: Museum Tusculanum Press, 2010.

Hahneman, Geoffrey. *The Muratorian Fragment and the Development of the Canon*. Oxford Theological Monographs. Oxford: Clarendon, 1992.

———. "The Muratorian Fragment and the Origins of the New Testament Canon." In *The Canon Debate*, edited by Lee Martin McDonald and James A. Sanders, 405–15. Peabody, MA: Hendrickson, 2002.

Halévy, Joseph. *Tëëzâza sanbat (Commandements du sabbat), accompagné de six autres écrits pseudo-épigraphiques admis par les Falachas ou Juifs d'Abyssinie*. Bibliothèque de l'École des hautes études Sciences historiques et philologiques 137. Paris: Bouillon, 1902.

Halm, Heinz. *Die islamische Gnosis: Die Extreme Schia und die 'Alawiten*. Die Bibliothek des Morgenlandes. Zürich: Artemis, 1982.

Harkavy, Abraham. "Leben Jesus." *Hebräische Bibliographie* 15 (1875) 15.

Harnack, Adolf von. *Marcion, Das Evangelium vom fremden Gott: Eine Monographie zur Geschichte der Grundlegung der katholischen Kirche*. 2nd expanded and improved ed. TUGAL 45. Leipzig: Hinrichs, 1924. English translation: *Marcion: The Gospel of the Alien God*. Translated by John E. Steely and Lyle D. Bierma. Grand Rapids: Baker, 1990.

———. *Zur Quellenkritik der Geschichte des Gnosticismus*. Leipzig: Bidder, 1873.

Heal, Kristian S. "Corpora, eLibraries and Databases: Locating Syriac Studies in the 21st Century." *Hugoye* 15.1 (2012) 65–78.

———. Review of Brent Landau, *Revelation of the Magi: The Lost Tale of the Wise Men's Journey to Bethlehem*. *Hugoye* 14 (2011) 294–98.

Heath, Jane. Review of *Antike christliche Apokryphen in deutscher Übersetzung*, edited by Christoph Markschies and Jens Schröter. *JTS* 64 (2013) 239–43.

Hedrick, Charles W. "An Amazing Discovery." *BAR* 35.6 (2009) 44–48, 86.

———. "An Anecdotal Argument for the Independence of Thomas from the Synoptic Gospels." In *For the Children, Perfect Instruction. Studies in Honor of Hans-Martin Schenke on the Occasion of the Berliner Arbeitskreis für Koptisch-gnostische Studien's Thirtieth Year*, edited by Hans-Gebhard Bethge, Stephen Emmel, Karen King, and Imke Schletter, 113–26. NHMS 54. Leiden: Brill, 2002.

———. "The Apocalypse of Adam: A Literary and Source Analysis." In *The Society of Biblical Literature One Hundred Eighth Annual Meeting: Book of Seminar Papers, Friday–Tuesday, 1–5 September 1972 Century Plaza Hotel—Los Angeles, CA*, edited by Lane C. McGaughy, 2:581–90. 2 vols. Missoula, MT: Scholars, 1972.

———. "The Apocalypse of Adam: A Literary and Source Analysis." PhD diss., Claremont Graduate School, 1977.

———. *The Apocalypse of Adam: A Literary and Source Analysis*. SBLDS 46. 1980. Reprinted, Ancient Texts and Translations. Eugene, OR: Wipf & Stock, 2005.

———. "Caveats to a 'Righted Order' of the Gospel of the Savior." *HTR* 96 (2003) 229–38.

———. "Christian Motifs in the Gospel of the Egyptians: Method and Motive." *NovT* 23 (1981) 242–60.

———. "Conceiving the Narrative. Colors in Achilles Tatius and the Gospel of Mark." In *Ancient Fiction and Early Christian Narrative*, edited by Ronald F. Hock, J. Bradley Chance, and Judith Perkins, 177–97. Atlanta: Scholars, 1998.

———. "Dating the *Gospel of the Savior*: Response to Peter Nagel and Pierluigi Piovanelli." *Apocrypha* 24 (2013) 223–36.

———. "The Emergence of the Chaplaincy as a Professional Army Branch: A Survey and Summary of Selected Issues." *Military Chaplains' Review* (Winter 1990) 19–50.

———. "Eschatological Existence: The Meaning of Eschatology. A Study of Rudolf Bultmann's Understanding of Eschatology in the New Testament." MA thesis, University of Southern California, 1968.

———. "Evaluating Morton Smith: Hoaxer Outed or Colleague Slandered?" *PRSt* 37 (2010) 283–94.

———. "Flawed Heroes and Stories Jesus Told. The One about a Man Wanting to Kill." In *Individual Studies*. Vol. 4 of *Handbook for the Study of the Historical Jesus*, edited by Tom Holmén and Stanley E. Porter, 4:3023–56. 4 vols. Leiden: Brill, 2011.

———. "Gnostic Proclivities in the Greek *Life of Pachomius* and the *Sitz im Leben* of the Nag Hammadi Library." *NovT* 22 (1980) 78–94.

———. "Is Belief in the Divinity of Jesus Essential to Being Christian." *The Fourth R* 24.5 (2011) 15–20, 26.

———. "Jonah." In *The Crosby-Schøyen Codex. MS 193 in the Schøyen Collection*, edited by James E. Goehring, 217–59. CSCO 521, Subsidia 85. Leuven: Peeters, 1990.

———. "Kingdom Sayings and Parables of Jesus in the Apocryphon of James: Tradition and Redaction." *NTS* 29 (1983) 1–24.

———. "A Monastic Exorcism Text." *Journal of Coptic Studies* 7 (2005) 17–21, plates 2–3.

———, ed. *Nag Hammadi Codices XI, XII, XIII*. NHS 28. Leiden: Brill, 1990.

———. "Narrator and Story in the Gospel of Mark: *Hermeneia* and *Paradosis*." *PRSt* 14.3 (1987) 239–58.

———. "A New Coptic Fragment of the Book of Hebrews." In *Go to the Land I Will Show You: Studies in Honor of Dwight W. Young*, edited by Joseph Coleson and Victor H. Matthews, 243–46. Winona Lake, IN: Eisenbrauns, 1996.

———. "Newly Identified Fragments of Coptic Acts and the Apocalypse." *Journal of Coptic Studies* 4 (2002) 127–32, plates 16–18.

———. "On Foreign Soil: The Tragedy of a Civilianized Chaplaincy during the Mexican-American War." *Military Chaplains' Review* (Winter 1992) 61–85.

———. "On Wearing Two Hats While Standing on a Banana Peel: Confessional Statements in Theological Education." *PRSt* 11.2 (Summer 1984) 105–14.

———. "Paul's Conversion/Call: A Comparative Analysis of the Three Reports in Acts." *JBL* 100 (1981) 415–32.

———. "The Parables and the Synoptic Problem." In *New Studies in the Synoptic Problem. Essays in Honour of Christopher M. Tuckett*, edited by Paul Foster, Andrew Gregory, John S. Kloppenborg, and Joseph Verheyden, 321–45. BETL 239. Leuven: Peeters, 2011.

———. "A Preliminary Report on Coptic Codex P.Berol. Inv. 22220." In *Ägypten und Nubien in spätantiker und christlicher Zeit: Akten des 6. Internationalen Koptologenkongresses Münster, 20.–26. Juli 1996*, edited by Stephen Emmel, Martin Krause, Siegfried G. Richter, and Sofia Schaten, 2:127–30. 2 vols. Sprachen und Kulteren des Christlichen Orients 6. Wiesbaden: Reichert, 1999.

———. "Religion and Public Education: The Bible in the Bible Belt." *Bulletin of the Council of Societies for the Study of Religion* 31.4 (2002) 90–94.

———. "Representing Prayer in Mark and Chariton's *Chaereas and Callirhoe*." *PRSt* 22 (1995) 239–57.

———. "A Revelation Discourse of Jesus." *Journal of Coptic Studies* 7 (2005) 13–15, plate 1.

———. "The (Second) Apocalypse of James (V, 4) 44,11–63,32." In *Nag Hammadi Codices V, 2–5 and VI with Papyrus Berolinensis 8502, 1 and 4*, edited by Douglas M. Parrott, 105–49. NHS 11. Leiden: Brill, 1977.

———. "The Second Apocalypse of James (V, 4)." In *The Nag Hammadi Library in English*, edited by James M. Robinson, 249–55. San Francisco: Harper & Row, 1977.

———. "The Secret Gospel of Mark: Stalemate in the Academy." *JECS* 11 (2003) 133–45.

———. *Secret Mark*: Moving on from Stalemate." In *Ancient Gospel or Modern Forgery? The Secret Gospel of Mark in Debate. Proceedings of 2011 York University Christian Apocrypha Symposium*, edited by Tony Burke, 30–66. Eugene, OR: Cascade Books, 2012.

———. "Some Techniques in the Placement of Papyrus Fragments." *BASP* 13 (December/1976) 3–5.

———. "The 34 Gospels: Diversity and Division among the Earliest Christians." *BRev* 18.3 (2002) 20–31, 46–47.

———. "Thomas and the Synoptics: Aiming at a Consensus." *SecCent* 7 (1989) 39–56.

———. "The Treasure Parable in Matthew and Thomas." *Forum* 2.2 (1986) 41–56.

———. *Unlocking the Secrets of the Gospel according to Thomas: A Radical Faith for a New Age*. Eugene, OR: Cascade Books, 2010.

———. "An Unpublished Coptic Fragment of the Gospel of Matthew." *Journal of Coptic Studies* 3 (2001) 149–151, plate 18.

———. "Vestiges of an Ancient Codex Containing a Psalm *Testimonia* and a Gospel Homily." *Journal of Coptic Studies* 8 (2006) 1–41, plates 1–9.

Hedrick, Charles W., and Robert Hodgson, Jr., eds. *Nag Hammadi, Gnosticism, and Early Christianity*. 1983. Reprinted, Eugene, OR: Wipf & Stock, 2005.

Hedrick, Charles W., and Paul A. Mirecki. *Gospel of the Savior: A New Ancient Gospel*. California Classical Library. Santa Rosa, CA: Polebridge, 1999.

Hedrick, Charles W., and Nikolaos Olympiou. "Secret Mark: New Photographs, New Witnesses." *The Fourth R* 13.5 (2000) 3–11, 14–16.

Henderson, William. *Notes on the Folk Lore of the Northern Counties of England and the Borders* (with an *Appendix on Household Stories* by Sabine Baring-Gould). London: Longmans, Green, 1866.

Hennecke, Edgar. *Neutestamentliche Apokryphen in Verbindung mit Fachgelehrten in deutscher Überstzung*. Tübingen: Mohr/Siebeck, 1904.

Hennecke, Edgar, and Wilhelm Schneemelcher, eds. *Neutestamentliche Apokryphen in deutscher Übersetzung*. 3rd ed. 2 vols. Tübingen: Mohr/Siebeck, 1959–1964. English translation: *New Testament Apocrypha*. Translated by R. McLachlan Wilson. 2 vols. Philadelphia: Westminster, 1963–1965.

Herrenschmidt, Clarisse and Francis Schmidt. "Présentation." In Jean-Claude Picard, *Le continent apocryphe: essai sur les littératures apocryphes juive et chrétienne*, xi–xxxiii. Instrumenta Patristica et Mediaevalia 36. Turnhout: Brepols, 1999.

Herold, Johannes Basilius. *Orthodoxographa theologiae sacrosanctae ac synceriorisfidei doctores numero LXXVI, etc.* Basel: ex officina Henricpetriana, 1555.

Hilgenfeld, Adolf. *Die Ketzergeschichte des Urchristentums*. Leipzig: Fues/Reisland, 1884.

Hills, Julian V. "The *Acts of Paul* and the Legacy of the Lukan Acts." *Semeia* 80 (1997) 145–58.

———. "The Acts of the Apostles in the *Acts of Paul.*" SBLSP 33 (1994) 24–54.
———. *Tradition and Composition in the* Epistula Apostolorum. HDR 24. Minneapolis: Fortress, 1980.
Himmelfarb, Martha. "*Sefer Eliyyahu:* Jewish Eschatology and Christian Jerusalem." In *Shaping the Middle East: Jews, Christians, and Muslims in an Age of Transition, 400–800 C.E.*, edited by Kenneth G. Holum and Hayim Lapin, 223–38. Studies and Texts in Jewish History and Culture 20. Bethesda, MD: University Press of Maryland, 2011.
Holdenried, Anke. *The Sibyl and Her Scribes: Manuscripts and Interpretation of the Latin Sibylla Tiburtina c. 1050–1500*. Church, Faith, and Culture in the Medieval West. Aldershot, UK: Ashgate, 2006.
Hone, William. *The Apocryphal New Testament*. London: Printed for William Hone, Ludgate Hill, 1820.
Horbury, William. "A Critical Examination of the Toledoth Jeshu." PhD diss., University of Cambridge, 1971.
———. "The Strasbourg Text of the *Toledot.*" In *Toledot Yeshu ("The Life Story of Jesus") Revisited: A Princeton Conference*, edited by Peter Schäfer, Michael Meerson, and Yaacov Deutsch, 49–59. TSAJ 143. Tübingen: Mohr/Siebeck, 2011.
———. "The Trial of Jesus in Jewish Tradition." In *The Trial of Jesus: Cambridge Studies in Honour of C. F. D. Moule*, edited by Ernst Bammel, 116–21. Studies in Biblical Theology 2/13. Naperville, IL: Allenson, 1970.
Horn, Cornelia, ed. *The Bible, the Qur'an, and Their Interpretation: Syriac Perspectives*. Eastern Mediterranean Texts and Contexts 1. Warwick, RI: Abelian Academic, 2013.
Hovhanessian, Vahan S., ed. *The Canon of the Bible and the Apocrypha in the Churches of the East*. Bible in the Christian Orthodox Tradition 2. New York: Lang, 2012.
Hoyland, Robert G. *Seeing Islam as Others Saw It: A Survey and Evaluation of Christian, Jewish and Zoroastrian Writings on Early Islam*. Studies in Late Antiquity and Early Islam 13. Princeton: Darwin, 1997.
Hubai, Péter. *Koptische Apokryphen aus Nubien. Der Qasr el-Wizz Kodex*. Translated by Angelika Balog. TUGAL 163. Berlin: de Gruyter, 2009. Originally published as *A Megváltó a keresztről: Kopt apokrifek Núbiából (A Kasr El-Wizz kódex)*. Budapest: Szent István Társulat, 2006.
Hull, Robert F., Jr. *The Story of the New Testament Text: Movers, Materials, Motives, Methods, and Models*. Resources for Biblical Studies 58. Atlanta: Society of Biblical Literature, 2010.
Huskinson, Janet M. *Concordia Apostolorum: Christian Propaganda at Rome in the Fourth and Fifth Centuries*. Bibilical Archaeological Reports International Series 148. Oxford: British Archaeological Reports, 1982.
Irmscher, Johannes, and Georg Strecker. "The Pseudo-Clementines." In *The New Testament Apocrypha*. Vol. 2, *Writings Relating to the Apostles, Apocalypses, and Related Writings*, edited by Wilhelm Schneemelcher, 483–541. Revised ed. translated by R. McL. Wilson. Louisville: Westminster John Knox, 1992.
Ivanow, Wladimir. "Исмаилитские рукописи Азиатского музея (Собрание И. Зарубина, 1916 г.) (Ismā'īlī Manuscripts in the Asiatic Museum of the Russian Academy of Sciences, Collection of I. Zarubin [1916])." *Bulletin de l'Académie Impériale des Sciences de Russie* 6 II (1917) 359–386.

———. "Notes sur l'*Ummu'l-kitāb* des Ismaëliens de l'Asie Centrale." *Revue des Études Islamiques* 6 (1932) 419–81.

———. "Ummu'l-kitāb." *Der Islam* 23 (1936) 1–132.

Izydorczyk, Zbigniew. "The Earliest Printed Versions of the *Evangelium Nicodemi* and Their Manuscript Sources." *Apocrypha* 21 (2010) 121–32.

———. *Manuscripts of the Evangelium Nicodemi: A Census*. Toronto: Pontifical Institute of Mediaeval Studies, 1993.

———, ed. *The Medieval Gospel of Nicodemus: Texts, Intertexts, and Contexts in Western Europe*. Medieval and Renaissance Texts and Studies 158. Tempe, AZ: Medieval and Renaissance Texts and Studies, 1997.

Izydorczyk, Zbigniew and Charlotte Fillmore-Handlon. "The Modern Life of an Ancient Text: The *Gospel of Nicodemus* in Manitoba." *Apocrypha* 21 (2010) 113–20.

Izydorczyk, Zbigniew and Rémi Gounelle. "Thematic Bibliography of the *Acts of Pilate*." In *The Medieval Gospel of Nicodemus: Texts, Intertexts, and Contexts in Western Europe*, edited by Zbigniew Izydorczyk, 419–532. Medieval and Renaissance Texts and Studies 158. Tempe, AZ: Medieval and Renaissance Texts and Studies, 1997.

———. "A Thematic Bibliography of the *Acts of Pilate*. Addenda et corrigenda." *Apocrypha* 11 (2000) 259–92.

Izydorczyk, Zbigniew, and Wiesław Wydra, eds. *A Gospel of Nicodemus Preserved in Poland*. CCSA Instrumenta 3. Turnhout: Brepols, 2007.

James, M. R. *The Apocryphal New Testament*. 1924. Reprinted, Oxford: Clarendon, 1953.

Jenott, Lance. "Clergy, Clairvoyance, and Conflict: The Synod of Latopolis and the Problem with Pachomius' Visions." In *Beyond the Gnostic Gospels: Studies Building on the Work of Elaine Pagels*, edited by Eduard Iricinschi et al., 320–34. Studies and Texts in Antiquity and Christianity 89. Tübingen: Mohr/Siebeck, 2013.

———. "Recovering Adam's Lost Glory: Nag Hammadi Codex II in Its Egyptian Monastic Environment." In *Jewish and Christian Cosmogony in Late Antiquity*, edited by Lance Jenott and Sarit K. Gribetz, 222–36. TSAJ 155. Tübingen: Mohr/Siebeck, 2013.

Jenson, Robert W. *Canon and Creed*. Interpretation. Louisville: Westminster John Knox, 2010.

Jeremias, Joachim. *Die Gleichnisse Jesu*. 6th rev. ed. Göttingen: Vandenhoeck & Ruprecht, 1962.

———. *Unknown Sayings of Jesus*. Translated by R. H. Fuller. 1957^1. 2nd ed. London: SPCK, 1964. Originally published as *Unbekannte Jesusworte*. 1948^1. 1951^2. 3rd ed. Gütersloh: Gerd Mohn, 1963.

Johnson, Luke Timothy. *The Real Jesus: The Misguided Quest for the Historical Jesus and the Truth of the Traditional Gospels*. San Francisco: HarperCollins, 1996.

Jonas, Hans. *The Gnostic Religion: The Message of the Alien God and the Beginnings of Christianity*. Boston: Beacon Press, 1958. 3rd ed. 2001.

Jones, F. Stanley. *An Ancient Jewish Christian Source on the History of Christianity: Pseudo-Clementine "Recognitions" 1.27–71*. SBLTT 37, Christian Apocrypha Series 2. Atlanta: Scholars, 1995.

———. "From Toland to Baur: Tracks of the History of Research into Jewish Christianity." In *The Rediscovery of Jewish Christianity: From Toland to Baur*, edited by F. Stanley Jones, 123–36. SBLHBS 5. Atlanta: Society of Biblical Literature, 2012.

———. "Marcionism in the *Pseudo-Clementines*." In *Poussières de christianisme et de judaïsme antiques: Études réunies en l'honneur de Jean-Daniel Kaestli et Éric Junod*, edited by Albert Frey and Rémi Gounelle, 225–44. Publications de l'Institut romand des sciences bibliques 5. Lausanne: Zèbre, 2007. Reprinted in F. Stanley Jones, *Pseudoclementina Elchasaiticaque inter Judaeochristiana: Collected Studies*, 152–71. OLA 203. Leuven: Peeters, 2012.

———. "Photius's Witness to the *Pseudo-Clementines*." In *Nouvelles intrigues pseudo-clémentines*, edited by Frédéric Amsler, et al., 93–101. Publications de l'Institut romand des sciences bibliques 6. Lausanne: Éditions du Zèbre, 2008. Reprinted in F. Stanley Jones, *Pseudoclementina Elchasaiticaque inter Judaeochristiana: Collected Studies*, 345–55. OLA 203. Leuven: Peeters, 2012.

———. *Pseudoclementina Elchasaiticaque inter Judaeochristiana: Collected Studies*. OLA 203. Leuven: Peeters, 2012.

———. "The Pseudo-Clementines: A History of Research." *SecCent* 2 (1982) 1–33, 63–96. Reprinted with corrections in F. Stanley Jones, *Pseudoclementina Elchasaiticaque inter Judaeochristiana: Collected Studies*, 50–113. OLA 203. Leuven: Peeters, 2012.

———. *The Syriac "Pseudo-Clementines": An Early Version of the First Christian Novel*. Apocryphes 14. Turnhout: Brepols, 2014.

Junod, Éric. "Apocryphes du Nouveau Testament ou apocryphes chrétiens anciens? Remarques sur la désignation d'un corpus et indications bibliographiques sur les instruments de travail récents." *ETR* 59 (1983) 409–21.

———. "'Apocryphes du Nouveau Testament': une appellation erronée et une collection artificielle. Discussion de la nouvelle définition proposée par W. Schneemelcher." *Apocrypha* 3 (1992) 17–46.

———. "Le mystère apocryphe ou les richesses cachées d'une littérature méconnue." In *Le mystère apocryphe*, edited by Jean-Daniel Kaestli and Daniel Marguerat, 9–25. Geneva: Labor et Fides, 1995.

———. Review of *En marge du canon. Études sur les textes apocryphes juifs et chrétiens. 65e congrès de l'Association catholique des études bibliques au Canada*, edited by André Gagné and Jean-François Racine. *Apocrypha* 24 (2013) 293–95.

Kaestli, Jean-Daniel. "Les écrits apocryphes chrétiens. Pour une approche qui valorise leur diversité et leurs attaches bibliques." In *Le mystère apocryphe*, edited by Jean-Daniel Kaestli and Daniel Marguerat, 27–42. Geneva: Labor et Fides, 1995.

———. "Mapping an Unexplored Second Century Apocryphal Gospel: The *Liber de Nativitate Salvatoris* (CANT 53)." In *Infancy Gospels: Stories and Identities*, edited by Claire Clivaz et al., 506–59. WUNT 1/281. Tübingen: Mohr/Siebeck, 2011.

———. "Recherches nouvelles sur les 'Évangiles latins de l'enfance' de M. R. James et sur un récit apocryphe mal connu de la naissance de Jésus." *ETR* 72 (1997) 219–33.

———. "Où en est l'étude de l'*Évangile de Barthélemy*?" *RB* 95 (1988) 5–33.

Kaestli, Jean-Daniel and Pierre Cherix, eds. *L'évangile de Barthélemy d'après deux écrits apocryphes. I: Questions de Barthélemy; II: Livre de la Résurrection de Jésus-Christ par l'apôtre Barthélemy*. Apocryphes 1. Turnhout: Brepols, 1993.

Kalin, Everett R. "Argument from Inspiration in the Canonization of the New Testament." ThD diss., Harvard University, 1967.

———. "The Inspired Community: A Glance at Canon History." *Concordia Theological Monthly* 42 (1971) 541–49.

Kampers, Franz. *Die deutsche Kaiseridee in Prophetie und Sage*. Munich: Lüneburg, 1896.

Karras, Ruth Mazo. "The Aerial Battle in the *Toledot Yeshu* and Sodomy in the Late Middle Ages." *Medieval Encounters* 19 (2013) 493–533.

Kasser, Rodolphe, and Gregor Wurst, eds. *The Gospel of Judas Together with the Letter of Peter to Philip, James, and a Book of Allogenes from Codex Tchacos. Critical Edition*. Washington, DC: National Geographic Society, 2007.

Kasser, Rodolphe, and Philippe Luisier. "Le Papyrus Bodmer XLI en édition princeps. L'épisode d'Éphèses des *Acta Pauli* en copte et en traduction." *Mus* 117.3 (2004) 281–384.

Kelley, Nicole. "On Recycling Texts and Traditions: The Pseudo-Clementine *Recognitions* and Religious Life in Fourth-Century Syria." In *The Levant: Crossroads of Late Antiquity. History, Religion and Archaeology—Le Levant: Carrefour de l'Antiquité tardive. Histoire, religion et archéologie*, edited by Ellen B. Aitken and John M. Fossey, 105–12. McGill University Monographs in Classical Archaeology and History 22. Leiden: Brill, 2013.

———. "Astrology in the Pseudo-Clementine *Recognitions*." *JEH* 59 (2008) 607–29.

———. "What Is the Value of Sense Perception in the Pseudo-Clementine Romance?" In *Nouvelles intrigues pseudo-clémentines—Plots in the Pseudo-Clementine Romance. Actes du deuxième colloque international sur la littérature apocryphe chrétienne, Lausanne—Genève, 30 août—2 septembre 2006*, edited by Frédéric Amsler et al., 361–69. Publications de l'Institut romand des sciences bibliques 6. Lausanne: Zèbre, 2008.

———. "The Theological Significance of Physical Deformity in the Pseudo-Clementine *Homilies*." *PRSt* 34 (2007) 77–90.

Kerchove, Anna Van den. Review of *The Emergence of Christianity*, by François Bovon. *Apocrypha* 25 (2014) 265–67.

———. Review of *Introduction to "Gnosticism": Ancient Voices, Christian Worlds*, by Nicola Denzey Lewis. *Apocrypha* 25 (2014) 291–96.

King, Karen L. *The Gospel of Mary of Magdala: Jesus and the First Woman Apostle*. Santa Rosa, CA: Polebridge, 2003.

———. "'Jesus said to them, "My wife . . ."': A New Coptic Papyrus Fragment." *HTR* 107 (2014) 131–59.

———. *Revelation of the Unknowable God*. Santa Rosa, CA: Polebridge, 1996.

———. *The Secret Revelation of John*. Cambridge: Harvard University Press, 2006.

———. *What Is Gnosticism?* Cambridge: Harvard University Press, 2003.

———. "Which Early Christianity?" In *The Oxford Handbook of Early Christian Studies*, edited by Susan Ashbrook Harvey and David G. Hunter, 66–84. New York: Oxford University Press, 2008.

Kinzig, Wolfram. "Wilhelm Schneemelcher." In *Neue Deutsche Bibliographie*, edited by Historische Kommission bei der Bayerischen Akademie der Wissenschaften, 23:283–84. 25 vols. Berlin: Duncker & Humblot, 1953–2013.

Klauck, Hans-Josef. *The Apocryphal Acts of the Apostles: An Introduction*. Translated by Brian J. McNeil. Waco, TX: Baylor University Press, 2008. Originally published as *Apokryphe Apostelakten: Eine Einführung*. Stuttgart: Katholisches Bibelwerk, 2005.

———. *The Apocryphal Gospels: An Introduction*. Translated by Brian J. McNeil. London: T. & T. Clark, 2003. Originally published as *Apokryphe Evangelien: Eine Einführung*. Stuttgart: Katholisches Bibelwerk, 2002.

———. *Die apokryphe Bibel: Ein anderer Zugang zum frühen Christentum*. Tria corda 4. Tübingen: Mohr/Siebeck, 2008.
Klauser Theodor, and Friedrich W. Deichmann. *Frühchristliche Sarkophage in Bild und Wort*. Antike Kunst 3. Olten: Urs Graf, 1966.
Klijn, A. F. J. *Seth in Jewish, Gnostic and Christian Literature*. NovTSup 46. Leiden: Brill, 1977.
Kline, Leslie L. *The Sayings of Jesus in the Pseudo-Clementine Homilies*. SBLDS 14. Missoula, MT: Scholars, 1975.
Kloppenborg, John S., "Alms, Debt and Divorce: Jesus' Ethics in Their Mediterranean Context." *TJT* 6.2 (1990) 182–200.
———, ed. *Apocalypticism, Anti-Semitism, and the Historical Jesus: Subtexts in Criticism*. In collaboration with John W. Marshall. JSNTSup 275. London: T. & T. Clark, 2005.
———. "A Dog among the Pigeons: The 'Cynic Hypothesis' as a Theological Problem." In *From Quest to Q: Festschrift James M. Robinson*, edited by Jon Ma. Asgeirsson, Kristin de Troyer, and Marvin W. Meyer, 73–117. BETL 146. Leuven: Peeters, 1999.
———. *The Formation of Q: Trajectories in Ancient Wisdom Collections*. SAC. Philadelphia: Fortress, 1987.
———. "Sources, Methods, and Discursive Locations in the Quest of the Historical Jesus." In *How to Study the Historical Jesus*. Vol. 1 of *Handbook of the Study of the Historical Jesus*, edited by Tom Holmén and Stanley E. Porter, 241–90. Leiden: Brill, 2011.
Köstenberger, Andreas J., and Michael J. Kruger. *The Heresy of Orthodoxy: How Contemporary Culture's Fascination with Diversity Has Reshaped Our Understanding of Early Christianity*. Wheaton, IL: Crossway, 2010.
Koester, Helmut. *Ancient Christian Gospels: Their History and Development*. Harrisburg, PA: Trinity, 1990.
———. "Apocryphal and Canonical Gospels." *HTR* 73 (1980) 105–30. Published in French as "Évangiles apocryphes et évangiles canoniques." In *Genèse de l'Écriture chrétienne*, edited by Helmut Koester and François Bovon, 59–106. Mémoires premières. Turnhout: Brepols, 1991.
———. "Conclusion: The Intention and Scope of Trajectories." In *Trajectories through Early Christianity*, edited by James M. Robinson and Helmut Koester, 269–79. 1971. Reprinted, Eugene, OR: Wipf & Stock, 2006.
———. "Epilogue: Current Issues in New Testament Scholarship." In *The Future of Early Christianity: Essays in Honor of Helmut Koester*, edited by Birger Pearson, 470–76. Minneapolis: Fortress, 1991.
———. "GNOMAI DIAPHORAI: The Origin and Nature of Diversification in the History of Early Christianity." In *Trajectories through Early Christianity*, edited by James M. Robinson and Helmut Koester, 114–57. 1971. Reprinted, Eugene, OR: Wipf & Stock, 2006.
———. "History and Development of Mark's Gospel: From Mark to Secret Mark and 'Canonical' Mark." In *Colloquy on New Testament Studies: A Time for Reappraisal and Fresh Approaches*, edited by Bruce C. Corley, 35–58. Macon, GA: Mercer University Press, 1983.

———. "An Intellectual Biography of James M. Robinson." In *From Quest to Q: Festschrift James M. Robinson*, edited by Jon Ma. Asgeirsson, Kristin de Troyer, and Marvin W. Meyer, xiii–xxi. Leuven: Peeters, 1999.

———. *Introduction to the New Testament*. 1982. 2nd ed. Berlin & New York: de Gruyter, 1995. Originally published as *Einführung in das Neue Testament im Rahmen der Religionsgeschichte und Kulturgeschichte der hellenistischen und römischen Zeit*. De Gruyter Lehrbuch. Berlin: de Gruyter, 1980.

———. "One Jesus and Four Primitive Gospels." In *Trajectories through Early Christianity*, edited by James M. Robinson and Helmut Koester, 158–204. 1971. Reprinted, Eugene, OR: Wipf & Stock, 2006.

———. *Synoptische Überlieferung bei den apostolischen Vätern*. TUGAL 65. Berlin: Akademie-Verlag, 1957.

———. "Thomas Jefferson, Ralph Waldo Emerson, the *Gospel of Thomas*, and the Apostle Paul." In *Paul and His World: Interpreting the New Testament in Its Context*, edited by Helmut Koester, 195–206. Minneapolis, MN: Fortress, 2007.

Kohlberg, Etan. "Authoritative Scriptures in Early Imami Shi'ism." In *Les retours aux Écriture: fondamentalismes présents et passés*, edited by Evelyne Patlagean and Alain Le Boulluec, 295–312. Bibliothèque de l'École des hautes études. Section des sciences religieuses 99. Leuven & Paris: Peeters, 1993.

———. "An Unusual Shīʿī *isnād*." *Israel Oriental Studies* 5 (1975) 142–49.

Konrad, Robert. *De ortu et tempore Antichristi: Antichristvorstellung und Geschichtsbild des Abtes Adso von Montier-en-Der*. Münchener historische Studien, Abteilung mittelalterliche Geschichte 1. Kallmünz: Lassleben, 1964.

Kraft, András. "The Last Roman Emperor Topos in the Byzantine Apocalyptic Tradition." *Byzantion* 82 (2012) 213–57.

Krauss, Samuel. "Fragments araméens de Toldot Yéschou." *REJ* 62 (1911) 28–37.

Kripal, Jeffrey. *Comparing Religions: Coming to Terms*. Malden, MA: Wiley Blackwell, 2014.

Landau, Brent. "'One Drop of Salvation from the House of Majesty': Universal Revelation, Human Mission, and Mythical Geography in the Syriac *Revelation of the Magi*." In *The Levant: Crossroads of Late Antiquity. History, Religion and Archaeology—Le Levant: Carrefour de l'Antiquité tardive. Histoire, religion et archéologie*, edited by Ellen B. Aitken and John M. Fossey, 83–103. McGill University Monographs in Classical Archaeology and History 22. Leiden: Brill, 2013.

———. "The *Revelation of the Magi* in the *Chronicle of Zuqnin*: The Magi from the East in the Ancient Christian Imagination." *Apocrypha* 19 (2008) 182–201.

———. *Revelation of the Magi: The Lost Tale of the Wise Men's Journey to Bethlehem*. New York: HarperOne, 2010.

———. "The Sages and the Star-Child: An Introduction to the *Revelation of the Magi*, An Ancient Christian Apocryphon." ThD diss., Harvard Divinity School, 2008.

Landes, Richard A., and Catherine Paupert. *Naissance d'Apôtre: Les origines de la Vita prolixior de Saint Martial de Limoges au XIe siècle*. Turnhout: Brepols, 1991.

Lange, Armin. "Oral Collection and Canon: A Comparison between Judah and Greece in Persian Times." In *Jewish and Christian Scripture as Artifact and Canon*, edited by Craig A. Evans and H. Daniel Zacharias, 9–47. Library of Second Temple Studies 13. London: T. & T. Clark, 2009.

———. "The Textual Plurality of Jewish Scriptures in the Second Temple Period in Light of the Dead Sea Scrolls." In *Qumran and the Bible: Studying the Jewish and

Christian Scriptures in Light of the Dead Sea Scrolls, edited by Nora David and Armin Lange, 43–96. CBET 57. Leuven: Peeters, 2010.

Layton, Bentley. *The Gnostic Scriptures. Ancient Wisdom for the New Age.* Anchor Bible Reference Library. Garden City, NY: Doubleday 1987.

Le Boulluec, Alain. "Écrits 'contestés,' 'inauthentiques' ou 'impies'?" In *Apocryphité: Histoire d'un concept transversal aux religions du livre. En hommage à Pierre Geoltrain,* edited by Simon Claude Mimouni, 153–65. Bibliothèque de l'École des Hautes Études. Sciences religieuses 113. Turnhout: Brepols, 2002.

Leslau, Wolf. *Falasha Anthology.* Yale Judaica Series 6. New Haven: Yale University Press, 1951.

Létourneau, Pierre. Review of *En marge du canon: Études sur les textes apocryphes juifs et chrétiens. 65e congrès de l'Association catholique des études bibliques au Canada,* edited by André Gagné and Jean-François Racine. *SR* 42 (2013) 393–97.

Lidzbarski, Mark. *Ginzā, Der Schatz, oder Das Große Buch der Mandäer.* Quellen der Religionsgeschichte 13, Gruppe 4. Göttingen: Vandenhoeck & Ruprecht, 1925.

Lim, Timothy H. *The Formation of the Jewish Canon.* New Haven: Yale University Press, 2013.

Lincicum, David. "F. C. Baur's Place in the Study of Jewish Christianity." In *The Rediscovery of Jewish Christianity: From Toland to Baur,* edited by F. Stanley Jones, 127–66. SBLHBS 5. Atlanta: Society of Biblical Literature, 2012.

Lipsius, Richard Adelbert. *Die Quellen der ältesten Ketzergeschichte.* Leipzig: Barth, 1875.

———. *Zur Quellenkritik des Epiphanios.* Vienna: Braumüller, 1865.

Lohfink, Gerhard. *The Conversion of St. Paul: Narrative and History in Acts.* Translated by Bruce J. Malina. Chicago: Franciscan Herald, 1976. Originally published as *Paulus vor Damaskus.* 3rd ed. SBS 4. Stuttgart: Katholisches Bibelwerk, 1967.

Lüdemann, Gerd. *Early Christianity according to the Traditions in Acts: A Commentary.* Translated by John Bowden. Minneapolis: Fortress, 1989. Translation of *Das frühe Christentum nach den Traditionen der Apostelgeschichte: Ein Kommentar.* Göttingen: Vandenhoeck & Ruprecht, 1987.

Lührmann, Dieter. *Die apokryph gewordenen Evangelien: Studien zu neuen Texten und neuen Fragen.* NovTSup 112. Leiden: Brill, 2004.

Luz, Ulrich. Review of *Ancient Christian Gospels,* by Helmut Koester. *Interpretation* 47 (1993) 87–88.

MacDonald, Dennis R. *Christianizing Homer: The Odyssey, Plato, and the Acts of Andrew.* Oxford: Oxford University Press, 1994.

———. *Does the New Testament Imitate Homer? Four Cases from the Acts of the Apostles.* New Haven: Yale University Press, 2003.

———. *The Homeric Epics and the Gospel of Mark.* New Haven: Yale University Press, 2010.

———. *The Legend and the Apostle: The Battle for Paul in Story and Canon.* Philadelphia: Fortress, 1983.

———. *There is No Male and Female: The Fate of a Dominical Saying in Paul and Gnosticism.* HDR 20. Philadelphia: Fortress, 1987.

Madelung, Wilferd. Review of *Ummu'l-Kitāb,* by Pio Filippani-Ronconi. *Oriens* 25–26 (1976) 352–58.

Magdalino, Paul. "The History of the Future and Its Uses: Prophecy, Policy, and Propaganda." In *The Making of Byzantine History: Studies Dedicated to Donald*

M. Nicol, edited by Roderick Beaton and Charlotte Roueché, 3–32. Centre for Hellenic Studies, King's College London Publications 1. Aldershot, UK: Variorum, 1993.

Mallette, Karla. *European Modernity and the Arab Mediterranean: Toward a New Philology and a Counter-Orientalism*. Philadelphia: University of Pennsylvania Press, 2011.

Mango, Cyril A. *Byzantium: The Empire of New Rome*. London: Weidenfeld & Nicolson, 1980.

Marguerat, Daniel. "The *Acts of Paul* and the Canonical Acts: A Phenomenon of Rereading." *Semeia* 80 (1997) 169–83.

Marguerat, Daniel, Enrico Norelli, and Jean-Michel Poffet, eds. *Jésus de Nazareth: Nouvelles approches d'une énigme*. Geneva: Labor et Fides, 1998.

Marjanen, Antii. "Is Thomas a Gnostic Gospel?" In *Thomas at the Crossroads: Essays on the Gospel of Thomas*, edited by Risto Uro, 107–39. SNTW. Edinburgh: T. & T. Clark, 1998.

Markschies, Christoph. "Die Fragen des Bartholomaeus." In *Antike christliche Apokryphen in deutscher Übersetzung, I. Band: Evangelien und Verwandtes*, edited by Christoph Markschies and Jens Schröter, 702–850. Tübingen: Mohr/Siebeck, 2012.

———. "Haupteinleitung." In *Antike christliche Apokryphen in deutscher Übersetzung, I. Band: Evangelien und Verwandtes*, edited by Christoph Markschies and Jens Schröter, 4–114. Tübingen: Mohr/Siebeck, 2012.

———. "'Neutestamentliche Apokryphen': Bemerkungen zu Geschichte und Zukunft einer von Edgar Hennecke im Jahr 1904 begründeten Quellensammlung." *Apocrypha* 9 (1998) 97–132.

———. *Valentinus Gnosticus? Untersuchungen zur valentinianischen Gnosis mit einem Kommentar zu den Fragmenten Valentins*. WUNT 1/65. Tübingen: Mohr/Siebeck, 1992.

———, "Was wissen wir über den Sitz im Leben der apokryphen Evangelien?" In *Jesus in den apokryphen Evangelienüberlieferungen. Beiträge zu außerkanonischen Jesusüberlieferungen aus verschiedenen Sprach- und Kulturtraditionen*, edited by Jörg Frey and Jens Schröter, 61–92. WUNT 254. Tübingen: Mohr/Siebeck, 2010.

Markschies, Christoph, and Jens Schröter, eds. *Antike christliche Apokryphen in deutscher Übersetzung*. Vol. 1. Tübingen: Mohr/Siebeck, 2012.

Martinez, Francisco Javier. "The Apocalyptic Genre in Syriac: The World of Pseudo-Methodius." In *IV Symposium Syriacum 1984: Literary Genres in Syriac Literature*, edited by Han J. W. Drijvers, René Lavenant, Corrie Molenberg, and Gerrit J. Reinink, 337–52. OrChrAn 229. Rome: Pontificale Institutum Studiorum Orientalium, 1987.

Marrou, Henri-Irénée. *A History of Education in Antiquity*. Translated by George Lamb. Madison: University of Wisconsin Press, 1956.

McAuliffe, Jane Dammen. "Text and Textuality: Q. 3:7 as a Point of Intersection." In *Literary Structures of Religious Meaning in the Qur'an*, edited by Issa J. Boullata, 56–76. London: Curzon, 2000.

McDonald, Lee Martin. *The Biblical Canon: Its Origin, Transmission, and Authority*. Grand Rapids: Baker Academic, 2011.

———. *Forgotten Scriptures: The Selection and Rejection of Early Religious Writings*. Louisville: Westminster John Knox, 2009.

———. *Formation of the Bible: The Story of the Church's Canon*. Peabody, MA: Hendrickson, 2012.

———. "Hellenism and the Biblical Canons: Is there a Connection?" In *Christian Origins and Hellenistic Judaism: Social and Literary Contexts for the New Testament*. Vol. 2 of *Early Christianity in Its Hellenistic Context*, edited by Stanley E. Porter and Andrew W. Pitts, 13–49. Texts and Editions for New Testament Study 10. Leiden: Brill, 2013.

———. Review of *Canon and Creed*, by Robert W. Jenson. *RBL* (posted 19 August 2011). http://www.bookreviews.org/bookdetail.asp?TitleId=7881&CodePage=7881.

———. Review of *The Canon of the Bible and the Apocrypha in the Churches of the East*, edited by Vahan S. Hovhanessian. *RBL* (posted 24 September 2013). http://www.bookreviews.org/bookdetail.asp?TitleId=8951&CodePage=8951.

———. Review of *The Goodly Fellowship of the Prophets: The Achievement of Association in Canon Formation*, by Christopher R. Seitz. *Interpretation* 64 (2010) 427–28.

McDonald, Lee Martin, and James H. Charlesworth, eds. *Non-Canonical Religious Texts in Early Judaism and Early Christianity*. T. & T. Clark Jewish and Christian Texts in Contexts 14. London: T. & T. Clark, 2012.

McGinn, Bernard. "Oracular Transformations: The 'Sibylla Tiburtina' in the Middle Ages." In *Sibille e linguaggi oracolari: mito, storia, tradizione: atti del convegno, Macerata-Norcia, settembre 1994*, edited by Ileana Chirassi Colombo and Tullio Seppilli, 603–44. Pisa: Istituti editoriali e poligrafici internazionali, 1998.

———. "*Teste David cum Sibylla*: The Significance of the Sibylline Tradition in the Middle Ages." In *Women of the Medieval World: Essays in Honor of John H. Mundy*, edited by Julius Kirshner and Susan F. Wemple, 7–35. Oxford: Blackwell, 1985.

———. *Visions of the End: Apocalyptic Traditions in the Middle Ages*. Records of Civilization, Sources and Studies 96. New York: Columbia University Press, 1979.

Mead, G. R. S. *The Hymn of the Robe of Glory*. Echoes from the Gnosis 10. 1908. Reprinted, Whitefish, MT: Kessinger, 1993.

Meeks, Wayne A. "The Image of the Androgyne: Some Uses of a Symbol in Early Christianity." *HR* 13 (1974) 165–208.

Meier, John P. *A Marginal Jew: Rethinking the Historical Jesus*. 4 vols. Anchor Bible Reference Library. New York: Doubleday, 1991–2009.

———. "The Present State of the Third Quest of the Historical Jesus: Loss and Gain." *Biblica* 80 (1999) 459–87.

Metzger, Bruce M. *The Bible in Translation: Ancient and English Versions*. Grand Rapids: Baker Academic, 2001.

———, trans. "The Fourth Book of Ezra." In *The Old Testament Peudepigrapha*. Vol. 1, *Apocalyptic Literature and Testaments*, edited by James H. Charlesworth, 517–59. Anchor Bible Reference Library. New York et al.: Doubleday, 1983.

Metzger, Bruce M., and Bart D. Ehrman. *The Text of the New Testament: Its Transmission, Corruption, and Restoration*. 4th ed. Oxford: Oxford University Press, 2005.

Meyer, Marvin et al., eds. *The Nag Hammadi Scriptures: The International Edition*. New York: HarperOne, 2008.

———. *Secret Gospels: Essays on Thomas and the Secret Gospel of Mark*. London: Continuum, 2003.

Miceli, Calogero. "An Account of the York University Christian Apocrypha Symposium Series: 'Ancient Gospel or Modern Forgery? The Secret Gospel of Mark in Debate' (Held at Vanier College on April 29th, 2011)." *Apocrypha* 22 (2011) 265–72.

Michel, Charles, and Paul Peeters, eds. *Évangiles apocryphes*. 2 vols. Textes et documents pour l'étude historique du Christianisme 13 and 18. Paris: Picard, 1911–1914.

Migne, Jacques-Paul. *Dictionnaire des Apocryphes, ou Collection de tous les livres apocryphes relatifs à l'Ancien et au Nouveau Testament*. 2 vols. Paris: Ateliers catholique, 1856–1858.

Mimouni, Simon C. "Les Apocalypses de la Vierge: État de la question." *Apocrypha* 4 (1993) 101–12.

———. *Les traditions anciennes sur la Dormition et l'Assomption de Marie: Études littéraires, historiques et doctrinales*. VCSup 104. Leiden: Brill, 2011.

Miller Parmenter, Dorina. "The Bible as Icon: Myths of the Divine Origins of Scripture." In *Jewish and Christian Scripture as Artifact and Canon*, edited by Craig A. Evans and H. Daniel Zacharias, 298–309. Library of Second Temple Studies 13. London: T. & T. Clark, 2009.

Miller, Robert J., ed. *The Apocalyptic Jesus: A Debate*. Santa Rosa, CA: Polebridge, 2001.

———. ed. *The Complete Gospels*. Rev. ed. Salem, OR: Polebridge, 2010.

———. *The Jesus Seminar and Its Critics*. Santa Rosa, CA: Polebridge, 1999.

Möhring, Hannes. *Der Weltkaiser der Endzeit: Entstehung, Wandel und Wirkung einer tausendjährigen Weissagung*. Mittelalter-Forschungen 3. Stuttgart: Thorbecke, 2000.

Morgan, Teresa. *Literate Education in the Hellenistic and Roman Worlds*. Cambridge Classical Studies. Cambridge: Cambridge University Press, 1998.

Mroczek, Eva. "'Gospel of Jesus' Wife' Less Durable Than Sexism Surrounding It." *Religion Dispatches*. Posted 6 May 2014. No pages. http://religiondispatches.org/gospel-of-jesus-wife-less-durable-than-sexism-surrounding-it/.

Naïmi, Mustapha. Review of *En marge du canon: Études sur les textes apocryphes juifs et chrétiens. 65e congrès de l'Association catholique des études bibliques au Canada*, edited by André Gagné and Jean-François Racine. *ASSR* 160 (2012) 176.

Navtanovich, Liudmila. "The Provenance of 2 Enoch: A Philological Perspective. A Response to C. Böttrich's Paper 'The "Book of the Secrets of Enoch" (2 En): Between Jewish Origins and Christian Transmission. An Overview.'" In *New Perspectives on 2 Enoch: No Longer Slavonic Only*, edited by Andrei A. Orlov and Gabriele Boccaccini, in association with Jason M. Zurawski, 69–82. Studia Judaeoslavica 4. Leiden: Brill, 2012.

———. "Second Enoch and the Tale of the Blessed Zerubbabel: Two Different Examples of Old Testament Slavonic Apocrypha." *JSP* 19 (2009) 109–26.

Neander, Michael. *Catechesis Martini Lutheri parua, Graecolatina, postremum recognita, etc.* 1564². 3rd ed. Basel: Oporini, 1567.

Neusner, Jacob. "Zaccheus/Zakkai." *HTR* 67 (1964) 67–69.

Newman, Hillel. "The Death of Jesus in the Toledot Yeshu Literature." *JTS* 50 (1999) 59–79.

Nicholson, Oliver. "Golden Age and End of the World: Myths of Mediterranean Life from Lactantius to Joshua the Stylite." In *The Medieval Mediterranean: Cross-Cultural Contacts*, edited by Marilyn J. Chiat and Katherine L. Reyerson, 11–18. Medieval Studies at Minnesota 3. St. Cloud, MN: North Star Press of St. Cloud, 1988.

Nicklas, Tobias. "'Écrits apocryphes chrétiens': ein Sammelband als Spiegel eines weitreichenden Paradigmenwechsels in der Apokryphenforschung." *VC* 61 (2007) 70–95.

---. "Semiotik—Intertextualität—Apokryphität: Eine Annäherung an den Begriff 'christlicher Apokryphen.'" *Apocrypha* 17 (2006) 55-78.

Nongbri, Brent. "The Use and Abuse of 𝔓52: Papyrological Pitfalls in the Dating of the Fourth Gospel." *HTR* 98 (2005) 23-48.

Norelli, Enrico. *Marie des apocryphes: Enquête sur la mère de Jésus dans le christianisme antique*. Christianismes antiques. Geneva: Labor et Fides, 2009.

---. "Que pouvons-nous reconstituer du *Syntagma* contre les hérésies de Justin? Un exemple." *RTP* 139 (2007) 167-81.

Olster, David. "Byzantine Apocalypses." In *The Encyclopedia of Apocalypticism*, edited by John J. Collins, Bernard McGinn, and Stephen J. Stein, 2:48-73. 3 vols. New York: Continuum, 1999.

Osthövener, Claus-Dieter. "Adolf von Harnack als Systematiker." *ZTK* 99 (2002) 296-331.

---. "Nachwort." In Adolf von Harnack, *Das Wesen des Christentums*, 259-92. 3rd enlarged ed. Tübingen: Mohr/Siebeck, 2012.

Pagels, Elaine. "Exegesis of Genesis 1 in the Gospels of Thomas and John." *JBL* 118 (1999) 477-96.

Painchaud, Louis. "À Propos de la (re)découverte de l'Évangile de Judas." *LTP* 62 (2006) 553-68. Republished in English as "On the (Re)Discovery of the Gospel of Judas." In *Rediscovering the Apocryphal Continent: New Perspectives on Early Christian and Late Antique Apocryphal Texts and Traditions*, edited by Pierluigi Piovanelli, Tony Burke, and Timothy Pettipiece, 119-36. WUNT 1/349. Tübingen: Mohr/Siebeck, 2015.

Palmer, Andrew. *The Seventh Century in West-Syrian Chronicles*. Translated Texts for Historians 15. Liverpool: Liverpool University Press, 1993.

Papandreou, Damaskinos, Wolfgang A. Bienert, and Knut Schäferdiek. *Oecumenica et Patristica: Festschrift für Wilhelm Schneemelcher zum 75. Geburtstag*. Stuttgart: Kohlhammer, 1989.

Parsons, Mikeal C., and Richard I. Pervo. *Rethinking the Unity of Luke and Acts*. Philadelphia: Fortress, 1993.

Pasquali, Giorgio. *Storia della tradizione e critica del testo*. Florence: Le Monnier, 1934. New ed., with a Foreword by Dino Pieraccioni. Bibliotheca 11. Florence: Le Lettere, 1988.

Patterson, Stephen J. "Apocalypticism or Prophecy and the Problem of Polyvalence: Lessons from the Gospel of Thomas." *JBL* 130 (2011) 795-817.

---. "The End of Apocalypse: Rethinking the Eschatological Jesus." *ThTo* 52 (1995) 29-48.

---. *The God of Jesus: The Historical Jesus and the Search for Meaning*. Philadelphia: Trinity Press International, 1998.

---. "The Gospel of Thomas and Christian Beginnings." In *The Gospel of Thomas in Recent Study*, edited by Jon Asgiersson, et al., 1-18. NHMS 59. Leiden: Brill, 2006.

---. *The Gospel of Thomas and Christian Origins: Essays on the Fifth Gospel*. NHMS 84. Leiden: Brill, 2013.

---. *The Gospel of Thomas and Jesus*. Foundations & Facets Reference Series. Sonoma, CA: Polebridge, 1993.

---. "The Gospel of Thomas within the Development of Early Christianity." PhD diss., Claremont Graduate School, 1988.

Paulissen, Lucie. "Jésus à l'école. L'enseignement dans l'Évangile de l'Enfance selon Thomas." *Apocrypha* 14 (2003) 153–75.
Peeters, Paul. *Bibliotheca hagiographica orientalis*. Subsidia Hagiographica 10. Brussels: Société des Bollandistes, 1910.
Pennec, Hervé. *Des jésuites au royaume du Prêtre Jean (Éthiopie). Stratégies, rencontres et tentatives d'implantation, 1495–1633*. Paris: Centre Culturel Calouste Gulbenkian, 2003.
Penner, Kenneth M. "Citation Formulae as Indices to Canonicity in Early Jewish and Early Christian Literature." In *Jewish and Christian Scriptures: The Function of 'Canonical' and 'Non-Canonical' Religious Texts*, edited by James H. Charlesworth and Lee Martin McDonald, 62–84. Jewish and Christian Texts in Contexts and Related Studies 7. London: T. & T. Clark, 2010.
Perrin, Norman. *Rediscovering the Teaching of Jesus*. New York: Harper & Row, 1967.
———. *Kingdom of God in the Teaching of Jesus*. Philadelphia: Westminster, 1963.
Pervo, Richard I. *Acts: A Commentary*. Hermeneia. Minneapolis: Fortress, 2009.
———. *Dating Acts: Between the Evangelists and the Apologists*. Santa Rosa, CA: Polebridge, 2006.
———. "A Hard Act to Follow: The *Acts of Paul* and the Canonical Acts." *Journal of Higher Criticism* 2/2 (1995) 3–32.
———. *Profit with Delight: The Literary Genre of the Acts of the Apostles*. Philadelphia: Fortress, 1987.
Pesce, Mauro. *Le parole dimenticate di Gesù*. Fondazione Lorenzo Valla. Milan: Mondadori, 2004.
Petersen, Erik. *Intellectum liberare Johann Albert Fabricius, en Humanist I Europa*. Danish Humanist Texts and Studies 18. Copenhagen: Museum Tusculanum Press, 1998.
———. "Learned Communication: Johann Albert Fabricius and the Literary Communities." In *Renaissance Readings of the Corpus Aristotelicum. Proceedings from the Conference Held in Copenhagen 23–25 April 1998*, edited by Marianne Pade, 287–94. Renaessance Studier 9. Copenhagen: Museum Tusculanum Press, 2001.
Pfister, Friedrich. *Alexander der Grosse in den Offenbarungen der Griechen, Juden, Mohammedaner und Christen*. Schriften der Sektion für Altertumswissenschaft, Deutsche Akademie der Wissenschaften zu Berlin 3. Berlin: Akademie, 1956.
Piazzesi, Vittorio, ed. *Acta Sanctae Sedis. In compendium opportune redacta ac illustrata*, Vol. 31. Rome: Congregatio de Propaganda Fide, 1898–1899.
Picard, Jean-Claude. *Le continent apocryphe. Essai sur les littératures apocryphes juive et chrétienne*. Instrumenta Patristica et Mediaevalia 36. Turnhout: Brepols, 1999.
Pick, Bernhard. *Apocryphal Acts of Paul, Peter, John, Andrew and Thomas*. 1909. Reprinted, Ancient Texts and Translations. Eugene, OR: Wipf & Stock, 2006.
———. *The Cabala and Its Influence on Judaism and Christianity*. Chicago: Open Court, 1913.
———. *The Extra-Canonical Life of Christ, Being a Record of the Acts and Sayings of Jesus of Nazareth Drawn from Uninspired Sources*. New York: Funk & Wagnall, 1903.
———. "History of the Printed Editions of the Old Testament, together with a Description of the Rabbinic and Polyglott Bibles." *Hebraica* 9 (1892–1893) 47–116.

———. *Jesus in the Talmud: His Personality, His Disciples and His Sayings.* 1913. Reprinted, Eugene, OR: Wipf & Stock, 2004.

———. *The Life of Jesus according to Extra-Canonical Sources.* New York: Alden, 1887.

———. *Paralipomena: Remains of Gospels and Sayings of Christ.* Chicago: Open Court, 1908.

———. *The Talmud: What It Is and What It Says about Jesus and the Christians.* Chicago: Open Court, 1887.

———. "The Vowel Points Controversy in the 16th and 17th Centuries." *Hebraica* 8.3/4 (1892) 150–73.

Piemonte, Gustavo A. "Recherches sur les *Tractatus in Matheum* attribués à Jean Scot." In *The Bible and Hermeneutics: Proceedings of the Ninth International Colloquium of the Society for the Promotion of Eriugenian Studies, Leuven—Louvain-la-Neuve, June 7–10, 1995*, edited by Gerd van Riel et al., 321–50. Ancient and Medieval Philosophy 1/20. Leuven: Leuven University Press, 1996.

Piovanelli, Pierluigi. "De l'usage polémique des récits de la Passion, ou: Là où les chemins qui auraient dû se séparer ont fini par se superposer." In *La croisée des chemins revisitée. Quand l'Église et la Synagogue se sont-elles distinguées? Actes du colloque de Tours, 18–19 juin 2010*, edited by Simon C. Mimouni and Bernard Pouderon, 123–59. Patrimoines, Judaïsme antique. Paris: Cerf, 2012.

———. "From Enoch to Seth: Primeval Patrons in Jewish-Apocalyptic and Christian-Gnostic Traditions." *Judaïsme ancien—Ancient Judaism* 2 (2014) 79–112.

———. "L'Enoch Seminar. Quelques considérations rétrospectives et prospectives de la part d'un 'vétéran.'" In *En marge du canon. Études sur les textes apocryphes juifs et chrétiens. 65e congrès de l'Association catholique des études bibliques au Canada*, edited by André Gagné and Jean-François Racine, 251–78. L'Écriture de la Bible 2. Paris: Cerf, 2012.

———. "In Praise of 'The Default Position,' or Reassessing the Christian Reception of the Jewish Pseudepigraphic Heritage." *NedTT* 61 (2007) 233–50.

———. "Livre du coq." In *Écrits apocryphes chrétiens*, vol. 2, edited by Pierre Geoltrain and Jean-Daniel Kaestli, 135–203. Bibliothèque de la Pléiade 516. Paris: Gallimard, 2005.

———. "La *Prière et Apocalypse de Paul* au sein de la littérature apocryphe d'attribution paulinienne." *Apocrypha* 15 (2004) 31–40.

———. "Qu'est-ce qu'un 'écrit apocryphe chrétien,' et comment ça marche? Quelques suggestions pour une herméneutique apocryphe." In *Pierre Geoltrain, ou comment "faire l'histoire" des religions. Le chantier des "origines," les méthodes du doute, et la conversation contemporaine entre disciplines*, edited by Simon C. Mimouni and Isabelle Ullern-Weité, 171–84. Bibliothèque de l'École des hautes études, Sciences religieuses 128. Turnhout: Brepols, 2006.

———. "Rabbi Yehuda versus Judas Iscariot: The Gospel of Judas and the Apocryphal Passion Stories." In *The Codex Judas Papers: Proceedings of the International Congress on the Tchacos Codex Held at Rice University, Houston Texas, March 13–16, 2008*, edited by April DeConick, 223–39. NHMS 71. Leiden: Brill, 2009.

———. "The Reception of Early Christian Texts and Traditions in Late Antiquity Apocryphal Literature." In *The Reception and Interpretation of the Bible in Late Antiquity: Proceedings of the Montréal Colloquium in Honour of Charles Kannengiesser, 11–13 October 2006*, edited by Lorenzo DiTommaso and Lucian Turcescu, 429–39. The Bible in Ancient Christianity 6. Leiden: Brill, 2008.

———. "Le recyclage des textes aprocryphes à l'heure de la petite 'mondialisation' de l'Antiquité tardive (ca. 325–451). Quelques perspectives littéraires et historiques." In *Poussières de christianisme et de judaïsme antiques: Études réunies en l'honneur de Jean-Daniel Kaestli et Éric Junod*, edited by Rémi Gounelle and Albert Frey, 277–95. Publications de l'Institut romand des sciences bibliques 5. Lausanne: Zèbre, 2007.

———. "Rewriting: The Path from Apocryphal to Heretical." In *Religious Conflict from Early Christianity to the Rise of Islam*, edited by Wendy Mayer and Bronwen Neil, 87–108. Arbeiten zur Kirchengeschichte 121. Berlin: de Gruyter, 2013.

———. "*Rewritten Bible* ou *Bible in progress*? La réécriture des traditions mémoriales bibliques dans le judaïsme et le christianisme ancien." *RTP* (2007) 295–310.

———. "Thursday Night Fever: Dancing and Singing with Jesus in the *Gospel of the Savior* and the *Dance of the Savior around the Cross*." *Early Christianity* 3 (2012) 229–48.

———. "The Toledot Yeshu and Christian Apocryphal Literature: The Formative Years." In *Toledot Yeshu ("The Life Story of Jesus") Revisited: A Princeton Conference*, edited by Peter Schäfer et al., 89–100. TSAJ 143. Tübingen: Mohr/Siebeck, 2011.

———. "What Is a Christian Apocryphal Text and How Does It Work? Some Observations on Apocryphal Hermeneutics." *NedTT* 59 (2005) 31–40.

Piovanelli, Pierluigi, Tony Burke, and Timothy Pettipiece, eds. *Rediscovering the Apocryphal Continent: New Perspectives on Early Christian and Late Antique Apocryphal Texts and Traditions*. WUNT 1/349. Tübingen: Mohr/Siebeck, 2015.

Platt, Rutherford Hayes, Jr. *The Lost Books of the Bible and the Forgotten Books of Eden*. Cleveland: World, 1963.

Podskalsky, Gerhard. *Byzantinische Reichseschatologie: die Periodisierung der Weltgeschichte in den vier Grossreichen (Daniel 2 und 7) und dem tausendjährigen Friedensreiche (Apok. 20) Eine motivgeschichtliche Untersuchung*. Münchener Universitäts-Schriften. Reihe der Philosophischen Fakultät 9. Munich: Fink, 1972.

Pöhner, Ralph. "Judas, der Held." *Facts* 1 (6 January 2005) 77–79.

Poirier, Paul-Hubert. *L'Hymne de la perle des Actes de Thomas: Introduction, texte, traduction, commentaire*. Homo Religiosus 8. Louvain-la-Neuve: Centre d'histoire des religions, 1981.

———. "Vers une redéfinition du champ apocryphe: Aperçus de la recherche récente consacrée aux apocryphes." In *En marge du canon: Études sur les textes apocryphes juifs et chrétiens. 65e congrès de l'Association catholique des études bibliques au Canada*, edited by André Gagné and Jean-François Racine, 85–106. L'Écriture de la Bible 2. Paris: Cerf, 2012.

Pratten, Benjamin P. *Syriac Documents Attributed to the First Three Centuries*. Edinburgh: T. & T. Clark, 1871.

Quantin, Jean-Louis. "Dodwell, Mill, Grabe et le problème du canon néo-testamentaire au tournant du XVIIe et du XVIIIe siècle." In *Apocryphité: Histoire d'un concept transversal aux religions du livre. En hommage à Pierre Geoltrain*, edited by Simon Claude Mimouni, 285–306. Bibliothèque de l'École des Hautes Études. Sciences religieuses 113. Turnhout: Brepols, 2002.

Quarry, John. "Notes, Chiefly Critical, on the Clementine Homilies and the Epistles Prefixed to Them." *Hermathena* 7 (1890) 67–104, 239–67; 8 (1893) 91–112, 133–60, 287–300.

Quispel, Gilles. *De bronnen van Tertullianus' Adversus Marcionem*. Leiden: Burgersdijk & Niermans, 1943.

Rangheri, Maurizio. "La 'Epistola ad Gerbergam reginam de ortu et tempore Antichristi' di Adsone di Montier-en-Der e le sue fonti." *Studi medievali* 14 (1973) 677–732.

Reed, Annette Y. "Beyond the Land of Nod: Syriac Images of Asia and the Historiography of 'The West.'" *HR* 49 (2009) 48–87.

————. "From Judaism and Hellenism to Christianity and Paganism: Cultural Identities and Religious Polemics in the Pseudo-Clementine *Homilies*." In *Nouvelles intrigues pseudo-clémentines—Plots in the Pseudo-Clementine Romance. Actes du deuxième colloque international sur la littérature apocryphe chrétienne, Lausanne—Genève, 30 août—2 septembre 2006*, edited by Frédéric Amsler et al., 425–35. Publications de l'Institut romand des sciences bibliques 6. Lausanne: Zèbre, 2008.

————. "Heresiology and the (Jewish-)Christian Novel: Narrativized Polemics in the Pseudo-Clementine *Homilies*." In *Heresy and Identity in Late Antiquity*, edited by Eduard Iricinschi and Holger M. Zellentin, 273–98. TSAJ 119. Tübingen: Mohr/Siebeck, 2008.

————. "'Jewish Christianity' as Counter-history? The Apostolic Past in Eusebius' *Ecclesiastical History* and the Pseudo-Clementine *Homilies*." In *Antiquity in Antiquity: Jewish and Christian Pasts in the Greco-Roman World*, edited by Gregg Gardner and Kevin L. Osterloh, 173–216. TSAJ 123. Tübingen: Mohr/Siebeck, 2008.

————. "The Modern Invention of 'Old Testament Pseudepigrapha.'" *JTS* 60 (2009) 403–36.

————. "Pseudepigraphy, Authorship, and the Reception of 'The Bible' in Late Antiquity." In *The Reception and Interpretation of the Bible in Late Antiquity: Proceedings of the Montréal Colloquium in Honour of Charles Kannengiesser, 11–13 October 2006*, edited by Lorenzo DiTommaso and Lucian Turcescu, 467–90. Bible in Ancient Christianity 6. Leiden: Brill, 2008.

————. Review of Brent Landau, *Revelation of the Magi: The Lost Tale of the Wise Men's Journey to Bethlehem*. *Sino Platonic Papers* 208 (2011) 36–54.

Reeves, John C. *Trajectories in Near Eastern Apocalyptic: A Postrabbinic Jewish Apocalypse Reader*. Resources for Biblical Studies 45. Leiden: Brill, 2006.

Rehm, Bernhard. "Zur Entstehung der pseudoclementinischen Schriften." *ZNW* 37 (1938) 77–184.

Reinhartz, Adele. "The Vanishing Jews of Antiquity: How Should One Translate the Greek Term *ioudaios*?" *Marginalia Review of Books*. Posted 24 June 2014. No pages. http://marginalia.lareviewofbooks.org/vanishing-jews-antiquity-adele-reinhartz/.

Reinink, Gerrit J. "Alexander the Great in Seventh-Century Syriac 'Apocalyptic Texts.'" *Byzantinorossica* 2 (2003) 150–78.

————. "'Pseudo-Ephraems 'Rede über das Ende' und die syrische eschatologische Literatur des siebten Jahrhunderts." *Aram* 5 (1993) 437–63.

————. "Pseudo-Methodius und die Legende vom römischen Endkaiser." In *The Use and Abuse of Eschatology in the Middle Ages*, edited by Werner Verbeke, Daniel Verhelst, and Andries Welkenhuysen, 82–111. Mediaevalia Lovaniensia Series 1, Studia 15. Leuven: Leuven University Press, 1988.

————. "Ps.-Methodius: A Concept of History in Response to the Rise of Islam." In *The Byzantine and Early Islamic Near East: Papers of the First Workshop on Late*

Antiquity and Early Islam, edited by Averil Cameron and Lawrence I. Conrad, 149–87. Studies in Late Antiquity and Early Islam 1. Princeton: Darwin, 1992.

———. "The Romance of Julian the Apostate as a Source for Seventh Century Syriac Apocalypses." In *La Syrie de Byzance à l'Islam: VIIe–VIIIe siècles*, edited by P. Canivet and J.-P. Rey-Coquais, 75–86. Damascus: Institut français de Damas, 1992.

———. "Die syrischen Wurzeln der mittelalterlichen Legende vom römischen Endkaiser." In *Non Nova, Sed Nova: Mélanges de civilisation médiévale dédiés à Willem Noomen*, edited by Martin Gosman and Jaap van Os, 195–209. Mediaevalia Groningana 5. Groningen: Bouma, 1984.

Resch, Alfred. *Agrapha: aussercanonische Schriftfragmente*. TUGAL 30. Leipzig: Hinrichs, 1906.

———. *Aussercanonische Paralleltexte zu den Evangelien*. 4 vols. TUGAL 10:1–4. Leipzig: Hinrichs, 1893–1896.

Ritter, Adolf Martin. *Stemmatisierungsversuche zum Corpus Dionysiacum Areopagiticum im Lichte des EDV-Verfahrens*. NAWG I. Philosophisch-historische Klasse, 6/1980. Göttingen: Vandenhoeck & Ruprecht, 1980.

Robinson, Gesine. "Codex Berolinensis P 20915. A Progress Report." In *Ägypten und Nubien in spätantiker und christlicher Zeit. Akten des 6. Internationalen Koptologenkongresses Münster, 20.–26. Juli 1996*, edited by Stephen Emmel, Martin Krause, Siegfried G. Richter, and Sofia Schaten, 2:167–77. 2 vols. Sprachen und Kulteren des Christlichen Orients 6. Wiesbaden: Reichert, 1999.

Robinson, James M., ed. *The Facsimile Edition of the Nag Hammadi Codices*. 11 vols. Leiden: Brill, 1972–1984.

———, ed. *The Secrets of Judas: The Story of the Misunderstood Disciple and His Lost Gospel*. San Francisco: HarperSanFrancisco, 2006.

———. "Theological Autobiography." In *The Craft of Religious Studies*, edited by Jon R. Stone, 117–50. New York: St. Martin's, 1998.

———, ed. *The Nag Hammadi Library in English*. San Francisco: Harper & Row, 1977.

Robinson, James M., and Helmut Koester. *Trajectories Through Early Christianity*. 1971. Reprinted, Eugene, OR: Wipf & Stock, 2006.

Robinson, James M., Paul Hoffmann, and John S. Kloppenborg, eds. *The Sayings Gospel Q in Greek and English, with Parallels from the Gospels of Mark and Thomas*. Minneapolis: Fortress, 2002.

Roessli, Jean-Michel. "Le VIe livre des *Oracles Sibyllins*." In *Les Sibylles: Actes des VIIIe Entretiens de La Garenne Lemot, Nantes 18–20 octobre 2001*, edited by Jackie Pigeaud, 203–30. Nantes: Université de Nantes, 2005.

———. "L'Introduction à la littérature judéo-hellénistique d'Albert-Marie Denis." *Apocrypha* 13 (2002) 257–79.

———. "The Passion Narrative in the *Sibylline Oracles*." In *Gelitten—Gestorben—Auferstanden: Passions- und Ostertraditionen im antiken Christentum*, edited by Tobias Nicklas, Andreas Merkt, and Joseph Verheyden, 299–327. WUNT 2/273. Tübingen: Mohr/Siebeck, 2010. Republished in French as "Le récit de la Passion dans les *Oracles sibyllins*." In *En marge du canon. Études sur les écrits apocryphes juifs et chrétiens*, edited by André Gagné and Jean-François Racine, 159–200. L'écriture de la Bible 2. Paris: Cerf, 2012.

———. "Sébastien Castellion et les *oracula Sibyllina*." In *Sébastien Castellion: Des Écritures à l'écriture. Actes du colloque international, Université de Paris-Ouest-

Nanterre-La Défense, 15–16 avril 2010, edited by Marie-Christine Gomez-Géraud, 223–38. Paris: Garnier, 2013.

Roessli, Jean-Michel and Tobias Nicklas, eds. *Christian Apocrypha: Receptions of the New Testament in Ancient Christian Apocrypha*. Novum Testamentum Patristicum 26. Göttingen: Vandenhoeck & Ruprecht, 2014.

Ropes, James Hardy. *Die Sprüche Jesu: die in den kanonischen Evangelien nicht überliefert sind: ein kritische Bearbeitung des von D. Alfred Resch gesammelten Materials*. Leipzig: Hinrichs, 1896.

Rordorf, Willy. "Im welchem Verhältnis stehen die apokryphen Paulusakten zur kanonischen Apostelgeschichte und zu den Pastoralbriefen?" In *Text and Testimony: Essays on New Testament and Apocryphal Literature in Honor of A. J. F. Klijn*, edited by Tjitze Baarda, 449–74. Kampen: Kok, 1988.

———. *Lex Orandi—Lex Credendi. Gesammelte Aufsätze zum 60. Geburtstag*. Paradosis 36. Freiburg: Universitätsverlag Freiburg in der Schweiz, 1993.

———. "Paul's Conversion in the Canonical Acts and in the *Acts of Paul*." Semeia 80 (1997) 137–44.

———. "Quelques jalons pour une interprétation symbolique des *Actes de Paul*." In *Early Christian Voices. In Texts, Traditions, and Symbols. Essays in Honor of François Bovon*, edited by David H. Warren, Ann Graham Brock, and David W. Pao, 251–65. Biblical Interpretation Series 66. Leiden: Brill, 2003.

———. "Terra Incognita: Recent Research on the Christian Apocryphal Literature, especially on some Acts of Apostles." In *Biblica et Apocrypha, Orientalia, Ascetica: Papers Presented at the Eleventh International Conference on Patristic Studies Held in Oxford 1991*, edited by Elizabeth A. Livingstone, 142–58. StPatr 25. Leuven: Peeters, 1993.

Rordorf, Willy, with Pierre Cherix and Rudolph Kasser. "Actes de Paul." In *Écrits apocryphes chrétiens*. Vol. 1, edited by François Bovon, and Pierre Geoltrain, 1117–77. Bibliothèque de la Pléiade 442. Paris: Gallimard, 1997.

Rose, Els. "Medieval Memories of the Apostolic Past: Reception and Use of the Apocryphal Acts in the Liturgical Commemoration of the Apostles." *Apocrypha* 19 (2008) 123–45.

———. *Ritual Memory: The Apocryphal Acts and Liturgical Commemoration in the Early Medieval West (c. 500–1215)*. Mittelalterliche Studien und Texte 40. Leiden: Brill, 2009.

Ross, E. Dennison. "Summary and Review of an Article by Ivanow on Ismailis." *JRAS* (1919) 429–35.

Rubinstein, Jeffrey L. *Stories of the Babylonian Talmud*. Baltimore: Johns Hopkins University Press, 2010.

Rudolph, Kurt. *Gnosis: The Nature and History of Gnosticism*. Translated by R. McL. Wilson. San Francisco: Harper & Row, 1983.

Ryle, Herbert E. *The Canon of the Old Testament*. London: Macmillan, 1904.

Salvador Gonzalez, José María. "The Death of the Virgin Mary (1295) in the Macedonian Church of the Panagia Peribleptos in Ohrid. Iconographic Interpretation from the Perspective of Three Apocryphal Writings." *Mirabilia: Electronic Journal of Antiquity and Middle Ages* 13 (2011) 237–68.

———. "La Dormición de la Virgen María en el arte bizantino durante la dinastía de los paleólogos. Estudios de cuatro casos." In *Imagen y cultura: La interpretación de las imágenes como historia cultural, 16–18 de octubre de 2007, Universitat*

Internacional de Gandía, Gandía, ed. Rafael García Mahíques and Vicent F. Zuriaga, 1:1425–36. 2 vols. Valencia: Biblioteca Valenciana, 2008.

———. "El Fresco de La Dormición de María en la iglesia de la Stma. Trinidad de Sopoçani a la luz de tres apócrifos asuncionistas." *Espéculo. Revista de Estudios Literarios* 47.8 (2011) 189–220.

———. "La presentación de María en el templo en la pintura italiana bajomedieval. Análisis iconográfico de cinco casos." *Espéculo. Revista de Estudios Literarios* 14.44 (2010). Pages 1–13. http://www.ucm.es/info/especulo/numero44/matemplo.html.

Sanders, E. P. *Jesus and Judaism*. Philadelphia: Fortress, 1985.

Sanders, James A. "Canon, Hebrew Bible." In *ABD* 1:837–52.

———. *Torah and Canon*. Philadelphia: Fortress, 1972¹. 2nd ed. Eugene, OR: Cascade Books, 2005.

Sandnes, Karl Olav. *The Challenge of Homer: School, Pagan Poets, and Early Christianity*. Library of New Testament Studies 400. London: T. & T. Clark, 2009.

Schäfer, Peter. *Jesus in the Talmud*. Princeton: Princeton University Press, 2009.

Schäfer, Peter, Michael Meerson, and Yaacov Deutsch, eds. *Toledot Yeshu ("The Life Story of Jesus") Revisited. A Princeton Conference*. TSAJ 143. Tübingen: Mohr/Siebeck, 2011.

Schleifer, Joel. *Die Erzählung der Sibylle: Ein Apokryph. Nach den karschunischen, arabischen und äthiopischen Handschriften zu London, Oxford, Paris und Rom*. Denkschriften der kaiserlichen Akad. der Wissensch. in Wien, Phil.-hist. Klasse 53.1. Vienna: Hölder, 1910.

Schmidt, Carl. *Acta Pauli aus der Heidelberger koptischen Papyrus-Handschrift Nr. 1*. 1904. 2nd enlarged ed. Leipzig: Hinrichs, 1905.

———. *Gespräche Jesu mit seinen Jüngern nach der Auferstehung: Ein katholisch-apostolisches Sendschreiben aus dem 2. Jahrhundert*. TU 43. Leipzig: Hinrichs, 1919.

Schmidt, Carl, and Wilhelm Schubart. *ΠΡΑΞΕΙΣ ΠΑΥΛΟΥ: Acta Pauli nach dem Papyrus der Hamburger Staats- und Universitätsbibliothek unter Mitarbeit von Wilhelm Schubart*. Hamburg: Augustin, 1936.

Schmidt, Daryl D. "The Greek New Testament as a Codex." In *The Canon Debate*, edited by Lee Martin McDonald and James A. Sanders, 469–84. Peabody, MA: Hendrickson, 2002.

Schneemelcher, Wilhelm. "Die Apostelgeschichte des Lukas und die *Acta Pauli*." In *Apophoreta: Festschrift für Ernst Haenchen zu seinem siebzigsten Geburtstag am 10. Dezember 1964*, edited by Walther Eltester and Franz Heinrich Kettler, 236–50. BZNW 30. Berlin: Töpelmann, 1964.

———. *Gesammelte Aufsätze zum Neuen Testament und zur Patristik*. Analekta Vlatadōn 22. Thessaloniki: Patriarchal Institute for Patristic Studies, 1974.

———, ed. *New Testament Apocrypha*. Translated by R. McL. Wilson. 2 vols. Louisville: Westminster John Knox, 1991–1992. Originally published as *Neutestamentliche Apokryphen in deutscher Übersetzung*. 6th ed. 2 vols. Tübingen: Mohr/Siebeck, 1990.

Schneemelcher, Wilhelm, and Rudolph Kasser. "Acts of Paul." In *The New Testament Apocrypha*. Vol. 2, *Writings Relating to the Apostles, Apocalypses, and Related Writings*, edited by Wilhelm Schneemelcher, 213–70. Rev. ed. Translated by R. McL. Wilson. Louisville: Westminster John Knox, 1991.

Schonfield, Hugh J. *According to the Hebrews*. London: Duckworth, 1937.

Schröter, Jens. *Erinnerung an Jesu Worte: Studien zur Rezeption der Logienüberlieferung in Markus, Q und Thomas.* WMANT 75. Neukirchen-Vluyn: Neukirchener, 1997.

Schwartz, Daniel R. "'Judaean' or 'Jew'? How Should We Translate *Ioudaios* in Josephus?" In *Jewish Identity in the Greco-Roman World/Jüdische Identität in Der Griechisch-Römischen Welt,* edited by Jörg Frey, Daniel R. Schwartz, and Stephanie Gripentrog, 3–27. Ancient Judaism and Early Christianity 71. Leiden: Brill, 2007.

Schwartz, Seth. "How Many Judaisms Were There? A Critique of Neusner and Smith on Definition and Mason and Boyarin on Categorization." *Journal of Ancient Judaism* 2 (2011) 208–38.

Scrivener, Frederick H. *Bezae Codex Cantabrigiensis: A Critical Introduction, Annotations, and Facsimiles.* London: Dell & Daldy, 1864.

Searby, Denis, and Bridget Morris. *The Revelations of St. Birgitta of Sweden, Volume I: Liber Caelestis, Books I–III.* Oxford: Oxford University Press, 2006.

Seitz, Christopher R. *The Goodly Fellowship of the Prophets: The Achievement of Association in Canon Formation.* Acadia Studies in Bible and Theology. Grand Rapids: Baker Academic, 2009.

Semler, Johann Salomo. *Abhandlung von freier Untersuchung des Canon.* Halle: Hemmerde, 1775.

Shepherd, William H. "Early Christian Apocrypha: A Bibliographic Essay." *Theological Librarianship* 3 (2010) 40–47.

Sheppard, Gerald T. "Canon." In *The Encyclopedia of Religion,* edited by Mircea Eliade, 3:62–69. New York: Macmillan, 1987.

Shoemaker, Stephen J. *The Death of a Prophet: The End of Muhammad's Life and the Beginnings of Islam.* Divinations: Rereading Late Ancient Religion. Philadelphia: University of Pennsylvania Press, 2012.

———. "Early Christian Apocryphal Literature." In *Oxford Handbook of Early Christian Studies,* edited by Susan Ashbrook Harvey and David G. Hunter, 521–48. Oxford: Oxford University Press, 2008.

———. "Epiphanius of Salamis, the Kollyridians, and the Early Dormition Narratives: The Cult of the Virgin in the Fourth Century." *JECS* 16 (2008) 371–401.

———. "Mary the Apostle: A New Fragment in Coptic and Its Place in the History of Marian Literature." In *Bibel, Byzanz und Christlicher Orient. Festschrift für Stephen Gerö zum 65. Geburtstag,* edited by Dmitrij Bumazhnov et al., 203–29. OLA 187. Leuven: Peeters, 2011.

———. "New Syriac Dormition Fragments from Palimpsests in the Schøyen Collection and the British Library: Presentation, Edition and Translation." *Mus* 124 (2011) 259–78.

———. "The Reign of God Has Come: Eschatology and Empire in Late Antiquity and Early Islam." *Arabica: Journal of Arabic and Islamic Studies* 61 (2014) 514–58.

Skarsaune, Oskar. *The Proof from Prophecy, A Study in Justin Martyr's Proof-Text Tradition: Text-Type, Provenance, Theological Profile.* NovTSup 56. Leiden: Brill, 1987.

Small, Jocelyn Penny. "Romulus et Remus." In *Lexicon Iconographum Mythologicae Classicae,* edited by John Boardman et al., 7.1: 644 and figs. 15, 20, 24, 25. 8 vols. Zurich: Artemis, 1981–2009.

Smelik, Willem F. "The Aramaic Dialect(s) of the *Toldot Yeshu* Fragments." *Aramaic Studies* 7 (2009) 39–73.

Smith, Dwight Moody. "John and the Apocryphal Gospels: Was John the First Apocryphal Gospel?" In *The Fourth Gospel in Four Dimensions: Judaism and Jesus, the Gospels and Scripture*, 156–65. Columbia: University of South Carolina Press, 2008. Originally published as "The Problem of John and the Synoptics in Light of the Relation between Apocryphal and Canonical Gospels." In *John and the Synoptics*, edited by Adelbert Denaux, 147–62. BETL 101. Leuven: Leuven University Press, 1992.

Smith, Jonathan Z. "The Garments of Shame." *HR* 5 (1965–1966) 217–38.

Smith, Morton. *Clement of Alexandria and a Secret Gospel of Mark*. Cambridge: Harvard University Press, 1973.

Snyder, Glenn E. *Acts of Paul: The Formation of a Pauline Corpus*. WUNT 2/352. Tübingen: Mohr/Siebeck, 2013.

Sokoloff, Michael. "The Date and Provenance of the Aramaic *Toledot Yeshu* on the Basis of Aramaic Dialectology." In *Toledot Yeshu ("The Life Story of Jesus") Revisited. A Princeton Conference*, edited by Peter Schäfer, Michael Meerson, and Yaacov Deutsch, 13–26. TSAJ 143. Tübingen: Mohr/Siebeck, 2011.

Souter, Alexander. *The Text and Canon of the New Testament*. Studies in Theology. London: Duckworth, 1917. Revised by C.S.C. Williams in 1954.

Spanheim, Friedrich. *Dubiorum evangelicorum*. 3 vols. Geneva: Chouët, 1639.

Speyer, Wolfgang. *Die literarische Fälschung im heidnischen und christlichen Altertum: Ein Versuch ihrer Deutung*. Handbuch der Altertumswissenschaft 1.2. Munich: Beck, 1971.

Stanislawski, Michael. "A Preliminary Study of a Yiddish 'Life of Jesus' (*Toledot Yeshu*): JTS Ms. 2211." In *Toledot Yeshu ("The Life Story of Jesus") Revisited. A Princeton Conference*, edited by Peter Schäfer, Michael Meerson, and Yaacov Deutsch, 79–87. TSAJ 143. Tübingen: Mohr/Siebeck, 2011.

Stern, David, ed. *The Anthology in Jewish Literature*. Oxford: Oxford University Press, 2004.

———. "On Canonization in Rabbinic Judaism." In *Homer, the Bible, and Beyond: Literary and Religious Canons in the Ancient World*, edited by Margalit Finkelberg and Guy G. Stroumsa, 227–52. Jewish Studies in Religion and Culture 2. Leiden: Brill, 2003.

Stökl Ben Ezra, Daniel. "An Ancient List of Christian Festivals in *Toledot Yeshu*: Polemics as Indication for Interaction." *HTR* 102 (2009) 481–96.

Stoyanov, Yuri. *Defenders and Enemies of the True Cross: The Sasanian Conquest of Jerusalem in 614 and Byzantine Ideology of Anti-Persian Warfare*. Österreichische Akademie der Wissenschaften, Philosophisch-Historische Klasse, Sitzungsberichte 819. Veröffentlichungen zur Iranistik 61. Vienna: Verlag der Österreichischen Akademie der Wissenschaften, 2011.

Strecker, Georg. "Eine Evangelienharmonie bei Justin und Pseudoklemens?" *NTS* 24 (1977–1978) 297–316.

———. *Das Judenchristentum in den Pseudoklementinen*. 2nd rev. ed. TUGAL 70. Berlin: Akademie, 1981.

Suciu, Alin. "Apocryphon Berolinense/Argentoratense (Previously Known as the Gospel of the Savior): Edition of P. Berol. 22220, Strasbourg Copte 5–7 and Qasr el-Wizz Codex ff. 12v–17r with Introduction and Commentary." PhD diss., Faculté de Théologie et de Sciences des religions, Université Laval, Québec, 2013.

Suermann, Harald. "Der byzantinische Endkaiser bei Pseudo-Methodius." *OrChr* 71 (1987) 140–55.

———. *Die geschichtstheologische Reaktion auf die einfallenden Muslime in der edessenischen Apokalyptik des 7. Jahrhunderts*. Europäische Hochschulschriften Reihe 23, Theologie 256. Frankfurt: Lang, 1985.

Sullivan, Ruth W. "Saints Peter and Paul: Some Ironic Aspects of Their Imaging." *AH* 17 (1994) 59–80.

Swete, Henry Barclay. *Introduction to the Old Testament in Greek*. Cambridge: Cambridge University Press, 1914.

Sykes, Norman. *William Wake, Archbishop of Canterbury, 1657–1737*. Cambridge: Cambridge University Press, 1957.

Talbert, Charles H. *Reading Luke–Acts in Its Mediterranean Milieu*. NovTSup 107. Leiden: Brill, 2003.

Tannehill, Robert C. *The Narrative Unity of Luke–Acts: A Literary Interpretation*. 2 vols. Philadelphia/Minneapolis: Fortress, 1986, 1990.

Tedros Abraha. "Some Philological Notes on the *Mäṣəḥafä ˁƷräfətä läMaryam* 'Liber Requiei' (*LR*)." *Apocrypha* 23 (2012) 223–45.

Theissen, Gerd, and Annette Merz. *The Historical Jesus: A Comprehensive Guide*. Translated by John Bowden. Minneapolis: Fortress, 1998.

Thilo, Johann Carl. *Codex apocryphus Novi Testamenti: Tomus primus, e libris et manuscriptis, maxime Gallicanis, Germanicis et Italicis, recensitus notisque et prolegominis illustratus*. Leipzig: Vogel, 1832.

Thomassen, Einar. "Some Notes on the Development of Christians Ideas about a Canon." In *Canon and Canonicity: The Formation and Use of Scripture*, edited by Einar Thomassen, 9–28. Copenhagen: Museum Tusculanum Press, 2010.

Tijdens, E. F. "Der mythologisch-gnostische Hintergrund des 'Umm al-kitāb.'" *Acta Iranica* 7 (1977) 241–526.

Till, Walter. *Die gnostischen Schriften des koptischen Papyrus Berolinensis 8502*. TU 60. Berlin: Akademie, 1955. 2nd ed., 1972, edited with Hans-Martin Schenke.

———. *Koptische Grammatik (Saïdischer Dialekt)*. Leipzig: Otto Harrassowitz, 1955.

Tischendorf, Constantin, ed. *Acta apostolorum apocrypha*. Leipzig: Mendelssohn, 1851.

———. *Apocalypses apocryphae*. Leipzig: Mendelssohn, 1866.

———. *Evangelia apocrypha*. Leipzig: Mendelssohn, 1853. 2nd ed. 1876.

Tite, Philip L. *The Apocryphal Epistle to the Laodiceans: An Epistolary and Rhetorical Analysis*. TENTS 7. Leiden: Brill, 2012.

———. *Valentinian Ethics and Paraenetic Discourse: Determining the Social Function of Moral Exhortation in Valentinian Christianity*. NHMS 67. Leiden: Brill, 2009.

Toland, John. *Nazarenus: Or, Jewish, Gentile, and Mahometan Christianity*. 2nd ed. London: Brotherton, Roberts & Dodd, 1718.

Townsend, John T. "The Date of Luke-Acts." In *Luke-Acts: New Perspectives from the Society of Biblical Literature Seminar*, edited by Charles H. Talbert, 47–62. New York: Crossroad, 1984.

Trocmé, Étienne. *Le livre des Actes et l'histoire*. EHPR 45. Paris: Presses Universitaires de France, 1957.

Tubach, Jürgen. "Seth and the Sethites in Early Syriac Literature." In *Eve's Children: The Biblical Stories Retold and Interpreted in Jewish and Christian Traditions*, edited by Gerard P. Luttikhuizen, 187–201. Themes in Biblical Narrative 5. Leiden: Brill, 2003.

Tyson, Joseph B. *Marcion and Luke-Acts: A Defining Struggle*. Columbia: University of South Carolina Press, 2006.
Ullmann, B. L. Review of *Storia della tradizione e critica del testo*, by Giorgia Pasquali. *CP* 32 (1937) 371–73.
Ulrich, Eugene. "The Canonical Process, Textual Criticism, and Later Stages in the Composition of the Bible." In *Sha'arei Talmon: Studies in the Bible, Qumran, and the Ancient Near East Presented to Shemaryahu Talmon*, edited by Michael A. Fishbane, et. al., 267–91. Winona Lake, IN: Eisenbrauns, 1992.
———. "The Notion and Definition of Canon." In *The Canon Debate*, edited by Lee Martin McDonald and James A. Sanders, 21–35. Peabody, MA: Hendrickson, 2002.
VanderKam, James C. *From Revelation to Canon: Studies in the Hebrew Bible and Second Temple Literature*. JSJSup 62. Leiden: Brill, 2002.
Van Voorst, Robert E. *Jesus Outside the New Testament: An Introduction to the Ancient Evidence*. Grand Rapids: Eerdmans, 2000.
Vardi, Amiel D. "Canons of Literary Texts at Rome." In *Homer, the Bible, and Beyond: Literary and Religious Canons in the Ancient World*, edited by Margalit Finkelberg and Guy G. Stroumsa, 131–52. Jewish Studies in Religion and Culture 2. Leiden: Brill, 2003.
Veltri, Giuseppe. *Libraries, Translations, and 'Canonic' Texts: The Septuagint, Aquila and Ben Sira in the Jewish and Christian Traditions*. JSJSup 109. Leiden: Brill, 2006.
Verhelst, Daniel. "La préhistoire des conceptions d'Adson concernant l'Antichrist." *RTAM* 40 (1973) 52–103.
Vööbus, Arthur. "The Oldest Extant Traces of the Syriac Peshitta." *Mus* 63 (1950) 191–204.
Vouaux, Léon. *Les Actes de Paul et ses lettres apocryphes. Introduction, textes, traduction, et commentaire*. Paris: Letouzey et Ané, 1913.
Waitz, Hans. *Die Pseudoklementinen, Homilien und Rekognitionen: Eine quellenkritische Untersuchung*. TUGAL n.s., 10.4. Leipzig: Hinrichs, 1914.
Wake, William. *Genuine Epistles of the Apostolic Fathers*. London: Hartford, Parsons & Hills, 1693.
Wasserstrom, Steve. "The Moving Finger Writes: Mughīra b. Sa'īd's Islamic Gnosis and the Myths of Its Rejection." *HR* 25 (1985) 1–29.
Weis-Liebersdorf, Johannes E. *Christus- und Apostelbilder: Einfluss des Apokryphen auf die ältesten Kunsttypen*. Freiburg: Herder, 1902.
Widengren, Geo. *The Ascension of the Apostle and the Heavenly Book*. Uppsala: Uppsala University Press, 1950.
Wilder, Amos. "New Testament Study in the Divinity School." *Harvard Divinity Bulletin* 25 (1961) 9–16.
Williams, Michael Allan. *Rethinking "Gnosticism": An Argument for Dismantling a Dubious Category*. Princeton: Princeton University Press, 1996.
Wilson, Robert McL. "The Gospel of Thomas Reconsidered." In *Divitiae Aegypti Koptologische und verwandte Studien zu Ehren von Martin Krause*, edited by Cäcilia Fluck, Lucia Langener, Siegfried Richter, Sofia Schaten, and Gregor Wurst, 331–36. Wiesbaden: Reichert, 1995.
Winter, Paul. "Matthew xi 27 and Luke x 22 from the First to the Fifth Century: Reflections on the Development of the Text." *NovT* 1 (1956) 112–48.

Wion, Anaïs. "Onction des malades, funérailles et commémorations: pour une histoire des textes et des pratiques liturgiques en Éthiopie chrétienne." *Afriques* 3 (2011) 1–57. http://afriques.revues.org/921.

Witakowski, Witold. "The Magi in Ethiopic Tradition." *Aethiopica* 2 (1999) 69–89.

———. "The Magi in Syriac Tradition." In *Malphono w-Rabo d-Malphone: Studies in Honor of Sebastian P. Brock*, edited by George A. Kiraz, 809–44. Gorgias Eastern Christian Studies 3. Piscataway, NJ: Gorgias, 2008.

Wordsworth, Christopher. *The Four Gospels, and Acts of the Apostles*. Vol. 1. of *The New Testament of our Lord and Saviour Jesus Christ: In the Original Greek*. London: Rivingtons, 1867.

Wortley, John. "The Literature of Catastrophe." *Byzantine Studies/Études byzantines* 4 (1977) 1–17.

Würthwein, Ernst. *The Text of the Old Testament*. Translated by Erroll F. Rhodes. 2nd ed. Grand Rapids: Eerdmans, 1995.

Wyrick, Jed. *The Ascension of Authorship: Attribution and Canon Formation in Jewish, Hellenistic, and Christian Traditions*. Cambridge: Harvard University Press, 2004.

Yingling, Erik. "Singing with the Savior: Reconstructing the Ritual Ring-dance in the *Gospel of the Savior*." *Apocrypha* 24 (2013) 255–79.

Zahn, Molly M. "Rewritten Scripture." In *The Oxford Handbook of The Dead Sea Scrolls*, edited by in Timothy H. Lim and John J. Collins, 323–36. Oxford Handbooks. Oxford: Oxford University Press, 2010.

Zuwiyya, Z. David, ed. *A Companion to Alexander Literature in the Middle Ages*. Brill's Companions to the Christian Tradition 29. Leiden: Brill, 2011.

Ancient Texts Index

HEBREW BIBLE/ OLD TESTAMENT

Genesis
1:27 — 183, 197

Leviticus
13—14 — 292

Deuteronomy
5 — 163
13:1-2 — 163
34:3 — 207, 295

Judges
14 — 295

1 Samuel
10:27 — 164
11:1 — 164

2 Kings
17:13 — 152
22:1 — 149

Chronicles
— 163

2 Chronicles
34:1 — 149

Ezra
3:2 — 152

5:1-2 — 152
7:6 — 152
7:10 — 152
7:12 — 152
9:10 — 152
10:3 — 152

Nehemiah
1:5-9 — 152
8:9-15 — 152
8:18 — 152
9:3 — 152
9:13-14 — 152
9:16 — 152

Psalms
— 140, 252
33 — 160
34 — 160
68:31 — 233-34, 236-38
78:65 — 235
110:1 — 264
119 — 158
139:16 — 151

Isaiah
— 252
35:5-6 — 300
54:4-6 — 253

Jeremiah
— 163, 164
23:6 — 237

345

Ezekiel

16:8	253
37:1	295

Daniel

	237, 241
2	227
7:13	166

Hosea

	253

DEUTEROCANONICAL WORKS

Wisdom of Solomon

	165
7:25–26	166

Sirach

44–49	152
49:10	153

2 Maccabees

3:1—4:6	287

4 Maccabees

3:19–4:14	287

Prayer of Manasseh

	152

OLD TESTAMENT PSEUDEPIGRAPHA

Apocalypse of Adam

	83–84

Apocalypse of Elijah

	230, 241
2.46–3.1	241

5 Baruch

	243

Cave of Treasures

	101, 236
24:24–26	236

1 Enoch

	97, 109, 143, 146, 150, 151, 171
1:9	166
17	151

2 Enoch

	109

4 Ezra

14:45–47	158

Jonah the Prophet

	83

Joseph and Aseneth

1—21	287

Jubilees

	163
2:23–24	158

Letter of Aristeas

	157

Life of Adam and Eve

	101

Odes of Solomon

	141, 150, 160

Psalms of Solomon

	140

Repentance of Adam

	115

History of Joseph

	xvii, 17, 271–78

Sibylline Oracles

	9, 23, 39, 41, 42, 44
6	44

Testament of Adam

	101

Testament of Job

3   287

Testament of Solomon

152

Testament of the Twelve Patriarchs

42, 151

DEAD SEA SCROLLS

Temple Scroll

163

Genesis Apocryphon

163
20   287

Reworked Pentateuch

163

OTHER JEWISH WRITINGS

Josephus

Against Apion

1:10–13   156
1:12   162
1:37–43   149, 158, 162

Antiquities

     39
1.6.1   240
10.49   149
20.161–71   287

Jewish War

2.254–63   287
7.7.4   240

Philo of Alexandria

De congressu eruditionis gratia

74–78   158

Legatio ad Gaium

3.244–45   158

Toledot Yeshu

xvii, 13, 15, 98, 111, 117–19, 264, 269
8.1–20   265
10   282

Tosefta *Chullin*

2:22–24   264

NEW TESTAMENT

Gospel of Matthew

66, 71, 86, 146, 163, 167, 170, 198, 217
2:1–2   44
5:22   211
10:28   210–11
11:25   214
11:27   208
12:26   208
13:16–17   154
18:3   188
18:9   211
18:10–14   195
19:1–9   197
19:12   184, 187, 196
19:17   211–13
22:37–38   213–14
23:13   215–16
25:30   208–209
25:41   208–209

Gospel of Mark

66, 71, 140, 141, 163, 167, 170, 217
1:1   164
1:8   181
3:28   188
4:9   154
4:11   181
5:31–32   197
5:45   202–205
10:1–10   197
10:3   197
10:11–12   188

10.13–16	189	7:58	283, 284, 287, 289
10:15	188	8	292
10:18	211–13	8:1	283, 284, 287, 289
11:27	205–207	8:3	283, 284, 287, 289
14:62	166	8:12	291
15:40	103	8:29—10:14	284
16:1	103	9:1–30	283, 284–94, 298–300
16:9–20	164	9:1–10a	17
		9:12	292

Gospel of Luke

66, 71, 154, 163, 167, 198, 217

1:1–3	163	9:10b–11	17
1:20	288	9:26	296
1:36	103	9:27	284
1:64	288	9:28–30	296
2:28	36	9:30	293
6:35–36	202–205	10	292
10:21	214	11:2–10	284
10:22	205	11:25	287, 293
11:52	215–16	11:30	287
12:4–5	210–11	12:25	287
14:35	154	13:1	287
15:3–7	195	13:2	287
16:18	197	13:4–12	289–90
17:20–21	176	13:7	287
18:19	211–13	13:9	285, 287
		13:21	287

Gospel of John

21, 63, 65, 66, 140, 151, 167, 170, 217

		14:8–10	265
		16:1–3	260
		16:9–20	284
1:6–8	178, 180	17:28	252
1:33	181	18:1–3	297
3:3	188	18:18–21	297
3:22	180	18:24–28	297
3:26	180	18:24	292
4:1	180	18:25	179
4:2	180, 181	19:1–7	297
14:6	255	19:3	179
		19:4	179

Acts

17, 86, 198, 245, 248, 260

		19:22	261
		19:24	293
		20:5—21:18	284
		21:17—22:29	283, 288
2:17–21	168	21:27–33	256
3:1–10	265	21:37—22:21	284
3:16	291	21:39	291, 293
4:12	291	21:40	287
5	292	22:2	287
5:1	292	22:3–21	283, 284–94, 298–300
5:34	116	22:3	116

22:4–5	287	4:10–11	296
22:6–8	286, 287	6:10	254
22:7	287	9:7	250
22:9–11	287	10:13	149
22:13	287	10:15	149
22:10–20	284	10:16	149
22:29—28:31	284	11:2–4	253
22:30—23:11	288	11:21–23	282
23–24	292	11:32–33	282, 287, 293
23:12–15	256	12:1–10	282
24:1–9	261		
25:13–26:32	283	## Galatians	
26:2–23	284–94, 298–300		17, 296
26:12–20a	284	1–2	286, 287
27:1–28:16	284	1:1	255
28:17–29	257	1:11–24	282
		1:11–12	255
## Romans		1:18	246
5:12–21	251	2:1–10	282
7:7	253	2:11–21	282
9:3–5	282	2:3–5	260
11:1–2a	282	2:6–9	255
12:10	254	2:19–20	296
13:5–7	254	2:11–14	246, 256, 265
15:9	254	3:27–28	177, 178, 182, 196
		6:14	249
## 1 Corinthians		6:16	149
1–4	179–80		
1:12–17	180	## Ephesians	
1:14–16	183		287
2:1	180	3:8	251
2:7	180	5:22–27	253
2:9	252	5:22–28	255
2:14–3:4	180	6:1	254
3:5–9	249	6:4	254
7:10–11	188, 196	6:5–6	255
9:1	282	6:9	255
11	196		
11:2–16	177, 178	## Philippians	
12:13	183	1:21–24	249
13	296	1:25–26	249
15:1–11	282	3:4b–6	282
15:9	251		
15:20–23	251	## Colossians	
15:45–49	251	1:15	255
		3:18–19	255
## 2 Corinthians		3:20	254
3:3–6	162	3:22–24	255
4:6	282	4:1	255

2 Thessalonians
2:15 — 250

1 Timothy
151, 170
1:4 — 143
1:5 — 254
1:17 — 255
1:20 — 261
4:7 — 143
6:8 — 254
6:17 — 254
6:20 — 143

2 Timothy
151, 170
1:1 — 296
2:17 — 261
2:22 — 254

Titus
151, 170

Philemon
255

Hebrews
86, 151, 160, 170, 172
1:1–13 — 92
1:3 — 166
10:7 — 166

1 Peter
16, 140, 160, 250, 254
2:9 — 254

James
151, 168, 172, 189
2:11–17 — 253
3:13—4:2 — 253
4:12–19 — 253
5:9–10 — 253

2 Peter
16, 140, 151, 160, 170, 250
1:13–14 — 253
3:14 — 253
3:15–16 — 260

1 John
151

2 John
151, 166, 170

3 John
151, 166, 170

Jude
140, 151, 160, 172
14 — 166

Revelation
72, 86, 151, 160, 170, 172, 218, 221
1:8 — 157
2:7 — 154
2:17 — 154
2:29 — 154
3:6 — 154
3:13 — 154
3:22 — 154
22:13 — 157

EARLY CHRISTIAN WRITINGS

3 Corinthians
141, 150, 152, 160

Act of Peter
137, 143, 287

Acts of Andrew
5, 70

Acts of John
48, 70
88–94 — 101
94–96 — 99, 136–37
97–102 — 99

Acts of Matthew and Andrew
275

Acts of Paul
17, 248, 262, 282–83, 289

1.7	259
3.3	266, 293
9	294
9.5–11	294–300

Acts of Peter

15, 139, 143, 246, 248, 261

6	246
20–21	101

Acts of Peter and the Twelve Apostles

13, 139

Acts of Philip

17, 57, 70, 96, 183, 198, 270

Acts of Pilate

30

Acts of the Holy Apostles Peter and Paul

2–4	258
2	260
5–10	259
21–22	259
23	259
24	260
29	253
26	254
57–59	255
60	255
61	255

Acts of Thomas

8, 134–36, 271, 275

143	101

Acts of Xanthippe and Polyxena

16

Adamantius

Dialogue on the Orthodox Faith

1.23	206

Allogenes

73

Antonius of Placenza

Itinerarium

18	241–42

1 Apocalypse of James

138

27.25—28.2 (Al-Minya Codex)

104

2 Apocalypse of James

84, 138

Apocalypse of Paul

9, 97, 275

Apocalypse of Paul (Coptic)

295

Apocalypse of Peter

72, 143, 151

Apocalypse of Pseudo-Methodius

228–44

5.9	229
10.6	229, 230
13.2	229, 230
13.11—14.6	228

Apocalypse of the Virgin

16, 98, 219

Apocryphon of James

20, 134, 138

Apocryphon of John

74, 134, 137, 138, 143

Apology of Phileas

160

Apostolic Constitutions

97

Ancient Texts Index

Apostolic Tradition
97

Aphrahat
Demonstrations
5	227
5.1	217

On Wars
13–14	227
24	227

Arabic Infancy Gospel
17–18, 125

Armenian Infancy Gospel
13, 111, 113, 119–24, 128, 130–31
6	114
9:3–4	114
11:9–23	100
19:1	115
19:3	115
19:4	115
20:1	116, 122
20:2	116, 122
20:3	114, 119, 120–21
20:6	116
20:7	123
20:8	123

Athanasius of Alexandria
39th Festal Letter
148, 150

Augustine
Confessions
8.12.29	35

De doctrina christiana
2.32–72	161

Book of the Resurrection of Jesus Christ by Bartholomew the Apostle
96, 98

Book of the Rooster
9, 11, 96, 98

Book of Thomas
138

Books of Jeu
137, 138

Chronicle of Zuqnin
100

1 Clement
42, 66, 71, 140
7.2	149

2 Clement
67, 71, 140
5.4	211
12.2	177

Clement of Alexandria
Excerpta ex Theodoto
14.3	211

Stromateis
3.13.92	177

Dance of the Savior
99

Decretum Gelasianum
41

Dialogue of the Savior
20, 138, 195

Didache
80, 97, 146, 150, 151
1:3	217

Didascalia Apostolorum
97, 261

Discourse of the Savior
99

Doctrine of Addai
49

Egerton Gospel
65–67, 73, 193

Epiphanius of Salamis

Ancoratus

39

De mensuribus et ponderibus

| 22–23 | 158 |

Panarion

30.16.5	216
30.16.6–9	282
33.10.5	205
34.18.10–11	212
39	167
42.11.6	214
42.11.17	212
66.22.4	205

Epistle of Barnabas
71, 72, 80, 140, 150, 151, 160

Epistle of Pseudo-Dionysius the Areopagite to Timothy
16

Epistle of the Apostles

67

4	113
9–10	103
29–34	282

Epistle to Marcellinus
140

Eusebius of Caesarea

Demonstratio evangelica

| 15, frag. 1 | 227 |

Historia ecclesiastica

1.13	39
2.1.13	233
3.25	45
3.25.1–7	150
3.25.1	167
3.25.2–3	166
4.18.9	207–209
4.26.13–14	152
5.16.3–4	168
6.12.3–6	167
6.25.1–14	149–150
6.25.3–6	167

Gospel of Barnabas
53

Gospel of Jesus' Wife
58, 75–76

Gospel of Judas
6, 8, 12, 73, 75, 88–90, 98, 108, 167

Gospel of Mary
5, 13, 74, 98, 137, 143, 195

Gospel of Nicodemus
10, 16, 17, 25, 47–48, 57, 96

Gospel of Peter
20, 21, 23, 65, 67, 69, 143, 167, 174, 193, 211

Gospel of Philip
141, 195, 197

| 32 | 98 |
| 55 | 98 |

Gospel of Pseudo-Matthew
16, 17, 100, 125

Gospel of the Ebionites
216

Gospel of the Egyptians
177, 189

Gospel of the Hebrews
72, 189, 193

Gospel of the Savior (Apocryphon Berolinense/ Argentoratense)
12, 87–88, 100, 137

Gospel of Thomas

xiii, 8, 13, 14, 20, 21, 62, 64, 65–67, 69, 73, 83, 87, 108, 133, 137, 138, 139, 141, 173, 175, 176, 189, 194–98

Prol.	133
2	140
3	140
5	140
18	140, 184, 196
19	140
22	14, 177, 184, 187–88, 196
31	140
37	183, 196
39	215
42	174
61	104
67	140
69	140
80	140
91	140
97	174
98	174
114	98

Gospel of Truth

20, 195

Haran Gawaita

179

Hippolytus of Rome

Refutatio omnium haeresium

7.30.6	212
8.12	168

History of the Blessed Virgin Mary

17–18

Hypostasis of the Archons

138

Infancy Gospel of Thomas

9, 13, 26, 69, 70, 100, 138

6–7	111, 115
6:2	116
14	111, 115

Irenaeus

Adversus haereses

1.10.1	149, 168
1.20.1	112–13
1.20.2	212
1.31.1	167
2.23.3	209
3.3.3	152
3.11.8	152
3.12.15	152
3.14.1–15	152
3.21.3–4	152
3.4.2	149, 168
4.6.1–3	208
4.6.2	207–208
5.26.3	209

Isidore of Seville

Origenes

6.3.3–4	157

Jerome

Epistulae

58.10	165
77.8	240

De viris illustribus

74.1	165

Justin Martyr

1 Apology

10.1–8	158
15.9	217
15.13	203–205
16.1–2	213
16.6	213–14
19.7	210–11
20.5	158
26.8	202
54.1–2	158
63.3	205–207

Dialogue with Trypho

	202
17.4	215–16

Ancient Texts Index 355

67	149, 153
76.4	213
76.5	208
96.3	203–205
101.2	211–13
120.6	213

Syntagma

15, 202, 204, 206, 207, 212–16

Letter from Heaven

219

Letter of Lentulus

25, 26, 41

Letter of Peter to Philip

138

Life of Constantine

39

Life of the Man of God

275

Manichean Psalm-Book

39.27	217

Martyrdom of St. Arethas and His Companions

39	242

Martyrdom of St. Julian

143

Melito of Sardis

Homily on the Passover

160

Nonnos of Panapolis

Paraphrase of the Gospel of John

39

Opus imperfectum in Matthaeum

100–101

Passion of the Holy Apostles Peter and Paul

1–2	257
3	260
5	253
8	252
36–38	255
39	255
40	255
41	255–56

Origen

De principis

1.3	151
4.35	151
4.1.31	151

Papyrus Oxyrhynchus 840

70

Petition of Euthalius

152

Pistis Sophia

13, 137, 138

Protevangelium of James

17, 42, 70, 141, 160, 198

Prudentius

Peristephanon

12.7–58	267

Pseudo-Abdias

37, 41

Pseudo-Clement

15, 96, 97, 127, 247

Homilies/Klementia

1.19.5–6	207
2	179
2.16–17	282
2.19–20	217
2.51.1	216
2.51.2	216
3.18.3	215

3.19.3	217
3.50.1	215
3.50.2	216
3.57	203–205
8.4.1	213
8.21	208
11.35–56	282
11.35.3	208
12.29.1	217
12.32.1	217
15.5.5	213
16.15.1	207
17.4–5	211
17.4.2–3	212
17.4.3	205
17.5.2	210–11
17.7.1	213–14
17.13–19	282
18.1–2	204
18.1.3	212
18.3.4	211–13
18.4.2	205–208
18.14–15	214
18.15	216
18.15.1	214
18.15.7	214
18.16.2	215
18.20.3	216
18.20.4	216
19.2.3	208
19.2.5	208–209
19.20.1	217

Recognitions/Recognition

1.39.1	216
1.16.5–6	207
1.54.7	214
1.71–72	282
2.30.1	215–16
2.45.5	207
2.46.3–4	216
2.46.3	214
2.47.3	205–208
3.4.6	209, 210–11
3.38	204
4.34	208
4.4.3	213
5.13.2	203–205

Pseudo-Cyril of Jerusalem

On the Life and Passion of Christ

	99, 101

Pseudo-Ephrem

Homily on the End

8	228

Pseudo-Linus

Martyrdom of Blessed Peter the Apostle

7	248
8	249, 250
9	250
10	250
12	250–51
14	251
15	251, 252

Pseudo-Narsai

Memre on Joseph

	272, 277

Pseudo-Prochorus

Acts of John

	40

Q

	15, 67, 73, 197
3:16	181
6:20b	189
7:35	180
10	190
10:21–22	181
11:39–52	191
12:10	188
16:18	188

Questions of Bartholomew

	96–98

Repose of the Evangelist John

	152

Ancient Texts Index 357

Revelation of the Magi
27, 69, 100–102

Right Ginza
7	181
8	181

Rufinus
Origenis in Numeros homiliae
28.2	151

Origenis in Jonam homiliae
6.42	151

Secret Gospel of Mark
xix, 3, 5, 9, 21, 25, 26, 50, 65, 67–68, 90–92, 180, 182

Shepherd of Hermas
42, 44, 71, 140, 146, 150, 151, 160, 168, 171, 188
4.1.6	188

Socrates Scholasticus
Historia ecclesiastica
1.17	265

Sophia of Jesus Christ
137, 143

Teaching of the Apostles
261–63

Tertullian
Adversus Marcionem
1.2.2	209
2.13.5	213
4.8.7	211
4.17.6	204
4.25.1	214
4.25.10	206
4.27–28	215

De praescriptione haereticorum
21.2	206

Theodoret
Historia ecclesiastica
4.19	39
6.18	39

Three Steles of Seth
138, 179

Tiburtine Sibyl
15, 49, 218–44
6–7	226
8–9	226
10	226–27, 235, 237
16	16

Transitus Mariae/ Liber Requiei
97, 98

Vengeance of the Savior
10

Vision of Paul
115

MEDIEVAL CHRISTIAN LITERATURE

Agapius of Menbidj
Kitab Al-'Unvan / Histoire universelle
2.1	263

Bandlet of Righteousness
102

Fifteen Oes
105–106

Revelation about the Passion of Christ
102, 104, 107–108

Revelation of Christ's Wounds
105

Story of the Passion of Christ
11, 102–108

Suda
39, 40

GRECO-ROMAN WRITINGS

Alexander Romance
239–40

Apuleius
Metamorphoses
11.1–30   287

Aristotle
Rhetorica
3.19.1   156

Chariton
5.6–8   289

Homer
Iliad
156–157

Odyssey
156–157

Lives of Ten Orators
156

Plato
Phaedrus
275   162

Xenophon
An Ephesian Tale
287

ISLAMIC LITERATURE

Umm al-kitâb
13, 111, 123
10   128
12–14   126–27
13   128, 129
21   128
32   128

Qur'ān
3:7   128
3:46   129
5:110   129
13:39   123
19:29   129
85:21–22   123, 128–29

Abū Jaʻfar Muhammad b. Jarīr al-Tabarī
Ta'rīkh al-rusul wa'l-mulūk
741   263

Lives of the Prophets
125, 126

Subject Index

Association catholique pour l'étude de la Bible au Canada (ACÉBAC), 26
Association pour l'étude de la littérature apocryphe chrétienne (AELAC), xi, xiv, xv, 1, 8, 9, 11, 18, 26, 28–33, 43, 48, 50, 52–57, 68, 95–96, 110
Aleppo Codex, 164
Alexander the Great, 157, 237, 238–40
Al-Minya Codex, 97, 104
ancient fiction, 85–86
apologetics (against Christian Apocrypha), 7, 22, 60, 133, 195–95
apocrypha,
  anthologies, 1–2, 4, 6, 11, 36–44, 55, 132, 139, 221
  artistic representations, 16, 48–49
  early dating of, xvi, 4, 60, 73, 108
  definition, xiv, xv, 20, 32, 34–36, 41, 45–46, 55, 65, 133, 220–21
  digital humanities and, xvii–xviii, 76, 270–81
  distinction from canonical texts, 69, 71, 74, 75, 76, 93–94
  Islam and, 123–31
  modern, 36
  re-use of, 95–110
Apollos, 179–80, 197, 249, 292
Apostolic Fathers, 43, 46, 62–63, 72, 80, 152, 168
Aristotle, 156
asceticism, 175, 177, 178, 191, 192, 196–97, 295

Athanasius of Alexandria, 72, 148, 159

Bauer Hypothesis, 3, 6–7, 18, 64–65

Canadian Society of Biblical Studies (CSBS), 26
canon, xiv, xv, xvii, 67, 141–42, 145–72
  Augustine and, 161
  Coptic, 141
  definition, 148–55
  Ethiopic, 141, 152
  Eusebius and, 149–51, 165–66
  Greco-Roman antecedents, 155–59
  Irenaeus and, 152, 155, 161, 167
  Josephus and, 158
  Martin Luther and, 171–72
  Melito of Sardis and, 152
  Muratorian Canon, 14, 150, 164–66, 167, 168
  Origen and, 150, 159, 161, 165, 167
  Stichometry of Nicephorus, 72, 172
  Syriac, 141
Cicero, 109
Claremont Graduate University, 5, 12, 18, 76, 81–84
Codex Alexandrinus, 71, 140
Codex Askewianus, 62, 137
Codex Berolinensis, 137, 143
Codex Bezae, 284
Codex Brucianus, 62, 137
Codex Panopolitanus, 143
Codex Sinaiticus, 71, 140, 151, 160, 164, 186

Codex Vaticanus, 151, 164
Constantine, emperor, 15, 39, 151, 171, 223–24, 226–27, 241
Coptic Gnostic Library Project, 5, 6, 8, 12, 82–84, 89
Coptic Library of Nag Hammadi series (BCNH), 8, 27
Corpus Christianorum Series Apocryphorum, 1, 9, 69, 70, 204, 271, 294
Crosby-Schøyen Codex MS 193, 83
Council of Nicea, 169, 171
Council of Trent, 152, 172

Da Vinci Code, The, 6, 22, 30
Dead Sea Scrolls, 163, 164
Diogenes of Sinope, 190–91
Dositheus, 179

Gnosticism (Gnostics), (see also Valentinus, Marcion, Marcos, and Sethianism), xiv, 5, 13, 27, 30, 64, 74, 81, 86–87, 98, 99, 112, 124, 132–44, 155, 167, 168, 177, 194
Gregory 1505 (manuscript), 160

Hadrian, emperor, 283
hagiography, 48, 49
Harvard Divinity School, xii, 3, 12, 18, 58–77
Hill Museum and Manuscript Library, 274, 279
Historical Jesus, xiii, 3, 4, 7, 14, 18, 21, 22, 25, 59, 63–64, 70, 73, 75, 173–99
Homer, 156–58, 186

Ignatius of Antioch, 42, 43, 67, 169
Islam, origins, 220, 228–34, 243–44

Jesus Seminar, 3–4, 14, 73, 173–74, 177, 184–85, 194–95
John the Baptist, 103, 178–80
Judas Iscariot, 98
Julian (emperor), 224, 236

Laval University, 8, 18, 27
Leningrad Codex, 164

Mandaeans, 63, 179–81
Mani, Manichaeans, 8, 205
Marcion, Marcionites, 7, 15, 154–55, 200–217,
Marcos, Marcosians, 112–13, 212
Mary Magdalene, 98, 102–4, 108
Mary (mother), 98, 114, 122, 125
Montanus, Montanism, 155, 168
More New Testament Apocrypha volumes, 3, 9, 15, 16, 18, 110

Nag Hammadi library, xiv, 5, 7, 8, 13, 12, 27, 37, 64, 73, 74, 76, 81–84, 85, 87, 97, 109, 134, 136, 137–39, 142–43
North American Society for the Study of Christian Apocryphal Literature (NASSCAL), 18

orthodoxy and heresy, 7, 64–65, 74, 133, 143, 168, 198
Oxyrhynchus Papyri, 24, 137–38, 186

Papias of Hierapolis, 67
papyri:
  P46, 151
  P52, 66
  P72, 140, 160
  P75, 161
Passion of the Christ, The (film), 32, 104
Paul (apostle), 16, 66, 127, 140, 154, 168, 170, 178, 179–80, 182–83, 197–98
  iconography of, 266–69
  conversion accounts of, 17, 255, 282–301
Peter (apostle), 16, 245–66
  iconography of, 266–69
Plato, 109, 133, 177
Priscilla and Aquila, 179, 294, 295, 297–98
Pseudepigrapha, xvi, 8, 14, 30, 43, 45, 46, 55, 109, 221, 272

Qasr el-Wizz Codex, 99

Salome, 103, 104, 108

Septuagint, 140, 159, 164, 299
Serapion, 167
Sethianism, 180
Simon the Magician, 127, 179, 211, 246, 252, 254–57, 259, 261
Society of Biblical Literature (SBL), xi, 2, 9, 13, 19, 88, 91, 158
Synoptic Gospels, xiii, 67, 72, 73, 163, 174–76, 178, 180, 182, 185, 186–91, 193, 195, 197

Tacitus, 109, 186
Tertullian of Carthage, 98, 168, 204–5
Thucydides, 109

Valentinus, Valentinianism, 99, 112, 134, 136
Victorinus of Pettau, 150, 165

York Christian Apocrypha Symposium Series, 1, 10, 11–18, 33, 50, 77, 91, 287

Modern Authors Index

Aasgaard, Reidar, 111
Abrahamyan, Ashot G., 115
Adler, Elkan N., 117
Aerts, Willem J., 230, 231
Aghabeki, Karapet, 115
Aichele, George, 150, 162, 164
Alexander, Paul J., 218, 219–26, 229–44
Allison, Dale C., 175
Amersfoort, Jacobus van, 215
Amiot, François, 52
Amsler, Frédéric, 70, 201
Andrist, Patrick, 26
Anthony, Sean W., 111, 124–31
Armstrong, Jonathan J., 159, 165
Ashbrook Harvey, Susan, 244
Askeland, Christian, 75
Attridge, Harold, 4
Aune, David E., 20, 44, 189–90

Backus, Irena Dorota, 24, 38–42
Bagnall, Roger S., 66
Barnes, Timothy D., 262
Barnstone, Willis, 136, 143, 181
Barrett, David P., 160
Barth, Karl, xii, xiii
Barton, John, 154
Basset, René, 218, 232
Bauckham, Richard, 3, 25, 31, 103, 110, 163, 219, 283
Baudoin, Anne-Catherine, 19, 20
Bauer, Walter, 6–7, 36, 64–65, 171, 185
Baum, Armin Daniel, 44
Baur, Ferdinand Christian, 247

Bausi, Alessandro, 95
Bazzana, Giovanni, 186
Beasley, Jonathan, 75
Becker, Adam H., 33
Beckwith, Roger T., 166
Bédier, Joseph, 47
Bedjan, Paul, 272
Bedrosian, Robert, 115
Bekkum, Wout Jac van, 243
Bellinzoni, Arthur J., 202, 205, 208, 213
Betz, Hans Dieter, xii
Bianchi, Ugo, 135
Bickerman, Elias, 45
Bienert, Wolfgang A., xii
Bihlmeyer, Karl, 211
Bilby, Mark, 16
Bisson, Gisèle, 10
Blount, Justine Ariel, xv, 143
Bock, Darrell L., 3
Bockmuehl, Marcus, 127, 147
Bonnet, Maximilian, xvii, 70
Borg, Marcus, 175, 176
Böttrich, Christfried, 27
Bousset, Wilhelm, 206, 223
Boustan, Ra'anan S., 96
Bouvier, Bertrand, xiii, 70, 108
Bovini, Giuseppe, 269
Bovon, François, xi, xii, xiii, xviii, 1, 5, 7, 9, 11, 12, 17, 30, 31, 32–33, 34, 42, 52, 55, 59, 68–73, 74, 75, 76, 108, 109, 110, 142, 270
Boyarin, Daniel, 33, 117
Brakke, David, 134, 136
Brandes, Wolfram, 223, 244

Modern Authors Index

Bremmer, Jan, 30
Brock, Ann Graham, 5, 29, 31, 142
Brock, Sebastian P., 114, 228–29, 230, 271, 272
Broek, Roelof van den, 99, 101
Brossard-Dandré, Michèle, 10
Brown, Ian, 10
Brown, Scott G., 9
Bujanda, Jesús Martinez, 43
Bultmann, Rudolf, xii, xiii, xviii, 7, 62–63, 81, 178
Budge, E. A. Wallis, 103
Burke, Tony, xi, xviii, 2, 3, 7, 9–10, 19, 21, 22, 25, 26–27, 30, 31, 32, 33, 34, 46, 49, 56, 69, 70, 74, 76, 110, 111, 115, 116, 132, 138, 173, 186, 226
Burnet, Régis, 26
Burris, Catherine, 6
Burtea, Bogdan, 102
Buttrick, George Arthur, 89
Butts, Aaron, 272

Cadbury, Henry J., 283, 287
Callon, Callie, 10
Cameron, Averil, 244
Cameron, Ron, 4, 136
Campenhausen, Hans von, 145, 154–55
Cardinal, Pierre, 28
Carlson, Stephen C., 91
Cartlidge, David R., 49, 246, 269
Castalio, Sebastian, 42
Cazelais, Serge, 28
Cerquiglini, Bernard, 47
Charlesworth, James H., 21, 22, 23–24, 25, 47, 221
Cherix, Pierre, 96, 294
Chernetsov, Sevir, 102
Cirillo, Luigi, 53
Clark, Elizabeth A., xii
Clivaz, Claire, 278
Cobb, James Harrel, xii
Cohen, Leonardo, 218
Cohn, Norman, 218
Collins, John. J., 221
Comfort, Philip W., 160
Constantinou, Eugenia Scarvelis, 151

Conybeare, Frederick C., 115
Conzelmann, Hans, 252, 291
Côté, Dominique, 9, 96, 127
Cowley, Roger W., 152
Credner, Karl August, 200
Crossan, John Dominic, 4, 20, 21, 60, 64, 67–68, 73, 174–78, 184, 187–90, 193–95, 197
Cureton, William, 261, 262–63
Cwikla, Anna, 10
Czachesz, Istaván, 283

Daniel-Rops, Henri, 36, 52
Darrow, William R., 60–61
Davies, Stevan L., 184
Davila, James R., 3, 14, 31, 109, 110
Davis, Stephen J., 111
Debié, Muriel, 101
Deichmann, Friedrich W., 269
Denis, Albert-Marie, 45
Denzey Lewis, Nicola, xiv–xv, 6, 10, 13, 14, 27, 73, 112, 133, 143
Desreumaux, Alain, 19, 33, 52, 275
Detoraki, Marina, 242
Deutsch, Yaacov, 117
Dewey, Arthur J., 185
Dhorme, Édouard, 30
Dibelius, Martin, 283
Dilley, Paul, 99
Dillmann, August, 109
DiTommaso, Lorenzo, 8, 14, 49, 95, 108, 109
Donzel, Emeri J. van, 240
Drijvers, Han J. W., 135, 201, 206
Dubois, Jean-Daniel, 10, 19, 27, 33, 48–49, 52–53, 55
Dunderberg, Ismo, 134
Dunn, James D. G., 154
Dunn, Peter, 56
Dunning, Benjamin, 5
Dupont, Jacques, 283
Dupont-Sommer, André, 30
Duval, Rubens, 272
Dzon, Mary, 9, 10, 17, 48, 56

Eastman, David L., 16, 245, 266, 267
Ebied, Rifaat Y., 218

Ehrman, Bart D., 2, 6, 7, 30, 46, 97, 143, 161, 196
Elliott, J. Keith, 2, 3, 23, 27, 49, 138, 246, 269
Elliott, Ralph H., 81
Emerson, Ralph Waldo, 12, 61–62
Emmel, Stephen, 88
Epp, Eldon Jay, 81, 141, 163, 284
Erbetta, Mario, 16, 52, 138, 219
Erho, Ted, 109
Esbroeck, Michel van, 219
Evans, Craig A., 27
Evans, Ernest, 204

Fabricius, Johann Albertus, xv, xvi, 20, 23, 36, 37–38
Falk, Ze'ev W., 117
Fee, Gordon D., 180
Fiey, Jean Maurice, 274
Filippani-Ronconi, Pio, 124
Fillmore-Handlon, Charlotte, 48
Fitzmyer, Joseph A., 194, 198
Flower, Robin, 106, 107
Flusser, David, 226
Förster, Hans, 97
Förster, Niclas, 112
Foster, Paul, 21
Frankenberg, Wilhelm, 202
Frankfurter, David, 230, 241
Frémaux, Michel, 53
Frey, Albert, 10
Frilingos, Chris, 6, 111
Fritz, Kurt von, 44
Funk, Robert W., 4, 174, 184
Funk, Wolf-Peter, 2, 8
Fusella, Luigi, 103

Gagné, André, 8–9, 23, 28
Gagné, Hervé, 8
Galizzi, Flavio, 106
Gallagher, Edmon L., 159
Gardner-Smith, Percival, 21
Garstad, Benjamin, 230
Gasque, W. Ward, 283
Gaster, Moses, 218
Gathercole, Simon, 193
Gaudard, François, 104
Geerard, Maurice, 54

Geoltrain, Pierre, 1, 30, 32, 33, 34, 52, 56, 110
Gero, Stephen, 111, 116
Geyer, Paul, 242
Gieseler, J. K. L., 247
Ginzberg, Louis, 117
Goehring, James E., 83
Goldstein, Miriam, 118
Goldstein, Morris, 265
Goodacre, Mark, 15, 175, 186, 193, 197, 198
Goodspeed, Edgar J., xii, 36, 46, 145
Goodstein, Laurie, 76
Gounelle, Rémi, 10, 24, 47
Graffin, René, 227
Grafton, Anthony, 24
Gregory, Andrew, 278
Greisiger, Lutz, 238
Grenfell, Bernard P., 24, 137, 186
Gribetz, Sarit K., 98
Griffith, Sidney H., 228
Gros, Paul, 30
Grosjean, Jean, 30
Grosseteste, Robert, 42
Grynaeus, Johann J., 42
Guignard, Christophe, 47
Guillaumont, Antoine, 30

Haelewyck, Jean-Claude, 101
Haelst, Joseph van, 160
Haenchen, Ernst, 283, 291
Hagen, Joost L., 99
Hägg, Tomas, 156
Hahneman, Geoffrey, 164–65
Halévy, Joseph, 243
Halm, Heinz, 124, 125, 128
Hamidović, David, 278
Harkavy, Abraham, 117
Harnack, Adolf von, xii, 36, 43, 62, 145, 154–55, 201, 202, 204, 213
Harris, J. Rendell, 86
Heal, Kristian S., xvii, 2, 17, 27, 101, 271
Heath, Jane, 27, 43
Hedrick, Charles W., 4, 5, 12–13, 78–94, 97, 99, 283, 291
Heikel, Ivar A., 227
Henderson, William, 106

Modern Authors Index

Hennecke, Edgar, xii, xv–xvi, 25, 43, 52, 53, 65, 220–21
Herold, Johannes Basilius, 42
Herrenschmidt, Clarisse, 34
Hilberg, Isidor, 240
Hilgenfeld, Adolf, 201, 202
Hills, Julian V., 4, 113, 283
Himmelfarb, Martha, 243
Hock, Ronald F., 4, 6
Hoffmann, Johann Georg Ernst, 236
Hodgson, Roger, Jr., 86–87
Holdenried, Anke, 218, 219–20, 222
Hone, William, 46
Hoover, Roy W., 174, 184
Horbury, William, 117, 264
Horn, Cornelia, 13, 49, 56, 109
Hovhanessian, Vahan S., 152
Hoyland, Robert G., 228, 229
Hubai, Péter, 99
Hull, Robert F., Jr. 159, 161
Hunt, Arthur S., 24, 137, 186
Huskinson, Janet M., 246

Irmscher, Johannes, 179
Ivanow, Wladimir, 123–25, 127–29
Izydorczyk, Zbigniew, 10, 19, 47–48, 56

James, M. R., 2, 52, 133, 138
Jennings, Louis B., xii
Jenott, Lance, 97
Jenson, Robert W., 169
Jeremias, Joachim, 24–25, 176
Johnson, Scott, 271
Johnson, Luke Timothy, 60
Jonas, Hans, 132, 135
Jones, F. Stanley, xiii, 2, 4, 6, 15, 29, 56, 96, 201, 204, 206–7, 247
Jones, Jeremiah, 46
Junod, Éric, xv, 28, 33, 34, 48, 52, 55, 70, 96, 137, 221

Kaestli, Jean-Daniel, 1, 30, 31, 33, 34, 52, 55, 70, 96, 100, 110, 137
Kaler, Michael, 8
Kalin, Everett R., 168
Kampers, Franz, 223
Karras, Ruth Mazo, 118

Kasser, Rodolphe, 8, 89, 90, 104, 283, 294, 295, 296
Kelley, Nicole, 5, 96
Kenney, Theresa M., 48
Kerchove, Anna Van den, 27, 42
King, Karen L., 4, 5, 12, 59, 68, 73–75, 76, 134, 136
Kinzig, Wolfram, 43
Kiraz, George A., 272
Klauck, Hans-Josef, 21
Klauser Theodor, 269
Klijn, Albertus Frederik Johannes, 101
Kline, Leslie L., 202, 208, 209, 213, 216
Kloppenborg, John S., 4, 15, 176, 187, 188, 189, 190
Köstenberger, Andreas J., 7
Koester, Helmut, xii, xviii, 3–5, 7, 12, 21, 31, 59, 60, 62–68, 69, 71, 72, 73, 76, 171, 182, 194, 195
Kohlberg, Etan, 129
Konrad, Robert, 223, 233, 236
Kortekaas, Georgius A. A., 230, 231
Kraft, András, 231
Kraft, Robert A., 6, 192
Krauss, Samuel, 117
Kripal, Jeffrey, 61
Kroll, Wilhelm, 240
Kruger, Michael J., 7
Krupp, Michael, 118
Kübler, Bernhard Gustav Adolf, 240

Landau, Brent, xii, xviii, 2, 3, 5, 12, 19, 26–27, 30, 31, 33, 49, 56, 100–101, 110, 173, 226
Landes, Richard A., 49
Lange, Armin, 147, 163
Layton, Bentley, 4, 136, 143
Lazius, Wolfgang, 41
Le Boulluec, Alain, 19, 45, 50
Lefèvre d'Étaples, Jacques, 40
Leloir, Louis, 54
Leslau, Wolf, 243
Létourneau, Pierre, 28
Léturmy, Michel, 30
Lidzbarski, Mark, 181
Lim, Timothy H., 153
Lincicum, David, 247

Link, Samuel Wolf, 272
Lipsett, Diane, 6
Lipsius, Richard Adelbert, xvii, 53, 70, 202, 204
Lohfink, Gerhard, 283
Lüdemann, Gerd, 283, 291, 292
Lührmann, Dieter, 211
Luijendijk, AnneMarie, 5
Luisier, Philippe, 294, 295, 296
Luz, Ulrich, 68

MacDonald, Dennis R., 5, 157, 177, 178, 182, 283
Madelung, Wilferd, 124
Magdalino, Paul, 219, 244
Mahé, Jean-Pierre, 30
Marjanen, Antii, 140
Mallette, Karla, 109
Mango, Cyril A., 244
Margolis, Max L., 145
Marguerat, Daniel, 21, 283
Markschies, Christoph, xiv, xv–xvi, xvii, 1, 2, 27, 34, 43–44, 48, 97, 134
Marrassini, Paolo, 102
Martin, Anick, 50
Martinez, Francisco Javier, 230, 236, 238
Marrou, Henri-Irénée, 156
Matthews, Christopher R., 31, 70, 142
McAuliffe, Jane Dammen, 123
McDonald, Lee Martin, xvii, 13–14, 46–47, 147, 149, 151, 152, 154, 156, 158, 169
McGinn, Bernard, 218–19, 221, 223–24, 231, 233
McNamara, Martin, 70
Mead, G. R. S., 135
Meeks, Wayne A., 178, 182, 183
Meerson, Michael, 117
Meier, John P., 20, 189–90, 194, 198
Melikʻ-Ôhanjanyan, K. A., 115
Ménard, Jacques É., 8
Merz, Annette, 188, 193–94
Metzger, Bruce M., 141, 158, 161
Meyer, Marvin W., 4, 5, 104, 181
Miceli, Calogero, 26
Michaéli, Franck, 30

Michard, Jean-Pierre, 28
Michel, Charles, 52
Migne, Jacques-Paul, 24
Mimouni, Simon C., 97, 219
Miller Parmenter, Dorina, 147
Miller, Robert J., 4, 175, 182
Minov, Sergey, 272
Mirecki, Paul A., 88, 97
Möhring, Hannes, 223, 233, 239, 242
Morgan, Teresa, 156, 247
Morris, Bridget, 106
Mroczek, Eva, 76
Mueller, James R., 23

Naïmi, Mustapha, 28
Nausea, Friedrich, 41
Navtanovich, Liudmila, 109
Neander, Michael, xvi, 38–42
Neusner, Jacob, 127
Newman, Hillel, 264
Nicholson, Oliver, 244
Nicklas, Tobias, 23, 34
Niclós, José-Vicente, 117
Nock, Arthur Darby, 62
Nöldeske, Theodor, xii
Nongbri, Brent, 66
Norelli, Enrico, 21, 97, 202, 204

Olster, David, 219
Olympiou, Nikolaos, 90
Osthövener, Claus-Dieter, xiii
Ott, Claudia, 240

Pagels, Elaine, 4, 5, 6, 184, 194
Painchaud, Louis, 8
Palmer, Andrew, 228, 229, 235, 237
Panayatov, Alexander, 3, 31, 110
Pantuck, Allan, 91
Papandreou, Damaskinos, xii
Paupert, Catherine, 48–49
Parsons, Mikeal C., 283
Pasquali, Giorgio, 47, 108
Patterson, Stephen J., xiii, xvi, 4, 14–15, 73, 140, 173, 175, 176, 190, 192–99
Paulissen, Lucie, 111
Pearson, Birger, 91
Peeters, Paul, 52, 274

Pennec, Hervé, 107
Penner, Kenneth M., 166
Perrin, Norman, 176
Pervo, Richard I., 283, 284, 287, 289, 292
Pesce, Mauro, 24
Petersen, Erik, 20
Pettipiece, Timothy, 2, 8, 10
Pfister, Friedrich, 240
Phenix, Robert, 56
Philonenko, Marc, 30
Piazzesi, Vittorio, 106
Picard, Jean-Claude, 27, 33, 96
Pick, Bernhard, 34–36
Piemonte, Gustavo A., 101
Piovanelli, Pierluigi, xiii–xiv, 2, 9, 11–12, 19, 25, 28, 31–32, 33, 50, 56, 95, 96, 97, 98, 99, 101, 102, 103, 109, 110, 137, 243
Platt, Rutherford Hayes, Jr., 46
Playoust, Catharine, 5
Pleše, Zlatko, 6, 143
Podskalsky, Gerhard, 223, 227, 230
Poffet, Jean-Michel Poffet, 21
Pöhner, Ralph, 90
Poirier, Paul-Hubert, 8, 9, 10, 25, 28, 30, 135
Porter, Stanley E., 2
Porter, Wendy, 2
Pratten, Benjamin P., 261
Prieur, Jean-Marc, 52, 70

Quantin, Jean-Louis, 24
Quarry, John, 206
Quispel, Gilles, 204

Racine, Jean-François, 28
Rangheri, Maurizio, 223, 234, 242
Rappé, Donald, 4
Rasinnus, Tuomas, 8
Reed, Annette Y., 6, 15, 20, 27, 33, 37, 44, 45, 96, 101, 109, 110
Reeves, John C., 243
Rehm, Bernhard, 206
Reinhartz, Adele, 246
Reinink, Gerrit J., 228–29, 230, 231, 235–37, 239

Resch, Alfred, 24, 62, 202, 205, 208, 209, 213, 215
Ri, Su-Min, 236
Ritter, Adolf Martin, xviii
Roberge, Michael, 8
Robinson, Gesine, 87
Robinson, James M., xii, xiii, xviii, 5, 59, 64, 88, 90, 137, 171, 181
Robinson, Stephen E., 101
Roessli, Jean-Michel, xv, xvi, 2, 8–9, 10, 11, 23, 42, 45, 56, 95
Rompay, Lucas van, 272
Ropes, James Hardy, 12, 62
Rordorf, Willy, 34, 283, 294, 295
Rose, Els, 24, 41, 48
Ross, E. Dennison, 124
Rousseau, Adelin, 112, 209
Rubinstein, Jeffrey L., 264
Rudolph, Kurt, 179
Ryle, Herbert E., 145, 151

Sackur, Ernst, 222, 223–26, 231–41
Salvador Gonzalez, José María, 49
Sanders, James A., 150
Sanders, E. P., 188–89
Sandnes, Karl Olav, 157, 158
Santos Otero, Aurelio de, 52
Schäfer, Peter, xvii, 117, 264
Schaff, Philip, 227
Schäferdiek, Knut, xii
Schenke, Hans-Martin, 73
Schleifer, Joel, 218, 232
Schmidt, Andrea B., 240
Schmidt, Carl, 113, 283, 294, 295
Schmidt, Daryl D., 160
Schmidt, Francis, 34, 53
Schneemelcher, Wilhelm, xiv, xv–xvi, 25, 34, 43, 48, 52, 53, 65, 138, 220–21, 283, 296
Schonfield, Hugh J., 264, 265
Schroeder, Caroline, 18
Schröter, Jens, xvi, 1, 2, 27, 34, 43–44, 97, 190
Schubart, Wilhelm, 283, 294, 295
Schwartz, Daniel R., 246
Schwartz, Seth, 246
Schweitzer, Albert, 187
Scrivener, Frederick H., 284

Modern Authors Index 369

Searby, Denis, 106
Seitz, Christopher R., 154
Sellew, Philip H., 4
Semler, Johann Salomo, 247
Shepherd, William H., 32
Sheppard, Gerald T., 32, 149
Shoemaker, Stephen J., 2, 15–16, 21, 33, 48, 49, 56, 97, 109, 221, 243, 244
Sinkewicz, Robert, 9
Skarsaune, Oskar, 206
Small, Jocelyn Penny, 268
Smelik, Willem F., 117–18
Smith, Dwight Moody, 20–21
Smith, Geoffrey, 6
Smith, Jonathan Z., 183
Smith, Morton, 68, 91, 182
Snyder, Glenn E., 5, 17, 283, 297–99
Sokoloff, Michael, 117–18
Souter, Alexander, 151
Spanheim, Friedrich, 44
Speyer, Wolfgang, 45
Stanislawski, Michael, 118
Steindorff, Georg, 230, 241
Stendahl, Krister, 62
Stern, David, 37, 158
Stökl Ben Ezra, Daniel, 98
Stone, Michael E., 109
Stoneman, Richard, 240
Stoyanov, Yuri, 243, 244
Strecker, Georg, 64, 179, 202, 205, 206, 207–8, 215
Stuart, Moses A., 145
Suciu, Alin, 8, 99
Suermann, Harald, 228, 229, 231, 243
Sullivan, Lawrence, 141–42
Sullivan, Ruth W., 269
Sundberg, Albert, 164
Swete, Henry Barclay, 145, 151
Sykes, Norman, 46

Talbert, Charles H., 283, 286
Tannehill, Robert C., 283
Tannous, Jack, 271
Tedros Abraha, 97
Terian, Abraham, 100, 113–14, 115, 116, 120–21
Tesfa Gebre Selassie, 102–3

Thackeray, Henry St. John, 240
Theissen, Gerd, 188, 193–94
Thierry, Nicole, 48
Thilo, Johann Carl, 36
Thomassen, Einar, 150, 153
Tijdens, E. F., 128
Till, Walter, 137
Tischendorf, Constantin, xvii, 24, 53, 70, 132
Tite, Philip L., 10, 27
Toepel, Alexander, 100
Toland, John, 247
Tov, Emanuel, 162
Townsend, John T., 283
Trocmé, Étienne, 283
Tubach, Jürgen, 101
Turaiev, Boris A., 103
Turcescu, Lucien, 95
Turner, John D., 5, 84
Tyson, Joseph B., 283

Ullmann, B. L., 47
Ulrich, Eugene, 148

Valantasis, Richard, 4
VanderKam, James C., 159
Van Voorst, Robert E., 20
Van Seters, John, 158–59
Vardi, Amiel D., 147 48, 156
Vasiliev, Alexander, 263
Veltri, Giuseppe, 157
Verhelst, Daniel, 218
Vööbus, Arthur, 211
Vouaux, Léon, 283
Vuong, Lily, 17–18

Wace, Henry, 227
Wagenseil, Johannes Christophorus, 118
Waitz, Hans, 201, 206, 207–8
Wake, William, 46
Wasserstrom, Steve, 131
Weinberg, Magnus, 272
Weis-Liebersdorf, Johannes E., 269
Widengren, Geo, 147
Wildeboer, Gerrit, 145
Wilder, Amos N., 62
Williams, Michael Allan, 134, 136

Wilson, Robert McL., 140
Winter, Paul, 205
Wion, Anaïs, 102
Witakowski, Witold, 95, 101
Wolohojian, Albert Mugrdich, 240
Wordsworth, Christopher, 36
Wortley, John, 223, 231
Wurst, Gregor, 8, 90, 104
Wydra, Wiesław, 10
Wyrick, Jed, 157

Xystus, Betuleius, 42

Yingling, Erik, 99
Young, Michael J. L., 218

Zahn, Molly M., 163
Zahn, Theodore, 145, 154
Zamagni, Claudio, 95
Zeldes, Amir, 18
Zuwiyya, Z. David, 240

www.ingramcontent.com/pod-product-compliance
Lightning Source LLC
Chambersburg PA
CBHW022227010526
44113CB00033B/516